Second Edition

Computer System Architecture

M. MORRIS MANO

Professor of Engineering
California State University, Los Angeles

PRENTICE-HALL, INC., Englewood Cliffs, New Jersey 07632

Library of Congress Cataloging in Publication Data

MANO, M. MORRIS.
   Computer system architecture.

   Includes bibliographies and index.
   1. Computer architecture. I. Title.
QA76.9.A73M36 1982   621.3819'52   81-15799
ISBN 0-13-166611-8   AACR2

Editorial/Production Supervision: Nancy Moskowitz
Manufacturing Buyer: Joyce Levatino
Cover Design by Mario Piazza
Art Production by Margaret Mary Finnerty and Steven Frim

Printed in the United States of America

10 9 8 7 6 5 4

ISBN 0-13-166611-8

PRENTICE-HALL INTERNATIONAL, INC., *London*
PRENTICE-HALL OF AUSTRALIA PTY. LIMITED, *Sydney*
PRENTICE-HALL OF CANADA, LTD., *Toronto*
PRENTICE-HALL OF INDIA PRIVATE LIMITED, *New Delhi*
PRENTICE-HALL OF JAPAN, INC., *Tokyo*
PRENTICE-HALL OF SOUTHEAST ASIA PTE. LTD., *Singapore*
WHITEHALL BOOKS LIMITED, *Wellington, New Zealand*

Contents

Preface

Computer architecture is of concern to computer engineers who deal with the hardware design of computer systems, and computer scientists involved in the design of hardware dependent software systems. A computer system is a system that includes both hardware and software. This book is concerned mostly with the hardware aspects of computer systems, but the impact of software on the architecture of the computer has not been neglected.

Computer architecture is sometimes defined to include only those attributes of the computer that are of interest to the programmer. Here, we define computer architecture by considering what professional computer architects are supposed to know. Computer architects must be familiar with the basic hardware building blocks from which computers are constructed. They must have knowledge of the structure and behavior of computer systems and the way they are designed. Thus, computer architecture as defined in this book is concerned with the structural organization and hardware design of digital computer systems.

The physical organization of a particular processor including its registers, the data flow, the micro-operations and control functions are best described symbolically by means of a register transfer language. Such a language is developed in the book and its relation to the hardware organization and design of digital computers is fully explained. The register transfer language is used on many occasions to specify various computer operations in a concise and precise manner.

The plan of the book is to present the simpler material first and introduce the more advanced subjects later. The first six chapters cover material needed for the basic understanding of computer organization, design, and programming of a simple digital computer. The last six chapters present the separate functional units of digital computers with an emphasis on more advanced topics not covered in the earlier part.

The revisions for the second edition are in the last six chapters. Chapter 7, on the central processor unit and Chapter 11, on input-output organization have been completely rewritten. Chapter 8, on microprogram control and Chapter 12, on memory organization have been revised and new material added. The other chapters remain essentially the same as the first edition except for some minor reorganization.

Chapter 1 introduces the fundamental knowledge needed for the design of digital systems when they are constructed with individual gates and flip-flops. It covers Boolean algebra, combinational circuits, and sequential circuits. In order to keep the book within reasonable bounds, it is necessary to limit the discussion of this subject to one introductory chapter. The justification for this approach is that the design of digital computers takes on a different dimension when integrated circuit functions are employed instead of individual gates and flip-flops. The material included in the first chapter provides the necessary background for understanding the digital systems being presented.

Chapter 2 starts by enumerating the general properties of integrated circuits. It covers in detail some of the most basic digital functions such as registers, counters, decoders, multiplexers, random access memories, and read-only memories. The digital functions are used as building blocks for the design of larger units in the chapters that follow.

Chapter 3 presents the various data types found in digital computers and shows how they are represented in binary form in computer registers. The emphasis is on the representation of numbers employed in arithmetic computations and on the binary coding of symbols, such as the letters of the alphabet used in data processing, and other discrete symbols used for specific applications.

Chapter 4 defines a register transfer language and shows how it is used to express in symbolic form the micro-operation sequences among the registers of a digital computer. Symbols are defined for arithmetic, logic, and shift micro-operations as well as for control functions that initiate the micro-operations. The presentation goes to great lengths to show the hardware implications associated with the various symbols and register transfer statements.

Chapter 5 presents the organization and design of a small basic digital computer. The registers of the computer are defined and a set of computer instructions is specified. The computer description is formalized with register transfer statements that specify the micro-operations among the registers as well as the control functions that initiate the micro-operations. It is then shown that the set of micro-operations can be used to design the data processor part of the computer. The control functions in the list of register transfer statements supply the information for the design of the control unit.

Chapter 6 utilizes the twenty-five instructions of the basic computer defined in Chapter 5 to illustrate many of the techniques commonly used to program a computer. Programming examples in symbolic code are presented for many elementary data processing tasks. The relationships between binary programs, symbolic code programs, and high-level language programs are explained by examples. This leads into the necessity for translation programs such as assemblers and compilers. The basic operation of an assembler is presented together with other system programs. The purpose of this chapter is to introduce the basic ideas of computer software without going deeply into detail. Knowledge of software principles coupled with the hardware presentation should give the reader an overview of a total computer system which includes both hardware and software.

Chapter 7 deals with the central processor unit (CPU) of digital computers. A bus organized processor is presented and a specific arithmetic logic unit (ALU) is designed. The organization of a memory stack is explained with a demonstration of some of its applications. Various instruction formats are illustrated together with their addressing modes. The most common instructions found in a typical computer are enumerated with an explanation of their functions. The microprocessor which is a CPU enclosed in one integrated circuit package is then introduced and its internal and external characteristics analyzed. The chapter concludes with a section on parallel and pipeline processing.

Chapter 8 introduces the concept of microprogramming. A specific control unit is developed to show by example how to generate the microprogram for a typical set of computer instructions. A microprogram sequencer is developed to demonstrate the design procedure with LSI components of the bit-sliced variety. The last section discusses the advantages and applications of microprogramming.

Chapter 9 is devoted to the design of an arithmetic processor. It presents the algorithms for addition, subtraction, multiplication, and division of binary integer numbers in signed-magnitude representation. The arithmetic processor is designed using the register transfer language. The configuration ties the arithmetic processor to the computer designed in Chapter 5. A binary calculator is defined and used for demonstrating the method by which the arithmetic operations can be microprogrammed.

Chapter 10 presents other arithmetic algorithms. Algorithms are developed for signed-2's complement binary data, for floating-point data, and decimal data. The algorithms are presented by means of flow charts that use the register transfer language to specify the sequence of micro-operations and control decisions required for the implementation of the algorithms.

Chapter 11 explains the function of some commonly used input and output devices. The requirement of an interface between the processor and I/O devices is explained and the various configurations for I/O transfers are enumerated. This includes asynchronous transfer, direct memory access, and priority interrupt. Other topics covered are input-output processors, data communication processors, and multiprocessor system organization.

Chapter 12 introduces the concept of memory hierarchy, composed of cache memory, main memory, and auxiliary memory devices such as magnetic disks and tapes. The internal organization and external operation of associative memories is explained in detail. The concept of memory management is introduced through the presentation of the hardware requirements for a cache memory and a virtual memory system.

Every chapter includes a set of problems and a list of references. Some of the problems serve as exercises for the material covered in the chapter. Others are of a more advanced nature and are intended to provide some practice in solving problems associated with the area of digital computer hardware design. A *Solutions Manual* is available for the instructor from the publisher.

The book is suitable for a course in computer architecture in an electrical engineering, computer engineering, or computer science department. Parts of the book can be used in a variety of ways: (1) As a first course in computer hardware organization by covering Chapters 1 through 5 with additional material from Chapters 7, 8, or 9 as the instructor sees fit. (2) As a course in computer design with previous knowledge of digital logic design by reviewing Chapter 5 and then covering Chapters 7 through 12. (3) As a course in computer hardware systems that covers the five functional units of digital computers: processor (Chapter 7), control (Chapter 8), arthimetic (Chapter 10), input-output (Chapter 11), and memory (Chapter 12). The book is also suitable for self-study by computer engineers and scientists who need to acquire the basic knowledge of computer hardware architecture.

M. MORRIS MANO

Digital Logic Circuits

1-1 LOGIC GATES

A digital computer, as the name implies, is a digital system that performs various computational tasks. The word *digital* implies that the information in the computer is represented by variables that take a limited number of *discrete* or *quantized* values. These values are processed internally by components that can maintain a limited number of discrete states. The decimal digits 0, 1, 2, ..., 9, for example, provide 10 discrete values. In practice, digital computers function more reliably if only two states are used. Because of the physical restriction of components, and because human logic tends to be binary (i.e., *true* or *false*, *yes* or *no* statements), digital components that are constrained to take discrete values are further constrained to take only two values and are said to be *binary*.

Digital computers use the binary number system, which has two digits: 0 and 1. A binary digit is called a *bit*. Information is represented in digital computers in groups of bits. By using various coding techniques groups of bits can be made to represent not only binary numbers but also any other discrete symbols, such as decimal digits or letters of the alphabet. By judicious use of binary arrangements and by using various coding techniques, the binary digits or groups of bits may be used to develop complete sets of instructions for performing various types of computations.

In contrast to common decimal numbers that employ the base 10 system, binary numbers use a base 2 system. For example, the binary number 101101 represents a quantity that can be converted to a decimal number by multiplying each bit by the base 2 raised to an integer power as follows:

$$1 \times 2^5 + 0 \times 2^4 + 1 \times 2^3 + 1 \times 2^2 + 0 \times 2^1 + 1 \times 2^0 = 45$$

The six bits 101101 represent a binary number whose decimal equivalent is 45. However, the group of six bits could also represent a binary code for a letter of the alphabet or a control code for specifying some decision logic in a particular digital system. In other words, groups of bits in a digital computer are used to represent many different things. This is similar to the concept that the same letters of an alphabet are used to construct different languages, such as English and French.

Binary information is represented in a digital system by physical quantities called *signals*. Electrical signals such as voltages exist throughout a digital system in either one of two recongnizable values and represent a binary variable equal to 1 or 0. For example, a particular digital system may employ a signal of 3 V to represent a binary 1 and 0.5 V for binary 0. As shown in Fig. 1-1, each binary value has an acceptable deviation from the nominal. The intermediate region between the two allowed regions is crossed only during state transition. The input terminals of digital circuits accept binary signals within the allowable tolerances and the circuits respond at the output terminals with binary signals that fall within the specified tolerances.

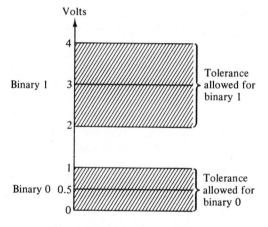

Fig. 1-1   Example of a binary signal.

Binary logic deals with binary variables and with operations that assume a logical meaning. It is used to describe, in algebraic or tabular form, the manipulation and processing of binary information. The manipulation of binary information is done by logic circuits called *gates*. Gates are blocks of hardware that produce signals of binary 1 or 0 when input logic requirements are satisfied. Various logic gates are commonly found in digital computer systems. Each gate has a distinct graphic symbol and its operation can be described by means of an algebraic function. The input-output relationship of the binary variables for each gate can be represented in tabular form in a *truth table*.

The names, graphic symbols, algebraic functions, and truth tables of eight logic gates are listed in Fig. 1-2. Each gate has one or two binary input variables designated by A and B and one binary output variable designated by x. The AND gate produces the AND logic junction: that is, the output is 1 if input a *and* input B are *both* binary 1; otherwise, the output is 0. These conditions are also specified in the truth table for the AND gate. The table shows that output x is 1 only when both input A and input B are 1. The algebraic operation symbol of the AND function is the same as the multiplication symbol of ordinary arithmetic. We can either use a dot between the variables or concatenate the variables without an operation symbol between them. AND gates may have more than two inputs and by definition, the output is 1 if and only if *all* inputs are 1.

The OR gate produces the inclusive-OR function, that is, the output is 1 if input A or input B or both inputs are 1; otherwise, the output is 0. The algebraic symbol of the OR function is $+$, similar to arithmetic addition. OR gates may have more than two inputs and by definition, the output is 1 if *any* input is 1.

The inverter circuit inverts the logic sense of a binary signal. It produces the NOT, or *complement*, function. The algebraic symbol used for the logic complement

Name	Graphic Symbol	Algebraic Function	Truth Table
AND	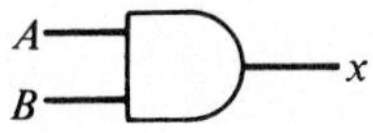 A — B — x	$x = A \cdot B$ or $x = AB$	$\begin{array}{cc\|c} A & B & x \\ \hline 0 & 0 & 0 \\ 0 & 1 & 0 \\ 1 & 0 & 0 \\ 1 & 1 & 1 \end{array}$
OR	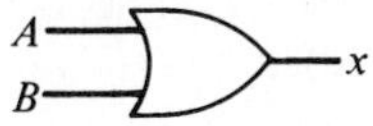 A — B — x	$x = A + B$	$\begin{array}{cc\|c} A & B & x \\ \hline 0 & 0 & 0 \\ 0 & 1 & 1 \\ 1 & 0 & 1 \\ 1 & 1 & 1 \end{array}$
inverter	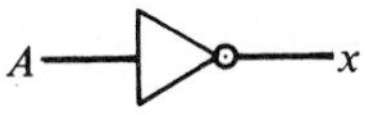 A — x	$x = A'$	$\begin{array}{c\|c} A & x \\ \hline 0 & 1 \\ 1 & 0 \end{array}$
buffer	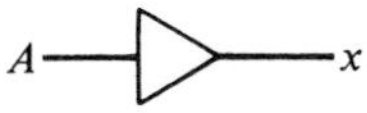 A — x	$x = A$	$\begin{array}{c\|c} A & x \\ \hline 0 & 0 \\ 1 & 1 \end{array}$
NAND	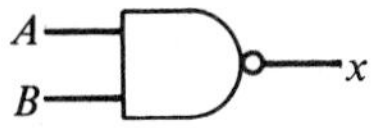 A — B — x	$x = (AB)'$	$\begin{array}{cc\|c} A & B & x \\ \hline 0 & 0 & 1 \\ 0 & 1 & 1 \\ 1 & 0 & 1 \\ 1 & 1 & 0 \end{array}$

Fig. 1-2 Digital logic gates.

Name	Graphic Symbol	Algebraic Function	Truth Table
NOR	A, B → x	$x = (A + B)'$	$A\ B\ \|\ x$ $0\ 0\ \|\ 1$ $0\ 1\ \|\ 0$ $1\ 0\ \|\ 0$ $1\ 1\ \|\ 0$
exclusive-OR (XOR)	A, B → x	$x = A \oplus B$ or $x = A'B + AB'$	$A\ B\ \|\ x$ $0\ 0\ \|\ 0$ $0\ 1\ \|\ 1$ $1\ 0\ \|\ 1$ $1\ 1\ \|\ 0$
exclusive-NOR or equivalence	A, B → x	$x = A \odot B$ or $x = A'B' + AB$	$A\ B\ \|\ x$ $0\ 0\ \|\ 1$ $0\ 1\ \|\ 0$ $1\ 0\ \|\ 0$ $1\ 1\ \|\ 1$

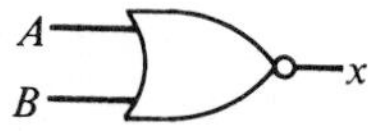

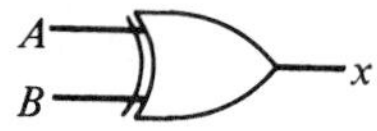

Fig. 1-2 (Continued).

is either a prime or a bar over the variable symbol. This book uses a prime for the logic complement of a binary variable, while a bar over the letter is reserved for designating a complement micro-operation as defined in Chap. 4.

The small circle in the output of the graphic symbol of an inverter designates a logic complement. A triangle symbol by itself designates a buffer circuit. A buffer does not produce any particular logic function since the binary value of the output is the same as the binary value of the input. This circuit is used merely for signal amplification. For example, a buffer that uses 3 V for binary 1 will produce an output of 3 V when its input is 3 V. However, the current supplied at the input is much smaller than the current produced at the output. This way, a buffer can drive many other gates requiring a large amount of current not otherwise available from the small amount of current applied to the buffer input.

The NAND function is the complement of the AND function, as indicated by the graphic symbol which consists of an AND graphic symbol followed by a small circle. The designation NAND is derived from the abbreviation of NOT-AND. A more proper designation would have been AND-invert since it is the AND function that is inverted. The NOR gate is the complement of the OR gate and uses an OR graphic symbol followed by a small circle. Both NAND and NOR gates may have more than two inputs, and the output is always the complement of the AND or OR function, respectively.

4

The exclusive-OR gate has a graphic symbol similar to the OR gate except for the additional curved line on the input side. The output of this gate is 1 if any input is 1 but excludes the combination when both inputs are 1. The exclusive-OR function has its own algebraic symbol or can be expressed in terms of AND, OR, and complement operations as shown in Fig. 1-2. The exclusive-NOR is the complement of the exclusive-OR as indicated by the small circle in the graphic symbol. The output of this gate is 1 only if both inputs have the same binary value. We shall refer to the exclusive-NOR function as the *equivalence* function. Since the exclusive-OR and equivalence functions are not always the complement of each other. A more fitting name for the exclusive-OR operation would be an *odd* function; i.e., its output is 1 if an odd number of inputs are 1. Thus, in a three-input exclusive-OR (odd) function, the output is 1 if only one input is 1 or if all three inputs are 1. The equivalence function is an *even* function; that is, its output is 1 if an even number of inputs are 0. For a three-input equivalence function, the output is 1 if none of the inputs are 0 (all inputs are 1) or if two of its inputs are 0 (one input is 1). Careful investigation will show that the exclusive-OR and equivalence functions are the complement of each other when the gates have an even number of inputs, but the two functions are equal when the number of inputs is odd. These two gates are commonly available with two inputs and only seldom are they found with three or more inputs.

1-2 BOOLEAN ALGEBRA

Boolean algebra is an algebra that deals with binary variables and logic operations. The variables are designated by letters such as A, B, x, and y. The three basic logic operations are *AND*, *OR*, and *complement*. A Boolean function is an algebraic expression formed with binary variables, the logic operation symbols, parentheses, and equal sign.For a given value of the variables, the Boolean function can be either 1 or 0. Consider, for example, the Boolean function

$$F = x + y'z$$

The function F is equal to 1 if x is 1 *or* if both y' and z are equal to 1; F is equal to 0 otherwise. But saying that $y' = 1$ is equivalent to saying that $y = 0$ since y' is the complement of y. Equivalently, we may say that F is equal to 1 if $x = 1$ or $yz = 01$. The relationship between a function and its binary variables can be represented in a truth table. To represent a function in a truth table we need a list of the 2^n combinations with 1's and 0's of the n binary variables. As shown in Fig. 1-3(a), there are eight possible distinct combinations for assigning bits to the three variables. The function F is equal to 1 for those combinations where $x = 1$ or $yz = 01$; it is equal to 0 for all other combinations.

A Boolean function can be transformed from an algebraic expression into

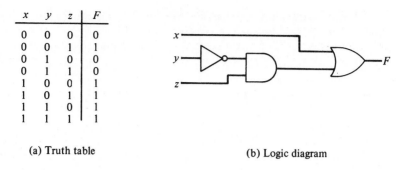

x	y	z	F
0	0	0	0
0	0	1	1
0	1	0	0
0	1	1	0
1	0	0	1
1	0	1	1
1	1	0	1
1	1	1	1

(a) Truth table   (b) Logic diagram

Fig. 1-3   Truth table and logic diagram for $F = x + y'z$.

a *logic diagram* composed of AND, OR, and inverter gates. The logic diagram for F is shown in Fig. 1-3(b). There is an inverter for input y to generate its complement y'. There is an AND gate for the term $y'z$ and an OR gate is used to combine the two terms. In a logic diagram, the variables of the function are taken to be the inputs of the circuit and the variable symbol of the function is taken as the output of the circuit.

The purpose of Boolean algebra is to facilitate the analysis and design of digital circuits. It provides a convenient tool to:

1. Express in algebraic form a truth table relationship between variables.

2. Express in algebraic form the input-output relationship of logic diagrams.

3. Find simpler circuits for the same function.

A Boolean function specified by a truth table can be expressed algebraically in many different ways. By manipulating a Boolean expression according to Boolean algebra rules, one may obtain a simpler expression that will require fewer gates. To see how this is done, we must first study the manipulative capabilities of Boolean algebra.

Table 1-1 lists the most basic relations of Boolean algebra. All the relations can be proven by means of truth tables. The first eight in Table 1-1 show the basic relationship between a single variable and itself, or in conjunction with the binary

TABLE 1-1   Basic Relations of Boolean Algebra

(1) $x + 0 = x$	(2) $x \cdot 0 = 0$
(3) $x + 1 = 1$	(4) $x \cdot 1 = x$
(5) $x + x = x$	(6) $x \cdot x = x$
(7) $x + x' = 1$	(8) $x \cdot x' = 0$
(9) $x + y = y + x$	(10) $xy = yx$
(11) $x + (y + z) = (x + y) + z$	(12) $x(yz) = (xy)z$
(13) $x(y + z) = xy + xz$	(14) $x + yz = (x + y)(x + z)$
(15) $(x + y)' = x'y'$	(16) $(xy)' = x' + y'$
(17) $(x')' = x$	

constants of 1 and 0. The next five relations (9 to 13) are similar to ordinary algebra. Relation 14 does not apply in ordinary algebra but is very useful in manipulating Boolean expressions. Relations 15 and 16 are called *DeMorgan's theorems* and are discussed below. The last relation states that if a variable is complemented twice, one obtains the original value of the variable. The relations listed in the table apply to single variables x, y, and z or to Boolean functions expressed by binary variables x, y, or z.

DeMorgan's theorem is very important in dealing with NOR and NAND gates. It states that a NOR gate that performs the $(x + y)'$ function is equivalent to the function $x'y'$. Similary, a NAND function can be expressed by either $(xy)'$ or by $x' + y'$. For this reason, the NOR and NAND gates have two distinct graphic symbols as shown in Figs. 1-4 and 1-5. Instead of representing a NOR gate with an OR graphic symbol followed by a circle, we can represent it by an AND graphic symbol preceded by circles in all inputs. The invert-AND symbol for the NOR gate follows from DeMorgan's theorem and from the convention that small circles denote complementation. Similary, the NAND gate has two distinct symbols as shown in Fig. 1-5.

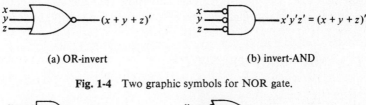

(a) OR-invert   (b) invert-AND

Fig. 1-4   Two graphic symbols for NOR gate.

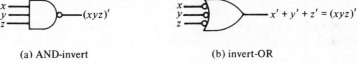

(a) AND-invert   (b) invert-OR

Fig. 1-5   Two graphic symbols for NAND gate.

To see how Boolean algebra manipulation is used to simplify digital circuits consider the logic diagram of Fig. 1-6(a). The output of the first NAND gate is, by DeMorgan's theorem, $(AB')' = A' + B$. The output of the circuit is the NAND operation of this term and B':

$$x = [(A' + B) \cdot B']'$$

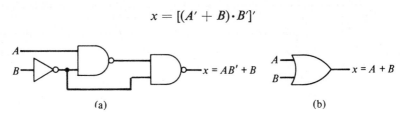

(a)   (b)

Fig. 1-6   Two logic diagrams for the same Boolean function.

Using DeMorgan's theorem twice more, we obtain

$$x = (A' + B)' + B = AB' + B$$

Note that DeMorgan's theorem has been applied three times (to demonstrate its use) but could have been applied only once as follows:

$$x = [(AB')' \cdot B']' = AB' + B$$

The expression for x can be simplified by application of the relations listed in Table 1-1.

$$x = AB' + B \qquad\qquad \textit{by relation}$$
$$= B + AB' \qquad\qquad (9)$$
$$= (B + A)(B + B') \qquad (14)$$
$$= (B + A) \cdot 1 \qquad\qquad (7)$$
$$= B + A = A + B \qquad (4), (9)$$

The final result produces an OR function and can be implemented with a single OR gate as shown in Fig. 1-6(b). One can show that the two circuits produce identical input-output binary relationships by obtaining the truth table of each.

1-3 MAP SIMPLIFICATION

The complexity of the logic diagram that implements a Boolean function is directly related to the complexity of the algebraic expression from which the function is implemented. The truth table representation of a function is unique but the function can appear in many different forms when expressed algebraically. The expression may be simplified using the basic relations of Boolean algebra. This procedure, however, is sometimes difficult because it lacks specific rules for predicting each succeeding step in the manipulative process. The map method provides a simple, straigthforward procedure for simplifying Boolean functions. This method may be regarded as a pictorial arrangement of the truth table which allows an easy interpretation for choosing the minimum number of variables needed to express the function algebraically. The map method is also known by the names *Karnaugh map* and *Veitch diagram*.

Each combination of the variables in a truth table is called a *minterm*. For example, the truth table of Fig. 1-3 contains eight minterms. A function of n variables when expressed by means of a truth table will have 2^n minterms, equivalent to the 2^n binary numbers obtained from n digits. A Boolean function will be equal to 1 for some minterms and to 0 for others. The information contained in a truth table may be expressed in compact form by listing the decimal equivalent of those minterms that produce a 1 for the function. For example, the truth table of Fig. 1-3 can be expressed as follows:

$$F(x, y, z) = \sum (1, 4, 5, 6, 7)$$

The letters in parentheses list the binary variables in the order that they appear in the truth table. The symbol $\sum$ stands for the sum of the minterms that follow in parentheses. The minterms that produce 1 for the function are listed in their decimal equivalent. The minterms missing from the list are the ones that produce 0 for the function.

The map is a diagram made up of squares, with each square representing one minterm. The squares corresponding to minterms that produce 1 for the function are marked by a 1 and the others are marked by a 0 or left empty. By recognizing various patterns and combining squares marked by 1's in the map, it is possible to derive alternative algebraic expressions for the function, from which the most convenient may be selected.

The maps for functions of two, three, and four variables are shown in Fig. 1-7. The number of squares in a map of n variables is 2^n minterms are listed by an equivalent decimal number for easy reference. The minterm numbers are assigned in an orderly arrangement such that adjacent squares represent minterms which differ by only one variable. The variable names are listed across both sides of the diagonal line in the corner of the map. The 0's and 1's marked along each row and each column designate the value of the variables. Each variable under brackets contains half of the squares in the map where that variable appears unprimed. The variable appears

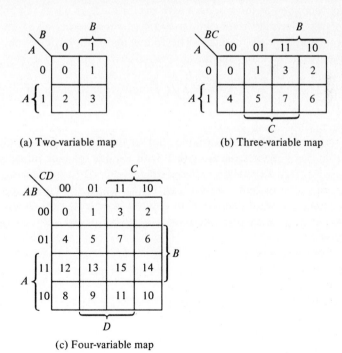

(a) Two-variable map

(b) Three-variable map

(c) Four-variable map

Fig. 1-7 Maps for two-, three-, and four-variable functions.

with a prime (complemented) in the remaining half of the squares. All the information appearing in the maps of Fig. 1-7 is not always needed; it is shown here for explanation only.

The minterm represented by a square is determined from the binary assignments of the variables along the left and top edges in the map. For example, minterm 5 in the three-variable map is 101 in binary which may be obtained from the 1 in the second row concatanated with the 01 of the second column. This minterm represents a value for the binary variables A, B, and C, with A and C being unprimed and B being primed (i.e., $AB'C$). On the other hand, minterm 5 in the four-variable map represents a minterm for four variables. The binary number contains the four digits 0101 and the corresponding term it represents is $A'BC'D$.

Minterms of adjacent squares in the map are identical except for one variable that appears complemented in one square and uncomplemented in the *adjacent* square. According to this definition of adjacency, the squares at the extreme ends of the same horizontal row are also to be considered adjacent. The same applies to the top and bottom squares of a column. As a result, the four corner squares of a map must also be considered to be adjacent.

A Boolean function represented by a truth table is entered into the map by inserting 1's in those squares where the function is 1. The squares containing 1's are combined in groups of adjacent squares. These groups must contain a number of squares which is an integral power of 2. Groups of combined adjacent squares may share one or more square with one or more group. Each group of squares represents an algebraic term, and the OR of those terms gives the simplified algebraic expression for the function. The following examples show the use of the map for simplifying Boolean functions.

> ***EXAMPLE 1:*** Simplify the Boolean function:
>
> $$F(A, B, C) = \sum (3, 4, 6, 7)$$
>
> The three-variable map for this function is shown in Fig. 1-8. There are four squares marked with 1's, one for each minterm that produces 1 for the function. These squares belong to minterms 3, 4, 6, and 7 and are recognized from Fig. 1-7(b). Two adjacent squares are combined in the third column. This column belongs to both B and C and produces the term BC. The remaining two squares with 1's in the two corners of

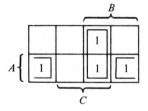

Fig. 1-8 Map for $F = \sum (3, 4, 6, 7)$
$= BC + AC'$.

the second row are adjacent and belong to row A and the two columns of C', so they produce the term AC'. The simplified algebraic expression for the function is the OR of the two terms:

$$F = BC + AC'$$

EXAMPLE 2: Simplify the Boolean function:

$$F(A, B, C) = \sum (0, 2, 4, 5, 6)$$

The five minterms are marked by 1's in the corresponding squares of the three-variable map shown in Fig. 1-9. The four squares in the first and fourth columns are adjacent and represent the term C'. The remaining square marked with a 1 for minterm 5 is combined with the square of minterm 4 to produce the term AB'. The simplified function is

$$F = C' + AB'$$

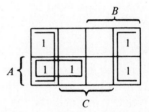

Fig. 1-9　Map for $F = \sum (0, 2, 4, 5, 6)$
　　　　　$= C' + AB'$.

EXAMPLE 3: Simplify the Boolean function:

$$F(A, B, C, D) = \sum (0, 1, 2, 6, 8, 9, 10)$$

The area in the map covered by this four-variable function consists of the squares marked with 1's in Fig. 1-10. The function contains 1's in

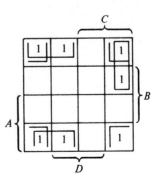

Fig. 1-10　Map for $F = \sum (0, 1, 2, 6, 8, 9, 10)$
　　　　　　$= B'D' + B'C' + A'CD'$.

the four corners that, when taken as a group, give the term $B'D'$. This is possible because these four squares are adjacent when the map is considered with top and bottom or left and right edges touching. The two 1's on the left of the top row are combined with the two 1's on the left of the bottom row to give the term $B'C'$. The remaining 1 in the square of minterm 6 is combined with minterm 2 to give the term $A'CD'$. The simplified function is

$$F = B'D' + B'C' + A'CD'$$

Product of Sums

The Boolean functions derived from the maps in the previous examples were expressed in *sum of products* form. The product terms are AND terms and the sum denotes the ORing of these terms. It is sometimes convenient to obtain the algebraic expression for the function in a *product of sums* form. The sums are OR terms and the product denotes the ANDing of these terms. With a minor modification, a product of sums form can be obtained from a map.

The procedure for obtaining a product of sums expression follows from the basic properties of Boolean algebra. The 1's in the map represent the minterms that produce 1 for the function. The squares not marked by 1 represent the minterms that produce 0 for the function. If we mark the empty squares by 0's and combine them into groups of adjacent squares, we obtain the complement of the function, F'. Using DeMorgan's theorem, we take the complement of F' [i.e., $(F')' = F$] and the function so obtained is in product of sums form. The best way to show this is by example.

> **EXAMPLE 4:** Simplify the following Boolean function in (a) sum of products form and (b) product of sums form:

$$F(A, B, C, D) = \sum (0, 1, 2, 5, 8, 9, 10)$$

The 1's marked in the map of Fig. 1-11 represent the minterms that produce a 1 for the function. The squares marked with 0's represent the

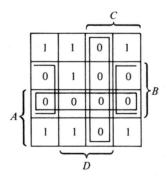

Fig. 1-11   Map for Example 4.

minterms not included in F, and therefore, denote the complement of F. Combining the squares with 1's gives the simplified function in sum of products form:

$$F = B'D' + B'C' + A'C'D$$

If the squares marked with 0's are combined, as shown in the diagram, one obtains the simplified complemented function:

$$F' = AB + CD + BD'$$

Applying DeMorgan's theorem, we obtain the simplified function in product of sums form:

$$F = (A' + B')(C' + D')(B' + D)$$

The logic diagrams of the simplified expressions obtained in Example 4 are shown in Fig. 1-12. The sum of products expression is implemented in Fig. 1-12(a) with a group of AND gates, one for each AND term. The outputs of the AND gates are connected to the inputs of a single OR gate. The same function is implemented in Fig. 1-12(b) in its product of sums form with a group of OR gates, one for each

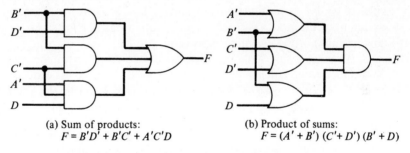

(a) Sum of products:
$F = B'D' + B'C' + A'C'D$

(b) Product of sums:
$F = (A' + B')(C' + D')(B' + D)$

Fig. 1-12   Logic diagrams for the function of Example 4.

OR term. The outputs of the OR gates are connected to the inputs of a single AND gate. In each case it is assumed that the input variables are directly available in their complement, so inverters are not included. The pattern established in Fig. 1-12 is the general form by which any Boolean function is implemented when expressed in one of the standard forms. AND gates are connected to a single OR gate when in sum of products form. OR gates are connected to a single AND gate when in product of sums form.

A sum of products expression can be implemented with NAND gates as shown in Fig. 1-13(a). Note that the second NAND gate is drawn with the graphic symbol of Fig. 1-5(b). There are three lines in the diagram with small circles at both ends. Two circles in the same line designate double complementation and since $(x')' = x$, the two circles can be removed and the resulting diagram is equivalent to the one shown in Fig. 1-12(a). Similarly, a product of sums expression can be implemented

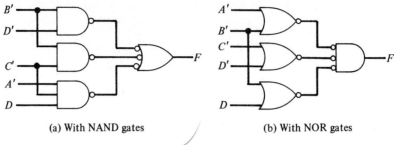

(a) With NAND gates

(b) With NOR gates

Fig. 1-13 Logic diagrams for the function of Example 4.

with NOR gates as shown in Fig. 1-13(b). The second NOR gate is drawn with the graphic symbol of Fig. 1-4(b). Again the two circles on both sides of each line may be removed and the diagram so obtained is equivalent to the one shown in Fig. 1-12(b).

Don't-Care Conditions

The 1's and 0's in the map represent the minterms that make the function equal to 1 or 0. There are occasions when it does not matter if the function produces 0 or 1 for a given minterm. Since the function may be either 0 or 1, we say that we don't-care what the function output is to be for this minterm. Minterms that may produce either 0 or 1 for the function are said to be *don't-care conditions* and are marked by an X in the map. These don't-care conditions can be used to provide further simplification of the algebraic expression.

When choosing adjacent squares for the function in the map, the X's may be assumed to be either 0 or 1, whichever gives the simplest expression. In addition, an X need not be used at all if it does not contribute to the simplification of the function. In each case, the choice depends only on the simplification that can be achieved.

EXAMPLE 5: Simplify the Boolean function:

$$F(A, B, C) = \sum (0, 2, 6)$$

having the don't-care conditions

$$d(A, B, C) = \sum (1, 3, 5)$$

The minterms listed with F produce a 1 for the function. The minterms of d may produce either a 0 or 1 for the function. The remaining minterms, i.e., 4 and 7, produce a 0 for the function. The map is shown in Fig. 1-14. The minterms of F are marked with 1's, those of d are marked by X's, and the remaining squares may be marked by 0's or left empty. The 1's and X's are combined in any convenient manner so as to enclose the maximum number of adjacent squares. It is not necessary to

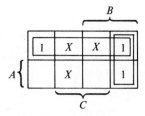

Fig. 1-14 Example of map with don't-care conditions.

include all or any of the X's but all the 1's must be included. By including the don't-care minterms 1 and 3 with the 1's in the first row we obtain the term A'. The remaining 1 for minterm 6 is combined with minterm 2 to obtain the term BC'. The simplified expression is

$$F = A' + BC'$$

Note that don't-care minterm 5 was not included because it does not contribute to the simplification of the expression. Note also that if don't-care minterms 1 and 3 were not included with the 1's, the simplified expression for F would have been

$$F = A'C' + BC'$$

This would require two AND gates and an OR gate, as opposed to the expression obtained previously which requires only one AND and one OR gate.

The function is completely determined once the X's are assigned to the 1's or 0's in the map. Thus, the expression

$$F = A' + BC'$$

when transferred to a truth table will have minterms 0, 1, 2, 3, and 6 produce a 1 for the function and minterms 4, 5, and 7 produce a 0. Since minterms 1, 3, and 5 were specified as being don't-care conditions, i.e., they can produce either a 0 or a 1 for the function, we have chosen minterms 1 and 3 to produce a binary 1 and minterm 5 to produce a 0 because this combination gives the simplest Boolean expression.

1-4 COMBINATIONAL CIRCUITS

A combinational circuit is a connected arrangement of logic gates with a set of inputs and outputs. At any given time, the binary values of the outputs are a function of the combination of 1's and 0's at the inputs. A block diagram of a combinational circuit is shown in Fig. 1-15. The n input variables come from an external source; the m output variables go to an external destination; and in between there is an interconnection of logic gates. A combinational circuit transforms binary information

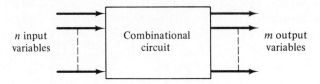

Fig. 1-15 Block diagram of a combinational circuit.

from the given input data to the required output data. Combinational circuits are employed in digital systems for generating binary control decisions and for providing digital functions required in data processing. Many digital functions are available commercially in small packages called integrated circuits. Chapter 2 introduces integrated circuits and a number of digital functions commonly found in integrated circuit packages.

A combinational circuit can be described by a truth table showing the binary relationships between the n input variables and the m output variables. There are 2^n possible combinations of binary input values. The truth table lists the corresponding output binary values for each of the 2^n input combinations. A combinational circuit also can be specified with m Boolean functions, one for each output variable. Each output function is expressed in terms of the n input variables.

Analysis Procedure

The analysis of a combinational circuit starts with a given logic circuit diagram and culminates with a set of Boolean functions or a truth table. If the digital circuit is accompanied by a verbal explanation of its function, then the Boolean functions or the truth table is sufficient for verification. If the function of the circuit is under investigation, then it is necessary to interpret the operation of the circuit from the derived Boolean functions or the truth table. The success of such investigation is enhanced if one has experience and familiarity with digital circuits. The ability to correlate a truth table or a set of Boolean functions with an information processing task is an art that one acquires with experience.

To illustrate with an example, let us investigate the combinational circuit shown in Fig. 1-16. The circuit has five input variables and two output variables.

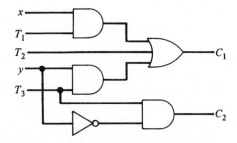

Fig. 1-16 Example of a combinational circuit.

Let us assume that input variables T_1, T_2, and T_3 are binary signals that occur in a time sequence. Thus, at a given time, variable $T_1 = 1$ while $T_2 = T_3 = 0$. During the next time period $T_1 = 0$, $T_2 = 1$, and $T_3 = 0$. The next time period produces $T_1 = T_2 = 0$ and $T_3 = 1$, and so on. The input binary variables x and y may represent results of previous operations. For example, variable x may be used to indicate that two numbers are equal ($x = 1$) or unequal ($x = 0$). Output variable C_1 (and C_2) may designate a control variable that enables a certain digital operation when $C_1 = 1$ and disables the operation when $C_1 = 0$.

The combinational circuit of Fig. 1-16 can be expressed with two Boolean functions as follows:

$$C_1 = xT_1 + T_2 + yT_3$$
$$C_2 = y'T_3$$

From the diagram or the Boolean functions it is possible to interpret the operation of the circuit. Control variable $C_1 = 1$ if $x = 1$ when timing variable $T_1 = 1$; or if timing variable $T_2 = 1$; or if $y = 1$ when timing variable $T_3 = 1$; otherwise, $C_1 = 0$, Similarly, $C_2 = 1$ if $y = 0$ and timing variable $T_3 = 1$; otherwise, $C_2 = 0$.

Binary control decisions in digital computers are generated in combinational circuits. The input variables for these circuits are internal timing sequences as well as binary variables from other operations. The digital functions being controlled are circuits that implement various data processing tasks, and these tasks are generated by means of other combinational circuits.

Design Procedure

The design of combinational circuits starts from the verbal outline of the problem and ends in a logic circuit diagram. The procedure involves the following steps:

1. The problem is stated.
2. The input and output variables are assigned letter symbols.
3. The truth table that defines the relationship between inputs and outputs is derived.
4. The simplified Boolean functions for each output are obtained.
5. The logic diagram is drawn.

To demonstrate the design of combinational circuits we will present three examples of digital arithmetic circuits. These circuits serve as basic building blocks for the construction of more complicated arithmetic digital functions.

Half-Adder

The most basic digital arithmetic function is the addition of two binary digits. A combinational circuit that performs the arithmetic addition of two bits is called a *half-adder*. One that performs the addition of three bits (two significant bits and a previous carry) is called a *full-adder*. The name of the former stems from the fact that two half-adders can be employed to implement a full-adder.

The input variables of a half-adder are called the *augend* and *addend* bits. The output variables are called the *sum* and *carry*. It is necessary to specify two output variables because the sum of $1 + 1$ is binary 10, which has two digits. We assign symbols x and y to the two input variables, and S (for sum) and C (for carry) to the two output variables. The truth table for the half-adder is shown in Fig. 1-17(a). The C output is 0 unless both inputs are 1. The S output represents the least significant bit of the sum. The Boolean functions for the two outputs can be obtained directly from the truth table:

$$S = x'y + xy' = x \oplus y$$
$$C = xy$$

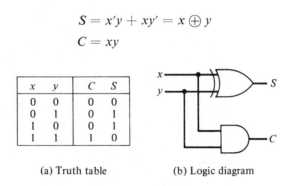

x	y	C	S
0	0	0	0
0	1	0	1
1	0	0	1
1	1	1	0

(a) Truth table   (b) Logic diagram

Fig. 1-17   Half-adder.

The logic diagram is shown in Fig. 1-17(b). It consists of an exclusive-OR gate and an AND gate.

Full-Adder

A full-adder is a combinational circuit that forms the arithmetic sum of three input bits. It consists of three inputs and two outputs. Two of the input variables, denoted by x and y, represent the two significant bits to be added. The third input, z, represents the carry from the previous lower significant position. Two outputs are necessary because the arithmetic sum of three binary digits ranges in value from 0 to 3, and binary 2 or 3 needs two digits. The two outputs are designated by the symbols S (for sum) and C (for carry). The binary variable S gives the value of the least significant bit of the sum. The binary variable C gives the output carry. The truth table of the full-adder is shown in Table 1-2. The eight rows under the input variables designate all possible combinations of 1's and 0's that these variables may have. The 1's and 0's for the output variables are determined from the arithmetic sum of the input bits. When all input bits are 0's the output is 0. The S output is equal to 1 when only one input is equal to 1 or when all three inputs are equal to 1. The C output has a carry of 1 if two or three inputs are equal to 1.

The maps of Fig. 1-18 are used to find algebraic expressions for each of the

TABLE 1-2 Truth Table for Full-Adder

Inputs			Outputs	
x	y	z	C	S
0	0	0	0	0
0	0	1	0	1
0	1	0	0	1
0	1	1	1	0
1	0	0	0	1
1	0	1	1	0
1	1	0	1	0
1	1	1	1	1

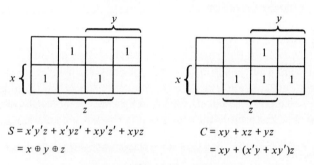

$$S = x'y'z + x'yz' + xy'z' + xyz$$
$$= x \oplus y \oplus z$$

$$C = xy + xz + yz$$
$$= xy + (x'y + xy')z$$

Fig. 1-18 Maps for full-adder.

output variables. The 1's in the squares for the maps of S and C are determined directly from the minterms in the truth table. The squares with 1's for the S output do not combine in groups of adjacent squares. But since the output is 1 when an odd number of inputs are 1, S is an odd function, and represents the exclusive-OR relation of the variables (see the discussion at the end of Sec. 1-1). The squares with 1's for the C output may be combined in a variety of ways. One possible expression for C is

$$C = xy + (x'y + xy')z$$

Realizing that $x'y + xy' = x \oplus y$, and including the expression for output S, we obtain the two functions for the full-adder:

$$S = x \oplus y \oplus z$$
$$C = xy + (x \oplus y)z$$

The logic diagram for the full-adder is drawn in Fig. 1-19(a). Note that the full-adder circuit consists of two half-adders and an OR gate.

The full-adder circuit is the most basic digital function for generating arith-

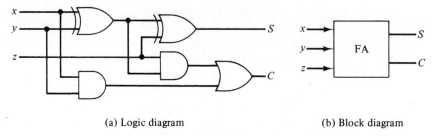

(a) Logic diagram   (b) Block diagram

Fig. 1-19   Full-adder circuit.

metic operations in digital computers. When used in subsequent chapters, the full-adder circuit will be designated by a block diagram symbol as shown in Fig. 1-19(b).

Full-Subtractor

A full-subtractor is a combinational circuit that performs a subtraction between two bits while taking into account the fact that a 1 may have been borrowed by a lower significant position. This circuit consists of three inputs and two outputs. The three inputs x, y, and z denote the minuend, subtrahend, and previous borrow, respectively. The two outputs D and K represent the difference and next borrow, respectively. The truth table for the circuit is shown in Table 1-3.

TABLE 1-3   Truth Table for Full-Subtractor

Inputs			Outputs	
x	y	z	K	D
0	0	0	0	0
0	0	1	1	1
0	1	0	1	1
0	1	1	1	0
1	0	0	0	1
1	0	1	0	0
1	1	0	0	0
1	1	1	1	1

The eight rows under the input variables designate all possible combinations of 1's and 0's that the binary variables may take. The 1's and 0's for the output variables are determined from the subtraction of $x - y$, taking into account that when $z = 1$, it signifies that a bit has been borrowed by the previous lower significant position. This borrow must be subtracted from the minuend bit x. For example, with $x = 0$, $y = 0$, and $z = 1$, we have to borrow a 1 from the next stage, which makes $K = 1$ and adds 2 to x. Since $z = 1$ signifies a previous borrow we must

20

subtract a 1 from x so that $2 - 1 = 1$. The value of y is then subtracted from x to give for the difference $D = 1 - 0 = 1$.

The simplified Boolean functions for the two outputs of the full-subtractor can be derived by means of maps. The output functions are

$$D = x \oplus y \oplus z$$
$$K = x'y + x'z + yz$$

We note that the logic function for output D in the full-subtractor is exactly the same as output S in the full-adder. Moreover, the output K resembles the function for C in the full-adder except that the input variable x is complemented. Because of these similarities, it is possible to convert a full-adder into a full-subtractor merely by complementing input x (the minuend) prior to its application to the gates that form the carry output. Subtractors are very seldom used as digital functions because, as we shall see in Chap. 3, a subtraction operation may be achieved by complementing the subtrahend and adding it to the minuend.

1-5 FLIP-FLOPS

There are two types of sequential circuits and their classification depends on the timing of their signals. A *synchronous* sequential circuit employs storage elements called *flip-flops* that are allowed to change their binary value only at discrete instants of time. An *asynchronous* sequential circuit is a system whose outputs depend upon the order in which its input variables change and can be affected at any instant of time. Gate-type asynchronous systems are basically combinational circuits with feedback paths. Because of the feedback among logic gates the system may, at times, become unstable. The instability problems encountered in asynchronous systems impose many difficulties and for this reason, they are very seldom used in the design of digital computer systems.

Synchronous sequential logic systems use logic gates and flip-flop storage devices. Synchronization is achieved by a timing device called a *clock pulse* generator. The clock pulses from the generator are distributed throughout the system in such a way that flip-flops are affected only with the arrival of the synchronization pulse. Clocked synchronous sequential circuits do not manifest instability problems and their timing is easily broken down into independent discrete steps, each of which may be considered separately. The sequential circuits discussed in this book are exclusively of the clocked synchronous type.

A flip-flop is a binary cell capable of storing one bit of information. It has two outputs, one for the normal value and one for the complement value of the bit stored in it. A flip-flop maintains a binary state until directed by a clock pulse to switch states. The difference among various types of flip-flops is in the number of inputs they possess and in the manner in which the inputs affect the binary state. The most common types of flip-flops are discussed below.

Basic Flip-Flop or Latch

An asynchronous flip-flop is constructed from two NAND gates or two NOR gates connected back to back. The circuit for the NAND version is shown in Fig. 1-20. The cross-coupled connections from the output of one gate to the input of the other gate constitutes a feedback path. For this reason, the circuit is classified as asynchronous. Each flip-flop has two outputs, Q and Q', and two inputs, *set* and *reset*. This type of flip-flop is called a *direct-coupled RS* flip-flop, the R and S being the first letters of the two input names. Another more popular name for this type of flip-flop is a *latch*. The latch forms a basic circuit upon which more complicated flip-flop types can be constructed.

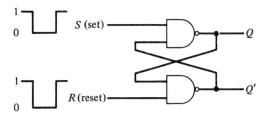

Fig. 1-20   Basic flip-flop (latch).

The NAND latch operates with both inputs normally at 1, unless the state of the circuit has to be changed. The application of a momentary 0 to the set input causes output Q to go to 1 and Q' to go to 0. The outputs of the circuit do not change when the set input returns to 1. A momentary 0 applied to the reset input causes an output of $Q = 0$ and $Q' = 1$. The state of the flip-flop is always taken from the value of its normal output Q. When $Q = 1$, we say that the flip-flop stores a 1 and is in the *set* state. When $Q = 0$, we say that the flip-flop stores a 0 and is in the *clear* state.

The latch circuit manifests an undesirable condition if *both* inputs go to 0 simultaneously. Investigation of the circuit will show that when both inputs are 0, outputs Q and Q' will go to 1, a condition which is normally meaningless in flip-flop operation. If both inputs are then returned to 1, the state of the flip-flop is unpredictable; either state may result, depending on which input remains in the 0 state for a longer period of time before the transition to 1.

RS Flip-Flop

By adding gates to the inputs of the latch, the flip-flop can be made to respond only during the occurrence of a clock pulse. The clocked *RS* flip-flop, shown in Fig. 1-21, consists of the basic latch and two other NAND gates. The outputs of gates 3 and

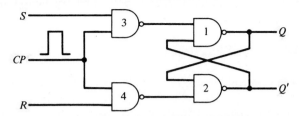

Fig. 1-21 Logic diagram of a clocked *RS* flip-flop.

4 remain at 1 as long as the clock pulse (abbreviated *CP*) is 0, regardless of the *S* and *R* input values. When the clock pulse goes to 1, information from the *S* and *R* inputs is allowed to reach the latch in gates 1 and 2. The set state is reached with $S = 1$, $R = 0$, and $CP = 1$. To change to the clear state, the inputs must be $S = 0$, $R = 1$, and $CP = 1$. With both $S = 0$ and $R = 0$, a *CP* of 1 does not affect the state of the flip-flop. *S* and *R* cannot be 1 during the occurrence of a clock pulse because the next state of the flip-flop is indeterminate.

The graphic symbol of the *RS* flip-flop is shown in Fig. 1-22. It has three inputs: *S*, *R*, and *CP*. The *CP* input is marked with a small triangle. The triangle is a symbol for a *dynamic indicator* and denotes the fact that the circuit responds to an input *transition* from 0 to 1.* The outputs of the flip-flop are given a variable name such as *Q* or any other convenient letter designation. The small right-angle triangle is a graphic symbol for a *polarity indicator*. It designates the complement output of the flip-flop which in this case is *Q'*.

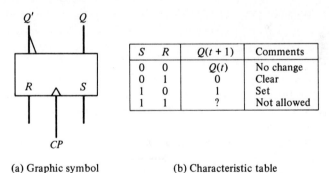

S	R	Q(t + 1)	Comments
0	0	Q(t)	No change
0	1	0	Clear
1	0	1	Set
1	1	?	Not allowed

(a) Graphic symbol (b) Characteristic table

Fig. 1-22 *RS* flip-flop.

The characteristic table shown in Fig. 1-22(b) summarizes the operation of the *RS* flip-flop in tabular form. $Q(t)$ is the binary state of the flip-flop at a given time (referred to as *present state*). The *S* and *R* columns give the binary values of the inputs. $Q(t + 1)$ is the state of the flip-flop after the occurrence of a clock pulse

---

*This graphic symbol and all other logic symbols in this book follow the recommendation of the American National Standard Institute *Graphic Symbols for Logic Diagrams* as specified in ANSI Y32.14–1973.

(referred to as *next state*). If $S = R = 0$, a pulse produces no change of state, that is, $Q(t + 1) = Q(t)$. If $S = 0$ and $R = 1$, the flip-flop goes to the 0 (clear) state. If $S = 1$ and $R = 0$ the flip-flop goes to the 1 (set) state. An *RS* flip-flop should not be pulsed when $S = R = 1$ since it produces an indeterminate next state.

D Flip-Flop

The *D* (data) flip-flop is a slight modification of the *RS* flip-flop. An *RS* flip-flop is converted to a *D* flip-flop by inserting an inverter between *S* and *R* and assigning the symbol *D* to the *S* input. The *D* input is sampled during the occurrence of a clock pulse and if it is 1, the flip-flop goes to the 1 state (because $S = 1$ and $R = 0$). If it is 0, a pulse changes the state of the flip-flop to 0 (because $S = 0$ and $R = 1$). The graphic symbol and characteristic table of the *D* flip-flop are shown in Fig. 1-23. Note that no input condition exists that will leave the state of the flip-flop unchanged. Although a *D* flip-flop has the advantage of having only one input (excluding the *CP*), it has the disadvantage that its characteristic table does not have a "no change" condition $Q(t + 1) = Q(t)$. The "no change" condition can be accomplished either by disabling the clock pulses with an external AND gate or by feeding the output back into the input so clock pulses keep the state of the flip-flop unchanged.

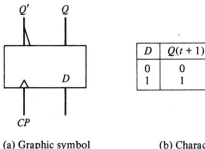

D	Q(t + 1)	Comments
0	0	Clear
1	1	Set

(a) Graphic symbol   (b) Characteristic table

Fig. 1-23   *D* flip-flop.

JK and T Flip-Flops

A *JK* flip-flop is a refinement of the *RS* flip-flop in that the indeterminate condition of the *RS* type is defined in the *JK* type. Inputs *J* and *K* behave like input *S* and *R* to set and clear the flip-flop, respectively. When inputs *J* and *K* are both equal to 1, a clock pulse switches the outputs of the flip-flop to its complement state, $Q(t + 1) = Q'(t)$. The graphic symbol and characteristic table of the *JK* flip-flop are shown in Fig. 1-24. Note that the *J* input is equivalent to the *set* condition while the *K* input produces the *clear* condition. In addition there are both *no change* and *complement* conditions in this type of flip-flop.

Another type of flip-flop found in textbooks is the *T* (toggle) flip-flop. This flip-flop, shown in Fig. 1-25, is obtained from a *JK* type when inputs *J* and *K*

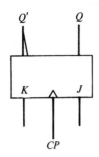

J	K	Q(t + 1)	Comments
0	0	$Q(t)$	No change
0	1	0	Clear
1	0	1	Set
1	1	$Q'(t)$	Complement

(a) Graphic symbol   (b) Characteristic table

Fig. 1-24   *JK* flip-flop.

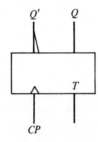

T	Q(t + 1)	Comments
0	$Q(t)$	No change
1	$Q'(t)$	Complement

(a) Graphic symbol   (b) Characteristic table

Fig. 1-25   *T* flip-flop.

are tied together. The T flip-flop, therefore, has only two conditions. When $T = 0$ ($J = K = 0$) a clock pulse does not change the state of the flip-flop. When $T = 1$ ($J = K = 1$) a clock pulse complements the state of the flip-flop.

Excitation Tables

The characteristic tables of flip-flops specify the next state when the inputs and the present state are known. During the design process we usually know the required transition from present state to next state and wish to find the flip-flop input conditions that will cause the required transition. For this reason we need a table that lists the required input combinations for a given change of state. Such a table is called a *flip-flop excitation table*.

Table 1-4 lists the excitation tables for the four types of flip-flops. Each table consists of two columns, $Q(t)$ and $Q(t + 1)$, and a column for each input to show how the required transition is achieved. There are four possible transitions from present state $Q(t)$ to next state $Q(t + 1)$. The required input conditions for each of these transitions are derived from the information available in the characteristic tables. The symbol X in the tables represents a don't-care condition; that is, it does not matter whether the input to the flip-flop is 0 or 1.

TABLE 1-4 Excitation Tables for the Four Types of Flip-Flops

$Q(t)$	$Q(t+1)$	S	R
0	0	0	X
0	1	1	0
1	0	0	1
1	1	X	0

(a) RS flip-flop

$Q(t)$	$Q(t+1)$	J	K
0	0	0	X
0	1	1	X
1	0	X	1
1	1	X	0

(b) JK flip-flop

$Q(t)$	$Q(t+1)$	D
0	0	0
0	1	1
1	0	0
1	1	1

(c) D flip-flop

$Q(t)$	$Q(t+1)$	T
0	0	0
0	1	1
1	0	1
1	1	0

(d) T flip-flop

The reason for the don't-care conditions in the excitation tables is that there are two ways of achieving the required transition. For example, in an RS flip-flop, a transition from present state of 0 to a next state of 0 can be achieved by having inputs S and R equal to 0 (to obtain *no change* when the clock pulse is applied), or by letting $S = 0$ and $R = 1$ to *clear* the flip-flop (although it is already cleared). In both cases S must be 0, but R is 0 in the first case and 1 in the second. Since the required transition will occur in either case, we mark the R input with an X and let the designer choose either 0 or 1 for the R input, whichever is more convenient.

1-6 SEQUENTIAL CIRCUITS

A sequential circuit is an interconnection of flip-flops and gates. The gates by themselves constitute a combinational circuit but when included with the flip-flops, the overall circuit is classified as a sequential circuit. A block diagram of a clocked sequential circuit is shown in Fig. 1-26. It consists of a combinational circuit and two JK clocked flip-flops. In general, any number or type of flip-flops may be encountered. The combinational circuit part receives binary signals from external inputs and from the outputs of flip-flops. It generates binary signals to external outputs and to inputs of flip-flops.

The gates in the combinational circuit determine not only the value of external outputs but also the binary value to be stored in the flip-flops after each clock pulse. The outputs of flip-flops, in turn, are applied to the combinational circuit inputs and determine the circuit's behavior. This process clearly demonstrates that the external outputs of a sequential circuit are functions of both external inputs and

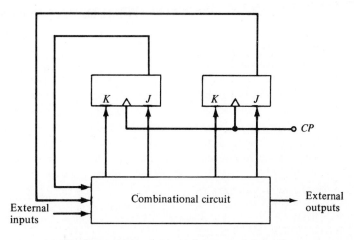

Fig. 1-26 Block diagram of a sequential circuit.

the present state of the flip-flops. Moreover, the next state of flip-flops is also a function of their present state and external inputs. Thus, a sequential circuit is specified by a time sequence of external inputs, external outputs, and internal flip-flop binary states.

Flip-Flop Input Functions

An example of a sequential circuit is shown in Fig. 1-27. It has one input variable x, one output variable y, and two clocked RS flip-flops. The AND gates and inverter form the combinational logic part of the circuit. The interconnections among the

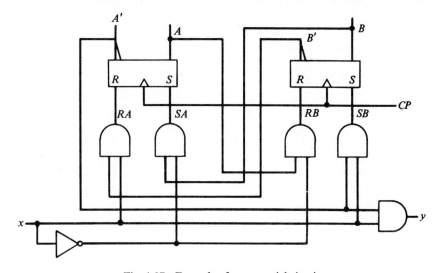

Fig. 1-27 Example of a sequential circuit.

gates in the combinational circuit can be specified by a set of Boolean functions. The part of the combinational circuit that generates the inputs to flip-flops are described by a set of Boolean functions called flip-flop *input functions* or *input equations*. We adopt the convention of using two letters to designate the binary variable of an input function. The first letter designates the type of flip-flop input and the second, the name of the flip-flop. Thus, in Fig. 1-27, we have four input functions designated by *RA*, *SA*, *RB*, *SB*. The first letter in each symbol denotes the *R* or *S* input of an *RS* flip-flop. The second letter is the symbol name of the flip-flop.

The input functions are Boolean functions for flip-flop input variables. They can be derived by inspection of the circuit. The output of the AND gate marked *RA* has inputs from B' and x. Since this output goes to the R input of flip-flop A, we write the input function as

$$RA = B'x$$

where RA is a binary variable having a two-letter symbol. Similarly, the other input functions are

$$SA = Bx'$$
$$RB = Ax'$$
$$SB = A'x$$

The sequential circuit also has an external output which is a function of the input variable and the state of one of its flip-flops. This output can be specified algebraically by the expression

$$y = A'x$$

From this example, we note that a flip-flop input function is a Boolean function for a combinational circuit. The two-letter designation is a binary variable name for an output of the combinational circuit. This output is always connected to a flip-flop input terminal.

State Table

The behavior of a sequential circuit is determined from the inputs, the outputs, and the state of its flip-flops. Both the outputs and next state are a function of the inputs and the present state. A sequential circuit is specified by a *state table* which relates outputs and next states as a function of inputs and present states. In clocked sequential circuits, the transition from present state to next state is activated by the presence of a clock pulse.

The state table for the sequential circuit of Fig. 1-27 is shown in Table 1-5. The present state designates the state of flip-flops before the occurrence of a clock pulse. At any given time, the present state of flip-flops A and B together with the input can be in one of eight possible binary values. These binary values are listed under the columns labeled present state and input. The next state lists the state of

TABLE 1-5 State Table for Circuit of Fig. 1-27

Present State		Input	Next State		Output
A	B	x	A	B	y
0	0	0	0	0	0
0	0	1	0	1	1
0	1	0	1	1	0
0	1	1	0	1	1
1	0	0	1	0	0
1	0	1	0	0	0
1	1	0	1	0	0
1	1	1	1	1	0

the flip-flops after the application of a clock pulse. The output column lists the value of the output variable.

The derivation of the state table is facilitated if the input functions of the flip-flops are obtained first. The input functions for the circuit have already been derived and are repeated again for convenience.

$$RA = B'x \qquad SA = Bx'$$
$$RB = Ax' \qquad SB = A'x$$

From these functions we note that flip-flop A is cleared if $Bx = 01$, it is set if $Bx = 10$, and remains unchanged otherwise. Going down column A in the next state, we write a 0 when $Bx = 01$, a 1 when $Bx = 10$ and transfer the value of A from the present state column to the next state column in the other rows. Similarly, from the input functions we note that flip-flop B is cleared if $Ax = 10$, set if $Ax = 01$, and unchanged otherwise. The binary values in the B column of the next state are derived from these conditions in a similar manner. By this procedure we can determine the next state values from knowledge of the present state and input values.

The entries for the output column are also a function of the present state and input. The output can be expressed by the Boolean function

$$y = A'x$$

which means that the output is equal to 1 if the present state of flip-flop A is 0 and if the input is 1. Output y is 0 otherwise. Therefore, y has a 1 in the two rows where $Ax = 01$ and a 0 in all other entries.

The state table of any sequential circuit is obtained by the procedure used in this example. In general, a sequential circuit with m flip-flops, n input variables, and p output variables will contain m columns for present state, n columns for inputs, m columns for next state, and p columns for outputs. The present state and input columns are combined and under them we list all the 2^{m+n} binary combinations of 1's and 0's. The next state and output columns are functions of the present state and input values and are derived directly from the circuit.

State Diagram

The information available in a state table may be represented graphically in a *state diagram*. In this diagram, a state is represented by a circle and the transition between states is indicated by directed lines connecting the circles. The state diagram of the sequential circuit of Fig. 1-27 is shown in Fig. 1-28. The binary number inside each

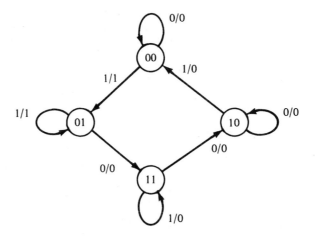

Fig. 1-28   State diagram for circuit of Fig. 1-27.

circle identifies the state of flip-flops A and B. The directed lines are labeled with two binary numbers separated by a slash. The input value that causes the state transition is labeled first; the number after the slash gives the value of the output during the present state. For example, the directed line from state 00 to 01 is labeled 1/1, meaning that the sequential circuit is in a present state 00 while $x = 1$ and $y = 1$. On the application of the next clock pulse, the circuit goes to next state 01. A directed line connecting a circle with itself indicates that no change of state occurs. The state diagram provides the same information as the state table and is obtained directly from Table 1-5.

   There is no difference between a state table and a state diagram except in the manner of representation. The state table is easier to derive from the circuit diagram and the state diagram follows directly from the state table. The state diagram gives a pictorial view of state transitions and is in a form suitable for human interpretation of the circuit operation. The state diagram is often used as the initial design specification of a sequential circuit.

Design Example

The procedure for designing sequential circuits will be demonstrated by a specific example. The design procedure consists of first translating the circuit specifications into a state diagram. The state diagram is then converted into a state table. From the state table we obtain the information for obtaining the circuit diagram.

We wish to design a clocked sequential circuit that goes through a sequence of repeated binary states 00, 01, 10, and 11 when an external input x is equal to 1. The state of the circuit remains unchanged when $x = 0$. This type of circuit is called a two-bit *binary counter* because the state sequence is identical to the count sequence of two binary digits. Input x is the control variable that specifies when the count should proceed.

The binary counter needs two flip-flops because two bits are specified for each state. The state diagram for the circuit is shown in Fig. 1-29. The diagram is drawn

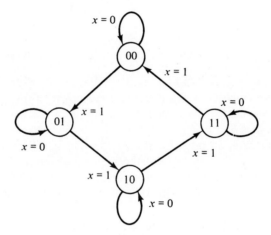

Fig. 1-29 State diagram for binary counter.

to show that the states of the circuit follow the binary count as long as $x = 1$. The state following 11 is 00 which causes the count to be repeated. If $x = 0$, the state of the circuit remains unchanged. This sequential circuit has no external outputs and therefore, only the input value is labeled in the diagram. The state of the flip-flops may be considered as the outputs of the circuit.

We have already assigned the symbol x to the input variable. Let us now assign the symbols A and B to the two flip-flops. The next state of A and B as a function of their present state and input x can be transferred from the state diagram into a state table. The first five columns of Table 1-6 constitute the state table. The entries for this table are obtained directly from the state diagram.

The *excitation table* of a sequential circuit is an extension of the state table. This extension consists of a list of flip-flop input excitations that will cause the required

TABLE 1-6 Excitation Table for Binary Counter

State table

Present State		Input	Next State		Flip-Flop Input Conditions			
A	B	x	A	B	JA	KA	JB	KB
0	0	0	0	0	0	X	0	X
0	0	1	0	1	0	X	1	X
0	1	0	0	1	0	X	X	0
0	1	1	1	0	1	X	X	1
1	0	0	1	0	X	0	0	X
1	0	1	1	1	X	0	1	X
1	1	0	1	1	X	0	X	0
1	1	1	0	0	X	1	X	1

Inputs of combinational circuit

Outputs of combinational circuit

state transitions. The flip-flop input conditions are a function of the type of flip-flop used. If we employ JK flip-flops we need columns for the J and K inputs of each flip-flop. We denote the inputs of flip-flop A by JA and KA, and those of flip-flop B by JB and KB.

The excitation table for the JK flip-flop specified in Table 1-4(b) is now used to derive the excitation table of the sequential circuit. For example, in the first row of Table 1-6, we have a transition for flip-flop A from 0 in the present state to 0 in the next state. In Table 1-4(b), we find that a transition of states from 0 to 0 requires that input $J = 0$ and input $K = X$. So 0 and X are copied in the first row under JA and KA, respectively. Since the first row also shows a transition for flip-flop B from 0 in the present state to 0 in the next state, 0 and X are copied in the first row under JB and KB. The second row of Table 1-6 shows a transition for flip-flop B from 0 in the present state to 1 in the next state. From Table 1-4(b) we find that a transition from 0 to 1 requires that input $J = 1$ and input $K = X$. So 1 and X are copied in the second row under JB and KB, respectively. This process is continued for each row of the table and for each flip-flop, with the input conditions as specified in Table 1-4(b) being copied into the proper row of the particular flip-flop being considered.

Let us now pause and consider the information available in an excitation table such as Table 1-6. We know that a sequential circuit consists of a number of flip-flops and a combinational circuit. Figure 1-26 shows two JK flip-flops and a box to represent the combinational circuit. From the block diagram, it is clear that the outputs of the combinational circuit go to flip-flop inputs. The inputs to the combinational circuit are the external inputs and the present state values of the flip-flops. Moreover, the Boolean functions that specify a combinational circuit are derived from a truth table that shows the input-output relations of the circuit.

The entries that list the combinational circuit *inputs* are specified under the present state and input columns and the combinational circuit *outputs* are specified under the flip-flop input columns. Thus, as shown in Table 1-6, an excitation table transforms a state diagram to a truth table needed for the design of the combinational circuit part of the sequential circuit.

The simplified Boolean functions for the combinational circuit can now be derived. The inputs are the variables A, B, and x; the outputs are the variables JA, KA, JB, and KB. The information from the excitation table is transferred into the maps of Fig. 1-30, where the four simplified flip-flop input functions are derived:

$$JA = Bx \qquad KA = Bx$$
$$JB = x \qquad KB = x$$

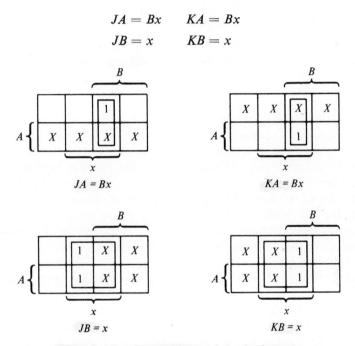

Fig. 1-30   Maps for combinational circuit of counter.

The logic diagram is drawn in Fig. 1-31 and consists of two flip-flops and an AND gate. Note that inputs J and K determine the transition that will occur when a clock pulse (CP) arrives. If both J and K are equal to 0, a clock pulse will have no effect, that is, the state of the flip-flops will not change. Thus, when $x = 0$, the state of the flip-flops remains unchanged even though clock pulses are continuously applied.

Design Procedure

The design of sequential circuits follows the outline described in the previous example. The behavior of the circuit is first formulated in a state diagram. The number of flip-flops needed for the circuit is determined from the number of bits listed within the circles of the state diagram. The number of inputs for the circuit is specified along

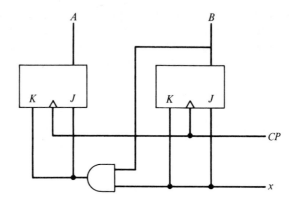

Fig. 1-31 Logic diagram of binary counter.

the directed lines between the circles. We then assign letters to designate all flip-flops and input variables and proceed to obtain the state table.

For m flip-flops and n inputs, the state table will consist of m columns for the present state, n columns for the inputs and m columns for the next state. The number of rows in the table will be up to 2^{m+n}, one row for each binary combination of present state and inputs. For each row we list the next state as specified by the state diagram.

Next, the flip-flop type to be used in the circuit is chosen. A two letter symbol for flip-flop inputs may be used to designate the outputs of the combinational circuit part of the circuit. By this convention, the first letter designates the type of input and the second letter the name of the flip-flop.

The state table is then extended into an excitation table by including columns for each input of each flip-flop. The excitation table for the type of flip-flop in use can be found in Table 1-4. From the information available in this table and by inspecting present to next state transitions in the state table, we obtain the information for the flip-flop input conditions in the excitation table.

The truth table for the combinational circuit part of the sequential circuit is available in the excitation table. The present state and input columns constitute the *inputs* in the truth table. The flip-flop input conditions constitute the *outputs* in the truth table. By means of map simplification techniques, we obtain a set of flip-flop input functions for the combinational circuit. Each flip-flop input function specifies a logic diagram whose output must be connected to one of the flip-flop inputs. The combinational circuit so obtained together with the flip-flops constitute the sequential circuit.

The outputs of flip-flops are often considered to be also the outputs of the sequential circuit. However, the combinational circuit may also contain external outputs. In such a case, the Boolean functions for the external outputs are derived from the state table by combinational circuit design techniques.

A set of flip-flop input functions specifies a sequential circuit in algebraic form. The procedure for obtaining the logic diagram from a set of flip-flop input functions

34

is a straightforward process. First draw the flip-flops (specified by the second letter of the two letter symbols) and label all their inputs and outputs. Then draw the combinational circuit from the Boolean functions given by the flip-flop input functions. Finally, connect outputs of flip-flops to inputs in the combinational circuit and outputs of the combinational circuit to flip-flop inputs.

1-7 CONCLUDING REMARKS

This chapter introduces the basic digital circuits that serve as building blocks for the construction of digital computers or any digital system. The chapter also presents the fundamental concepts needed for the design of digital systems, especially when they are constructed with individual gates and flip-flops.

In order to keep the book within reasonable bounds, it was necessary to limit the discussion of digital system design to one introductory chapter. The justification for this approach is that the design of digital computers takes on a different dimension when integrated circuits are employed instead of individual gates and flip-flops. Integrated circuits provide entire digital components in small packages so the designer does not have to deal with individual gates and flip-flops but instead with the interaction between integrated circuit components. The next chapter presents a number of digital functions useful in the design and construction of digital computers. The rest of the book uses these functions to investigate the organization and design of digital computers.

The basic concepts presented in this chapter are, nevertheless, important for the understanding of the functions that integrated circuits provide. Moreover, a computer designer with the responsibility of making hardware work must have extensive knowledge of digital system design concepts. Although the material presented in this chapter is sufficient for the understanding of the subject matter in this book, the reader interested in digital system design is advised to acquire more information from any of the books listed in the reference section.

REFERENCES

1. MANO, M. M., *Digital Logic and Computer Design*. Englewood Cliffs, N.J.: Prentice-Hall, Inc., 1979.

2. LEE, S. C., *Digital Circuits and Logic Design*. Englewood Cliffs, N.J.: Prentice-Hall, Inc., 1976.

3. RHYNE, V. T., *Fundamentals of Digital System Design*. Englewood Cliffs, N.J.: Prentice-Hall, Inc., 1973.

4. PEATMAN, J. B., *Digital Hardware Design*. New York: McGraw-Hill Book Company, 1980.

5. ROTH, C. H., JR., *Fundamentals of Logic Design*, 2nd ed. St. Paul, Minn.: West Publishing Co., 1979.

6. FLETCHER, W. I., *An Engineering Approach to Digital Design*. Englewood Cliffs, N.J.: Prentice-Hall, Inc., 1980.

7. BOOTH, T. L., *Digital Networks and Computer Systems*, 2nd ed. New York: John Wiley & Sons, Inc., 1978.

8. WINKEL, D., AND F. PROSSER, *The Art of Digital Design*. Englewood Cliffs, N.J.: Prentice-Hall, Inc., 1980.

PROBLEMS

1-1.   Obtain the truth tables for the logic diagrams of Fig. 1-6 and show that the two truth tables are identical.

1-2.   Verify the two DeMorgan's theorems by means of truth tables.

1-3.   (a) Show that the following circuit of NAND gates produces the exclusive-OR function.
        (b) Replace the NAND gates by NOR gates and show that the exclusive-NOR function (equivalence) is obtained.

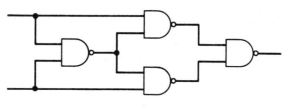

Fig. P1-3

1-4.   Using the Boolean algebra relations of Table 1-1, show that

$$x + xy = x$$

List the relation used in each step.

1-5.   Simplify the following Boolean functions algebraically.

		Answers
(a)	$xy + xy'$	x
(b)	$(x + y)(x + y')$	x
(c)	$xz + xyz'$	$x(y + z)$
(d)	$(A + B)'(A' + B')'$	0
(e)	$A + A'B + A'B'$	1

1-6.   Obtain the truth table for the function $F = AB' + B'C + A'C$.

1-7.   Simplify the following Boolean function in sum of products form by means of a four variable map. Draw the logic diagram with (a) AND-OR gates; (b) NAND gates.

$$F(w, x, y, z) = \Sigma\,(0, 2, 8, 9, 10, 11, 14, 15)$$

1-8. Simplify the following Boolean function in product of sums form by means of a four variable map. Draw the logic diagram with (a) OR-AND gates; (b) NOR gates.

$$F(A, B, C, D) = \Sigma (2, 3, 4, 5, 6, 7, 11, 14, 15)$$

1-9. Simplify F together with its don't-care condition d in (a) sum of products form; (b) product of sums form.

$$F(A, B, C, D) = \Sigma (0, 1, 2, 8, 9, 12, 13)$$
$$d(A, B, C, D) = \Sigma (10, 11, 14, 15)$$

1-10. Implement the following Boolean function with NAND gates. Use inverters to complement inputs.

$$F(x, y, z) = \Sigma (0, 2, 4, 5)$$

1-11. By algebraic manipulation show that the S output of a full-adder is the exclusive-OR (odd function) of its three inputs.

1-12. A majority function is a digital circuit whose output is 1 if and only if the majority of the inputs are 1. The output is 0 otherwise.
(a) Obtain the truth table of a three-input majority function.
(b) Show that the circuit of a majority function can be obtained with four NAND gates.
(c) Show that a full-adder circuit consists of a three-input exclusive-OR and a three-input majority function.

1-13. Two digital functions are enabled by control variables C_1 and C_2. The Boolean functions for the control signals are

$$C_1 = ABT_1 + A'B'T_2$$
$$C_2 = AT_1 + B'T_2$$

Under what conditions of input variables A, B and timing variables T_1, T_2 will the two digital functions be enabled at the same time?

1-14. Obtain the simplified Boolean functions of the full-adder in sum of products form and draw the logic diagram using NAND gates.

1-15. Design a combinational circuit that accepts a three-bit number and generates an output binary number equal to the square of the input number.

1-16. The difference between a full-adder and a full-subtractor is in the Boolean function that generates the carry or borrow. Use a control variable w and obtain the logic diagram of a circuit that functions as a full-adder when $w = 0$ and as a full-subtractor when $w = 1$.

1-17. A set-dominate flip-flop has set (S) and reset (R) inputs. It differs from a conventional RS flip-flop in that an input of $S = R = 1$ results in setting the flip-flop. Obtain the characteristic table and excitation table of the set-dominate flip-flop.

1-18. Show that a JK flip-flop can be converted to a D flip-flop with an inverter between the J and K inputs.

1-19. Design a two-bit countdown counter. This is a sequential circuit with two flip-flops and one input x. When $x = 0$, the state of the flip-flops does not change. When $x = 1$ the state sequence is 11, 10, 01, 00, 11, and so on.

1-20. Design the circuit and draw the logic diagram of the sequential circuit specified by the following state diagram. Use an RS flip-flop.

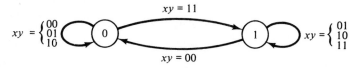

Fig. P1-20

1-21. A sequential circuit is specified by the following flip-flop input functions. Draw the logic diagram of the circuit.

$$JA = Bx' \qquad KA = Bx$$
$$JB = x \qquad KB = A \oplus x$$

Integrated Circuits
and Digital Functions

2-1 DIGITAL INTEGRATED CIRCUITS

An integrated circuit (IC) is a small silicon semiconductor crystal called a *chip* containing electrical components such as transistors, diodes, resistors, and capacitors. The various components are interconnected inside the chip to form an electronic circuit. The chip is mounted in a metal or plastic package and connections are welded to external pins to form the IC. Integrated circuits differ from conventional discrete component circuits in that individual components cannot be separated or disconnected and the circuit inside the IC package is accessed only through its external pins. The benefits derived from ICs as compared to circuits with discrete components are: (1) a substantial reduction in size, (2) a substantial reduction in cost, (3) a reduction in power requirements, (4) a higher reliability against failures, (5) an increase in operating speed, and (6) a reduction of externally wired connections.

Integrated circuits are classified as being in one of two general categories, *analog* or *digital*. Analog integrated circuits operate with continuous waveforms to provide electronic functions such as operational amplifiers, voltage comparators, and voltage regulators. Digital integrated circuits operate with binary signals and provide such digital functions as gates, flip-flops, registers, counters, adders, memories, and arithmetic calculators. Here we will be concerned only with digital integrated circuits.

Because of their many advantages, integrated circuits are used exclusively to provide various digital functions needed in the design of computer systems. In order to understand the architecture of computer systems it is very important that one should be familair with the different digital functions commonly encountered in integrated circuit packages. For this reason, the most basic functions are introduced in this chapter and many other IC digital functions are explained in succeeding chapters.

Logic Circuit Families

Digital integrated circuits are classified not only by their function but also by their being members of a specific logic circuit family. Each logic family has its own basic electronic circuit upon which more complex circuits and functions are developed. The basic circuit in each family is either a NOR or a NAND gate. The topology of this basic circuit, that is, the electronic components employed and their interconnection, is usually used to derive the name of the family. Many different logic families of digital integrated circuits have been introduced commercially. The ones that have achieved widespread popularity are:

TTL	Transistor-transistor logic
ECL	Emitter-coupled logic
MOS	Metal-oxide semiconductor
CMOS	Complementary metal-oxide semiconductor

TTL has an extensive list of digital functions and is the most popular logic family. ECL is used for systems requiring high-speed operation. MOS is used in circuits requiring high component density, and CMOS is used in systems requiring low power consumption.

The characteristics of digital logic families are usually compared by analyzing the circuit of the basic gate in each family. The most important parameters that are evaluated and compared are listed below.

1. *Fan-out* specifies the number of standard loads that the output of a standard gate can drive without impairing its normal operation. A standard load is usually defined to be the load (the amount of current) needed by an input of another similar standard gate.

2. *Power-dissipation* is the power consumed by the gate which must be available from the power supply.

3. *Propagation delay* is the average transition delay time for the signal to propagate from input to output when the binary signals change in value. The operating speed is inversely proportional to the propagation delay.

4. *Noise margin* is the minimum noise voltage that causes an undesirable change in the circuit output.

Transistor-Transistor Logic—TTL

The basic circuit for the TTL logic family is the NAND gate. There are many versions (sometimes referred to as *series*) of the TTL gate. The names of five versions are listed in Table 2-1 together with their respective propagation delay and power dissipation. The standard TTL gate was the first version of the TTL family. Additional improvements were added as TTL technology progressed. In the low-power version, the propagation delay is sacrificed to provide a reduced power dissipation. In the high-

TABLE 2-1 Characteristics of Five TTL Versions

Name of Version	Abbre-viation	Propaga-tion Delay (ns)	Power Dissipa-tion (mW)	Speed-Power Product (pJ)
Standard	TTL	10	10	100
Low-power	LTTL	33	1	33
High-speed	HTTL	6	22	132
Schottky	STTL	3	19	57
Low-power Schottky	LSTTL	9.5	2	19

speed version, the power dissipation is increased to reduce the propagation delay. The Schottky TTL is a later improvement that increases the speed of operation without excessive increases in dissipated power. Finally, the low-power Schottky version sacrifices some speed for reduced power dissipation. It compares favorably with the standard TTL in speed and requires considerably less power. The fan-out of TTL gates is 10 when the standard loads are of the same circuit version. The noise margin is better than 0.4 V with a typical value of 1 V.

Each of the five TTL versions comes in one of three output circuit configurations commonly referred to as:

1. Open-collector output.

2. Totem-pole output.

3. Tri-state output.

The open-collector gate needs an external resistor for proper operation. This resistor is connected to the IC package externally. Outputs of two or more collector gates can be connected to a common resistor to achieve an external AND function. This is shown in Fig. 2-1 for two open-collector NAND gates. The AND gate formed by connecting together the two outputs is called a *wire-AND* function. The AND gate is drawn with the lines going through the center of the gate to distinguish

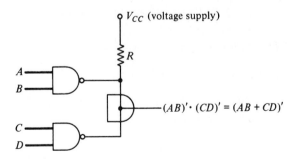

Fig. 2-1 Wire-AND connection of two open collector TTL NAND gates.

it from a conventional gate. The wire-AND gate is not a physical gate but only a symbol to designate the function obtained from the indicated connection. Note that two open-collector gates connected to a common resistor produce the so-called AND-OR-INVERT function $(AB + CD)'$.

The totem-pole output is the standard output of a TTL gate and is specifically designed to reduce the propagation delay in the circuit and to provide sufficient output power for a high fan-out. Totem-pole outputs cannot be connected together to form an AND function as in open-collector outputs.

The tri-state output exhibits three output-state conditions. Two of the states are signals equivalent to binary 1 and 0, similar to a conventional gate. The third state is a high-impedance state. This means, for all practical purposes, that the circuit behaves as if the output is disabled. As a consequence, the output cannot affect or be affected by any external signal at its terminals. The third state is controlled by a separate input as shown in Fig. 2-2. When the control input C is 1, the gate behaves like a

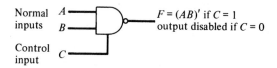

Normal inputs A, B

Control input C

$F = (AB)'$ if $C = 1$
output disabled if $C = 0$

Fig. 2-2 Symbol for tri-state NAND gate.

normal NAND gate providing states of 0 and 1. When the control input is 0, the output is disabled irrespective of the values of the normal inputs. Tri-state gates are also available with the control input having a complementary effect, that is, disabling the gate when the control input is 1 and enabling it when it is 0. The high-impedance state of a tri-state gate allows the possibility of making a direct wire connection from many outputs to a common bus line with only one output having access to the bus at any given time. The gate having access to the common output line will be the one whose control is enabled while all other outputs are disabled by their respective control inputs.

Emitter-Coupled Logic—ECL

The transistors in the ECL gates operate in a so-called *nonsaturation state*, a condition that allows the achievement of propagation delays of 1 to 2 ns. This logic family has the lowest propagation delay compared with any other logic family and is used mostly in systems requiring very high speed operation.

The basic circuit of the ECL logic family is a NOR gate, but many ECL ICs provide an output for the OR function as well. The symbol for the ECL gate is shown in Fig. 2-3. Two outputs are available, one for the NOR function and the other for

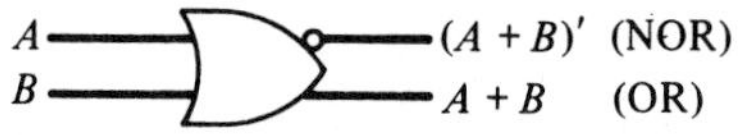

A, B

$(A + B)'$ (NOR)
$A + B$ (OR)

Fig. 2-3 Graphic symbol for ECL gate.

the OR function. The outputs of two or more ECL gates can be connected externally (with or without a resistor) to form a *wire-OR* function. This property may be utilized to form other logic functions by connecting the outputs of gates. As shown in Fig. 2-4, the wire-OR connection of two NOR gates produces an OR-AND-INVERT function.

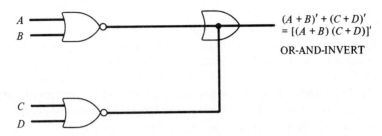

$(A + B)' + (C + D)'$
$= [(A + B)(C + D)]'$

OR-AND-INVERT

Fig. 2-4　Wire-OR connection in ECL gates.

The ECL logic family has a variety of versions. The propagation delay of a typical gate is between 1 and 2 ns, depending on the version used. The power dissipation is about 25 mW; the fan-out greater than 25. The noise margin is the lowest of all families and is about 0.2 V.

Metal-Oxide Semiconductor—MOS

MOS is a unipolar transistor that depends upon the flow of only one type of electronic carrier which may be electrons (N-channel) or holes (P-channel). This is in contrast to the bipolar transistor used in TTL and ECL gates, where both carriers exist during normal operation. A P-channel MOS, referred to as PMOS, requires negative voltages for its operation. An N-channel MOS, referred to as NMOS, requires positive voltages for its operation. Complementary MOS, or CMOS, uses one PMOS and one NMOS transistor, connected in a complementary fashion. CMOS requires positive voltages for its operation. The three most important advantages of MOS over bipolar are as follows.

1. High packing density that allows more circuits to be placed in a given chip area.

2. Simpler processing techniques when fabricated in integrated circuits and therefore more economical to manufacture.

3. MOS gate power consumption is much less than the bipolar gate. This makes MOS circuits more economical to operate.

PMOS and NMOS ICs do not come with individual gates; they are mostly used in ICs that provide digital functions such as memories and microprocessors, CMOS ICs come in a variety of functions similar to TTL and ECL.

Gate Complexity

Each digital logic family is recognized by its basic NOR or NAND gate. The basic gate is the building block from which more complex functions are constructed. For example, a latch circuit is constructed from two NAND gates or two NOR gates connected back to back. A master-slave flip-flop is obtained from the interconnection of nine basic gates. A register is obtained from the interconnection of flip-flops and NAND gates. Each logic family has a catalog of integrated circuit packages that lists the digital functions available in the logic family. It is customary to classify the gate complexity of an IC in one of the four following categories.

1. An SSI (small-scale integration) device has a complexity of less than 10 gates. These are ICs that contain several gates or flip-flops in one package.

2. An MSI (medium-scale integration) device has a complexity of 10 to 100 gates. These are ICs that provide elementary logic functions such as registers, counters, and decoders.

3. An LSI (large-scale integration) device has a complexity of more than 100 gates. Examples of LSI ICs are large memories, microprocessors, and calculator chips.

4. A VLSI (very large scale integration) device has a complexity of thousands of gates. Examples are large memory arrays and complex micoprocessor and microcomputer chips.

Three logic families, TTL, ECL, and CMOS, have a large number of SSI and MSI packages. SSI ICs are those that contain a small number of NAND, NOR, flip-flops, or other type gates, in one package. The limit on the number of digital circuits in SSI devices is the number of pins in the package. A 14 pin package for example, can accommodate only two-input NAND gates. This is because each gate requires three external pins (two for inputs and one for output), for a total of $4 \times 3 = 12$ pins. The remaining two pins are needed for supplying power to the circuits.

One will appreciate the variety of MSI functions available in IC packages by looking at a data book or catalog provided by a vendor. A typical data book may list over 100 different MSI functions. When these functions are divided into categories, one may find about 15 different arithmetic elements, over 20 types of registers, about 10 types of memories, 10 decorders, 5 multiplexers, 20 counters, and other assorted functions. The succeeding sections of this chapter present the most common digital functions encountered in IC packages. Other digital functions are explained in succeeding chapters.

TTL, ECL, and CMOS have many SSI and MSI functions and some LSI functions as well. On the other hand, MOS ICs very seldom come as SSI or even as MSI. Because of the high density of transistors that can be fabricated on a given area of silicon, MOS is mostly used to supply a variety of LSI functions. LSI functions available in MOS are shift registers, memory units, microprocessors, and electronic calculator chips.

IC Packages

Digital integrated circuits come in two types of packages, the *flat* package and the *dual-in-line* (DIP) package. The latter is the most widespread type used for digital ICs because of its low price and easy installation on printed circuit boards. The envelope of the IC package is usually made of plastic or ceramic. Most packages have standard sizes and the number of pins range from 14 to 64. Each IC has a numerical designation number which is printed on the surface of the package for identification. The numbers are assigned by the semiconductor manufacturer. Each vendor publishes a data book or catalog that provides the necessary information concerning the various products.

TTL ICs are usually distingushed by their numerical designation as the 5400 and 7400 series. The former has a wide operating temperature range, suitable for military use, and the latter has a narrower temperature range, suitable for industrial use. The numerical designation of 7400 series, for example, means that IC packages are numbered as 7400, 7401, 7402,..., 74181, and so on. Some vendors make available TTL ICs with different numerical designation such as 9000 or 8000 series.

The most common ECL version is designated by the 10000 series. That of CMOS is the 4000 series (also known as COS/MOS, or complementary symmerty MOS). Other versions of CMOS ICs are the 54C00 and 74C00 series. The ICs in these series are compatible with the TTL series and are pin-to-pin replaceable with their TTL counterpart 5400 and 7400 numbers.

In summary, a digital integrated circuit is identified by all of the following designations:

1. The logic circuit family type.

2. The circuit function name, such as register, memory, and so on.

3. The circuit complexity, that is, SSI, MSI, or LSI.

4. The type of package and number of pins.

5. The IC identification number and the name of the vendor.

2-2 IC FLIP-FLOPS AND REGISTER

The digital function commonly used for holding binary information in a digital computer is called a *register*. A register is a group of binary storage cells. A group of flip-flops constitutes a register since a flip-flop is a binary cell capable of storing one bit of information. In addition to the flip-flops, a register may have combinational gates that perform certain data processing tasks. In its broadest definition, a register con-sists of a group of flip-flops and the gates that effect their transition. The flip-flops hold binary information while the gates control when and how the information is transferred into the register.

Master-Slave Flip-Flop

The flip-flops in integrated circuit registers are usually constructed internally from two separate flip-flop circuits. One circuit serves as a master and the other as a slave and the overall circuit is referred to as a *master-slave* flip-flop. The logic diagram of an *RS* master-slave flip-flop is shown in Fig. 2-5. It consists of a master flip-flop, a slave flip-flop and an inverter. When the clock pulse *CP* is 0, the output of the inverter is 1. Since the clock input of the slave (the terminal marked with a small triangle) is 1, the flip-flop is enabled and output Q is equal to Y while Q' is equal to Y'. The master flip-flop is disabled because $CP = 0$. When the pulse becomes 1, the information then at the external R and S inputs is transmitted to the master flip-flop. The slave flip-flop however is isolated as long as the pulse is at its 1 level because the output of the inverter is 0. When the pulse returns to 0, the master flip-flop is isolated, pre-venting the external inputs from affecting it. The slave flip-flop then goes to the same state as the master flip-flop.

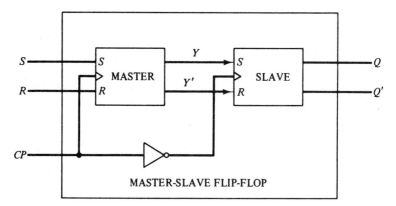

Fig. 2-5   Logic diagram of a master-slave flip-flop.

The timing relations shown in Fig. 2-6 illustrate the sequence of events that occur in a master-slave flip-flop. Assume that the flip-flop is in the clear state prior to the occurrence of a pulse so that $Y = 0$ and $Q = 0$. The input conditions are $S = 1$, $R = 0$, and the next clock pulse should change the flip-flop to the set state with $Q = 1$. During the pulse transition from 0 to 1, the master flip-flop is set and changes Y to 1. The slave flip-flop is not affected because its CP input is 0. Since the master flip-flop is an internal circuit, its change of state is not noticeable in the outputs Q and Q'. When the pulse returns to 0, the information from the master is allowed to pass through to the slave making the external output $Q = 1$. Note that the external S input can be

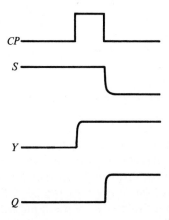

Fig. 2-6 Timing relations in a master-slave flip-flop.

changed at the same time that the pulse goes to 0. This is because once the *CP* reaches 0, the master is disabled and its *R* and *S* inputs have no influence until the next clock pulse occurs. Thus, in a master-slave flip-flop, it is possible to switch the output of the flip-flop and its input information with the same clock pulse.

Now consider a digital system containing many master-slave flip-flops with outputs of some flip-flops going to inputs of other flip-flops. Assume that clock pulse inputs to all flip-flops are synchronized and occur at the same time. At the beginning of each clock pulse, some of the master elements will change state, but all flip-flop outputs will remain at their previous values. After the clock pulse returns to 0, some of the outputs will change state and none of these new states will have an effect on any of the master elements until the next clock pulse. Thus the state of flip-flops in the system can be changed simultaneously during the same clock pulse even though outputs of flip-flops are connected to inputs of flip-flops. This is possible because the new state appears at the output terminals only after the clock pulse has returned to 0. Therefore, the binary content of one register can be transferred to a second register and the content of the second register transferred to the first, and both transfers can occur during the same clock pulse.

The behavior of the master-slave flip-flops just described dictates that state changes in all registers coincide with the 1 to 0 transition of clock pulses. However, some IC master-slave flip-flops change state on the 0 to 1 transition of clock pulses. This happens in registers whose master-slave flip-flops receive the complement of the clock pulse (through a second inverter) so that a 1 to 0 pulse transition affects the master and a 0 to 1 transition affects the slave.

Other IC Flip-Flops

Another type of flip-flop that synchronizes the state change during a clock pulse transition is the *edge-triggered* flip-flop. In this type of flip-flop, output transitions occur at a specific level of the clock pulse. When the pulse input level exceeds this threshold level, the inputs are locked out so that the flip-flop is unresponsive to further changes in inputs until the clock pulse returns to 0 and another pulse occurs. Some edge-triggered flip-flops cause a transition on the rising edge of the clock pulse (0 to 1 transition) and others cause a transition on the falling edge (1 to 0 transition). Flip-flops commonly available in IC form are of the above four varieties. Most digital systems are constructed using master-slave and edge-triggered flip-flops having one type of transition so complete synchronization is achieved. For the sake of uniformity, this book assumes that all flip-flops are of the master-slave type with output transitions during the falling edge of the clock pulse.

Flip-flops available in IC packages will sometimes provide special input terminals for setting or clearing the flip-flop asynchronously. These inputs are usually called "preset" and "clear." They affect the flip-flop on a positive (or negative) swing of the input signal without the need of a clock pulse. These inputs are useful for bringing the flip-flops to an initial state prior to its clocked operation.

Register with Parallel Load

It was mentioned previously that a register is a group of flip-flops together with gates that affect the flip-flop transitions. The number of flip-flops in the register dictates the number of bits stored in it. An n-bit register consists of n flip-flops and can store any binary information containing n bits. An example of a four-bit register is shown in Fig. 2-7. It consists of four flip-flops and a variety of gates. When included in an IC package it will have four outputs A_1 to A_4, four inputs I_1 to I_4 and three common control inputs. Each control input has a buffer (a noninverting amplifier) whose purpose is to reduce the loading of the input control signal. This is because each control input is connected to only one buffer input instead of to the four gate inputs that would have been required if the buffer gate were not present.

The *clear* input goes to a special terminal in each flip-flop (marked with a circle). When this terminal goes to 0, the flip-flop is cleared asynchronously, that is, without the requirement of a clock pulse. This input is useful for bringing all flip-flops in the register to an initial cleared state prior to its clocked operation. The clear input must go to the 1 state during normal clocked operations.

The clock pulse input of the register receives continuous synchronized pulses which are applied to all flip-flops. The CP input in each flip-flop is marked by a small triangle. The small circle below the triangle indicates that flip-flop output transitions occur during the falling edge of the clock pulse (1 to 0 transition). However, whether an output transition occurs or not is dictated by the *load* input and the state of inputs I_1 through I_4.

The two AND gates and inverter in each flip-flop determine the values of the R and S inputs. If the *load* input is 0, both R and S are 0 and no change of state can occur with any clock pulse. Thus, the *load* input is a control variable which can prevent any information change in the register as long as its input is 0. When the *load* input goes to 1, the inputs I_1 to I_4 determine what binary information will be transferred into the register on the next clock pulse. For each I that is equal to 1, the corresponding flip-

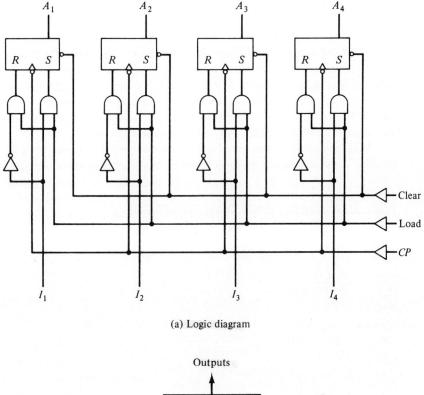

(a) Logic diagram

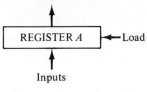

(b) Block diagram

Fig. 2-7 Four-bit register with parallel load.

flop inputs are maintained at $S = 1$ and $R = 0$. For each I that is equal to 0, the corresponding flip-flop inputs are $R = 1$ and $S = 0$. This information is transferred into the register, provided the *load* input is 1, the *clear* input is 1, and a clock pulse occurs. This type of transfer is designated as a *parallel load* transfer because all bits of the register are loaded simultaneously.

When this register is enclosed inside an IC package it will have four output terminals, four input terminals, three control terminals, and two or three power supply terminals. It can, therefore, be enclosed in a standard 14-pin package. The register can be expanded to five bits in a 16-pin package or to nine bits in a 24-pin package. If more than four bits are needed for the register, two or more 14-pin ICs will have to be used. Thus, an 8-bit register requires two ICs and a 16-bit register requires four ICs.

Digital computers use a considerable number of registers with parallel load capabilities. To avoid drawing the logic diagram of the register every time it is encountered, we will adopt the convention of drawing its block diagram instead. As shown in Fig. 2-7(b), the block diagram consists of a rectangular box with the name of the register written inside. One line is used to designate the inputs and one line to designate the outputs. The number of bits of the register will be evident from its function within the computer. The *CP* and clear terminals are not shown in the block diagram but they will be assumed to be included in all registers requiring clocked operations and an initial cleared state. The *load* input is included in the diagram to specify the type of control available in this particular register. It will be shown subsequently that it is possible to have registers with more or different types of control inputs.

2-3 DECODERS AND MULTIPLEXERS

A *decoder* is a digital function that converts binary information from one coded form to another. For example, a BCD-to-seven-segment decoder converts a decimal digit in BCD (binary-coded decimal) into seven outputs for the selection of the set of segments needed to display a decimal digit. The decoders presented in this section are called n-to-2^n line decoders and their purpose is to generate the 2^n minterms of n input variables. These decoders form a combinational circuit with n input variables and 2^n output variables. For each binary input combination of 1's and 0's there is one, and only one, output line that assumes the value of 1. This type of decoder is found in many applications and is used extensively in the design of digital systems.

Decoders

An example of a 2 by 4 decoder is shown in Fig. 2-8. It consists of four AND gates and two inverters. A decoder has as many outputs as there are possible binary input

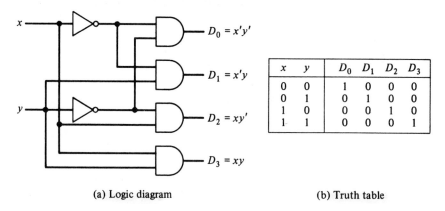

x	y	D_0	D_1	D_2	D_3
0	0	1	0	0	0
0	1	0	1	0	0
1	0	0	0	1	0
1	1	0	0	0	1

(a) Logic diagram   (b) Truth table

Fig. 2-8 2 by 4 decoder.

combinations. In this particular example, the two inputs x and y can be in one of four possible binary values, as shown in the truth table accompanying the diagram. Observe that the output variables are mutually exclusive and that only one output can be equal to 1 at any one time. The output whose value is equal to 1 represents the minterm combination in the input lines.

Integrated circuit decoders may use NAND or NOR gates instead of AND gates. In such a case, the outputs are the complement of the values listed in the truth table. The minterm combination of the input variables is then distingushed by the output whose value is 0 while all other outputs are equal to 1.

It is sometimes convenient to include an enable input with a decoder to control the circuit operation. For example, a 3 by 8 decoder with an enable input is shown in Fig. 2-9. All outputs will be equal to 0 if the enable input is 0. This occurs because a 0

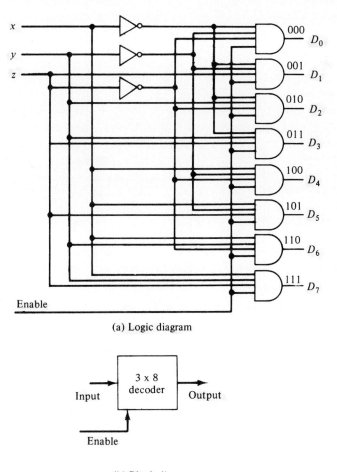

(a) Logic diagram

(b) Block diagram

Fig. 2-9　3 by 8 decoder with enable input.

input to an AND gate produces a 0 output, no matter what the other input values are. When the enable input is 1, the circuit operates as a conventional decoder. Decoders will be used extensively in subsequent discussion. In order to avoid drawing the logic diagram every time a decoder is needed, we will draw its block diagram instead, as shown in Fig. 2-9(b). The enable input may or not be included in the block diagram, depending on the particular application.

The size of a decoder in an IC package is usually depending on the number of external pins in the package. For example, two 2 by 4 decoders can be inserted in a 14-pin package. One 3 by 8 decoder with an enable input can be inserted in a 14-pin package (eight outputs, three inputs, one enable, and two pins for power supply). It is possible to provide three enable inputs if the package contains 16 pins.

Binary information stored in a register is said to be decoded if there exist 2^n distinct output lines, one for each of the states that the register can assume. The binary information held in a four-bit register can be decoded with a 4 by 16 decoder. It is also possible to employ two 3 by 8 decoders with enable inputs and connect them to the register as shown in Fig. 2-10. The register has four outputs labeled A_0 to A_3, with

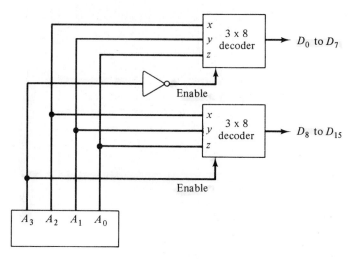

Fig. 2-10   A 4 by 16 decoder constructed with two 3 by 8 decoders.

A_3 holding the high-order bit. When $A_3 = 0$, the enable input of the bottom decoder is 0 and the top is 1. This condition enables the outputs of the top decoder but produces 0's in the outputs of the bottom decoder. The top eight outputs then generate minterms 0000 to 0111. When $A_3 = 1$, the enable conditions are reversed and the bottom decoder outputs generate minterms 1000 to 1111. Thus, two 3 by 8 decoders with enable inputs can be used to generate a 4 by 16 decoder function. This example demonstrates the usefulness of the enable inputs in ICs. In general, the enable lines are convenient for expanding two or more IC packages into a digital function of larger capacity.

Demultiplexers

A decoder with one or more enable inputs can function as a demultiplexer. A *demulti-plexer* is a digital function that receives information on a single line and transmits this information in one of 2^n possible output lines. The output line being selected is determined from the bit combination of n selection lines. The decoder of Fig. 2-9 will function as a demultiplexer if the enable line is taken as the data input and the decoder inputs x, y, and z are taken as the selection lines. The single input variable (available in the enable line) has a path to all eight outputs, but the input information is directed to only one of the output lines as specified by the binary combination of the three selection lines. For example, if the selection lines $xyz = 000$, output D_0 will be the same as the input information in the enable line while all other outputs will be main-tained at 0. Because of the similarity of decoders and demultiplexers, these circuits are usually referred to as *decoder/demultiplexer* circuits.

Multiplexers

The function of a demultiplexer is to receive binary information from a single source and steer it to any of 2^n outputs under control of the selection lines. A digital multi-plexer performs the reverse operation. A *multiplexer* is a digital function that receives binary information from 2^n lines and transmits information on a single output line. The one input line being selected is determined from the bit combination of n selec-tion lines. An example of a 4 by 1 multiplexer is shown in Fig. 2-11. The four input

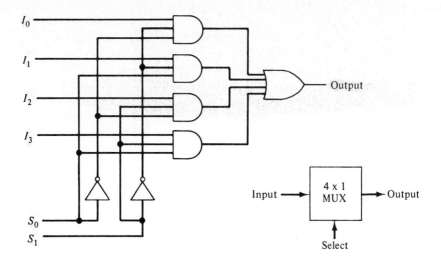

(a) Logic diagram   (b) Block diagram

Fig. 2-11 4 by 1 multiplexer.

lines are applied to four AND gates whose outputs go to a single OR gate. Only one input line has a path to the output at any particular time. The selection lines S_1 and S_0 determine which input is selected to have a direct path to the output. Thus, with $S_1S_0 = 10$, the AND gate associated with input I_2 has two of its inputs equal to 1. If $I_2 = 1$ the output of the gate is also 1; if $I_2 = 0$, the output is 0. All other AND gates have an output of 0. The output of the OR gate will be equal to the output value of the AND gate associated with input I_2. A multiplexer is also called a *data selector* since it selects one of multiple input data lines and steers the binary information to the output line.

The AND gates in a multiplexer resemble a decoder circuit and indeed, they decode the input selection lines. In general, a multiplexer circuit is constructed from an n by 2^n decoder by adding one input line to each AND gate and applying all AND gate outputs to a single OR gate. The size of a multiplexer is specified by the number of its inputs, 2^n. It is then implied that it also contains one output line and n selection line. A multiplexer may have one or more enable lines, as in a decoder. The enable lines can then be used to expand two or more multiplexer ICs to a digital multiplexer with a larger number of inputs.

2-4 BINARY COUNTERS

A register that goes through a predetermined sequence of states upon the application of input pulses is called a *counter*. The input pulses may be clock pulses or may originate from an external source. They may occur at uniform intervals of time or at random. Counters are found in almost all equipment containing digital logic. They are used for counting the number of occurrences of an event and are usful for generating timing signals to control the sequence of operations in digital computers. The sequence of state of a counter may follow a binary count or any other sequence. A wide variety of different types of counters are available in integrated circuit packages.

Counters may be operated synchronously or asynchronously. The signals that affect the flip-flops in an asynchronous counter are generated in output transitions of other flip-flops. Asynchronous counters are sometimes called *ripple* counters. This is because flip-flop transitions ripple through from one flip-flop to the next in sequence until all flip-flops reach a new state. In a synchronous counter, all the flip-flops receive the same clock pulse and as a consequence, all flip-flops change state synchronously with the pulse. We will consider here synchronous counters only.

Binary Counter Sequence

Of the various sequences a counter may follow, the straight binary sequence is the simplest and most straightforward. A counter that follows the binary number sequence is called a *binary counter*. An n-bit binary counter is a register of n flip-flops and associated gates that follows a sequence of states according to the binary count of n bits, from 0 to $2^n - 1$. The design of binary counters can be carried out by the procedure outlined in Sec. 1-6. A simpler alternate design procedure may be carried out from a direct inspection of the sequence of states that the register must undergo in order to achieve a straight binary count. Going through a sequence of binary numbers, as shown in Table 2-2, we note that the lower-order bit is complemented after every

TABLE 2-2   Complement Conditions for Binary Counter

Count Sequence $A_2\ A_1\ A_0$	Flip-Flops to Be Complemented for Next Count
0 0 0	A_0
0 0 1	A_0, A_1 because $A_0 = 1$
0 1 0	A_0
0 1 1	A_0, A_1 because $A_0 = 1$, A_2 because $A_1 A_0 = 11$
1 0 0	A_0
1 0 1	A_0, A_1 because $A_0 = 1$
1 1 0	A_0
1 1 1	A_0, A_1 because $A_0 = 1$, A_2 because $A_1 A_0 = 11$

count and every other bit is complemented from one count to the next if and only if all its lower-order bits are equal to 1. If the table is extended to four-bit numbers we will find that the binary number 1000 is obtained from its preceding number 0111 by: (1) complementing the low-order bit; (2) complementing the second-order bit (because the first bit is 1); (3) complementing the third bit (because the first two are 1's); and (4) complementing the fourth bit (because the first three bits are all 1's).

A counter circuit will usually employ flip-flops with complementing capabilities. Both T-type and JK-type flip-flops have this property. The flip-flop in a binary counter that holds the low-order bit is complemented with every clock pulse. Every other flip-flop in the register is complmented if and only if all its lower order flip-flops contain 1's.

The logic diagram of a four-bit binary counter using T-type flip-flops is shown in Fig. 2-12. Flip-flop A_0 (holding the low-order bit) is complemented with each pulse arriving in the CP terminal. This occurs because the T input of the flip-flop is main-

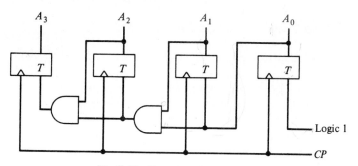

Fig. 2-12   Four-bit binary counter.

tained at 1 permanently. A_1 is complemented with a pulse if $A_0 = 1$. A_2 is complemented if $A_1 A_0 = 11$ and A_3 is complemented if $A_2 A_1 A_0 = 111$. For every clock pulse, the state of the register goes to a next state dictated by the binary count sequence from 0000 to 1111. The next state after 1111 is 0000 because all flip-flops will be complemented after the 1111 state. A binary counter can be expanded to any number of bits by providing one flip-flop and one AND gate for each additional bit and connecting them in cascade according to the pattern shown in the diagram.

Binary Down-Counter

A binary counter with a reverse count is called a binary *down-counter*. In a down-counter the binary count is reduced by one with every input pulse. The state of the flip-flops in a four-bit down-counter starts from binary 15 and continues to binary states 14, 13, 12, . . . , 0 and then back to 15. Going through a descending sequence of binary numbers, one will find that the low-order bit is complemented with each down-count and every other bit is complemented if and only if all of its lower order bits are equal to 0. This means that a register will operate as a binary down-counter if each flip-flop in the register is complemented when its lower-order flip-flops are equal to 0, except for the first, which is complemented with every pulse. The logic diagram of a four-binary down-counter is shown in Fig. 2-13. It is similar to the *up-counter* of Fig. 2-12 except that the AND gates receive inputs from the complement outputs of flip-flops.

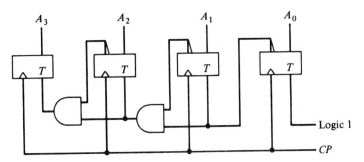

Fig. 2-13   Four-bit binary down-counter.

Binary Counter with Parallel Load

The counters just described will count the input pulses arriving in the CP terminal every time a pulse occurs. It is sometimes necessary to control the count sequence by a control signal so that clock pulses affect the counter only if the control signal is enabled. This was done in the two-bit counter designed in Sec. 1-6. If we refer back to Fig. 1-29 we will find that the input control designated by x determines whether the counter goes to the next state (when $x = 1$) or remains in its present state (when $x = 0$). Furthermore, counters employed in digital computers quite often require a parallel load capability for transferring an initial binary number into the register prior to its operation as a counter. Figure 2-14 shows the logic diagram of a register that

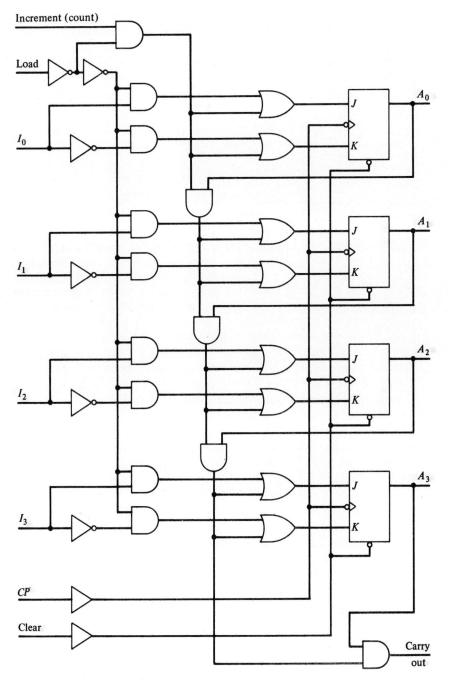

Fig. 2-14 Binary counter with parallel load.

has a parallel load capability and can also operate as a counter when enabled by a control input. This is a very useful register and will be used extensively in succeeding chapters. The input *load* control, when equal to 1, disables the count sequence and causes a transfer of data from inputs I_0 to I_3 into flip-flops A_0 to A_3, respectively. If the load input is 0 and the increment input control is 1, the register operates as a counter and the next clock pulse causes the state of the flip-flops to go to the next binary count sequence. If both control inputs are 0, clock pulses do not change the state of the register.

The operation of the register is summarized in Table 2-3. The four control inputs *clear, CP load,* and *increment* determine the next output state. The clear input is

TABLE 2-3   Control Functions in Register of Fig. 2-14

Clear	CP	Load	Increment	Outputs A_0–A_3
0	X	X	X	All 0's
1	X	0	0	No change
1	↓	1	X	Receive inputs I_0–I_3
1	↓	0	1	Count to next value

asynchronous and, when equal to 0, causes the register to be cleared irrespective of the presence of clock pulses or other inputs. This is indicated in the table by the X entries, which symbolize don't-care conditions for the other control inputs, so their values may be either 0 or 1. The clear input must go to the 1 state for clocked operations. With both the load and increment inputs at 0, the outputs of the register will not change, whether a pulse is applied or not. A load input of 1 causes a transfer from inputs I_0 to I_3 into the register during the falling edge of an input pulse. The input information is transferred into the register when the load input is 1 irrespective of the value of the increment input. If the load input is maintained at 0, the increment input controls the count sequence. A count occurs with every clock pulse if the increment input is 1 and no change of state occurs if the increment input is 0.

The carry-out terminal in the register will be 1 if all flip-flops are equal to 1. This is the condition for complementing the flip-flop holding the next higher-order bit. This output is useful for expanding the counter to more than four bits. The speed of the counter can be increased if the two-input AND gates that propagate the carry are replaced with AND gates whose inputs are connected directly to all previous flip-flop outputs. Thus, the AND gate associated with flip-flops A_1, A_2, and A_3 will have two, three, and four inputs, respectively. The AND gate associated with the carry output will have five inputs, one from the increment control and one from each of the flip-flop outputs. This type of arrangement is called a *look-ahead* carry.

The four-bit register shown in Fig. 2-14 can be enclosed in a 16-pin IC package. Two ICs are necessary for the construction of an eight-bit register, four ICs for a 16-bit register, and so on. The carry output of one IC must be connected to the increment input of the IC holding the four next-higher-order bits of the register.

Counters with parallel load capability having a specified number of bits will be used in succeding chapters to design digital computers. We will refer to them by means of the block diagram shown in Fig. 2-15. The clear and *CP* inputs are not included in the block diagram since their presence will be implied in all registers. The data input variables are represented by a single line and so are the data output lines. The two control inputs *load* and *increment* and the carry output labeled are along horizontal lines with arrows going into or out of the register.

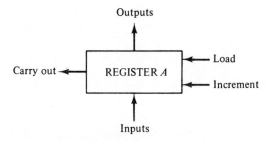

Fig. 2-15 Block diagram of a register with increment and parallel load capabilities.

2-5 SHIFT REGISTERS

A register capable of shifting its binary information either to the right or to the left is called a *shift register*. An *n*-bit shift register consists of *n* flip-flops and the gates that control the shift operation. A block diagram of a shift- right register is shown in Fig. 2-16. It has a *shift-right* control input whose purpose is to enable shift operation. The *serial input* is a single line going to the input of the leftmost flip-flop of the register. The *serial output* is a single line from the output of the rightmost flip-flop of the register. The parallel output consists of *n* lines, one for each of the flip-flops in the register.

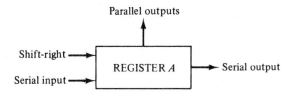

Fig. 2-16 Block diagram of a shift-right register.

The reason for calling some lines *serial* and others *parallel* will become evident from the operation of a four-bit shift-right register as depicted in Table 2-4. The initial binary information stored in the register is 0111. The parallel outputs have one line for each flip-flop, so the information stored in the register can be inspected through these lines all at once. The serial output is a single line coming from the output of the

TABLE 2-4   Serial Input and Output in a Four-Bit Shift-Right Register

Clock Pulse	Serial Input Bit	State of Register (parallel outputs)	Serial Output Bit
Initial	1	0 1 1 1	1
1	1	1 0 1 1	1
2	0	1 1 0 1	1
3	1	0 1 1 0	0
4	X	1 0 1 1	1

rightmost flip-flop, so that the four bits stored in the register can come out through this line one at a time. Similarly, the serial input is a single line where binary information can enter the register one bit at a time during four consecutive clock pulses. Information is transferred serially in and out when the register is shifted to the right.

Suppose that we want to transfer the binary number 1011 into the register in a serial fashion and, at the same time, in serial fashion extract the stored 0111 information. Since there is only one serial input line, the binary information must be applied at this input one bit at a time. The least significant bit of the input information is brought into the serial input line prior to the arrival of the clock pulse that causes the shift. At the same time, the bit in the rightmost flip-flop of the register is extracted from the serial output line. As the input bit is transferred into the leftmost flip-flop (with a clock pulse), the other bits of the register are shifted to the right, bringing the second bit into the serial output line. The other three input bits are shifted in a similar fashion. After four shift pulses, the input number 1011 is shifted into the register (lower-order bit first) and the previously stored number 0111 is shifted out, one bit at a time. At the same time, the parallel output lines give the state of the register after each shift. However, a shift register may or may not have external pins for the parallel output lines, and their use depends on the particular application.

Computers may operate in a serial mode, a parallel mode, or in a combination of both. The parallel outputs of registers are not needed if the computer operates in a serial mode only. Information is transferred into shift registers through their serial input lines and information is taken out of registers through their serial output lines. Serial operations are slower than parallel operations because of the time it takes to transfer information in and out of shift registers. Serial computers, however, require less hardware to perform other operations because one common circuit can be used over and over again to manipulate the bits coming out of shift registers in a sequential manner.

Most computers operate in a parallel mode because this is a faster mode of operation. But even parallel computers need to perform shift operations. For example, the multiplication of two numbers is implemented in digitial computers by successive additions and shifts. Division is done by successive subtractions and shifts. When shift registers are used in parallel computers, the output is taken from the parallel output lines. The serial input and serial output lines are needed for cascading IC registers into shift registers with more bits and for entering data into the extreme flip-flops of the register.

Registers may have either shift-right or shift-left capabilities, or both. Some shift registers may also provide parallel input lines for parallel loading of information into the register. The most general shift register will have all the capabilities listed below. Others may have only some of these capabilities with at least one shift operation.

1. A *clear* control to clear the register to 0.

2. A *CP* input for clock pulses to synchronize all operations.

3. A *shift-right* control to enable the shift-right operation and the *serial input* and *output* lines associated with the shift-right operation.

4. A *shift-left* control to enable the shift-left operation and the *serial input* and *output* lines associated with the shift-left operation.

5. A *parallel-load* control to enable the parallel transfer of *n input* lines.

6. *n* parallel output lines.

In addition, there may be a control state that leaves the information in the register unchanged even though clock pulses are continuously applied to the inputs of the flip-flops.

The logic diagram of a three-bit shift register with all the capabilities mentioned above is shown in Fig. 2-17. It consists of three D-type flip-flops, a number of gates for controlling the various operations, and a 2 by 4 decoder. The two-mode control lines H_1 and H_0 determine the operation that occurs in the register during the falling edge of a clock pulse. When $H_1 H_0 = 00$, output D_0 of the decoder is equal to 1 and the other three decoder outputs are equal to 0. This condition forms a path from the output of each flip-flop, through the leftmost gate, and into the input of the flip-flop. The next clock pulse will transfer into each flip-flop the binary value it held previously and no change of state will result. When $H_1 H_0 = 01$, output D_1 causes a shift-right operation. When $H_1 H_0 = 10$, output D_2 causes a shift-left operation. Finally, when $H_1 H_0 = 11$, the binary information in the parallel input lines I_1, I_2, I_3 is transferred into the flip-flops in parallel. Table 2-5 summarizes the effect of the mode control lines on the operation of the register.

TABLE **2-5** Effect of Mode Control on the Shift Register of Fig. 2-17

Mode Control $H_1 H_0$	Decoder Output	Register Operation
0 0	D_0	No change in register
0 1	D_1	Shift-right
1 0	D_2	Shift-left
1 1	D_3	Parallel-load I_1–I_3

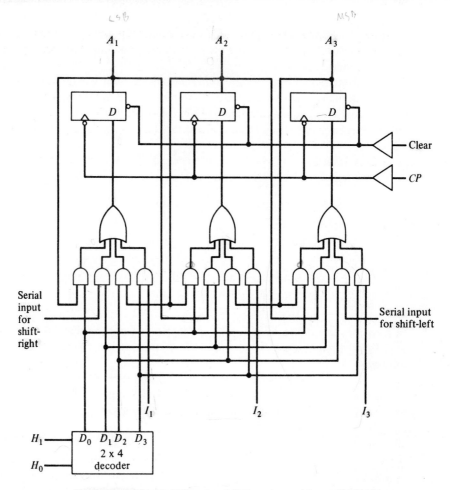

Fig. 2-17 Three-bit bidirectional shift-register with parallel load.

2-6 RANDOM-ACCESS MEMORIES (RAM)

A memory unit is a collection of storage registers, together with the associated circuits needed to transfer information in and out of the registers. Memory registers can be accessed for information transfer as required and hence the name *random-access memory*, abreviated RAM.

A memory unit stores binary information in groups of bits called *words*. Each word is stored in one memory register. A word in memory is an entity of n bits that move in and out of the memory unit. A word of eight bits is sometimes called a *byte*.

62

A memory word is a group of 0's and 1's and may represent a number, an instruction code, alphanumeric characters, or any other binary-coded information.

The communication between a memory unit and its environment is achieved through control lines, address selection lines, and data input and output lines. The control signals specify the direction of transfer required, that is, whether a word is to be stored in a memory register or whether a word previously stored is to be transferred out of a memory register. The address lines specify the particular word chosen out of hundreds or thousands available. The input lines provide the information to be stored in memory and the output lines supply the information coming out of memory. A block diagram of a memory unit is shown in Fig. 2-18.

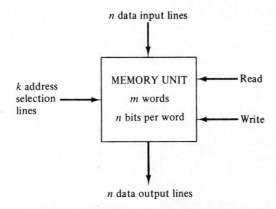

Fig. 2-18   Block diagram of a memory unit.

A memory unit is specified by the number of words it contains and the number of bits in each word. The address selection lines select one particular memory word out of the m words available. Each word in a memory is assigned an identification number, called an *address*, starting from 0 and continuing with 1, 2, 3, and up to m — 1. The selection of a specific word inside the memory is done by inserting its binary address value into the selection lines. A decoder inside the memory unit accepts this address and opens the paths needed to select the word specified. Thus, k address bits can select any one of $2^k = m$ words. Computer memories may range from 1024 words, requiring an address of 10 bits, to $1,048,576 = 2^{20}$ words, requiring 20 address bits. It is customary to refer to the number of words in a memory unit with the unit K. K refers to $1024 = 2^{10}$ words: thus $1K = 1024$ words, $4K = 4096$ words, and $64K = 2^{16}$ words.

The two control signals are called *read* and *write*. A write signal specifies a transfer-in operation; a read signal specifies a transfer-out operation. On accepting one of the control signals, the internal control circuits inside the memory unit provide the desired function. When the memory unit receives a *write* control signal, the internal control transfers the n data input bits into the word specified by the address lines.

With a *read* control signal, the word selected by the address lines appears in the *n* data output lines.

IC RAM

Integrated circuit memories sometimes have a single line for the read/write control. One binary state, say 1, specifies a read operation and the other binary state specifies a write operation. In addition, one or more enable lines may be included in each IC package to provide means for expanding several packages into a memory unit with a larger number of words.

The internal construction of a random-access memory of *m* words with *n* bits per word consists of *m* × *n* binary storage cells and the associated logic needed to select a word for writing or reading. The binary storage cell is the basic building block of a memory unit. The logic diagram of a binary cell that stores one bit of information is shown in Fig. 2-19. Although the cell is shown to include five gates and a flip-flop, internally it is constructed with a two-transistor flip-flop having multiple inputs. The binary cell of a memory unit must be very small in order to be able to pack as many cells as possible in the semiconductor area available in the chip. The binary cell is shown to have three input lines and one output line. The purpose of the select input is to select one cell out of the many available. With the select line at 1, a 1 in the read/write terminal forms a path from the output of the flip-flop to the output terminal. With the read/write terminal at 0, the bit in the input line is transferred into the flip-flop. Both the input and output are disabled when the select line is 0. Note that the flip-flop operates without a clock pulse and that its purpose is to store the information bit in the binary cell.

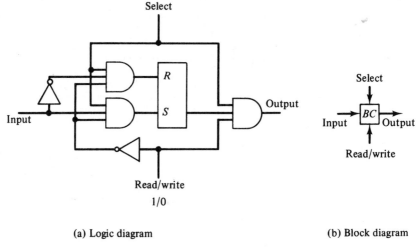

(a) Logic diagram   (b) Block diagram

Fig. 2-19 Memory cell.

The configuration of a 4 by 3 RAM is shown in Fig. 2-20. It consists of four words of three bits each for a total of 12 binary storage cells. Each small box labeled *BC* in the diagram includes within it the circuit of a binary cell. The four lines included with each *BC* box designate the three inputs and one output as specified in the diagram of Fig. 2-19.

The two address lines go through a 2 by 4 decoder with an enable input. When the memory enable is 0, all the outputs of the decoder are 0 and none of the memory words are selected. With the memory enable input at 1, one of the four words is selected, depending on the bit combination of the two address lines. Now, with the read/write control at 1, the bits of the selected word go through the three OR gates to the output terminals. The non-selected binary cells produce 0's in the inputs of the OR

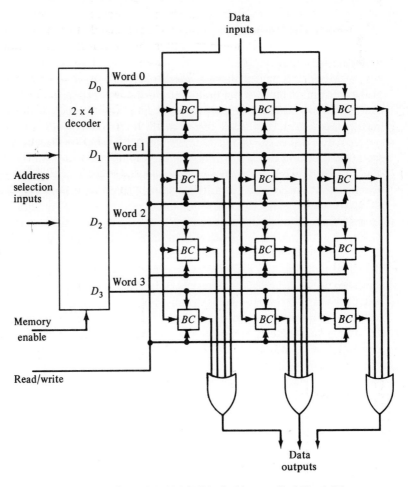

Fig. 2-20   4 by 3 IC RAM (BC is the binary cell of Fig. 2-19).

gate and have no effect on the outputs. With the read/write control at 0, the information available in the input lines is transferred into the flip-flops of the selected word. The non-selected binary cells in the other words are disabled by their selection line so their previous values remain unchanged. Thus, with the memory enable at 1, the read/write control initiates the required read and write operations for the memory unit. An inhibit operation is obtained by maintaining the memory enable at 0. This condition leaves the contents of all words in memory as they were, irrespective of the value of the read/write control.

IC RAMs sometimes employ binary cells whose outputs can be tied to form a wire-OR or a wire-AND function. Other IC RAMs provide tri-state outputs. These outputs are convenient when two or more ICs are connected to form a memory unit with a larger number of words since they eliminate the need for external OR gates that would otherwise be needed.

Magnetic Core Memory

IC memories retain the binary information when a word is read from memory. This type of memory is said to have a *non-destructive-read* property because the content of the word in memory is not destroyed during the reading process. Another component commonly used as a binary storage cell in memory units in the *magnetic core.* A magnetic core is a very small toroid made of ferromagnetic material. The physical quantity that makes the magnetic core suitable for binary storage is its magnetic property. One direction of magnetization is used to represent a 0 and the other to represent a 1. Reading out the binary information stored in a core requires that its direction of magnetization be forced into the 0 state. Therefore, a magnetic core memory has a *destructive-read* property; it loses the previously stored information after the reading process. Because of its destructive-read property, a magnetic core memory must provide additional control functions to restore the original contents of the word just read. A *read* control signal applied to a magnetic core memory transfers the contents of the addressed word into an *external register* and, at the same time, the memory register is automatically cleared. The sequence of internal control in a magnetic core memory then provides appropriate signals to cause the restoration of the word into the memory register. This is done by writing back the information from the external register into the same word memory. Similarly, in order to write new information into a word in a magnetic core memory, the bits of the selected word are first cleared to 0's. The binary information from the input lines is then transferred into the selected word by setting those bits that need 1 and not changing the bits that need 0. Again, this double operation is automatically taken care of by the internal control inside the memory unit.

Memory Operations

The internal control sequence of a memory unit is a function of its components and the type of control lines provided with the unit. Moreover, address and input information may come from many sources and output information may go to many destinations.

The operation of a memory unit is simplified if we associate with it two external registers and assume the availability of two control signals as shown in Fig. 2-21. The address lines of the memory unit are permanently connected to the outputs of a single external register called the Memory Address Register, abbreviated MAR. Binary information is transferred between words of memory and the external environment through one common external register called the Memory Buffer Register, abbreviated MBR (other names are: *information register*, *storage register*, and *data register*.) Input information is always transferred to MBR, and output information is always taken from MBR.

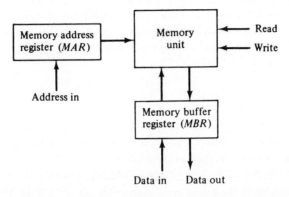

Fig. 2-21   Block diagram of memory and associated registers.

When the memory receives a *write* command, the internal control interprets the contents of the buffer register as the information bits of the word to be stored. With a *read* command, the internal control transfers the word from memory into the buffer register. In each case, the contents of the address register specify the particular word in memory referenced for writing or reading. If a magnetic core memory is used, its internal control sequence *automatically* restores the word into memory after a read operation.

   The sequence of *external* operations needed to communicate with the memory unit for the purpose of transferring a word out to the external environment are as follows:

   1. Transfer the address bits of the required word into MAR.

   2. Activate the *read* control input.

The binary information stored in the memory word specified by MAR will then be found in MBR. The content of the word read from the memory will not be destroyed.

   The sequence of *external* operations needed to store a word into memory are:

   1. Transfer the address bits of the required word into MAR.

   2. Transfer the data bits of the word into the MBR.

   3. Activate the write signal.

The information from *MBR* is then stored in the memory word specified by *MAR*. The previous contents of the word are, obviously, destroyed.

Special Characteristics

Access time is defined as the time differential between the time a memory unit receives a read signal and the time when the information read from memory is available in its outputs. In a destructive-read memory, such as magnetic core, information read out is physically destroyed by the reading process. It is, however, automatically restored; but this requires an additional time. The sum of access time and restoration time is called *cycle time*. In a non-destructive-read memory, the cycle time is equal to the access time because no restoration is necessary. Typical cycle times of memory units range from about 100 ns to 1 μs.

The mode of access of a memory unit is determined by the type of components used. In a *random-access* memory, the memory registers may be thought of as being separated in space, with each register occupying one particular spatial location as in an IC RAM or magnetic core memory. In a *sequential-access* memory, the information stored in some medium is not immediately accessible but is available only at certain intervals of time. A shift-register memory is of this type. Shift registers are used as serial memories and are available in MOS/LSI packages. The contents of the memory are recirculated via a feedback loop from the output to the input. An *m* words by *n* bits sequential-access memory is obtained from *n* shift registers in synchronization, with each shift register representing one bit of the word. The length of the shift register determines the number of words. Recirculating shift registers used as memories derive their address from an auxiliary counter which determines the word just emerging from the output terminals. Each word passes the output terminals in turn and the information is read out when the requested word is available in the output terminals.

In a random-access memory, the access time is always the same regardless of the word's particular location in space. In a sequential memory, the access time depends on the position of the word at the time of the request. If the word is just emerging from storage at the time it is requested, the access time is the time necessary to read it. If the word happened to be in a different position, the access time also includes the time required for all the other words to move past the output terminals. Thus, access time in a sequential memory is variable.

Memory units whose components lose stored information with time or when the power is turned off are said to be *volatile*. IC memories are volatile since their binary cells require external power to maintain the stored information. By contrast, a *non-volatile* memory unit such as magnetic core or magnetic disk retains its stored information after power is removed. This is because the stored information in magnetic components is manifested by the direction of magnetization, which is retained when power is turned off. A nonvolatile property is desirable in digital computers because many useful programs are left permanently in the memory unit. When power is turned off and then on again, the previously stored programs and other information are not lost but continue to reside in memory. Computers with volatile memories may solve the problem of power failure by using backup batteries or special power supplies that continue to deliver power for some time after a power interruption occurs.

2-7 READ-ONLY MEMORIES (ROM)

A read-only memory (ROM), as the name implies, is a memory unit that performs the read operation only; it does not have a write capability. This implies that the binary information stored in a ROM is made permanent during the hardware production of the unit and cannot be altered by writing different words into it. While a RAM is a general-purpose device whose contents can be altered during the computational process, a ROM is restricted to reading words that are permanently stored within the unit.

An m by n ROM is an array of binary cells organized into m words of n bits each. As shown in the block diagram of Fig. 2-22, a ROM has k address lines to select one

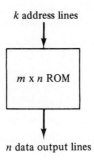

k address lines

m x n ROM

n data output lines

Fig. 2-22   Block diagram of a read-only memory (ROM).

of $2^k = m$ words of memory, and n output lines, one for each bit of the word. An IC ROM may also have one or more enable lines for expanding a number of IC packages into a ROM with larger capacity. The ROM does not need a read-control line since at any given time, the output lines automatically provide the 1's and 0's of the n bits of the word selected by the address value. Because the outputs are a function of only the present inputs (the address lines)a ROM is classified as a combinational circuit. In fact, a ROM is constructed internally with decoders and a set of OR gates. There is no need for providing storage capabilities as in a RAM, since the values of the bits in the ROM are permanently fixed.

Consider the logic diagram of a 4 by 3 ROM as depicted in Fig. 2-23. The unit contains a 2 by 4 decoder to decode the two address lines. The OR gates provide the three outputs. If each minterm output of the decoder is connected to the input of each OR gate, the circuit outputs will all be 1 no matter what word is selected by the address

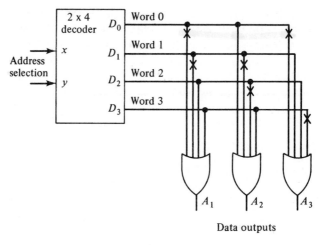

(a) Logic diagram

Address		Outputs		
x	y	A_1	A_2	A_3
0	0	0	1	0
0	1	0	0	1
1	0	1	0	1
1	1	1	1	0

(b) Truth table

Fig. 2-23 An example of a 4 by 3 ROM.

lines. Suppose we want the ROM to contain the bit combinations listed in the truth table accompanying the diagram. The truth table specifies a bit combination of 010 for word 0. This bit combination is obtained by breaking two wires (marked with a cross) between word 0 and the leftmost inputs of the OR gates. In other words, when the input address is 00, the D_0 output of the decoder is equal to 1 and all other outputs of the decoder are equal to 0. Only the OR gate associated with output A_2 receives an input of 1 because the other two wires are broken. Therefore, the output lines will provide an output $A_1 A_2 A_3 = 010$ (assuming that an open wire to the OR gate behaves as a 0 input). Similarly, all other wires marked with crosses indicate broken wires and when these wires are removed from the diagram, the logic diagram so obtained will implement the truth table listed for the ROM.

An IC ROM is fabricated first with outputs all being 1 (or all 0, depending on the particular IC). The particular pattern of 1's and 0's is then obtained by providing a *mask* in the last fabrication step. Each cell in a ROM incorporates a link (in the position of the cross in the diagram of Fig. 2-23) that can be fused during the last fabrication process. A broken link in a cell defines one binary state and an unbroken link represents the other state. The procedure involved in fabricating a ROM requires that the customer fill out the truth table he wishes the ROM to satisfy. The manufacturer then makes the corresponding mask for the links to produce the 1's and 0's of each word desired. This process is called *custom* or *mask programming*. It is a hardware procedure even though the word *programming* is used.

For small quantities it is more convenient to use a *programmable* ROM, referred to as PROM. When ordered, PROMs contain all 0's (or all 1's) in every word. Each cell in a PROM incorporates a link that can be fused by application of a high current pulse. A broken link in a cell defines one binary state and an unbroken link represents the other state. The procedure is usually irreversible and, once fused, the output for that bit is permanent. This allows the user to program the unit in his own laboratory by breaking those links which must be opened to achieve the desired relationship between input address and output data. Erasable PROMs are also available. Such ROMs have special procedures for restructuring the links back to their initial value (all 0's or all 1's) even though they have been programmed previously. In any case, all procedures for programming or erasing ROMs are *hardware* procedures. Digital applications that use ROMs specify a fixed-word pattern. The programming aspect of ROMs is concerned with the procedures for obtaining the desired fixed pattern.

ROMs find a wide range of applications in the design of digital systems. Basically, a ROM generates an input-output relation specified by a truth table. As such, it can implement any combinational circuit with k inputs and n outputs. A ROM can also be used in the design of sequential circuits. This is because a sequential circuit can be subdivided into a group of flip-flops and a combinational circuit (see Sec. 1-6). A register can be used for the group of flip-flops and a ROM for the combinational circuit.

Another type of LSI circuit that implements a complex combinational circuit is the *Programmable Logic Array* (PLA). A PLA is similar to a ROM in concept except that it does not provide full decoding of the input lines. Thus, in a PLA, the decoder in Fig. 2-23 is replaced by a group of AND gates each of which can be programmed to produce an AND term of the input variables. The AND and OR gates inside the PLA are initially fabricated without interconnections. The specific functions desired are implemented in the last processing step and involve a mask for linking the input lines to the AND gates and the outputs of the AND gates to the inputs of the OR gates.

ROMs are widely used for converting one binary code to another, for lookup tables needed in mathematical functions, for the display of characters, and in many other applications requiring a large number of inputs and outputs. They are also employed in the design of control units for digitial computers. As such they are used to store coded information that represents the sequence of internal control variables needed for enabling the various operations in the computer. A control unit that utilizes a ROM to store binary control information is called a microprogrammed control unit. Chapter 8 discusses this subject in more detail.

REFERENCES

1. MANO, M. M., *Digital Logic and Computer Design*. Englewood Cliffs, N.J.: Prentice-Hall, Inc., 1979.

2. *The TTL Data Book for Design Engineers*, 2nd ed. Dallas, Tex.: Texas Instruments, Inc.

3. BLAKESLEE, T. R., *Digital Design with Standard MSI and LSI*, 2nd ed. New York: Wiley-Interscience, 1979.

4. FLETCHER, W. I., *An Engineering Approach to Digital Design*. Englewood Cliffs, N.J.: Prentice-Hall, Inc., 1980.

5. PEATMAN, J. B., *Digital Hardware Design*. New York: McGraw-Hill Book Company, 1980.

6. LEE, S. C., *Digital Circuits and Logic Design*. Englewood Cliffs, N.J.: Prentice-Hall, Inc., 1976.

7. WINKEL, D., AND F. PROSSER, *The Art of Digital Design*. Englewood Cliffs, N.J.: Prentice-Hall, Inc., 1980.

8. TAUB, H., AND D. SCHILLING, *Digital Integrated Electronics*. New York: McGraw-Hill Book Company, 1977.

PROBLEMS

2-1. TTL SSI come mostly in 14-pin IC packages. Two pins are reserved for power supply and the other pins are used for input and output terminals. How many circuits are included in one such package if it contains the following type of circuits: (a) inverters; (b) 2-input exclusive-OR gates; (c) 3-input OR gates; (d) 4-input AND gates; (e) 5-input NOR gates; (f) 8-input NAND gates; (g) clocked JK flip-flops with asynchronous clear.

2-2. ECL SSI gates come in 16-pin packages. Three pins are reserved for power supply and the other pins are used for input and output terminals.
   (a) Draw four ECL gates (Fig. 2-3) and include them in an IC package. How would you resolve the problem that the package has a smaller number of pins than gate terminals?
   (b) Repeat part (a) with each pair of gates connected internally as shown in Fig. 2-4.

2-3. List in tabular form the fan-out, power dissipation, propagation delay, and noise margin for the following digital IC logic families: TTL, STTL, ECL, CMOS.

2-4. Consider two master-slave JK flip-flops Q_1 and Q_2. The output of Q_1 is connected to both the J and K inputs of Q_2 and the output of Q_2 is connected to both the J and K inputs of Q_1. Prior to the occurrence of a pulse $Q_1 = 1$ and $Q_2 = 1$. Draw the timing relations of the master and slave elements of each flip-flop during the clock pulse. What is the advantage of using master-slave flip-flops for this type of application?

2-5. What modifications should be made to the register of Fig. 2-7 so that the outputs of the master-slave flip-flops change state during the *rising edge* of the input clock pulse from the *CP* terminal? The change of state should occur only if the *load* input is 0.

2-6.   Redraw the register of Fig. 2-7 with NOR gates instead of the AND gates and show that the number of gates does not change.

2-7.   For the following MSI registers, draw the logic diagram and assign pins to the IC package.
       (a) A 6-bit register with D-type flip-flops with six inputs, six outputs, one common CP terminal, and one common asynchronous clear terminal.
       (b) A 4-bit register with D-type flip-flops having a parallel-load capability and tri-state gates in the four outputs. Use a common CP and a common clear terminal.

2-8.   Draw the logic diagram of a 2 by 4 decoder with an enable input using (a) NAND gates; (b) NOR gates. Show that with NAND gates it is more convenient to distinguish the selected output with a value of 0.

2-9.   Show the circuit of a 5 by 32 decoder constructed with four 3 by 8 decoders (with enable inputs) and one 2 by 4 decoder.

2-10. (a) Draw the logic diagram of a 4 by 1 multiplexer with an enable input.
       (b) Show how two 4 by 1 multiplexers with enable inputs can be connected to provide an 8 by 1 multiplexer. Would it be advantageous to provide a wire-OR capability to the outputs of the multiplexers?

2-11. Draw the logic diagram of a 4-bit up-down binary counter with an enable input terminal and up-down control terminals. Provide carry outputs for both the up and down count.

2-12. Show the external connections of four IC binary counters with parallel load (Fig. 2-14) to produce a 16-bit register with increment and load capabilities. Use a block diagram for each IC.

2-13. Show how the binary counter with parallel load of Fig. 2-14 can be made to operate as a divide-by-N counter, that is, a counter that counts from 0000 to N $-$ 1 and back to 0000. Specifically show the circuit for a divide-by-ten counter. Use an external AND gate.

2-14. Expand the bidirectional shift-register of Fig. 2-17 into four bits. Remove the decoder shown in the diagram and include the decoding function within the AND gates by providing three inputs for each AND gate.

2-15. Show the external connections of four IC bidirectional shift registers (Fig. 2-17) to produce a 12-bit bidirectional shift register. Use a block diagram for each IC and neglect the parallel inputs.

2-16. Obtain a table similar to Table 2-4 to show the timing sequence for serial input of 1110 and serial output of 0110.

2-17. Show how a shift register with parallel load can be used to convert serial input to parallel output and parallel input to serial outputs.

2-18. (a) Show how the read and write signals of Fig. 2-21 must be connected to the enable and read/write control inputs of the RAM in Fig. 2-20.
       (b) Show how the MBR of Fig. 2-21 can be included with the RAM of Fig. 2-20. Use a register with parallel load and a multiplexer.

2-19. When the number of words in a memory is too large it is convenient to use binary storage cells with two select inputs: one X (horizontal) and one Y (vertical) select input.

(a) Draw a binary storage cell similar to Fig. 2-19 with an X and a Y select input.

(b) Show how the select inputs are to be connected internally in a 256 by 1 RAM. Use two 4 by 16 decoders.

2-20.   A TTL 64-bit RAM is organized as 16 words with four bits per word and open collector outputs. The function table for the memory is given below.

(a) Draw a block diagram of the RAM listing the number of data input lines, data output lines, address selection lines, and control inputs.

(b) Show the external connections of two ICs that will produce a 16 by 8 RAM.

(c) Show the external connections of two ICs that will produce a 32 by 4 RAM.

(d) Show the external connections of eight ICs that will produce a 64 by 8 RAM. Use a 2 by 4 decoder constructed with NAND gates.

Enable Control	Read/ Write	Operation	Condition of Outputs
0	0	Write	All 1's
0	1	Read	Value of selected word
1	X	Inhibit	All 1's

2-21.   (a) A magnetic core memory has a capacity of 8192 words of 24 bits each. How many flip-flops are needed for the *MAR* and *MBR* (Fig. 2-21)?

(b) How many words would a memory unit contain if it has an *MAR* of 15 bits?

2-22.   Draw the logic diagram of an 8 by 2 ROM that produces the full-adder function (see Table 1-2), Indicate with crosses the links that must be broken.

2-23.   (a) Draw the block diagram of a 32 by 8 ROM with an *enable* input. How many address lines and output lines are needed?

(b) Show the external connections of two such ROMs in order to produce a 64 by 8 ROM.

2-24.   List the truth table of a 16 by 4 ROM that multiplies two binary numbers, each two bits long, and forms a 4-bit product.

Data Representation

3-1 DATA TYPES

Binary information in digitial computers is stored in memory or processor registers. Registers contain either data or control information. Control information is a bit or a group of bits used to specify the sequence of command signals needed for manipulation of the data in other registers. Data are numbers and other binary-coded information that are operated on to achieve required computational results. This chapter presents the most common types of data found in digital computers and shows how the various data types are represented in binary-coded form in computer registers.

The data types found in the registers of digital computers may be classified as being one of the following categories: (1) numbers used in arithmetic computations; (2) letters of the alphabet used in data processing; and (3) other discrete symbols used for specific purposes. All types of data, except binary numbers, are represented in computer registers in binary-coded form. This is because registers are made up of flip-flops and flip-flops are two-state devices that can store only 1's and 0's. The binary number system is the most natural system to use in a digital computer. But sometimes it is convenient to employ different number systems, especially the decimal number system, since it is used by people to perform arithmetic computations.

Number Systems

A number system of *base*, or *radix*, *r* is a system that uses distinct symbols for *r* digits. Numbers are represented by a string of digit symbols. To determine the quantity that the number represents, it is necessary to multiply each digit by an integer power of *r*, and then form the sum of all weighted digits. For example, the decimal number system in everyday use employs the radix 10 system. The 10 symbols are: 0, 1, 2, 3, 4, 5, 6, 7, 8, and 9. The string of digits 724.5 is interpreted to represent the quantity

$$7 \times 10^2 + 2 \times 10^1 + 4 \times 10^0 + 5 \times 10^{-1}$$

that is, 7 hundreds, plus 2 tens, plus 4 units, plus 5 tenths. Every decimal number can be similarly interpreted to find the quantity it represents.

The *binary* number system uses the radix 2. The two digit symbols used are 0 and 1. The string of digits 101101 is interpreted to represent the quantity

$$1 \times 2^5 + 0 \times 2^4 + 1 \times 2^3 + 1 \times 2^2 + 0 \times 2^1 + 1 \times 2^0 = 45$$

In order to distinguish between different radix numbers, the digits will be enclosed in parentheses and the radix of the number inserted as a subscript. For example, to show the equality between decimal and binary forty-five we will write $(101101)_2 = (45)_{10}$.

Besides the decimal and binary number systems, the *octal* (radix 8) and *hexadecimal* (radix 16) are important in digital computer work. The eight symbols of the octal system are 0, 1, 2, 3, 4, 5, 6, and 7. The sixteen symbols of the hexadecimal system are 0, 1, 2, 3, 4, 5, 6, 7, 8, 9, A, B, C, D, E, and F. The last six symbols are, unfortunately, identical to the letters of the alphabet and can cause confusion at times. However, this is the adopted convention and the symbols A, B, C, D, E, F, when used to represent hexadecimal digits, correspond to the decimal numbers 10, 11, 12, 13, 14, 15, respectively.

A number in radix r can be converted to the familiar decimal system by forming the sum of the weighted digits. For example, octal 736.4 is converted to decimal as follows:

$$(736.4)_8 = 7 \times 8^2 + 3 \times 8^1 + 6 \times 8^0 + 4 \times 8^{-1}$$
$$= 7 \times 64 + 3 \times 8 + 6 \times 1 + 4/8 = (478.5)_{10}$$

The equivalent decimal number of hexadecimal F3 is obtained from the following calculation:

$$(F3)_{16} = F \times 16 + 3 = 15 \times 16 + 3 = (243)_{10}$$

The conversion from decimal to its equivalent representation in radix r system is carried out by separating the number into its *integer* and *fraction* parts and converting each part separately. The conversion of a decimal integer into a base r representation is done by successive divisions by r and accumulation of the remainders. The conversion of a decimal fraction to radix r representation is accomplished by successive multiplications by r and accumulation of the integer digits so obtained. Figure 3-1 demonstrates these procedures.

The conversion of decimal 41.6875 into binary is done by first separating the number into its integer part 41 and fraction part .6875. The integer part is converted by dividing 41 by $r = 2$ to give an integer quotient of 20 and a remainder of 1. The quotient is again divided by 2 to give a new quotient and remainder. This process is repeated until the integer quotient becomes 0. The coefficients of the binary number are obtained from the remainders with the first remainder giving the low-order bit of the converted binary number.

```
Integer = 41                          Fraction = 0.6875
41                                        0.6875
20  | 1                                        2
10  | 0                                   1.3750
 5  | 0                                     x 2
 2  | 1                                   0.7500
 1  | 0                                     x 2
 0  | 1                                   1.5000
                                           x 2
                                         1.0000
   (41)₁₀ = (101001)₂            (0.6875)₁₀ = (0.1011)₂

         (41.6875)₁₀ = (101001.1011)₂
```

Fig. 3-1 Conversion of decimal 41.6875 into binary.

The fraction part is converted by multiplying it by $r = 2$ to give an integer and a fraction. The new fraction (*without* the integer) is multiplied again by 2 to give a new integer and a new fraction. This process is repeated until the fraction part becomes zero or until the number of digits obtained gives the required accuracy. The coefficients of the binary fraction are obtained from the integer digits with the first integer computed being the digit to be placed next to the binary point. Finally, the two parts are combined to give the total required conversion.

Binary, Octal, and Hexadecimal Representation

The conversion from and to binary, octal, and hexadecimal representation plays an important part in digital computers. Since $2^3 = 8$ and $2^4 = 16$, each octal digit corresponds to three binary digits and each hexadecimal digit corresponds to four binary digits. The conversion from binary to octal is easily accomplished by partitioning the binary number into groups of three bits each. The corresponding octal digit is then assigned to each group of bits and the string of digits so obtained gives the octal equivalent of the binary number. Consider for example a 16-bit register. Physically, one may think of the register as composed of 16 binary storage cells, with each cell capable of holding either a 1 or a 0. Suppose that the bit configuration stored in the register is as shown in Fig. 3-2. Since a binary number consists of a string of 1's and 0's, the 16-bit register can be used to store any binary number from 0 to $2^{16} - 1$. For the particular example shown, the binary number stored in the register is the equivalent of decimal 44899. Starting from the low-order bit, we partition the register into groups of three bits each (the sixteenth bit remains in a group by itself). Each group of three bits is assigned its octal equivalent and placed on top of the register. The string of octal digits so obtained represents the octal equivalent of the binary number.

```
 1   2    7    5    4    3      Octal
 1 0 1 0 1 1 1 1 0 1 1 0 0 0 1 1   Binary
   A     F      6    3      Hexadecimal
```

Fig. 3-2 Binary, octal, and hexadecimal conversion.

Conversion from binary to hexadecimal is similar except that the bits are divided into groups of four. The corresponding hexadecimal digit for each group of four bits is written as shown below the register of Fig. 3-2. The string of hexadecimal digits so obtained represents the hexadecimal equivalent of the binary number. The corresponding octal digit for each group of three bits is easily remembered after studying the first eight entries listed in Table 3-1. The correspondence between a hexadecimal digit and its equivalent 4-bit code can be found in the first 16 entries of Table 3-2.

TABLE 3-1   Binary-Coded Octal Numbers

Octal Number	Binary-Coded Octal	Decimal Equivalent	
0	000	0	
1	001	1	
2	010	2	Code
3	011	3	for one
4	100	4	octal
5	101	5	digit
6	110	6	
7	111	7	
10	001 000	8	
11	001 001	9	
12	001 010	10	
24	010 100	20	
62	110 010	50	
143	001 100 011	99	
370	011 111 000	248	

Table 3-1 lists a few octal numbers and their representation in registers in binary-coded form. The binary code is obtained by the procedure explained above, Each octal digit is assigned a 3-bit code as specified by the entries of the first eight digits in the table. Similarly, Table 3-2 lists a few hexadecimal numbers and their representation in registers in binary-coded form. Here the binary code is obtained by assigning to each hexadecimal digit the 4-bit code listed in the first 16 entries of the table.

Comparing the binary-coded octal and hexadecimal numbers with their binary number equivalent we find that the bit combination in all three representations is exactly the same. For example, decimal 99, when converted to binary, becomes 1100011. The binary-coded octal equivalent of decimal 99 is 001 100 011 and the binary-coded hexadecimal of decimal 99 is 0110 0011. If we neglect the leading zeros in these three binary representations we find that their bit combination is identical. This should be so because of the straightforward conversion that exists between binary numbers and octal or hexadecimal. The point of all this is that a string of 1's and 0's stored in a register could represent a binary number, but this same string of bits may be interpreted as holding an octal number in binary-coded form (if we divide the bits in groups

TABLE 3-2 Binary-Coded Hexadecimal Numbers

Hexadecimal Number	Binary-Coded Hexadecimal	Decimal Equivalent	
0	0000	0	↑
1	0001	1	
2	0010	2	
3	0011	3	
4	0100	4	
5	0101	5	
6	0110	6	Code
7	0111	7	for one
8	1000	8	hexadecimal
9	1001	9	digit
A	1010	10	
B	1011	11	
C	1100	12	
D	1101	13	
E	1110	14	
F	1111	15	↓
14	0001 0100	20	
32	0011 0010	50	
63	0110 0011	99	
F8	1111 1000	248	

of three) or as holding a hexadecimal number in binary-coded form (if we divide the bits in groups of four).

The registers in a digital computer contain many bits. Specifying the content of registers by their binary values will require a long string of binary digits. It is more convenient to specify content of registers by their octal or hexadecimal equivalent. The number of digits is reduced by one-third in the octal designation and by one-fourth in the hexadecimal designation. For example, the binary number 1111 1111 1111 has 12 digits. It can be expressed in octals as 7777 (four digits) or in hexadecimal as FFF (three digits). Computer manuals invariably choose either the octal or the hexadecimal designation for specifying contents of registers.

Decimal Representation

The binary number system is the most natural system for a computer, but people are accustomed to the decimal system. One way to solve this conflict is to convert all input decimal numbers into binary numbers, let the computer perform all arithmetic operations in binary and then convert the binary results back to decimal for the human user to understand. However, it is also possible for the computer to perform arithmetic operations directly with decimal numbers provided they are placed in registers in a coded form. Decimal numbers enter the computer usually as binary-coded alphanumeric characters. These codes, introduced later, may contain from six to eight bits for each decimal digit. When decimal numbers are used for internal arithmetic computations, they are converted to a binary code with four bits per digit.

A binary code is a group of n bits that assume up to 2^n distinct combinations of 1's and 0's with each combination representing one element of the set that is being coded. For example, a set of four elements can be coded by a two-bit code with each element assigned one of the following bit combinations; 00, 01, 10, or 11. A set of eight elements requires a 3-bit code, a set of 16 elements requires a 4-bit code, and so on. A binary code will have some unassigned bit combinations if the number of elements in the set is not a multiple power of 2. The 10 decimal digits form such a set. A binary code that distinguishes among 10 elements must contain at least four bits, but six combinations will remain unassigned. Numerous different codes can be obtained by arranging four bits in 10 distinct combinations. The bit assignment most commonly used for the decimal digits is the straight binary assignment listed in the first 10 entries of Table 3-3. This particular code is called *binary-coded decimal* and is commonly referred to by its abbreviation BCD. Other decimal codes are sometimes used and a few of them are given in Sec. 3-4.

TABLE 3-3   Binary-Coded Decimal (BCD) Numbers

Decimal Number	Binary-Coded Decimal (BCD) Number	
0	0000	↑
1	0001	
2	0010	
3	0011	Code
4	0100	for one
5	0101	decimal
6	0110	digit
7	0111	
8	1000	
9	1001	↓
10	0001 0000	
20	0010 0000	
50	0101 0000	
99	1001 1001	
248	0010 0100 1000	

It is very important to understand the difference between the *conversion* of decimal numbers into binary and the *binary coding* of decimal numbers. For example, the decimal number 99, when *converted* to a binary number, is represented by the string of bits 1100011, but when represented in BCD, it becomes 1001 1001. The *only* difference between a decimal number represented by the familiar digit symbols 0, 1, 2, . . . , 9 and the BCD symbols 0001, 0010, . . . , 1001 is in the symbols used to represent the digits—the number itself is exactly the same. A few decimal numbers and their representation in BCD are listed in Table 3-3.

Alphanumeric Representation

Many applications of digital computers require the handling of data that consist not only of numbers, but also of the letters of the alphabet and certain special characters. An *alphanumeric character set* is a set of elements that includes the 10 decimal digits, the 26 letters of the alphabet and a number of special characters, such as $, +, and =. Such a set contains between 32 and 64 elements (if only uppercase letters are included) or between 64 and 128 (if both uppercase and lowercase letters are included). In the first case, the binary code will require six bits and in the second case, seven bits. The standard alphanumeric binary code is the ASCII (American National Standard Code for Information Interchange) which uses seven bits to code 128 characters. The binary code for the uppercase letters, the decimal digits, and a few special characters is listed in Table 3-4. Note that the decimal digits in ASCII can be converted to BCD by removing the three high-order bits, 011.

Binary codes play an important part in digital computer operations. The codes must be in binary because registers can only hold binary information. One must real-

TABLE 3-4 American National Standard Code for Information Interchange (ASCII)

Character	Binary Code	Character	Binary Code
A	100 0001	0	011 0000
B	100 0010	1	011 0001
C	100 0011	2	011 0010
D	100 0100	3	011 0011
E	100 0101	4	011 0100
F	100 0110	5	011 0101
G	100 0111	6	011 0110
H	100 1000	7	011 0111
I	100 1001	8	011 1000
J	100 1010	9	011 1001
K	100 1011		
L	100 1100		
M	100 1101	blank	010 0000
N	100 1110	.	010 1110
O	100 1111	(	010 1000
P	101 0000	+	010 1011
Q	101 0001	$	010 0100
R	101 0010	*	010 1010
S	101 0011	)	010 1001
T	101 0100	—	010 1101
U	101 0101	/	010 1111
V	101 0110	,	010 1100
W	101 0111	=	011 1101
X	101 1000		
Y	101 1001		
Z	101 1010		

ize that binary codes merely change the symbols, not the meaning of the discrete elements they represent. The operations specified for digital computers must take into consideration the meaning of the bits stored in registers so that operations are performed on operands of the same type. In inspecting the bits of a computer register at random, one is likely to find that it represents some type of coded information rather than a binary number.

Binary codes can be formulated for any set of discrete elements: the colors of the spectrum, musical notes, and chess pieces and their positions on the chessboard. Binary codes are also used to formulate instructions that specify control information for the computer. This chapter is concerned with *data* representation. Instruction codes are discussed in Chap. 5.

3-2   FIXED-POINT REPRESENTATION

Numbers used in scientific calculations are designated by a sign, the magnitude of the number and sometimes a decimal point. The sign is needed for arithmetic operations as it shows whether the number is positive or negative. The position of the decimal (or binary) point is needed to represent fractions or mixed integer-fraction numbers.

The sign of a number may be considered as a set of two elements, *plus* and *minus*. This two-element set can be assigned a binary code of one bit. The convention is to represent a plus with a 0 and a minus with a 1. To represent a signed binary number in a register we need $n + 1$ bits; n bits for the number and one bit for the sign. The sign bit is customarily placed in the leftmost position of the register.

The representation of the decimal (or binary) point in a register is complicated by the fact that it is characterized by a *position* between two flip-flops in the register. There are two ways of specifying the position of the decimal point in a register: by giving it a *fixed* position or by employing a *floating-point* representation. The fixed-point method assumes that the decimal point is always fixed in one position. The two positions most widely used are: (1) a decimal point in the extreme left of the register to make the stored number a fraction, and (2) a decimal point in the extreme right of the register to make the stored number an integer. In either case, the decimal point is not actually present but its presence is assumed from the fact that the number stored in the register is treated as a fraction or as an integer. The floating-point representation uses a second register to store a number that designates the position of the decimal point in the first register. Floating-point representation is discussed further in the next section.

Before proceeding to show how fixed-point numbers are represented in registers, it is necessary to define the *complement* of a number. Complements are used in digital computers to represent negative numbers because this representation facilitates arithmetic manipulations. There are two types of complements for each radix r number system: (1) the r's complement and (2) the $(r - 1)$'s complement. When the radix number is substituted for r, the two types receive the names 2's and 1's complement for binary numbers, or 10's and 9's complement for decimal numbers.

The $(r - 1)$'s Complement

The $(r - 1)$'s complement of a number in radix r is obtained by subtracting each digit of the number from $(r - 1)$. For decimal numbers, $(r - 1) = 9$ and for binary numbers, $(r - 1) = 1$. Thus, the 9's complement of decimal 835 is 164 and is obtained by subtracting each digit from 9. The 1's complement of the binary number 1010 is 0101 and is obtained by subtracting each digit from 1. However, when subtracting binary digits from 1, we can have either $1 - 0 = 1$ or $1 - 1 = 0$. In either case, the digit obtained by subtracting it from 1 is the complement of its original value. In other words, the 1's complement of a binary number is identical to the bit-by-bit logic complement operation. An easier way to obtain the 1's complement is to change all 1's to 0's and all 0's to 1's. Since the logic complement and 1's complement are identical operations for binary digits, we will sometimes drop the designation 1's and call it just *complement*.

The $(r - 1)$'s complement of octal or hexadecimal numbers are obtained by subtracting each digit from 7 or F (decimal 15), respectively. When these numbers are binary coded, the complement is obtained by changing 1's to 0's and 0's to 1's.

The r's Complement

The r's complement of a number in radix r is obtained by adding 1 to the low-order digit of its $(r - 1)$'s complement. Thus, the 10's complement of the decimal 835 is $164 + 1 = 165$ and is obtained by adding 1 to its 9's complement value. The 2's complement of binary 1010 is $0101 + 1 = 0110$ and is obtained by complementing each bit and adding 1.

The 2's complement can be formed also by leaving all least significant 0's and the first 1 unchanged, and then complementing the remaining digits. For example, the 2's complement of 10100 is 01100 and is obtained by leaving the two low-order 0's and the first 1 unchanged, and then complementing the two most significant bits.

Binary Fixed-Point Representation

When a fixed-point binary number is positive, the sign is represented by 0 and the magnitude by a positive binary number. When the number is negative, the sign is represented by 1 but the rest of the number may be represented in one of three possible ways. These are:

1. Signed-magnitude representation, or
2. Signed-1's complement representation, or
3. Signed-2's complement representation.

In the signed-magnitude representation of a negative number the magnitude of the number is inserted next to its negative sign. In the other two representations, the negative number is represented as either the 1's or 2's complement of its position value designation. As an example, consider the number 9 stored in a 7-bit register. $+9$ is represented by a sign bit of 0 in the leftmost position followed by the binary equivalent of 9: 0 001001. Note that each of the seven bits of the register must have a value and therefore, 0's must be inserted in the two most significant positions following the sign bit. Although there is only one way to represent $+9$, there are three different ways to represent -9. These representations are shown below:

In signed-magnitude representation	1 001001
In signed-1's complement representation	1 110110
In signed-2's complement representation	1 110111

The signed-magnitude representation of -9 is obtained from $+9$ (0 001001) by complementing *only* the sign bit. The signed-1's complement representation of -9 is obtained by complementing *all* the bits of 0 001001 ($+9$), including the sign bit. The signed-2's complement designation is obtained by taking the 2's complement of the positive number, *including* its sign bit.

Arithmetic Addition

The reason for using the signed-complement representation for negative numbers will become apparent after we consider the steps involved in forming the sum of two signed numbers. The signed-magnitude representation is the one used in everyday calculations. For example, $+23$ and -35 are represented with a sign, followed by the magnitude of the number. To add these two numbers, it is necessary to subtract the smaller magnitude from the larger and to use the sign of the larger number for the sign of the result, that is: $(+23) + (-35) = - (35 - 23) = -12$. The process of adding two signed numbers when negative numbers are represented in signed-magnitude form requires that we compare their signs. If the two signs are the same, we add the two magnitudes. If the signs are not the same, we compare the relative magnitudes of the numbers and then subtract the smaller from the larger. It is necessary also to determine the sign of the result. This is a process that, when implemented with digital hardware, requires a long sequence of control decisions as well as circuits that can compare, add, and subtract numbers.

Now compare the above procedure with the procedure that forms the sum of two signed binary numbers when negative numbers are in signed-2's complement representation. This procedure is very simple and can be stated as follows:

Add the two numbers, including their sign bit, and discard any carry out of the leftmost (sign) bit.

Numerical examples for addition of two binary numbers with negative numbers in their signed-2's complement representation are shown below. Note that negative numbers must be initially in signed-2's complement representation and the sum obtained after the addition, if negative, is also in its signed-2's complement representation. The two numbers in the four examples are added, including their sign bit, and any carry out of the sign bit is discarded.

$$
\begin{array}{lll}
+6 & 0\ 000110 \\
  & \qquad + \\
+9 & 0\ 001001 \\ \hline
+15 & 0\ 001111
\end{array}
\qquad
\begin{array}{lll}
-6 & 1\ 111010 \\
  & \qquad + \\
+9 & 0\ 001001 \\ \hline
+3 & 0\ 000011
\end{array}
$$

$$
\begin{array}{lll}
+6 & 0\ 000110 \\
  & \qquad + \\
-9 & 1\ 110111 \\ \hline
-3 & 1\ 111101
\end{array}
\qquad
\begin{array}{lll}
-9 & 1\ 110111 \\
  & \qquad + \\
-9 & 1\ 110111 \\ \hline
-18 & 1\ 101110
\end{array}
$$

This procedure is much simpler than the one used for signed-magnitude numbers. It requires only one control decision and a circuit for adding two numbers. The procedure requires that negative numbers be initially stored in registers in their 2's complement form. This can be easily accomplished by complementing and then incrementing the positive number.

The procedure that forms the sum of two binary numbers when negative numbers are in signed-1's complement form is similar and can be stated as follows:

Add the two numbers, including their sign bit. If there is a carry out of the most significant (sign) bit, the result is incremented by 1 and the carry discarded.

The two examples shown below demonstrate this procedure. Note that all negative numbers, including results, are in their signed-1's complement form. The carry out of the sign bit, when 1, is returned and added to the least significant bit. This is referred to as *end-around carry*.

$$
\begin{array}{lll}
+6 & 0\ 000110 \\
  & \qquad + \\
-9 & 1\ 110110 \\ \hline
-3 & 1\ 111100
\end{array}
\qquad
\begin{array}{lll}
-6 & 1\ 111001 \\
  & \qquad + \\
+9 & 0\ 001001 \\ \hline
  & 1\ 0\ 000010 \\
  & \qquad\qquad + \\
  & \qquad\qquad 1 \\ \hline
+3 & 0\ 000011
\end{array}
$$

The advantage of the signed-2's complement representation over the signed-1's complement form (and the signed-magnitude form) is that it contains only one type of zero. The other two representations have both a positive zero and a negative zero. For example, adding $(+9)$ to (-9) in the 1's complement representation, one obtains:

$$
\begin{array}{ll}
+9 & 0\ 001001 \\
-9 & 1\ 110110 \\
\hline
-0 & 1\ 111111
\end{array}
$$

and the result is a negative zero, that is, the complement of 0 000000 (positive zero).

A zero with an associated sign bit will appear in a register in one of the following forms, depending on the representation used for negative numbers:

	$+0$	-0
In signed-magnitude	0 0000000	1 0000000
In signed-1's complement	0 0000000	1 1111111
In signed-2's complement	0 0000000	none

Both the signed-magnitude and the 1's complement representation have associated with them the possibility of a negative zero. The signed-2's complement representation has only a positive zero. This occurs because the 2's complement of 0 000000 (positive zero) is 0 000000 and may be obtained from the 1's complement plus 1 (i.e., 1 111111 + 1) provided the end-carry is discarded.

The range of binary integer numbers that can be accommodated in a register of $n = k + 1$ bits is $\pm(2^k - 1)$, where k bits are reserved for the number and one bit for the sign. A register with eight bits can store binary numbers in the range $\pm(2^7 - 1) = \pm127$. However, since the signed-2's complement representation has only one zero, it should accommodate one more number than the other two representations. Consider the representation of the largest and smallest numbers:

	Signed-1's Complement	Signed-2's Complement
$+126 = 0\ 1111110$	$-126 = 1\ 0000001$	$= 1\ 0000010$
$+127 = 0\ 1111111$	$-127 = 1\ 0000000$	$= 1\ 0000001$
$+128$ (impossible)	-128 (impossible)	$= 1\ 0000000$

In the signed-2's complement representation, it is possible to represent -128 with eight bits. In general, the signed-2's complement representation can accommodate numbers in the range $+(2^k - 1)$ to -2^k, where $k = n - 1$ and n is the number of bits in the register.

Arithmetic Subtraction

Subtraction of two signed binary numbers when negative numbers are in the 2's complement form is very simple and can be stated as follows:

Take the 2's complement of the subtrahend (including the sign bit) and add it to the minuend (including sign bit).

This procedure utilizes the fact that a subtraction operation can be changed to an addition operation if the sign of the subtrahend is changed. This is demonstrated by the following relations (B is the subtrahend):

$$(\pm A) - (-B) = (\pm A) + (+B)$$
$$(\pm A) - (+B) = (\pm A) + (-B)$$

But changing a positive number to a negative number is easily done by taking its 2's complement (including the sign bit). The reverse is also true because the complement of the complement restores the number to its original value.

The subtraction with 1's complement numbers is similar except for the end around carry. Subtraction with signed-magnitude numbers is more complicated and is covered in detail in Sec. 9-3.

Because of the availability of simple procedures for adding and subtracting numbers when negative numbers are in the signed-2's complement form, many computers adopt this representation over the more familiar signed-magnitude form. The reason 2's complement is usually chosen over 1's complement is to avoid the occurrence of a negative zero.

Overflow

When two numbers of n digits each are added and the sum occupies $n + 1$ digits, we say that an *overflow* occurs. This is true for binary numbers or decimal numbers, whether signed or unsigned. When one performs the addition with paper and pencil, an overflow in not a problem, since we are not limited by the width of the page to write down the sum. An overflow is a problem in a digital computer because the lengths of all registers, including memory registers, are of finite length. A result of $n + 1$ bits cannot be accommodated in a register of standard length n. For this reason, many computers check for the occurrence of an overflow, and when it occurs, they set an overflow flip-flop for the user to check.

An overflow cannot occur after an addition if one number is positive and the other is negative, since adding a positive number to a negative number produces a result (positive or negative) which is smaller than the larger of the two original numbers. An overflow may occur if the two numbers are added and both are positive or both are negative. When two numbers in sign-magnitude representation are added, an overflow can be easily detected from the carry out of the number bits. When two numbers in signed-2's complement representation are added, the sign bit is treated as part of the number and the end carry does not necessarily indicate an overflow.

The algorithm for adding two numbers in signed-2's complement representation, as previously stated, gives an incorrect result when an overflow occurs. This arises because an overflow of the number of bits always changes the sign of the result and gives an erroneous n-bit answer. To see how this happens, consider the following example. Two signed binary numbers, 70 and 80, are stored in two eight-bit registers. The maximum capacity of the register is $(2^7 - 1) = 127$ and the minimum capacity is $-2^7 = -128$. Since the sum of the numbers is 150, it exceeds the capacity of the register. This is true if the numbers are both positive or both negative. The operations in binary are shown below together with the last two carries of the addition:

	carries: 0 1			carries: 1 0
$+$ 70	0 1000110		$-$ 70	1 0111010
$+$ 80	0 1010000		$-$ 80	1 0110000
$+150$	1 0010110		-150	0 1101010

In the first case, the 8-bit result that should have been positive has a negative sign bit. In the second case, the 8-bit result that should have been negative has a positive sign bit. Note that if the carry out of the sign-bit position is taken as the sign of the result, then the 9-bit answer so obtained will be correct. However, a 9-bit number cannot be accommodated in a system with standard 8-bit registers. Obviously, the 8-bit binary answer is incorrect and the algorithm for adding binary numbers in signed-2's complement, as stated previously, fails to give correct results when an overflow occurs.

From the examples above we see that an overflow occurs if the two numbers are positive and the sum contains a negative sign or if the two numbers are negative and the sum contains a positive sign. In other words, an overflow produces an erroneous sign reversal.

An overflow condition can be detected by observing the carry *into* the sign-bit position and the carry *out* of the sign-bit position. If these two carries are not equal, an overflow condition will occur. This is indicated in the two examples above, where these two carries are explicitly shown. If the two carries are applied to an exclusive-OR gate, an overflow would be detected when the output of the gate is 1. The effect of the overflow condition on signed-2's complement arithmetic is discussed further in Sec 10-2.

Decimal Fixed-Point Representation

The representation of decimal numbers in registers is a function of the binary code used to represent a decimal digit. A 4-bit decimal code requires four flip-flops for each decimal digit. The representation of $+4385$ in BCD requires at least 17 flip-flops, one flip-flop for the sign and four for each digit. This number will be represented in a register with 25 flip-flops as follows:

$$+ \quad 0 \qquad 0 \qquad 4 \qquad 3 \qquad 8 \qquad 5$$
$$0 \quad 0\,0\,0\,0 \quad 0\,0\,0\,0 \quad 0\,1\,0\,0 \quad 0\,0\,1\,1 \quad 1\,0\,0\,0 \quad 0\,1\,0\,1$$

By representing numbers in decimal we are wasting a considerable amount of storage space since the number of flip-flops needed to store a decimal number in a binary code is greater than the number of flip-flops needed for its equivalent binary representation. Also, the circuits required to perform decimal arithmetic are more complex. However, there are some advantages in the use of decimal representation because computer input and output data are generated by people who use the decimal system. Some applications such as electronic calculators or business data processing require small amounts of arithmetic computations compared to the amount required for input and output of data. For this reason, some computers and all calculators will perform arithmetic computations directly on decimal data (in binary code) and thus eliminate the need for conversion to binary and back to decimal. Large scale computer systems usually have hardware for arithmetic calculations with both binary and decimal data. The user can specify by programmed instructions whether he wants the computer to perform calculations on binary or decimal data.

There are three ways to represent negative fixed-point decimal numbers. They are similar to the three representations of a negative binary number except for the radix change:

1. Signed-magnitude representation, or

2. Signed-9's complement representation, or

3. Signed-10's complement representation.

For all three representations, a positive decimal number is represented by 0 for plus followed by the magnitude of the number. It is in regard to negative numbers that the representations differ. The sign of a negative number is represented by 1 and the magnitude of the number is positive in signed-magnitude representation. In the other two representations the number is represented by the 9's or 10's complement form. The sign of the decimal number is sometimes represented by a 4-bit code to conform with the 4-bit representation of digits. For example, the code 1100 (not assigned to a BCD digit) may be used to represent a plus and 1101 to represent a minus.

Arithmetic addition and subtraction of decimal numbers employs the same procedures as binary numbers except for the difference in the radix. The 2's complement procedures of binary numbers, described previously, apply also to decimals when negative numbers are represented in their signed-10's complement form. The sign is represented by 0 or 1 and placed in the leftmost position of the number. The sign bit is added together with the other digits. A corresponding similarity exists with the other two representations.

3-3 FLOATING-POINT REPRESENTATION

The floating-point representation of a number needs two parts. The first part represents a signed, fixed-point number called the *mantissa*. The second part designates the position of the decimal (or binary) point and is called the *exponent*. The fixed-point mantissa may be a fraction or an integer. For example, the decimal number $+6132.789$ is represented in floating point as follows:

sign		*sign*	
0	.6132789	0	04
	mantissa		exponent

The mantissa has a 0 in the leftmost position to denote a plus. The mantissa here is considered to be a fixed-point *fraction*, so the decimal point is assumed to be at the left of the most significant digit. The decimal mantissa, when stored in a register, requires at least 29 flip-flops: four flip-flops for each BCD digit and one for the sign. The decimal point is not physically indicated in the register; it is only assumed to be there. The exponent contains the decimal number $+04$ (in BCD) to indicate that the *actual* position of the decimal point is four decimal positions to the right of the *assumed* decimal point. This representation is equivalent to the number expressed as a fraction times 10 to an exponent, that is, $+.6132789 \times 10^{+04}$. Because of this analogy, the mantissa is sometimes called the *fraction part*.

In the previous example, we have assumed that the mantissa is a fixed-point fraction and that the exponent is associated with a radix of 10. Some computers assume a fixed-point integer for the mantissa. Moreover, the assumed radix for the exponent is a function of the number system that is being represented in the register. Consider, for example, a computer that assumes integer representation for the mantissa and radix 8 for the numbers. The octal number $+36.754 = 36754 \times 8^{-3}$, in its floating-point representation, will look like this:

sign		*sign*	
0	36754.	1	03
	mantissa		exponent

When this number is represented in a register, in its binary-coded form, the actual value of the register becomes

$$0 \; 011 \; 110 \; 111 \; 101 \; 100 \qquad 1 \; 000 \; 011$$

The register needs 23 flip-flops. The circuits that operate on such data must recognize the flip-flops assigned to the bits of the mantissa and exponent and their associated signs. Note that if the exponent is increased by one (to -2) the *actual* point of the mantissa is shifted to the right by three bits (one octal digit).

Floating-point is always interpreted to represent a number in the following form:

$$m \times r^e$$

Only the mantissa m and the exponent e are physically represented in the register (including their signs). The radix r and the radix-point position of the mantissa are always *assumed*. The circuits that manipulate the floating-point numbers in registers must conform with these two assumptions if correct computational results are to be achieved. A floating-point binary number is represented in a similar manner except that the radix assumed is 2. For example, the number $+1001.11$ is represented in a 16-bit register as follows:

$$
\begin{array}{cc}
\textit{sign} & \textit{sign} \\
0 \quad \underbrace{100111000} & 0 \quad \underbrace{00100} \\
\text{mantissa} & \text{exponent}
\end{array}
$$

with the mantissa occupying ten bits and the exponent six bits. The mantissa is assumed to be a fixed-point fraction. If the mantissa is assumed to be an integer, the exponent will be 1 00101 (-5).

A floating-point number is said to be *normalized* if the most significant position of the mantissa contains a nonzero digit. For example, the mantissa 035 is not normalized but 350 is. When 350 is represented in BCD, it becomes 0011 0101 0000 and although two 0's seem to be present in the two most significant positions, the mantissa *is* normalized. Because the bits represent a *decimal* number, not a binary number, and decimal numbers in BCD must be taken in groups of four bits, the first digit is 3 and is nonzero.

When the mantissa is normalized, it has no leading zeros and therefore contains the maximum possible number of significant digits. Consider, for example, a register that can accommodate a mantissa of five decimal digits and a sign. The number $+.35746 \times 10^2 = 35.746$ is normalized because the mantissa has a nonzero digit 3 in its most significant position. The number can be represented in an unnormalized form as $+.00357 \times 10^4 = 35.7$. This unnormalized number contains two most significant zeros and therefore the mantissa can accommodate only three significant digits. The two least significant digits, 4 and 6, that were accommodated in the normalized form, have no room in the unnormalized form because the register can only accommodate five digits.

A zero cannot be normalized because it does not contain a nonzero digit. A zero is represented in floating-point by all 0's in the mantissa and exponent, including their signs. It is then necessary to check for an all 0 quantity before deciding whether the number can be normalized.

Arithmetic operations with floating-point numbers are more complicated than arithmetic operations with fixed-point numbers and their execution takes longer and requires more complex hardware. However, floating-point representation is a must for scientific computations because of the scaling problems involved with fixed-point computations. Many computers and all electronic calculators have built-in capability of performing floating-point arithmetic operations. Computers that do not have hardware for floating-point computations have a set of subroutines to help the user program his scientific problems with floating-point numbers. Floating-point numbers are called *real* numbers when specified in a Fortran program. Arithmetic operations with floating-point numbers are discussed in Sec. 10-4.

3-4 OTHER BINARY CODES

The previous sections introduced the most common types of binary-coded data found in digital computers. Other binary codes for decimal numbers and alphanumeric characters are sometimes used. Digital computers also employ other binary codes for special applications. A few additional binary codes encountered in digital computers are presented in this section.

Gray Code

Digital systems can process data in discrete form only. Many physical systems supply continuous output data. The data must be converted into digital form before it can be used by a digital computer. Continuous, or analog, information is converted into digital form by means of an analog-to-digital converter. The reflected binary or *Gray* code, shown in Table 3-5, is sometimes used for the converted digital data. The advantage of the Gray code over straight binary numbers is that the Gray code changes by only one bit as it sequences from one number to the next. In other words, the change from any number to the next in sequence is recognized by a change of only one bit from 0 to 1 or from 1 to 0. A typical application of the Gray code occurs when the analog data is represented by the continuous change of a shaft position. The shaft is partitioned into segments with each segment assigned a number. If adjacent segments

TABLE 3-5   4-Bit Gray Code

Binary Code	Decimal Equivalent	Binary Code	Decimal Equivalent
0000	0	1100	8
0001	1	1101	9
0011	2	1111	10
0010	3	1110	11
0110	4	1010	12
0111	5	1011	13
0101	6	1001	14
0100	7	1000	15

are made to correspond to adjacent Gray code numbers, ambiguity is reduced when the shaft position is in the line that separates any two segments.

Gray code counters are sometimes used to provide the timing sequences that control the operations in a digital system. A Gray code counter is a counter whose flip-flops go through a sequence of states as specified in Table 3-5. Gray code counters remove the ambiguity during the change from one state of the counter to the next because only one bit can change during the state transition.

Other Decimal Codes

Binary codes for decimal digits require a minimum of four bits. Numerous different codes can be formulated by arranging four or more bits in 10 distinct possible combinations. A few possibilities are shown in Table 3-6.

TABLE 3-6   Four Different Binary Codes for the Decimal Digit

Decimal Digit	BCD 8421	2421	Excess-3	Excess-3 Gray
0	0000	0000	0011	0010
1	0001	0001	0100	0110
2	0010	0010	0101	0111
3	0011	0011	0110	0101
4	0100	0100	0111	0100
5	0101	1011	1000	1100
6	0110	1100	1001	1101
7	0111	1101	1010	1111
8	1000	1110	1011	1110
9	1001	1111	1100	1010
	1010	0101	0000	0000
Unused	1011	0110	0001	0001
bit	1100	0111	0010	0011
combi-	1101	1000	1101	1000
nations	1110	1001	1110	1001
	1111	1010	1111	1011

The BCD (binary-coded decimal) has been introduced before. It uses a straight assignment of the binary equivalent of the digit. The six unused bit combinations listed have no meaning when BCD is used, just as the letter H has no meaning when decimal digit symbols are written down. For example, saying that 1001 1110 is a decimal number in BCD is like saying that 9H is a decimal number in the conventional symbol designation. Both cases contain an invalid symbol and, therefore, designate a meaningless number.

One disadvantage of using BCD is the difficulty encountered when the 9's complement of the number is to be computed. On the other hand, the 9's complement is easily obtained with the 2421 and the excess-3 codes listed in Table 3-6. These two codes have a self-complementing property which means that the 9's complement of a decimal number, when represented in one of these codes, is easily obtained by changing 1's to 0's and 0's to 1's. This property is useful when arithmetic operations are done in signed-complement representation.

The 2421 is an example of a *weighted* code. In a weighted code, the bits are multiplied by the weights indicated and the sum of the weighted bits gives the decimal digit.

For example, the bit combination 1101, when weighted by the respective digits 2421, gives the decimal equivalent of $2 \times 1 + 4 \times 1 + 2 \times 0 + 1 + 1 = 7$. The BCD code can be assigned the weights 8421 and for this reason it is sometimes called the 8421 code.

The excess-3 code is a decimal code that has been used in older computers. This is an unweighted code. Its binary code assignment is obtained from the corresponding BCD equivalent binary number after the addition of binary 3 (0011).

From Table 3-5 we note that the Gray code is not suited for a decimal code if we were to choose the first 10 entries in the table. This is because the transition from 9 back to 0 involves a change of three bits (from 1101 to 0000). To overcome this difficulty, we choose the 10 numbers starting from the third entry 0010 up to the twelfth entry 1010. Now the transition from 1010 to 0010 involves a change of only one bit. Since the code has been shifted up three numbers, it is called the excess-3 Gray. This code is listed with the other decimal codes in Table 3-6.

Other Alphanumeric Codes

The ASCII code (Table 3-4) is the standard code commonly used for the transmission of binary information. Each character is represented by a 7-bit code and usually an eighth bit is inserted for parity (see Sec. 3-5). The code consists of 128 characters. 95 characters represent *graphic symbols* that include upper and lower case letters, numerals zero to nine, punctuation marks and special symbols. Twenty-three characters represent *format effectors* which are functional characters for controlling the layout of printing or display devices such as carriage return, line feed, horizontal tabulation, and back space. The other 10 characters are used to direct the data communication flow and report its status.

Another alphanumeric (sometimes called *alphameric*) code used in IBM equipment is the EBCDIC (Extended BCD Interchange Code). It uses eight bits for each character (and a ninth bit for parity). EBCDIC has the same character symbols as ASCII but the bit assignment to characters is different.

When alphanumeric characters are used internally in a computer for data processing (not for transmission purposes) it is more convenient to use a 6-bit code to represent 64 characters. A 6-bit code can specify the 26 upper-case letters of the alphabet, numerals zero to nine, and up to 28 special characters. This set of characters is usually sufficient for data processing purposes. Using fewer bits to code characters has the advantage of reducing the memory space needed to store large quantities of alphanumeric data.

When alphanumeric information is transferred to the computer via punched cards, the alphanumeric characters use a 12-bit code. Programs and data are often prepared on punched cards for input to a computer. Of the different cards that are in use, the *Hollerith card* is the most common. A punched card consists of 80 columns and 12 rows. Each column represents an alphanumeric character of 12 bits by punching holes in the appropriate rows. A hole is sensed as a 1 and the absence of a hole is sensed as a 0. The 12 rows are marked starting from the top, as 12, 11, 0, 1, 2, . . . , 9 punch. The first three are called the *zone* punch and the last nine are called the *numeric* punch. The decimal digits are represented by a single hole in a numeric punch. The letters of the alphabet are represented by two holes, one in a zone and the other in a numeric punch. Special characters are represented by one, two or three holes; the zone is always used, and the other two holes, if used, are in a numeric punch with the 8 punch most commonly used. The 12-bit card is code inefficient with respect to the number of bits used. Most computers convert the input 12-bit card code into an internal 6-bit code to conserve bits of memory.

3-5 ERROR DETECTION CODES

Binary information transmitted through some form of communication medium is subject to external noise that could change bits from 1 to 0, and vice versa. An error detection code is a binary code that detects digital errors during transmission. The detected errors cannot be corrected but their presence is indicated. The usual procedure is to observe the frequency of errors. If errors occur infrequently at random, the particular erroneous informatiom is transmitted again. If the error occurs too often, the system is checked for malfunction.

The most common error detection code used is the *parity bit*. A parity bit is an extra bit included with a binary message to make the total number of 1's either odd or even. A message of three bits and two possible parity bits is shown in Table 3-7.

TABLE 3-7   Parity Bit Generation

Message xyz	P(odd)	P(even)
000	1	0
001	0	1
010	0	1
011	1	0
100	0	1
101	1	0
110	1	0
111	0	1

The P(odd) bit is chosen in such a way as to make the sum of 1's (in all four bits) odd. The P(even) bit is chosen to make the sum of all 1's even. In either case, the sum is taken over the message and the P bit. In any particular application, one or the other type of parity will be adopted. The even parity scheme has the disadvantage of having a bit combination of all 0's, while in the odd parity there is always one bit (of the four bits that constitute the message and P) that is 1. Note that the P(odd) is the complement of the P(even).

During transfer of information from one location to another, the parity bit is handled as follows. At the sending end, the message (in this case three bits) is applied to a *parity generator*, where the required parity bit is generated. The message, including the parity bit, is transmitted to its destination. At the receiving end, all the incoming bits (in this case, four) are applied to a *parity checker* that checks the proper parity adopted (odd or even). An error is detected if the checked parity does not conform to the adopted parity. The parity method detects the presence of one, three, or any odd number of errors. An even number of errors is not detected.

Parity generator and checker networks are logic circuits constructed with exclusive-OR functions. This is because, as mentioned in Sec. 1-1, the exclusive-OR function of three or more variables is by definition an odd function. An odd function is a logic funcion whose value is binary 1 if, and only if, an odd number of variables are equal to 1. According to this definition, the P(even) function is the exclusive-OR of x, y, and z because it is equal to 1 when either one or all three of the variables are equal to 1 (Table 3-7). The P(odd) function is the complement of the P(even) function.

As an example, consider a 3-bit message to be transmitted with an odd parity bit. At the sending end, the odd parity bit is generated by a parity generator circuit. As shown in Fig. 3-3, this circuit consists of one exclusive-OR and one exclusive-

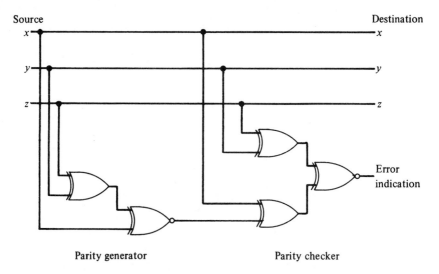

Fig. 3-3 Error detection with odd parity bit.

NOR gate. Since P(even) is the exclusive-OR of x, y, z, and P(odd) is the complement of P(even), it is necessary to employ an exclusive-NOR gate for the needed complementation. The message and the odd parity bit are transmitted to their destination where they are applied to a parity checker. An error has occurred during transmission if the parity of the four bits received is even, since the binary information transmitted was originally odd. The output of the parity checker would be 1 when an error occurs, that is, when the number of 1's in the four inputs is even. Since the exclusive-OR function of the four inputs is an odd function, we again need to complement the output by using an exclusive-NOR gate.

It is worth noting that the parity generator can use the same circuit as the parity checker if the fourth input is permanently held at a logic-0 value. The advantage of this is that the same circuit can be used for both parity generation and parity checking.

It is evident from the example above that even parity generators and checkers can be implemented with exclusive-OR functions. Odd parity networks need an exclusive-NOR at the output to complement the function. Parity generator/checker circuits are available in IC packages.

REFERENCES

1. MANO, M. M., *Digital Logic and Computer Design.* Englewood Cliffs, N.J.: Prentice-Hall, Inc., 1979.

2. RHYNE, V. T., *Fundamentals of Digital System Design.* Englewood Cliffs, N.J.: Prentice-Hall, Inc., 1973.

3. FLETCHER, W. I., *An Engineering Approach to Digital Design.* Englewood Cliffs, N.J.: Prentice-Hall, Inc., 1980.

4. BOOTH, T. L., *Digital Networks and Computer Systems*, 2nd ed. New York: John Wiley & Sons, Inc., 1978.

5. ROTH, C. H., JR., *Fundamentals of Logic Design*, 2nd ed. St. Paul, Minn.: West Publishing Co., 1979.

PROBLEMS

3-1.   Give the decimal equivalent of $(11010.111)_2$, $(736.5)_8$, and $(3FA.8)_{16}$.

3-2.   Convert the following decimal numbers to binary: 12.0625, 10^4, 673.23, and 1998.

3-3.   Convert decimal 225.225 to octal and hexadecimal.

3-4.   Show the value of all cells of a 12-bit register that hold the number equivalent to $(215)_{10}$ in (a) binary; (b) binary-coded octal; (c) binary-coded hexadecimal; (d) BCD.

3-5.   Represent your first name, middle initial, and last name in binary using ASCII (Table 3-4). Include blanks between names and a period after the middle initial.

3-6.   Why do you suppose people adopted the decimal number system for everyday use? If you had to propose another number system so as to facilitate arithmetic computations, what radix would you choose? As a computer architect, what radix would you recommend?

3-7.   A computer has been proposed based on the radix 3 system.
       (a) What type of storage cells are needed for memory and registers?
       (b) What type of logic system is needed to replace the two-valued Boolean algebra?
       (c) How many combinations will be unassigned in a radix 3 code for the ten decimal digits?

3-8.   Show the bit configuration of a 24-bit register when its content represents the decimal equivalent of 295 in: (a) binary; (b) BCD; (c) ASCII.

3-9.   Assign a binary code in some orderly manner to the 52 playing cards.

3-10.   Obtain the 1's and 2's complement of the following binary numbers: 1010101, 0111000, 0000001, 10000, and 0000.

3-11.   Obtain the 9's and 10's complement of the following decimal numbers: 13579, 09900, 90090, 10000, and 0000. Show their representation in BCD.

3-12.   Obtain the 7's and 8's complement of the following octal numbers: 770, 1263, 00010, and 0000. Show their representation in binary-coded form.

3-13.   Obtain the 15's and 16's complement of the following hexadecimal numbers: FF0, 1234, ABCD, and 0000. Show their representation in binary-coded form.

3-14.   Represent the binary equivalent of −86 in three different ways using a register of 10 bits.

3-15.   Represent −8620 in BCD in three different ways.

3-16.   The binary numbers listed below have a sign bit in the leftmost position. Negative numbers are in their signed-2's complement form. Perform the arithmetic operations indicated and leave results, if negative, in the signed-2's complement form. Verify your results.

$$
\begin{array}{ll}
001110 + 110010 & \qquad 010101 - 000111 \\
010101 + 000011 & \qquad 001010 - 111001 \\
111001 + 001010 & \qquad 111001 - 001010 \\
101011 + 111000 & \qquad 101011 - 100110
\end{array}
$$

3-17.   Repeat Prob. 3-16 assuming that negative numbers are in signed-1's complement representation.

3-18.   Perform the arithmetic operations $(+35) + (+40)$ and $(-35) + (-40)$ with binary numbers in signed-2's complement representation. Use seven bits to accommodate each number together with its sign. Show that overflow occurs in both cases, that the last two carries are unequal, and that there is a sign reversal. Interpret the 7-bit result obtained in each case.

3-19.   What is the difference (if any) between fixed-point numbers (in any representation) and binary-coded octal or binary-coded hexadecimal numbers? Would arithmetic calculations give the same results? From your answer to the above, how could you explain a statement from a computer manufacturer who says that his computer is an octal machine rather than a binary machine?

3-20.   The procedure for adding and subtracting decimal numbers when negative numbers are in signed-10's complement form is similar to the procedure used for binary numbers when negative numbers are in signed-2's complement representation. Formulate this procedure and apply it to the following decimal computations: $(-638) + (+785)$ and $(-638) - (+185)$.

3-21.   A 36-bit floating-point binary number has 8 bits plus a sign for the exponent. The mantissa is assumed to be a normalized fraction. Negative numbers in the mantissa and exponent are in signed-magnitude representation. What are the largest and smallest positive quantities that can be represented, excluding zero?

3-22. A 30-bit register holds a decimal floating-point number represented in BCD. The mantissa occupies 21 bits of the register and is assumed to be a normalized integer. Negative numbers in the mantissa and exponent are in signed-10's complement representation. What are the largest and smallest positive quantities that can be represented, excluding zero?

3-23. Represent the number $(+47.5)_{10}$ with a normalized integer manitissa of 13 bits and an exponent of 7 bits:
(a) As a binary number (assumed radix of 2).
(b) As a binary-coded octal (assumed radix of 8).
(c) As a binary-coded hexadecimal (assumed radix of 16).
Show that the mantissa is the same in all three cases (except for left or right zeros) but that the value of the exponent changes. Determine the largest positive number that the 20-bit register can hold in each of the three representations. What is the advantage of using radix 8 (or 16) over radix 2 for floating-point numbers in registers?

3-24. Show that a decimal digit in BCD has the corresponding weights of 8421.

3-25. The Gray code is sometimes called a *reflected* code because the bit values are reflected on both sides of any 2^n value. For example, as shown in Table 3-5, the values of the three low-order bits are reflected over a line drawn between 7 and 8 ($8 = 2^3$). Using this property of the Gray code obtain:
(a) The Gray code numbers for 16 to 31 as a continuation of Table 3-5.
(b) The excess-3 Gray code for decimals 10 to 19 as a continuation of Table 3-6, column 5.

3-26. Obtain the 9's complement of 1763 in BCD. Add it to BCD 8391 and interpret the result obtained.

3-27. Represent decimal $+3984$ in the 2421 code of Table 3-6. Complement all bits and show that the result is -3984 in signed-9's complement representation with the 2421 code.

3-28. Generate an even parity bit for all ASCII characters listed in Table 3-4 and place it in the most significant position. List the 8-bit code obtained for each character as a two-digit hexadecimal.

3-29. Look at the special characters of a typewriter and find about ten more special characters that are not included in Table 3-4.

3-30. How would you convert the 7-bit code of the characters listed in Table 3-4 to a 6-bit code?

3-31. Hollerith cards with a 12-bit code are inefficient with respect to the number of bits used.
(a) Why do you suppose that it is the most widely used?
(b) How would you formulate a more efficient card code?

3-32. Show that the exclusive-Or function $x = A \oplus B \oplus C \oplus D$ is an odd function. One way to show this is to obtain the truth table for $y = A \oplus B$ and for $z = C \oplus D$ and then formulate the truth table for $x = y \oplus z$.

3-33. Prove that the generation of P(even) for any number of message bits is obtained by the exclusive-OR function of all message bits. Prove that P(odd) is always the complement of P(even).

3-34. Draw the circuit of an 8-bit parity generator/checker having eight inputs and two outputs, one for even and the other for odd parity. What should be the value of the eighth input when the circuit is used to generate an even parity bit for seven message bits?

Register Transfer
and Micro-Operations

4

4-1 REGISTER TRANSFER LANGUAGE

A digital system is an interconnection of digital hardware modules that accomplish a specific information processing task. Digital systems vary in size and complexity from a few integrated circuits to a complex of interconnected and interacting digital computers. Digital computer design invariably uses a modular approach. The modules are constructed from such digital functions as registers, decoders, arithmetic elements, and control logic. The various modules are interconnected with common data and control paths to form a digital computer system.

Each digital module is best defined by the registers it contains and the operations that are performed on the data stored in them. The operations executed on data stored in registers are called *micro-operations*. A micro-operation is an elementary operation, performed during one clock pulse, on the information stored in one or more registers. The result of the operation may replace the previous binary information of a register or may be transferred to another register. Examples of micro-operations are shift, count, clear, and load. Some of the IC digital functions introduced in Chap. 2 are registers that implement micro-operations. For example, a counter with parallel load is capable of performing the micro-operations increment and load. A bidirectional shift-register is capable of performing the shift-right and shift-left micro-operations.

The organization of a digital computer is best defined by specifying:

1. The set of registers it contains and their function.

2. The sequence of micro-operations performed on the binary information stored in the registers.

3. The control functions that initiate the sequence of micro-operations.

It is possible to specify the sequence of micro-operations in a computer by explaining every operation in words, and though sometimes done, this procedure usually involves a lengthy explanation. It is more convenient to adopt a suitable symbology to describe the sequence of transfers between registers and the various arithmetic and logic micro-operations associated with the transfers. The use of symbols, instead of a narrative explanation, provides an organized and concise manner for listing the micro-operation sequences in registers and the control functions that initiate them.

The symbolic notation used to describe the micro-operation transfers among registers is called a *register transfer language*. The term *register transfer* implies the availability of hardware logic circuits that can perform a stated micro-operation and transfer the result of the operation to the same or another register. The word *language* is borrowed from programmers who apply this term to programming languages. A programming language is a procedure for writing symbols to specify a given computational process. Similarly, a natural language such as English is a system for writing symbols and combining them into words and sentences for the purpose of communication between people. A register transfer language is a system for expressing in symbolic form the micro-operation sequences among the registers of a digital module. It is a convenient tool for describing the internal organization of digital computers in concise and precise manner. It can also be used to facilitate the design process of digital systems.

At this time no standard symbology exists for a register transfer language since different sources adopt different conventions. The register transfer language adopted here is believed to be as simple as possible, so it should not take very long to memorize. We will proceed to define symbols for various types of micro-operations, and at the same time, describe associated hardware that can implement the stated micro-operations. Unlike a programming language, a register-transfer language is directly related to and cannot be separated from the registers and other hardware that it defines.

The symbolic designation introduced in this chapter will be utilized in subsequent chapters to specify the register transfers, the micro-operations and the control functions that describe the architecture of digital computers. Other symbology in use can be easily learned once this language has become familiar, for most of the differences between register transfer languages consist of variations in detail rather than in overall purpose.

4-2 INTER-REGISTER TRANSFER

Computer registers are designated by capital letters (sometimes followed by numerals) usually chosen so as to denote the function of the register. For example, the register that holds the address of a memory unit is usually called the *memory address register* and is designated by the capital letters *MAR*. Other designations for registers are: *A*, *AC*, *R*3, and *MBR*. The cells (flip-flops) of an *n*-bit register are numbered in sequence from 1 to *n* (or from 0 to *n* − 1) starting either from the left or from the right. Figure 4-1 shows four ways of drawing the block diagram of a register. In (a) we use a rectangular box with the name of the register inside the box. The numbering of cells from left to right in an 8-bit register is indicated in (b). The individual cells are shown in (c) with each cell assigned a subscript number under A—the letter that designates the name of the register. A 12-bit register is partitioned into two parts in (d). Bits 1 to 4 of the register are assigned the function name *OP* (for *operation*) and bits 5 to 12 are assigned the function name *AD* (for *address*). The symbol *MBR* refers to the 12-bit register. The symbol *MBR(OP)* or *MBR* (1–4) refers to the first four bits of the register while *MBR(AD)* or *MBR* (5–12) refers to bits 5 to 12 of the register.

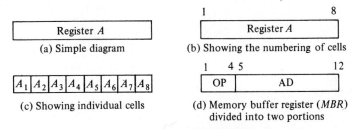

Fig. 4-1   Block diagram for registers.

Data transfer among registers is accomplished by means of *inter-register transfer* micro-operations. These micro-operations perform a direct transfer of binary information from one register to another. The destination register that receives the information assumes the previous value of the source register. The value of the source register does not change because of the transfer.

Parallel Transfer

Information transfer from one register to another can be performed either in parallel or in serial. Parallel transfer is a simultaneous transfer of all bits from the source register to the destination register and is accomplished during one clock pulse. This micro-operation is designated in symbolic form as follows:

$$A \leftarrow B$$

and denotes a transfer of the *content* of register B into register A.

The statement of the transfer $A \leftarrow B$ implies that circuits are available from the outputs of register B to the cell inputs of register A. Normally we do not want this transfer to occur with every clock pulse but only under a predetermined condition. The binary condition that determines when the transfer is to occur is called a *control function*. A control function is a binary function. This means that it can be equal to either 0 or 1. The control function is included with the transfer micro-operation by modifying the symbology as follows:

$$P: \quad A \leftarrow B$$

The control function P (followed by a colon) symbolizes the fact that the stated micro-operation is executed by the hardware only if $P = 1$.

Figure 4-2 shows the hardware for implementing the micro-operation $P: A \leftarrow B$. The outputs of register B are connected to the inputs of register A. Register A has a parallel load capability, that is, the transfer occurs only if the load input is equal to 1. Although not shown, it is assumed that register A has an additional input that accepts continuous synchronized clock pulses (see Fig. 2-7). The control function P is generated in a control logic network and applied to the load input of the register. It is assumed that the control logic is also synchronized by the clock pulses so output P becomes 1 right after the falling edge of a clock pulse. During the next clock pulse, the load input is in the 1 state and the transfer from B to A occurs right after the falling edge of this clock pulse. The timing relations conform with the state transition adopted in Sec. 2-2 for master-slave flip-flops.

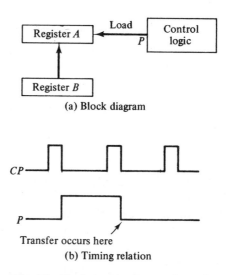

(a) Block diagram

(b) Timing relation

Fig. 4-2 Hardware implementation of the statement $P: A \leftarrow B$.

The basic symbols for the register transfer language are listed in Table 4-1. As mentioned before, capital letters are used to denote registers and subscripts denote individual cells of the register. Parentheses are used to define a portion of a register. The arrow must be present in every micro-operation statement and denotes a transfer of the *content* of the register listed on the right side of the arrow into the register listed on the left side of the arrow. The colon denotes a control function and the comma is used to separate two or more micro-operations when executed at the same time. For example,

$$E: \quad A \leftarrow B, \quad C \leftarrow B$$

TABLE 4-1 Basic Symbols for Register Transfer Language

Symbol	Description	Examples
capital letters and numerals	denotes a register	A, MBR, $R3$
subscript	denotes a bit of a register	A_2, B_l
parentheses ( )	denotes portion of a register	$I(1\text{-}5)$, $MBR(AD)$
arrow ←	denotes transfer of information	$A \leftarrow B$
colon :	denotes termination of control function	$P:$
comma ,	separates two micro-operations	$A \leftarrow B, B \leftarrow A$

specifies two transfers that occur simultaneously provided $E = 1$. It is also possible to swap the contents of two registers during one clock pulse. This is designated in symbolic form by the statement

$$F: \quad A \leftarrow B, \quad B \leftarrow A$$

This simultaneous operation is possible if the registers contain master-slave or edge-triggered flip-flops.

Serial Transfer

For serial transfer, both the source and destination registers are shift-registers. The information is transferred one bit at a time by shifting the bits out of the source register into the destination register. In order not to lose the information stored in the source register it is necessary that the information shifted out of the source register be circulated and shifted back at the same time.

The serial transfer of information from register B to register A is done with shift registers as shown in the block diagram of Fig. 4-3. Each register contains four cells as indicated by the numbers on top of the box. The serial output of register B comes from the output of the rightmost flip-flop B_4. The serial input of register A goes into the leftmost flip-flop A_1. When the shift-right control S is 1, and a clock pulse occurs, the contents of registers A and B are shifted once to the right and the value of B_4 transferred to flip-flops A_1 and B_1. This causes the transfer of one bit of information from register B to register A and, at the same time, one bit is circulated back in register B. This transfer can be expressed by means of symbolic notation as follows:

$$S: \quad A_1 \leftarrow B_4, B_1 \leftarrow B_4, A_i \leftarrow A_{i-1}, B_i \leftarrow B_{i-1} \quad i = 2, 3, 4$$

The control function S is terminated by a colon and designates a Boolean condition; i.e., the register micro-operations listed after the colon are performed only if $S = 1$.

The micro-operations are separated by a comma and are performed simultaneously during one clock pulse. The subscript i denotes the individual cells of the register. Note that a micro-operation, by definition, is executed during one clock pulse. Therefore, the symbolic statement above designates a transfer of one bit only. For a complete transfer of four bits, the control function S must remain 1 for a period of four clock pulses. This time period is called a *word-time* and is depicted in the timing diagram of Fig. 4-3.

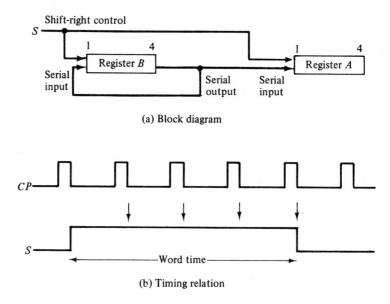

(a) Block diagram

(b) Timing relation

Fig. 4-3   Serial transfer with shift registers.

The statement for serial transfer above is cumbersome to write because it mentions each bit of each register. For serial computers, it may be convenient to redefine a mirco-operation as an operation that takes a word-time for execution (instead of a bit-time). If this convention is adopted, the serial transfer can be stated as

$$S: \quad A \leftarrow B, \quad B \leftarrow B$$

A third symbolic designation for serial transfer uses the *shift* micro-operation (to be introduced in Sec. 4-5).

The registers in serial digital systems are shift registers. The external circuits that perform micro-operations receive the bits from registers sequentially. The time interval between adjacent bits is called the *bit-time*, and the time required to shift the entire content of registers is called the *word-time*. These timing sequences are generated by the control section of the system. In a parallel computer, a control function is enabled during one clock pulse interval. Transfers into registers are in parallel and occur upon the application of a single clock pulse. In a serial computer, the control function must be enabled during one word-time period. The pulse applied every bit-time transfers the results of micro-operations one at a time into a shift register.

Bus Transfer

In a system with many registers, the transfer from each register to another requires that lines be connected from the output of each flip-flop in one register to the input of each flip-flop in all the other registers. Consider, for example, the requirement for transfer among three registers as shown in Fig. 4-4. There are six data paths between registers. If each register consists of n flip-flops, there is a need for $6n$ lines for parallel transfer from each register to each other register. As the number of registers increases, the number of lines increases considerably. However, if we restrict the transmission of data between registers to one at a time, the number of paths among all registers can be reduced to just one per flip-flop for a total of n lines. This is shown in Fig. 4-5, where the output and input of each flip-flop are connected to a common line through an electronic circuit that acts like a switch. All the switches are normally open until a transfer is required. For a transfer from F_1 to F_3, for example, switches S_1 and S_4 are closed to form the required path. This scheme can be extended to registers with n flip-flops and requires n common lines since each flip-flop of the register must be connected to one common line.

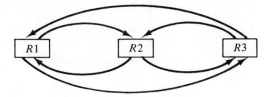

Fig. 4-4 Transfer among three registers.

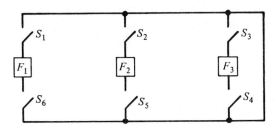

Fig. 4-5 Transfer through one common line.

A group of wires through which binary information is transferred among registers is called a *bus*. For a parallel transfer, the number of wires in the bus is equal to the number of flip-flops in the register. The idea of a bus transfer is analogous to a central transportation system used to bring commuters from one point to another. Instead of each commuter using his own private car to go from one location to another, a bus system is used with each commuter waiting in line until transportation is available.

A bus system is formed with multiplexer circuits. A digital multiplexer selects data from many lines and directs it to a single output line. Figure 4-6 shows how four registers are connected through multiplexers to form one set of common bus lines. Each register has four bits. Each 4 by 1 multiplexer (see Fig. 2-11) has four data input lines, two selection lines, and one output line. The first cell in each register is connected to one of the inputs of the leftmost multiplexer, the second cell to the second multiplexer and so on. The selection lines are connected in parallel to input selection variables x and y. With $xy = 00$, multiplexer inputs I_0 are selected and applied to the outputs that form the bus. The bus lines receive the contents of register A since this register is connected to the I_0 inputs of the multiplexers. Similarly, register B is selected if $xy = 01$, and so on. To simplify the diagram, the lines from

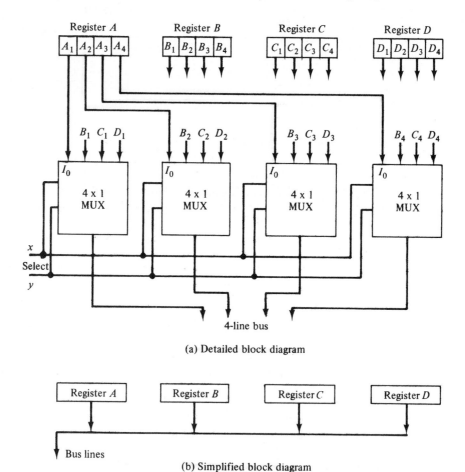

(a) Detailed block diagram

(b) Simplified block diagram

Fig. 4-6 A bus system for four registers.

registers *B*, *C*, and *D* are not drawn, but their connections are indicated by labels at the multiplexer inputs. It is sometimes necessary to simplify the block diagram shown in Fig. 4-6(a) into the one shown in Fig. 4-6(b). The multiplexers are assumed to be part of the bus system although they are not drawn in the block diagram of part (b). The multiplexers may sometimes have an enable line to prevent any register from communicating with the bus.

A bus system can be constructed without multiplexers if the outputs of the registers have tri-state outputs. Outputs of tri-state gates can be connected directly without affecting each other (see Fig. 2-2). The register that communicates with the bus is selected by enabling the control input associated with its tri-state gates. The selection can be controlled by activating the individual tri-state control lines in each register.

The transfer of information from a bus into one of many destination registers can be accomplished by connecting the bus lines to the inputs of all registers and activating the *load* control of the particular destination register selected. As shown in Fig. 4-7, the bus lines are connected to the data inputs of all registers. Activating the load input of a particular register will cause a transfer of information from the bus into the register. The load inputs of the registers can be decoded to reduce the number of selection lines from four to two.

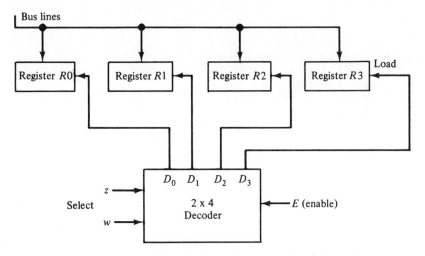

Fig. 4-7 Transfer of information from bus to one of multiple registers.

Transfer through a bus is limited to one transmission at a time. If two transfers are required at the same time, two buses must be used. A large digital system will normally employ a number of buses with each of its registers being connected to one or more buses to form the various paths needed for the transfer of information.

The symbolic statement for a bus transfer may mention the bus and the control functions, or their presence may be implied in the statement. When the bus and control functions are included in the statement, the register transfer is symbolized as follows:

$$xy': \qquad BUS \leftarrow C$$
$$z'wE: \qquad R1 \leftarrow BUS$$

where x and y are the control selection lines for the source register (see Fig. 4-6) and z, w, and E (enable) are the control lines for the destination register (see Fig. 4-7). When selection lines $xy = 10$, register C is selected to communicate with the bus. When selection lines $zw = 01$ and $E = 1$, register $R1$ is selected to accept the information from the bus.

The transfer from register C, through the bus, to register $R1$ can be executed during one clock pulse. To indicate the fact that the two micro-operations are done simultaneously we separate them by a comma as follows:

$$BUS \leftarrow C, \qquad R1 \leftarrow BUS$$

with the control functions being implied or, if necessary, included in the statement.

If the bus is known to exist in the system, it may be convenient to just state on transfer

$$R1 \leftarrow C$$

and from that, the designer knows the values to be inserted for x, y, z, w, and E. This is convenient when the control functions are generated in a control memory as explained in Chap. 8.

Memory Transfer

The operation of a memory unit was described in Sec. 2-6 in conjuction with Fig. 2-21. The transfer of information from memory to the external environment is called a *read* operation. The transfer of new information into the memory is called a *write* operation. In both operations, the particular memory word selected must be specified by an address.

A memory register or word will be symbolized by the letter M. The particular memory register among the many available in a memory unit is selected by the memory address during the transfer. It is necessary to specify the address of M when writing memory transfer statements. In some applications, a memory address register MAR is connected to the address terminals of the memory. In other applications the address lines form a common bus system to allow many registers to specify an address. When only one register is connected to the memory address, we know that this register specifies the address and we can adopt a convention that will simplify the notation. If the letter M stands by itself in a statement, it will always designate a memory register selected by the address presently in MAR. Otherwise, the register that specifies the address will be enclosed within square brackets after the symbol M.

Consider a memory unit associated with a single address register MAR as shown in Fig. 4-8(a). The diagram also shows a memory buffer register MBR used to transfer data into and out of memory. A *read* micro-operation is a transfer from the selected memory register M into MBR. This is designated symbolically by the statement

$$MBR \leftarrow M$$

This causes a transfer of one word into MBR from the selected memory register M as specified by the address in MAR.

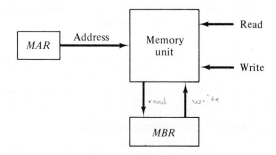

(a) Using a single address register MAR

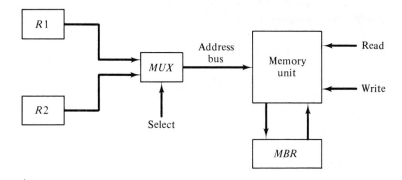

(b) Using an address bus

Fig. 4-8. Connection of address to a memory unit.

A *write* micro-operation is a transfer from MBR to the selected memory word M. This is designated by the statement

$$M \leftarrow MBR$$

This causes the transfer of a word from MBR into the memory register M selected by the address presently available in MAR. Note that address register MAR is implied in both statements.

In many systems, the memory unit receives its address from any one of a number of registers connected to a common bus. Consider the case depicted in Fig. 4-8(b). Two registers, named $R1$ and $R2$, are connected to a common bus that supplies the address to the memory. The address bus can be constructed using multiplexers or tri-state gates. A memory word is specified in such a system by the symbol M followed by a register enclosed in square brackets. The content of the register named within the square brackets specify the address for M. For example, the memory transfer specified by the statement

$$MBR \leftarrow M[R1]$$

denotes a read operation from the memory word whose address is specified by the value presently available in register $R1$. The memory transfer

$$M[R2] \leftarrow MBR$$

denotes a write operation with register $R2$ specifying the address of the memory word. It should be obvious from the definitions above that the statements

$$MBR \leftarrow M \quad \text{and} \quad M \leftarrow MBR$$

constitute an alternate notation for the statements

$$MBR \leftarrow M[MAR] \quad \text{and} \quad M[MAR] \leftarrow MBR$$

respectively. The shorter notation will be used every time the memory address is attached to a single register called MAR.

Summary of Inter-Register Micro-Operations

Table 4-2 summarizes the symbols to be used for the various inter-register transfers. Note the notation used for transferring parts of registers such as $MBR(AD)$. The transfer of a constant value into a register is symbolized by specifying the constant in binary, octal, decimal, or hexadecimal. If there is more than one bus in the system, it is necessary to give each bus a different symbol name such as $ABUS$ or $RBUS$. If there is more than one memory address register in the system, it is necessary to specify the memory address within square brackets after the letter M.

TABLE 4-2 Inter-register Micro-operations

Symbolic designation	Description
$A \leftarrow B$	Transfer content of register B into register A
$MAR \leftarrow MBR(AD)$	Transfer content of AD portion of register MBR into register MAR
$A \leftarrow$ constant	Transfer binary (code) constant into register A
$ABUS \leftarrow R1,$ $R2 \leftarrow ABUS$	Transfer content of $R1$ into bus A and, at the same time, transfer content of bus A into $R2$
MAR	Memory address register: holds the address of the memory unit
MBR	Memory buffer register: holds the data transferred in or out of the memory unit
$M[R]$	Denotes the memory word specified by the address presently available in register R
M	Denotes the memory word specified by the address in an implied register MAR; equivalent to $M[MAR]$
$MBR \leftarrow M$	Memory *read* operation: transfers content of memory word specified by MAR into MBR
$M \leftarrow MBR$	Memory *write* operation: transfers content of MBR into memory word specified by MAR

4-3 ARITHMETIC MICRO-OPERATIONS

The inter-register transfer micro-operations discussed thus far do not change the information content when the binary information moves from the source register to the destination register. All other micro-operations change the information content during the transfer. For example, the arithmetic micro-operation defined by the statement:

$$R3 \leftarrow R1 + R2$$

specifies an *add* micro-operation. It states that the content of register $R1$ is to be added to the content of $R2$ and the sum transferred to $R3$. This is an operational statement and requires for its implementation not only the three registers, but also the logic circuits that perform the stated arithmetic function.

The logic circuit that forms the arithmetic sum of two bits and a previous carry is called a *full-adder* (see Fig. 1-19). Two binary numbers can be added serially by shifting pairs of significant bits sequentially through a full-adder. The sum bit out of the full-adder is shifted into the register that holds the sum. The carry out of the full-adder is stored in a special flip-flop. This flip-flop then provides the carry for the next pair of significant bits coming out of the shift registers that hold the augend and addend.

A *binary parallel-adder* is a digital function that produces the arithmetic sum of two binary numbers in parallel. It consists of full-adders connected in cascade, with the output-carry from one full-adder connected to the input-carry of the next full-adder.

Figure 4-9 shows the interconnections of four full-adders (FA) to provide a four-bit parallel adder. The augend bits of A and the addend bits of B are designated by subscript numbers from right to left with subscript 1 denoting the low-order bit. The carries are connected in a chain through the full-adders. The S outputs of the full-adders generate the required sum bits. When the 4-bit full-adders circuit is enclosed within an IC package, it has four terminals for the augend bits, four terminals for the addend bits, four terminals for the sum bits and two terminals for the input- and output-carries C_1 and C_5.

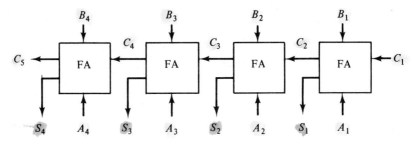

Fig. 4-9   Four-bit full-adders.

An n-bit binary parallel-adder requires n full-adders. It can be constructed from 4-bit full-adders ICs by cascading several packages. The output-carry from one package must be connected to the input-carry of the one with the next-higher-order bits. The block diagram of an n-bit binary parallel-adder is shown in Fig. 4-10.

The following numerical example demonstrates the operation of the parallel-adder:

Subscript i	4	3	2	1	
Input carry	0	1	1	0	C_i
Augend	1	0	1	1	A_i
Addend	0	0	1	1	B_i
Sum	1	1	1	0	S_i
Output carry	0	0	1	1	$C_i + 1$

The bits are added starting from the least significant position (subscript 1) to form the sum bit and carry bit. The input-carry C_1 in the least significant position must be 0. The value of $C_i + 1$ in a given significant position is the output-carry of the full-adder. This value is transferred into C_i (input-carry of full-adder) one higher

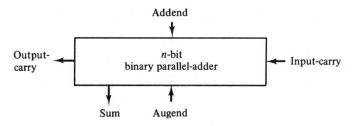

Fig. 4-10 Binary parallel-adder block diagram.

significant position to the left. The sum bits are thus generated starting from the right-most position and are available as soon as the corresponding previous carry bits are generated.

An *add* micro-operation may employ two or three different registers. The micro-operation symbolized by the statement

$$P: \quad A \leftarrow A + B$$

specifies two registers, A and B. It also specifies a parallel-adder needed for obtaining the arithmetic sum, and the paths for loading the sum back into register A. This implementation is shown in Fig. 4-11. The diagram also includes a flip-flop, labeled E, that accepts the output-carry from the parallel-adder. If we use the symbol EA to designate the combined register formed by cascading E and A, we can modify the micro-operation statement by writing

$$P: \quad EA \leftarrow A + B$$

which takes care of the output-carry transfer.

Note that the sum bits and the output-carry are available at the output terminals of the parallel-adder at all times, since the parallel-adder is a combinational circuit. The micro-operation is executed by control function P, and only after $P = 1$ do

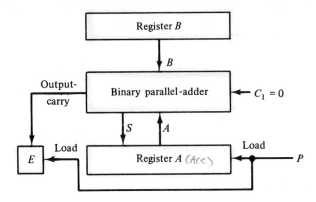

Fig. 4-11 Block diagram for $P: \quad EA \leftarrow A + B$.

we see a change in the contents of register A. When $P = 1$, the load control of the EA register is activated, so on the next clock pulse, the outputs of the parallel-adder are transferred into the destination register. As long as $P = 0$, register A holds the augend and although the sum is available in the S outputs of the parallel-adder, the sum is not transferred into register A.

Other Arithmetic Micro-Operations

The most basic arithmetic micro-operations are listed in Table 4-3. Arithmetic addition has been defined. Arithmetic subtraction implies the availability of a binary parallel-subtractor composed of full-subtractor circuits connected in cascade. Subtraction is most often implemented through complementation and addition as explained below.

TABLE 4-3 Arithmetic Micro-Operations

Symbolic Designation	Description
$A \leftarrow A + B$	Addition: content of A plus B transferred to A
$A \leftarrow A - B$	Subtraction: content of A minus B transferred to A
$A \leftarrow A + 1$	Increment the content of A by one (count-up)
$A \leftarrow A - 1$	Decrement the content of A by one (count-down)
$A \leftarrow \bar{A}$	Complement register A (1's complement)
$A \leftarrow \bar{A} + 1$	Form the 2's complement of register A
$A \leftarrow A + \bar{B}$	Transfer the content of A plus the 1's complement of B into register A
$A \leftarrow A + \bar{B} + 1$	Transfer the content of A plus the 2's complement of B into register A (equivalent to subtraction)

The increment and decrement micro-operations are specified symbolically by a *plus one* or *minus one* operation executed on the contents of the register. These micro-operations are implemented with hardware by providing a count-up or count-down control to the register (see Sec. 2-4). The symbol for the complement micro-operation is a bar over the letter (or letters) that symbolize the register. It denotes the complementation of *all* bits of the register. This is in contrast to the complement operation used in expressing Boolean functions, where the prime symbol is used to denote the complementation of a *single* binary variable. The complement micro-operation is implemented with hardware by providing a complement control to the register.

The 2's complement of a binary number is obtained by complementing each bit of the number and adding 1 to the least significant position. However, the statement

$$P: \quad A \leftarrow \bar{A} + 1$$

implies that the 2's complement of the number stored in register A is executed during one clock pulse period. The control gates associated with the register that has such a capability are shown in Fig. 4-12. The gates are derived from the alternate procedure for obtaining the 2's complement. By this procedure we leave any least significant zeros and the first one unchanged, and then complement all other bits. The first low-order bit A_1 is never complemented because it is either a 0 or the first 1 so a 0 is applied to the T input of the flip-flop holding this bit (by connecting the input carry to 0). Each other flip-flop is complemented provided $P = 1$ and one of the previous flip-flops is 1. The four-bit register can be expanded to more bits by connecting the carry out of A_4 to the carry-in of the next stage.

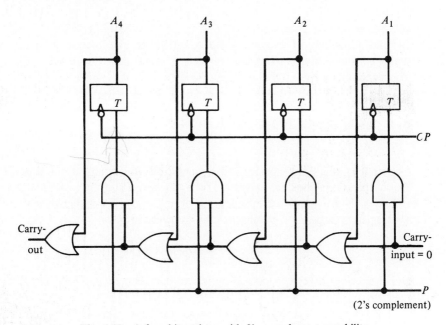

Fig. 4-12 A four-bit register with 2's complement capability.

The 2's complement micro-operation can be executed during two clock pulses provided the register has a complement and increment capability. When such a register is available, we can save the gates of Fig. 4-12 and specify the 2's complement operation by two consecutive micro-operation statements:

$$T_1: \quad A \leftarrow \bar{A}$$
$$T_2: \quad A \leftarrow A + 1$$

where T_1 and T_2 are two consecutive control functions. When $T_1 = 1$ the register is complemented, forming the 1's complement of the number stored in it. When $T_2 = 1$, the register is incremented to form the 2's complement.

It was stated in Sec. 3-2 that two binary numbers can be subtracted by adding the minuend to the 2's complement of the subtrahend. This micro-operation can be stated as follows:

$$A \leftarrow A + \bar{B} + 1$$

and implies that the hardware forms the 2's complement of B and loads the sum into register A, all during one clock pulse period. If circuits are not available to do all these operations simultaneously, it is possible to break the statement into three individual micro-operations. For example, the three consecutive micro-operations

$$T_1: \quad B \leftarrow \bar{B}$$
$$T_2: \quad B \leftarrow B + 1$$
$$T_3: \quad A \leftarrow A + B$$

will accomplish a subtraction of B from A. The statements imply that register B has the capability of executing the complement and increment micro-operations, that a parallel-adder is available between A and B and that register A has a parallel-load capability.

4-4 LOGIC MICRO-OPERATIONS

Logic micro-operations specify binary operations for strings of bits stored in registers. These operations consider each bit of the register separately and treat them as binary variables. For example, the exclusive-OR micro-operation between the contents of two registers A and B is symbolized by the statement:

$$P: \quad A \leftarrow A \oplus B$$

and it specifies a logic micro-operation to be executed on the individual bits of the registers.

As a numerical illustration, assume that each register has four cells. Let the content of A be 1010 and the content of B be 1100. The exclusive-OR micro-operation stated above symbolizes the following logic computation:

$$
\begin{array}{ll}
1010 & \text{content of } A \\
\underline{1100} & \text{content of } B \\
0110 & \text{content of } A \text{ after } P = 1
\end{array}
$$

The content of A, after the execution of the micro-operation, is equal to the bit-by-bit exclusive-OR operation on pairs of bits in B and previous values of A.

When the bits of the registers are designated by a subscript number, the above micro-operation can be stated as:

$$P: \quad A_i \leftarrow A_i \oplus B_i \qquad i = 1, 2, 3, \ldots, n$$

which emphasizes the fact that the logic operation is done on pairs of bits treated as binary variables.

Special symbols will be adopted for the logic micro-operations OR, AND, and complement, in order to distinguish them from the corresponding symbols used to express Boolean functions. The symbol $\vee$ will be used to denote an OR micro-operation and the symbol $\wedge$ to denote an AND micro-operation. The complement micro-operation is the same as the 1's complement and uses a bar on top of the letter (or letters) that denotes the register. By using different symbols, it will be possible to differentiate between a logic micro-operation and a control (or Boolean) function. Another reason for adopting two sets of symbols is to be able to distinguish the symbol $+$, when used to symbolize an arithmetic plus, from a logic OR operation. Although the $+$ symbol has two meanings, it will be possible to distinguish between them by noting where the symbol occurs. When the symbol $+$ occurs in a micro-operation, it will denote an arithmetic plus. When it occurs in a control (or Boolean) function, it will denote a binary OR operation. We will never use it to symbolize an OR micro-operation. For example, in the statement

$$T_1 + T_2: \quad A \leftarrow A + B, \quad C \leftarrow D \vee F$$

the $+$ between T_1 and T_2 is an OR operation between two binary variables of a control function. The $+$ between A and B specifies an *add* micro-operation. The OR micro-operation is designated by the symbol $\vee$ between registers D and F.

Logic micro-operations are seldom used in scientific computations, but they are very useful for bit manipulation of binary data and for making logical decisions. By having bits of registers perform logic operations, it is possible to program logical functions that are not otherwise built in the hardware. As an extreme case, consider a hypothetical computer that has logic micro-operations but no arithmetic micro-operations. We can nevertheless program the computer to simulate the truth table of a full-adder by means of logic micro-operations. This simulation will provide a capability for performing arithmetic operations through a long sequence of logic micro-operations.

A List of Logic Micro-operations

There are 16 different logic operations that can be performed with two binary variables. They can be determined from all possible truth tables obtained with two binary variables. The 16 truth tables are derived in Table 4-4. In this table, each of the 16

TABLE 4-4   Truth Tables for 16 Functions of Two Variables

x y	F_0	F_1	F_2	F_3	F_4	F_5	F_6	F_7	F_8	F_9	F_{10}	F_{11}	F_{12}	F_{13}	F_{14}	F_{15}
0 0	0	0	0	0	0	0	0	0	1	1	1	1	1	1	1	1
0 1	0	0	0	0	1	1	1	1	0	0	0	0	1	1	1	1
1 0	0	0	1	1	0	0	1	1	0	0	1	1	0	0	1	1
1 1	0	1	0	1	0	1	0	1	0	1	0	1	0	1	0	1

columns, F_0 to F_{15}, represents a truth table of one possible Boolean function for the two variables x and y. Note that the functions are determined from the 16 binary combinations that can be assigned to F.

The 16 Boolean functions of two variables x and y are expressed in algebraic form in the first column of Table 4-5. The 16 logic micro-operations are derived from

TABLE 4-5 Sixteen Logic Micro-operations

Boolean Function	Micro-Operation	Name
$F_0 = 0$	$F \leftarrow 0$	Clear
$F_1 = xy$	$F \leftarrow A \wedge B$	AND
$F_2 = xy'$	$F \leftarrow A \wedge \bar{B}$	
$F_3 = x$	$F \leftarrow A$	Transfer A
$F_4 = x'y$	$F \leftarrow \bar{A} \wedge B$	
$F_5 = y$	$F \leftarrow B$	Transfer B
$F_6 = x \oplus y$	$F \leftarrow A \oplus B$	Exclusive-OR
$F_7 = x + y$	$F \leftarrow A \vee B$	OR
$F_8 = (x + y)'$	$F \leftarrow \overline{A \vee B}$	NOR
$F_9 = (x \oplus y)'$	$F \leftarrow \overline{A \oplus B}$	Exclusive-NOR
$F_{10} = y'$	$F \leftarrow \bar{B}$	Complement B
$F_{11} = x + y'$	$F \leftarrow A \vee \bar{B}$	
$F_{12} = x'$	$F \leftarrow \bar{A}$	Complement A
$F_{13} = x' + y$	$F \leftarrow \bar{A} \vee B$	
$F_{14} = (xy)'$	$F \leftarrow \overline{A \wedge B}$	NAND
$F_{15} = 1$	$F \leftarrow$ all 1's	Set to all 1's

these functions by replacing the single variable x by the binary content of register A and that of y by the binary content of register B. Table 4-5 lists all 16 micro-operations and also names some of them. The destination register chosen for the micro-operations is a register denoted by the letter F, but either A or B or any other register could be designated. Note that the symbols used for OR, AND, and complement in micro-operations are $\vee$, $\wedge$, and a bar, respectively.

It is important to realize that the Boolean functions listed in the first column of Table 4-5 represent a relation between two binary variables x and y. The logic micro-operations listed in the second column represent a relation between the binary content of two registers A and B. Each bit of the register is treated as a binary variable and the micro-operation is performed on the string of bits stored in the registers.

Hardware Implementation

The hardware implementation of logic micro-operations requires that logic gates be inserted for each bit or pair of bits in the registers to perform the required logic function. Some logic micro-operations can be implemented directly with flip-flops. For example, the clear micro-operation

$$P_1: \quad A \leftarrow 0$$

can be implemented with JK flip-flops for the A register by applying control function P_1 directly to all the K inputs of the flip-flops. The complement micro-operation

$$P_2: \quad A \leftarrow \bar{A}$$

can be implemented by applying P_2 to both the J and K inputs. The gates for the other logic micro-operations can be derived by means of sequential circuit theory (see Sec. 1-6).

When the destination register is also one of the source registers, the digital system can be considered as a sequential circuit and its behavior tabulated in a state or excitation table. The bit content of the source register corresponds to the present state values in the excitation table. The content of the same register after the micro-operation is executed corresponds to the next state values in the table. For example, the micro-operation

$$P_3: \quad A \leftarrow A \lor B$$

uses register A as both a source and a destination. The bits of A prior to the execution of the micro-operation are the present state values. The bits of A after the execution are the next state values.

Figure 4-13 lists the excitation tables for one typical stage i for the logic micro-operations OR, AND, and XOR. The source registers are A and B; the destination register is A. The value of bit A_i is listed in both the present and next state columns. The bit of B_i is considered as an input to the sequential circuit. From the change of present to next state, we obtain the flip-flop input values. These values are obtained from the JK flip-flop excitations listed in Table 1-4(b). The maps accompanying each table derive the simplified Boolean functions for JA_i (J input of flip-flop A_i) and KA_i (K input of flip-flop A_i).

Using the results obtained from the excitation tables, we draw the logic diagram of Fig. 4-14. Each control function P_j must be ANDed with the condition derived in the maps of Fig. 4-13. For example, the OR micro-operation requires that the J input of A_i be excited if $B_i = 1$ and the K input be left at binary value 0. This function is controlled by P_3 so when $P_3 = 1$ and $B_i = 1$, the J input receives a 1 and the K input is maintained at 0 because all other P's are equal to 0.

Some Applications

Logic micro-operations are very useful for manipulating individual bits or a portion of a word stored in a register. They can be used to change bit values, delete a group of bits or insert new bit values into a register. The following examples show how the bits of one register (designated by A) are manipulated by logic micro-operations as a function of the bits of another register (designated by B). In a typical application,

Present State A_i	Input B_i	Next State A_i	Flip-flop Inputs JA_i	KA_i
0	0	0	0	X
0	1	1	1	X
1	0	1	X	0
1	1	1	X	0

(a) Logic OR

Present State A_i	Input B_i	Next State A_i	Flip-flop Inputs JA_i	KA_i
0	0	0	0	X
0	1	0	0	X
1	0	0	X	1
1	1	1	X	0

(b) Logic AND

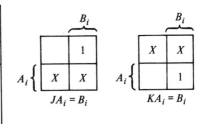

Present State A_i	Input B_i	Next State A_i	Flip-flop Inputs JA_i	KA_i
0	0	0	0	X
0	1	1	1	X
1	0	1	X	0
1	1	0	X	1

(c) Logic exclusive-OR (XOR)

Fig. 4-13 Excitation tables for the micro-operations.

register A is a processor register and the bits of register B constitute a logic operand extracted from the memory unit and placed in register B.

The *selective-set* operation sets the bits in register A where there are corresponding 1's in register B. It does not affect bit positions which have 0's in B. The following numerical example clarifies this operation.

$$
\begin{array}{ll}
1010 & A \text{ before} \\
1100 & B \\
\hline
1110 & A \text{ after}
\end{array}
$$

The two leftmost bits of B are 1's and so the corresponding bits of A are set. One of these two bits was already set and the other has been changed from 0 to 1. The

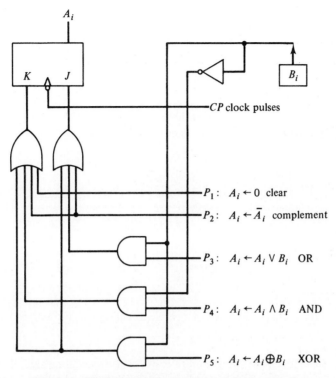

Fig. 4-14 Hardware implementation of logic operations when the destination register is also a source register.

two bits of A with corresponding 0's in B remain unchanged. The above example serves as a truth table since it has all four possible combinations of two binary variables. From the truth table we note that the bits of A after the operation are obtained from the logic-OR operation of bits in B and previous values of A. Therefore, the OR micro-operation can be used to selectively set bits of a register.

The *selective-complement* operation complements bits in A where there are corresponding 1's in B. It does not affect bit positions which have 0's in B. For example,

$$
\begin{array}{ll}
1010 & A \text{ before} \\
\underline{1100} & B \\
0110 & A \text{ after}
\end{array}
$$

Again the two leftmost bits of B are 1's and so the corresponding bits of A are complemented. This example again can serve as a truth table from which one can deduce that the selective-complement operation is just an exclusive-OR micro-operation. Therefore, the exclusive-OR micro-operation can be used to selectively complement bits of a register.

The *selective-clear* operation clears the bits in A only where there are corresponding 1's in B. For example,

1010	A before
1100	B
0010	A after

Again the two leftmost bits of B are 1's and so the corresponding bits of A are cleared to 0. One can deduce that the logic operation performed on the individual bits is $A_i B_i'$. The corresponding logic micro-operation is

$$A \leftarrow A \wedge \bar{B}$$

The *mask* operation is similar to the selective-clear operation except that the bits of A are cleared only where there are corresponding 0's in B. The mask operation is an AND micro-operation as seen from the following numerical example:

1010	A before
1100	B
1000	A after masking

The two rightmost bits of A are cleared because the corresponding bits of B are 0's. The two leftmost bits are left unchanged because the corresponding bits of B are 1's.

The mask operation is more convenient to use than the selective-clear operation because most computers provide an AND instruction and only few provide an instruction that executes the micro-operation for selective-clear. The mask operation can be considered as a *delete* operation. Theoretically, a delete operation will delete selected bits of a word stored in a register. However, because register cells are binary, they can be either 0 or 1 and nothing else. There is really no way of making "deletions" from registers, but by changing a group of bits to all 0's we can assume that the previous content of the bits has been "deleted."

The *insert* operation inserts a new value into a group of bits. This is done by first masking (deleting) the bits and then ORing them with the required value. For example, suppose an A register contains eight bits, 0110 1010. To replace the four leftmost bits by the value 1001 we first mask the four unwanted bits

0110	1010	A before
0000	1111	B (mask)
0000	1010	A after masking

and then insert the new value

0000	1010	A before
1001	0000	B (insert)
1001	1010	A after insertion

The mask operation is an AND micro-operation and the insert operation is an OR micro-operation.

The *compare* operation compares the words in A and B and produces all 0's in A if the two words are equal. This operation is achieved by an exclusive-OR micro-operation as shown by the following example:

$$
\begin{array}{ll}
1010 & A \\
\underline{1010} & B \\
\overline{0000} & A \leftarrow A \oplus B
\end{array}
$$

When both A and B are equal, the two corresponding bits are either both 0 or both 1. In either case the exclusive-OR function produces a 0. The all 0's result is then checked to determine if the words were equal.

The *packing* of binary coded information such as characters is an operation that groups two or more characters in one word. For example, three binary-coded characters that occupy seven bits each in ASCII (Table 3-4) can be packed into one 21-bit word. To pack the three characters "MAY" into a 21-bit processor register A, we read the characters from memory one at a time and perform the following logic micro-operations:

Micro-Operation	Register A
Clear A	0000000 0000000 0000000
OR with "M" = 100 1101	0000000 0000000 1001101
Shift-left seven times	0000000 1001101 0000000
OR with "A" = 100 0001	0000000 1001101 1000001
Shift-left seven times	1001101 1000001 0000000
OR with "Y" = 101 1001	1001101 1000001 1011001

It is assumed that the binary-coded characters are stored in a 21-bit memory word with the 14 high-order bits all 0's. The words are read from memory into MBR and the contents of A are ORed with MBR. A shift with 0's inserted in the empty spaces is considered as a logical shift (see next section). The final packed word of three characters can be stored in a single memory word.

The *unpacking* of binary-coded information is a reverse operation from packing. It separates two or more characters stored in one word into three separate characters. The unpacking is accomplished by masking the unwanted characters in the register.

Logic micro-operations are very useful for data processing of alphanumeric data. They can change, remove, delete, and modify characters. *Editing* operations are performed by a sequence of logical operations such as masking, insertion, and shift. An example of a financial edit of alphanumeric characters is one that provides output data in a special format. Such a format may require the insertion of a leading dollar sign, the deletion of leading zeros, the insertion of commas and periods and the conversion of the algebraic sign to special symbols. For example, a financial edit on the string of characters $+00023598$ might yield as output $23,598.00 CREDIT, but on -00023598 might yield $23,598.00 DEBIT.

4-5 SHIFT MICRO-OPERATIONS

Shift micro-operations transfer binary information between registers in serial computers. They are also used in parallel computers for arithmetic, logic, and other data processing operations. While the bits of a register are shifted, the extreme flip-flop receives information from the serial input of the register. The extreme flip-flop is in the leftmost position of the register during a right-shift micro-operation and in the rightmost position during a left-shift micro-operation. The information transferred into the extreme flip-flop determines the type of shift implemented. There are four types of shifts: serial transfer shift, logical shift, circular shift and arithmetic shift.

Serial transfer was discussed in Sec. 4-2. The serial input in the destination register receives the bit from the source register. The source register is circulated to restore the information being shifted out. We adopt the symbols *shl* and *shr* to indicate a shift-left and a shift-right micro-operation, respectively. The symbols *cil* and *cir* will be used for circular left-shift and circular right-shift, respectively. A serial transfer from register B into register A can be symbolized by the following statement (see Fig. 4-3):

$$S: \quad shr\ A, \quad cir\ B. \quad A_1 \leftarrow B_n$$

where n denotes the number of bits in the registers. B_n is the rightmost cell of B, and A_1 the leftmost cell of A.

A *logical shift* is one that inserts a 0 into the extreme flip-flop. Therefore, the serial input of the shift-register must contain a 0 during a logical shift micro-operation. The symbols *shl* and *shr* can be used to indicate a logical shift when the information inserted into the extreme flip-flop is not specified explicitly. Thus, the statement:

$$L: \quad shl\ A$$

specifies a logical shift-left micro-operation for register A, and the statement

$$S: \quad shr\ A$$

specifies a logical shift-right micro-operation. Note that the first statement does not specify what goes into the right-most flip-flop A_n, nor does the second statement specify what goes into A_1. Therefore, we conclude that these extreme flip-flops receive a 0.

A *circular shift* circulates the bits of the register around the two ends. This is accomplished by connecting the serial output of the shift register into its serial input. The statement

$$P: \quad cil\ A, \quad cir\ B$$

specifies that register A is to be circulated to the left and register B circulated to the right.

An *arithmetic shift* is a micro-operation that shifts a *signed* number to the left or the right. This type of shift is also called *scaling* or *shift with sign extention*.

The binary information in the register during an arithmetic shift is considered to be an arithmetic operand holding a fixed-point number or the mantissa of a floating-point number. An arithmetic left-shift multiplies a signed binary number by two, and an arithmetic right shift divides it by two. Remember that the leftmost flip-flop in the register holds the sign bit and that negative numbers may be represented in one of three different ways. Arithmetic shifts must leave the sign bit unchanged because the sign of the number remains the same when it is multiplied or divided by 2. For positive numbers and negative numbers in signed-magnitude representation, the added bits during the shift are 0's. This is equivalent to a logical shift among the $n - 1$ bits that represent the number, excluding the sign bit which remains unchanged. When a negative number in 2's complement representation is shifted left, the added bits from the right are 0's but the sign bit is not shifted out. During a right shift, the sign bit is shifted into the high-order bit position of the number. For negative numbers in signed 1's complement representation, all bits shifted into the extreme flip-flops that represent the number (excluding the sign bit) are 1's. The rules for arithmetic shifts are summarized in Table 4-6.

The symbols for six shift micro-operations are listed in Table 4-7. Note that

TABLE 4-6   Arithmetic Shifts for Signed Binary Numbers

Representation	Sign Bit	Number Bits
Positive number	Unchanged	All added bits are 0's
Negative number in signed-magnitude	Unchanged	All added bits are 0's
Negative number in signed-2's complement	Unchanged	Added bits are 0's for left-shift Added bits are 1's for right-shift
Negative number in signed-1's complement	Unchanged	All added bits are 1's

TABLE 4-7   Shift Micro-Operations

Symbolic Designation	Description
shl A	Shift-left register A, content of right-most flip-flop becomes 0 unless specified otherwise
shr A	Shift-right register A, content of left-most flip-flop becomes 0 unless specified otherwise
cil A	Circulate left contents of register A
cir A	Circulate right contents of register A
ashl A	Arithmetic shift-left contents of register A
ashr A	Arithmetic shift-right contents of register A

arithmetic shifts are symbolized by *ashl* and *ashr*. The hardware implementation of these micro-operations depends on the type of data stored in the register and the type of representation adopted for negative numbers.

4-6 CONTROL FUNCTIONS

The timing for all registers in a synchronous digital system is controlled by a master clock generator, whose clock pulses are applied to all flip-flops in the system. The continuous clock pulses applied to a register do not change the state of the register unless its specific function is enabled. The binary variables that control the enable inputs of registers are called *control functions*. We have used control functions in previous examples. This section defines them more precisely and considers their hardware implementation.

The hardware control network that generates control functions can be organized in one of three different ways: (1) as a sequential circuit, (2) as a sequence of timing signals coupled with control conditions, or (3) as a control memory.

A control logic network designed as a sequential circuit requires that it be specified by a state diagram or a state table and designed by sequential circuit theory methods. The disadvantages of this method are threefold: (1) The number of states in a control logic network for a typical digital computer is very large. Design methods that use state and excitation tables can be used in theory, but in practice they are cumbersome and difficult to manage. (2) The final control circuit obtained by this method is irregular and requires an excessive number of SSI gates and flip-flops. Constructing digital circuits with SSI integrated circuits is inefficient with respect to the number of packages used and the number of wires that must be interconnected. (3) It is difficult for a person to familiarize himself with the sequence of events that the control logic undergoes and as a consequence, it is difficult to service and maintain the equipment. For these reasons, the method is seldom used for controlling the operations of digital computers and therefore, this method is not discussed any further here. The interested reader can find more information in the references listed at the end of Chap. 1.

The second method provides a sequence of timing signals. These signals are combined with various other control conditions to generate the required control functions. This method solves the first and third difficulties listed above but the second difficulty is improved only slightly since this method also requires a large number of SSI gates. The hardware that generates timing signals and the control functions obtained by this method are discussed in this section.

The third method uses a special memory unit, usually a ROM, to store the 1's and 0's of the control functions for all registers. By reading words from control memory in a prescribed sequence, it is possible to activate the necessary registers and execute the micro-operations for the system. This is the most efficient method of control organization for a digital system. Assigning the 1's and 0's for the words in a control memory is called *microprogramming*. Because of its importance, all of Chap. 8 is devoted to this topic.

Timing Sequences

Timing signals that control the sequence of operations in a digital computer can be generated with a ring counter or a binary counter and a decoder. A *ring counter* is a circular shift register with only one flip-flop being set at any particular time; all others are cleared. The single bit is shifted from one flip-flop to the other to produce the sequence of timing signals. Figure 4-15(a) shows the block diagram of a ring counter that produces four timing signals. The initial value of the shift register T is 1000. The single bit is shifted right with every clock pulse and circulated back

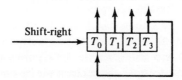

(a) Four-bit ring counter (initial value of $T = 1000$)

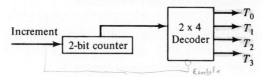

(b) Counter decoder block diagram

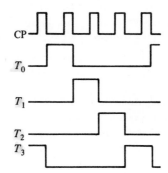

(c) A sequence of four timing signals

Fig. 4-15   Generation of four consecutive timing signals.

from T_3 to T_0. Each flip-flop is in the 1 state once every four clock pulses and produces one of the four timing signals shown in Fig. 4-15(c). Each output becomes 1 at the falling edge of a clock pulse and remains 1 during the next pulse. Thus, each clock pulse is associated with one of the timing variables. The timing signals can be generated also by continuously incrementing a binary counter and applying its outputs to a decoder as shown in Fig. 4-15(b). This type of circuit will also generate the required timing signals.

Small digital computers provide a timing sequence of 8 to 16 repetitive timing signals. The time of one repetitive sequence is called a *computer cycle*. Each computer cycle is synchronized with the memory cycle and initiates the control functions for the micro-operations associated with each access to memory. Large computer systems have multiple timing sequences with each sequence providing control to a different module in the system. Timing sequences in a synchronous system are synchronized with the master clock generator. In an asynchronous system each timing signal is generated after the completion of the previous micro-operation.

The timing signals shown in Fig. 4-15, when enabled by the clock pulses, will provide multiple phase clock pulses. For example, if T_0 is ANDed with CP, the output of the AND gate will generate clock pulses at one-fourth the frequency of the master clock pulses. Multiple phase clock pulses can be used for controlling different registers with different time scales.

Generation of Control Functions

Each computer cycle is associated with a sequence of micro-operations. These micro-operations are controlled by the timing signals and other binary conditions in the system. The Boolean functions that generate the control decisions are the control functions that we have been using. For example, a digital computer may require that a word be read from memory during time T_1 of every computer cycle. This is symbolized by the statement

$$T_1: \quad MBR \leftarrow M$$

In other words, timing variable T_1 serves as a read-control input for the memory unit. As another illustration, suppose that the content of register B is to be transferred to register A every time a signal F is 1 during time T_1 or if another signal R is 0 during time T_3. This is symbolized by the statement

$$FT_1 + R'T_3: \quad A \leftarrow B$$

The control function, being a Boolean function, can be generated with logic gates as shown in Fig. 4-16. The gates that generate the control function go to the *load* input of register A to initiate the transfer. Other conditions from other statements may also require the same transfer. Moreover, flip-flops F and R themselves are set or reset according to other conditions dictated by other control functions.

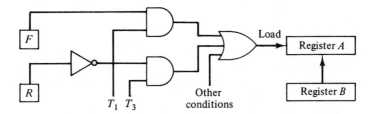

Fig. 4-16 Hardware for the symbolic statement $FT_1 + R'T_3$: $A \leftarrow B$.

Conditional Control Statements

It is sometimes convenient to specify a control function by a conditional statement. A *conditional control* statement is symbolized by an *if–then* statement in the following way:

$$P: \quad \text{If (condition) then (micro-operation(s))}$$

and is interpreted to mean that if the condition stated within the parentheses after the word *if* is met, then the micro-operation, or micro-operations, enclosed within the parentheses after the word *then* are executed. In addition, the control function P must be 1. If the condition is not met, or if $P = 0$, the micro-operation is not executed.

As an example, consider a 4-bit binary counter, denoted by the symbol C, which is initially set to all 1's. The counter is decremented with timing signal T_7. During the next time sequence, at T_8, we want to check the content of the counter, and if it is 0, set a flip-flop labeled F. Since C is initially set to all 1's (binary 15) it is necessary that T_7 appears 15 times for the binary down-counter to reach the value of 0. The two micro-operations just described are stated symbolically below. The second statement is a conditional control statement.

$$T_7: \quad C \leftarrow C - 1$$
$$T_8: \quad \text{If } (C = 0) \text{ then } (F \leftarrow 1)$$

During T_7, the counter is decremented and during T_8, its content is checked for 0. If the value stored in C is 0, F is set to 1 during T_8; if not, F is not changed. The hardware implementation of the statements above is shown in Fig. 4-17. T_7 decrements the counter and T_8 sets flip-flop F if $x = 1$. The Boolean function for x is derived from the condition $(C = 0)$. This condition is met if all four flip-flops of C are 0. The condition is expressed by the Boolean function:

$$x = C_1'C_2'C_3'C_4' = (C_1 + C_2 + C_3 + C_4)'$$

The second form is derived from DeMorgan's theorem. Therefore, signal x can be generated by a NOR gate with all cells of the register as inputs. The above condi-

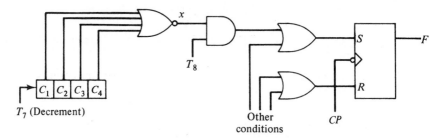

Fig. 4-17 Hardware for conditional control statement
T_8: If $(C = 0)$ then $(F \leftarrow 1)$.

tional control statement can be stated without the *if–then* statement as follows:

$$xT_8: \quad F \leftarrow 1$$

provided we define the binary variable x by the Boolean function above.

When using a conditional control statement one must realize that the condition specified in the statement is a control condition that must be generated with hardware and incorporated with the associated control function. The necessary hardware must be deduced from the stated control condition after the word *if*.

Tabular Summary of Control Functions

Table 4-8 lists the symbols used to specify control functions. The Boolean operators AND, OR and complement are used to express control functions. This is in contrast to the symbols used to express logic micro-operations of the same type. A control

TABLE 4-8   Control Functions

Symbolic Designation	Description
$+$	Denotes logic OR in a control function
$\cdot$	(or absence of operator) denotes logic AND in a control function
′ (prime)	Denotes logic complement in a control function
$xT_1 + y'T_2:$	Denotes control function terminated by a colon
If $(SC = 0)$ then $(A \leftarrow B)$	Conditional control statement with control condition specified in parentheses after the word *If*

function is terminated by a colon (:) and is implemented by a digital circuit composed of logic gates. Control information can be specified by control functions or conditional control statements. Although not shown here, a control network constructed around a control memory is specified by a *microprogram* instead of control functions. This procedure is discussed in Chap.8.

REFERENCES

1. MANO, M. M., *Digital Logic and Computer Design*. Englewood Cliffs, N.J.: Prentice-Hall, Inc., 1979.

2. CHU, Y., *Computer Organization and Microprogramming*. Englewood Cliffs, N.J.: Prentice-Hall, Inc., 1972.

3. BELL, C. G., AND A. NEWELL, *Computer Structures: Readings and Examples*. New York: McGraw-Hill Book Company, 1971.

4. BARTEE, T. C., I. L. LEBOW, AND I. S. REED, *Theory and Design of Digital Machines*. New York: McGraw-Hill Book Company, 1962.

5. BOOTH, T. L., *Digital Networks and Computer Systems*, 2nd ed. New York: John Wiley & Sons, Inc., 1978.

6. SLOAN, M. E., *Computer Hardware and Organization*. Chicago: Science Research Associates, 1976.

7. BARBACCI, M. R., "A Comparison of Register Transfer Languages for Describing Computers and Digital Systems," *IEEE Trans. on Computers*, Vol. C-24 (February 1975), pp. 137–150.

8. *Computer*, special issue on Computer Hardware Description Languages, Vol. 7, No. 12 (December 1974).

9. *Computer*, special issue on Hardware Description Language Applications, Vol. 10, No. 16 (June 1977).

PROBLEMS

4-1. List the micro-operations that transfer bits 1–8 of register A to bits 9–16 of register B and bits 1–8 of register B to bits 9–16 of register A. Draw a block diagram of the hardware.

4-2. Show the block diagram that executes the statement

$$T: \quad A \leftarrow B, B \leftarrow A$$

4-3. Show the hardware for transferring the binary-coded hexadecimal F3 into register A. This is stated symbolically as

$$P: \quad A \leftarrow (F3)_{16}$$

4-4. An 8-bit register A has one binary input x. The register operation can be described symbolically as follows:

$$P: \quad A_8 \leftarrow x, A_i \leftarrow A_{i+1} \quad i = 1, 2, \ldots, 7$$

What is the function of the register? The cells are numbered from left to right.

4-5. A serial computer employs 32-bit registers and clock pulses at a rate of one million per second. What is the bit time and the word time of the computer?

4-6. (a) Show the block diagram of a 4-bit register with tri-state inverters at each cell output. The register should have one common control input to enable all tri-state gates.

(b) Show the block diagram of four such registers connected to a common bus. Include a decoder for selecting the register that communicates with the bus.

✓ 4-7. Draw a block diagram of a bus system connected to four registers with information transferred *serially* from any register to any other register. Use a decoder and a multiplexer to select the source register and a decoder to select the destination register.

4-8. What should be the values of x and y in Fig. 4-6 and z, w, and E in Fig. 4-7 to initiate the following transfers?
(a) $R3 \leftarrow D$
(b) $R0 \leftarrow B$
(c) $R2 \leftarrow C$
(d) $R1 \leftarrow A$

4-9. Draw the block diagram of a bus system connected to 8 registers with 8 bits in each register.

4-10. A digital system has 16 registers, each with 32 bits. It is necessary to provide parallel data transfer from each register to each other register.
(a) How many lines are needed for direct parallel transfer?
(b) How many lines are needed for transfer along a common bus?
(c) If the registers form a scratch-pad memory, how is information transferred from one register to another? Let the registers in the memory be designated by $R0$ to $R15$. List the sequence of micro-operations for a transfer of the content of $R6$ into $R13$.

✓ 4-11. Draw a block diagram for the *add* micro-operation when implemented in a serial computer. Include two shift registers, one full-adder and a flip-flop to store the carry. Assume that the carry flip-flop is initially cleared.

4-12. Register A in Fig. 4-11 holds the number 1011 and register B holds 0111.
(a) Determine the values of each S and C output of the four full-adders in the binary parallel adder.
(b) Repeat part (a) after register A is enabled by the control function P.

✓ 4-13. (a) Draw the logic diagram of a full-subtractor from the Boolean functions derived in Sec. 1-4.
(b) Draw a block diagram of a binary parallel-subtractor composed of four full-subtractors. Let A be the minuend and B the subtrahend.
(c) If the minuend A is 1010 and the subtrahend B is 0111, determine the values of each D (difference) and each K (borrow) output of the four full-subtractors.

4-14. Draw the logic diagram of a 4-bit register with clocked JK flip-flops having control inputs for the increment, complement, and parallel transfer micro-operations. Show how the 2's complement can be implemented in this register.

4-15. (a) Modify the circuit of Fig. 4-12 by using JK flip-flops and including control inputs for a parallel transfer as well as the 2's complement micro-operation.
(b) Let this register be register B in Fig. 4-11. List the micro-operation sequence that subtracts the content of B from the content of A and places the difference in register A.

4-16. The content of register A is 1101 and that of B is 0110. Show that either one of the micro-operation sequences listed below produce the difference 0111.

(a) T_1: $B \leftarrow \bar{B}$ (b) T_1: $B \leftarrow \bar{B}$
T_2: $B \leftarrow B + 1$ T_2: $EA \leftarrow A + B$
T_3: $A \leftarrow A + B$ ET_3: $A \leftarrow A + 1$

4-17. Derive a combinational circuit that selects and generates any one of the 16 functions listed in Table 4-4.

4-18. Design a typical stage (similar to Fig. 4-14) that implements the following logic micro-operations.

$$P_6:\quad A \leftarrow A \vee \bar{B} \qquad P_8:\quad A \leftarrow \overline{A \vee B}$$
$$P_7:\quad A \leftarrow \bar{A} \wedge B \qquad P_9:\quad A \leftarrow \overline{A \wedge B}$$

4-19. List the sequence of logic micro-operations required for packing the six alphanumeric characters "HI-LO" into a 48-bit register. Use 8 bits per character, obtained from the 7 ASCII bits (Table 3-4) and an even parity bit in the most significant position.

4-20. How would you convert decimal digits represented by a 7-bit ASCII into a 4-bit BCD and pack the BCD digits in one register?

4-21. Show that the statement

$$A \leftarrow A + A$$

symbolizes a shift-left micro-operation.

4-22. (a) Show the representation of $+12$ in binary in a 7-bit register. Divide and multiply this number by 2 and show how it can be done by means of arithmetic shift micro-operations.

(b) Repeat part (a) for -12 when it is in (1) signed-magnitude representation; (2) signed-1's complement representation; and (3) signed-2's complement representation.

(c) From the results above, justify the entries of Table 4-6.

4-23. Show that an n-bit binary counter connected to an n by 2^n decoder is equivalent to a ring counter with 2^n flip-flops. Show the block diagram of both circuits for $n = 3$. How many timing signals are generated?

4-24. Include an enable input to the decoder of Fig. 4-15(b) and connect it to the master clock pulse generator. Draw the sequence of timing signals [similar to Fig. 4-15(c)] that are now generated at the outputs of the decoder.

4-25. Show the hardware, including the logic gates for the control function, that implements the statement

$$xy'T_0 + T_1 + x'yT_2:\quad A \leftarrow A + 1$$

4-26. Prove that the following conditional control statement

$$P:\quad \text{If } (C = 1001) \text{ then } (C \leftarrow 0), \text{ If } (C \neq 1001) \text{ then } (C \leftarrow C + 1)$$

symbolizes a one-decade BCD counter.

4-27. What is wrong with the following register transfer statements? The T variables are timing signals as in Fig. 4-15.

(a) xT_1: $A \leftarrow \bar{A}, A \leftarrow 0$

(b) $(C = 0)FT_3$: $PC \leftarrow R$

(c) $T_1 \vee yT_2$: $MAR \leftarrow MBR + PC$

(d) yT_0T_2: $A \leftarrow A + \bar{B} + 1$

(e) FR': $F'R \leftarrow FR'$

4-28. A digital system has three registers: AR, BR, and PR. Three flip-flops provide the control functions for the system: S is a flip-flop which is enabled by an external signal to start the system's operation; F and R are used for sequencing the micro-operations. A fourth flip-flop, D, is set by the digital system when the operation is completed. The function of the system is described by the following register transfer operations:

$$S: \quad PR \leftarrow 0, S \leftarrow 0, D \leftarrow 0, F \leftarrow 1$$

$$F: \quad F \leftarrow 0, \text{ if } (AR = 0) \text{ then } (D \leftarrow 1), \text{ if } (AR \neq 0) \text{ then } (R \leftarrow 1)$$

$$R: \quad PR \leftarrow PR + BR, AR \leftarrow AR - 1, R \leftarrow 0, F \leftarrow 1$$

(a) Show that the digital system multiplies the contents of AR and BR and places the product in PR.

(b) Draw a block diagram of the hardware implementation. Include a *start* input to set flip-flop S and a *done* output from flip-flop D.

Basic Computer
Organization and Design

5

5-1 INSTRUCTION CODES

The internal organization of a digital system is defined by the sequence of micro-operations it performs on data stored in its registers. In a *special purpose* digital system, the sequence of micro-operations is fixed by the hardware and the system performs the same specific task over and over again. Once a special purpose system is built, its sequence of micro-operations is not subject to alterations. Examples of special purpose digital systems can be found in numerous peripheral control units, one of which is a magnetic tape controller. Such a unit controls the movement of a magnetic tape transport and the transfer of binary information between the tape and its external environment. The unit cannot perform any operations other than the special task for which it was designed.

A digital computer is a *general purpose* digital system. A general-purpose digital computer is capable of executing various micro-operations and, in addition, can be instructed as to what specific sequence of operations it must perform. The user of such a system can control the process by means of a *program*, that is, a set of instructions that specify the operations, operands and the sequence by which processing has to occur. The data processing task may be altered simply by specifying a new program with different instructions or specifying the same instructions with different data. A computer instruction is a binary code that specifies a sequence of micro-operations for the computer. Instruction codes together with data are stored in memory. The control reads each instruction from memory and places it in a control register. The control then interprets the binary code of the instruction and proceeds to execute the instruction by issuing a sequence of control functions. Every general-purpose computer has its own unique instruction repertoire. The ability to store and execute instructions, the stored program concept, is the most important property of a general-purpose computer.

An *instruction code* is a group of bits that tell the computer to perform a specific operation. It is usually divided in parts, each having its own particular interpretation. The most basic part of an instruction code is its operations part. The *operation code* of an instruction is a group of bits that define such operations as add, subtract, multiply, shift, and complement. The set of operations formulated for a computer depends on the processing it is intended to carry out. The total number of operations thus obtained determines the set of machine operations. The number of bits required for the operation part of an instruction code is a function of the total number of operations used. It must consist of at least n bits for a given 2^n (or less) distinct operations. As an illustration, consider a computer with 32 distinct operations, one of them being an ADD operation. The operation code consists of five bits, with a bit configuration 10010 assigned to the ADD operation. When this operation code is received by the control unit, it issues control functions which read an operand from memory and add the operand to a processor register.

At this point we must recognize the relation between an operation and a micro-operation. An operation is part of an instruction stored in computer memory. It is a binary code that tells the computer to perform a specific operation. The control unit receives the instruction from memory and interprets the operation code bits. It then issues a sequence of control functions that perform micro-operations in internal computer registers. For every operation code, the control issues a sequence of micro-operations needed for the hardware implementation of the specified operation. For this reason, an operation code is sometimes called a *macro-operation* because it specifies a set of micro-operations.

The operation part of an instruction code specifies the operation to be performed. This operation must be executed on some data stored in memory and/or processor registers. An instruction code, therefore, must specify not only the operation, but also the registers and/or the memory words where the operands are to be found, as well as the register or memory word where the result is to be stored. Memory words can be specified in instruction codes by their address. Processor registers can be specified by assigning to the instruction another binary code of k bits that specifies one of 2^k registers. There are many variations for arranging the binary code of instructions and each computer has its own particular instruction code format. Instruction code formats are conceived by computer designers who specify the architecture of the computer. There are as many instruction code formats as there are computers on the market. In this chapter we choose a particular instruction code to explain the basic organization of digital computers.

The simplest way to organize a computer is to have one processor register and an instruction code format with two parts. The first part specifies the operation to be performed and the second specifies an address. The address tells the control where to find an operand in memory. This operand is read from memory and used as the data to be operated on together with the data stored in the processor register.

Figure 5-1 depicts this type of organization. Instructions are stored in one section of memory and data in another. For a memory unit with 4096 words we need 12 bits to specify an address since $2^{12} = 4096$. If we store each instruction code in one 16-bit memory word, we have available four bits to specify one out of 16 possible operations and 12 bits to specify the address of an operand. The control reads a 16-bit instruction from the program portion of memory. It uses the 12-bit address part of the instruction to read an operand from the data portion of memory. It then executes the operation by means of micro-operations between the operand and the processor register. Computers that have a single processor register usually assign to it the name *accumulator* and label it *AC*.

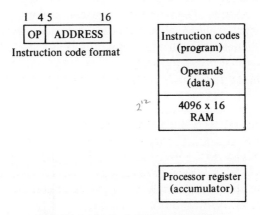

Fig. 5-1   Stored program organization.

If an operation in an instruction code does not need an operand from memory, the rest of the bits in the instruction can be used for other purposes. For example, operations such as clear *AC*, complement *AC*, and increment *AC* operate on data stored in the *AC* register. They do not need an operand from memory. For these types of operations, the second part of the instruction code (bits 5 to 16) is not needed for specifying a memory address and can be used to specify other operations for the computer.

It is sometimes convenient to use the address bits of an instruction code not as an address but as the actual operand. When the second part of an instruction code specifies an operand, the instruction is said to have an *immediate* operand. When the second part specifies the address of an operand, the instruction is said to have a *direct* address. This is in contrast to a third possibility called *indirect* address, where the bits in the second part of the instruction designate an address of a memory word in which the *address of the operand* is found. It is customary to use one bit in the instruction code to distinguish between a direct and an indirect address.

As an illustration of this concept, consider the instruction code format shown in Fig. 5-2(a). It consists of a three-bit operation code designated by OP, a six-bit address part designated by *AD*, and an indirect-address mode bit designated by *I*.

The mode bit is 0 for a direct address and 1 for an indirect address. A direct address instruction is shown in Fig. 5-2(b). It is placed in address 2 in memory. The *I* bit is 0, so the instruction is recognized (by the control) as a direct address instruction. Since the address part *AD* is equal to the binary equivalent of 9 (001001), the control finds the operand in memory at address 9. The instruction in address 2 shown in Fig. 5-2(c) has a mode bit *I* = 1. Therefore, it is recognized as an indirect address instruction. The address part is the binary equivalent of 9. The control goes to address 9 to find the *address of the operand*. This address is in the address portion of the word and is designated by *M(AD)*. Since *M(AD)* contains 14 (binary 001110), the control finds the operand in memory at address 14. The indirect address instruction needs two references to memory to fetch an operand. The first reference is needed to read the address of the operand; the second is for the operand itself.

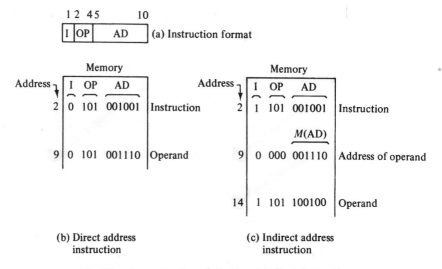

Fig. 5-2 Demonstration of direct and indirect instructions.

5-2 COMPUTER INSTRUCTIONS

Computer instructions are normally stored in consecutive memory locations and are executed sequentially one at a time. The control reads an instruction from a specific address in memory and executes it. It then continues by reading the next instruction in sequence and executes it, and so on. This type of instruction sequencing needs a counter to calculate the address of the next instruction after the execution of the current instruction is completed. Moreover, memory words cannot communicate with processor registers directly without going through an address and buffer register. It is also necessary to provide a register in the control unit for storing operation codes after they are read from memory. These requirements dictate the register configuration shown in Fig. 5-3. This register configuration will be used to describe the internal organization of a basic digital computer.

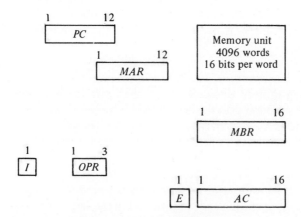

Fig. 5-3 Basic computer registers.

The memory unit has a capacity of 4096 words and each word contains 16 bits. Twelve bits of an instruction word are needed to specify the address of an operand. This leaves four bits for the operation part of the instruction. However, only three bits are used to specify an operation code. The fourth bit is used to specify a direct or indirect addressing mode. The memory buffer register (MBR) consists of 16 bits, as does the AC (accumulator) register. The E flip-flop is an extension of the AC. It is used during shifting operations, it receives the end-carry during addition, and otherwise is a useful flip-flop that can simplify the data processing capabilities of the computer. The I register has a single cell for storing the mode bit and the operation register (OPR) stores the three-bit operation code read from memory.

The memory address register MAR has 12 bits since this is the length of a memory address. The program counter (PC) also has 12 bits and it holds the address of the next instruction to be read from memory after the current instruction is executed. This register goes through a counting sequence and causes the computer to read sequential instructions previously stored in memory. Instruction words are read and executed in sequence unless a branch instruction is encountered. A branch instruction has an operation part that calls for a transfer to a nonconsecutive instruction in memory. The address part of a branch instruction is transferred to PC to become the address of the next instruction. To read an instruction, the content of PC is transferred to MAR, a memory read cycle initiated, and PC is incremented by one. This places the instruction code into MBR and prepares PC for the address of the next instruction. The operation code is transferred to OPR, the mode bit into I and the address part into MAR. A memory read operation places the operand (if $I = 0$) into MBR. The AC

and the *MBR* are used as the source registers for the micro-operations specified by the operation code. The result of the operation is stored in the *AC*.

However, an instruction may have an indirect bit *I* equal to 1, or may not require an operand from memory, or may be a branch instruction. In each of these cases, the control must issue a different set of control functions to execute different types of register transfers. In order to investigate the role that the control unit plays in executing instructions it is necessary to define the computer instructions and their code formats.

The basic computer has three different instruction code formats, as shown in Fig. 5-4. The operation part of the instruction contains three bits; the meaning of the remaining thirteen bits depends on the operation code encountered. A *memory-reference* instruction uses the last 12 bits to specify an address and the first bit to specify the mode *I*. A *register-reference* instruction specifies an operation on or a test of the *AC* or *E* register. An operand from memory is not needed; therefore, the last 12 bits are used to specify the operation or test to be executed. A register-reference instruction is recognized by the operation code 111 with a 0 in the first bit of the instruction. Similarly, an input-output instruction does not need a reference to memory and is recognized by the operation code 111 with a 1 in the first bit of the instruction. The remaining 12 bits are used to specify the type of input-output operation or test performed. Note that the first bit of the instruction code is not used as a mode bit when the last 12 bits are not used to designate an address.

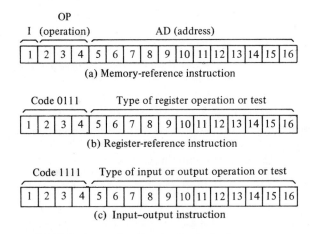

Fig. 5-4 Instruction formats for the basic computer.

Only three bits of the instruction are used for the operation code. It may seem that the computer is restricted to a maximum of eight distinct operations. However, since register-reference and input-output instructions use the remaining 12 bits as part of the operation code, the total number of instructions can exceed eight. In fact, the total number of instruction chosen for the basic computer is equal to 25.

The instructions for the computer are listed in Table 5-1. The symbol designation is a three-letter word and represents an abbreviation intended for programmers and users. The hexadecimal code is equal to the equivalent hexadecimal number of the binary code used for the instruction. By using the hexadecimal equivalent we reduced the 16 bits of an instruction code to four digits with each hexadecimal digit being equivalent to four bits. A memory-reference instruction has an address part of 12 bits. The address part is denoted by the symbol AD and must be specified by three hexadecimal digits. The first bit of the instruction is designated by the symbol I. When $I = 0$, AD is the address of the operand. In this case, the first four bits of an instruction have a hexadecimal designation from 0 to 6 since the first bit is 0. When $I = 1$, AD is an address where the address of the operand is to be found in memory. The hexadecimal digit equivalent of the first four bits of the instruction ranges from 8 to E since the first bit is 1.

Register-reference instructions use 16 bits to specify an operation. The first four bits are always 0111, which is equivalent to hexadecimal 7. The other three hexadecimal digits give the binary equivalent of the remaining 12 bits. The input-output instructions also use all 16 bits to specify an operation. The first four bits are always 1111 which is equivalent to hexadecimal F. The three X's following the F for an input-output instruction are digits that distinguish between the different I/O instructions. These digits are specified later in Table 5-5.

TABLE 5-1   Computer Instructions

Symbol	Hexadecimal Code			Description
	$I = 0$	$I = 1$	Address	
AND	0	8	AD	AND memory word to AC
ADD	1	9	AD	Add memory word to AC
LDA	2	A	AD	Load AC from memory
STA	3	B	AD	Store AC into memory
BUN	4	C	AD	Branch unconditionally
BSA	5	D	AD	Branch and save return address
ISZ	6	E	AD	Increment and skip if zero
CLA	7800			Clear AC
CLE	7400			Clear E
CMA	7200			Complement AC
CME	7100			Complement E
CIR	7080			Circulate right E and AC
CIL	7040			Circulate left E and AC
INC	7020			Increment AC
SPA	7010			Skip if AC is positive
SNA	7008			Skip if AC is negative
SZA	7004			Skip if AC is zero
SZE	7002			Skip if E is zero
HLT	7001			Halt computer
I/O	FXXX			Input-output instructions (see Table 5-5)

Before investigating the operations performed by the instructions, let us discuss the type of instructions that must be included in a practical computer. A computer should have a set of instructions that allows the user to formulate any conceivable data processing task. To ensure this, the computer must include a sufficient number of instructions in each of the following categories:

1. Arithmetic, logic, and shift instructions.
2. Instructions for moving information to and from memory and processor registers.
3. Instructions that check status information to provide decision making capabilities.
4. Input and output instructions.
5. The capability of stopping the computer.

Arithmetic, logic, and shift instructions provide computational capabilities for processing the type of data that the user may wish to employ. The bulk of the binary information in a digital computer is stored in memory but all computations are done in processor registers. Therefore, the user must have the capability of moving information between these two units. Decision-making capabilities are an important aspect of digital computers. For example, two numbers can be compared; however, if the first is greater than the second, it may be necessary to proceed differently than if the second is greater than the first. Logical decisions are provided in computers by instructions that check status conditions after a computation. The branch instructions are then used to branch to a different set of instructions depending on the status condition encountered. Input and output instructions are needed for communication between the computer and the user. Programs and data must be transferred into memory and results of computations must be transferred back to the user. Finally, there must be an instruction that will halt further computer operations when necessary.

The instructions listed in Table 5-1 constitute a minimum set that provides all the capabilities mentioned above. There are three arithmetic instructions: ADD, complement AC (CMA), and increment AC (INC). With these three instructions we can add and subtract binary numbers when negative numbers are in signed-2's complement representation. The circulate instructions, CIR and CIL, can be used for arithmetic shifts to provide multiplication and division operations as well as any other type of shifts desired. There are three logic operations: AND, complement AC (CMA), and clear AC (CLA). With these operations, it is possible to obtain the 16 logic operations listed in Table 4-5.

Moving information from memory to AC is accomplished by the load AC (LDA) instruction. Storing information from AC into memory is done by the store AC (STA) instruction. The branch instructions BUN and BSA, the ISZ instruction, the four skip instructions, and the instructions associated with the E register provide capabilities for making logical decisions. These instructions will be explained further in Sec. 5-4 and their capabilities will be demonstrated in the programming examples of

Chap. 6. The input-output instructions are explained in Sec. 5-5. Finally, the halt (HLT) instruction is provided to stop the computer by programming means.

The detailed function of each instruction and the micro-operations needed for their execution are presented in Sec. 5-4. We delay this discussion because we must first consider the control unit and understand its internal organization.

5-3 TIMING AND CONTROL

The digital computer operates in discrete steps. Micro-operations are performed during each step. Instructions are read from memory and executed in registers by a sequence of micro-operations. Once a start switch is activated, the computer sequence follows a basic pattern. An instruction whose address is in the *PC* register is read from memory into *MBR*. Its operation part is transferred into *OPR* and the mode bit into the *I* register. The operation part is decoded in the control unit. If it is a memory reference type that needs an operand from memory, control checks the bit in *I*. If $I = 0$, the memory is accessed again to read the operand. If $I = 1$, the memory is accessed to read the address of the operand and again to read the operand. Thus a word read from memory into *MBR* may be an instruction, an operand, or an address of an operand. When an instruction is read from memory, the computer is said to be in an instruction *fetch* cycle. When the word read from memory is an address of an operand the computer is in an *indirect* cycle. When the word read from memory is an operand, the computer is in a data *execute* cycle. It is the function of the control to keep track of the various cycles.

The control unit uses two flip-flops to distinguish between the three cycles. These flip-flops are denoted by the letters *F* and *R*. A 2 by 4 decoder associated with these flip-flops provides four outputs, three of which can be used to differentiate between the above-mentioned cycles. The computer has a fourth cycle to be introduced in Sec. 5-5. Table 5-2 lists the binary values of *F* and *R* and the decoder variable c_i that is equal to 1 for each of the four cycles.

The block diagram of the control unit for the basic computer is shown in Fig. 5-5. The timing in the computer is generated by a 2-bit sequence counter (*SC*) and a 2 by 4 decoder. The timing signals out of the decoder are designated by t_0, t_1, t_2 and t_3. We will assume that the memory cycle is shorter than the time interval between

TABLE 5-2 Computer Cycle Control

Flip-Flops		Decoder	
F	*R*	*Output*	*Computer Cycle*
0	0	c_0	Fetch cycle (read instruction)
0	1	c_1	Indirect cycle (read address of operand)
1	0	c_2	Execute cycle (read operand)
1	1	c_3	Interrupt cycle (see Sec. 5-5)

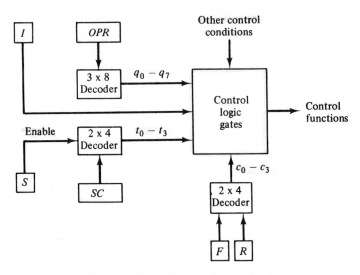

Fig. 5-5 Block diagram of control unit.

two clock pulses. According to this assumption, a memory read or write cycle initiated by the falling edge of one timing variable will be completed by the time the next clock pulse arrives [see Fig. 4-15(c)]. This is not common in most computers because a memory cycle is usually longer than the interval between two clock pulses. We make this assumption here to facilitate the presentation. The four timing variables employed in this computer are sufficient for the execution of any instruction during two or three cycles.

The operation code part of the instruction in OPR is decoded into eight outputs q_0 to q_7, the subscript number being equal to the binary equivalent of the operation code. The cycle control flip-flops F and R are decoded into four outputs c_0 to c_3 as specified in Table 5-2. The control logic gates generate the various control functions for the micro-operations in the computer. Each control function includes with it a timing variable t_i and a cycle designation c_i. During the execute cycle, the control function will also include a q_i variable. The I variable and other control conditions are also needed for the generation of control functions.

The control block diagram shows a start-stop flip-flop S connected to the enable input of the timing decoder. All micro-operations are conditioned on the timing signals. The timing signals are generated only when $S = 1$. When $S = 0$, none of the variables t_0 to t_3 are equal to 1 and therefore the control sequence stops and the computer halts. The S flip-flop can be set or cleared from switches in the computer console, or cleared by the HLT (halt) instruction. It is necessary to ensure that when S is set by a start switch, signal t_0 is the first to occur; and when S is cleared by a stop switch, the current instruction is completed before the computer halts.

We are now ready to specify in symbolic notation the sequence of control functions and micro-operations for the computer. Each symbolic statement consists of a control function followed by a colon, followed by one or more micro-operations.

All statements are to be interpreted in accordance with the symbolic notation defined in Chap. 4.

Fetch Cycle

An instruction is read from memory during the instruction fetch cycle. The register transfer relations that specify this process are:

predicates   *Assignments*

$c_0 t_0$:	$MAR \leftarrow PC$	Transfer instruction address
$c_0 t_1$:	$MBR \leftarrow M, PC \leftarrow PC + 1$	Read instruction and increment PC
$c_0 t_2$:	$OPR \leftarrow MBR(OP), I \leftarrow MBR(I)$	Transfer OP code and mode bit
$q_7' I c_0 t_3$:	$R \leftarrow 1$	Go to indirect cycle
$(q_7 + I') c_0 t_3$:	$F \leftarrow 1$	Go to execute cycle

The fetch cycle is recognized by variable c_0. The four timing signals that occur during this cycle initiate the sequence of micro-operations for the fetch cycle. The address, which is in PC, is transferred into MAR. The memory reads the instruction and places it in MBR. At the same time, the program counter is incremented by one to prepare it for the address of the next instruction. The operation part and the mode bit of the instruction are transferred from MBR into OPR and I, respectively. Note that the address part of the instruction remains in MBR.

At time t_3 control makes a decision as to what should be the next computer cycle. If the operation code contains 111, the instruction is either a register-reference or input-output instruction. Therefore, if $q_7 = 1$, the F flip-flop is set and control goes to the execute cycle. If $q_7 = 0$, the instruction is a memory-reference instruction. Now, if $I = 0$, it signifies that the instruction is a direct instruction so control goes to the execute cycle by setting F to 1. If $I = 1$, it is an indirect instruction. Control goes to the indirect cycle by setting R to 1. Note that the condition for going to the execute cycle is the complement of the condition for going to the indirect cycle, that is, $(q_7' I)' = q_7 + I'$.

Remember that F and R are 0 during the fetch cycle. Setting R to 1 results in $FR = 01$. Setting F to one results in $FR = 10$. The timing variable that becomes 1 after t_3 is t_0. When the next t_0 becomes 1 the computer may be either in the execute or in the indirect cycle.

Indirect Cycle

The indirect cycle is recognized by variable c_1. During this cycle, control reads the memory word where the address of the operand is to be found. The register transfer micro-operations for the indirect cycle are:

$c_1 t_0$:	$MAR \leftarrow MBR(AD)$	Transfer address part of instruction
$c_1 t_1$:	$MBR \leftarrow M$	Read address of operand
$c_1 t_2$:		Nothing
$c_1 t_3$:	$F \leftarrow 1, \ R \leftarrow 0$	Go to execute cycle

The address part of the instruction is in $MBR(5\text{--}16)$. These 12 bits are symbolized by $MBR(AD)$. They are transferred into MAR and a memory cycle is initiated. Bits 5–16 of the word just read from memory contain the address of the operand. Now that the address of the operand is in $MBR(AD)$, control goes to the execute cycle by setting F and clearing R. Note that nothing is done during time t_2. Changing F and R should be avoided during this time because timing variable t_3 that follows t_2 will find the computer in a different cycle. Changes from one cycle to another must be done at time t_3 so the next cycle can start with timing variable t_0.

Control Flow Chart

Control reaches the execute cycle from two different paths, after the fetch cycle or after the indirect cycle. The flow chart of Fig. 5-6 illustrates the various paths available in the control unit. It summarizes the discussion up to this point and indicates the paths that the control tasks during the execute cycle. A flow chart is a block diagram connected by directed lines. The directed lines between blocks designate the path to be taken from one step to the other. The two major types of blocks are (1) function blocks that show the operations to be performed (rectangular boxed), and (2) decision blocks that have two or more alternative paths dependent on the status of the condition indicated within a diamond-shaped box.

As shown in the flow chart, the start switch clears the cycle control flip-flops. This puts the computer in the fetch cycle. An instruction is read from memory and its operation and mode bits placed in control registers. If $q_7 = 1$, or if $q_7 = 0$ and $I = 0$, control goes to the execute cycle by setting F to 1. If $q_7 = 0$ and $I = 1$, it goes to the indirect cycle by setting R to 1. During the indirect cycle, control reads the address of the operand and moves to the execute cycle.

At the beginning of the execute cycle, the operation code of the instruction is in OPR, the first bit of the instruction is in I, and $MBR(5\text{--}16)$ holds the rest of the instruction. If $q_7 = 0$, $MBR(5\text{--}16)$ contains the *effective address*. This is the actual address of the operand and may have come from either the address part of the instruction (when $I = 0$) or from the indirect cycle (when $I = 1$). In either case, this address part in MBR is designated by $MBR(AD)$. Control reads the operand found in the effective address and executes the memory reference instruction. If $q_7 = 1$, the bits in $MBR(5\text{--}16)$ are part of the operation code. Control checks the bit in I to determine whether the instruction is a register-reference or an input-output type. It then checks the bits of $MBR(5\text{--}16)$ to decide which specific instruction to execute. Cycle control flip-flop F is cleared after the execution of the instruction. This causes a return to the fetch cycle to start all over again to read and execute the next instruction.

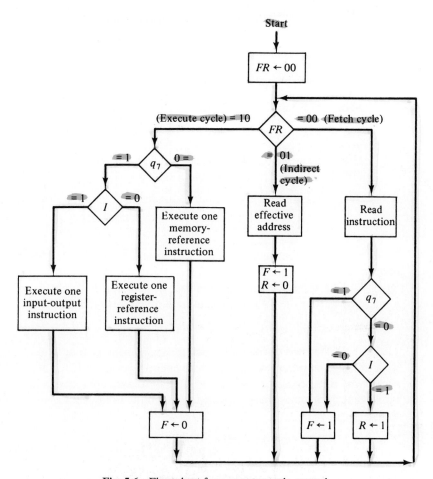

Fig. 5-6 Flow chart for computer cycle control.

5-4 EXECUTION OF INSTRUCTIONS

In order to specify the micro-operations needed for the execution of each instruction, it is necessary that the function that they are intended to perform be defined precisely. Looking back to Table 5-1, where the instructions are listed, we find that some instructions have an ambiguous description. This is because the explanation of an instruction in words is usually lengthy, and not enough space is available in the table for such a lengthy explanation. We will now show that the function of computer instructions can be defined precisely by means of symbolic notation.

Table 5-3 lists the seven memory-reference instructions and their functions. The q_i variable in the operation decoder that belongs to each instruction is included

TABLE 5-3 Memory Reference Instructions

Symbol	Operation Decoder	Effective Address	Memory Word	Symbolic Designation
AND	q_0	m	M	$AC \leftarrow AC \wedge M$
ADD	q_1	m	M	$EAC \leftarrow AC + M$
LDA	q_2	m	M	$AC \leftarrow M$
STA	q_3	m	M	$M \leftarrow AC$
BUN	q_4	m	—	$PC \leftarrow m$
BSA	q_5	m	M	$M \leftarrow PC, PC \leftarrow m + 1$
ISZ	q_6	m	M	$M \leftarrow M + 1$, if $(M + 1 = 0)$ then $(PC \leftarrow PC + 1)$

in the table. The effective address of the instruction is designated by the letter m. This address specifies a word in memory (the operand) and this word is designated by the letter M. The symbolic function for each instruction is a *macro-operation* and not a micro-operation. It is not a micro-operation because the statement

$$AC \leftarrow AC + M$$

cannot be performed during one clock pulse. Remember that data stored in memory words cannot be processed directly with external registers. The data must be read out of memory into processor registers where their binary content can be operated on. To implement the macro-operation above we need the following *sequence* of micro-operations:

$$MAR \leftarrow m$$
$$MBR \leftarrow M$$
$$AC \leftarrow AC + MBR$$

The effective address must be placed in MAR. A memory read operation reads the operand into MBR. Only after the operand is in MBR can the control initiate the ADD micro-operation between two processor registers.

When writing a statement in symbolic notation, one must distinguish between a macro-operation and a micro-operation. As long as this distinction is recognized, there is no reason why one cannot use a register transfer language to specify the macro-operations defined by computer instructions.

We now explain the function of each instruction separately and list the micro-operations and control functions associated with each.

AND to AC

This is an instruction that performs the AND logic operation on pairs of bits in the AC and the memory word specified by the effective address. The result of the operation remains in the AC. The micro-operations that execute this instruction are:

$q_0 c_2 t_0$: $MAR \leftarrow MBR(AD)$ Transfer effective address

$q_0 c_2 t_1$: $MBR \leftarrow M$ Read operand

$q_0 c_2 t_2$: $AC \leftarrow AC \wedge MBR$ AND with AC

$c_2 t_3$: $F \leftarrow 0$ Go to fetch cycle

[handwritten margin note: $MBR \leftarrow M[MBR(AD)]$ *;* $AC \leftarrow AC \wedge M[MBR(AD)]$ *]*

The control functions for this instruction need variables q_0 and c_2. The first recognizes the code of the AND operation and the second recognizes the execute cycle. Three of the timing variables that occur during the execute cycle initiate the micro-operations for reading the operand from memory and performing the AND micro-operation. At time t_3, F is cleared to 0. The timing signal that occurs after t_3 is t_0, so this t_0 finds the computer in the fetch cycle. Note that q_0 is not used with t_3. The condition for returning to the fetch cycle is common to all instructions and belongs at the end of the execute cycle no matter what instruction has been processed. As a consequence, the last statement in the above sequence will not be repeated again in the list of statements for the other instructions.

The reader should be reminded that the program counter (PC) is incremented during the fetch cycle at the same time the current instruction is read from memory. Therefore, when control returns to the fetch cycle after executing the current instruction, it finds in PC the address of the next instruction.

ADD to *AC*

This operation adds the content of the memory word specified by the effective address to the present value of the AC. The sum is transferred into the AC and the end-carry into the E flip-flop (EAC represents a register that combines the E and AC registers). The sign bit in the left-most position is treated as any other bit according to the signed-2's complement addition rule stated in Sec. 3-2. The micro-operations that execute this instruction are:

$q_1 c_2 t_0$: $MAR \leftarrow MBR(AD)$ Transfer effective address

$q_1 c_2 t_1$: $MBR \leftarrow M$ Read operand

$q_1 c_2 t_2$: $EAC \leftarrow AC + MBR$ Add to AC and store carry in E

LDA: Load to *AC*

This instruction transfers the memory word (specified by the effective address) into the AC. The word read from memory into MBR can be transferred to the AC by the micro-operation $AC \leftarrow MBR$. Such a statement defines a direct path from MBR to AC. However, we can utilize the existing path through the parallel-adder that is provided for the implementation of the *add* micro-operation. This path can be used if the AC is cleared prior to the transfer. Using the adder path, we specify the micro-operations for the LDA instruction as follows:

$$q_2 c_2 t_0: \quad MAR \leftarrow MBR(AD) \qquad \text{Transfer effective address}$$

$$q_2 c_2 t_1: \quad MBR \leftarrow M, AC \leftarrow 0 \qquad \text{Read operand, clear } AC$$

$$q_2 c_2 t_2: \quad AC \leftarrow AC + MBR \qquad \text{Add to } AC$$

The operand is read into MBR and the AC is cleared. The addition of MBR to the zero content of the AC results in the transfer of the content of MBR into the AC. Note that the carry is not transferred to E. We do not want to disturb the value of E in a direct transfer.

STA: Store *AC*

This instruction stores the present content of the AC in the memory word specified by the effective address. The micro-operations that execute this instruction are:

$$q_3 c_2 t_0: \quad MAR \leftarrow MBR(AD) \qquad \text{Transfer effective address}$$

$$q_3 c_2 t_1: \quad MBR \leftarrow AC \qquad \text{Transfer data to } MBR$$

$$q_3 c_2 t_2: \quad M \leftarrow MBR \qquad \text{Store word in memory}$$

BUN: Branch Unconditionally

This instruction transfers the program to the instruction specified by the effective address. The instruction is listed with the memory-reference instructions because it has an address part. However, it does not need a reference to memory to read an operand (it may need a reference to memory to read the effective address if $I = 1$). Remember that PC holds the address of the instruction to be read from memory at the next fetch cycle. Normally, the PC is incremented to give the address of the next instruction sequence. The programmer has the prerogative of specifying any other instruction out of sequence by using the BUN instruction. This instruction informs the control to take the effective address and transfer it into PC. During the next fetch cycle, this address becomes the address of the instruction that is read from memory. The micro-operation that performs this function is:

$$q_4 c_2 t_0: \quad PC \leftarrow MBR(AD) \qquad \text{Transfer effective address to } PC$$

Timing variables t_1 and t_2 are not used for this instruction and will not initiate any micro-operations.

The instructions discussed thus far are not difficult to comprehend compared to the function of the next two instructions. The next two memory-reference instructions require a slightly more complicated sequence of micro-operations. The usefulness of these two instructions will be demonstrated by the programming examples in the next chapter.

BSA : Branch and Save Return Address

This instruction is useful for branching to a portion of the program called a *subroutine*. When executed, the instruction stores the address of the next instruction held in *PC* (called the *return address*) into the word specified by the effective address *m*. The content of *m* plus 1 is transferred into *PC* to serve as the address of the instruction for the next fetch cycle (the beginning of the subroutine). The return from the subroutine to the program at the saved address is accomplished by means of an indirect BUN instruction. This instruction, when placed at the end of the subroutine, causes the program to transfer back to the position it left when it branched to the subroutine.

This process is depicted in the example of Fig. 5-7. The BSA instruction performs the macro-operations (see Table 5-3)

$$M \leftarrow PC, \quad PC \leftarrow m + 1$$

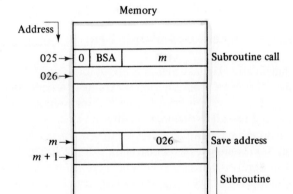

Fig. 5-7 Demonstration of subroutine call and return.

Suppose that the BSA instruction read during the fetch cycle is at address 25. During the execute cycle, *PC* contains 26, since it was incremented during the fetch cycle. The content of *PC* is transferred into the memory word specified by address *m*, and *m* + 1 is placed in *PC*. The next fetch cycle finds *PC* with the value *m* + 1, so control continues to execute the subroutine program. The last instruction in the subroutine is an indirect (*I* = 1) BUN instruction with an address *m*. When this instruction is executed, control goes to the indirect cycle to read the effective address at location *m*. It finds the previously saved address 26, and places it into *PC*. (Note that here the effective address is 26 and not *m*.) The next fetch cycle finds *PC* with the value 26 so control continues to execute the instruction at the return address. The BSA instruction performs the function usually referred to as a subroutine *call*. The last instruction in the subroutine performs the function referred to as a subroutine *return*.

The macro-operations for the BSA instruction are implemented in computer registers by a sequence of micro-operations as follows:

$q_5 c_2 t_0$:	$MAR \leftarrow MBR(AD)$,	Transfer m to MAR
	$MBR(AD) \leftarrow PC$,	Transfer PC to be stored
	$PC \leftarrow MBR(AD)$	Transfer m to PC
$q_5 c_2 t_1$:	$M \leftarrow MBR$	Store previous content of PC
$q_5 c_2 t_2$:	$PC \leftarrow PC + 1$	Increment m in PC

Three simultaneous micro-operations are performed during t_0. The contents of PC and $MBR(AD)$ are swapped, and the effective address transferred to MAR. At this time, m is in MAR and the previous content of PC in MBR. A memory write operation results in the implementation of $M \leftarrow PC$. The previous value of m, stored in PC, is incremented at time t_2 to implement $PC \leftarrow m + 1$.

ISZ: Increment and Skip-if-Zero

The increment and skip instruction is useful for address modification and for counting the number of times a program loop is executed. A negative number previously stored in memory at address m is read by the ISZ instruction. This number is incremented by 1 and stored back into memory. If, after it is incremented, the number reaches zero. the next instruction is skipped. Thus, at the end of a program loop one inserts an ISZ instruction followed by a BUN instruction. If the stored number does not reach zero, the program returns to execute the loop again. If it reaches zero, the next instruction (BUN) is skipped and the program continues to execute instructions out of the loop.

The function of the ISZ instruction as stated in Table 5-3 is symbolized by the macro-statements

$$M \leftarrow M + 1$$
$$\text{If } (M + 1 = 0) \text{ then } (PC \leftarrow PC + 1)$$

The sequence of micro-operations that implement the function are as follows:

$q_6 c_2 t_0$:	$MAR \leftarrow MBR(AD)$	Transfer effective address
$q_6 c_2 t_1$:	$MBR \leftarrow M$	Read memory word
$q_6 c_2 t_2$:	$MBR \leftarrow MBR + 1$	Increment value
$q_6 c_2 t_3$:	$M \leftarrow MBR$,	Restore incremented word
	if $(MBR = 0)$ then $(PC \leftarrow PC + 1)$	Skip if zero

The memory word specified by the effective address is read from memory at time t_1. It is incremented in MBR at t_2. (Remember that no processing can be done with memory words; they must be read into a processor register such as MBR to be incremented.) At t_3, the incremented word is restored to memory, and PC is incremented if the word in MBR is zero. Incrementing PC during the execute cycle causes a skip of one instruction in the program because it is incremented during the fetch cycle also.

Register-Reference Instructions

Register-reference instructions are recognized by the control when $q_7 = 1$ and $I = 0$. These instructions use the other 12 bits of the code to specify one of 12 different micro-operations. These 12 bits are available in $MBR(5$–$16)$ during the execute cycle.

The micro-operation statements for the register-reference instructions are listed in Table 5-4. These instructions are executed with timing variable t_3, although any other

TABLE 5-4   Register-Reference Instructions

Symbol	Hexadecimal Code	Control Function	Micro-Operation
		$r = q_7 I' c_2 t_3$	
		$B_i = MBR(i)$	
CLA	7800	rB_5:	$AC \leftarrow 0$
CLE	7400	rB_6:	$E \leftarrow 0$
CMA	7200	rB_7:	$AC \leftarrow \overline{AC}$
CME	7100	rB_8:	$E \leftarrow \bar{E}$
CIR	7080	rB_9:	cir EAC
CIL	7040	rB_{10}:	cil EAC
INC	7020	rB_{11}:	$EAC \leftarrow AC + 1$
SPA	7010	rB_{12}:	If $(AC(1) = 0)$ then $(PC \leftarrow PC + 1)$
SNA	7008	rB_{13}:	If $(AC(1) = 1)$ then $(PC \leftarrow PC + 1)$
SZA	7004	rB_{14}:	If $(AC = 0)$ then $(PC \leftarrow PC + 1)$
SZE	7002	rB_{15}:	If $(E = 0)$ then $(PC \leftarrow PC + 1)$
HLT	7001	rB_{16}:	$S \leftarrow 0$

timing variable could be used (except for the HLT instruction). Each control function needs the Boolean relation $q_7 I' c_2 t_3$ which we designate for convenience by the symbol r. The control function is distinguished by the one bit in $MBR(5$–$16)$ which is equal to 1. By assigning the symbol B_i to bit i of MBR, all control functions can be simply denoted by rB_i. For example, the instruction CLA has the hexadecimal code 7800 which gives the binary equivalent 0111 1000 0000 0000. The first bit is a zero and is recognized from I'. The next three bits constitute the operation code and are recognized from decoder output q_7. Bit 5 in MBR is 1 and is recognized from B_5. The control function that initiates the micro-operation for this instruction is $q_7 I' c_2 t_3 B_5 = rB_5$. Note that, since the register-reference instructions operate on a single register, they can be specified by micro-operation statements.

The first seven register-reference instructions perform clear, complement, circular shift, and increment micro-operations on the AC and/or E registers. The next four instructions cause a skip of the next instruction in sequence when a stated condition is satisfied. The skipping of the instruction is achieved by incrementing PC once again (in addition to the incrementing during the fetch cycle). The condition control statements must be recognized as part of the control requirement. The AC is positive when its sign bit $AC(1) = 0$; it is negative when $AC(1) = 1$. The content of AC is zero ($AC = 0$) if all cells of the register are zero. The HLT instruction clears the start-stop flip-flop S and stops the timing sequences.

5-5 INPUT-OUTPUT AND INTERRUPT

A computer can serve no useful purpose unless it communicates with the external environment. Instruction and data stored in memory must come from some input device. Computational results must be transmitted to the user through some output device. Commerical computers include many different types of input and output devices. To demonstrate the most basic requirements for input and output communication, we will use as an illustration a teletypewriter unit for the basic computer. Further discussion of input-output organization can be found in Chap. 11.

A teletypewriter, also known by its trade name *Teletype*, has an electric typewriter keyboard, a printer, a paper-tape reader, and a paper-tape punch. The input device consists of either the typewriter keyboard or the paper-tape reader, with a manual switch available for selecting the one to be used. The output device consists of the typewriter printer or the paper-tape punch, with another switch available for selecting either device. The unit has a facility for producing a series of pulses equivalent to a binary code of the character whose key is struck. These pulses are transmitted into a shift register and constitute the input character. Serial pulses of an alphanumeric character code are sent to the printer where they are decoded to determine the character to be printed. The speed of the Teletype is very slow, usually about ten characters per second.

Instructions and data are transferred into the computer either in symbolic form through the keyboard or in binary form through the paper-tape reader. A 16-bit instruction or binary data word can be prepared on paper tape in two rows of eight bits each. The first punched row represents half of the word and the second row supplies the other half of the word. The two parts can be packed into one 16-bit computer word and stored in memory.

Input-Output Registers

The teletypewriter sends and receives serial information. Each quantity of information has eight bits of an alphanumeric code. The serial information from the keyboard is shifted into an input register. The serial information for the printer is stored in an output register. These two registers communicate with the teletypewriter serially and with the AC in parallel. The register configuration is shown in Fig. 5-8.

The input register $INPR$ consists of eight bits and holds an alphanumeric input

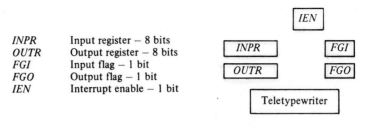

INPR	Input register − 8 bits
OUTR	Output register − 8 bits
FGI	Input flag − 1 bit
FGO	Output flag − 1 bit
IEN	Interrupt enable − 1 bit

Fig. 5-8   Registers for input, output, and interrupt.

information. The one-bit input flag *FGI* is a control flip-flop. The flag bit is set when new information is available in the input device and cleared when the information is accepted by the computer. The flag is needed to synchronize the timing rate differential between the input device and the computer. The process of information transfer is as follows: Initially, the input flag *FGI* is cleared. When a key is struck, an eight-bit code is shifted into *INPR* and the input flag is set to 1. As long as the flag is set, the information in *INPR* cannot be changed by striking another key. The computer checks the flag bit; if it is 1, the information from *INPR* is transferred in parallel into the *AC* and *FGI* is cleared. Once the flag is cleared, new information can be shifted into *INPR* by striking another key.

The output register *OUTR* works similarly but the direction of information flow is reversed. Initially, the output flag (*FGO*) is set to 1. The computer checks the flag bit; if it is 1, the information from *AC* is transferred in parallel to *OUTR* and *FGO* is cleared. The output device accepts the coded information, prints the corresponding character, and when the operation is completed, it sets *FGO* to 1. The computer does not load a new character into *OUTR* when *FGO* is 0 because this condition indicates that the output device is in the process of printing the character.

The process of communication just described is referred to as program controlled transfer. The computer keeps checking the flag bit and when it finds it set, it initiates an information transfer. The difference of information flow rate between the processor and that unit of the input-output device makes this type of transfer inefficient. To see why this is inefficient, consider a computer that can go through the fetch and execute cycles in 10 μs. The input-output device can transfer information at a maximum rate of 10 characters per second. This is equivalent to one character every 100,000 μs. Two instructions are executed when the computer checks the flag bit and decides not to transfer the information. This means that, at the maximum rate, the computer will check the flag 5,000 times between each transfer. The computer is wasting time while checking the flag instead of doing some other useful processing task.

An alternative to program-controlled procedure is to let the external device inform the computer when it is ready for the transfer. In the meantime the processor can be busy with other tasks. This type of transfer uses the interrupt facility. While the computer is running a program, it does not check the flags. However, when a flag is set the computer is momentarily interrupted from proceeding with the current program and is informed of the fact that a flag has been set. The computer deviates momentarily from what it is doing to take care of the input or output transfer. It then returns to the current program to continue what it was doing before the interrupt. The hardware that takes care of this procedure is explained below. At this time we explain the function of the interrupt enable flip-flop shown in Fig. 5-8.

The interrupt enable flip-flop (*IEN*) can be set and cleared by two instructions. When it is cleared, the flags cannot interrupt the computer and are neglected. When *IEN* is set, the computer can be interrupted. This flip-flop provides the programmer with a capability for making a decision whether to use the interrupt facility or not. If he issues an instruction to clear *IEN*, then he is saying in effect that he does not want his program to be interrupted. If he sets it, he has available the interrupt facility at his disposal.

Input-Output Instructions

Input and output instructions are needed for transferring information to and from the *AC* register, for checking the flag bits, and for controlling the interrupt enable flip-flop. These instructions are listed in Table 5-5. They have an operation code 111

TABLE 5-5 Input-Output Instructions

Symbol	Hexadecimal Code	Description	Function
INP	F800	Input character to *AC*	$AC\,(9\text{–}16) \leftarrow INPR,\ FGI \leftarrow 0$
OUT	F400	Output character from *AC*	$OUTR \leftarrow AC(9\text{–}16),\ FGO \leftarrow 0$
SKI	F200	Skip on input flag	If $(FGI = 1)$ then $(PC \leftarrow PC + 1)$
SKO	F100	Skip on output flag	If $(FGO = 1)$ then $(PC \leftarrow PC + 1)$
ION	F080	Interrupt on	$IEN \leftarrow 1$
IOF	F040	Interrupt off	$IEN \leftarrow 0$

with $I = 1$, which gives for the first digit of the instruction the hexadecimal digit F. The remaining 12 bits contain a single 1 and eleven 0's for each instruction. The INP instruction transfers the input information into the eight low-order bits of the *AC* and also clears the input flag. The OUT instruction transfers eight bits into the output registers and clears the flag. The next two instructions check the status of the flags and cause a skip of the next instruction if the flag is 1. The instruction that is skipped will normally be a branch instruction to return and check the flag again. This instruction is not skipped if the flag is 0. If the flag is 1, the branch instruction is skipped and an input or output intsruction is executed. The last two instructions set and clear the interrupt enable bit, respectively.

The micro-operations needed to execute each instruction are listed under the function column in Table 5-5. They are executed by the control during the execute cycle c_2 at time t_3. The input-output instructions are recognized by variable $q_7 I$ and the bit B_i in *MBR* that is equal to 1. Thus, the INP instruction is executed with the following control function:

$$q_7 Ic_2 t_3 B_5: \qquad AC(9–16) \longleftarrow INPR, FGI \longleftarrow 0$$

The other instructions have a similar control function, except for the B_i variable which is different in each.

Interrupt Cycle

So far we have shown three cycles for the computer: fetch, indirect, and execute. When the cycle control flip-flops F and R are both 1's, the computer goes to an interrupt cycle. This cycle is recognized by the cycle decoder output c_3 (see Table 5-2). It is initiated from the execute cycle after the current instruction is completed. Previously we have assumed that the last micro-operation in the execute cycle is

$$c_2 t_3: \qquad F \longleftarrow 0$$

which returns control to the fetch cycle. We now modify this condition as shown in the flow-chart of Fig. 5-9. *IEN* is checked at the end of each execute cycle. If it is 0, it indicates that the programmer does not want to use the interrupt, so control goes to the next fetch cycle by clearing F. If *IEN* is 1, control checks the flag bits. If both flags are 0, it indicates that neither the input nor the output registers are ready for transfer of information. In this case, control goes back to the fetch cycle. If any flag is set to 1, control goes to the interrupt cycle by setting R to 1 (F is already set to 1 during the execute cycle).

The interrupt cycle is a hardware implementation of a branch and save address operation. The current address in *PC* is stored in a specific location where it can be found later when the program returns to the instruction at which it was interrupted. This location may be a processor register or a memory location. We choose here the memory location at address 0 as the word for storing the return address. Control then inserts address 1 into *PC* and moves to the next fetch cycle. It also clears *IEN* so no more interruptions can occur until the interrupt request from the flag has been serviced.

At the beginning of the next fetch cycle, the instruction that is read from memory is in address 1 since this is the content of *PC*. At memory address 1, the programmer must store a branch instruction that sends the computer to a service program where it checks the flags, determines which flag is set and then transfers the required input or output information. Once this is done, the instruction ION is executed to set *IEN* to 1 (to enable other interrupts), and the next instruction executed returns the program to the location where it was interrupted. The instruction that returns the computer to the original program is

I	BUN	0
1	100	0000 0000 0000

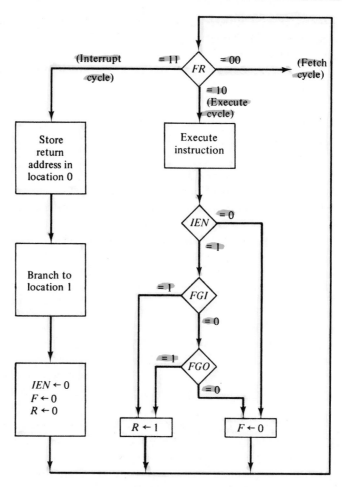

Fig. 5-9 Flow chart for interrupt cycle.

This is a branch indirect instruction with an address part of 0. After this instruction is read during the fetch cycle, control goes to the indirect cycle (because $I = 1$) to read the effective address. But the effective address is in location 0 and is the return address that was stored there during the previous interrupt cycle. The execution of the above instruction results in placing into PC the return address from location 0.

We are now ready to list the register transfer relations for the interrupt cycle. The interrupt cycle is initiated at the end of the execute cycle by the following micro-operations:

c_2t_3: If $[IEN \land (FGI \lor FGO) = 1]$ then $(R \leftarrow 1)$
If $[IEN \land (FGI \lor FGO) = 0]$ then $(F \leftarrow 0)$

The symbols $\land$ and $\lor$ stand for logic AND and OR, respectively. These conditional control statements replace the previously assumed micro-operation that cleared F unconditionally. These statements are in accordance with the requirements specified in the flow chart of Fig. 5-9.

Note that when the ION (interrupt on) instruction is executed by control, it is done during time t_3 as follows:

$$q_7 I c_2 B_9 t_3: \qquad IEN \leftarrow 1$$

The micro-operation may be executed at the same time that the conditional micro-operation listed above is executed because they have common variables in their control functions. If this occurs, and $IEN = 0$ during t_3, the computer goes to the fetch cycle and IEN does not become 1 until the next t_0 (in the fetch cycle). So an ION instruction would not cause an interrupt (if a flag is on) until the end of the *next* execute cycle. This ensures that the return address is placed in PC before another interrupt can occur.

The interrupt cycle occurs when $F = R = 1$ which makes variable $c_3 = 1$. The micro-operations for the interrupt cycle are:

$c_3 t_0$:	$MBR(AD) \leftarrow PC, PC \leftarrow 0$	Transfer return address and clear PC
$c_3 t_1$:	$MAR \leftarrow PC, PC \leftarrow PC + 1$	Transfer 0 to MAR, set PC to 1
$c_3 t_2$:	$M \leftarrow MBR, IEN \leftarrow 0$	Store return address and clear interrupt enable
$c_3 t_3$:	$F \leftarrow 0, R \leftarrow 0$	Go to fetch cycle

The return address is in PC and must be transferred to MBR for storage in memory. The PC is cleared and then transferred to MAR. At time t_2, MAR contains 0 and MBR has the return address. A memory-write operation stores the return address in location 0. PC is incremented at t_1 so it will contain address 1 at the beginning of the next fetch cycle. IEN is cleared and control returns to the fetch cycle.

5-6 DESIGN OF COMPUTER

The basic computer consists of a memory unit, a teletypewriter, a master clock generator, eight registers, eight flip-flops, three decoders, and a number of control logic gates. The memory and teletypewriter are standard units that can be purchased as finished products. The master clock generator is a common clock pulse source, usually an oscillator, that generates a periodic train of pulses. These pulses are fanned out by means of inverters and buffers and distributed over the entire system. Each pulse must reach every register and flip-flop at the same instant. Phasing delays are sometimes needed intermittently so that difference in transmission delays is uniform throughout.

The other components in the computer are decoders and registers which are available in standard MSI ICs. Flip-flops and gates are available in standard SSI ICs. From the list of register transfer statements developed for the computer, it is possible to determine the registers, flip-flops, and gates that are needed for the design of the computer. To illustrate with a specific example, consider the operation register *OPR* and its associated register transfer statement:

$$c_0t_2: \quad OPR \leftarrow MBR(OP)$$

This statement implies that the computer needs an AND gate with inputs c_0 and t_2 coming from the cycle decoder and timing decoder, respectively. The output of the gate must go to the load input of a 3-bit register with parallel-load capability. The data inputs to *OPR* are bits 2, 3, and 4 of *MBR*.

The control functions and micro-operations for the entire computer are summarized in Table 5-6. This table describes in a very concise form the internal organiza-

TABLE 5-6 Control Functions and Micro-operations for the Basic Computer

fetch	c_0t_0:	$MAR \leftarrow PC$
	c_0t_1:	$MBR \leftarrow M, PC \leftarrow PC + 1$
	c_0t_2:	$OPR \leftarrow MBR(OP), I \leftarrow MBR(I)$
	$q_7' Ic_0t_3$:	$R \leftarrow 1$
	$(q_7 + I')c_0t_3$:	$F \leftarrow 1$
indirect	c_1t_0:	$MAR \leftarrow MBR(AD)$
	c_1t_1:	$MBR \leftarrow M$
	c_1t_3:	$F \leftarrow 1, R \leftarrow 0$
interrupt	c_3t_0:	$MBR(AD) \leftarrow PC, PC \leftarrow 0$
	c_3t_1:	$MAR \leftarrow PC, PC \leftarrow PC + 1$
	c_3t_2:	$M \leftarrow MBR, IEN \leftarrow 0$
	c_3t_3:	$F \leftarrow 0, R \leftarrow 0$
execute	c_2t_3:	If $[IEN \wedge (FGI \vee FGO) = 1]$ then $(R \leftarrow 1)$,
		If $[IEN \wedge (FGI \vee FGO) = 0]$ then $(F \leftarrow 0)$
AND	$q_0c_2t_0$:	$MAR \leftarrow MBR(AD)$
	$q_0c_2t_1$:	$MBR \leftarrow M$
	$q_0c_2t_2$:	$AC \leftarrow AC \wedge MBR$
ADD	$q_1c_2t_0$:	$MAR \leftarrow MBR(AD)$
	$q_1c_2t_1$:	$MBR \leftarrow M$
	$q_1c_2t_2$:	$EAC \leftarrow AC + MBR$
LDA	$q_2c_2t_0$:	$MAR \leftarrow MBR(AD)$
	$q_2c_2t_1$:	$MBR \leftarrow M, AC \leftarrow 0$
	$q_2c_2t_2$:	$AC \leftarrow AC + MBR$
STA	$q_3c_2t_0$:	$MAR \leftarrow MBR(AD)$
	$q_3c_2t_1$:	$MBR \leftarrow AC$
	$q_3c_2t_2$:	$M \leftarrow MBR$
BUN	$q_4c_2t_0$:	$PC \leftarrow MBR(AD)$
BSA	$q_5c_2t_0$:	$MAR \leftarrow MBR(AD), PC \leftarrow MBR(AD), MBR(AD) \leftarrow PC$
	$q_5c_2t_1$:	$M \leftarrow MBR$
	$q_5c_2t_2$:	$PC \leftarrow PC + 1$
ISZ	$q_6c_2t_0$:	$MAR \leftarrow MBR(AD)$
	$q_6c_2t_1$:	$MBR \leftarrow M$
	$q_6c_2t_2$:	$MBR \leftarrow MBR + 1$
	$q_6c_2t_3$:	$M \leftarrow MBR$, if $(MBR = 0)$ then $(PC \leftarrow PC + 1)$

TABLE 5-6 Cont.

	$q_7I'c_2t_3 = r$	(common for all register-reference instructions)
	$MBR(i) = B_i$	$i = 5, 6, \ldots, 16$
CLA	$rB_5:$	$AC \leftarrow 0$
CLE	$rB_6:$	$E \leftarrow 0$
CMA	$rB_7:$	$AC \leftarrow \overline{AC}$
CME	$rB_8:$	$E \leftarrow \bar{E}$
CIR	$rB_9:$	cir EAC
CIL	$rB_{10}:$	cil EAC
INC	$rB_{11}:$	$EAC \leftarrow AC + 1$
SPA	$rB_{12}:$	If $(AC(1) = 0)$ then $(PC \leftarrow PC + 1)$
SNA	$rB_{13}:$	If $(AC(1) = 1)$ then $(PC \leftarrow PC + 1)$
SZA	$rB_{14}:$	If $(AC = 0)$ then $(PC \leftarrow PC + 1)$
SZE	$rB_{15}:$	If $(E = 0)$ then $(PC \leftarrow PC + 1)$
HLT	$rB_{16}:$	$S \leftarrow 0$
	$q_7Ic_2t_3 = p$	(common for all input-output instructions)
	$MBR(i) = B_i$	$i = 5, 6, \ldots, 10$
INP	$pB_5:$	$AC(9\text{–}16) \leftarrow INPR, FGI \leftarrow 0$
OUT	$pB_6:$	$OUTR \leftarrow AC(9\text{–}16), FGO \leftarrow 0$
SKI	$pB_7:$	If $(FGI = 1)$ then $(PC \leftarrow PC + 1)$
SKO	$pB_8:$	If $(FGO = 1)$ then $(PC \leftarrow PC + 1)$
ION	$pB_9:$	$IEN \leftarrow 1$
IOF	$pB_{10}:$	$IEN \leftarrow 0$

tion of the basic computer. It also gives all the information that is needed for designing the logic circuits of the computer. The control functions and conditional control statements listed in the table formulate the Boolean functions for the gates in the control unit. The list of micro-operations specifies the type of control inputs needed for the registers. A register transfer language is useful not only for describing the internal organization of a digital system but also for specifying the logic circuits needed for its design.

Accumulator Register

The design process will be illustrated by going through the procedure for designing the accumulator register (AC). This is the most complicated register in the computer because it serves as a processor register. The first step in the design is to scan the register transfer statements and retrieve all those statements that change the content of the AC. A micro-operation that changes the content of a register is recognized by the presence of its symbol on the left side of the arrow. To recognize the micro-operations belonging to the AC we scan Table 5-6 and retrieve all those statements that have the AC symbol on the left side of the arrow. The micro-operations for the other registers are obtained in a similar manner.

The register transfer statements that change the content of AC are listed below:

$q_0c_2t_2$:	$AC \leftarrow AC \wedge MBR$	AND with MBR
$q_1c_2t_2 + q_2c_2t_2$:	$AC \leftarrow AC + MBR$	Add
$q_2c_2t_1 + rB_5$:	$AC \leftarrow 0$	Clear
rB_7:	$AC \leftarrow \overline{AC}$	Complement
rB_9:	shr $AC, AC(1) \leftarrow E$	Shift-right
rB_{10}:	shl $AC, AC(16) \leftarrow E$	Shift-left
rB_{11}:	$AC \leftarrow AC + 1$	Increment
pB_5:	$AC(9\text{--}16) \leftarrow INPR$	Transfer $INPR$

Note that the *add* micro-operation occurs twice, and the two control functions are combined by a Boolean OR operation. They are also combined for the *clear* micro-operation. The circular shifts are separated from E and converted to shift micro-operations with E entering the serial input of the AC. The transfer from $INPR$ is to the eight low-order bits of the AC.

The control functions associated with the AC are generated by logic gates. The accumulator register itself is a general purpose register that requires eight different control inputs in addition to clock pulses. Such a register is available in integrated circuit form. (Such as *IC* Type 74281.)

Part of the hardware implementation for the AC is shown in Fig. 5-10. The rest of the implementation is illustrated in Fig. 5-11. Two diagrams are needed because of the large number of functions associated with this register. The total implementation is the combination of these two diagrams.

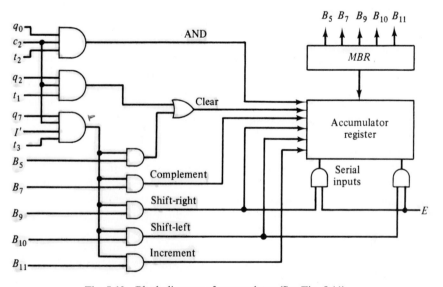

Fig. 5-10   Block diagram of accumulator (See Fig. 5-11).

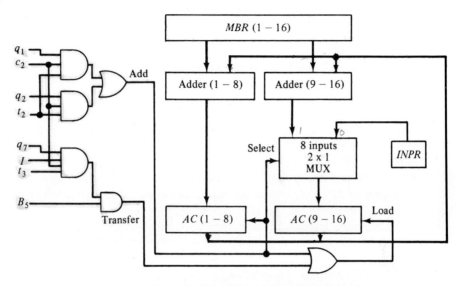

Fig. 5-11 Block diagram of accumulator (See Fig. 5-10).

Figure 5-10 shows the gates that generate six of the control functions for the *AC*. They are derived directly from the control functions listed with the register transfer statements above. The outputs of *MBR* are needed for the AND micro-operation and for the control functions that generate the register-reference and input-output micro-operations. Note that the *E* variable is applied to the serial inputs of the *AC* register during the shift micro-operations.

Figure 5-11 shows the circuit that implements the *add* and *transfer* micro-operations. The *AC* and parallel-adder are divided into two parts with eight bits in each. An 8-input, 2 by 1 multiplexer is inserted at the inputs of the eight low-order bits of the *AC*. The multiplexer chooses the eight outputs of *INPR* when its single select line is 0, and the outputs of the parallel-adder when the select line is 1. An *add* micro-operation loads all 16 bits from the parallel-adder.

Note that the outputs of *MBR* for the AND micro-operation (shown in Fig. 5-10) do not have to go through the multiplexer if the AND micro-operation is implemented as in Fig. 4-14 (Sec. 4-4). This implementation requires that the complements of *MBR* be ANDed with the AND control function and then applied to the *K* inputs of each *JK* flip-flop in the *AC* register. Figure 4-14 also shows the internal implementation of the *clear* and *complement* micro-operations. The *shift* micro-operations dictate that the *AC* be a bidirectional shift-register. The *increment* micro-operation specifies that the *AC* acts also as a counter.

Other Registers

The other registers in the computer can be designed in a similar manner. The register transfer statements for a particular register are first retrieved from Table 5-6 and listed separately. The list of control functions so obtained specifies the logic gates that control the register. The list of micro-operations specifies the types of digitial function that must be incorporated within the register.

There are eight registers and eight single flip-flops in the basic computer. The registers are $AC, PC, MAR, MBR, OPR, SC, INPR$, and $OUTR$. The flip-flops are F, R, E, I, S, IEN, FGI, and FGO. The list of register transfer statements from Table 5-6 that change the contents of PC include the three micro-operations: $PC \leftarrow PC + 1$, $PC \leftarrow 0$, and $PC \leftarrow MBR(AD)$. This implies that the PC must be a counter with clear and parallel load capabilities. Such a counter is shown in Fig. 2-14. The micro-operations that change the contents of MAR are: $MAR \leftarrow PC$ and $MAR \leftarrow MBR(AD)$. This implies the need for twelve 2×1 multiplexers to select the data between PC and $MBR(AD)$. The 12 output lines from the multiplexers are applied to the inputs of MAR. MAR can be implemented with a register having a parallel load capability similar to the one shown in Fig. 2-7.

The other registers in the computer require a load, or both load and increment control inputs. It is possible to choose an integrated circuit digital function that will implement all the registers in the computer except the AC. One possibility is IC type 74163, which consists of a 4-bit register with parallel load and has an increment and synchronous clear capabilities. The 12-bit registers, PC and MAR, will need three such ICs. The 16-bit MBR will need four ICs. The 8-bit registers, $INPR$ and $OUTR$, will require two such ICs and OPR together with I can use one IC. The 2-bit counter SC can be constructed with JK flip-flops as in Fig. 1-31. All eight single flip-flops can be constructed with JK- or D-type flip-flops.

5-7 CONCLUDING REMARKS

The basic computer whose internal organization is described in this chapter is a modified version of the PDP-8 computer. Although the basic computer is simple, it is far from useless. Its scope is quite limited when compared to commerical computer systems, yet it encompasses enough functional capabilities to demonstrate the power of a stored program, general purpose digital computer. It is suitable for construction in the laboratory with ICs, and the finished product can be a useful system capable of processing any type of binary data.

This chapter demonstrates that a register transfer language is a convenient tool when dealing with the architecture of computers. Specifically it can be used for the following tasks.

1. Defining computer instructions precisely by macro-operation statements.
2. Defining the internal organization of a computer by a sequence of micro-operations and control functions.
3. Designing a computer from a specified list of register transfer relations.

Each sequence of statements listed in this chapter is preceeded and followed by an explanation in words. The explanatio ns are not necessary once a statement is written down because the statement itself tells the whole story. The explanations are included for those readers who are not thoroughly familiar with the register transfer symbology. In an industrial situation, the specifications for the basic computer could be condensed to a few pages. All that would be needed is to specify the registers, tabulate the instructions and their format, define the control network, and list the control functions and micro-operations as they appear in Table 5-6.

The architecture of a computer is influenced by its intended use, i.e., by the type of programs that are written for it. Knowing how the computer is used may help to understand its internal organization. For this reason, Chap. 6 is devoted to the study of the programming aspects of digital computers.

The computer introduced in this chapter provides the basic concepts from which one can proced to study more advanced and complex computer systems. These advanced concepts are introduced in the chapters that follow.

Chapter 7 presents a more realistic organization of a processor unit in modern digital computers. The instruction formats for the basic computer are too simple and are oriented towards a processor unit with one accumulator register. Commercial computers have multiple processor registers and use more complicated instruction word formats.

The control unit of a computer is more efficiently implemented by means of a control memory and a microprogram. This type of control organization is presented in Chap. 8.

The only arithmetic instruction in the basic computer is the addition of two binary numbers. In Chap. 9 we show the procedure for including other arithmetic operations such as subtraction, multiplication, and division. In Chap. 10 we show how to include arithmetic operations for floating-point and decimal data.

The input, output, and interrupt in the basic computer are very crude compared to what is available in commercial computers. Chapter 11 discusses a more realistic input-output organization and interrupt facility.

Finally, the memory unit in most computers communicates not only with the processor but also with other external devices. Large computer systems have a memory hierachy that communicates with many processor units. Chapter 12 discusses the memory organization in computer systems.

REFERENCES

1. MANO, M. M., *Digital Logic and Computer Design*. Englewood Cliffs, N.J.: Prentice-Hall, Inc., 1979.

2. *Small Computer Handbook*. Maynard, Mass.: Digital Equipment Corp., 1973.

3. BOOTH, T. L., *Digital Networks and Computer Systems*, 2nd ed. New York: John Wiley & Sons, Inc., 1978.

4. HILL, F. J., AND G. R. PETERSON, *Digital Systems: Hardware Organization and Design*, 2nd ed. New York: John Wiley & Sons, Inc., 1978.

5. FOSTER C. C., *Computer Architecture*, 2nd ed. New York: Van Nostrand Reinhold Co., 1977.

6. BELL, C. G., J. GRASON, AND A. NEWELL, *Designing Computers and Digital Systems.* Maynard, Mass.: Digital Press, 1972.

7. DIETMEYER, D., *Logic Design of Digital Systems*, 2nd ed. Boston: Allyn and Bacon, 1978.

8. WINKEL, D., AND F. PROSSER, *The Art of Digital Design.* Englewood Cliffs, N.J., Prentice-Hall, Inc., 1980.

PROBLEMS

5-1. A memory unit has a capacity of 65,536 words of 25 bits each. It is used in conjunction with a general-purpose computer. The instruction code is divided into four parts: an indirect mode bit, operation code, two bits that specify a processor register, and an address part.
   (a) What is the maximum number of operations that can be incorporated in the computer if an instruction is stored in one memory word?
   (b) Draw the instruction word format indicating the number of bits and the function of each part.
   (c) How many processor registers are there in the computer and how many bits in each?
   (d) How many bits are there in *MBR*, *MAR*, and *PC*?

5-2. Suppose that the word in address 14 of Fig. 5-2(c) is an instruction and the word at memory address 36 contains the binary equivalent of 9. What is the operand?

5-3. What is the difference between an immediate, a direct, and an indirect address instruction? How many references to memory are needed for each type of instruction to bring an operand into a processor register?

5-4. Show that the logic operations AND, complement, and clear are sufficient to implement the logic operations listed in Table 4-5.

5-5. Show that the instruction CIR (circulate right *E* and *AC*) together with other instructions can be used to implement (a) a logic shift-right of the *AC*, (b) an arithmetic shift-right of the content of the *AC* when negative numbers are in signed-2's complement representation (the sign bit is in bit 1 of *AC* and the binary number may be positive or negative).

5-6. What are the two instructions needed in the basic computer to set the *E* register to 1?

5-7. A digital computer has a memory unit with a capacity of 8192 words, 36 bits per word. The instruction code format consists of 5 bits for the operation part and 13 bits for the address part (no indirect mode bit). Two instructions are packed in one memory word and a 36 bit instruction register *IR* is available in the control unit. Formulate the fetch and execute cycles for the computer.

5-8. A computer is available *without* a program counter (*PC*). Instead, all instructions contain three parts: an operation code, an address of an operand, and the address of the next instruction. The operation code consists of 6 bits and the computer has a memory unit of 8192 words.
   (a) How many bits must be in a memory word if an instruction is stored in one word? Show the instruction word format.

(b) What other register is needed in the control unit besides an operation register?

(c) List the micro-operations for the instruction fetch cycle of this computer. Use any register specified in part (b).

5-9.   List the eight registers and eight single flip-flops in the basic computer. Give their abbreviated name and full name. State the number of bits in each register. State, in one sentence for each, the function of each register and flip-flop.

5-10.   An instruction in address $(021)_{16}$ in the basic computer has a mode bit $I = 0$, an operation code of the AND instruction, and an address part equal to $(083)_{16}$. The memory word at address $(083)_{16}$ contains the operand $(B8F2)_{16}$ and the content of the AC is $(A937)_{16}$. Go over the fetch and execute cycles and determine the content of the following registers at the end of the execute cycle: PC, MAR, MBR, AC, and OPR. Repeat the problem six more times starting with the operation code of another memory reference instruction.

5-11.   The content of the AC in the basic computer is $(A937)_{16}$ and the content of E is 1. Determine the content of the AC, E, PC, and MBR after the execution of the CLA instruction. Repeat eleven more times starting from each one of the register-reference instruction. The initial value of PC is $(021)_{16}$.

✕ 5-12.   A computer similar to the basic computer has six timing signals t_0–t_5 and only one flip-flop F for cycle control. When $F = 0$, control performs the fetch and indirect cycle (if necessary). When $F = 1$, it executes the instruction. List the control functions and micro-operations for the computer when $F = 0$.

5-13.   Some of the instructions for the computer specified in Prob. 5-12 are listed below. List the control functions and micro-operations that execute these instructions. Use any convenient set of micro-operations that are known to be implemented by hardware.

	Operation Code	Symbolic Function	Description
(a)	000	$AC \leftarrow AC \oplus M$	Exclusive OR to AC.
(b)	001	If $(AC > 0)$ then $(PC \leftarrow m)$	Branch if AC positive and non-zero.
(c)	010	$M \leftarrow M + AC$	Add AC to memory. AC doesn't change.
(d)	011	$AC \leftarrow AC - M$	Subtract memory operand from AC.
(e)	100	$M \leftarrow AC, AC \leftarrow M$	Swap AC and memory word.
(f)	101	If $(M = AC)$ then $(PC \leftarrow PC + 1)$	Skip next instruction if AC is equal to M. AC doesn't change.

✕ 5-14.   It is possible to reduce the time it takes the control to process a register-reference instruction in the basic computer. Show that if the register-reference instructions are executed with timing variable t_3 during the fetch cycle, the control will process them in half the time it now takes. Show the register transfer relations for the fetch cycle that will take care of this proposed change.

5-15.   It is possible to combine two register-reference instruction codes to produce a new code for a different instruction. For example:
(a) A "2's complement AC" instruction can use the code 7220.
(b) A "set E to 1" instruction can use the code 7500.
(c) A "set AC to all 1's" instruction can use the code 7A00.
What changes must be made in the control functions for realizing these additional capabilities?

5-16.   Draw a diagram similar to Fig. 5-7 to demonstrate the interrupt cycle. What is the difference between the BSA instruction and the interrupt cycle? Explain why the BSA instruction cannot fulfill the function of the interrupt cycle.

5-17.   The control of the basic computer (Fig. 5-5) is to be modified as follows. Remove F and R and their associated decoder. Change SC and its decoder to a 4-bit counter and a 4×16 decoder with outputs t_0 through t_{15}. SC is to be cleared to 0 for a return to the fetch cycle.
(a) List those control functions and micro-operations for the modified computer that fetch and execute the BSA instruction. Minimize the number of clock cycles.
(b) Include in the list of part (a) the register transfer statements for handling a possible interrupt request.

✗ 5-18.   (a) Obtain the list of register transfer statements from Table 5-6 that change the contents of MAR.
(b) Combine the control functions for each common micro-operation.
(c) Show the hardware implementation associated with MAR using four AND gates, two OR gates, 12 multiplexers, and a register with parallel load.

✓ 5-19.   The list of register transfer statements from Table 5-6 that change the contents of PC can be reduced to three micro-operations and three control functions:

$$X_1: \quad PC \leftarrow PC + 1$$
$$X_2: \quad PC \leftarrow MBR(AD)$$
$$X_3: \quad PC \leftarrow 0$$

(a) Determine the control functions X_1, X_2, and X_3. You may want to define certain variables by a single letter to facilitate the writing of the three Boolean functions.
(b) Show the hardware implementation associated with PC using a register with parallel load, increment, and clear capabilities.

✗ 5-20.   (a) Obtain the list of register transfer statements from Table 5-6 that change the contents of MBR.
(b) Obtain the simplified control functions for each of the micro-operations.
(c) Draw the hardware implementation of MBR showing (1) the gates that generate the simplified control functions, (2) the type of control inputs in the register and their connection to the control functions, and (3) all multiplexer input and output connections as well as the connections between the control functions and multiplexer selection lines. For part (3) you have a choice of using tri-state buffers instead of multiplexers.

5-21.   Obtain the combine control function that sets flip-flop F to 1, and the combine control function that clears F to 0. [You may want to define $X = IEN \land (FGI \lor FGO)$ for convenience.] Using a JK-type flip-flop and gates, draw the hardware implementation of F.

5-22.   Repeat Prob. 5-21 for flip-flop R.

5-23.   Extract the six control functions from Table 5-6 that affect flip-flop E together with the corresponding micro-operations that show how E is changed. Note that E is also affected during the addition, increment, and circulate instructions. Using a JK-type flip-flop for E, draw the logic diagram showing all the control gates associated with the J and K terminals of the flip-flop.

Computer Software

6

6-1 INTRODUCTION

A total computer system includes both *hardware* and *software*. Hardware consists of the physical components and all associated equipment. Software refers to the programs that are written for the computer. It is possible to be familiar with various aspects of computer software without being concerned with details of how the computer hardware operates. It is also possible to design parts of the hardware without a knowledge of its software capabilities. However, those concerned with computer architecture should have a knowledge of both hardware and software because the two branches influence each other.

Writing a program for a computer consists of specifying, directly or indirectly, a sequence of machine instructions. Machine instructions inside the computer form a binary pattern which is difficult, if not impossible, for people to work with and understand. It is preferable to write programs with the more familiar symbols of the alphanumeric character set. As a consequence, there is a need for translating user-oriented symbolic programs into binary programs recognized by the hardware.

A program written by a user may be either dependent or independent of the physical computer that runs his program. For example, a program written in standard Fortran is machine independent because most computers provide a translator program that converts the standard Fortran program to the binary code of the computer available in the particular installation. But the translator program itself is machine dependent because it must translate the Fortran program to the binary code recognized by the hardware of the particular computer used.

This chapter introduces some elementary programming concepts and shows their relation to the hardware representation of instructions. The first part presents the basic operation and structure of a program that translates a user's symbolic program into an equivalent binary program. The discussion emphasizes the important concepts of the translator rather than the details of actually producing the program itself. The usefulness of various machine instructions is then demonstrated by means of several basic programming examples. The last section presents a brief discussion of the software components commonly found in computer systems.

The instruction set of the basic computer, whose hardware organization was explored in Chap. 5, will be used in this chapter to illustrate many of the techniques commonly used to program a computer. In this way, it will be possible to explore the relationship between a program and the hardware operations that execute the instructions.

The 25 instructions of the basic computer are repeated in Table 6-1 to provide an easy reference for the programming examples that follow. Each instruction is assigned a three-letter symbol to facilitate writing symbolic programs. The first seven instructions are memory-reference instructions and the other eighteen are register-reference and input-output instructions. A memory-reference instruction has three parts: a mode bit, an operation code of three bits, and a 12-bit address. The first hexadecimal digit of a memory-reference instruction includes the mode bit and the operation code. The other three digits specify the address. In an indirect address

TABLE 6-1   Computer Instructions

Symbol	Hexadecimal code	Description
AND	0 or 8	AND M to AC
ADD	1 or 9	Add M to AC, carry to E
LDA	2 or A	Load AC from M
STA	3 or B	Store AC in M
BUN	4 or C	Branch unconditionally to m
BSA	5 or D	Save return address in m and branch to $m + 1$
ISZ	6 or E	Increment M and skip if zero
CLA	7800	Clear AC
CLE	7400	Clear E
CMA	7200	Complement AC
CME	7100	Complement E
CIR	7080	Circulate right E and AC
CIL	7040	Circulate left E and AC
INC	7020	Increment AC, carry to E
SPA	7010	Skip if AC is positive
SNA	7008	Skip if AC is negative
SZA	7004	Skip if AC is zero
SZE	7002	Skip if E is zero
HLT	7001	Halt computer
INP	F800	Input information and clear flag
OUT	F400	Output information and clear flag
SKI	F200	Skip if input flag is on
SKO	F100	Skip if output flag is on
ION	F080	Turn interrupt on
IOF	F040	Turn interrupt off

instruction the mode bit is 1 and the first hexadecimal digit ranges in value from 8 to *E*. In a direct mode, the range is from 0 to 6. The other eighteen instructions have a 16-bit operation code. The code for each instruction is listed as a 4-digit hexadecimal number. The first digit of a register-reference instruction is always 7. The first digit of an input-output instruction is always *F*. The symbol *m* used in the description column denotes the effective address. The letter *M* refers to the memory word (operand) found at the effective address.

6-2 PROGRAMMING LANGUAGES

A program is a list of instructions or statements for directing the computer to perform a required data processing task. There are various types of programming languages that one may *write* for a computer but the computer can *execute* programs only when they are represented internally in binary form. Programs written in any other language must be translated to the binary representation of instructions before they can be executed by the computer. Programs written for a computer may be in one of the following categories:

1. *Binary code*. This is a sequence of instructions and operands in binary that list the exact representation of instructions as they appear in computer memory.

2. *Octal or hexadecimal code*. This is an equivalent translation of the binary code to octal or hexadecimal representation.

3. *Symbolic code*. The user employs symbols (letters, numerals, or special characters) for the operation part, the address part, and other parts of the instruction code. Each symbolic instruction can be translated into one binary coded instruction. This translation is done by a special program called an *assembler*. Because an assembler translates the symbols, this type of symbolic program is referred to as an *assembly-language* program.

4. *High-level programming languages*. These are special languages developed to reflect the procedures used in the solution of a problem rather than be concerned with the computer hardware behavior. An example of a high-level programming language is *Fortran*. It employs problem-oriented symbols and formats. The program is written in a sequence of statements in a form that people prefer to think in when solving a problem. However, each statement must be translated into a sequence of binary instructions before the program can be executed in a computer. The program that translates a high-level language program to binary is called a *compiler*.

Strictly speaking, a *machine-language* program is a binary program of category (1). Because of the simple equivalency between binary and octal or hexadecimal representation, it is customary to refer to category (2) as machine language. Because of the one-to-one relationship between a symbolic instruction and its binary equivalent, an assembly language is considered to be a machine-level language.

In computer science, the term *programming languages* refers to the study of the structure of various high-level programming languages. This study is carried out independent of any particular computing device and its hardware. Since we are interested in the relation between software and hardware, the term as used here has a different connotation since it includes machine-level languages.

We now use the basic computer to illustrate the relation between the various programming languages. Consider the binary program listed in Table 6-2. The first

TABLE 6-2   Binary Program to Add Two Numbers

Location	Instruction Code
0	0010 0000 0000 0100
1	0001 0000 0000 0101
10	0011 0000 0000 0110
11	0111 0000 0000 0001
100	0000 0000 0101 0011
101	1111 1111 1110 1001
110	0000 0000 0000 0000

column gives the memory location (in binary) of each instruction or operand. The second column lists the binary content of these memory locations. (The *location* is the address of the memory word where the instruction is stored. It is important to differentiate it from the address part of the instruction itself.) The program can be stored in the indicated portion of memory, and then executed by the computer starting from address 0. The hardware of the computer will execute these instructions and perform the intended task. However, a person looking at this program will have a difficult time understanding what is to be achieved when this program is executed. Nevertheless, the computer hardware recognizes *only* this type of instruction code.

Writing 16 bits for each instruction is tedious because there are too many digits. We can reduce the number of digits per instruction if we write the octal equivalent of the binary code. This will require six digits per instruction. On the other hand, we can reduce each instruction to four digits if we write the equivalent hexadecimal code as shown in Table 6-3. The hexadecimal representation is convenient to use; however, one must realize that each hexadecimal digit must be converted to its equivalent 4-bit number when the program is entered into the computer. The advantage of writing binary programs in equivalent octal or hexadecimal form should be evident from this example.

The program in Table 6-4 uses the symbolic names of instructions (listed in Table 6-1) instead of their binary or hexadecimal equivalent. The address parts of memory-reference instructions, as well as operands, remain in their hexadecimal

TABLE 6-3 Hexadecimal Program to Add Two Numbers

Location	Instruction
000	2004
001	1005
002	3006
003	7001
004	0053
005	FFE9
006	0000

TABLE 6-4 Program with Symbolic Operation Codes

Location	Instruction	Comments
000	LDA 004	Load first operand into AC
001	ADD 005	Add second operand to AC
002	STA 006	Store sum in location 006
003	HLT	Halt computer
004	0053	First operand
005	FFE9	Second operand (negative)
006	0000	Store sum here

value. Note that location 005 has a negative operand because the sign bit in the left-most position is 1. The inclusion of a column for comments provides some means for explaining the function of each instruction. Symbolic programs are easier to handle and as a consequence, it is preferable to write programs with symbols. These symbols can be converted to their binary code equivalent to produce the binary program.

We can go one step further and replace each hexadecimal address by a symbolic address and each hexadecimal operand by a decimal operand. This is convenient because one usually does not know exactly the numeric memory location of operands while writing a program. If the operands are placed in memory following the instructions, and if the length of the program is not known in advance, the numerical location of operands is not known until the end of the program is reached. In addition, decimal numbers are more familiar than their hexadecimal equivalents.

The program in Table 6-5 is the assembly-language program for adding two numbers. The symbol ORG followed by a number is not a machine instruction. Its purpose is to specify an *origin*, that is, the memory location of the next instruction below it. The next three lines have symbolic addresses. Their value is specified by their being present as a label in the first column. Decimal operands are specified following the symbol DEC. The numbers may be positive or negative, but if negative, they must be converted to binary in the signed-2's complement representation. The last line has the symbol END indicating the end of the program. The symbols ORG,

TABLE 6-5　Assembly-Language Program to Add Two Numbers

	ORG 0	/Origin of program is location 0
	LDA A	/Load operand from location *A*
	ADD B	/Add operand from location *B*
	STA C	/Store sum in location *C*
	HLT	/Halt computer
A,	DEC 83	/Decimal operand
B,	DEC −23	/Decimal operand
C,	DEC 0	/Sum stored in location *C*
	END	/End of symbolic program

DEC, and END are called *pseudo-instructions* and will be defined in the next section. Note that all comments are preceded by a slash.

The equivalent Fortran program for adding two integer numbers is listed in Table 6-6. The two values for *A* and *B* may be specified by an input statement or by a data statement. The arithmetic operation for the two numbers is specified by one simple statement. The translation of this Fortran program into a binary program consists of assigning three memory locations, one each for the augend, addend, and sum, and then deriving the sequence of binary instructions that form the sum. Thus, a compiler program translates the symbols of the Fortran program into the binary values listed in the program of Table 6-2.

TABLE 6-6　Fortran Program to Add Two Numbers

```
INTEGER A, B, C
DATA A,83 / B,−23
C = A + B
END
```

6-3 ASSEMBLY LANGUAGE

A programming language is defined by a set of rules. The user must conform with all format rules of the language if he wants his program to be translated correctly. Almost every commercial computer has its own particular assembly language. The rules for writing assembly-language programs are documented and published in manuals which are usually available from the computer manufacturer.

The basic unit of an assembly-language program is a line of code (when the input is from a teletypewriter, although it could just as well be a punched card). The specific language is defined by a set of rules that specify the symbols that can be used and how they may be combined to form a line of code. We will now formulate the rules of an assembly language for writing symbolic programs for the basic computer.

Rules of the Language

Each line of an assembly-language program is arranged in three columns called fields. The fields specify the following information.

1. The *label* field may be empty or it may specify a symbolic address.

2. The *instruction* field specifies a machine instruction or a pseudo-instruction.

3. The *comment* field may be empty or it may include a comment.

A symbolic address consists of one, two, or three, but not more than three alphanumeric characters. The first character must be a letter; the next two may be letters or numerals. The symbol can be chosen arbitrarily by the programmer. A symbolic address in the label field is terminated by a comma so it will be recognized as a label by the assembler.

The instruction field in an assembly-language program may specify one of the following items:

1. A memory-reference instruction (MRI).

2. A register-reference or input-output instruction (non-MRI).

3. A pseudo-instruction with or without an operand.

A memory-reference instruction occupies two or three symbols separated by spaces. The first must be a three-letter symbol defining an MRI operation code from Table 6-1. The second is a symbolic address. The third symbol, which may or may not be present, is the letter I. If I is missing, the line denotes a direct address instruction. The presence of the symbol I denotes an indirect address instruction.

A non-MRI is defined as an instruction that does not have an address part. A non-MRI is recognized in the instruction field of a program by any one of the three-letter symbols listed in Table 6-1 for the register-reference and input-output instructions.

The following is an illustration of the symbols that may be placed in the instruction field of a program.

CLA	non-MRI
ADD OPR	direct address MRI
ADD PTR I	indirect address MRI

The first three-letter symbol in each line must be one of the instruction symbols of the computer and must be listed in Table 6-1. A memory-reference instruction, such as ADD, must be followed by a symbolic address. The letter I may or may not be present.

A symbolic address in the instruction field specifies the memory location of an operand. This location must be defined somewhere in the program by appearing again as a label in the first column. In order to be able to translate an assembly-language program to a binary program, it is absolutely necessary that each symbolic address that is mentioned in the instruction field *must* occur again in the label field.

A pseudo-instruction is not a machine instruction but rather an instruction to the assembler giving information about some phase of the translation. Four pseudo-instructions that are recognized by the assembler are listed in Table 6-7. (Other

TABLE 6-7   Definition of Pseudo-Instructions

Symbol	Information for the Assembler
ORG N	Hexadecimal number N is the memory location for the instruction or operand listed in the following line.
END	Denotes the end of symbolic program.
DEC N	Signed decimal number N to be converted to binary.
HEX N	Hexadecimal number N to be converted to binary.

assembly-language programs recognize many more pseudo-instructions.) The ORG (origin) pseudo-instruction informs the assembler that the instruction or operand in the following line is to be placed in a memory location specified by the number next to ORG. It is possible to use ORG more than once in a program to specify more than one segment of memory. The END symbol is placed at the end of the program to inform the assembler that the program is terminated. The other two pseudo-instructions specify the radix of the operand and tell the assembler how to convert the listed number to a binary number.

The third field in a program is reserved for comments. A line of code may or may not have a comment, but if it has, it must be preceeded by a slash for the assembler to recognize the beginning of a comment field. Comments are useful for explaining the program and are helpful in understanding the step by step procedure taken by the program. Comments are inserted for explanation purposes only and are neglected during the binary translation process.

An Example

The program of Table 6-8 is an example of an assembly-language program. The first line has the pseudo-instruction ORG to define the origin of the program at memory location $(100)_{16}$. The next six lines define machine instructions and the last four have pseudo-instructions. Three symbolic addresses have been used and each is listed in column one as a label and in column two as an address of a memory-reference instruction. Three of the pseudo-instructions specify operands and the last one signifies the END of the program.

When the program is translated into binary code and executed by the computer it will perform a subtraction between two numbers. The subtraction is performed by adding the minuend to the 2's complement of the subtrahend. The subtrahend is a negative number. It is converted into a binary number in signed-2's complement rep-

TABLE 6-8 Assembly-Language Program to Subtract Two Numbers

	ORG 100	/Origin of program is location 100.
	LDA SUB	/Load subtrahend to *AC*.
	CMA	/Complement *AC*.
	INC	/Increment *AC*.
	ADD MIN	/Add minuend to *AC*.
	STA DIF	/Store difference.
	HLT	/Halt computer.
MIN,	DEC 83	/Minuend.
SUB,	DEC −23	/Subtrahend.
DIF,	HEX 0	/Difference stored here.
	END	/End of symbolic program.

resentation because we dictate that all negative numbers be in their 2's complement form. When the 2's complement of the subtrahend is taken (by complementing and incrementing the *AC*), −23 converts to +23 and the difference is 83 + (2's complement of −23) = 83 + 23 = 106.

Translation to Binary

The translation of the symbolic program into binary is done by a special program we have called an *assembler*. The tasks performed by the assembler will be better understood if we first perform the translation on paper. The translation of the symbolic program of Table 6-8 into an equivalent binary code may be done by scanning the program and replacing the symbols by their machine code binary equivalent. Starting from the first line, we encounter an ORG pseudo-instruction. This tells us to start the binary program from hexadecimal location 100. The second line has two symbols. It must be a memory-reference instruction to be placed in location 100. Since the letter I is missing, the first bit of the instruction code must be 0. The symbolic name of the operation is LDA. Checking Table 6-1 we find that the first hexadecimal digit of the instruction should be 2. The binary value of the address part must be obtained from the address symbol SUB. We scan the label column and find this symbol in line 9. To determine its hexadecimal value we note that line 2 contains an instruction for location 100 and every other line specifies a machine instruction or an operand for sequential memory locations. Counting lines, we find that label SUB in line 9 corresponds to memory location 107. So the hexadecimal address of the instruction LDA must be 107. When the two parts of the instruction are assembled, we obtain the hexadecimal code 2107. The other lines representing machine instructions are translated in a similar fashion and their hexadecimal code is listed in Table 6-9.

Two lines in the symbolic program specify decimal operands with the pseudo-instruction DEC. A third specifies a zero by means of a HEX pseudo-instruction (DEC could be used as well). Decimal 83 is converted to binary and placed in location 106 in its hexadecimal equivalent. Decimal −23 is a negative number and must

TABLE 6-9   Listing of Translated Program of Table 6-8

Hexadecimal Code		Symbolic Program	
Location	Content		
			ORG 100
100	2107		LDA SUB
101	7200		CMA
102	7020		INC
103	1106		ADD MIN
104	3108		STA DIF
105	7001		HLT
106	0053	MIN,	DEC 83
107	FFE9	SUB,	DEC −23
108	0000	DIF,	HEX 0
			END

be converted into binary in signed-2's complement form. The hexadecimal equivalent of the binary number is placed in location 107. The END symbol signals the end of the symbolic program telling us that there are no more lines to translate.

The translation process can be simplified if we scan the entire symbolic program twice. No translation is done during the first scan. We merely assign a memory location to each machine instruction and operand. The location assignment will define the address value of labels and facilitate the translation process during the second scan. Thus in Table 6-9, we assign location 100 to the first instruction after ORG. We then assign sequential locations for each line of code that has a machine instruction or operand up to the end of the program. (ORG and END are not assigned a numerical location because they do not represent an instruction or an operand.) When the first scan is completed, we associate with each label its location number and form a table that defines the hexadecimal value of each symbolic address. For this program, the address symbol table is as follows:

Address Symbol	Hexadecimal Address
MIN	106
SUB	107
DIF	108

During the second scan of the symbolic program we refer to the address-symbol table to determine the address value of a memory-reference instruction. For example, the line of code LDA SUB is translated during the second scan by getting the hexadecimal value of LDA from Table 6-1 and the hexadecimal value of SUB from the address-symbol table listed above. We then assemble the two parts into a 4-digit hexadecimal instruction. The hexadecimal code can be easily converted to binary if we wish to know exactly how this program resides in computer memory.

When the translation from symbols to binary is done by an assembler program, the first scan is called the *first pass*, and the second is called the *second pass*.

6-4 THE ASSEMBLER

An assembler is a program that accepts a symbolic-language program and produces its binary machine language equivalent. The input symbolic program is called the *source program* and the resulting binary program is called the *object program*. The assembler is a program that operates on character strings and produces an equivalent binary interpretation.

Representation of Symbolic Program in Memory

Prior to starting the assembly process, the symbolic program must be stored in memory. The user types the symbolic program on a Teletype (or prepares it in punched cards). A loader program is used to input the characters of the symbolic program into memory. Since the program consists of symbols, its representation in memory must use an alphanumeric character code. In the basic computer, each character is represented by an 8-bit code. The high-order bit is always 0 and the other seven bits are as specified by ASCII. The hexadecimal equivalent of the character set is listed in Table 6-10. Each character is assigned two hexadecimal digits which can be easily converted to their equivalent 8-bit code. The last entry in the table does not print a

TABLE 6-10 Hexadecimal Character Code

Character	Code	Character	Code	Character	Code	
A	41	Q	51	6	36	
B	42	R	52	7	37	
C	43	S	53	8	38	
D	44	T	54	9	39	
E	45	U	55	space	20	
F	46	V	56	(	28	
G	47	W	57	)	29	
H	48	X	58	*	2A	
I	49	Y	59	+	2B	
J	4A	Z	5A	,	2C	
K	4B	0	30	—	2D	
L	4C	1	31	.	2E	
M	4D	2	32	/	2F	
N	4E	3	33	=	3D	
O	4F	4	34	CR	0D	(carriage
P	50	5	35			return)

character but is associated with the physical movement of the carriage in the Teletype. The code for CR is produced when the "carriage-return" key is depressed. This causes the carriage to return to its initial position to start typing a new line. The assembler recognizes a CR code as the end of a line of code.

A line of code is stored in consecutive memory locations with two characters in each location. Two characters can be stored in each word since a memory word has a capacity of 16 bits. A label symbol is terminated with a comma. Operation and address symbols are terminated with a space and the end of the line is recognized by the CR code. For example, the following line of code:

$$PL3, \qquad LDA\ SUB\ I$$

is stored in seven consecutive memory locations as shown in Table 6-11. The label PL3 occupies two words and is terminated by the code for comma (2C). The instruc-

TABLE 6-11   Computer Representation of the Line of Code: PL3, LDA SUB I

Memory Word	Symbol	Hexadecimal Code	Binary Representation
1	P L	50 4C	0101 0000 0100 1100
2	3 ,	33 2C	0011 0011 0010 1100
3	L D	4C 44	0100 1100 0100 0100
4	A	41 20	0100 0001 0010 0000
5	S U	53 55	0101 0011 0101 0101
6	B	42 20	0100 0010 0010 0000
7	I CR	49 0D	0100 1001 0000 1101

tion field in the line of code may have one or more symbols. Each symbol is terminated by the code for space (20) except for the last symbol which is terminated by the code of carriage-return (0D). If the line of code has a comment, the assembler recognizes it by the code for a slash (2F). The assembler neglects all characters in the comment field and keeps checking for a CR code. When this code is encountered, it replaces the space code after the last symbol in the line of code.

The input for the assembler program is the user's symbolic language program in ASCII. This input is scanned by the assembler twice to produce the equivalent binary program. The binary program constitutes the output generated by the assembler. We will now describe briefly the major tasks that must be performed by the assembler during the translation process.

First Pass

A two-pass assembler scans the entire symbolic program twice. During the first pass, it generates a table that correlates all user-defined address symbols with their binary equivalent value. The binary translation is done during the second pass.

In order to keep track of the location of instructions, the assembler uses one memory word called a *location counter* (abbreviated LC). The content of LC stores the value of the memory location assigned to the instruction or operand presently being processed. The ORG pseudo-instruction initializes the location counter to the value of the first location. Since instructions are stored in sequential locations, the content of LC is incremented by 1 after processing each line of code. To avoid ambiguity in case ORG is missing, the assembler sets the location counter to 0 initially.

The tasks performed by the assembler during the first pass are described in the flow chart of Fig. 6-1. LC is initially set to 0. A line of symbolic code is analyzed to determine if it has a label (by the presence of a comma). If the line of code has no label, the assembler checks the symbol in the instruction field. If it contains an ORG pseudo-instruction, the assembler sets LC to the number that follows ORG and goes back to process the next line. If the line has an END pseudo-instruction, the assembler terminates the first pass and goes to the second pass. (Note that a line with ORG or END should not have a label.) If the line of code contains a label, it is stored in the address-symbol table together with its binary equivalent number specified by the content of LC. Nothing is stored in the table if no label is encountered. LC is then incremented by 1 and a new line of code is processed.

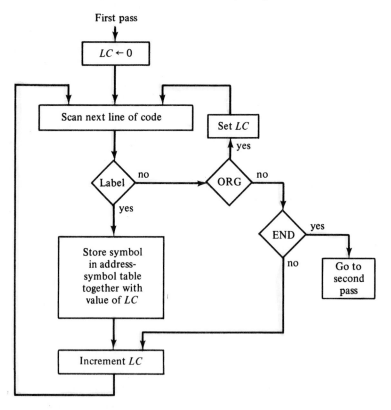

Fig. 6-1 Flow chart for first pass of assembler.

For the program of Table 6-8, the assembler generates the address symbol table listed in Table 6-12. Each label symbol is stored in two memory locations and is terminated by a comma. If the label contains less than three characters, the memory locations are filled with the code for space. The value found in LC while the line was processed is stored in the next sequential memory location. The program has three symbolic addresses: MIN, SUB, and DIF. These symbols represent 12-bit addresses equivalent to hexadecimal 106, 107, and 108, respectively. The address-symbol table occupies three words for each label symbol encountered and constitutes the output data that the assembler generates during the first pass.

TABLE 6-12   Address Symbol Table for Program in Table 6-8

Memory Word	Symbol or (LC)*	Hexadecimal Code	Binary Representation
1	M I	4D 49	0100 1101 0100 1001
2	N ,	4E 2C	0100 1110 0010 1100
3	(LC)	01 06	0000 0001 0000 0110
4	S U	53 55	0101 0011 0101 0101
5	B ,	42 2C	0100 0010 0010 1100
6	(LC)	01 07	0000 0001 0000 0111
7	D I	44 49	0100 0100 0100 1001
8	F ,	46 2C	0100 0110 0010 1100
9	(LC)	01 08	0000 0001 0000 1000

*(LC) designates content of location counter.

Second Pass

Machine instructions are translated during the second pass by means of table-lookup procedures. A table-lookup procedure is a search of table entries to determine whether a specific item matches one of the items stored in the table. The assembler uses four tables. Any symbol that is encountered in the program must be available as an entry in one of these tables; otherwise, the symbol cannot be interpreted. We assign the following names to the four tables:

1. Pseudo-instruction table.

2. MRI table.

3. Non-MRI table.

4. Address symbol table.

The entries of the pseudo-instruction table are the four symbols ORG, END, DEC, and HEX. Each entry refers the assembler to a subroutine that processes the pseudo-instruction when encountered in the program. The MRI table contains the seven symbols of the memory-reference instructions and their 3-bit operation code equivalent. The non-MRI table contains the symbols for the 18 register-reference and input-output instructions and their 16-bit binary code equivalent. The address-symbol table is generated during the first pass of the assembly process. The assembler searches these tables to find the symbol that it is currently processing in order to determine its binary value.

The tasks performed by the assembler during the second pass are described in the flow chart of Fig. 6-2. LC is initially set to 0. Lines of code are then analyzed one at a time. Labels are neglected during the second pass so the assembler goes immediately to the instruction field and proceeds to check the first symbol encountered. It first checks the pseudo-instruction table. A match with ORG sends the assembler to a subroutine that sets LC to an initial value. A match with END terminates the translation process. An operand pseudo-instruction causes a conversion of the operand into binary. This operand is placed in the memory location specified by the content of LC. The location counter is then incremented by 1 and the assembler continues to analyze the next line of code.

If the symbol encountered is not a pseudo-instruction, the assembler refers to the MRI table. If the symbol is not found in this table, the assembler refers to the non-MRI table. A symbol found in the non-MRI table corresponds to a register reference or input-output instruction. The assembler stores the 16-bit instruction code into the memory word specified by LC. The location counter is incremented and a new line analyzed.

When a symbol is found in the MRI table, the assembler extracts its equivalent 3-bit code and inserts it in bits 2-4 of a word. A memory reference instruction is specified by two or three symbols. The second symbol is a symbolic address and the third, which may or may not be present, is the letter I. The symbolic address is converted to binary by searching the address symbol table. The first bit of the instruction is set to 0 or 1, depending on whether the letter I is absent or present. The three parts of the binary instruction code are assembled and then stored in the memory location specified by the content of LC. The location counter is incremented and the assembler continues to process the next line.

One important task of an assembler is to check for possible errors in the symbolic program. This is called *error diagnostics*. One such error may be an invalid machine-code symbol which is detected by its being absent in the MRI and non-MRI tables. The assembler cannot translate such a symbol because it does not know its binary equivalent value. In such a case, the assembler prints an error message to inform the programmer that his symbolic program has an error at a specific line of code. Another possible error may occur if the program has a symbolic address that did not appear also as a label. The assembler cannot translate the line of code properly because the binary equivalent of the symbol will not be found in the address-symbol table generated during the first pass. Other errors may occur and a practical assembler should detect all such errors and print an error message for each.

It should be emphasized that a practical assembler is much more complicated than the one explained here. Most computers give the programmer more flexibility in writing assembly-language programs. For example, the user may be allowed to

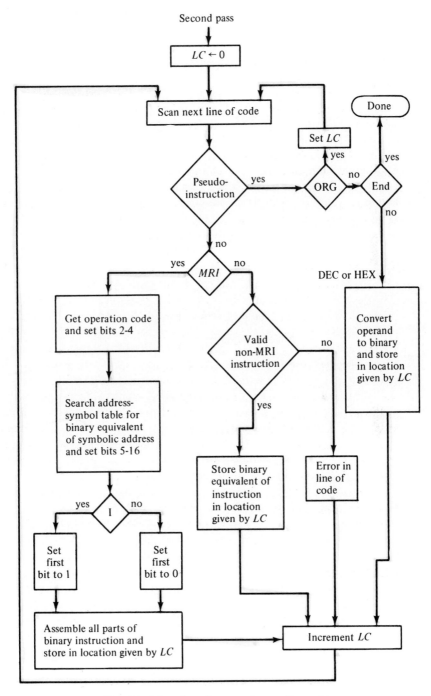

Fig. 6-2 Flow chart for second pass of assembler.

use either a number or a symbol to specify an address. Many assemblers allow the user to specify an address by an arithmetic expression. Many more pseudo-instructions may be specified to facilitate the programming task. As the assembly language becomes more sophisticated, the assembler becomes more complicated.

6-5 PROGRAM LOOPS

A program loop is a sequence of instructions that are executed many times, each time with a different set of data. Program loops are specified in Fortran by a DO statement. The following is an example of a Fortran program that forms the sum of 100 integer numbers.

$$
\begin{aligned}
&\text{DIMENSION} \quad \text{A(100)} \\
&\text{INTEGER} \quad \text{SUM, A} \\
&\text{SUM} \quad = \quad 0 \\
&\text{DO} \quad 3 \quad \text{J} = 1, \quad 100 \\
3 \quad &\text{SUM} = \text{SUM} + \text{A(J)}
\end{aligned}
$$

Statement number 3 is executed 100 times, each time with a different operand A(J) for $J = 1, 2, \ldots, 100$.

A system program that translates a program written in a high-level programming language such as the above to a machine-language program is called a *compiler*. A compiler is a more complicated program than an assembler and requires knowledge of systems programming to fully understand its operation. Nevertheless, we can demonstrate the basic functions of a compiler by going through the process of translating the program above to an assembly-language program. A compiler may use an assembly language as an intermediate step in the translation or may translate the program directly to binary.

The first statement in the Fortran program is a DIMENSION statement. This statement instructs the compiler to reserve 100 words of memory for 100 operands. The value of the operands is determined from an input statement (not listed in the program). The second statement informs the compiler that the numbers are integers. If they were of the *real* type, the compiler would have to reserve locations for floating-point numbers and generate instructions that perform the subsequent arithmetic with floating-point data. These two statements are nonexecutable and are similar to the pseudo-instructions in an assembly language. Suppose that the compiler reserves locations $(150)_{16}$ to $(1B3)_{16}$ for the 100 operands. These reserved memory words are listed in lines 19 to 118 in the translated program of Table 6-13. This is done by the ORG pseudo-instruction in line 18 which specifies the origin of the operands. The first and last operands are listed with a specific decimal number although

TABLE 6-13   Symbolic Program to Add 100 Numbers

Line			
1		ORG 100	/Origin of program is HEX 100.
2		LDA ADS	/Load first address of operands.
3		STA PTR	/Store in pointer.
4		LDA NBR	/Load minus 100.
5		STA CTR	/Store in counter.
6		CLA	/Clear accumulator.
7	LOP,	ADD PTR I	/Add an operand to *AC*.
8		ISZ PTR	/Increment pointer.
9		ISZ CTR	/Increment counter.
10		BUN LOP	/Repeat loop again.
11		STA SUM	/Store sum.
12		HLT	/Halt.
13	ADS,	HEX 150	/First address of operands.
14	PTR,	HEX 0	/This location reserved for a pointer.
15	NBR,	DEC −100	/Constant to initialized counter.
16	CTR,	HEX 0	/This location reserved for a counter.
17	SUM,	HEX 0	/Sum is stored here.
18		ORG 150	/Origin of operands is HEX 150.
19		DEC 75	/First operand.
.			
.			
.			
118		DEC 23	/Last operand.
119		END	/End of symbolic program.

these values are not known during compilation. The compiler just reserves the data space in memory and the values are inserted later when an input data statement is executed. The line numbers in the symbolic program are for reference only and are not part of the translated symbolic program.

The indexing of the DO statement is translated into the instructions in lines 2–5 and the constants in lines 13–16. The address of the first operand (150) is stored in location ADS in line 13. The number of times that Fortran statement number 3 must be executed is 100. So −100 is stored in location NBR. The compiler then generates the instructions in lines 2–5 to initialize the program loop. The address of the first operand is transferred to location PTR. This corresponds to setting A(J) to A(1). The number −100 is then transferred to location CTR. This location acts as a counter with its content incremented by one every time the program loop is executed. When the value of the counter reaches zero, the 100 operations will be completed and the program will exit from the loop.

Some compilers will translate the statement SUM = 0 into a machine instruction that initializes location SUM to zero. A reference to this location is then made every time Fortran statement number 3 is executed. A more intelligent compiler will realize that the sum can be formed in the accumulator and only the final result stored in location SUM. This compiler will produce an instruction in line 6 to clear the *AC*. It will also reserve a memory location symbolized by SUM (in line 17) for storing the value of this variable at the termination of the loop.

The program loop specified by the DO statement is translated to the sequence of instructions listed in lines 7–10. Line 7 specifies an indirect ADD instruction because it has the symbol I. The address of the current operand is stored in location PTR. When this location is addressed indirectly the computer takes the content of PTR to be the address of the operand. As a result, the operand in location 150 is added to the accumulator. Location PTR is then incremented with the ISZ instruction in line 8 so its value changes to the value of the address of the next sequential operand. Location CTR is incremented in line 9 and if it is not zero, the computer does not skip the next instruction. The next instruction is a branch (BUN) instruction to the beginning of the loop so the computer returns to repeat the loop once again. When location CTR reaches zero (after the loop is executed 100 times), the next instruction is skipped and the computer executes the instructions in lines 11 and 12. The sum formed in the accumulator is stored in SUM and the computer halts. The halt instruction is inserted here for clarity; actually, the program will branch to a location where it will continue to execute the rest of the program or branch to the beginning of another program. Note that ISZ in line 8 is used merely to add 1 to the address pointer PTR. Since the address is a positive number, a skip will never occur.

The program of Table 6-13 introduces the idea of a pointer and a counter which can be used, together with the indirect address operation, to form a program loop. The pointer points to the address of the current operand and the counter counts the number of times that the program loop is executed. In this example we use two memory locations for these functions. In computers with more than one processor register, it is possible to use one processor register as a pointer, another as a counter and a third as an accumulator. When processor registers are used as pointers and counters they are called *index registers*. Index registers are discussed in Sec. 7-5.

6-6 PROGRAMMING ARITHMETIC AND LOGIC OPERATIONS

The number of instructions available in a computer may be a few hundred in a large system or a few dozen in a small one. Some computers perform a given operation with one machine instruction; others may require a large number of machine instructions to perform the same operation. As an illustration, consider the four basic arithmetic operations. Some computers have machine instructions to add, subtract, multiply, and divide. Others, such as the basic computer, have only one arithmetic instruction such as ADD. Operations not included in the set of machine instructions must be implemented by a program. We have shown in Table 6-8 a program for subtracting two numbers. Programs for the other arithmetic operations can be developed in a similar fashion.

Operations that are implemented in a computer with one machine instruction are said to be implemented by hardware. Operations implemented by a set of instructions that constitute a program are said to be implemented by software. Some computers provide an extensive set of hardware instructions designed to speed up common tasks. Others contain a smaller set of hardware instructions and depend more heavily on the software implementation of many operations. Hardware implementation is more costly because of the additional circuits needed to implement the operation. Software implementation results in long programs both in number of instructions and in execution time.

This section demonstrates the software implementation of a few arithmetic and logic operations. Programs can be developed for any arithmetic operation and not only for fixed-point binary data but for decimal and floating-point data as well. The hardware implementation of arithmetic operations is carried out in Chaps. 9 and 10.

Multiplication Program

We now develop a program for multiplying two numbers. To simplify the program, we neglect the sign bit and assume positive numbers. We also assume that the two binary numbers have no more than eight significant bits so their product cannot exceed the word capacity of 16 bits. It is possible to modify the program to take care of the signs or use 16-bit numbers. However, the product may be up to 31 bits in length and will occupy two words of memory.

The program for multiplying two numbers is based on the procedure we use to multiply numbers with paper and pencil. As shown in the numerical example of Fig. 6-3, the multiplication process consists of checking the bits of the multiplier Y and adding the multiplicand X as many times as there are 1's in Y, provided the value of X is shifted left from one line to the next. Since the computer can add only two numbers at a time, we reserve a memory location, denoted by P, to store intermediate sums. The intermediate sums are called partial products since they hold a partial product until all numbers are added. As shown in the numerical example under P, the partial product starts with zero. The multiplicand X is added to the content of P for each bit of the multiplier Y that is 1. The value of X is shifted left after checking each bit of the multiplier. The final value in P forms the product. The numerical example has numbers with four significant bits. When multiplied, the product contains eight significant bits. The computer can use numbers with eight significant bits to produce a product of up to 16 bits.

The flow chart of Fig. 6-3 shows the step-by-step procedure for programming the multiplication operation. The program has a loop that is traversed eight times, once for each significant bit of the multiplier. Initially, location X holds the multiplicand and location Y holds the multiplier. A counter CTR is set to -8 and location P is cleared to zero.

The multiplier bit can be checked if it is transferred to the E register. This is done by clearing E, loading the value of Y into the AC, circulating right E and AC

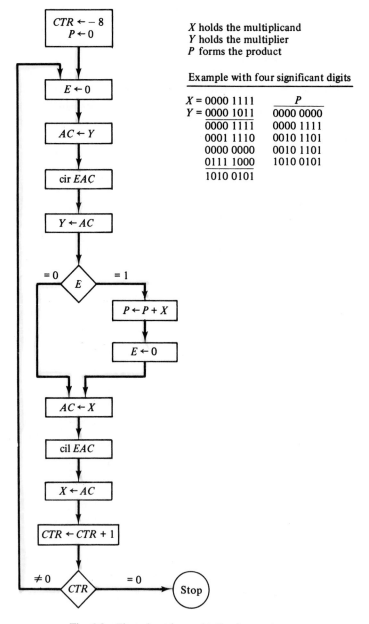

X holds the multiplicand
Y holds the multiplier
P forms the product

Example with four significant digits

$X = 0000\ 1111$	P
$Y = 0000\ 1011$	0000 0000
0000 1111	0000 1111
0001 1110	0010 1101
0000 0000	0010 1101
0111 1000	1010 0101
1010 0101	

Fig. 6-3   Flow chart for multiplication program.

and storing the shifted number back into location Y. This bit stored in E is the low-order bit of the multiplier. We now check the value of E. If it is 1, the multiplicand X is added to the partial product P. If it is 0, the partial product does not change. We then shift the value of X once to the left by loading it into the AC and circulating left E and AC. The loop is repeated eight times by incrementing location CTR and checking when it reaches zero. When the counter reaches zero, the program exits from the loop with the product stored in location P.

The program in Table 6-14 lists the instructions for multiplying two unsigned numbers. The initialization is not listed but should be included when the program is loaded into the computer. The initialization consists of bringing the mulitiplicand and multiplier into locations X and Y, respectively; initializing the counter to -8; and initializing location P to zero. If these locations are not initialized, the program may run with incorrect data. The program itself is straightforward and follows the steps listed in the flow chart. The comments may help in following the step-by-step procedure.

TABLE 6-14   Program to Multiply Two Positive Numbers

	ORG 100	
LOP,	CLE	/Clear E
	LDA Y	/Load multiplier
	CIR	/Transfer multiplier bit to E
	STA Y	/Store shifted multiplier
	SZE	/Check if bit is zero
	BUN ONE	/Bit is one; go to ONE
	BUN ZRO	/Bit is zero; go to ZRO
ONE,	LDA X	/Load multiplicand
	ADD P	/Add to partial product
	STA P	/Store partial product
	CLE	/Clear E
ZRO,	LDA X	/Load multiplicand
	CIL	/Shift left
	STA X	/Store shifted multiplicand
	ISZ CTR	/Increment counter
	BUN LOP	/Counter not zero; repeat loop
	HLT	/Counter is zero; halt
CTR,	DEC -8	/This location serves as a counter
X,	HEX 000F	/Multiplicand stored here
Y,	HEX 000B	/Multiplier stored here
P,	HEX 0	/Product formed here
	END	

This example has shown that if a computer does not have a machine instruction for a required operation, the operation can be programmed by a sequence of machine instructions. Thus, we have demonstrated the software implementation of the multiplication operation. The corresponding hardware implementation is presented in Sec. 9-4.

Double-Precision Addition

When two 16-bit unsigned numbers are multiplied, the result is a 32-bit product that must be stored in two memory words. A number stored in two memory words is said to have double precision. When a partial product is computed, it is necessary that a double-precision number be added to the shifted multiplicand which is also a double-precision number. For greater accuracy, the programmer may wish to employ double-precision numbers and perform arithmetic with operands that occupy two memory words. We now develop a program that adds two double-precision numbers.

One of the double-precision numbers is placed in two consecutive memory locations, AL and AH, with AL holding the 16 low-order bits. The other number is placed in BL and BH. The program is listed in Table 6-15. The two low-order

TABLE 6-15 Program to Add Two Double-Precision Numbers

	LDA AL	/Load A low
	ADD BL	/Add B low, carry in E
	STA CL	/Store in C low
	CLA	/Clear AC
	CIL	/Circulate to bring carry into $AC(16)$
	ADD AH	/Add A high and carry
	ADD BH	/Add B high
	STA CH	/Store in C high
	HLT	
AL,	—	/Location of operands
AH,	—	
BL,	—	
BH,	—	
CL,	—	
CH,	—	

portions are added and the carry transferred into E. The AC is cleared and the bit in E is circulated into the least significant position of the AC. The two high-order portions are then added to the carry and the double-precision sum is stored in CL and CH.

Logic Operations

The basic computer has three machine instructions that perform logic operations: AND, CMA, and CLA. The LDA instruction may be considered as a logic operation that transfers a logic operand into the AC. In Sec. 4-4 we listed 16 different logic operations. All 16 logic operations can be implemented by software means because any logic function can be implemented using the AND and complement operations. For example, the OR operation is not available as a machine instruction in the basic computer. From DeMorgan's theorem we recognize the relation $x + y = (x'y')'$.

The second expression contains only AND and complement operations. A program that forms the OR operation of two logic operands A and B is as follows:

LDA A	/Load first operand A
CMA	/Complement to get $\bar{A}$
STA TMP	/Store in a temporary location
LDA B	/Load second operand B
CMA	/Complement to get $\bar{B}$
AND TMP	/AND with $\bar{A}$ to get $\bar{A} \wedge \bar{B}$
CMA	/Complement again to get $A \vee B$

The other logic operations can be implemented by software in a similar fashion.

Shift Operations

The circular-shift operations are machine instructions in the basic computer. The other shifts of interest are the logical shifts and arithmetic shifts. These two shifts can be programmed with a small number of instructions.

The logical shift requires that zeros be added to the extreme positions. This is easily accomplished by clearing E and circulating the AC and E. Thus for a logical shift-right operation we need the two instructions:

$$\text{CLE}$$
$$\text{CIR}$$

For a logical shift-left operation we need the two instructions:

$$\text{CLE}$$
$$\text{CIL}$$

The arithmetic shifts depend on the type of representation of negative numbers. For the basic computer we have adopted the signed-2's complement representation. The rules for arithmetic shifts are listed in Table 4-6 of Sec. 4-5. For an arithmetic right-shift it is necessary that the sign bit in the leftmost position remain unchanged. But the sign bit itself is shifted into the high-order bit position of the number. The program for the arithmetic right-shift requires that we set E to the same value as the sign bit and circulate right, thus:

CLE	/Clear E to 0
SPA	/Skip if AC is positive; E remains 0
CME	/AC is negative; set E to 1
CIR	/Circulate E and AC

For arithmetic shift-left it is necessary that the added bit in the least significant position be 0. This is easily done by clearing E prior to the circulate-left operation. The sign bit must not change during this shift. With a circulate instruction, the sign bit moves into E. It is then necessary to compare the sign bit with the value of E after the operation. If the two values are equal, the arithmetic shift has been correctly implemented. If they are not equal, an overflow occurs. An overflow indicates that the unshifted number was too large. When multiplied by 2 (by means of the shift), the number so obtained exceeds the capacity of the AC.

6-7 SUBROUTINES

Frequently the same piece of code must be written over again in many different parts of a program. Instead of repeating the code every time it is needed, there is an obvious advantage if the common instructions are written only once. A set of common instructions that can be used in a program many times is called a *subroutine*. Each time that a subroutine is used in the main part of the program, a branch is executed to the beginning of the subroutine. After the subroutine has been executed, a branch is made back to the main program.

A subroutine consists of a self-contained sequence of instructions that carries out a given task. A branch can be made to the subroutine from any part of the main program. This poses the problem of how the subroutine knows which location to return to, since many different locations in the main program may make branches to the same subroutine. It is therefore necessary to store the return address somewhere in the computer for the subroutine to know where to return. Because branching to a subroutine and returning to the main program is such a common operation, all computers provide special instructions to facilitate subroutine entry and return.

In the basic computer, the link between the main program and a subroutine is the BSA instruction (branch and save return address). To explain how this instruction is used, let us write a subroutine that shifts the content of the accumulator four times to the left. Shifting a word four times is a useful operation for processing binary-coded decimal numbers or alphanumeric characters. Such an operation could have been included as a machine instruction in the computer. Since it is not included, a subroutine is formed to accomplish this task. The program of Table 6-16 starts by loading the value of X into the AC. The next instruction encountered is BSA SH4. The BSA instruction is in location 101. Subroutine SH4 must return to location 102 after it finishes its task. When the BSA instruction is executed, the control unit stores the return address 102 into the location defined by the symbolic address SH4 (which is 109). It also transfers the value of SH4 + 1 into the program counter. After this instruction is executed, memory location 109 contains the binary equivalent of hexadecimal 102 and the program counter contains the binary equivalent of hexadecimal 10A. This action has saved the return address and the subroutine is now executed starting from location 10A (since this is the content of *PC* in the next fetch cycle).

TABLE 6-16 Program to Demonstrate the Use of Subroutines

Location			
		ORG 100	/Main program
100		LDA X	/Load X
101		BSA SH4	/Branch to subroutine
102		STA X	/Store shifted number
103		LDA Y	/Load Y
104		BSA SH4	/Branch to subroutine again
105		STA Y	/Store shifted number
106		HLT	
107	X,	HEX 1234	
108	Y,	HEX 4321	
			/Subroutine to shift left 4 times
109	SH4,	HEX 0	/Store return address here
10A		CIL	/Circulate left once
10B		CIL	
10C		CIL	
10D		CIL	/Circulate left fourth time
10E		AND MSK	/Set AC(13–16) to zero
10F		BUN SH4 I	/Return to main program
110	MSK,	HEX FFF0	/Mask operand
		END	

The computation in the subroutine circulates the content of AC four times to the left. In order to accomplish a logical shift operation, the four low-order bits must be set to zero. This is done by masking FFF0 with the content of AC. A mask operation is a logic AND operation that clears the bits of the AC where the mask operand is zero and leaves the bits of the AC unchanged where the mask operand bits are 1's.

The last instruction in the subroutine returns the computer to the main program. This is accomplished by the indirect branch instruction with an address symbol identical to the symbol used for the subroutine name. The address to which the computer branches is not SH4 but the value found in location SH4 because this is an indirect address instruction. What is found in location SH4 is the return address 102 which was previously stored there by the BSA instruction. The computer returns to execute the instruction in location 102. The main program continues by storing the shifted number into location X. A new number is then loaded into the AC from location Y, and another branch is made to the subroutine. This time location SH4 will contain the return address 105 since this is now the location of the next instruction after BSA. The new operand is shifted and the subroutine returns to the main program at location 105.

From this example we see that the first memory location of each subroutine serves as a link between the main program and the subroutine. The procedure for branching to a subroutine and returning to the main program is referred to as a subroutine *linkage*. The BSA instruction performs an operation commonly called subroutine *call.* The last instruction of the subroutine performs an operation commonly called subroutine *return.*

The procedure used in the basic computer for subroutine linkage is commonly found in computers with only one processor register. Many computers have multiple processor registers and some of them are assigned the name *index registers.* In such computers, an index register is usually employed to implement the subroutine linkage. A branch-to-subroutine instruction stores the return address in an index register. A return-from-subroutine instruction is effected by branching to the address presently stored in the index register.

Subroutine Parameters and Data Linkage

When a subroutine is called, the main program must transfer the data it wishes the subroutine to work with. In the previous example, the data was transferred through the accumulator. The operand was loaded into the AC prior to the branch. The subroutine shifted the number and left it there to be accepted by the main program. In general, it is necessary for the subroutine to have access to data from the calling program and to return results to that program. The accumulator can be used for a single input parameter and a single output parameter. In computers with multiple processor registers, more parameters can be transferred this way. Another way to transfer data to a subroutine is through the memory. Data are often placed in memory locations following the call. They can also be placed in a block of storage. The first address of the block is then placed in the memory location following the call. In any case, the return address always gives the link information for transferring data between the main program and the subroutine.

As an illustration, consider a subroutine that performs the logic OR operation. Two operands must be transferred to the subroutine and the subroutine must return the result of the operation. The accumulator can be used to transfer one operand and to receive the result. The other operand is inserted in the location following the BSA instruction. This is demonstrated in the program of Table 6-17. The first operand in location X is loaded into the AC. The second operand is stored in location 202 following the BSA instruction. After the branch, the first location in the subroutine holds the number 202. Note that in this case, 202 is not the return address but the address of the second operand. The subroutine starts performing the OR operation by complementing the first operand in the AC and storing it in a temporary location TMP. The second operand is loaded into the AC by an indirect instruction at location OR. Remember that location OR contains the number 202. When the instruction refers to it indirectly, the operand at location 202 is loaded into the AC. This operand is complemented and then ANDed with the operand stored in TMP. Complementing the result forms the OR operation.

The return from the subroutine must be manipulated so the main program continues from location 203 where the next instruction is located. This is accomplished by incrementing location OR with the ISZ instruction. Now location OR holds the number 203 and an indirect BUN instruction causes a return to the proper place.

TABLE 6-17 Program to Demonstrate Parameter Linkage

Location			
		ORG 200	
200		LDA X	/Load first operand into *AC*
201		BSA OR	/Branch to subroutine OR
202		HEX 3AF6	/Second operand stored here
203		STA Y	/Subroutine returns here
204		HLT	
205	X,	HEX 7B95	/First operand stored here
206	Y,	HEX 0	/Result stored here
207	OR,	HEX 0	/Subroutine OR
208		CMA	/Complement first operand
209		STA TMP	/Store in temporary location
20A		LDA OR I	/Load second operand
20B		CMA	/Complement second operand
20C		AND TMP	/AND complemented first operand
20D		CMA	/Complement again to get OR
20E		ISZ OR	/Increment return address
20F		BUN OR I	/Return to main program
210	TMP,	HEX 0	/Temporary storage
		END	

It is possible to have more than one operand following the BSA instruction. The subroutine must increment the return address stored in its first location for each operand that it extracts from the calling program. Moreover, the calling program can reserve one or more locations for the subroutine to return results that are computed. The first location in the subroutine must be incremented for these locations as well, before the return. If there is a large amount of data to be transferred, the data can be placed in a block of storage and the address of the first item in the block is then used as the linking parameter.

A subroutine that moves a block of data starting at address 100 into a block starting with address 200 is listed in Table 6-18. The length of the block is 16 words. The first instruction is a branch to subroutine MVE. The first part of the subroutine transfers the three parameters 100, 200 and −16 from the main program and places them in its own storage location. The items are retrieved from their blocks by the use of two pointers. The counter insures that only 16 items are moved. When the subroutine completes its operation, the required data is in the block starting from the location 200. The return to the main program is to the HLT instruction.

Fortran Subroutines

The relation between machine language and a high-level programming language such as Fortran can be demonstrated by writing the equivalent Fortran program for the MVE subroutine. A subroutine is defined in Fortran by a SUBROUTINE statement. The last statement is always a RETURN statement. The MVE subroutine

TABLE 6-18   Subroutine to Move a Block of Data

		/Main program
	BSA MVE	/Branch to subroutine
	HEX 100	/First address of source data
	HEX 200	/First address of destination data
	DEC −16	/Number of items to move
	HLT	
MVE,	HEX 0	/Subroutine MVE
	LDA MVE I	/Bring address of source
	STA PT1	/Store in first pointer
	ISZ MVE	/Increment return address
	LDA MVE I	/Bring address of destination
	STA PT2	/Store in second pointer
	ISZ MVE	/Increment return address
	LDA MVE I	/Bring number of items
	STA CTR	/Store in counter
	ISZ MVE	/Increment return address
LOP,	LDA PT1 I	/Load source item
	STA PT2 I	/Store in destination
	ISZ PT1	/Increment source pointer
	ISZ PT2	/Increment destination pointer
	ISZ CTR	/Increment counter
	BUN LOP	/Repeat 16 times
	BUN MVE I	/Return to main program
PT1,	—	
PT2,	—	
CTR,	—	

is written as follows:

SUBROUTINE MOVE (SOURCE, DEST, N)

DIMENSION SOURCE(N), DEST(N)

DO 20 I = 1, N

20   DEST(I) = SOURCE(I)

RETURN

END

The parameters are enclosed in parentheses after the name of the subroutine. When this subroutine is compiled, it produces a machine-language program similar to the one listed in Table 6-18.

The CALL statement is used to link the main program with the subroutine. It is equivalent to the BSA instruction. The CALL statement in this case is:

CALL MOVE (X, Y, 16)

X and Y are array identifiers whose dimension are defined by the DIMENSION statement. Note that the names of the parameters in the CALL statement can be different from the names used in the SUBROUTINE statement. However, the compiler correlates X with SOURCE, Y with DEST, and 16 with N.

6-8 INPUT-OUTPUT PROGRAMMING

The user of the computer writes his program with symbols that are defined by the programming language he employs. The symbols are strings of charaters and each character is assigned an 8-bit code so it can be stored in computer memory. A binary-coded character enters the computer when an INP (input) instruction is executed. A binary-coded character is transferred to the output device when an OUT (output) instruction is executed. The output device detects the binary code and types the corresponding character.

Table 6-19(a) lists the instructions needed to input a character and store it in

TABLE 6-19 Programs to Input and Output One Character

(a) Input a character:		
CIF,	SKI	/Check input flag
	BUN CIF	/Flag=0, branch to check again
	INP	/Flag=1, input character
	OUT	/Print character
	STA CHR	/Store character
	HLT	
CHR,	—	/Store character here
(b) Output one character:		
	LDA CHR	/Load character into AC
COF,	SKO	/Check output flag
	BUN COF	/Flag=0, branch to check again
	OUT	/Flag=1, output character
	HLT	
CHR,	HEX 0057	/Character is "W"

memory. The SKI instruction checks the input flag to see if a character is available for transfer. The next instruction is skipped if the input flag bit is 1. The INP instruction transfers the binary-coded character into $AC(9–16)$. The character is then printed by means of the OUT instruction. A Teletype unit that communicates directly with a computer does not print the character when a key is depressed. To type it, it is necessary to send an OUT instruction for the printer. In this way, the user is insured that the correct transfer has occurred. If the SKI instruction finds the flag bit at 0, the next instruction in sequence is executed. This instruction is a branch to return and check the flag bit again. Because the input device is much slower than the computer, the two instructions in the loop will be executed many times before a character is transferred into the accumulator.

Table 6-19(b) lists the instructions needed to print a character initially stored in memory. The character is first loaded into the *AC*. The output flag is then checked. If it is 0, the computer remains in a two-instruction loop checking the flag bit. When the flag changes to 1, the character is transferred from the accumulator to the printer.

Character Manipulation

A computer is not just a calculator but also a symbol manipulator. The binary-coded characters that represent symbols can be manipulated by computer instructions to achieve various data processing tasks. One such task may be to pack two characters in one word. This is convenient because each character occupies 8 bits and a memory word contains 16 bits. The program in Table 6-20 lists a subroutine named IN2

TABLE 6-20   Subroutine to Input and Pack Two Characters

IN2,	—	/Subroutine entry
FST,	SKI	
	BUN FST	
	INP	/Input first character
	OUT	
	BSA SH4	/Shift left four times
	BSA SH4	/Shift left four more times
SCD,	SKI	
	BUN SCD	
	INP	/Input second character
	OUT	
	BUN IN2 I	/Return

that inputs two characters and packs them into one 16-bit word. The packed word remains in the accumulator. Note that subroutine SH4 (Table 6-16) is called twice to shift the accumulator left eight times.

In the discussion of the assembler it was assumed that the symbolic program is stored in a section of memory which is sometimes called a *buffer*. The symbolic program being typed enters through the input device and is stored in consecutive memory locations in the buffer. The program listed in Table 6-21 can be used to input a symbolic program from the teletypewriter, pack two characters in one word and store them in the buffer. The first address of the buffer is 500. The first double character is stored in location 500 and all characters are stored in sequential locations. The program uses a pointer for keeping track of the current empty location in the buffer. No counter is used in the program so characters will be read as long as they are available, or until the buffer reaches location 0 (after location FFFF). In a practical situation it may be necessary to limit the size of the buffer and a counter may be used for this purpose. Note that subroutine IN2 of Table 6-20 is called to input and pack the two characters.

TABLE 6-21 Program to Store Input Characters in a Buffer

	LDA ADS	/Load first address of buffer
	STA PTR	/Initialize pointer
LOP,	BSA IN2	/Go to subroutine IN2 (Table 6-20)
	STA PTR I	/Store double character word in buffer
	ISZ PTR	/Increment pointer
	BUN LOP	/Branch to input more characters
	HLT	
ADS,	HEX 500	/First address of buffer
PTR,	HEX 0	/Location for pointer

In discussing the second pass of the assembler in Sec. 6-4 it was mentioned that one of the most common operations of an assembler is table lookup. This is an operation that searches a table to find out if it contains a given symbol. The search may be done by comparing the given symbol with each of the symbols stored in the table. The search terminates when a match occurs or if none of the symbols match. When a match occurs, the assembler retrieves the equivalent binary value. A program for comparing two words is listed in Table 6-22. The comparison is

TABLE 6-22 Program to Compare Two Words

	LDA WD1	/Load first word
	CMA	
	INC	/Form 2's complement
	ADD WD2	/Add second word
	SZA	/Skip if AC is zero
	BUN UEQ	/Branch to "unequal" routine
	BUN EQL	/Branch to "equal" routine
WD1,	—	
WD2,	—	

accomplished by forming the 2's complement of a word (as if it were a number) and arithmetically adding it to the second word. If the result is zero, the two words are equal and a match occurs. If the result is not zero, the words are not the same. This program can serve as a subroutine in a table-lookup program.

Program Interrupt

The running time of input and output programs is primarily made up of the time spent by the computer in waiting for the external device to set its flag. The waiting loop that checks the flag keeps the computer occupied with a task that wastes a large amount of time. This waiting time can be eliminated if the interrupt facility is used to notify the computer when a flag is set. The advantage of using the interrupt is that the information transfer is initiated upon request from the external device. In the meantime, the computer can be busy performing other useful tasks. Obviously, if no other program resides in memory, there is nothing for the computer to do so it might as well check for the flags. The interrupt facility is useful in a multiprogram environment when two or more programs reside in memory at the same time.

Only one program can be executed at any given time even though two or more programs may reside in memory. The program currently being executed is referred to as the running program. The other programs are usually waiting for input or output data. The function of the interrupt facility is to take care of the data transfer of one (or more) program while another program is currently being executed. The running program must include an ION instruction to turn the interrupt on. If the interrupt facility is not used, the program must include an IOF instruction to turn it off. (The *start* switch of the computer should also turn the interrupt off.)

The interrupt facility allows the running program to proceed until the input or output device sets its ready flag. Whenever a flag is set to 1, the computer completes the execution of the instruction in progress and then acknowledges the interrupt. The result of this action is that the return address is stored in location 0. The instruction in location 1 is then performed; this initiates a service routine for the input or output transfer. The service routine can be stored anywhere in memory provided a branch to the start of the routine is stored in location 1. The service routine must have instructions to perform the following tasks:

1. Save contents of processor registers.

2. Check which flag is set.

3. Service the device whose flag is set.

4. Restore contents of processor registers.

5. Turn the interrupt facility on.

6. Return to the running program.

The contents of processor registers before the interrupt and after the return to the running program must be the same; otherwise, the running program may be in error. Since the service routine may use these registers, it is necessary to save their contents at the beginning of the routine and restore them at the end. The sequence by which the flags are checked dictates the priority assigned to each device. Even though two or more flags may be set at the same time, the devices nevertheless are serviced one at a time. The device with higher priority is serviced first followed by the one with lower priority.

The occurrence of an interrupt disables the facility from further interrupts. The service routine must turn the interrupt on before the return to the running program. This will enable further interrupts while the computer is executing the running program. The interrupt facility should not be turned on until after the return address is inserted into the program counter.

An example of a program that services an interrupt is listed in Table 6-23. Location 0 is reserved for the return address. Location 1 has a branch instruction to the beginning of the service routine SRV. The portion of the running program

TABLE 6-23   Program to Service an Interrupt

Location			
0	ZRO,	—	/Return address stored here
1		BUN SRV	/Branch to service routine
100		CLA	/Portion of running program
101		ION	/Turn on interrupt facility
102		LDA X	
103		ADD Y	/Interrupt occurs here
104		STA Z	/Program returns here after interrupt
.		.	
.		.	/Interrupt service routine
200	SRV,	STA SAC	/Store content of *AC*
		CIR	/Move *E* into *AC*(1)
		STA SE	/Store content of *E*
		SKI	/Check input flag
		BUN NXT	/Flag is off, check next flag
		INP	/Flag is on, input character
		OUT	/Print character
		STA PT1 I	/Store it in input buffer
		ISZ PT1	/Increment input pointer
	NXT,	SKO	/Check output flag
		BUN EXT	/Flag is off, exit
		LDA PT2 I	/Load character from output buffer
		OUT	/Output character
		ISZ PT2	/Increment output pointer
	EXT,	LDA SE	/Restore value of *AC*(1)
		CIL	/Shift it to *E*
		LDA SAC	/Restore content of *AC*
		ION	/Turn interrupt on
		BUN ZRO I	/Return to running program
	SAC,	—	/*AC* is stored here
	SE,	—	/*E* is stored here
	PT1,	—	/Pointer of input buffer
	PT2,	—	/Pointer of output buffer

listed has an ION instruction that turns the interrupt on. Suppose that an interrupt occurs while the computer is executing the instruction in location 103. The interrupt cycle stores the binary equivalent of hexadecimal 104 in location 0 and branches to location 1. The branch instruction in location 1 sends the computer to the service routine SRV.

The service routine performs the six tasks mentioned above. The contents of *AC* and *E* are stored in special locations. (These are the only processor registers in the basic computer.) The flags are checked sequentially, the input flag first and the output flag second. If any or both flags are set, an item of data is transferred to or from the corresponding memory buffer. Before returning to the running program the previous contents of *E* and *AC* are restored and the interrupt facility is turned on. The last instruction causes a branch to the address stored in location 0. This is the return address previously stored there during the interrupt cycle. Hence the running program will continue from location 104 where it was interrupted.

A typical computer may have many more input and output devices connected to the interrupt facility. Furthermore, interrupt sources are not limited to input and output transfers. Interrupts can be used for other purposes such as internal processing errors or special alarm conditions. Further discussion of interrupts and some advanced concepts concerning this important subject can be found in Sec. 11-5.

6-9 SYSTEM SOFTWARE

A computer system is composed of its hardware components and the system software available for its use. The system software of a computer consists of a collection of operative programs whose purpose is to make the use of the computer more effective. The programs included in a system software package are called *system programs*. They are distinguished from *application programs* written by computer users for the purpose of solving particular problems. For example, a Fortran program written by a scientist to solve his particular research problem is an application program but the compiler that translates the Fortran program to a machine-language executable program is a system program. Most of the system programs are distributed by the computer manufacturer. The customer who buys or leases a computer system would usually receive, in addition to the hardware, any available software needed for the effective operation of his computer. The system software is an indispensable part of a total computer system. Its function is to compensate for the differences that exist between the user needs and the capabilities of the hardware. A computer without some kind of system software would be very ineffective and most likely impossible to operate.

The production of system programs is a complex undertaking requiring extensive knowledge and considerable specialized training in computer science. System programs offer several advantages and conveniences to application programmers and computer users in general. A brief summary of the major components that system programs offer is included in this section.

Software systems can be subdivided into six different categories as follows.

1. Language processors that convert programs from user-oriented languages to machine language.
2. Library programs that provide standard routines for the application programmer.
3. Utility programs to facilitate the communication among computer components and between computer and user.

4. Loader programs to facilitate the reading of various programs into memory.

5. Diagnostic programs to facilitate the maintenance of the computer.

6. An operating system that supervises all other programs and controls their execution.

Language Processors

A language processor is a system program that translates a *source* program written by the user to an *object* program which is meaningful to the hardware of the computer. We have already discussed two language processors: assemblers and compilers. An *assembler* is a system program that translates an assembly-language program to an equivalent binary machine language program. A *compiler* is a system program that translates a high-level language program to machine language. Two other language processors widely used and worth mentioning are macro-assemblers and interpreters.

A *macro* is a pseudo-instruction that defines a group of machine instructions. A *macro-assembler* translates assembly-language programs with macro facility. When employing a macro, the programmer essentially defines a symbolic name to represent a sequence of instructions. For every occurrence of this macro, or symbolic name, the macro-assembler substitutes the defined sequence of instructions. For example, a program that computes the average value of two positive numbers consists of four machine instructions which can be defined by a macro routine as follows:

```
AVG,      MACRO   OP1   OP2
          LDA     OP1
          ADD     OP2
          CLE
          CIR
          END     MACRO
```

In the above program, a macro routine is defined by the symbolic name AVG. The instructions following the macro definition, when executed, will add two operands (OP1 and OP2) and divide their sum by 2 (by shifting right) to obtain the average value. Now, if we want to compute the average of two positive operands, say X and Y, it is not necessary to rewrite the four instructions again. We can use the macro symbol already defined and write only one line of code as follows:

```
AVG X Y
```

The macro-assembler will substitute the instructions defined by the macro routine but with the new specified operands. In other words, the macro-assembler will produce the binary code equivalent to the following instruction sequence:

LDA X

ADD Y

CLE

CIR

A macro is a special type of subroutine, usually with very few instructions, that is included in the main program whenever the instructions are needed. To differentiate between a macro and a normal subroutine, it is customary to refer to a macro as an *open* subroutine and to a normal subroutine as a *closed* subroutine. An open subroutine is different from a closed one in that all instructions defined by a macro name are inserted in the main program every time the macro symbolic name is encountered. Thus, if the same open subroutine were used four times, it would appear in four different places in the main program. A closed subroutine resides outside of the main program and control transfers to the subroutine by means of a *call* instruction. The closed subroutine uses less overall storage space for instructions but takes longer to execute because of the additional instructions for subroutine and parameter transfer.

An *interpreter* is a language processor that translates each statement of a high-level language program and then immediately executes it. Translation and execution alternate for each statement encountered. This differs from a compiler which merely translates the entire source program and is not involved in its execution. The advantage of the interpreter over a compiler is fast response to changes in the source program. This is useful in a time sharing environment where the user can type part of his program and ask the interpreter to execute it. He does not have to type the entire program first as required by a conventional compiler. The interpreter, however, is a time-consuming translation method because each statement must be translated every time it is executed from the source program.

Library Programs

Library programs are available in a computer system for the purpose of simplifying the drudgery of repetitious programming. Routines that are repetitious and similar to previously written ones become standard routines and conventions are adopted for each computer so that any user has access to a library of routines. These routines are typically prepared by computer users and distributed by an association of computer users or by the manufacturer.

In the area of scientific applications, the usual types of library routines available are the mathematical functions such as square root and exponential functions. Other operations of various types are also encountered such as matrix inversion and statistical analysis. In the area of commercial data processing applications, the most widely used library routines are *sort* and *merge*. Sort programs are used to arrange data into a specified sequence. For example, business transactions may be stored in a computer in the order in which they occur. The transactions may be sorted by different items such as by account number to identify the customer or by salesman's name to calculate the commission to be paid. Merge programs are used to combine two or more sets of sorted data into one file containing all the items from both of the original sets. Sort and merge are sometimes categorized as utility programs.

Utility Programs

Utility programs are a collection of commonly used routines that the programmer may use to perform specific tasks, thereby reducing his own programming effort. Each computer installation will have its own library of utility programs and a well-informed programmer would know how and when to use them. A few examples of utility programs commonly available in a computer system are text editors, debugging aids, and input-output routines.

A *text editor* is a program that facilitates the creation of corrected and well-organized text. The text being edited could be an English language letter, but most often, it is a symbolic-language program typed by the user. The text editor program does not interpret the meaning of the text but has the capability of changing it when special commands are issued by the user. For example, when a symbolic language program is being entered into a computer memory via a Teletype terminal, the programmer may use the facility of a text editor program to correct his typing errors by issuing commands to insert, delete, or replace characters in his source program. A time-sharing service which provides remote access to a computer via a typewriter terminal will have available a text editor system so that users can prepare programs and correct them with relative ease.

Debugging aids are programs that help the user correct logical mistakes in his program. Debugging is a process for locating and correcting logical mistakes in a program after it has been executed. These mistakes are called *bugs* and correcting them is referred to as debugging. Debugging procedures begin after the machine-language program is executed and results are not as expected.

A *dynamic debugging* program is a system program which allows the programmer to execute his binary program in the computer while using a Teletype keyboard to control program execution. He can examine contents of registers, change contents of registers and memory, make alterations to the binary program, and other similar functions. By using the facilities of a dynamic debugging program the user can detect and correct logical errors in his program.

A *memory dump* is a system program that selects specified locations in memory, taken at some particular point during the program execution, and prints their content. A memory dump typically shows both the program and operand data. By inspecting both program and data, and comparing it with what it should have been if the program had run correctly, the programmer is able to find his mistakes.

A *trace* is a system program that allows the user to trace the flow of his program while it is executed. He can request, for example, that the contents of certain registers or memory locations be printed every time a branch is executed or when certain memory locations are changed. This allows the user to get a picture of what his program is doing and thus be able to correct mistakes in his program.

In many computer systems, input and output procedures are quite complicated and writing effective input and output programs becomes a cumbersome process. For that reason, the computer manufacturer will provide ready made utility routines in the form of macros or subroutines to relieve the user of the drudgery of programming in detail his own input-output requirements. Other utility routines facilitate interchange among peripheral units. Peripheral transfer routines make possible the copying of data from one unit, for instance, magnetic tape, to another unit, for instance magnetic disk. This results in a more efficient utilization of the data preparation equipment. In a large computer system, all input-output and peripheral interchange is handled by the operating system.

Loaders

A loader is a system program that places other programs into memory and prepares them for execution. The simplest type of loader is called an *absolute* loader. In this scheme the binary program produced by an assembler is punched on cards or paper tape instead of being placed directly in memory after translation. The function of the loader is to accept the machine-language program and place it in memory in the locations specified by the user by means of established pseudo-instructions such as ORG.

A more efficient scheme is to use a *relocating* loader. Such a loader does not allow the programmer to specify the memory space for his binary program. The task of a relocating loader is to adjust programs and subroutines so they can be placed in arbitrary memory locations in an efficient manner. A relocating loader performs four basic functions. It allocates space in memory for the binary program. It links symbolic references between the main program and its subroutines. It relocates memory addresses to correspond to the allocated memory space. And it places the program and data into the allocated memory space. An application program submitted by the user will be processed in a computer system by running it three times. In the first run the program will be translated to a binary program by means of a language processor. In the second run the binary program will be loaded into memory and prepared for execution by a relocating loader. Only in the third run will the program be executed.

A *bootstrap* loader is a program whose function is to start the computer when "cold," when nothing meaningful is in its memory. A bootstrap loader performs a process similar to the initial operation involved in starting an idle engine. To start the operation of a computer, it is not enough to turn the power on; it is necessary also that an initial program be resident in memory so it can be used to load other programs. Once the initial program is loaded in a nonvolatile magnetic core memory, it will stay there even after power is turned off and on again. But if this program is destroyed, or if a volatile memory is employed, or if the computer just came out of production, the bootstrap program must be loaded into memory to start the operation of the computer. Since initially no programs reside in memory, this process must be implemented by special hardware whose sole purpose is to transfer the bootstrap routine from an external source into memory. The bootstrap process is sometimes referred to as *initial program load* (IPL) or *cold start.*

In small computers, the binary instructions of the bootstrap routine are loaded into memory by means of console switches. A more practical method is to store the bootstrap routine in a read-only memory (ROM) where it can never be destroyed. A special switch can be used to initiate the transfer of the content of ROM into a predetermined space in main memory. In some systems, the binary bootstrap routine is punched on a single card which is then placed in a card reader. When the operator activates an IPL switch, the hardware of the computer reads the card and transfers its contents to a number of predetermined words in memory starting from location 0. Then, starting the computer from location 0 causes the execution of this program. The bootstrap program is then used to read other cards containing other programs. In large systems, the common procedure is to store the bootstrap routine together with the operating system in a peripheral unit such as a magnetic disk. A special switch in the computer console causes the transfer of an initial routine from disk to memory.

Diagnostic Programs

The purpose of the diagnostic programs is to exercise selected parts of the hardware and check for malfunctions. A diagnostic program exercises a portion of the hardware and then checks the results obtained against known correct results. In this way, functional failures can be detected and failure messages printed out. Diagnostic programs assist field engineers in equipment maintenance work. They are useful for checking whether parts of the computer hardware are operating properly. In addition, diagnostic programs are frequently run at fixed intervals, usually at a time when the computer load is light, to make sure that the equipment is functioning correctly.

Operating System

An operating system is a collection of programs that control the operation of the computer for the purpose of obtaining an efficient performance. It is basically a software control program which resides in memory at all times and supervises all other programs that run in the computer. An operating system places a considerable demand on the hardware available in the computer and the benefit derived from using it increases as the range and complexity of the hardware increases. For this reason, the most comprehensive and powerful operating systems are used with the largest computers. Smaller computers often run with a very rudimentary operating system which is referred to as a *monitor, supervisor,* or *executive* program.

An operating system includes all the systems programs mentioned previously as well as other programs that control and supervise the operations of all programs residing in the computer. The analysis and design of operating systems is a subject that by itself can fill an entire volume. All we can do in this section is justify its need.

A brief examination of some functions performed by an operating system may help clarify its usefulness. An operating system allocates memory space and loads programs for execution. It provides services for obtaining input data and producing output data. In addition, it provides automatic recovery from many types of errors, for example, input read error or arithmetic overflow. In a *multiprogram* system, many programs can reside simultaneously in the computer. The operating system allocates various computer resources to selected programs and keeps switching resources back and forth. For example, while one program is being executed in the central processor, another program may be receiving input data from a magnetic tape and a third may be in the process of printing its output. In a *time-sharing* system, many users communicate with the computer system via remote terminal devices. The operating system allocates to each job a time-slice on a priority basis. A *job* is a unit of specified work as applied to the execution of a data processing task. A *time slice* is a given amount of time assigned to a job. In any given time slice, the operating system causes the computer to process a job until one of the following four conditions occurs: (1) the job is completed; (2) an error is detected; (3) an input or output is required; or (4) the time-slice runs out. In each case the processor is assigned to the job with the next highest priority. In the first two cases, the job may be removed from memory. In the last two, the job is only temporarily suspended.

The operating system contributes to a more efficient use of the hardware by managing memory resources. For example, if a program, because of its size, cannot be entirely accomodated in main memory, the operating system will partition the program into pieces called *pages* or *segments*. It then transfers segments back and forth between the main memory and an auxilliary memory such as magnetic drum. This gives the operating system further control over multiprogram and time-sharing operations.

The effect of the operating system on the management of the computer system is to improve its efficiency. Efficiency in computer systems is measured by throughput. *Throughput* is the amount of processing that the system accomplishes during a specified interval of time, such as an hour or a day. In general, throughput is a measure of both hardware speed and software facilities. Operating systems contribute to greater throughput by providing an efficient software facility.

In conclusion, it must be emphasized that computer software is a field of study in its own right. The presentation in this chapter was merely an overview of the subject. The introductory software concepts presented here constitute a bare minimum of knowledge necessary for understanding the concept of a total computer system.

REFERENCES

1. DONOVAN, J. J., *System Programming*. New York: McGraw-Hill Book Company, 1972.

2. *Introduction to Programming*. Maynard, Mass.: Digital Equipment Corp., 1973.

3. BOOTH, T. L., *Digital Networks and Computer Systems*, 2nd ed. New York: John Wiley & Sons, Inc., 1978.

4. GEAR, C. W., *Computer Organization and Programming*, 3rd ed. New York: McGraw-Hill Book Company, 1980.

5. CORBATO, F. J., J. W. PODUSKA, AND J. H. SALZER, *Advanced Computer Programming*. Cambridge, Mass.: The M.I.T. Press, 1963.

6. CHAPIN, N., *Computers—A System Approach*. New York: Van Nostrand Reinhold Co., 1971.

7. SOUCEK, B., *Minicomputers in Data Processing and Simulation*. New York: John Wiley & Sons, Inc., 1972.

8. MADNICK, S. E., AND J. J. DONOVAN, *Operating Systems*. New York: McGraw-Hill Book Company, 1974.

PROBLEMS

6-1.   The following program is stored in the memory unit of the basic computer. Show the contents of the AC, PC, and OPR (in hexadecimal), at the end, after each instruction is executed. All numbers listed below are in hexadecimal.

Location	Instruction
010	CLA
011	ADD 016
012	BUN 014
013	HLT
014	AND 017
015	BUN 013
016	C1A5
017	93C6

6-2.   The following program is a list of instructions in hexadecimal code. The computer executes the instructions starting from address 100. What is the content of the AC and the memory word at address 103 when the computer halts?

Location	Instruction
100	5103
101	7200
102	7001
103	0000
104	7800
105	7020
106	C103

6-3.   List the assembly-language program (of the equivalent binary instructions) generated by a compiler from the following Fortran program. Assume integer variables.

$$SUM = 0$$
$$SUM = SUM + A + B$$

$$DIF = DIF - C$$

$$SUM = SUM + DIF$$

6-4. Can the letter I be used as a symbolic address in the assembly-language program defined for the basic computer? Justify the answer.

6-5. What happens during the first pass of the assembler (Fig. 6-1) if the line of code that has a pseudo-instruction ORG or END also has a label? Modify the flow chart to include an error message if this occurs.

6-6. A line of code in an assembly language program is as follows:

DEC −35

(a) Show that four memory words are required to store the line of code and give their binary content.
(b) Show that one memory word stores the binary translated code and give its binary content.

6-7. (a) Obtain the address symbol table generated for the program of Table 6-13 during the first pass of the assembler.
(b) List the translated program in hexadecimal.

6-8. The pseudo-instruction BSS N (block started by symbol) is sometimes employed to reserve N memory words for a group of operands. For example, the line of code

A, BSS 10

informs the assembler that a block of 10 (decimal) locations is to be left free, starting from location A. This is similar to the Fortran statement DIMENSION A(10). Modify the flow chart of Fig. 6-1 to process this pseudo-instruction.

6-9. Modify the flow chart of Fig. 6-2 to include an error message when a symbolic address is not defined by a label.

6-10. Show how the MRI and non-MRI tables can be stored in memory.

6-11. List the assembly-language program (of the equivalent binary instructions) generated by a compiler for the following IF statement:

IF(A − B) 10, 20, 30

The program branches to statement 10 if $A − B < 0$; to statement 20 if $A − B = 0$; and to statement 30 if $A − B > 0$.

6-12. (a) Explain in words what the following program accomplishes when it is executed. What is the value of location CTR when the computer halts?
(b) List the address symbol table obtained during the first pass of the assembler.
(c) List the hexadecimal code of the translated program.

ORG 100

CLE

CLA

```
            STA CTR
            LDA WRD
            SZA
            BUN ROT
            BUN STP
   ROT,  CIL
            SZE
            BUN AGN
            BUN ROT
   AGN,  CLE
            ISZ CTR
            SZA
            BUN ROT
   STP,   HLT
   CTR,   HEX 0
   WRD,   HEX 62C1
            END
```

6-13. Write a program loop, using a pointer and a counter, that clears to 0 the contents of hexadecimal locations 500 through 5FF.

6-14. Write a program to multiply two positive numbers by a repeated addition method. For example, to multiply 5×4, the program evaluates the product by adding 5 four times, or $5 + 5 + 5 + 5$.

6-15. The multiplication program of Table 6-14 is not initialized. After the program is executed once, location CTR will be left with zero. Show that if the program is executed again starting from location 100, the loop will be traversed 65536 times. Add the needed instructions to initialize the program.

6-16. Write a program to multiply two unsigned positive numbers, each with 16 significant bits, to produce an unsigned double-precision product.

6-17. Write a program to multiply two signed numbers with negative numbers being initially in signed-2's complement representation. The product should be single-precision and signed-2's complement representation if negative.

6-18. Write a program to subtract two double-precision numbers.

6-19. Write a program that evaluates the logic exclusive-Or of two logic operands.

6-20. Write a program for the arithmetic shift-left operation. Branch to OVF if an overflow occurs.

6-21. Write a subroutine to subtract two numbers. In the calling program, the BSA instruction is followed by the subtrahend and minuend. The difference is returned to the main program in the third location following the BSA instruction.

6-22. Write a subroutine to complement each word in a block of data. In the calling program, the BSA instruction is followed by two parameters: the starting address of the block and the number of words in the block.

6-23. Write a subroutine to circulate E and AC four times to the right. If AC contains hexadecimal 079C and $E = 1$, what are the contents of AC and E after the subroutine is executed?

6-24. Write a program to accept input characters, pack two characters in one word and store them in consecutive locations in a memory buffer. The first address of the buffer is $(400)_{16}$. The size of the buffer is $(512)_{10}$ words. If the buffer overflows, the computer should halt.

6-25. Write a program to unpack two characters from location WRD and store them in bits 9–16 of locations CH1 and CH2. Bits 1–8 should contain zeros.

6-26. Obtain a flow chart for a program to check for a CR code (hexadecimal 0D) in a memory buffer. The buffer contains two characters per word. When the code for CR is encountered, the program transfers it to bits 9–16 of location LNE without disturbing bits 1–8.

6-27. Translate the service routine SRV from Table 6-23 to its equivalent hexadecimal code. Assume that the routine is stored starting from location 200.

6-28. Define a macro routine that subtracts two numbers and leaves the difference in the AC. Show how the macro can be used to perform $A - B$.

6-29. Write an interrupt service routine that performs all the required functions but the input device is serviced only if a special location, MOD, contains all 1's. The output device is serviced only if location MOD contains all 0's.

6-30. What is a bootstrap loader and why must every computer have one? List four ways for loading a bootstrap routine into a computer.

6-31. What is the difference between an application program and a system program? Can an application program run in a computer if the computer has no system programs? List about 10 different system programs and explain their usefulness.

Central Processor Organization

7

7-1 PROCESSOR BUS ORGANIZATION

The part of a computer that performs the bulk of data processing operations is called the *central processor unit* and is referred to as the CPU. The CPU contains the hardware components for processing instructions and data. It is comprised of a control unit and a processor unit which together supervise and implement the various data processing tasks in the central part of a computer system. If we remove the memory and Teletype units from the basic computer of Chap. 5, what remains can be classified as a CPU.

Computers with a limited number of registers in the CPU employ a single accumulator for implementing micro-operations. With the availability of integrated circuits, registers and other digital circuits are not as expensive as when constructed with discrete components. Consequently, most computers employ a large number of processor registers and route information among them through common buses.

In the programming examples of Chap. 6, we have shown that memory locations are needed for storing pointers, counters, return addresses, temporary results, and partial products during multiplication. Having to refer to memory locations for such applications is time consuming because memory access is the most time-consuming micro-operation in a CPU. It is more convenient and more efficient to store these intermediate values in processor registers. When a large number of registers are included in a processor unit, it is most efficient to connect them through a bus system or arrange them as a small local memory with very fast access time. The registers communicate with each other not only for direct data transfers, but also while performing various micro-operations. Hence, it is necessary to provide a common unit that can perform all the arithmetic, logic, and shift micro-operations in the processor.

A bus organization for seven CPU registers is shown in Fig. 7-1. The output of each register is connected to two multiplexers (MUX) to form input buses *A* and *B*. The selection lines in each multiplexer select one register or the input data

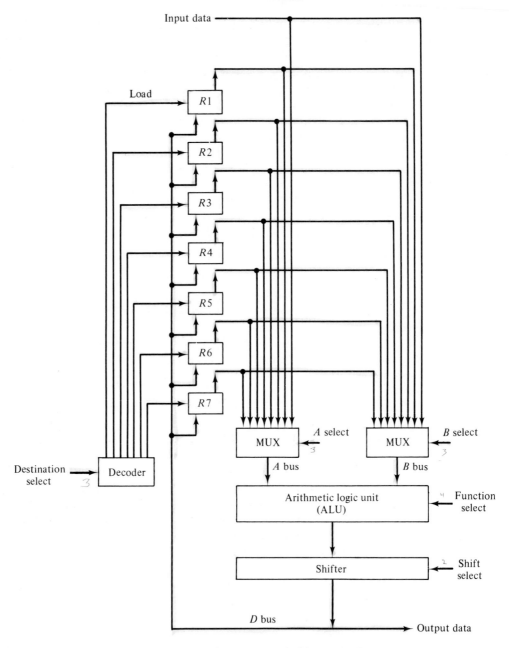

Fig. 7-1 CPU registers connected with common buses.

for the particular bus. The A and B buses form the inputs to a common arithmetic logic unit (ALU). The function selected in the ALU determines the arithmetic or logic micro-operation that is to be performed. The shift micro-operations are implemented in the shifter. The shifter unit is attached to the output of the ALU to provide a postshift capability. The shifter unit could be placed in the input of the ALU to provide a preshift capability, or it may be independent of the ALU to facilitate parallel operations. The result of the micro-operation is available for output data and also goes through the destination bus and into the inputs of all registers. The destination register that receives the information from the D bus is selected by a decoder. The decoder activates one of the register load inputs, thus providing a transfer path between the data in the D bus and the inputs of the selected destination register.

The operation of the multiplexers, the buses, and the destination decoder is explained in Sec. 4-2 in conjunction with Figs. 4-6 and 4-7. The arithmetic logic unit and the shifter are discussed in the next section.

The control unit that operates the CPU bus system directs the information flow through the ALU by selecting the various components in the system. For example, to perform the micro-operation

$$R1 \leftarrow R2 + R3$$

the control must provide binary selection variables to the following selector inputs:

1. *MUX A selector:* to place the contents of $R2$ into bus A.
2. *MUX B selector:* to place the contents of $R3$ into bus B.
3. *ALU function selector:* to provide the arithmetic operation $A + B$.
4. *Shift selector:* for direct transfer from the output of the ALU into output bus D (no shift).
5. *Decoder destination selector:* to transfer the contents of bus D into $R1$.

The five control selection variables must be generated simultaneously and must be available during one clock pulse interval. The binary information from the two source registers propagates through the combinational gates in the multiplexers, the ALU, and the shifter, to the output bus, and into the inputs of the destination register, all during one clock pulse interval. Then, when the next clock pulse arrives, the binary information on the output bus is transferred into $R1$. To achieve a fast response time, the ALU is constructed with high-speed circuits and the shifter is implemented with combinational gates.

7-2 ARITHMETIC LOGIC UNIT (ALU)

An arithmetic logic unit is a digital circuit that performs a set of arithmetic micro-operations and a set of logic micro-operations. The ALU has a number of selection lines to select a particular micro-operation in the unit. The selection variables are decoded within the ALU so that k selection variables can specify up to 2^k distinct micro-operations.

The internal operation of an ALU is better understood if it is separated into its arithmetic and logic parts. We will proceed by first explaining the operation of a typical arithmetic circuit that performs eight arithmetic micro-operations. A second circuit will then be shown for implementing four logic micro-operations. Finally, the two circuits will be combined to form an arithmetic logic unit.

Arithmetic Circuit

The binary parallel-adder, described in Sec. 4-3, is an arithmetic circuit that adds two binary numbers. Additional arithmetic micro-operations can be obtained by augmenting the parallel-adder with certain selection logic circuits. Figure 7-2 demonstrates the arithmetic micro-operations obtained when one set of inputs to a parallel-adder is controlled externally. The straight arithmetic addition is achieved when one set of inputs receives a binary number A, the other set of inputs receives a binary number B, and the input carry C_1 is maintained at 0. This case is shown in Fig. 7-2(a), where the output of the circuit designated by F produces the *add* micro-operation $F = A + B$. By making the input carry $C_1 = 1$ as in Fig. 7-2(b), it is possible to add 1 to the sum to produce an output $F = A + B + 1$.

Different arithmetic micro-operations can be obtained by controlling the data entering the inputs at B as indicated in the other six diagrams of Fig. 7-2. Complementing all the bits of input B results in a micro-operation $F = A + \bar{B}$, which is the sum of A plus the 1's complement of B. Adding 1 to this sum by making the input carry $C_1 = 1$, we obtain $F = A + \bar{B} + 1$, which produces the sum of A plus the 2's complement of B. This is equivalent to the subtraction operation $F = A - B$. Next, consider forcing all 0's into the B terminals of the parallel-adder. Since B is now zero, the sum produced at the output becomes $F = A$, which transfers input A into output F. Adding 1 through the input carry C_1 as shown in Fig. 7-2(f), we obtain $F = A + 1$, which is the increment micro-operation. The condition illustrated in Fig. 7-2(g) inserts all 1's into the B terminals of the parallel-adder. A binary number with all 1's represents the 2's complement of unity. Consider, for example, a parallel-adder of 4 bits. The 2's complement of the binary number 0001 is 1111. Adding a number A to the 2's complement of unity produces an output $F = A + 2$'s complement of $1 = A - 1$, which is the decrement micro-operation.

One stage of an arithmetic circuit that provides the micro-operations listed above is shown in Fig. 7-3. The full-adder circuit represents one state of the parallel-adder. The two selection lines S_1 and S_0 control the data path between the B terminal and one input of the full-adder circuit. When $S_1 S_0 = 00$, the controlled input of the full-adder is always 0. When $S_1 S_0 = 01$, the input receives the value of B_i. When $S_1 S_0 = 10$, the input receives the complement value of B_i. With $S_1 S_0 = 11$, the input is always equal to 1. These conditions can be verified by deriving the truth table of the selection logic. Note that the two selection variables S_1 and S_0 control the input path in the B terminal according to the four conditions illustrated in Fig. 7-2.

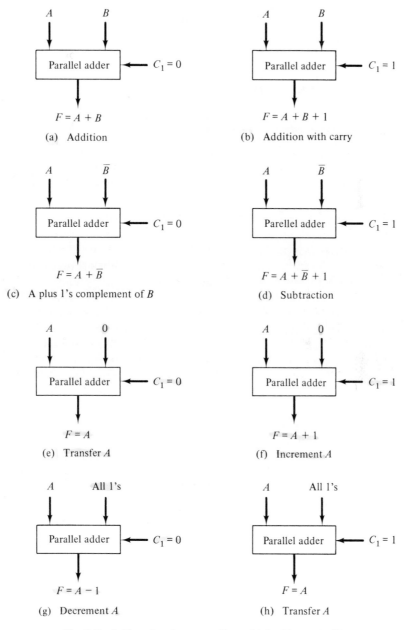

Fig. 7-2 Arithmetic micro-operations obtained by controlling one set of inputs to a parallel adder.

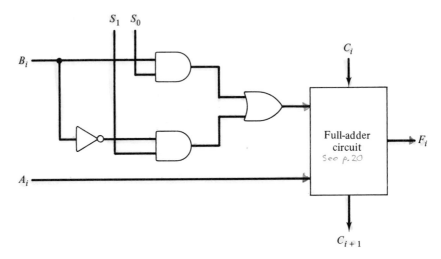

Fig. 7-3 One stage of arithmetic circuit.

Just as in a parallel-adder, the arithmetic circuit can be partitioned into stages, one for each pair of bits of the input operands. For operands with n bits, the arithmetic circuit consists of n identical stages. Figure 7-4 shows the block diagram of an arithmetic circuit partitioned into n stages. Each stage is identical to the circuit shown in Fig. 7-3. The bits of inputs A and B are designated by subscript numbers from right to left with subscript 1 denoting the low-order bit. The carries are connected in a chain through the stages. The function selection lines S_1, S_0, and C_1 select the arithmetic micro-operation and the F terminals generate the output function. Note that C_1 is the input carry to the first stage and its effect is to add 1 to the low-order pair of bits. S_1 and S_0 control the inputs to the B terminals in each stage.

The micro-operations implemented in the arithmetic circuit are listed in Table 7-1.

TABLE 7-1 Function Table for Arithmetic Circuit

Function Select				Correspond to Fig. 7-2
S_1	S_0	C_1	Output	Function Diagram
0	0	0	$F = A$	(e) Transfer A
0	0	1	$F = A + 1$	(f) Increment A
0	1	0	$F = A + B$	(a) Addition
0	1	1	$F = A + B + 1$	(b) Addition with carry
1	0	0	$F = A + \bar{B}$	(c) A plus 1's complement of B
1	0	1	$F = A + \bar{B} + 1$	(d) Subtraction
1	1	0	$F = A - 1$	(g) Decrement A
1	1	1	$F = A$	(h) Transfer A

222

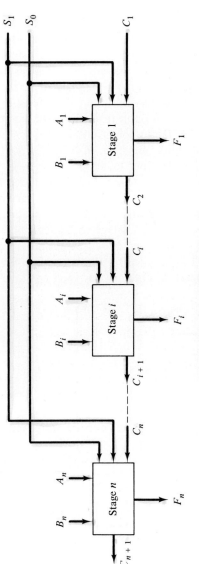

Fig. 7-4 Arithmetic circuit partitioned into n stages.

The eight operations listed in the table follow directly from the function diagrams illustrated in Fig. 7-2.

Logic Circuit

The logic micro-operations manipulate the bits of the operands by treating each bit as a binary variable. In Table 4-5 there is a list of 16 logic micro-operations that can be performed with two binary variables. The 16 logic operations can be generated in a circuit and each operation can be selected by means of four selection variables. However, there are essentially only four basic logic operations from which all others can be derived by means of Boolean algebra. They are the AND, OR, XOR (exclusive-OR), and complement micro-operations.

Figure 7-5(a) shows one stage of a logic circuit. It consists of four gates and a multiplexer. Each of the four logic operations AND, OR, XOR, and complement are generated with a gate that performs the required logic. The outputs of the gates are applied to a multiplexer with two selection variables S_1 and S_0. These selection variables choose one of the multiplexer inputs and direct its value to the output. The diagram shows one typical stage with subscript i. For a logic circuit with n bits, the diagram of Fig. 7-5(a) must be repeated n times for $i = 1, 2, 3, \ldots, n$. The selection variables must be applied to all stages. The function table in Fig. 7-5(b) lists the logic micro-operation obtained for each combination of the selection variables.

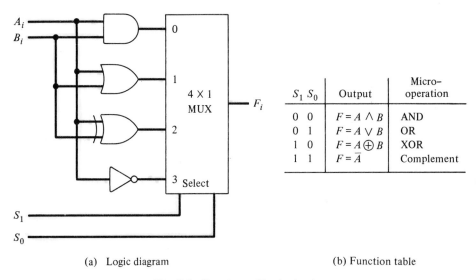

$S_1 \, S_0$	Output	Micro-operation
0 0	$F = A \wedge B$	AND
0 1	$F = A \vee B$	OR
1 0	$F = A \oplus B$	XOR
1 1	$F = \overline{A}$	Complement

(a) Logic diagram   (b) Function table

Fig. 7-5 One stage of logic circuit.

Arithmetic Logic Unit

The logic circuit can be combined with the arithmetic circuit to produce an arithmetic logic unit commonly referred to as an ALU. Selection variables S_1 and S_0 can be common to both circuits provided that we use a third selection variable to differentiate between the two. The configuration of a one-stage ALU is illustrated in Fig. 7-6. The outputs of the arithmetic and logic circuits in each stage are applied to a multiplexer with selection variable S_2. When $S_2 = 0$, the arithmetic output is selected, but when $S_2 = 1$, the logic output is selected. Note that the diagram shows just one typical stage of the ALU. The circuit of Fig. 7-6 must be repeated n times for an n-bit ALU. The output carry C_{i+1} of a given stage must be connected to the input carry C_i of the next-higher-order stage. The input carry to the first stage is designated by C_1 and provides a selection variable for the arithmetic micro-operations. Input C_1 has no effect on the logic micro-operations.

An ALU with individual stages as defined in Fig. 7-6 will provide 8 arithmetic and 4 logic micro-operations, for a total of 12 micro-operations. Each micro-operation is selected through the variables S_2, S_1, S_0, and C_1. The input carry C_1 is used for the selection of arithmetic micro-operations only.

Table 7-2 lists the 12 micro-operations of the ALU. The first eight listed (with $S_2 = 0$) are identical to the arithmetic micro-operations of Table 7-1. The input carry during the four logic operations (when $S_2 = 1$) has no effect on the operation of the unit, so the entries under the C_1 column for the logic micro-operations are marked with don't-care X's.

TABLE 7-2   Function Table for ALU

| Function Select | | | | | |
S_2	S_1	S_0	C_1	Output	Function
0	0	0	0	$F = A$	Transfer A
0	0	0	1	$F = A + 1$	Increment A
0	0	1	0	$F = A + B$	Addition
0	0	1	1	$F = A + B + 1$	Add with carry
0	1	0	0	$F = A + \bar{B}$	A plus 1's complement of B
0	1	0	1	$F = A + \bar{B} + 1$	Subtraction
0	1	1	0	$F = A - 1$	Decrement A
0	1	1	1	$F = A$	Transfer A
1	0	0	X	$F = A \wedge B$	AND
1	0	1	X	$F = A \vee B$	OR
1	1	0	X	$F = A \oplus B$	XOR
1	1	1	X	$F = \bar{A}$	Complement A

The Shifter

The shifter attached to the bus system transfers the output of the ALU into the output bus. The shifter may transfer the information directly or may shift it to the right or left. Provision is sometimes available for no transfer from ALU to the output bus. The latter case is sometimes needed, for example, when two numbers are compared to determine their relative magnitude. This is done by placing one number in bus A, the other in bus B and the selection lines of the ALU for $F = A + \bar{B}$. The output carry of the ALU gives the information concerning the relative magnitude.

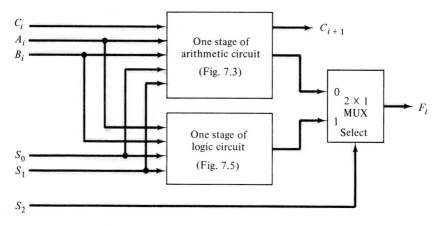

Fig. 7-6 One stage of arithmetic logic unit (ALU).

The result of the operation $A + \bar{B}$ need not be transferred anywhere if a comparison is all that is required.

The most obvious circuit for a shifter is a bidirectional shift-register with parallel load (see Fig. 2-17). The control inputs in the register shift the content of the register to the left or right or not at all. Shifting by means of a register delays the information transfer from the ALU to the output bus by a number of clock pulse periods equal to the number of shifts executed. One additional clock pulse is needed for loading the outputs of the ALU into the register.

The transfer from the source registers to the destination register can be done with one clock pulse if the shifter is implemented with a *position scaler*. A position scaler is a shifter made up of gates without the use of flip-flops. It is classified as a combinational circuit since only gates are included in the digital function. In a combinational circuit shifter, the signals from the ALU terminals to the output bus propagate without a need of a clock pulse. Hence, the only clock pulse needed in the system is for loading the data from the output bus into the destination register.

Figure 7-7 shows the logic diagram of a combinational circuit shifter. It has two control lines H_1 and H_0 for selecting the type of operation. The control lines specify four different operations for the shifter. The diagram shows only the first and last stages and a typical stage. The shifter, of course, must consist of n such identical stages.

Table 7-3 lists the four functions of the shifter selection control. When $H_1 H_0 = 00$, no shift is executed and the signals from the F lines go directly into the D lines. Two control input combinations cause a shift-right and shift-left operation. When $H_1 H_0 = 11$, all three decoder outputs are equal to zero. As a consequence, the D outputs are also equal to zero, blocking the transfer of information from the ALU to the output bus. The shifting to the right or left is for one bit position. Inputs I_R and I_L serve as serial inputs for the last and first stage during a shift-right or shift-left operation.

TABLE 7-3   Shift Selection Control

H_1	H_0	Function
0	0	No shift, transfer F to D
0	1	Shift-right F to D
1	0	Shift-left F to D
1	1	No transfer from F to D

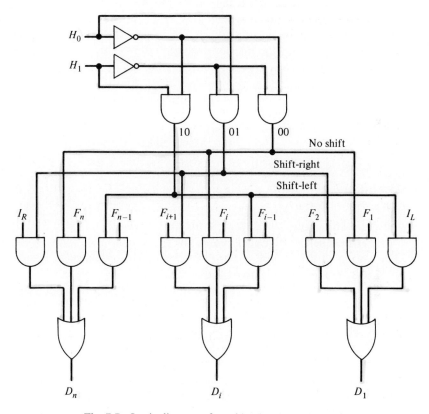

Fig. 7-7   Logic diagram of combinational circuit shifter.

Control Word

The selection variables in the processor unit of Fig. 7-1 control the micro-operation that is executed with every clock pulse. The selection variables control the buses, the ALU, the shifter, and the destination register. The source register for the A bus is selected with three bits which are applied to the A select inputs of the multiplexer. When the three bits are equal to 000, the bus selects the input data. Otherwise, the binary selection value chooses one of the registers. Thus 001 selects register $R1$ and

010 selects register $R2$ up to 111, which selects register $R7$. The source register for the B bus is selected with three other bits in a similar fashion. The destination register is also selected with three bits which are applied to the inputs of the selection decoder. The input combination 000 in the decoder does not select a register and this combination can be used when the contents of the D bus are diverted to the output data terminals. The ALU function select needs four bits as specified in Table 7-2 and the shift select needs two bits as specified in Table 7-3. Thus a total of 15 bits are required to select a micro-operation in the bus organized CPU of Fig. 7-1.

The total number of bits that select a micro-operation in a bus organized system is called a *control word*. This is in contrast to a control function which can be expressed as a Boolean function and constitutes one binary variable. For example, the control word that implements the micro-operation

$$R1 \leftarrow R2 + R3$$

consists of 15 bits to select the various components as follows:

A	B	ALU	Shift	Destination
010	011	0010	00	001

010 selects register $R2$ for bus A; 011 selects $R3$ for bus B; 0010 selects the add micro-operation for the ALU (Table 7-2); 00 selects no shift through the shifter (Table 7-3); and 001 selects $R1$ for the destination register.

The sequence of control words for the system is stored in a control memory. The output of the control memory is applied to the selection variables of the processor. By reading consecutive control words from memory, it is possible to sequence the micro-operations in the CPU. Thus, the entire design can be specified by means of a set of register transfer statements together with the corresponding control words. This design procedure is commonly referred to as the *microprogramming* method. This method of controlling the processor unit is demonstrated in Chap. 8.

7-3 STACK ORGANIZATION

A very useful feature that is included in the CPU of many computers is a *stack* or *last-in first-out* (LIFO) list. A stack is a storage device which stores information in such a manner that the item stored last is the first item retrieved. The operation of a stack can be compared to a stack of trays. The last tray placed on the stack is the first to be taken off.

The stack in digital computers is essentially a memory unit with an address register that can only count; no other value is ever loaded into the address register. This type of address register is called a *stack pointer* because its value always points to the address of the top word in the stack. Contrary to a stack of trays where the tray itself may be taken out or inserted, the physical registers of a memory stack are always available for reading or writing. It is the *item*, the content of the word, that is inserted or deleted. The stack pointer always holds the address of the last item inserted in the stack.

The two operations of a stack are the insertion and deletion of items. The operation of insertion is called *push* (or *push-down*) because it can be thought of as the result of pushing a new item on top. The operation of deletion is called *pop* (or *pop-up*) because it can be thought of as the result of moving each item up one register so that the top pops out. However, nothing is pushed or popped in a computer stack. These operations are simulated by incrementing or decrementing the stack pointer register.

Figure 7-8 shows the organization of a 64-word memory stack. The stack pointer register *SP* contains a binary number whose value is equal to the address of the word which is currently on top of the stack. Three items are placed in the stack, *A*, *B*, and *C*, in that order. Item *C* is on top of the stack so that the content of *SP* is now binary address 3. To remove the top item, the stack is popped by reading the memory word at address 3 and decrementing the content of *SP*. Item *B* is now on top of the stack since *SP* holds address 2. To insert a new item, the stack is pushed by incrementing *SP* and writing a word in the next higher location in the stack. Note that item *C* has been read out but not physically removed. This does not matter because when the stack is pushed, a new item is written in its place.

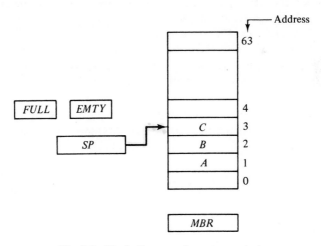

Fig. 7-8 Block diagram of a memory stack.

In a 64-word memory stack, the stack pointer contains 6 bits since $2^6 = 64$. The one-bit registers *FULL* and *EMTY* are set when the stack is full or empty of items, respectively. The *MBR* is the memory buffer register that holds the binary item to be written into or read out of the memory stack.

Initially, *SP* is cleared and *EMTY* is set, so that *SP* points to the word at address 0 and the stack is marked empty. If the stack is not full (if *FULL* = 0), a new item is inserted by a *push* operation. The push operation is implemented with the following sequence of micro-operations:

$SP \leftarrow SP + 1$ Increment stack pointer

$M[SP] \leftarrow MBR$ Write item on top of the stack

If $(SP = 0)$ then $(FULL \leftarrow 1)$ Check if stack is full

$EMTY \leftarrow 0$ Mark the stack not empty

The stack pointer is incremented so it points to the address of the next higher word. A memory *write* micro-operation inserts the word from *MBR* into the top of the stack. Note that *SP* holds the address of the top of the stack and that $M[SP]$ denotes the memory word specified by the address presently available in *SP*. If *SP* becomes zero, the stack is full of items so *FULL* is set to 1. This condition is reached if the last item was in location 63 and by incrementing *SP*, the new item is stored in location 0. Once an item is stored in location 0, there are no more empty registers in the stack. If an item is written in the stack, obviously the stack cannot be empty, so *EMTY* is cleared.

A new item is deleted from the stack if the stack is not empty (if $EMTY = 0$). The *pop* operation consists of the following sequence of micro-operations:

$MBR \leftarrow M[SP]$ Read item from the top of the stack

$SP \leftarrow SP - 1$ Decrement stack pointer

If $(SP = 0)$ then $(EMTY \leftarrow 1)$ Check if stack is empty

$FULL \leftarrow 0$ Mark the stack not full

The top item is read from the stack into *MBR*. The stack pointer is then decremented. If its value reaches zero, the stack is empty so *EMTY* is set to 1. This condition is reached if the item read was in location 1. Once this item is read out, all the registers in the stack are empty. Note that if a pop operation reads the item from location 0 and then *SP* is decremented, *SP* changes to all 1's which is equivalent to binary 63. In this configuration, the word in address 0 receives the last item in the stack. Note also that an erroneous operation will result if the stack is pushed when *FULL* = 1 or popped when $EMTY = 1$.

The two operations for either push or pop stack are (1) an access to memory through *SP*, and (2) updating *SP*. Which of the two operations is done first and whether *SP* is updated by incrementing or decrementing depends on the organization of the stack. In Fig. 7-8, the stack grows by *increasing* the memory address. The stack may be made to grow by *decreasing* the memory address. In such a case, *SP* is decremented for the push operation and incremented for a pop operation. A stack may be organized so that *SP* points at the next *empty* location on top of the stack. In this case, the sequence of operations of updating *SP* and memory access must be interchanged.

Memory Stack

A stack can exist as a stand-alone unit or can be implemented in a random-access memory attached to a CPU. The implementation of a stack in the CPU is done by assigning a portion of the computer memory to a stack operation and using a dedicated processor register as a stack pointer. This configuration is shown in Fig. 7-9.

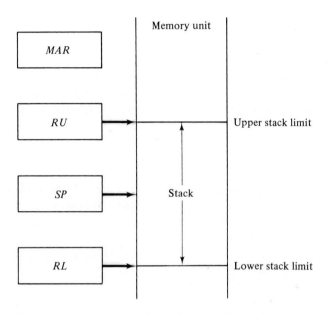

Fig. 7-9 Implementation of a stack in a random access memory.

Any word in the memory unit can be accessed by means of the memory address register *MAR*. However, a portion of memory is assigned exclusively to operate as a stack. In conjunction with the stack there are three processor registers: *RL*, *RU*, and *SP*. The *RL* register holds the address of the lower limit of the stack, the *RU* register holds the address of the upper limit of the stack, and *SP* is the stack pointer. To pop the stack, the address in *SP* is used to access memory to read the item on top of the stack. *SP* is then decremented and compared with *RL* to check if it reached the bottom stack limit. To push the stack, *SP* is incremented and its address is then used to access the memory to write a new item on top of the stack. *SP* is then compared with *RU* to check if it reached the upper stack limit. In this configuration, the CPU can perform random-access memory operations as well as stack operations.

Some older computers do not include a stack pointer register in the CPU and therefore do not provide a memory stack. All recent computers include a stack pointer as well as instructions to push and pop the memory stack. Only few computers, however, provide the stack limit registers *RL* and *RU* as part of the CPU hardware. When these registers are not available, it becomes the responsibility of the user to ensure that the stack limits are not exceeded.

Polish Notation

A stack organization is very effective for evaluating arithmetic expressions. The common mathematical method of writing arithmetic expressions imposes difficulties when evaluated by a computer. The common arithmetic expressions are written in *infix* notation, with each operator written *between* the operands. Consider the simple arithmetic expression

$$A * B + C * D$$

The star (denoting multiplication) is placed between two operands A and B or C and D. The plus is between the two products. To evaluate this arithmetic expression it is necessary to compute the product $A * B$, store this product while computing $C * D$ and then sum the two products. From this example we see that to evaluate arithmetic expressions in infix notation it is necessary to scan back and forth along the expression to determine the next operation to be performed.

The Polish mathematician Lukasiewicz showed that arithmetic expressions can be represented in *prefix* notation. This representation, often referred to as *Polish* notation, places the operator before the operands. The *postfix* notation, referred to as *reverse Polish* notation, places the operator after the operands. The following examples demonstrate the three representations:

$A + B$	Infix notation
$+AB$	Prefix or Polish notation
$AB+$	Postfix or reverse Polish notation

The reverse Polish notation is in a form suitable for stack manipulation. The expression

$$A * B + C * D$$

is written in reverse Polish notation as

$$AB * CD * +$$

and is evaluated as follows: Scan the expression from left to right. When an operator is reached, perform the operation with the two operands found on the left side of the operator. Remove the two operands and the operator and replace them by the number obtained from the result of the operation. Continue to scan the expression and repeat the procedure for every operator encountered until there are no more operators.

For the above expression we find the operator $*$ after A and B. We perform the operation $A * B$ and replace A, B, and $*$ by the product to obtain

$$(A * B) \, CD * +$$

where $(A * B)$ is a *single* quantity obtained from the product. The next operator is a $*$ and its previous two operands are C and D, so we perform $C * D$ and obtain an expression with two operands and one operator:

$$(A * B) (C * D) +$$

The next operator is $+$ and the two operands to be added are the two products, so we add the two quantities to obtain the result.

The conversion from infix notation to reverse Polish notation must take into consideration the operational hierarchy adopted for infix notation. This hierarchy dictates that we first perform all arithmetic inside inner parentheses, then inside outer parentheses, and do multiplication and division operations before addition and subtraction operations. Consider the expression

$$(A + B) * [C * (D + E) + F]$$

To evaluate the expression we must first perform the arithmetic inside the parentheses $(A + B)$ and $(D + E)$. Next we must calculate the expression inside the square brackets. The multiplication of $C * (D + E)$ must be done prior to the addition of F since multiplication has precedence over addition. The last operation is the multiplication of the two terms between the parentheses and brackets. The expression can be converted to reverse Polish notation, without the use of parentheses, by taking into consideration the operation hierarchy. The converted expression is

$$AB + DE + C * F + *$$

Proceeding from left to right, we first add A and B, then add D and E. At this point we are left with

$$(A + B)(D + E)C * F + *$$

where $(A + B)$ and $(D + E)$ are each a *single* number obtained from the sum. The two operands for the next $*$ are C and $(D + E)$. These two numbers are multiplied and the product added to F. The final $*$ causes the multiplication of the two terms.

Evaluation of Arithmetic Expressions

Reverse Polish notation, combined with a stack arrangement of registers, is the most efficient way known for evaluating arithmetic expressions. This procedure is employed in some electronic calculators and also in some computers. The stack is particulary useful for handling long, complex problems involving chain calculations.

It is based on the fact that any arithmetic expression can be expressed in parentheses-free Polish notation.

The procedure consists of first converting the arithmetic expression into its equivalent reverse Polish notation. The operands are pushed into the stack in the order that they appear. The initiation of an operation depends on whether we have a calculator or a computer. In a calculator, the operators are entered through the keyboard. In a computer, they must be initiated by instructions that contain an operation field (no address field is required). The following micro-operations are executed with the stack when an operation is entered in a calculator or issued by the control in a computer: (1) the two top-most operands in the stack are used for the operation, and (2) the stack is popped and the result of the operation replaces the lower operand. By continuously pushing the operands into the stack and performing the operations as defined above, the expression is evaluated in the proper order and the final result remains on top of the stack.

The following numerical example may clarify this procedure. Consider the arithmetic expression

$$(3 * 4) + (5 * 6)$$

In reverse Polish notation, it is expressed as

$$3\ 4 * 5\ 6 * +$$

Now consider the stack operations shown in Fig. 7-10. Each box represents one stack operation and the arrow always points to the top of the stack. Scanning the expression from left to right, we encounter two operands. First the number 3 is pushed into the stack, then the number 4. The next symbol is the multiplication operator *. This

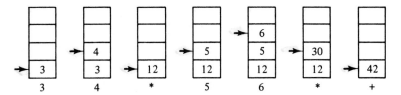

Fig. 7-10   Stack operations to evaluate $3 * 4 + 5 * 6$.

causes a multiplication of the two topmost items in the stack. The stack is then popped and the product is placed on top of the stack, replacing the two original operands. Next we encounter the two operands 5 and 6, so they are pushed into the stack. The stack operation that results from the next * replaces these two numbers by their product. The last operation causes an arithmetic addition of the two topmost numbers in the stack to produce the final result of 42.

Scientific calculators that employ an internal stack require that the user convert the arithmetic expressions into reverse Polish notation. Computers that use a stack organized CPU provide a system program to perform the conversion for the user.

Most compilers, irrespective of their CPU organization, convert all arithmetic expressions into Polish notation anyway because this is the most efficient method for translating arithmetic expressions into machine-language instructions. So in essence, a stack organized CPU may be more efficient in some applications than a CPU without a stack.

Stack-Organized CPU

In a stack-organized CPU, the top two locations of the stack are processor registers. The rest of the stack is stored in the memory unit. In this way, the operations that must be performed with the top two items of the stack are available in processor registers for manipulation. If the top of the stack happens to be in the second register, the stack must be adjusted to bring an operand from memory into a processor register.

A stack-organized CPU is depicted in Fig. 7-11(a). The two processor registers are labeled A and B. The rest of the stack remains in memory with the memory stack pointer MSP pointing to the top item in memory, not to the top of the entire stack which is at register A. Consider the case depicted in the fifth box of Fig. 7-10 and repeated in Fig. 7-11(b). Since register A is the top of the stack, it contains the number 6. Register B holds the next item, which is number 5. The third number

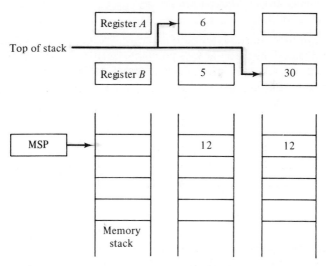

(a) General configuration   (b) Need for stack adjustment

Fig. 7-11   Stack organized CPU.

(12) is stored in the memory stack where MSP is currently pointing. A multiply operation multiplies the two numbers in A and B, and places the product in register B. Register B is now the top of the stack. In order to perform the arithmetic addition of the two remaining numbers, 30 and 12, it is necessary that the stack be adjusted.

This adjustment consists of popping the memory stack so that the number 30 moves into register *A* and 12 into register *B*.

Now that the two operands are in processor registers, they can be arithmetically added to provide the final result in register *B*. A stack adjustment operation is automatically carried out by the hardware in a stack-organized CPU.

7-4 INSTRUCTION FORMATS

The physical and logical structure of computers is normally described in reference manuals provided with the system. Such manuals explain the internal construction of the CPU, including the processor registers available and their logical capabilities. They list all hardware-implemented instructions, specify their binary code format, and provide a precise definition of each instruction. A computer will usually have a variety of instruction code formats. It is the function of the control unit within the CPU to interpret each instruction code and provide the necessary control functions needed to process the instruction.

The format of an instruction is usually depicted in a rectangular box symbolizing the bits of the instruction as they appear in memory words or in a control register. The bits of the instruction are divided into groups called fields. The most common fields found in instruction formats are:

1. An operation code field that specifies the operation to be performed.

2. An address field that designates a memory address or a processor register.

3. A mode field that specifies the way the operand or the effective address is determined.

Other special fields are sometimes employed under certain circumstances, as for example a field that gives the number of shifts in a shift-type instruction.

The operation code field of an instruction is a group of bits that define various processor operations, such as add, subtract, complement, and shift. The most common operations available in computer instructions are enumerated and discussed in Sec. 7-6. The bits that define the mode field of an instruction code specify a variety of alternatives for choosing the operands from the given address. The various addressing modes that have been formulated for digital computers are presented in Sec. 7-5. In this section we will be concerned with the address field of an instruction format and consider the effect of including multiple address fields in an instruction.

Operations specified by computer instructions are executed on some data stored in memory or processor registers. Operands residing in memory are specified by their memory address. Operands residing in processor registers are specified with a register address. A register address is a binary number of k bits that defines one of 2^k registers in the CPU. Thus, a CPU with 16 processor registers $R0$ through

$R15$ will have a register address field of four bits. The binary number 0101, for example, will designate register $R5$.

Computers may have instructions of several different lengths containing varying number of addresses. The number of address fields in the instruction format of a computer depends upon the internal organization of its registers. Most computers fall in one of three types of CPU organizations:

1. Single accumulator organization.

2. General register organization.

3. Stack organization.

An example of an accumulator-type organization is the basic computer presented in Chap. 5. All operations are performed with an implied accumulator register. The instruction format in this type of computer uses one address field. For example, the instruction that specifies an arithmetic addition is defined by an assembly-language instruction as

$$\text{ADD} \quad \text{X}$$

where X is the address of the operand. The ADD instruction in this case results in the operation $AC \leftarrow AC + M[X]$. AC is the accumulator register and $M[X]$ symbolized the memory word located at address X.

An example of a general register type of organization was presented in Fig. 7-1. The instruction format in this type of computer needs three register address fields. Thus, the instruction for an arithmetic addition may be written in an assembly language as

$$\text{ADD} \quad \text{R1, R2, R3}$$

to denote the operation $R1 \leftarrow R2 + R3$. The number of address fields in the instruction can be reduced from three to two if the destination register is the same as one of the source registers. Thus, the instruction

$$\text{ADD} \quad \text{R1, R2}$$

would denote the operation $R1 \leftarrow R1 + R2$. Only register addresses for $R1$ and $R2$ need be specified in this instruction.

Computers with multiple processor registers use the move instruction with a mnemonic MOV to symbolize a transfer instruction. Thus, the instruction

$$\text{MOV} \quad \text{R1, R2}$$

denotes the transfer $R1 \leftarrow R2$ (or $R2 \leftarrow R1$, depending on the particular computer). Thus, transfer-type instructions need two address fields to specify the source and the destination.

General register-type computers employ two or three address fields in their instruction format. Each address field may specify a processor register or a memory word. An instruction symbolized by

$$\text{ADD} \qquad R1, X$$

would specify the operation $R1 \leftarrow R1 + M[X]$. It has two address fields, one for register $R1$ and the other for the memory address X.

The stack-organized CPU was presented in Fig. 7-11. Computers with stack organization would have PUSH and POP instructions which require an address field. Thus, the instruction

$$\text{PUSH} \qquad X$$

will push the word at address X to the top of the stack. The stack pointer is automatically updated. Operation-type instructions do not need an address field in stack-organized computers. This is because the operation is performed on the two items which are on top of the stack. The instruction

$$\text{ADD}$$

in a stack computer consists of an operation code only with no address field. This operation has the effect of popping the two top numbers from the stack, adding the numbers, and pushing the sum into the stack. There is no need to specify operands with an address field since all operands are implied to be in the stack.

Most computers fall in one of the three types of organizations that have just been described. Some computers combine features from more than one organizational structure. For example, the Intel 8080 microprocessor has seven CPU registers, one of which is an accumulator register. As a consequence, the processor has some of the characteristics of a general register type and some of the characteristics of an accumulator type. All arithmetic and logic instructions, as well as the load and store instructions, use the accumulator register, so these instructions have only one address field. On the other hand, instructions that transfer data among the seven processor registers have a format that contains two register address fields. Moreover, the Intel 8080 processor has a stack pointer and instructions to push and pop from a memory stack. The processor, however, does not have the zero-address-type instructions which are characteristic of a stack-organized CPU.

To illustrate the influence of the number of addresses on computer programs, we will evaluate the arithmetic statement

$$X = (A + B) * (C + D)$$

using zero, one, two, or three address instructions.

We will use the symbols ADD, SUB, MUL, and DIV for the four arithmetic operations; MOV for the transfer-type operation; and LOAD and STORE for transfers to and from memory and *AC* register. We will assume that the operands are in memory addresses *A*, *B*, *C*, and *D*, and the result must be stored in memory at address *X*.

Three-Address Instructions

Computers with three-address instruction formats can use each address field to specify either a processor register or a memory operand. The program in assembly language that evluates $X = (A + B) * (C + D)$ is shown below, together with comments that explain the register transfer operation of each instruction.

ADD	R1, A, B	$R1 \leftarrow M[A] + M[B]$
ADD	R2, C, D	$R2 \leftarrow M[C] + M[D]$
MUL	X, R1, R2	$M[X] \leftarrow R1 * R2$

It is assumed that the computer has two processor registers *R1* and *R2*. The symbol *M[A]* denotes the operand at memory address symbolized by *A*.

The advantage of the three-address format is that it results in short programs when evaluating arithmetic expressions. The disadvantage is that the binary-coded instructions require too many bits to specify three addresses. An example of a commercial computer that uses three-address instructions is the Cyber 170. The instruction formats in the Cyber 170 computer are restricted to either three register address fields or two register address fields and one memory address field.

Two-Address Instructions

Two-address instructions are the most common in commercial computers. Here again each address field can specify either a processor register or a memory word. The program to evaluate $X = (A + B) * (C + D)$ is as follows:

MOV	R1, A	$R1 \leftarrow M[A]$
ADD	R1, B	$R1 \leftarrow R1 + M[B]$
MOV	R2, C	$R2 \leftarrow M[C]$
ADD	R2, D	$R2 \leftarrow R2 + M[D]$
MUL	R1, R2	$R1 \leftarrow R1 * R2$
MOV	X, R1	$M[X] \leftarrow R1$

The MOV instruction moves or transfers the operands to and from memory and processor registers. The first symbol listed in an instruction is assumed to be both a source and the destination where the result of the operation is transferred.

An example of a commercial computer that uses two-address instructions is the PDP-11. The two address fields in the PDP-11 computer instructions always specify processor registers. However, depending on the addressing mode (explained in the next section) the specified register may contain the operand or may contain the address of a memory operand.

One-Address Instructions

One-address instructions use an implied accumulator (AC) register for all data manipulation. For multiplication and division there is a need for a second register, as explained in Sec. 9-6. However, here we will neglect the second register and assume that the AC contains the result of all operations. The program to evaluate $X = (A + B) * (C + D)$ is

LOAD	A	$AC \leftarrow M[A]$
ADD	B	$AC \leftarrow AC + M[B]$
STORE	T	$M[T] \leftarrow AC$
LOAD	C	$AC \leftarrow M[C]$
ADD	D	$AC \leftarrow AC + M[D]$
MUL	T	$AC \leftarrow AC * M[T]$
STORE	X	$M[X] \leftarrow AC$

All operations are done between the AC register and a memory operand. T is the address of a temporary memory location required for storing the intermediate result. An example of a commercial computer that uses one-address instructions is the PDP-8.

Zero-Address Instructions

A stack-organized computer does not use an address field for the instructions ADD and MUL. The PUSH and POP instructions, however, need an address field to specify the operand that communicates with the stack. The following program shows how $X = (A + B) * (C + D)$ will be written for a stack-organized computer. (TOS stands for top of stack.)

PUSH	A	$TOS \leftarrow A$
PUSH	B	$TOS \leftarrow B$
ADD		$TOS \leftarrow (A + B)$
PUSH	C	$TOS \leftarrow C$
PUSH	D	$TOS \leftarrow D$
ADD		$TOS \leftarrow (C + D)$
MUL		$TOS \leftarrow (C + D) * (A + B)$
POP	X	$M[X] \leftarrow TOS$

In order to evaluate arithmetic expressions in a stack computer, it is necessary to convert the expression into reverse Polish notation. The name zero-address is given to this type of computer because of the absence of an address field in the computational instructions. An example of a stack-organized commercial computer is the Burroughs-6700.

7-5 ADDRESSING MODES

The operation field of an instruction specifies the operation to be performed. This operation must be executed on some data stored in computer registers or memory words. The way the operands are chosen during program execution is dependent on the *addressing mode* of the instruction. The addressing mode specifies a rule for interpreting or modifying the address field of the instruction before the operand is actually referenced. An example of an address mode field is the I bit in the basic computer of Chap. 5, which is used to distinguish between a direct and an indirect address.

Computers use addressing mode techniques for the purpose of accommodating one or both of the following provisions:

1. To give programming versatility to the user by providing such facilities as pointers, counters, indexing, and program relocation.

2. To reduce the number of bits in the address field of the instruction.

To the inexperienced user, the variety of addressing modes in some computers may seem excessively complicated. However, the availability of different addressing schemes gives the experienced programmer flexibility for writing programs that are more efficient with respect to the number of instructions and execution time.

Although most addressing modes modify the address field of the instruction, there are two modes that need no address field at all. These are the implied and immediate modes.

Implied Mode: In this mode the operands are specified implicitly in the definition of the instruction. For example, the instruction "complement accumulator" is an implied-mode instruction because the operand in the accumulator register is implied in the definition of the instruction. In fact, all register reference instructions that use an accumulator are implied-mode instructions. Zero-address instructions in a stack-organized computer are implied-mode instructions since the operands are implied to be on top of the stack.

Immediate Mode: In this mode the operand is specified in the instruction itself. In other words, an immediate-mode instruction has an operand field rather than an address field. The operand field contains the actual operand to be used in conjunction with the operation specified in the instruction. Immediate-mode instructions are useful for initializing registers to a constant value.

It was mentioned previously that the address field of an instruction may specify either a memory word or a processor register. When the address field specifies a processor register, the instruction is said to be in the register mode.

Register Mode: In this mode the operands are in registers which reside within the CPU. The particular register is selected from a register field in the instruction. A k-bit field can specify any one of 2^k registers.

Register-Indirect Mode: In this mode the instruction specifies a register in the CPU whose contents give the address of the operand in memory. In other words, the selected register contains the address of the operand rather than the operand itself. Before using a register-indirect mode instruction, the programmer must ensure that the memory address of the operand is placed in the processor register with a previous instruction. A reference to the register is then equivalent to specifying a memory address. The advantage of a register-indirect mode instruction is that the address field of the instruction uses fewer bits to select a register than would have been required to specify a memory address directly.

Autoincrement or Autodecrement Mode: This is similar to the register-indirect mode except that the register is incremented or decremented after (or before) its value is used to access memory. When the address stored in the register refers to a table of data in memory, it is necessary to increment or decrement the register after every access to the table. This can be achieved by using the increment or decrement instruction. However, because it is such a common requirement, some computers incorporate a special mode which automatically increments or decrements the content of the register after data access.

The address field of an instruction is used by the control unit in the CPU to obtain the operand from memory. Sometimes the value given in the address field is the address of the operand, but sometimes it is just an address from which the address of the operand is calculated. To differentiate among the various addressing modes it is necessary to distinguish between the address part of the instruction and the effective address used by the control when executing the instruction. The *effective address* is defined to be the memory address obtained from the computation dictated by the given addressing mode. The effective address is the address of the operand in a computational-type instruction. It is the address where control branches in response to a branch-type instruction. We have already defined two addressing modes in Chapter 5. They are summarized here for reference.

Direct-Address Mode: In this mode the effective address is equal to the address part of the instruction. The operand resides in memory and its address is given directly by the address field of the instruction. In a branch-type instruction the address field specifies the actual branch address.

Indirect-Address Mode: In this mode the address field of the instruction gives the address where the effective address is stored in memory. Control fetches the instruction from memory and uses its address part to access memory again to read the effective address. The indirect address mode is also explained in Sec. 5-1 in conjunction with Fig. 5-2.

A few addressing modes require that the address field of the instruction be added to the content of a specific register in the CPU. The effective address in these modes is obtained from the following computation:

$$\text{Effective address} = \text{Address part of instruction}$$
$$+ \text{Content of CPU register}$$

The CPU register used in the computation may be the program counter, an index register, or a base register. In either case we have a different addressing mode which is used for a different application.

Relative Address Mode: In this mode the content of the program counter is added to the address part of the instruction in order to obtain the effective address. The address part of the instruction is usually a signed number (in 2's complement representation) which can be either positive or negative. When this number is added to the content of the program counter, the result produces an effective address whose position in memory is relative to the address of the next instruction. To clarify with an example, assume that the program counter contains the number 825 and the address part of the instruction contains the number 24. The instruction at location 825 is read from memory during the fetch cycle and the program counter is then incremented by one to 826. The effective address computation for the relative address mode is $826 + 24 = 850$. This is 24 memory locations forward from the address of the next instruction. Relative addressing is often used with branch-type instructions when the branch address is in the area surrounding the instruction word itself. It results in a shorter address field in the instruction format since the relative address can be specified with a smaller number of bits compared to the number of bits required to designate the entire memory address.

Indexed Addressing Mode: In this mode the content of an index register is added to the address part of the instruction to obtain the effective address. The index register is a special CPU register that contains an index value. The address field of the instruction defines the beginning address of a data array in memory. Each operand in the array is stored in memory relative to the beginning address. The distance between the beginning address and the address of the operand is the index value stored in the index register. Any operand in the array can be accessed with the same instruction provided the index register contains the correct index value.

The index register can be incremented to facilitate the access to consecutive operands. Note that if an index-type instruction does not include an address field in its format, the instruction converts to the register-indirect mode of operation.

Some computers dedicate one CPU register to function solely as an index register. This register is involved implicitly when the index-mode instruction is used. In computers with many processor registers, any one of the CPU registers can contain the index number. In such a case, the register must be specified explicitly in a register field within the instruction format.

Base Register Addressing Mode: In this mode the content of a base register is added to the address part of the instruction to obtain the effective address. This is similar to the indexed addressing mode except that the register is now called a base register instead of an index register. The difference between the two modes is in the way they are used, rather than in the way that they are computed. An index register is assumed to hold an index number which is relative to the address part of the instruction. A base register is assumed to hold a base address and the address field of the instruction gives a displacement relative to this base address. The base register addressing mode is used in computers to facilitate the relocation of programs in memory. When programs and data are moved from one segment of memory to another, as required in multiprogramming systems, the address values of instructions must reflect this change of position. With a base register, the displacement values of instructions do not have to change. Only the value of the base register requires updating to reflect the beginning of a new memory segment.

In some computers, the addressing mode of the instruction is specified with a distinct binary code, just like the operation code is specified. Other computers use a single binary code that designates both the operation and the mode of the instruction. Instructions may be defined with a variety of addressing modes. Sometimes, two or more addressing modes are combined in one instruction. In order to appreciate the interrelation between the addressing modes and the formulation of computer instructions we present two examples from commercial computers.

Example from the IBM-370 Computer

The IBM-370 computer uses a memory unit with a capacity of 2^{24} bytes. (A byte is equal to 8 bits.) It has 16 processor registers in the CPU. Each register can be used for data manipulation, as an index register, or as a base register. An effective address for memory must have 24 bits. A processor register is specified with a register field of 4 bits. The computer has five different instruction formats, one of which is shown in Fig. 7-12. This format is called the *RX* format; *R* is for register and *X* stands for index. This type of instruction combines three addressing modes: register addressing, index addressing, and base register addressing.

The instruction format shown in Fig. 7-12(a) has 32 bits. It is divided into five fields: an operation code field of eight bits, three register fields of four bits each,

8	4	4	4	12
Opcode	R	XR	BR	D

(a) Instruction format: R = register; XR = index register; BR = base register; D = displacement address

5A	8	6	4	430

(b) Format for the add instruction: $R8 \leftarrow R8 + M[R4 + D + R6]$

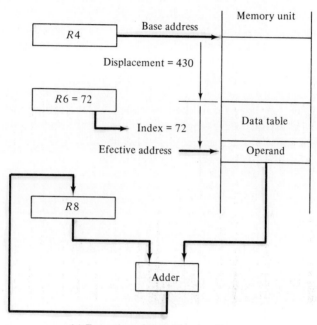

(c) Execution of the add instruction

Fig. 7-12 IBM-370 RX instruction format.

and a displacement address field of 12 bits. The R field designates a register number for an operand, the XR field designates an index register, and the BR field specifies a base register. The address field D gives a 12-bit displacement number relative to the base address in BR.

Figure. 7-12(b) shows the format of the add instruction. The operation code is equivalent to the hexadecimal number 5A. The three registers used are: $R8$ for the operand, $R6$ for the index, and $R4$ for the base address. This is a two-address instruction symbolized by the register transfer statement

$$R8 \leftarrow R8 + M[R4 + D + R6]$$

One of the operands is in register $R8$ and the second operand is in memory. The way the operand is found in memory is shown in Fig. 7-12(c). $R4$ is the base register, so its content gives a base address in memory. The 12-bit displacement address number is added to the 24-bit content of the base register to find the beginning of a table of numbers. Index register $R6$ is assumed to contain an index number equal to 72. The index number is added to the base-plus-displacement value to obtain the effective address. The operand at the effective address is added to the operand in register $R8$ and the sum transferred back to $R8$.

Addressing on the PDP-11 Computer

The PDP-11 uses a memory unit with 2^{16} bytes. A memory word consists of two bytes or 16 bits. The computer has eight CPU registers of 16 bits each. Therefore, a memory address must have 16 bits and a processor register must be specified with a register address of three bits. The computer has a variety of instruction formats, one of which is shown in Fig. 7-13(a). This is a two-address instruction format. It consists of 16 bits divided into five fields: an operation code field of four bits, two mode fields of three bits each, and two register fields of three bits each. The first mode field specifies the addressing mode for the source register. The second mode field specifies the addressing mode for the destination register. The source and destination registers are specified in the SR and DR fields, respectively.

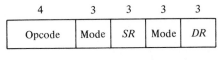

4	3	3	3	3
Opcode	Mode	SR	Mode	DR

(a) Instruction format: SR = source register;
DR = destination register

0110	001	100	000	101

(b) Format for add instruction: $R5 \leftarrow R5 + M[R4]$

Fig. 7-13 Format of a PDP-11 two-address instruction.

Figure. 7-13(b) shows the format of an add instruction. The operation code is 0110. The registers used are $R4$ ($SR = 100$) for the source and $R5$ ($DR = 101$) for the destination. As will be shown subsequently, code 001 designates a register indirect mode for the source and code 000 designates register mode for the destination. This instruction is written in the PDP-11 assembly language as

ADD (R4), R5

The first register $R4$ is the source and the parentheses enclosing it designate a register indirect mode. The second register $R5$ is the other source register as well as the destination register. This two-address instruction performs the operation:

$$R5 \leftarrow R5 + M[R4]$$

One of the operands is in register $R5$ and the other operand is in memory at the address given by the content of register $R4$.

The three bits in the mode field provide a code for specifying eight different addressing modes. The eight modes used in the PDP-11 are listed in Table 7-4. The

TABLE 7-4   PDP-11 Addressing Modes

Binary Code	Mode	Name	Assembler Symbolic	Location of Operand
000	0	Register	R	R
001	1	Register indirect	(R)	$M[R]$
010	2	Autoincrement	$(R)+$	$M[R]$ then $R \leftarrow R + 2$
100	4	Autodecrement	$-(R)$	$R \leftarrow R - 2$ then $M[R]$
110	6	Index (two words)	$X(R)$	$M[R + X]$
011	3	Autoincrement indirect	$@(R)+$	$M[M[R]]$ then $R \leftarrow R + 2$
101	5	Autodecrement indirect	$@-(R)$	$R \leftarrow R - 2$ then $M[M[R]]$
111	7	Index indirect (two words)	$@X(R)$	$M[M[R + X]]$

assembler symbolic column shows the way the addressing modes are symbolized in the assembly language of the PDP-11. R is the selected register associated with the mode field. The location of the operand is given in symbolic form. $M[R]$ designates the memory word whose address is given by the content of register R.

In the register mode, the operand is in the selected register R. In the register indirect mode, the effective address is in the selected register R. The operand is in memory at the address given by the value in R. The autoincrement mode is similar to the register indirect except that the register is incremented after it is used to access memory for the operand. If the operand is a byte, the register is incremented by 1, but if the operand is a 16-bit word (two bytes), R is incremented by 2. Table 7-4 shows R incremented by 2 assuming word operands.

The autodecrement mode is also similar to the register indirect mode except that the register is now decremented *before* it is used to access memory. The index-mode instruction consists of two words. The first is the 16-bit instruction code and the second is a 16-bit address field designated by X. The selected register R is now considered as an index register. Its index number is added to the address field X to obtain the effective address. If both mode fields in the instruction specify an index mode, the instruction would need three words with two address fields, one for each operand. Note that here X is the address field of the instruction and not the index register.

The last three modes listed in the table are an extension of the previous three modes in that they provide a memory indirect addressing capability. The autoincrement indirect and the autodecrement indirect modes include both register indirect and memory indirect capabilities. The memory transfer $M[M[R]]$ symbolizes a double access to memory. First, the value in R is used as an address to access memory to read the effective address. Symbolizing the effective address by EA, we have $EA = M[R]$. The effective address is then used to access memory to read the operand. In symbolic form the operand $= M[EA]$, that is, the memory word given by the effective address.

The index indirect mode combines both the index and the indirect addressing modes in one instruction. The index value in the selected register R is added to the address field X to obtain an address. This address is then used to access memory to read the effective address. The effective address is then used to access memory again to read the operand.

7-6 DATA TRANSFER AND MANIPULATION

Computers provide an extensive set of instructions to give the user the flexibility to carry out various computational tasks. The instruction set of different computers differ from each other mostly in the way the operands are determined from the address and mode fields. The actual operations available in the instruction set are not very different from one computer to another. It so happens that the binary code assignments in the operation code field is different in different computers, even for the same operation. It may also happen that the symbolic name given to instructions in the assembly language notation is different in different computers, even for the same instruction. Nevertheless, there is a set of basic operations that most, if not all, computers include in their instruction repertoire. The basic set of operations available in a typical computer is the subject that will be covered in this and the next section.

Most computer instructions can be classified into three categories:

1. Data transfer instructions.
2. Data manipulation instructions.
3. Program control instructions.

Data transfer instructions cause transfer of data from one location to another without changing the binary information content. Data manipulation instructions are those that perform arithmetic, logic, and shift operations. Program control instructions provide decision-making capabilities and change the path taken by the program when executed in the computer. The instruction set of a particular computer determines the register-transfer operations and control decisions that are available to the user.

Data Transfer Instructions

Data transfer instructions move data from one place in the computer to another without changing the data content. The most common transfers are between memory and processor registers, between processor registers and input or output, and between the processor registers themselves. Table 7-5 gives a list of eight data transfer instruc-

TABLE 7-5 Typical Data Transfer Instructions

Name	Mnemonic
Load	LD
Store	ST
Move	MOV
Exchange	XCH
Input	IN
Output	OUT
Push	PUSH
Pop	POP

tions used in many computers. Accompanying each instruction is a mnemonic symbol. This is the assembly language abbreviation recommended by a proposed standard (reference 8). It must be realized that different computers use different mnemonics for the same instruction name.

The *load* instruction has been used mostly to designate a transfer from memory to a processor register, usually an accumulator. The *store* instruction designates a transfer from a processor register into memory. The *move* instruction has been used in computers with multiple CPU registers to designate a transfer from one register to another. It has also been used for data transfers between CPU registers and memory or between two memory words. The *exchange* instruction swaps information between two registers or a register and a memory word. The *input* and *output* instructions transfer data among processor registers and input or output terminals. The *push* and *pop* instructions transfer data between processor registers and a memory stack.

It must be realized that the instructions listed in Table 7-5, as well as in subsequent tables in this section, are often associated with a variety of addressing modes. Some assembly-language convertions modify the mnemonic symbol to differentiate between the different addressing modes. For example, the mnemonic for *load immediate* becomes LDI. Other assembly-language conventions use a special character to designate the addressing mode. For example, the immediate mode is recognized from a pound sign # placed before the operand. In any case, the important thing is to realize that each instruction can occur with a variety of addressing modes. As an example, consider the *load to accumulator* instruction when used with eight different addressing modes. Table 7-6 shows the recommended assembly-language convention and the actual transfer accomplished in each case. *ADR* stands for an

TABLE 7-6   Eight Addressing Modes for the Load Instruction

Mode	Assembly Convention	Register Transfer
Direct address	LD ADR	$AC \leftarrow M[ADR]$
Indirect address	LD @ADR	$AC \leftarrow M[M[ADR]]$
Relative address	LD $ADR	$AC \leftarrow M[PC + ADR]$
Immediate operand	LD #NBR	$AC \leftarrow NBR$
Index addressing	LD ADR(X)	$AC \leftarrow M[ADR + XR]$
Register	LD R1	$AC \leftarrow R1$
Register indirect	LD (R1)	$AC \leftarrow M[R1]$
Autoincrement	LD (R1)+	$AC \leftarrow M[R1], R1 \leftarrow R1 + 1$

address, NBR is a number or operand, X is an index register, $R1$ is a processor register, and AC is the accumulator register. The @ character symbolizes an indirect address. The $ character before an address makes the address relative to the program counter PC. The # character precedes the operand in an immediate-mode instruction. An indexed mode instruction is recognized by a register which is placed in parentheses after the symbolic address. The register mode is symbolized by giving the name of a processor register. In the register-indirect mode, the name of the register that holds the memory address is enclosed in parentheses. The autoincrement mode is distinguished from the register-indirect mode by placing a plus after the parenthesized register. The autodecrement mode would use a minus instead. To be able to write assembly-language programs for a computer, it is necessary to know the type of instructions available and also to be familiar with the addressing modes used in the particular computer.

Data Manipulation Instructions

Data manipulation instructions perform operations on data and provide the computational capabilities for the computer. The data manipulation instructions in a typical computer are usually divided into three basic types:

1. Arithmetic instructions.
2. Logical and bit manipulation instructions.
3. Shift instructions.

A list of data manipulation instructions will look very much like the list of micro-operations given in Chap. 4. It must be realized, however, that each instruction when executed in the computer must go through the fetch cycle to read its binary code value from memory. The operands must also be brought into processor registers according to the rules of the instruction addressing mode. The last step is to execute the instruction in the processor. This last step is implemented by means of micro-operations as explained in Chap. 4 or through an ALU and shifter as shown in Fig. 7-1. Some of the arithmetic instructions need special circuits for their implementation.

Arithmetic Instructions

The four basic arithmetic operations are addition, subtraction, multiplication, and division. Most computers provide instructions for all four operations. Some small computers have only addition and possibly subtraction instructions. The multiplication and division must then be generated by means of software subroutines. The four basic arithmetic operations are sufficient for formulating solutions to scientific problems when expressed in terms of numerical analysis methods.

A list of typical arithmetic instructions is given in Table 7-7. The increment

TABLE 7-7   Typical Arithmetic Instructions

Name	Mnemonic
Increment	INC
Decrement	DEC
Add	ADD
Subtract	SUB
Multiply	MUL
Divide	DIV
Add with carry	ADDC
Subtract with borrow	SUBB
Negate (2's complement)	NEG

instruction adds 1 to the value stored in a register or memory word. One common characteristic of the increment operations when executed in processor registers is that a binary number of all 1's when incremented produces a result of all 0's. The decrement instruction subtracts 1 from a value stored in a register or memory word. A number with all 0's, when decremented, produces a number with all 1's.

The add, subtract, multiply, and divide instructions may be available for different types of data. The data type assumed to be in processor registers during the execution of these arithmetic operations is included in the definition of the operation code. An arithmetic instruction may specify fixed-point or floating-point data, binary or decimal data, single-precision or double-precision data. The various data types are presented in Chap. 3.

It is not uncommon to find computers with three or more add instructions: one for binary integers, one for floating-point operands, and one for decimal operands. The mnemonics for three add instructions that specify different data types are shown below.

ADDI   Add two binary integer numbers

ADDF   Add two floating-point numbers

ADDD   Add two decimal numbers in BCD

The design of an arithmetic unit for integers is carried out in Chap. 9. Algorithms for floating-point and decimal arithmetic operations are developed in Chap. 10.

The number of bits in any register is of finite length and therefore the results of arithmetic operations are of finite precision. Some computers provide hardware double-precision operations where the length of each operand is taken to be the length of two memory words. Most small computers provide special instructions to facilitate double-precision arithmetic. A special carry flip-flop is used to store the carry from an operation. The instruction "add with carry" performs the addition on two operands plus the value of the carry from the previous computation. Similarly, the "subtract with borrow" instruction subtracts two words and a borrow which may have resulted from a previous subtract operation. The negate instruction forms the 2's complement of a number, effectively reversing the sign of an integer when represented in the signed-2's complement form.

Logical and Bit Manipulation Instructions

Logical instructions perform binary operations on strings of bits stored in registers. They are useful for manipulating individual bits or a group of bits that represent binary-coded information. The logical instructions consider each bit of the operand separately and treat it as a Boolean variable. By proper application of the logical instructions it is possible to change bit values, to clear a group of bits, or to insert new bit values into operands stored in registers or memory words.

Some typical logical and bit manipulation instructions are listed in Table 7-8.

TABLE 7-8 Typical Logical and Bit
Manipulation Instructions

Name	Mnemonic
Clear	CLR
Complement	COM
AND	AND
OR	OR
Exclusive-OR	XOR
Clear carry	CLRC
Set carry	SETC
Complement carry	COMC
Enable interrupt	EI
Disable interrupt	DI

The clear instruction causes the specified operand to be replaced by 0's. The complement instruction produces the 1's complement by inverting all the bits of the operand. The AND, OR, and XOR instructions produce the corresponding logical operations on individual bits of the operands. Although they perform Boolean operations, when used in computer instructions, the logical instructions should be considered as performing bit manipulation operations. There are three bit manipulation operations possible: a selected bit can be cleared to 0, or can be set to 1, or can be complemented. The three logical instructions are usually applied to do just that.

The AND instruction is used to clear a bit or a selected group of bits of an operand. For any Boolean variable x, the relationships $x \cdot 0 = 0$ and $x \cdot 1 = x$ dictate that a binary variable ANDed with a 0 produces a 0; but the variable does not change in value when ANDed with a 1. Therefore, the AND instruction can be used to selectively clear bits of an operand by ANDing the operand with another operand that has 0's in the bit positions that must be cleared. The AND instruction is also called a *mask* because it masks or inserts 0's in a selected portion of an operand.

The OR instruction is used to set a bit or a selected group of bits of an operand. For any Boolean variable x, the relationships $x + 1 = 1$ and $x + 0 = x$ dictate that a binary variable ORed with a 1 produces a 1; but the variable does not change when ORed with a 0. Therefore, the OR instruction can be used to selectively set bits of an operand by ORing it with another operand with 1's in the bit positions that must be set to 1.

Similarly, the XOR instruction is used to selectively complement bits of an operand. This is because of the Boolean relationships $x \oplus 1 = x'$ and $x \oplus 0 = x$. Thus, a binary variable is complemented when XORed with a 1 but does not change in value when XORed with a 0. Numerical examples showing the three logic operations can be found in Sec. 4-4.

A few other bit manipulation instructions are included in Table 7-8. Individual bits such as a carry can be cleared, set, or complemented with appropriate instructions. Another example is a flip-flop that controls the interrupt facility and is either enabled or disabled by means of bit manipulation instructions.

Shift Instructions

Instructions to shift the content of an operand are quite useful and are often provided in several variations. Shifts are operations in which the bits of a word are moved to the left or right. The bit shifted in at the end of the word determines the type of shift used. Shift instructions may specify either logical shifts, arithmetic shifts, or rotate-type operations. In either case the shift may be to the right or to the left.

Table 7-9 lists four types of shift instructions. The logical shift inserts 0 to the end bit position. The end position is the leftmost bit for shift right and the rightmost bit position for the shift left. Arithmetic shifts usually conform with the rules for signed-2's complement numbers. These rules are given in Table 4-6. The arithmetic shift-right instruction must preserve the sign bit in the left-most position. The sign bit is shifted to the right together with the rest of the number, but the sign bit itself remains unchanged. This is a shift-right operation with the end bit remaining the same. The arithmetic shift-left instruction inserts 0 to the end position and is identical to the logical shift-left instruction. For this reason many computers do not provide a distinct arithmetic shift-left instruction when the logical shift-left instruction is already available.

TABLE 7-9   Typical Shift Instructions

Name	Mnemonic
Logical shift right	SHR
Logical shift left	SHL
Arithmetic shift right	SHRA
Arithmetic shift left	SHLA
Rotate right	ROR
Rotate left	ROL
Rotate right through carry	RORC
Rotate left through carry	ROLC

The rotate instructions produce a circular shift. Bits shifted out at one end of the word are not lost as in a logical shift but are circulated back into the other end. The rotate through carry instruction treats a carry bit as an extension of the register whose word is being rotated. Thus, a rotate left through carry instruction transfers the carry bit into the rightmost bit position of the register, transfers the leftmost bit position into the carry, and at the same time, shifts the entire register to the left.

Some computers have a multiple-field format for the shift instructions. One field contains the operation code and the others specify the type of shift and the number of times that an operand is to be shifted. A possible instruction code format of a shift instruction may include five fields as follows:

$$\text{OP} \quad \text{REG} \quad \text{TYPE} \quad \text{RL} \quad \text{COUNT}$$

Here OP is the operation code field; REG is a register address that specifies the location of the operand; TYPE is a 2-bit field specifying the four different types of shifts; RL is a 1-bit field specifying a shift right or left; and COUNT is a k-bit field specifying up to $2^k - 1$ shifts. With such a format, it is possible to specify the type of shift, the direction, and the number of shifts, all in one instruction.

7-7 PROGRAM CONTROL

Instructions are always stored in successive memory locations. When processed in the CPU, the instructions are fetched from consecutive memory locations and executed. Each time an instruction is fetched from memory, the program counter is incremented so that it contains the address of the next instruction in sequence. After the execution of a data transfer or data manipulation instruction, control returns to the fetch cycle with the program counter containing the address of the instruction next in sequence. On the other hand, a program control-type instruction, when executed, may change the address value in the program counter and cause the flow of control to be altered. In other words, program control instructions specify conditions for altering the content of the program counter, while data transfer and manipulation instructions specify conditions for data processing operations. The change in value of the program counter as a result of the execution of a program control instruction causes a break in the sequence of instruction execution. This is an important feature in digital computers, as it provides control over the flow of program execution and a capability for branching to different program segments.

Some typical program control instructions are listed in Table 7-10. The branch and jump instructions are used interchangeably to mean the same thing, but sometimes

TABLE 7-10   Typical Program Control Instructions

Name	Mnemonic
Branch	BR
Jump	JMP
Skip	SKP
Call	CALL
Return	RET
Compare (by subtraction)	CMP
Test (by ANDing)	TST

they are used to denote different addressing modes. The branch is usually a one-address instruction. It is written in assembly language as BR ADR, where ADR is a symbolic name for an address. When executed, the branch instruction causes a transfer of the value of ADR into the program counter. Since the program counter contains the address of the instruction to be executed, the next instruction will come from location ADR.

Branch and jump instructions may be conditional or unconditional. An unconditional branch instruction causes a branch to the specified address without any conditions. The conditional branch instruction specifies a condition for the branch such as branch if positive or branch if zero. If the condition is met, the program counter is loaded with the branch address and the next instruction is taken from this address. If the condition is not met, the program counter is not changed and the next instruction is taken from the next location in sequence.

The skip instruction does not need an address field and is, therefore, a zero-address instruction. A conditional skip instruction will skip the next instruction if the condition is met. This is accomplished by incrementing the program counter during the execute cycle in addition to its being incremented during the fetch cycle. If the condition is not met, control proceeds with the next instruction in sequence where the programmer inserts an unconditional branch instruction. Thus, a skip-branch pair of instructions causes a branch if the condition is not met, while a single conditional branch instruction causes a branch if the condition is met.

The call and return instructions are used in conjunction with subroutines. Their performance and implementation is discussed later in this section. The compare and test instructions do not change the program sequence directly. They are listed in

Table 7-10 because of their application in setting conditions for subsequent conditional branch instructions. The compare instruction performs a subtraction between two operands but the result of the operation is not retained. However, certain status bit conditions are set as a result of the operation. Similarly, the test instruction performs the logical AND of two operands and updates certain status bits without retaining the result or changing the operands. The status bits of interest are the carry bit, the sign bit, a zero indication, and an overflow condition. The generation of these status bits will be discussed first and then we will show how they are used in conditional branch instructions.

Status Bit Conditions

It is sometimes convenient to supplement the ALU circuit in the CPU with a status register where status bit conditions can be stored for further analysis. Status bits are also called *condition-code* bits or *flag* bits. Figure 7-14 shows the block diagram.

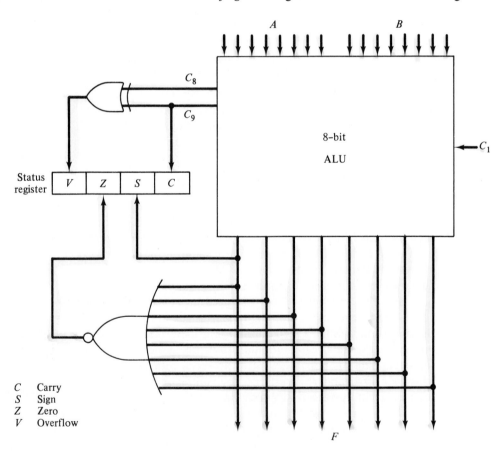

Fig. 7-14 Setting bits in status register.

of an 8-bit ALU with a 4-bit status register. The four status bits are symbolized by $C, S, Z,$ and $V.$ The bits are set or cleared as a result of an operation performed in the ALU.

1. Bit C is set if the output carry of the ALU is 1. It is cleared if the output carry is 0.

2. Bit S is set if the highest-order bit of the result in the output of the ALU (the sign bit) is 1. It is cleared if the highest-order bit is 0.

3. Bit Z is set if the output of the ALU contains all 0's, and cleared otherwise. $Z = 1$ if the result is zero, and $Z = 0$ if the result is nonzero.

4. Bit V is set if the exclusive-OR of carries C_8 and C_9 is 1, and cleared otherwise. This is the condition for overflow when the numbers are in signed-2's complement representation (see Sec. 3-2). For the 8-bit ALU, V is set if the result is greater than 127 or less than $-128.$

The status bits can be checked after an ALU operation to determine certain relationships that exist between the values of A and $B.$ If bit V is set after the addition of two signed numbers, it indicates an overflow condition. If Z is set after an exclusive-OR operation, it indicates that $A = B.$ This is so because $x \oplus x = 0,$ and the exclusive-OR of two equal operands gives an all-0's result which sets the Z bit. A single bit in A can be checked to determine if it is 0 or 1 by masking all bits except the bit in question and then checking the Z status bit. For example, let $A = 101x1100,$ where x is the bit to be checked. The AND operation of A with $B = 00010000$ produces a result $000x0000.$ If $x = 0,$ the Z status bit is set, but if $x = 1,$ the Z bit is cleared since the result is not zero. The AND operation can be generated with the TEST instruction listed in Table 7-10 if the original content of A must be preserved.

Conditional Branch Instructions

Table 7-11 gives a list of the most common branch instructions. Each mnemonic is constructed with the letter B (for branch) and an abbreviation of the condition name. When the opposite condition state is used, the letter N (for no) is inserted to define the 0 state. Thus, BC is Branch on Carry, and BNC is Branch on No Carry. If the stated condition is true, then program control is transferred to the address specified by the instruction. If not, control continues with the instruction that follows. The conditional instructions can be associated also with the jump, skip, call, or return type of program control instructions.

   The zero status bit is used for testing if the result of an ALU operation is equal to zero or not. The carry bit is used to check if there is a carry out of the most significant bit position of the ALU. It is also used in conjunction with the rotate instructions to check the bit shifted from the end position of a register into the carry position. The sign bit reflects the state of the most significant bit of the output from the ALU. $S = 0$ denotes a positive sign and $S = 1,$ a negative sign. Therefore, a branch on

TABLE 7-11 Conditional Branch Instructions

Mnemonic	Branch condition	Tested condition
BZ	Branch if zero	$Z = 1$
BNZ	Branch if not zero	$Z = 0$
BC	Branch if carry	$C = 1$
BNC	Branch if no carry	$C = 0$
BP	Branch if plus	$S = 0$
BM	Branch if minus	$S = 1$
BV	Branch if overflow	$V = 1$
BNV	Branch if no overflow	$V = 0$
Unsigned compare conditions $(A - B)$		
BHI	Branch if higher	$A > B$
BHE	Branch if higher or equal	$A \geq B$
BLO	Branch if lower	$A < B$
BLOE	Branch if lower or equal	$A \leq B$
BE	Branch if equal	$A = B$
BNE	Branch if not equal	$A \neq B$
Signed compare conditions $(A - B)$		
BGT	Branch if greater than	$A > B$
BGE	Branch if greater or equal	$A \geq B$
BLT	Branch if less than	$A < B$
BLE	Branch if less or equal	$A \leq B$
BE	Branch if equal	$A = B$
BNE	Branch if not equal	$A \neq B$

plus checks for a sign bit of 0 and a branch on minus checks for a sign bit of 1. It must be realized, however, that these two conditional branch instructions can be used to check the value of the most significant bit whether it represents a sign or not. The overflow bit is used in conjunction with arithmetic operations done on signed numbers in 2's complement representation.

As stated previously, the compare instruction performs a subtraction of two operands, say $A - B$. The result of the operation is not transferred into a destination register, but the status bits are affected. The status register provides information about the relative magnitude of A and B. Some computers provide conditional branch instructions that can be applied right after the execution of a compare instruction. The specific conditions to be tested depend on whether the two numbers A and B are considered to be unsigned or signed numbers. Table 7-11 gives a list of such conditional branch instructions. Note that we use the words higher and lower to denote the relations between unsigned numbers, and greater and less than for signed numbers. The relative magnitude shown under the tested condition column in the table seems to be the same for unsigned and signed numbers. However, this is not the case since each must be considered separately as explained in the following numerical example.

Consider an 8-bit ALU as shown in Fig. 7-14. The largest unsigned number that can be accommodated in 8 bits is 255. The range of signed numbers is between $+127$ and -128. The subtraction of two numbers is the same whether they are unsigned or in signed-2's complement representation (see Sec. 3-2). Let $A = 11110000$ and $B = 00010100$. To perform $A - B$, the ALU takes the 2's complement of B and adds it to A.

$$
\begin{array}{rl}
A: & 11110000 \\
\bar{B} + 1: & +11101100 \\
\hline
A - B: & 11011100 \qquad C = 1 \qquad S = 1 \qquad V = 0 \qquad Z = 0
\end{array}
$$

The compare instruction updates the status bits as shown. $C = 1$ because there is a carry out of the last stage. $S = 1$ because the left-most bit is 1. $V = 0$ because the last two carries are both equal to 1, and $Z = 0$ because the result is not equal to 0.

If we assume unsigned numbers, then the decimal equivalent of A is 240 and that of B is 20. The subtraction in decimal is $240 - 20 = 220$. The binary result 11011100 is indeed the equivalent of decimal 220. Since $240 > 20$, we have that $A > B$ and $A \neq B$. These two relations can also be derived from the fact that status bit C is equal to 1 and bit Z is equal to 0. The instructions that will cause a branch after this comparison are BHI (branch if higher), BHE (branch if higher or equal), and BNE (branch if not equal).

If we assume signed numbers, then the decimal equivalent of A is -16. This is because the sign of A is negative and 11110000 is the 2's complement of 00010000, which is the decimal equivalent of $+16$. The decimal equivalent of B is $+20$. The subtraction in decimal is $(-16) - (+20) = -36$. The binary result 11011100 (the 2's complement of 00100100) is indeed the equivalent of decimal -36. Since $(-16) < (+20)$ we have that $A < B$ and $A \neq B$. These two relations can be derived also from the fact that status bits $S = 1$ (negative), $V = 0$ (no overflow), and $Z = 0$ (not zero). The instructions that will cause a branch after this comparison are BLT (branch if less than), BLE (branch if less or equal), and BNE (branch if not equal).

It should be noted that the instruction BNE ahd BNZ (branch if not zero) are identical. Similarly, the two instructions BE (branch if equal) and BZ (branch if zero) are also identical. Each is repeated three times in Table 7-11 for the purpose of clarity and completeness.

It should be obvious from the example that the relative magnitude of two unsigned numbers can be determined (after a compare instruction) from the values of status bits C and Z (see Prob. 7-30). The relative magnitude of two signed numbers can be determined from the values of S, V, and Z (see Prob. 7-31).

Some computers consider the C bit to be a borrow bit after a subtraction operation $A - B$. A borrow does not occur if $A \geq B$, but a bit must be borrowed from the next most significant position if $A < B$. The condition for a borrow is the complement of the carry obtained when the subtraction is done by taking the 2's complement of *B*. For this reason, a processor that considers the *C* bit to be a borrow after a subtraction will complement the *C* bit after adding the 2's complement of the subtrahend and denote this bit a borrow.

Subroutine Call and Return

A subroutine is a self-contained sequence of instructions that performs a given computational task. During the execution of a program, a subroutine may be called to perform its function many times at various points in the main program. Each time a subroutine is called, a branch is executed to the beginning of the subroutine to start executing its set of instructions. After the subroutine has been executed, a branch is made back to the main program.

The instruction that transfers program control to a subroutine is known by different names. The most common names used are *call subroutine, jump to subroutine, branch to subroutine,* or *branch and save address.* A call subroutine instruction consists of an operation code together with an address that specifies the beginning of the subroutine. The instruction is executed by performing two operations: (1) the address of the next instruction available in the program counter (the return address) is stored in a temporary location so the subroutine knows where to return, and (2) control is transferred to the beginning of the subroutine. The last instruction of every subroutine, commonly called *return from subroutine*, transfers the return address from the temporary location into the program counter. This results in a transfer of program control to the instruction whose address was originally stored in the temporary location.

Different computers use a different temporary location for storing the return address. Some store the return address in the first memory location of the subroutine, some store it in a fix location in memory, some store it in a processor register, and some store it in a memory stack. The most efficient way is to store the return address in a memory stack. The advantage of using a stack for the return address is that when a succession of subroutines is called, the sequential return addresses can be pushed into the stack. The return from subroutine instruction causes the stack to pop and the contents of the top of the stack transferred to the program counter. In this way, the return is always to the program which last called a subroutine. A subroutine call is implemented with the following micro-operations:

$SP \leftarrow SP + 1$	Increment stack pointer
$M[SP] \leftarrow PC$	Push content of *PC* onto the stack
$PC \leftarrow$ Effective address	Transfer control to the subroutine

If another subroutine is called by the current subroutine, the new return address is pushed into the stack, and so on. The instruction that returns from the last subroutine is implemented by the micro-operations:

$PC \leftarrow M[SP]$ Pop stack and transfer to PC

$SP \leftarrow SP - 1$ Decrement stack pointer

By using a subroutine stack, all return addresses are automatically stored by the hardware in one unit. The programmer does not have to be concerned or remember where the return address was stored.

A *recursive* subroutine is a subroutine that calls itself. If only one register or memory location is used to store the return address, and the recursive subroutine calls itself, it destroys the previous return address. This is undesirable because vital information is destroyed. This problem can be solved if different storage locations are employed for each use of the subroutine while another higher level use is still active. When a stack is used, each return address can be pushed into the stack without destroying any previous values. This solves the problem of recursive subroutines because the next subroutine to exit is always the last subroutine that was called.

Program Interrupt

The concept of program interrupt is used to handle a variety of problems which arise out of normal program sequence. Program interrupt refers to the transfer of program control from a currently running program to another service program as a result of an external or internal generated request. Control returns to the original program after the service program is executed.

The interrupt procedure is, in principle, quite similar to a subroutine call except for three variations: (1) The interrupt is usually initiated by an internal or external signal rather than from the execution of an instruction (except for software interrupt as explained later). (2) The address of the interrupt service program is determined by the hardware rather than from the address field of an instruction. (3) An interrupt procedure usually stores all the information necessary to define the state of the CPU rather than storing only the program counter. These three procedural concepts are clarified further below.

After a program has been interrupted and the service routine been executed, the CPU must return to exactly the same state that it was when the interrupt occurred. Only if this happens will the interrupted program be able to resume exactly as if nothing had happened. The state of the CPU at the end of the execute cycle (when the interrupt is recognized) is determined from:

1. The content of the program counter.

2. The content of all processor registers.

3. The content of certain status conditions.

The collection of all status bit conditions in the CPU is sometimes called a *program status word* or PSW. The PSW is stored in a separate hardware register and contains the status information that characterizes the state of the CPU. Typically, it includes the status bits from the last ALU operation, it specifies the interrupts that are allowed to occur, and whether the CPU is operating in a supervisor or user mode. Many computers have a resident operating system that controls and supervises all other programs in the computer. When the CPU is executing a program which is part of the operating system, it is said to be in the supervisor or system mode. Certain instructions are privileged and can be executed in this mode only. The CPU is normally in the user mode when executing user programs. The mode that the CPU is operating at any given time is determined from special status bits in the PSW.

Some computers store only the program counter when responding to an interrupt. The service program must then include instructions to store status and register content before these resources are used. Only few computers store both program counter and all status and register content in response to an interrupt. Most computers just store the program counter and the PSW. In some cases, there exist two sets of processor registers within the computer, one for each CPU mode. In this way, when the program switches from the user to the supervisor mode (or vice versa) in response to an interrupt, it is not necessary to store the contents of processor registers as each mode uses its own set of registers.

The hardware procedure for processing an interrupt is very similar to the execution of a subroutine call instruction. The state of the CPU is pushed into a memory stack and the beginning address of the service routine is transferred to the program counter. The beginning address of the service routine is determined by the hardware rather than the address field of an instruction. Some computers assign one memory location where interrupts are always transferred. The service routine must then determine what caused the interrupt and proceed to service it. Some computers assign a memory location for each possible interrupt. Sometimes, the hardware interrupt provides its own address that directs the CPU to the desired service routine. In any case, the CPU must possess some form of hardware procedure for selecting a branch address for servicing the interrupt.

The CPU does not respond to an interrupt until the end of an instruction execution. Just before going to the next fetch cycle, control checks for any interrupt signals. If an interrupt is pending, control goes to a hardware interrupt cycle. During this cycle, the contents of PC and PSW are pushed onto the stack. The branch address for the particular interrupt is then transferred to PC and a new PSW is loaded into the status register. The service program can now be executed starting from the branch address and having a CPU mode as specified in the new PSW.

The last instruction in the service program is a *return from interrupt* instruction. When this instruction is executed, the stack is popped to retrieve the old PSW and the return address. The PSW is transferred to the status register and the return address to the program counter. Thus, the CPU state is restored and the original program can continue executing.

Types of Interrupts

There are three major types of interrupts that cause a break in the normal execution of a program. They can be classified as:

1. External interrupts.
2. Internal interrupts.
3. Software interrupts.

External interrupts come from input-output (I/O) devices, from a timing device, from a circuit monitoring the power supply, or from any other external source. Examples that cause external interrupts are: I/O device requesting transfer of data, I/O device finished transfer of data, elapsed time of an event, or power failure. Time-out interrupt may result from a program that is in an endless loop and thus exceeded its time allocation. Power failure interrupt may have as its service routine a program that transfers the complete state of the CPU into a nondestructive memory in the few milliseconds before power ceases.

Internal interrupts arise from illegal or erroneous use of an instruction or data. Internal interrupts are also called *traps*. Examples of interrupts caused by internal error conditions are register overflow, attempt to divide by zero, an invalid operation code, stack overflow, and protection violation. These error conditions usually occur as a result of a premature termination of the instruction execution. The service program that processes the internal interrupt determines the corrective measure to be taken.

The difference between internal and external interrupts is that the internal interrupt is initiated by some exceptional condition caused by the program itself rather than an external event. Internal interrupts are synchronous with the program while external interrupts are asynchronous. If the program is rerun, the internal interrupts will occur in the same place each time. External interrupts depend on external conditions which are independent of the program being executed at the time.

External and internal interrupts are initiated from signals that occur in the hardware of the CPU. A software interrupt is initiated by executing an instruction. Software interrupt is a special call instruction that behaves like an interrupt rather than a subroutine call. It can be used by the programmer to initiate an interrupt procedure at any desired point in the program. The most common use of software interrupt is associated with a supervisor call instruction. This instruction provides means for switching from a CPU user mode to the supervisor mode. Certain operations in the computer may be assigned to the supervisor mode only, as for example, a complex input or output transfer procedure. A program written by a user must run in the user mode. When an input or output transfer is required, the supervisor mode is requested by means of a supervisor call instruction. This instruction causes a software interrupt which stores the old CPU state and brings in a new PSW which belongs to the supervisor mode. The calling program must pass information to the operating system in order to specify the particular task requested.

7-8 MICROPROCESSOR ORGANIZATION

A CPU can be designed and constructed by combining various digital functions, such as registers, ALU, multiplexers, and decoders. Such a custom-made system has the advantage that it can be tailored to the needs of the particular application. However, because a CPU is a widely used digital computer component, it is also available in standard integrated circuit packages. A *microprocessor* is a central processor unit (CPU) enclosed in one integrated circuit (IC) packge. Unlike the custom-designed CPU, the functional characteristics of a microprocessor are fixed by the internal architecture of the device. The only access available to a microprocessor is through the terminals of the package; no direct connection can be made to the registers, the ALU, or any other internal component. Microprocessors have all the characteristic features introduced in this chapter. What makes the microprocessor unique is that the entire CPU is enclosed in one small package and therefore, it is much smaller and costs much less than a custom-made unit.

Because of their small size and low cost, microprocessors have revolutionized the digital computer system design technology, giving the designer the capability to create structures that were previously uneconomical. Microprocessors are used in a wide range of applications. They function as a CPU in a general-purpose computer or as a processor unit in a special-purpose dedicated system. Microprocessor applications extend across a wide product line, such as personal home computers, traffic control, test instrumentation, the control of automobile ignition system, and numerous business applications, such as the automation of retail store sales and inventory.

Microcomputer Organization

A microprocessor combined with memory and input-output capabilities becomes a microcomputer. The word *micro* is used to indicate the small physical size of the components involved. The second part of the word in microprocessor and microcomputer is what really sets them apart. The word *processor* is an abbreviation for the central processor unit. The term *microcomputer* is used to indicate a complete computer system, consisting of the three basic units: CPU, memory, and input-output. To understand how a microprocessor operates, it is necessary to be familiar with its interaction with other components in a microcomputer system.

Figure 7-15 shows a block diagram of a microcomputer system. Typically, the microcomputer has a single microprocessor. If many processors are included, then we have a multiprocessor system. The RAM (random-access memory) and ROM (read-only memory) provide the memory for the computer. The interface units communicate with input-output devices through the I/O bus. At any given time, the microprocessor selects one of the units through its address bus. Data are transferred to and

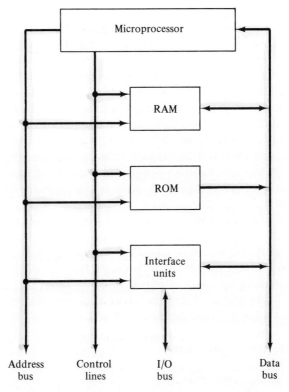

Fig. 7-15 Microcomputer system block diagram.

from the selected unit and the microprocessor via the data bus. Control information is transferred through individual lines each specifying a particular control function.

The RAM is a read/write memory type and consists of a number of IC packages connected together. It is used to store data, variable parameters, and intermediate results that need updating and are subject to change. The ROM consists of a number of IC packages and is used for storing programs and tables of constants that are not subject to change once the production of the microcomputer system is completed. The method of connecting memory chips to the microprocessor is described in Sec. 12-2.

The interface units provide the necessary paths for transferring information between the microprocessor and external input and output devices connected to the I/O bus. The microprocessor receives status and data information from external devices through the interface. It responds by sending control and data information for the external devices through the interface. This communication is specified by programmed instructions that direct data through the buses in the microcomputer system. An example of an interface unit can be found in Fig. 11-5.

The communication between the components in a microcomputer takes place via the address and data buses. The address bus is unidirectional from the microprocessor to the other units. The binary information that the microprocessor places on the address bus specifies a particular memory word in RAM or ROM. The address bus is also used to select one of many interface units connected to the system or to a particular register within an interface unit. A memory word and an interface register may be distinguished by assigning a different address to each. Alternatively, a control signal may be used to specify whether the address on the bus is for a memory word or for an interface register. The number of lines available in the address bus determines the maximum memory size that can be accommodated in the system. For n lines, the address bus can specify up to 2^n words of memory. The typical length of a microprocessor address bus is 16, providing a maximum memory capacity of $2^{16} = 65,536$ words. The amount of memory employed in a microcomputer system depends on the particular application and quite often is less than the maximum available in the address bus.

The data bus transfers data to and from the microprocessor and the memory or interface which is selected by the address bus. The data bus is bidirectional, which means that the binary information can flow in either direction. A bidirectional data bus is used to save pins in the IC package. If a unit did not use a bidirectional data bus, it would be necessary to provide separate input and output terminals in the IC package. The number of lines in the microprocessor data bus ranges from 4 to 16, with 8 and 16 lines being the most common.

Microprocessor Bus

One of the most important differences between a conventional computer system and a microcomputer system is the physical interconnection between components. The component interconnection in a conventional computer system is essentially hidden to anyone outside the inner group of people who designed the system. In contrast, the component boundaries between processor, memory, and input-output in a micro-computer-based system represent actual interfaces and most users must be familiar with them. Because the component interconnection are visible, the user must be familiar with the microcomputer system bus as a link between the various components.

The bus system in a microprocessor is commonly implemented by means of bus buffers constructed with tri-state gates. A tri-state gate is a digital circuit that exhibits three output states. Two of the states are signals equivalent to binary 1 and 0 as in conventional gates. The third state is called a *high-impedance* state. The high-impednace state behaves as if the output is disabled or "floating," which means that it cannot affect or be affected by an external signal at the terminal.

The graphic symbol of a tri-state buffer gate is shown in Fig. 7-16. It has a normal input and a control input that determines the output state. When the control input is equal to binary 1, the gate behaves as any conventional buffer, with the output equal to the normal input. When the control input is 0, the output is disabled and the gate goes to the high-impedance state, regardless of the value in the normal input. The high-impedance state of a tri-state gate provides a feature not available in other gates. Because of this feature, a large number of tri-state gate outputs can be connected with wires to form a common bus line without endangering loading effects. However, no more than one gate may be in the active state at any given time. The connected gates must be controlled so that one tri-state gate has access to the bus line while all other gates are in a high-impedance state.

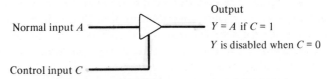

Normal input A Output

$Y = A$ if $C = 1$

Y is disabled when $C = 0$

Control input C

Fig. 7-16 Graphic symbol for tri-state buffer gate.

A bidirectional bus can be constructed with bus buffers to control the direction of information flow. One line of a bidirectional bus is shown in Fig. 7-17. The bus control has two selection lines, s_i for input transfer and s_o for output rtansfer. These selection lines control two tri-state buffers. When $s_i = 1$ and $s_o = 0$, the bottom buffer is enabled and the top buffer is disabled by going to a high-impedance state. This forms a path for input data coming from the bus to pass through the bottom buffer and into the system. When $s_o = 1$ and $s_i = 0$, the top buffer is enabled and the bottom buffer goes to a high-impedance state. This forms a path for output data coming from the system to pass through the upper gate and out to the bus line. The bus line can be disabled by making s_i and s_o both 0. This puts both buffers into a high-impedance state, which prevents any input or output transfer of information through the bus line. This condition must exist when an external source is using the common bus line to communicate with some other component. The two selection lines can be used to inform the external modules connected to the bus of the state in which the bidirectional bus is at any given time.

In most cases, the drive capability of a microprocessor bus is limited; that is,

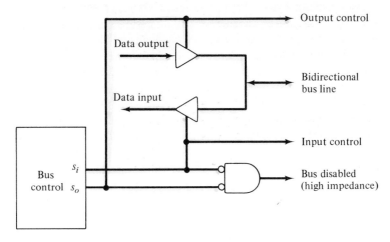

Fig. 7-17 Bidirectional bus buffer.

it can drive only a small number of external loads. When the bus is connected to a large number of external units, the drive capability of the microprocessor must be enhanced with external bus buffers, which are also available in IC form. Furthermore, any component that has separate input and output terminals must be connected to the microcomputer bus system through external bus buffers in order to isolate the component when it is not communicating with the bus. Thus, a microcomputer system quite often needs external bus buffers between the microprocessor and the other components and between certain components and the common-bus system.

Microprocessor Control Signals

Proper operation of a microprocessor requires that certain control and timing signals be provided to accomplish specific functions and that other control lines be monitored to determine the state of the microprocessor. A typical set of control lines available in most microprocessors is shown in Fig. 7-18. For completion, the diagram also shows the data bus, address bus, and power supply input to the unit. The power requirement for a particular microprocessor is specified by the voltage level and current consumption that must be supplied to operate the IC.

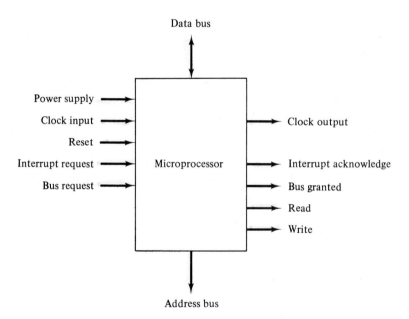

Fig. 7-18   Control signals in a microprocessor.

The *clock* input is used by the microprocessor to generate multiphase clock pulses that provide timing and control for internal functions. Some microprocessors require an external clock generator to supply the clock pulses. In this case, the output clock is available from the clock generator rather than from the microprocessor itself. Some units generate the clock within the chip but require an external crystal or circuit to control the frequency of the clock. The clock pulses are used by external modules to synchronize their operations with the operations of the microprocessor.

The *reset* input is used to reset and start the microprocessor after power is turned on or any time the user wants to start the process from the beginning. The effect of a reset signal is to initialize the microprocessor by forcing a given address into the program counter. The program then starts executing with the first instruction at this address. The simplest way to initiate a reset is to clear the program counter and start the program from address zero. Some microprocessors respond to the reset signal by transferring the contents of a specified memory location into the program counter. The designer must then store the beginning address of the program at the adopted memory location.

The *interrupt request* into the microprocessor typically comes from an interface module to inform the microprocessor that it is ready to transfer information. When the microprocessor is ready to respond to the interrupt, it enables the *interrupt acknowledge* output. The interface then provides an address, through the data bus, for the beginning of the service program. The microprocessor suspends the execution of the current program and branches to the program that services the interface module. At the completion of the service routine, the microprocessor returns to the previous program. The interrupt facility is included to provide a change in program sequence as a result of external conditions. The connection of I/O devices to the interrupt request and acknowledge lines is discussed in Sec. 11-5.

The *bus request* control input is a request to the microprocessor to temporarily suspend its operation and drive all buses into their high-impedance state. When the request is acknowledged, the microprocessor responds by enabling the *bus granted* control output line. Thus, when an external device wishes to transfer information directly to memory, it requests that the microprocessor relinquish control of the common buses. Once the buses are disabled by the microprocessor, the device that originated the request takes control of the address and data buses to conduct memory transfers without processor intervention. This feature is called direct memory access and is discussed in Sec. 11-4.

The *read* and *write* are control lines that inform the component selected by the address bus of the direction of transfer expected in the data bus. The read line informs the selected unit that the data bus is in an input mode and that the microprocessor will accept data from the data bus. The write line indicates that the microprocessor is in an output mode and that valid data are available on the data bus. When the buses are disabled, these two control lines are in a high-impedance state; thus, the external unit in control of the buses can specify the read and write operations.

The control signals enumerated in Fig. 7-18 constitute a minimum set of control functions for a microprocessor. Most microprocessors have additional control features for special functions. Different units may use different names for identical control functions, and not necessarily the names used here.

Microprocessor Example

In order to guarantee a wide range of acceptability, most microprocessors provide an internal organization suited for a wide range of applications. Microprocessors have some properties in common, although every unit differs from all others in its internal architecture. The basic function of a microprocessor is to interpret instruction codes received from an external source such as a memory unit and perform arithmetic, logic, and control operations on data stored in internal registers. A microprocessor usually includes a number of registers, an ALU, a bus system, and timing and control logic. Externally, it provides a bus system for transferring instructions, addresses, and data between the CPU and the other modules connected to it.

The characteristics of particular microprocessors are described in reference manuals published by the manufacturers. These manuals invariably assume that the reader is familiar with the basic concepts of computer hardware and software architecture. There are a wide variety of microprocessor units available commercially. Although the architectures are different, all microprocessors have one property in common: they are organized as a central processor unit. This means that the CPU components introduced in this chapter are also found in microprocessors. The control logic of a microprocessor may be organized through a sequence of timing signals and control functions as described in Chap. 5 or by means of a microprogram as explained in Chap. 8. The communication with the external environment is implemented by means of interface logic as presented in Chap. 11.

To appreciate the tasks performed by a microprocessor, it will be instructive to investigate the internal organization of a typical unit. Figure 7-19 shows the block diagram of the Intel 8080 microprocessor. The unit is enclosed in a 40-pin integrated circuit and can be purchased for less than \$20. Externally, it provides a bidirectional data bus, an address bus, and a number of control lines. The data bus consists of eight lines. The information contained in the data bus is called a *byte*, which is the name used to denote an 8-bit word. The address bus consists of 16 lines to specify $2^{16} = 64K$ ($K = 1024$) possible addresses. Thus, the microprocessor is capable of communicating with a memory unit of 64K bytes.

Internally, the microprocessor has seven registers labeled A (for accumulator), B, C, D, E, H, and L. These registers are eight bits wide and can accommodate a byte. The ALU operates on the data stored in the accumulator and a temporary register. The byte in the temporary register comes from any one of the other six registers or from memory through the data bus and the internal bus. The flag flip-flops are status bits that reflect the result of the last ALU operation. The flag (status) bits used in the 8080 microprocessor are Z (zero), C (carry), S (sign), P (parity), and AC (auxiliary carry). The auxiliary carry comes out of the fourth significant bit of an ALU operation and is useful for the addition of decimal numbers in BCD (binary-coded decimal).

The operation code of an instruction read from memory during the fetch cycle is transferred to the instruction register. It is then decoded by the control to determine the sequence of micro-operations needed to execute the instruction. The timing and

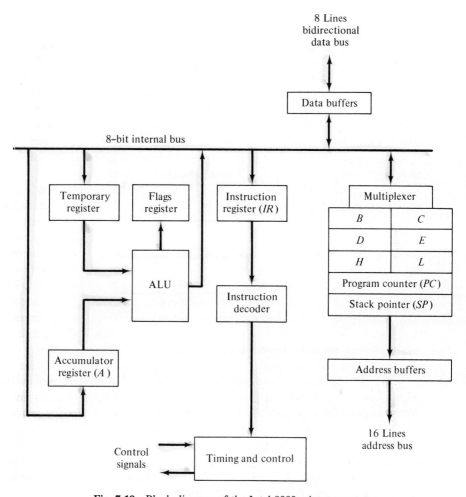

Fig. 7-19 Block diagram of the Intel 8080 microprocessor.

control unit supervises all internal operations in the CPU and activates the external buses and control lines in the microprocessor.

The address buffers can receive information from three sources: the program counter (*PC*), the stack pointer (*SP*), or a pair of processor registers. *PC* maintains the memory address of the current program instruction and is incremented after every instruction fetch. *SP* is used in conjunction with a memory stack. A pair of processor registers can be used to store an address. Three pairs can be formed to provide a 16-bit address. They are labeled with the combined register symbols *BC*, *DE*, and *HL*. Each processor register contains 8 bits and, when combined with the one adjacent to it, forms a register pair of 16 bits. Registers *B*, *C*, *D*, and *E* are usually used for processing data and register pair *HL* is used to specify an address for register indirect-mode instructions.

Microprocessor Memory Cycle

The interaction between the microprocessor and memory is through the address and data buses. The read and write control signals determine the type of memory cycle requested. The connection between the microprocessor and memory is shown in Fig. 7-20. Typically, the memory unit consists of both RAM and ROM. *ABUS* specifies the address for memory. The bidirectional *DBUS* transfers the binary information in the direction specified by the *RD* or *WR* control.

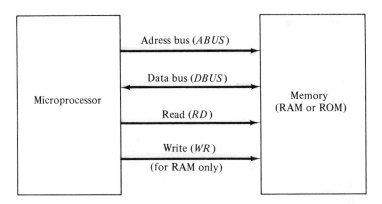

Fig. 7-20 Communication between microprocessor and memory.

In the read cycle, the microprocessor places an address in *ABUS* and enables control line *RD*. The memory responds by reading a byte and placing it in *DBUS*. The microprocessor accepts the byte and transfers it to an internal register. To express the read cycle symbolically, assume that the microprocessor is in the fetch cycle so the address comes from the program counter *PC* and the instruction code is transferred to the instruction register *IR*.

$ABUS \leftarrow PC, RD \leftarrow 1$ Address in bus for reading

$DBUS \leftarrow M[ABUS]$ Memory reads byte

$IR \leftarrow DBUS, RD \leftarrow 0$ Byte transferred to register

First, the microprocessor places the memory address into *ABUS* and informs the memory that a valid address is available for reading. The memory responds to *RD* by reading the word at the address given by *ABUS* and placing it in *DBUS*. The microprocessor then accepts the word from *DBUS* and transfers it to *IR*. At the same time, control signal *RD* is disabled, indicating the end of the memory read cycle.

The sequence of micro-operations listed above can be combined into one statement:

$$IR \leftarrow M[PC]$$

This is a read operation that transfers the memory word specified by the address in *PC* into *IR*.

In the write cycle, the microprocessor places an address in *ABUS* and the data in *DBUS*. The control signal *WR* is then enabled. The memory responds to *WR* by writing the byte available in *DBUS* into a memory location given by the address in *ABUS*. To express the write cycle symbolically, assume that the microprocessor is executing a *store accumulator* instruction using register pair *HL* for the address.

$$ABUS \leftarrow HL \qquad\qquad \text{Address in bus}$$
$$DBUS \leftarrow A, WR \leftarrow 1 \qquad\qquad \text{Data in bus for writing}$$
$$M[ABUS] \leftarrow DBUS, WR \leftarrow 0 \qquad\qquad \text{Memory writes word}$$

This states that the content of accumulator *A* is transferred to a memory location specified by the address in register pair *HL*. Again, it is possible to write the sequence of micro-operations with one statement

$$M[HL] \leftarrow A$$

Memory transfers to and from the microprocessor must conform with certain timing relationships that must exist between the control signals and the information on the buses. These timing relationships are specified in timing waveforms that are included with the product specifications of the units involved. The time interval of a memory cycle is a function of the internal clock frequency of the microprocessor and the access time of the memory. Once the microprocessor sends an address, it expects a response within a given interval of time. A memory that is capable of responding within the processor time interval can be directly controlled by the microprocessor memory cycle.

If the microprocessor communicates with a slow memory, it may take longer to access the memory than the allowable timing interval. To be able to use slow memories, a microprocessor must be able to delay the transfer until the memory access is completed. One way is to extend the microprocessor clock period by reducing the clock frequency to fit the access time of the memory. Some microprocessors provide a special control input called *ready* to allow the memory to set its own memory cycle time. If, after sending an address out, the microprocessor does not receive a *ready* input from memory, it enters a *wait* state for as long as the ready line is in the 0-state. When the memory access is completed, the ready line goes to the 1-state to indicate that the memory is ready for the specified transfer.

7-9 PARALLEL PROCESSING

Parallel processing is a term used to denote simultaneous computations in the CPU for the purpose of increasing its computational speed. Instead of processing each instruction sequentially as in conventional computers, a parallel processor performs concurrent data processing tasks to achieve faster execution time. For example, while an instruction is being executed in the ALU, the next instruction can be read from memory. If two or more ALUs are included within the processor unit, it may be possible to execute two or more instructions at the same time. The purpose of parallel processing is to speed up the computer processing capability and increase its throughput, that is, the amount of processing that can be accomplished during a given interval of time. The amount of hardware increases with parallel processing and with it, the cost of the system increases. However, tecnhological developments have reduced hardware costs to the point where certain parallel processing techniques are economically feasible.

The normal operation of a CPU is to fetch instructions from memory and execute them in the processor. The steps associated with reading instructions from memory can be viewed as forming an *instruction stream*. The various operations performed on the data in the processor form a *data stream*. Parallel processing may occur in the instruction stream, in the data stream, or both. If a single instruction stream causes parallel execution of the incoming data, the system is said to operate with a single instruction stream and multiple data stream or SIMD. Another possibility is MISD, which is a system with a multiple instruction stream and a single data stream. In most cases, parallel processing exhibits parallelism in both the instruction and data streams, forming a multiple-instruction multiple data stream or MIMD. These terms are sometimes used to distinguish between parallel processing in the instruction or data portions of the CPU. However, the best way to categorize simultaneous processing is in the way the hardware units are organized. There are two major ways to introduce parallelism. A set of functional units can be organized to compute in parallel, or we can use a technique known as pipeline processing.

Pipeline Processing

Pipeline is a technique of decomposing a sequential process into subprocesses with each subprocess being executed in a special dedicated segment that operates concurrently with all other segments. A pipeline can be visualized as a collection of processing segments through which binary information flows. Each segment performs partial processing dictated by the way the task is partitioned. The result obtained from the computation in each segment is transferred to the next segment in the pipeline. The final result is obtained after the data have passed through all segments. The name "pipeline" implies a flow of information analogous to an industrial assembly line. It is characteristic of pipelines that several computations can be in progress in distinct segments at the same time. The overlapping of computation is made possible by associating a register with each segment in the pipeline. The registers provide isolation between each segment so that each can operate on distinct data simultaneously.

Perhaps the simplest way of viewing the basic pipeline structure is to imagine that each segment consists of an input register followed by a combinational circuit. The register holds the data and the combinational circuit performs the subprocess in the particular segment. The output of the combinational circuit in a given segment is connected to the input register of the next segment. A clock pulse is applied to all input registers after enough time is elapsed to perform all segment activity. In this way, the binary information flows through the pipeline one step at a time with every clock pulse.

The pipeline concept will be demonstrated by means of a very simple example. This example is of no practical value and is used merely for illustrative purposes. Suppose that we want to subtract a series of numbers:

$$C_i = A_i - B_i \qquad \text{for } i = 1, 2, 3, \dots, n$$

Each subtraction will be performed with a sequence of three suboperations: (1) complement B_i; (2) increment to get the 2's complement; and (3) add the 2's complement to A_i. Each suboperation is to be implemented in a segment within a pipeline. Each segment has one or two registers and a combinational circuit as shown in Fig. 7-21(a). $R1$ through $R5$ are registers that receive new input data with every clock pulse. The complementer, incrementer, and adder are combinational circuits. The suboperations performed in each segment of the pipeline are as follows:

$$R1 \leftarrow B_i, \qquad \qquad \text{Input } B_i$$
$$R2 \leftarrow \overline{R1} \qquad \qquad \text{Complement}$$
$$R3 \leftarrow R2 + 1, R4 \leftarrow A_i \qquad \text{Increment and input } A_i$$
$$R5 \leftarrow R3 + R4 \qquad \qquad \text{Add to get } A_i + \bar{B}_i + 1$$

The five registers are loaded with new data every clock pulse. The effect of each clock pulse is shown in Fig. 7-21(b). It takes four clock pulses to fill up the pipe and retrieve the first output from register $R5$. From there on, each clock pulse produces a new output and moves the data one step down the pipeline. This happens as long as new input data flow into the system. When no more input data are available, the clock pulses must continue until the last output emerges out of the pipeline.

Note that a pipeline processor performs simultaneous operations in each segment. No matter how many segments there are in the system, once the pipe is full, it takes only one clock pulse to obtain an output, no matter how many steps are required to execute it. If the time it takes to process the suboperation in each segment is an interval t, and if there are k segments, then each computation is executed in $k \times t$ intervals. However, since successive operations are overlapped in the pipeline, results are always delivered at every t interval after a setup time of $k \times t$ that it takes to fill up the pipe.

Any operation that can be decomposed into a sequence of suboperations of about the same complexity can be implemented by a pipeline processor. The procedure is efficient only in those applications where the same computation must be repeated on a stream of input data. Pipeline processing has been applied mostly to floating-point arithmetic operations. These operations are easily decomposed into consecutive suboperations as demonstrated in Sec. 10-4. For example, the floating-point addition

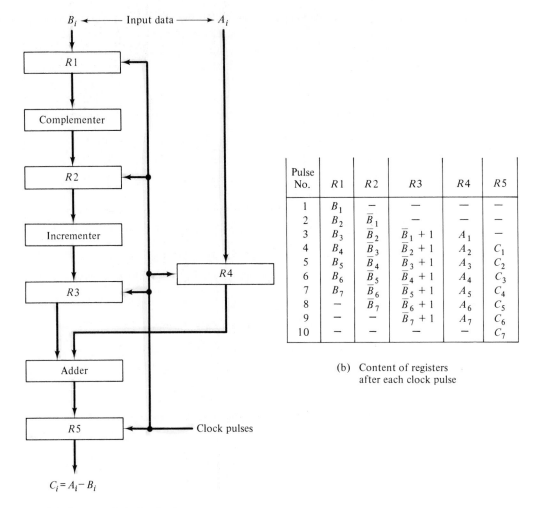

(b) Content of registers
after each clock pulse

$C_i = A_i - B_i$

(a) Segmented pipeline hardware

Fig. 7-21 A simple example demonstrating pipeline processing.

can be divided into three consecutive suboperations:

1. Align the mantissas.
2. Add the mantissas.
3. Normalize the result.

The floating-point add hardware can be structured as a pipeline with three segments. This is demonstrated in Fig. 7-22. The internal operation of each segment is demonstrated by means of a numerical example. Two floating-point numbers X and Y are

276

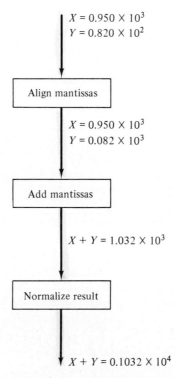

$X = 0.950 \times 10^3$
$Y = 0.820 \times 10^2$

Align mantissas

$X = 0.950 \times 10^3$
$Y = 0.082 \times 10^3$

Add mantissas

$X + Y = 1.032 \times 10^3$

Normalize result

$X + Y = 0.1032 \times 10^4$

Fig. 7-22   Pipeline processing of floating-point addition.

aligned by shifting one of their mantissas until their two exponents are equal. Adding the mantissas may cause an overflow. This is adjusted by normalizing the result so that the sum is always a fraction with a nonzero first digit. New sets of numbers can enter the pipeline as the information moves along the three segments to form the sum.

Instruction Pipeline

Pipeline processing can occur not only in the data stream but in the instruction stream as well. An instruction pipeline reads consecutive instructions from memory while previous instructions are being executed in the processor. This causes the instruction fetch and execute cycles to overlap and perform simultaneous operations. An instruction pipeline is also known by the name of *instruction look-ahead* buffer, as it reads instructions ahead of their use by the processor. The only digression associated with such a scheme is that one of the instructions may cause a branch out of sequence. In that case, the pipe must be emptied and all the instructions that have been read from memory must be discarded.

An instruction pipeline can be implemented by means of a first-in first-out (FIFO) buffer. This is a type of unit that forms a queue rather than a stack. Whenever the execute cycle is not using the memory, the control increments the program counter and uses its address value to read consecutive instructions from memory. The instructions are inserted in the FIFO buffer so that they can be executed on a first-in first-out basis. Thus, an instruction stream can be placed in a queue, waiting for decoding and execution by the processor.

The instruction stream queuing mechanism provides an efficient way for reducing the average access time to memory for reading instructions. Whenever there is space in the buffer, the processor executes an instruction fetch cycle. The buffer acts as a queue from which control extracts instructions for execution. If the CPU executes an instruction that transfers control to a location out of normal sequence, the buffer is reset and the pipeline is declared empty. Control then fetches the instruction from the branch address and begins to refil the buffer from the new location. Often, branch instructions form a small fraction of the total number of instructions executed, so throughput can be increased by this kind of instruction pipeline.

The instruction pipeline can be extended to include other processor cycles. As an example, Fig. 7-23 shows how the instruction cycle in the CPU can be processed with a four-segment pipeline. While an instruction is executed in the ALU, the next instruction in sequence is busy fetching an operand from memory. The effective address may be calculated for the third instruction and, whenever the memory is available, the fourth and all subsequent instructions can be fetched and placed in an instruction pipeline. Thus, up to four suboperations in the instruction cycle can overlap and up to four different instructions can be in progress of being processed at the same time.

Once in a while, an instruction in the sequence may be a program control type that causes a branch out of normal sequence. In that case, the pending operations in the last two segments are completed and all information stored in the first two segments is deleted. The pipeline then restarts from the new value stored in PC. Similarly, an interrupt request, when acknowledged, will cause the pipeline to empty and start again from a new address value.

There are certain difficulties that will prevent a CPU pipeline from operating at its maximum rate. Different segments may take different times to operate on the incoming data. Some segments are skipped for certain instructions. For example, a register mode instruction does not need an effective address calculation. Two or more segments may require memory access at the same time, causing one segment to wait until another is finished with the memory. Memory access conflicts are sometimes resolved by using a memory unit with multiple modules as explained below.

Memory Interleaving

In order to carry out two or more simultaneous accesses to memory, the memory must be partitioned into separate modules which are independent of each other. A memory module is a memory array together with its own address and buffer registers. Figure 7-24 shows a memory unit organized in four modules. Each memory array has its own address register MAR and buffer or data register MBR. The address registers receive information from a common address bus and the buffer registers communicate with a bidirectional data bus. The two least significant bits of the address can be used to distinguish between the four modules. The modular system permits one module to

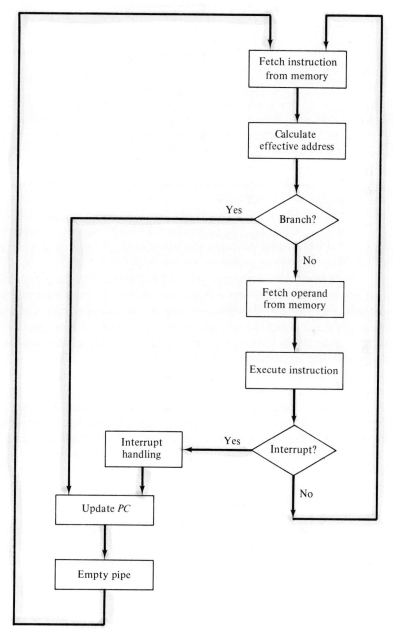

Fig. 7-23 Four-segment CPU pipeline.

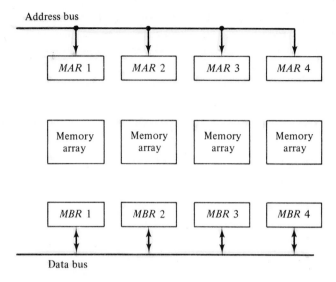

Fig. 7-24 Multiple module memory organization.

be accessed while other modules are in a process of reading or writing a word since each module can honor a memory request independent of the state of other modules.

The advantage of a modular memory is that it allows the use of a technique called *interleaving*. In an interleaved memory, consecutive addresses are assigned to different memory modules. For example, in a two-module memory system, the even addresses are in one module and the odd addresses in the other. The control can fetch two consecutive instructions from two modules and place them in an instruction buffer. With *m*-way interleaving *m* consecutive instructions can be fetched from *m* different modules. By staggering the memory access, the effective memory cycle time can be reduced by a factor somewhat less than the number of modules.

A modular memory is also useful in systems with pipeline processing. If instructions and operands are placed in two different modules, the instruction fetch cycle and reading of the operand may be overlapped. A pipelined organized CPU can take advantage of multiple memory modules so that each segment in the pipeline can access memory independent of memory requests from other segments.

Multiple Functional Units

Parallel processing can be achieved through separate functional units that perform identical or different operations simultaneously. Parallel processing is established by distributing the data among the multiple functional units. For example, floating-point arithmetic operations can be implemented using two functional units, one for the exponents and the other for the mantissas. The multiplication of two floating-point numbers requires that we multiply the mantissas and add the exponents. These two operations can be done concurrently in the two separate functional units. Another possibility is to separate the arithmetic, logic, and shift operations into separate units and divert operands to each unit under the supervision of a special control unit.

Any possible parallelism associated with programs can be exploited by using a multifunction processor unit. Figure 7-25 shows one possible way of separating an

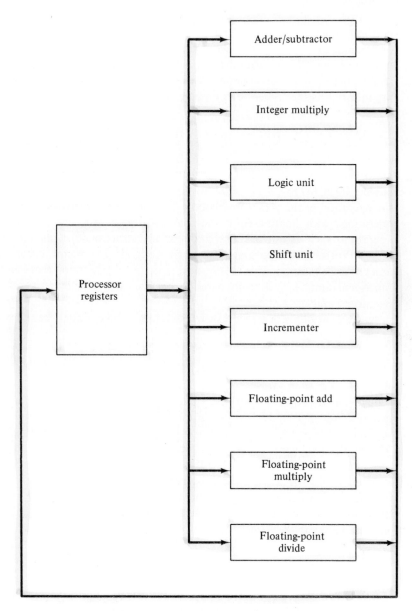

Fig. 7-25 Processor with multiple functional units.

arithmetic logic unit into eight functional units operating in parallel. The operands in the registers are applied to one of the units depending on the operation specified by the instruction associated with the operands. The operation performed in each functional unit is shown in each block. The adder and integer multiplier perform the arithmetic operations with fixed-point numbers. The floating-point operations are separated into three parallel circuits. The logic, shift, and increment operations can perform concurrently on different data. All units are independent of each other, so one number may be shifting while another number is being incremented. A multi-function organization must have a complex control unit to coordinate all the activities among the various components. An example of a processor that uses this type of organization is the Cyber-70 computer.

Vector Processor

A vector processor includes vector operations in its instruction set in addition to the conventional set of instructions normally found in a CPU. A typical vector instruction has the form $C(I) = A(I) * B(I)$ for $I = 1$ through n, where the symbol $*$ represents the operation of the vector instruction. Typical vector instructions include arithmetic operations with floating-point data, logical operations, compare and test, matrix operations such as dot product, and search instructions for maximum or minimum values. Vector processors are especially designed to execute complex instructions quickly and efficiently. This is done by an internal organization that combines multiple functional units operating in parallel together with pipeline processing within the functional units.

As an example of a vector instruction execution consider the following DO loop:

$$DO \quad I = 1, 50$$
$$C(I) = A(I) + B(I)$$

This defines a program loop that adds 50 sets of numbers. For most computers, the machine-language equivalent of the above DO loop is a sequence of instructions that read a pair of operands from the A and B arrays and perform a floating-point addition. The loop control variables are then updated and the steps repeated 50 times. A vector processor eliminates the overhead associated with the time it takes to fetch and execute the instructions in the program loop. This is because a vector instruction includes the initial addresses of the operands, the length of the vectors, and the operation to be performed, all in one composite instruction. Two operands $A(I)$ and $B(I)$ are read simultaneously from an interleaved memory and directed to a pipeline processor that performs the floating-point addition. After the first sum $C(1)$ emerges from the pipeline, it is stored in a third interleaved memory module while succeeding operations are being performed within the pipeline.

A processor suitable for vector processing is sometimes called an *array* processor. This is because the processor is capable of performing parallel computations on large arrays of data. The name "array" is also used to signify a special type of parallel organization. Here the array designates a hardware connection of a number of identical processing units connected together with direct paths between each unit and its neighbors.

A measure used to evaluate fast computers in their ability to perform a given number of floating-point operations per second is referred to as FLOPS. For vector processing, the term MFLOPS is used to denote "million floating-point operations per second." A typical vector processor has a basic cycle time of about 20 ns. If the processor can produce a floating-point answer through the pipeline each cycle time, it will have the ability to perform 50 MFLOPS. This rate would be sustained from the time the first answer is produced and does not include the initial setup time or the time it takes to empty the pipeline.

Vector processors are not suitable for normal everyday processing in a typical computer installation. They are limited to a small number of scientific applications, such as nuclear research, seismic analysis, and weather prediction and modeling. The number of vector processors available commercially is very small. The three most commonly cited examples are Gray-1, Cyber 205, and Burroughs Scientific processor (reference 14).

The Gray-1 computer uses a vector processor with 13 distinct functional units operating in parallel. Each functional unit is fully segmented to process the incoming data through a pipeline. All the functional units can operate concurrently with inter-mediate results stored in the large number (over 150) of internal CPU registers. A floating-point operation can be performed on two sets of 64-bit operands during one clock pulse period of 12.5 ns. This gives a rate of 80 MFLOPS during the time that the data are processed through the pipeline. The Gray-1 computer memory has a capacity of 4 million 64-bit words. The memory is divided into 16 interleaved arrays called "banks," with each bank having a 50-ns cycle time. This means that when all 16 banks are accessed simultaneously, the memory transfer rate becomes $16/(50 \times 10^{-9}) = 320$ million words per second.

Control Data Cyber 205 is an improved version of the STAR-100 (STring ARray) processor. Its vector processor contains two floating-point pipeline arithmetic units with an option providing two additional pipeline units, for a total of four. A stream control unit manages the data stream between the memory unit and the vector pipe-lines. Arithmetic operations are performed on 64-bit operands with a clock period of 20 ns. When the pipeline is fed with data to keep it full, the processor can achieve a rate of 50 MFLOPS. The memory capacity is 4 million 64-bit words with access time of 80 ns. The memory is four-way interleaved for an effective cycle time of 20 ns and a maximum transfer rate of 50 million words per second.

The Burroughs Scientific Processor (BSP) evolved from experience gained implementing the Illiac IV array processor. It contains 16 arithmetic units operating in parallel and driven synchronously by a single instruction stream. The data from any one of 16 memory arrays may be routed to any one of the 16 arithmetic units. The basic arithmetic instruction execution time is 320 ns. When all 16 arithmetic units are operating simultaneously, the processor operates at a rate of 50 MFLOPS. The main memory capacity is 8 million 48-bit words with access time of 160 ns. The memory is 16-way interleaved for an effective cycle time of 10 ns and a maximum transfer rate of 100 million words per second.

REFERENCES

1. MANO, M. M., *Digital Logic and Computer Design*. Englewood Cliffs, N.J.: Prentice-Hall, Inc., 1979.

2. LIPPIATT, A. G., *The Architecture of Small Computer Systems*. London: Prentice-Hall International, 1979.

3. GEAR, C. W., *Computer Organization and Programming*, 3rd ed. New York: McGraw-Hill Book Company, 1980.

4. TANENBAUM, A. S., *Structured Computer Organization*. Englewood Cliffs, N.J.: Prentice-Hall, Inc., 1976.

5. HAYES, J. P., *Computer Architecture and Organization*. New York: McGraw-Hill Book Company, 1978.

6. HAMACHER, V. C., Z. G. VRANESIC, AND S. G. ZAKY, *Computer Organization*. New York: McGraw-Hill Book Company, 1978.

7. STONE, H. S., ed., *Introduction to Computer Architecture*. Chicago: Science Research Assoc., 1975.

8. FISCHER, W. P., "Microprocessor Assembly Language Draft Standard," *Computer*, Vol. 12 (December 1979), pp. 96–109.

9. IBM CORP., *IBM System/370 Principles of Operation*, Publ. GA22-7000-5, Poughkeepsie, N.Y., 1976.

10. DIGITAL EQUIPMENT CORP., *PDP-11 Processor Handbook*. Maynard, Mass., 1975.

11. INTEL CORP., *MCS-80/85 User's Manual*. Santa Clara, Calif., 1979.

12. LEVENTHAL, L. A., *Introduction to Microprocessors*. Englewood Cliffs, N.J.: Prentice-Hall, Inc., 1978.

13. RAMAMOORTHY, C. V., AND H. F. LI, "Pipeline Architecture," *ACM Comp. Surv.*, Vol. 9 (March 1977), pp. 61–102.

14. KOZDROWICKI, E. W., AND D. J. THEIS, "Second Generation of Vector Supercomputers," *Computer*, Vol. 13 (November 1980), pp. 71–83.

15. BAER, J. L., *Computer Systems Architecture*, Potomac, Maryland: Computer Science Press, 1980.

PROBLEMS

7-1. A bus-organized CPU as shown in Fig. 7-1 contains 30 processor registers. How many selection lines are needed for each multiplexer and for the destination decoder?

7-2. Formulate a binary code for the 3-bit destination select inputs to the decoder of Fig. 7-1. What would you choose for the binary code 000, and why?

7-3. Instead of using registers, multiplexers, and a decoder as shown in Fig. 7-1, some processors use a small fast memory which is connected to the ALU and shifter. Draw a block diagram showing the general organization and selection variables for such a processor unit that incorporates a 16-word memory.

7-4. Determine the arithmetic operations obtained in the eight diagrams of Fig. 7-2 if, in each case, input A is changed to $\bar{A}$ (complement of A).

7-5. Design a 4-bit arithmetic circuit with one selection variable S and two 4-bit data inputs A and B. When $S = 0$ the circuit performs the addition $A + B$. When $S = 1$ the circuit performs the subtractions $A - B$ by taking the 2's complement of B.

7-6. An arithmetic circuit has two selection variables S_1 and S_0. The arithmetic operations available in the unit are listed below. Determine the circuit that must be incorporated with a full adder in each stage of the arithmetic unit. (An example of a circuit associated with a full-adder is shown in Fig. 7-3.)

S_1	S_0	$C_1 = 0$	$C_1 = 1$
0	0	$F = A + B$	$F = A + B + 1$
0	1	$F = A$	$F = A + 1$
1	0	$F = \bar{B}$	$F = \bar{B} + 1$
1	1	$F = A + \bar{B}$	$F = A + \bar{B} + 1$

7-7. Design a logic circuit that performs the four logic operations of exclusive-OR, equivalence, NOR, and NAND. Use two selection variables. Show the logic diagrams of one typical stage.

7-8. What modification is needed in the circuit of Fig. 7-7 so that both input combinations 00 and 11 of $H_1 H_0$ will cause a no-shift condition?

7-9. The control unit that operates the CPU bus system of Fig. 7-1 provides a 15-bit control word to select the various components in the system. (See the end of Sec. 7-2 for an example of a control word.) List the 15-bit control words that initiate the following micro-operations:
(a) $R2 \leftarrow R1 + 1$
(b) $R3 \leftarrow R4 + R5$
(c) $R6 \leftarrow \bar{R6}$
(d) $R4 \leftarrow R5$
(e) $R1 \leftarrow R1 \oplus R2$
(f) shr $R5$

7-10. List the micro-operations for popping and pushing a stack simulated with a random access memory (see Fig. 7-9).

7-11. Two operations of a stack organized CPU (Fig. 7-11) are concerned with stack adjustments. A *pop-stack adjustment* brings the top element of the stack to register A. A *push-stack adjustment* pushes the contents of A and B into the memory stack. Let the B register be the memory buffer register and use two flip-flops, YA and YB, so that when $YA = 1$, register A is full and is on top of the stack. If $YA = 0$ and $YB = 1$, register B is the top of the stack. When both are 0, the top of the stack is in the memory part. Draw a flow chart showing the micro-operations needed for the two stack adjustment operations as a function of the values of YA and YB. Neglect any overflow.

7-12. Convert the following arithmetic expressions into reverse Polish notation:
(a) $A + B + C$
(b) $A * B + A * (B * D + C * E)$
(c) $A * B/C + D$

7-13. Give the infix notation of the following reverse Polish expressions:
(a) $ABCDE * / - +$
(b) $AB * CD * + EF * +$
(c) $AB + C * D +$

7-14. Convert the following numerical expression into reverse Polish notation and show the stack operations for evaluating the numerical result.

$$(3 + 4)[10(2 + 6) + 8]$$

7-15. A *first-in first-out* (FIFO) is a memory unit that stores information in such a manner that the item first in is the item first out. Show how a FIFO memory operates with three counters: a write counter WC that holds the address for the memory write operation; a read counter RC that holds the address for the read operation; and an available storage counter ASC that indicates the number of items stored. ASC is incremented for every item stored and decremented for every item that is retrieved. The memory unit communicates with MAR and MBR.

7-16. Write the programs to evaluate the arithmetic statement

$$X = (A + B * C)/(D - E * F + G * H)$$

(a) Using a general-register-type computer with three-address instructions.
(b) Using a general-register-type computer with two-address instructions.
(c) Using an accumulator-type computer with one-address instructions.
(d) Using a stack organized computer with zero-address operation instructions.

7-17. Let the address stored in the program counter of a computer be designated by the symbol $X1$. The instruction stored in location $X1$ has an address part $X2$. The operand needed to execute the instruction is stored in the memory word whose address is $X3$. An index register contains the value $X4$. What should be the relationship between the various addresess if the addressing mode of the instruction is (a) direct; (b) indirect; (c) relative; (d) indexed?

7-18. A relative mode branch instruction is stored in memory at an address equivalent to decimal 620. The branch is made to an address equivalent to decimal 530.
(a) What should be the value of the relative address field of the instruction in binary? (Use a 10-bit relative address field.)
(b) Show that the binary value in PC after the fetch cycle plus the binary value of the relative address calculated in part (a) is equal to the binary value of 530.

7-19. How many times does the control unit need to refer to memory when it fetches and executes an indirect address-mode instruction if the instruction is: (a) a computational type requiring an operand; (b) a branch type?

7-20. What is the condition that must exist in an index-mode instruction to make it the same as a register indirect-mode instruction?

7-21. Consider a computer similar to the basic computer developed in Chap. 5 with registers PC, MAR, and MBR. In addition, the computer has an index register XR and two bits in the instruction code to specify four addressing modes: direct, indirect, indexed, and relative. The addressing mode bits are decoded into four outputs, a_0, a_1, a_2, and a_3, respectively. The control checks the direct address decoder output a_0 at the end of the fetch cycle. If $a_0 = 1$, control goes to the execute cycle; but if $a_0 = 0$, control goes to the "address computation" cycle to evaluate the effective address. Formulate the control functions and micro-operations for the address computation cycle in this computer. Assume that the computer has a separate adder for address calculations, and show the hardware necessary to implement the listed micro-operations.

7-22. The contents of the base and index registers in the IBM-370 processor are 004AF6C0 and 0000164E. (All numbers are in hexadecimal.)
   (a) Find the effective address of an RX format instruction with a displacement D equal to 2F2.
   (b) What should be the value of D for the effective address to be (1) 4B0D8D; (2) 4B1F18?

7-23. Register $R7$ in the PDP-11 processor is actually the program counter. When PC is specified in the register field of the instruction, the modes defined in Table 7-4 convert into different modes. Show that the following mode conversions are possible:
   (a) The autoincrement mode with $R7$ as the register converts into the immediate mode.
   (b) The autoincrement indirect mode with $R7$ as the register converts into the direct address mode.
   (c) The index mode with $R7$ as the register converts into the relative mode.

7-24. Register $R6$ in the PDP-11 processor is used as the stack pointer register in conjuction with a memory stack that grows with decreasing address values. Show that the auto-decrement mode with $R6$ as the register can be used for a push stack operation and the autoincrement mode with $R6$ as the register can be used for a pop stack operation.

7-25. Assuming an 8-bit microprocessor, show the multiple precision subtraction of the two 32-bit unsigned numbers listed below using the subtract with borrow instruction. Each byte is expressed as a 2-digit hexadecimal number.

$$6E\ C3\ 56\ 7A\ -\ 13\ 25\ 6B\ 84$$

7-26. Perform the logic AND, OR, and XOR with the two numbers 10011100 and 10101010.

7-27. (a) An 8-bit register contains the value 01111011 and the carry bit is equal to 1. Perform the eight shift operations listed in Table 7-9, each time starting from the initial value given above.
   (b) Repeat part (a) for 11000111 and a carry bit of 0.

7-28. An 8-bit computer has a register R. Determine the values of status bits C, S, Z, and V (Fig. 7-14) after each of the following instructions. The initial value of register R in each case is hexadecimal 72. The numbers below are also in hexadecimal.
   (a) Add immediate operand C6 to R.
   (b) Add immediate operand 1E to R.
   (c) AND immediate operand 8D to R.
   (d) Exclusive-OR R with R.

7-29. Consider the two 8-bit binary numbers $A = 01000001$ and $B = 10000100$.

(a) Give the decimal equivalent of each number assuming (1) that they are unsigned and (2) that they are signed numbers in 2's complement representation.

(b) Add the two binary numbers and interpret the result assuming that the numbers and the sum are (1) unsigned and (2) signed. What would the values of status bit C, S, Z, and V be?

(c) Subtract $A - B$ and interpret the result assuming that the numbers and the difference are (1) unsigned and (2) signed. List those instructions from Table 7-11 which will cause a branch as a result of the subtraction.

(d) Subtract $B - A$ and repeat part (c).

7-30. Two unsigned numbers A and B are compared by subtracting $A - B$. The carry status bit is considered as a borrow bit after a compare instructions in most commercial computers so that $C = 1$ if $A < B$. Status bit Z is set to 1 if $A - B = 0$. Show that the relative magnitude of A and B can be determined from inspection of status bits C and Z as specified below. (See also Table 7-11.)

Relation	Condition of status bits
$A > B$	C or $Z = 0$
$A \geq B$	$C = 0$
$A < B$	$C = 1$
$A \leq B$	C or $Z = 1$
$A = B$	$Z = 1$
$A \neq B$	$Z = 0$

7-31. Two signed numbers A and B represented in signed-2's complement form are compared by subtracting $A - B$. Status bits S, V, and Z are set or cleared depending on the result of the operation. (Note that there is a sign reversal if an overflow occurs—see Sec. 3-3 under *overflow*.) Show that the relative magnitude of A and B can be determined from inspection of the status bits as specified below. (See also Table 7-11.)

Relation	Condition of status bits
$A > B$	Z or $(S \oplus V) = 0$
$A \geq B$	$(S \oplus V) = 0$
$A < B$	$(S \oplus V) = 1$
$A \leq B$	Z or $(S \oplus V) = 1$
$A = B$	$Z = 1$
$A \neq B$	$Z = 0$

7-32. It is necessary to design a digital circuit with four inputs C, S, Z, and V and 10 outputs, one for each of the branch conditions listed in Probs. 7-30 and 7-31. (The equal and unequal conditions are common to both tables.) Draw the logic diagram of the circuit using two OR gates, one XOR gate, and five inverters.

7-33. The memory stack in a 16-bit computer contains 5A14 (all numbers are in hexadecimal). The stack pointer contains 3A56. A two-word call subroutine instruction is located at memory address 013E followed by the branch address of 67AE at memory address 013F. What are the contents of PC, SP, and the memory stack:

(a) Before the call instruction is executed?
(b) After the call instruction is executed?
(c) After the return from subroutine?
(d) After a second return from subroutine following the one in part (c)?

7-34. Give five examples of external interrupts and five examples of internal interrupts. What is the difference between software interrupt and a subroutine call?

7-35. (a) Why does the control in a digital computer wait until the end of the execute cycle to check for an interrupt request? What would happen if it responds at any other time?

(b) A computer is interrupted while processing the instruction in location 325 in memory. What is the state of the processor that must be stored before responding to the interrupt?

7-36. (a) Microprocessors are typically categorized as being 4-bit, 8-bit, or 16-bit. What does the number of bits imply?

(b) Why is the data bus in most microprocessors bidirectional while the address bus is unidirectional?

(c) What is the difference between RAM and ROM? What function does each serve in a microcomputer system?

(d) What is the difference between a microprocessor and a microcomputer?

7-37. A microprocessor data bus has 16 lines and its address bus contains 20 lines. What is the maximum memory capacity that can be connected to the microprocessor? How many bytes can be stored in memory?

7-38. A 16-bit microprocessor has a single 16-bit bus which is shared for transferring either a 16-bit address or a 16-bit data word. Explain why an external address latch or register would be required to store the address for the memory unit. Formulate a possible set of control signals for communicating between the microprocessor and memory. List the sequence of transfers for a memory read and a memory write cycles.

7-39. In certain scientific computations it is necessary to perform the combined multiply and add operation $X_i + Y_i * Z_i$ with a high-speed stream of numbers. Specify a pipeline configuration to carry out this task. List the contents of all registers in the pipe-time for $i = 1$ through 6.

Microprogram Control Organization

8

8-1 CONTROL MEMORY

The function of the control unit in a digital system is to initiate sequences of micro-operations. The number of different micro-operations available in a given system is finite. The complexity of the digital system is derived from the fact that a large number of micro-operations are performed in a given time sequence. When the control functions are generated by hardware using conventional logic design techniques, the control unit is said to be *hard-wired*. Microprogramming is a second alternative for designing the control unit of a digital computer. The principle of microprogramming is an elegant and systematic method for generating the micro-operation sequences in a digital system.

The control function that specifies a micro-operation is a binary variable. When it is in the 1 state, the corresponding micro-operation is executed. A control variable in its 0 state does not affect the state of the registers in the system. There are occasions when the state of control variables are defined in reverse with the 0 state initiating the micro-operation and the 1 state being the idle state. In a bus-organized system, the control signals that specify micro-operations are groups of bits that select the paths in multiplexers, decoders, and arithmetic logic units.

The control unit initiates a series of sequential steps of micro-operations. During any given time interval, certain micro-operations are to be initiated while all others remain idle. Thus the micro-operation steps in each time interval can be represented by a string of 1's and 0's called a *control word*. As such, control words can be programmed to initiate the various components of the system in a prescribed fashion. A control unit whose micro-operation steps are stored in a memory is called a *microprogrammed control unit*. Each control word of memory is called a *microinstruction* and a sequence of words is called a *microprogram*. Since alterations of the microprogram are seldom needed, the memory can be a read-only memory (ROM). The concept of microprogramming was not practical to implement until fast read-only memories became available commercially. The utilization of a microprogram involves placing all micro-operation steps in words of ROM for use by the control unit through successive read operations. The content of the words in ROM are fixed and cannot be altered by simple programming since no writing capability is available in the ROM. ROM words are made permanent during the hardware production of the unit. Although sometimes programmable read-only memories (PROM) are used, the programming procedure is a hardware process requiring the opening of fused links. Once a PROM is programmed it cannot be altered by simple programming.

A more advanced development known as *dynamic* microprogramming permits a prescribed microprogram to be loaded initially from either the computer console or from an auxiliary memory. Control units that use dynamic microprogramming employ a *writable control memory* (WCM). This memory has the capability of writing (to change the microprogram) but is used mostly for reading. A read-only memory or a writable control memory when used in the control unit of a computer is referred to as a *control memory*.

A computer that employs a microprogrammed control unit will have two separate memories: a main memory and a control memory. The main memory is available to the user for storing his programs. The contents of main memory may alter when the program is executed and every time the program is changed. The user's program in main memory consists of machine instructions and data. The control memory holds a fixed microprogram that cannot be altered by the occasional user. The microprogram consists of microinstructions that specify various internal control signals for execution of register micro-operations. Each machine instruction initiates a series of microinstructions in control memory. These microinstructions generate the micro-operations to (1) fetch the instruction from main memory; (2) evaluate the effective address of the operand; (3) execute the operation specified by the instruction; and (4) return control to the beginning of the fetch cycle to repeat the sequence again for the next instruction.

Figure 8-1 illustrates the general configuration of the microprogrammed control unit. The control memory is assumed to be a ROM, within which all control information is permanently stored. The control address register specifies the word read from control memory. It must be realized that a ROM operates as a combinational circuit

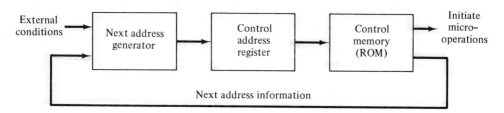

Fig. 8-1 Microprogram control organization.

with the address value as the input and the corresponding word as the output. The content of the specified word remains in the output wires as long as the address value remains in the address register. No *read* signal is needed as in a random-access memory. The word content of ROM should be transferred to a buffer register if the address register changes while the ROM word is still in use. If the change in address and ROM word can occur simultaneously, no buffer register is needed.

The word read from control memory represents a microinstruction. The microinstruction specifies one or more micro-operations for the components in the computer. Once these micro-operations are executed, the control unit must determine its next address. The location of the next microinstruction may be the one next in sequence or, it may be located somewhere else in the control memory. For this reason, it is necessary to use some bits of the microinstruction to control the generation of the address for the next microinstruction. A given microinstruction may also have special bits that specify explicitly the address of the next microinstruction. While the micro-operations are being executed in the processor, the next address is computed in the next address generator circuit and then transferred into the control address register to read the next microinstruction. Thus, a microinstruction contains bits for controlling the micro-operations in the digital system and bits that determine the address sequence of the control memory itself. We shall consider the problem of address sequencing first and then demonstrate the microprogram method by means of an example.

8-2 ADDRESS SEQUENCING

Microinstructions are stored in control memory in groups, with each group specifying a *routine*. Each computer instruction has its own routine in control memory to generate the micro-operations that execute the instruction. The hardware that controls the address sequencing of the control memory must be capable of sequencing the microinstructions within a routine and be able to branch from one routine to another.

Figure 8-2 shows a block digram of a control memory and the associated hardware needed for selecting the next microinstruction address. The microinstruction in control memory contains a set of control bits to specify the method by which the next ROM address is obtained. It may also contain an address field to specify the next address explicitly. The diagram shows four different paths from which the control address register can receive the next address. In order to appreciate the address sequencing in a microprogram control unit, let us enumerate the steps that the control must undergo during the execution of a single computer instruction.

An initial address is loaded into the control address register when a start switch is activated in the computer console. This address is usually the address of the first microinstruction that activates the instruction fetch routine. The fetch cycle routine may be

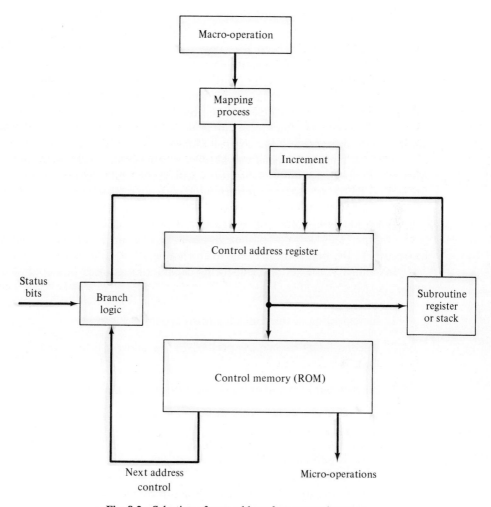

Fig. 8-2 Selection of next address for a control memory.

sequenced by incrementing the control address register through the rest of its micro-instructions. At the end of the fetch routine, the machine instruction would be in the instruction register of the computer.

The control memory next must go through the routine that determines the effective address of the operand. A machine instruction may have bits that specify various addressing modes such as indirect address and index registers. The effective address computation routine in control memory can be reached through a branch micro-instruction which is conditioned upon the status of the mode bits of the instruction.

293

When the effective address computation routine is completed, the address of the operand is available in the memory address register.

The next step is to generate the micro-operations that execute the instruction fetched from memory. The micro-operation steps to be generated in processor registers depend on the operation code part of the instruction, the macro-operation. Each macro-operation has its own routine stored in a given space of control memory. The transformation from the macro-operation bits to the bits of the first ROM address where the routine is stored is referred to as a *mapping* process. A mapping procedure is a rule that transforms the macro-operation into a ROM address. Once the required routine is reached, the microinstructions that execute the macro-operation may be sequenced by incrementing the control address register but sometimes the sequence of micro-operations will depend on values of certain status bits in processor registers. Microprograms that employ subroutines will require an external register or stack for storing the return address. Return addresses cannot be stored in ROM because the unit has no writing capability.

When the execution of the instruction is completed, control must return to the fetch routine. This is accomplished by executing an unconditional branch microinstruction to the first address of the fetch routine.

In summary, the address sequencing capabilities required in a control memory are:

1. Incrementing of the control address register.

2. Unconditional branch as specified by the address field of the microinstruction.

3. Conditional branch depending on status bits in the registers of the computer.

4. A mapping process from the bits of the macro-operation to the required bits of a ROM address.

5. A facility for subroutine calls and returns.

In a microprogrammed device with short control words, a program counter can be used to select the next sequential address by incrementing it by 1 just as the program counter is incremented in a typical computer. However, it is not necessary to provide a separate register for this function since the control address register itself can be incremented. The existence of an increment operation in the address register carries with it the implication that the next address will be selected automatically by counting, unless something is done to override this procedure. This saves bits of ROM because there is no need to have the address bits presented at the output of the control memory except when an out-of-sequence address is desired.

In microprogram devices with longer words, each microinstruction contains the address of the next microinstruction, even for sequential addresses. This eliminates the need for incrementing the control address register because the address field available in each microinstruction specifies the address of the next microinstruction.

Conditional Branch

The branch logic of Fig. 8-2 provides decision making capabilities in the control unit. The status conditions are special bits in the system that provide parameter information such as overflow indication, adder carry out, the sign bit of a register, the mode bits of an instruction, and input or output status conditions. Information in these bits can be tested and actions initiated based on their condition, i.e., whether their value is 1 or 0. The status bits, together with the bits in the microinstruction devoted to determining the next address, control the conditional branch decisions generated in the branch logic. The branch logic hardware may be implemented in a variety of ways. The simplest way is to test the specified condition and branch to the indicated address if the condition is met; otherwise, the address register is incremented. This can be implemented with a multiplexer as shown in Fig. 8-3. Suppose that we have eight status bit conditions to consider. Three bits in the microinstruction are used to specify any one of eight conditions. These three bits provide the selection variables for a multiplexer. If the selected status bit is in the 1 state, the output of the multiplexer is a 1; otherwise it is a 0. A 1 output in the multiplexer generates a control signal to load the address bits of the microinstruction into the address register. A 0 output in the multiplexer causes the address register to be incremented by 1. In this configuration, the control address register acts as a counter with parallel-load capability.

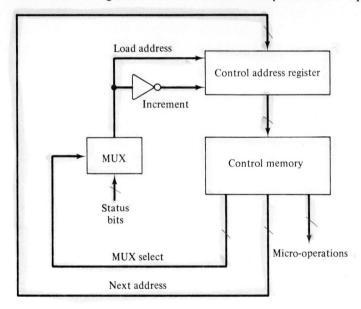

Fig. 8-3 Conditional branch logic.

An unconditional branch microinstruction can be implemented by loading the next address from control memory into the control address register. This can be accomplished with the circuit of Fig. 8-3 by fixing the value of one status bit at the input of the multiplexer so it is always equal to 1. A reference to this status bit by the MUX select lines causes the next address to be loaded into the control address register unconditionally.

The address bits in the microinstruction can be eliminated if a skip condition is used. If the control address register is permitted to count up in steps of one or two, a skip microinstruction will increment the address register by 1 if the condition is not satisfied and by 2 if it is satisfied. An unconditional branch microinstruction in the next word will transfer control to any address if the condition is not satisfied.

Control memories that do not increment the control address register include the address of the next microinstruction in the bits of the current microinstruction. This provides a capability for specifying a sequential address or an address for an unconditional branch. In a conditional branch microinstruction it is necessary to specify two branch locations, one for when the condition is satisfied and the other when it is not. One possibility would be to include two addresses in the branch microinstruction, but this requires an excessive number of control word bits. The second address can be avoided if the conditional branch microinstruction employs an address field with a 0 in the least significant bit position. The branch logic transfers the status bit tested into the last bit of the address register, causing a two way branch. If the status bit is 0, the address register receives an even-numbered address with zero in the last position. If the status bit is 1, a branch to the odd-numbered location would be forced, because the last bit would be a 1. It is possible to have a four-way branch if the last two bits of the address field in the microinstruction contain zeros. Two status bits can be tested simultaneously and forced into the address register. The result is a branch to an address ending with bits 00, 01, 10, or 11, depending on the two status bits tested.

Mapping of Macro-Operation

A special type of branch exists when a microinstruction specifies a branch to the first word in control memory where a routine for a macro-operation is located. The address bits for this type of branch are a function of the bits used in the operation part of the machine instruction. For example, a computer with a simple instruction format as shown in Fig. 8-4 has an operation code of four bits which can specify up to 16 distinct macro-operations. Assume further that the control memory has 128 words requiring an address of seven bits. For each macro-operation there exists a routine in control memory that executes the macro-operation. One specific mapping process that converts the 4-bit operation code to a 7-bit address is shown in Fig. 8-4. This mapping consists of clearing the most significant address bit to 0, transferring the operation-code bits, and clearing the two least significant bits of the control address register. This gives each macro-operation routine a capacity of four microinstructions. If the routine

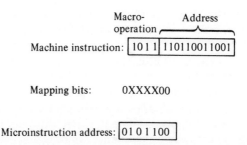

Machine instruction: | 101 1 | 110110011001 |

Mapping bits: 0XXXXX00

Microinstruction address: | 01 0 1 100 |

Fig. 8-4 A mapping process from macro-operation to a microinstruction address.

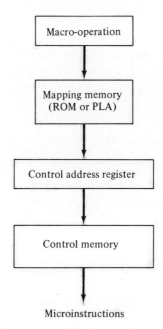

Microinstructions

Fig. 8-5 Mapping memory for transforming a macro-operation to a control memory address.

needs more than four microinstructions, it can use addresses 1000000 through 1111111. If it uses less than four microinstructions, the unused memory locations would be available for other routines.

One can extend this concept to a more general mapping rule by having the mapping function stored in the microinstruction that specifies the branch. A totally flexible scheme is one that uses a second ROM to specify the mapping bits as shown in Fig. 8-5. In this configuration, the bits in the macro-operation specify the address of a mapping memory. The contents of the mapping memory give the bits for the control memory address. In this way, the routine that executes the macro-operation can be placed in any desired location in control memory. The mapping concept provides a flexibility for adding instructions or macro-operations for control memory as the need arises.

The mapping memory is sometimes implemented by means of an integrated circuit called *programmable logic array* (PLA). A PLA is similar to ROM in concept except that it uses internal AND and OR gates instead of a decoder. The interconnection between PLA inputs, AND gates, OR gates, and outputs can be programmed as in a ROM. A mapping function that can be expressed in terms of simplified Boolean expressions can be conveniently implemented with a PLA.

Subroutines

Subroutines are programs to be used by other routines to accomplish a particular task. These routines can be called from any point within the main body of the microprogram. Frequently, many microprograms contain identical sections of code. Microinstructions can be saved by employing subroutines that use common sections of microcode. For example, the sequence of micro-operations needed to generate the effective address of the operand for a machine instruction is common to all memory reference instructions. This sequence could be a subroutine which is called from within many other routines to execute the effective address computation. Microprograms that use subroutines must have a provision for storing the return address during a subroutine call and restoring the address during a subroutine return. This may be accomplished by placing the output from the control address register into a special register and branching to the beginning of the subroutine. This subroutine storage register can then become the address source for setting the address register for the return to the main routine. The best way to structure a register file that stores addresses for subroutines is to organize the registers in a last-in first-out (LIFO) stack. The use of a stack in subroutine calls and returns is explained in more detail in Sec 7-7.

8-3 MICROPROGRAM EXAMPLE

Once the configuration of a computer and its microprogrammed control unit is established, the designer's task is to generate the microcode for the control memory. This code generation is called microprogramming and is a process very similar to conventional machine-language programming. In order to appreciate this process, we present here a simple general-purpose computer and show how it is microprogrammed.

Computer Configuration

The block diagram of the computer is shown in Fig. 8-6. It consists of two memory units: a main memory for storing instructions and data; and a control memory for

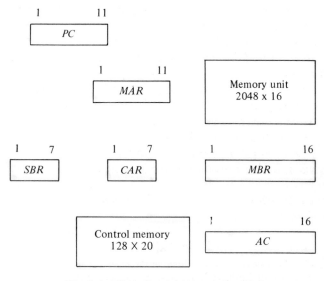

Fig. 8-6 Block diagram of the computer.

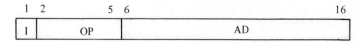

(a) Instruction code format

Symbol	Op-code	Function
ADD	0000	$AC \leftarrow AC + M$
BRANCH	0001	if $(AC < 0)$ then $(PC \leftarrow EA)$
STORE	0010	$M \leftarrow AC$

EA is the effective address.
M is the memory word specified by EA

(b) Operation code (macro-operation)

Fig. 8-7 Computer instructions.

storing the microprogram. Four of the registers are associated with the processor unit and two with the control unit. The processor registers are: program counter *PC*, memory address register *MAR*, memory buffer register *MBR*, and accumulator register *AC*. The function of these registers is similar to the basic computer introduced in Chap 5. The control unit has a control address register *CAR* and a subroutine return register *SBR*. The control memory and its registers are organized as a micro-programmed control unit similar to Fig. 8-2.

The computer instruction format is depicted in Fig. 8-7(a). It consists of three fields: a 1-bit field for indirect addressing symbolized by I, a 4-bit operation code symbolized by OP, and an 11-bit address field AD. Figure 8-7(b) lists three of sixteen possible memory-reference instructions. The ADD instruction adds the content of the operand found in the effective address to the content of the *AC*. The BRANCH instruction causes a branch to the effective address if the operand in the *AC* is negative. Control goes to the next consecutive address if the *AC* is not negative. The *AC* is negative if its sign bit (the bit in the leftmost position of the register) is a 1. The STORE instruction transfers the content of the *AC* into the memory word specified by the effective address.

It will be shown subsequently that each machine instruction must be microprogrammed. In order not to complicate the microprogramming example, only three computer instructions are considered here. It should be realized that thirteen other instructions can be included and each instruction must be microprogrammed by the procedure outlined below.

Microinstruction Format

The microinstruction format for the control memory is shown in Fig. 8-8(a). The 20 bits of the microinstruction are divided into four functional fields. The micro-ops fields specify micro-operations for the computer. The CD field selects status bit conditions, the BR field specifies the type of branch, and the ADF field contains an address. The address field is seven bits long since the control memory has $128 = 2^7$ words.

The *micro-ops* field is subdivided into three subfields F1, F2, and F3, of three bits each. The three bits in each field are encoded to specify seven distinct micro-operations as listed in Fig. 8-8(b). This gives a total of 21 micro-operations. No more than three micro-operations can be chosen for a microinstruction, one from each field. If less than three micro-operations are used, one or more of the fields will use the binary code 000 for no operation. As an illustration, a microinstruction can specify the two simultaneous micro-operations

$$MBR \leftarrow M \qquad \text{with} \qquad F2 = 100$$
$$\text{and} \quad PC \leftarrow PC + 1 \qquad \text{with} \qquad F3 = 101$$

and none from F1. The nine bits of the micro-ops fields will then be 000 100 101.

Note that each micro-operation in Fig. 8-8(b) is defined with a register transfer statement and is assigned a mnemonic for use in a symbolic microprogram. All transfer-type micro-operations symbols use five letters. The first two letters designate the source register, the third letter is always a T, and the last two letters designate the destination register. For example, the micro-operation that specifies the transfer *AC* ← *MBR* (F1 = 100) has the symbol BRTAC, which stands for (*M*)*BR* to *AC*.

The CD (condition) field consists of two bits which are encoded to specify four status bit conditions as listed in Fig. 8-8(c). The first condition is always a 1 so that

(a) Microinstruction format (20 bits):

3	3	3	2	2	7
F1	F2	F3	CD	BR	AD

— Micro-ops →

F1	Micro-operation	Symbol
000	None	NOP
001	$AC \leftarrow AC + MBR$	ADD
010	$AC \leftarrow 0$	CLRAC
011	$AC \leftarrow AC + 1$	INCAC
100	$AC \leftarrow MBR$	BRTAC
101	$MAR \leftarrow MBR (AD)$	BRTAR
110	$MAR \leftarrow PC$	PCTAR
111	$M \leftarrow MBR$	WRITE

F2	Micro-operation	Symbol
000	None	NOP
001	$AC \leftarrow AC - MBR$	SUB
010	$AC \leftarrow AC \vee MBR$	OR
011	$AC \leftarrow AC \wedge MBR$	AND
100	$MBR \leftarrow M$	READ
101	$MBR \leftarrow AC$	ACTBR
110	$MBR \leftarrow MBR + 1$	INCBR
111	$MBR (AD) \leftarrow PC$	PCTBR

F3	Micro-operation	Symbol
000	None	NOP
001	$AC \leftarrow AC \oplus MBR$	XOR
010	$AC \leftarrow \overline{AC}$	COM
011	shl AC	SHL
100	shr AC	SHR
101	$PC \leftarrow PC + 1$	INCPC
110	$PC \leftarrow MBR (AD)$	BRTPC
111	Reserved	—

(b) Micro-operation fields bit assignment:

CD	Condition	Symbol	Comments
00	1	U	Unconditional (always = 1)
01	$MBR (I)$	I	Indirect address bit
10	$AC (S)$	S	Sign bit of AC
11	$AC = 0$	Z	Zero value in AC

(c) CD (condition) field bit assignment:

BR	Symbol	Function
00	JMP	$CAR \leftarrow ADF$ if condition = 1 $CAR \leftarrow CAR + 1$ if condition = 0
01	CALL	$CAR \leftarrow ADF$, $SBR \leftarrow CAR + 1$ if condition = 1 $CAR \leftarrow CAR + 1$ if condition = 0
10	RET	$CAR \leftarrow SBR$ (Return from subroutine)
11	MAP	$CAR (2-5) \leftarrow MBR (OP)$, $CAR (1, 6, 7) \leftarrow 0$ (Micro-operation mapping)

(d) BR (branch) field bit assignment:

Fig. 8-8 Microinstruction format and bit assignment.

a reference to CD = 00 will always find the conditions to be true. When this condition is used in conjunction with the BR (branch) field, it provides an unconditional branch operation. The indirect bit I is available from bit 1 of the *MBR* after an instruction is read from memory. The sign bit of the *AC* provides the next status bit. The zero value symbolized by Z is a binary variable whose value is equal to 1 if all the bits in the *AC* are equal to zero. We will use the symbols U, I, S, and Z for the four status bits when we write microprograms in symbolic form.

The BR (branch) field consists of two bits. It is used, in conjunction with the address field ADF, to choose the address of the next microinstruction. As shown in the table of Fig. 8-8(d), when BR = 00, the control performs a jump (JMP) operation (which is similar to a branch) and when BR = 01, it performs a call to subroutine (CALL). The two operations are identical except that a call microinstruction stores the return address in the subroutine register *SBR*. The jump and call operations depend on the value of the CD field. If the status bit condition specified in the CD field is equal to 1, then the next address in ADF is transferred to the control address register *CAR*. Otherwise, *CAR* is incremented by 1.

The return from subroutine is accomplished with a BR field equal to 10. This causes the transfer of the return address form *SBR* to *CAR*. The mapping from the macro-operation bits to *CAR* is accomplished when the BR field is equal to 11. This mapping is as depicted in Fig. 8-4. The macro-operation is specified by the operation code bits of the instruction. These bits are in *MBR(OP)* after an instruction is read from memory. Note that the last two conditions in the BR field are independent of the values in the CD and ADF fields.

Symbolic Microinstructions

The symbols defined in Fig. 8-8 can be used to specify microinstructions in symbolic form. A symbolic microprogram can be translated into its binary equivalent by means of an assembler. A microprogram assembler is similar in concept to a conventional computer assembler as defined in Sec. 6-3. The simplest and most straightforward way to formulate an assembly language for a microprogram is to define symbols for each field of the microinstruction and to give the user a capability for defining his own symbolic names and addresses.

Each line of the assembly language program defines a symbolic microinstruction. Each symbolic microinstruction is divided into six fields: label, micro-ops, CD, BR, ADF, and comments. The fields specify the following information.

1. The *label* field may be empty or it may specify a symbolic address. A label is terminated with a colon (:).

2. The *micro-ops* field consists of one, two, or three symbols, separated by commas, from those defined in Fig. 8-8(b). There may be no more than one symbol from each F field. The NOP symbol is used when the microinstruction has no micro-operations. This will be translated by the assembler to nine zeros.

3. The *CD* field will have one of the letters U, I, S, or Z as defined in Fig. 8-8(c).

4. The *BR* field contains one of the four symbols defined in Fig. 8-8(d).

5. The *ADF* field specifies a value for the address field of the microinstruction in one of three possible ways:
   a. With a symbolic address which must also appear as a label:
   b. With the symbol NEXT to designate the next address in sequence:
   c. When the BR field contains a RET or MAP symbol, the ADF field is left empty and is converted to seven zeros by the assembler.

6. The *comment* field may be empty or it may include a comment preceded by a slash.

We will use also the pseudo-instruction ORG to define the origin, or first address, of a microprogram routine. Thus, the symbol ORG 64 informs the assembler to place the next microinstruction in control memory at decimal address 64, which is equivalent to binary address 1000000.

The Fetch Cycle

The control memory has 128 words, and each word contains 20 bits. To microprogram the control memory, it is necessary to determine the bit values of each of the 128 words. The first 64 words (addresses 0 to 63) are to be occupied by the routines for the 16 macro-operations. The last 64 words may be used for any other purpose. A convenient starting location for the fetch cycle routine is address 64. The microinstructions needed for the fetch routine are:

$$MAR \leftarrow PC$$

$$MBR \leftarrow M, \ PC \leftarrow PC + 1$$

$$MAR \leftarrow MBR(AD), \ CAR(2-5) \leftarrow MBR(OP), \ CAR(1, 6, 7) \leftarrow 0$$

The address of the instruction is transferred from *PC* to *MAR* and the instruction is then read from memory into *MBR*. Since no instruction register is available, the instruction code remains in *MBR*. The address part is transferred to *MAR* and then control is transferred to one of 16 micro-routines by mapping the operation code part of the instruction from *MBR(OP)* into *CAR*.

The fetch cycle routine needs three microinstructions which are placed in control memory at addresses 64, 65, and 66. Using the assembly language conventions defined previously, we can write the symbolic microprogram for the fetch routine as follows:

```
           ORG 64
FETCH:   PCTAR          U  JMP   NEXT   /PC to MAR
         READ, INCPC    U  JMP   NEXT   /Read instruction, inc PC
         BRTAR          U  MAP           /MBR(AD) to MAR, map to
                                         macro-operation routine
```

The translation of the symbolic program by an assembler produces the following binary microprogram: The bit values are obtained from Fig. 8-8.

Binary address	Micro-ops	CD	BR	ADF
1000000	110 000 000	00	00	1000001
1000001	000 100 101	00	00	1000010
1000010	101 000 000	00	11	0000000

The three microinstructions that constitute the fetch cycle are listed above in three different representations. The register transfer representation shows the internal register transfer operations that each microinstruction implements. The symbolic representation is useful for writing microprograms in an assembly language format. The binary representation is the actual internal content that must be stored in control memory. It is customary to write microprograms in symbolic form and then use an assembler program to obtain an automatic translation to binary.

Symbolic Microprogram

The execution of the third (MAP) microinstruction in the fetch cycle results in a branch to address 0XXXX00, where XXXX are the four bits of the macro-operation. For example, if MBR has an ADD instruction whose operation code is 0000, the MAP micro-instruction will transfer to CAR the address 0000000, which is the start address for the ADD routine. The first address for the BRANCH and STORE routines are 0 0001 00 (decimal 4) and 0 0010 00 (decimal 8), respectively. The first address for the other thirteen routines are at address values 12, 16, 20, . . . , 60. This gives four words for each routine.

In each routine we must provide microinstructions for evaluating the effective address and for executing the instruction. The indirect address mode is associated with all memory-reference instructions. A saving in the number of control memory words may be achieved if the microinstructions for the indirect address are stored as a subroutine. This subroutine, symbolized by INDRCT, is located right after the fetch cycle, as shown in Table 8-1. The table also shows the symbolic microprogram for the fetch cycle and the microinstruction routines that execute three computer instructions.

To see how the transfer and return from the indirect subroutine occurs, assume that the MAP microinstruction at the end of the fetch cycle caused a branch to address 0, where the ADD routine is stored. The first microinstruction in the ADD routine calls subroutine INDRCT, conditioned on status bit I. If $I = 1$, a branch to INDRCT occurs and the return address (address 1 in this case) is stored in the subroutine register SBR. The INDRCT subroutine has two microinstructions:

TABLE 8-1 Symbolic Microprogram (Partial)

Label	Micro-ops	CD	BR	ADF
	ORG 0			
ADD:	NOP	I	CALL	INDRCT
	READ	U	JMP	NEXT
	ADD	U	JMP	FETCH
	ORG 4			
BRANCH:	NOP	S	JMP	OVER
	NOP	U	JMP	FETCH
OVER:	NOP	I	CALL	INDRCT
	BRTPC	U	JMP	FETCH
	ORG 8			
STORE:	NOP	I	CALL	INDRCT
	ACTBR	U	JMP	NEXT
	WRITE	U	JMP	FETCH
	ORG 64			
FETCH:	PCTAR	U	JMP	NEXT
	READ, INCPC	U	JMP	NEXT
	BRTAR	U	MAP	
INDRCT:	READ	U	JMP	NEXT
	BRTAR	U	RET	

INDRCT:	READ	U	JMP	NEXT	$/MBR \leftarrow M$
	BRTAR	U	RET		$/MAR \leftarrow MBR(AD), CAR \leftarrow SBR$

Remember that an indirect address considers the address part of the instruction as the address where the effective address is stored rather than the address of the operand. Therefore, the memory has to be accessed to get the effective address, which is then transferred to MAR. The return from subroutine (RET) transfers the address from SBR to CAR, thus returning to the second micro-instruction of the ADD routine.

The execution of the ADD instruction is carried out by the microinstructions at addresses 1 and 2. These two microinstructions read the operand from memory into MBR, perform an add micro-operation with the content of the AC and then cause a jump back to the beginning of the fetch routine.

The BRANCH instruction should cause a branch to the effective address if $AC < 0$. The AC will be less than zero if its sign is negative, which is detected from status bit S being a 1. The Branch routine in Table 8-1 starts by checking the value of S. If S is equal to 0, no jump occurs and the next microinstruction causes a jump back to the fetch routine without altering the content of PC. If S is equal to 1, the first JMP microinstruction transfers control to location OVER. The microinstruction at this location calls the INDRCT subroutine if $I = 1$. The effective address is then transferred to PC and the microprogram jumps back to the fetch routine.

The STORE routine again uses the INDRCT subroutine if $I = 1$. The content of the AC is transferred into MBR. A memory-write operation is initiated to store the content of MBR in a location specified by the effective address.

Note that Table 8-1 contains a partial list of the microprogram. Only three out of 16 possible computer instructions have been microprogrammed. Also, control memory words at locations 69 to 127 have not been used. Instructions such as multiply, divide, and others that require a long sequence of micro-operations will need more than four microinstructions for their execution. Control memory words 69 to 127 can be used for this purpose.

Binary Microprogram

The symbolic microprogram is a convenient format for writing microprograms in a way that people can read and understand. But this is not the way that the microprogram is stored in memory. The symbolic microprogram must be translated to binary either by means of an assembler program, or by the user himself if the microprogram is simple enough, as in this example.

The equivalent binary form of the microprogram is listed in Table 8-2. The address for control memory is given both in decimal and binary. The binary content of each microinstruction is derived from the symbols and their equivalent binary values as defined in Fig. 8-8. Table 8-2 constitutes the truth table that specifies the binary content of the control memory.

Note that address 3 has no equivalent in the symbolic microprogram since the ADD routine has only microinstructions at addresses 0, 1, and 2. The next routine starts at address 4. Even though address 3 is not used, something must be specified for each word in control memory. We could have specified all 0's in the word since this location will never be used. However, if some unforeseen error occurs, or if a noise signal sets CAR to the value of 3, it will be wise to jump to address 64, which is the beginning of the fetch routine.

Implementation

The microprogram listed in Table 8-2 specifies the word content of the control memory. When a ROM is used for the control memory, the microprogram binary list provides the truth table for fabricating the unit. This fabrication is a hardware process and consists of creating a mask for the ROM so as to produce the 1's and 0's for each word. The bits of ROM are fixed once the links are fused during the hardware production. The ROM is made of IC packages that can be removed if necessary and replaced by other packages. To modify the instruction set of the computer, it is necessary to generate a new microprogram and mask a new ROM. The old one can be removed and the new one inserted in its place.

TABLE 8-2 Binary Microprogram for Control Memory (Partial)

Micro Routine	Address Decimal	Address Binary	Microinstruction Micro-ops	CD	BR	ADF	Micro-operations and Next Address
ADD	0	0000000	000000000	01	01	1000011	If $I = 1$ go to 67, $SBR \leftarrow 1$ If $I = 0$ go to 1
	1	0000001	000100000	00	00	0000010	$MBR \leftarrow M$, go to 2
	2	0000010	001000000	00	00	1000000	$AC \leftarrow AC + MBR$, go to 64
	3	0000011	000000000	00	00	1000000	Nothing, go to 64
BRANCH	4	0000100	000000000	10	00	0000110	If $AC(S) = 1$ go to 6 If $AC(S) = 0$ go to 5
	5	0000101	000000000	00	00	1000000	Go to 64
	6	0000110	000000000	01	01	1000011	If $I = 1$ go to 67, $SBR \leftarrow 7$ If $I = 0$ go to 7
	7	0000111	000000110	00	00	1000000	$PC \leftarrow MBR(AD)$, go to 64
STORE	8	0001000	000000000	01	01	1000011	If $I = 1$ go to 67, $SBR \leftarrow 9$ If $I = 0$ go to 9
	9	0001001	000101000	00	00	0001010	$MBR \leftarrow AC$, go to 10
	10	0001010	111000000	00	00	1000000	$M \leftarrow MBR$, go to 64
	.	.	.				.
	.	.	.				.
	.	.	.				.
FETCH	64	1000000	110000000	00	00	1000001	$MAR \leftarrow PC$, go to 65
	65	1000001	000100101	00	00	1000010	$MBR \leftarrow M$, $PC \leftarrow PC + 1$, go to 66
	66	1000010	101000000	00	11	0000000	$MAR \leftarrow MBR(AD)$, go to specified routine
INDRCT	67	1000011	000100000	00	00	1000100	$MBR \leftarrow M$, go to 68
	68	1000100	101000000	00	10	0000000	$MAR \leftarrow MBR(AD)$, $CAR \leftarrow SBR$

If a writable control memory is employed, the ROM is replaced by a RAM. The advantage of employing a RAM for the control memory is that the microprogram can be altered by simply writing a new pattern of 1's and 0's without resorting to hardware procedures. A writable control memory possesses the flexibility of choosing the instruction set of a computer dynamically, that is, by changing the microprogram under processor control. However, most microprogrammed systems use a ROM for the control memory because it is cheaper and faster than a RAM and also to prevent the occasional user from changing the architecture of the system.

The example has shown that the microprogram stored in a control memory contains the binary variables that control the hardware components of the system. The control information is stored in a memory and executed as a stored program. This gives microprogramming a software as well as a hardware flavor, so the term *firmware* is sometimes used.

8-4 MICROPROGRAM SEQUENCER

A microprogram control unit should be viewed as consisting of two parts: the control memory that stores the microinstructions and the associated circuits that control the generation of the next address. The address-generation part is called a microprogram sequencer, since it sequences the microinstructions in control memory. A microprogram sequencer can be constructed with digital functions to suit a particular application. However, just as there are large ROM units available in integrated circuit packages, so are general purpose sequencers suited for the construction of microprogram control units. To guarantee a wide range of acceptability, an integrated circuit sequencer must provide an internal organization that can be adapted to a wide range of applications.

The purpose of a microprogram sequencer is to present an address to the control memory so that a microinstruction may be read and executed. The next address logic of the sequencer determines the specific address source to be loaded into the control address register. The choice of the address source is guided by the next address information bits that the sequencer receives from the present microinstruction. Commercial sequencers include within the unit an internal register stack used for temporary storage of addresses during microprogram looping and subroutine calls. Some sequencers provide an output register which can function as the address register for the control memory.

To illustrate the internal structure of a typical microprogram sequencer we will show a particular unit which is suitable for use in the microprogram computer example developed in the preceding section. The block diagram of the microprogram sequencer is shown in Fig. 8-9. The control memory is included in the diagram to show the interaction between the sequencer and the memory attached to it. There are two multiplexers in the circuit. The first multiplexer selects an address from one of four sources and routes it into a control address register CAR. The second multiplexer tests the value of a selected status bit and the result of the test is applied to an input logic circuit. The output from CAR provides the address for the control memory. The content of CAR is incremented and applied to one of the multiplexer inputs and to the subroutine register SBR. The other three inputs to multiplexer number 1 come from the address field of the present microinstruction, from the output of SBR, and from an

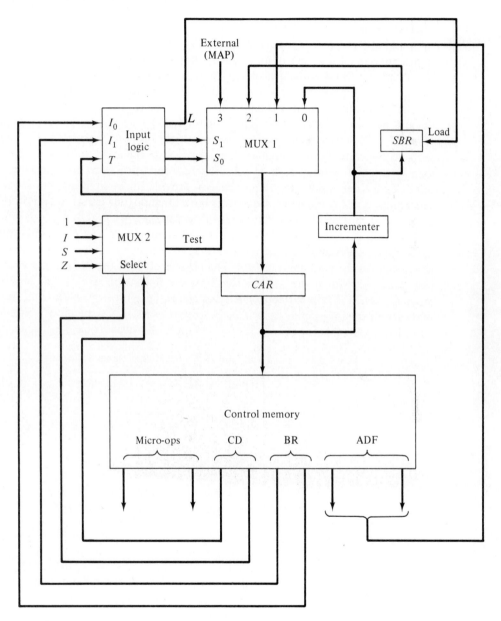

Fig. 8-9 Microprogram sequencer for a control memory.

external source that maps the macro-operation. Although the diagram shows a single subroutine register, a typical sequencer will have a register stack about four to eight levels deep. In this way, a number of subroutines can be active at the same time. A push and pop operation, in conjunction with a stack pointer, stores and retrieves the return address during the call and return microinstructions.

The CD (condition) field of the microinstruction selects one of the status bits in the second multiplexer. If the selected bit is equal to 1, then the T (test) variable is equal to 1; otherwise, it is equal to 0. The T value together with the two bits from the BR (branch) field go to an input logic circuit. The input logic in a particular sequencer will determine the type of operations that are available in the unit. Typical sequencer operations are: increment, branch or jump, call and return from subroutine, load an external address, push or pop the stack, and other address sequencing operations. With three inputs, the sequencer can provide up to eight address sequencing operations. Some commercial sequencers have three or four inputs in addition to the T input and thus provide a wider range of operations.

The input logic circuit in Fig. 8-9 has three inputs, I_0, I_1, and T, and three outputs, S_0, S_1, and L. Variables S_0 and S_1 select one of the source addresses for CAR. Variable L enables the load input in SBR. The binary values of the two selection variables determine the path in the multiplexer. For example, with $S_1 S_0 = 10$, multiplexer input number 2 is selected and establishes a transfer path from SBR to CAR. Note that each of the four inputs as well as the output of MUX 1 contains a 7-bit address.

The truth table for the input logic circuit is shown in Table 8-3. Inputs I_1 and

TABLE 8-3   Input Logic Truth Table for Microprogram Sequencer

BR Field	Input I_1 I_0 T	MUX 1 S_1 S_0	Load SBR L
0 0	0 0 0	0 0	0
0 0	0 0 1	0 1	0
0 1	0 1 0	0 0	0
0 1	0 1 1	0 1	1
1 0	1 0 X	1 0	0
1 1	1 1 X	1 1	0

I_0 are identical to the bit values in the BR field. The function listed in each entry was defined in Fig. 8-8(d). The bit values for S_1 and S_0 are determined from the stated function and the path in the multiplexer that establishes the required transfer. The subroutine register is loaded with the incremented value of CAR during a call microinstruction (BR = 01) provided the status bit condition is satisfied ($T = 1$). The truth table can be used to obtain the simplified Boolean functions for the input logic circuit:

$$S_1 = I_1$$
$$S_0 = I_1 I_0 + I_1' T$$
$$L = I_1' I_0 T$$

The circuit can be constructed with three AND gates, an OR gate, and an inverter.

Note that the incrementer circuit in the sequencer of Fig. 8-9 is not a counter constructed with flip-flops but rather a combinational circuit constructed with gates. A combinational circuit incrementer can be designed by cascading a series of half-adder circuits (see Fig. 1-17). The output carry from one stage must be applied to the input of the next stage. One input in the first least significant stage must be equal to 1 to provide the increment-by-1 operation.

Bit-Sliced Microprocessor

The central processor unit (CPU) of a digital computer can be divided into two distinct but interactive functional units: the processor unit and the control unit. When the entire CPU is constructed within a single IC package, we call the unit a microprocessor (see Sec. 7-8). An alternative design procedure is to construct the CPU with IC components such as processor unit, microprogram sequencer, and control memory. A CPU structured in this manner is called a bit-sliced microprocessor.

A single IC microprocessor has a predefined and fixed architecture, and therefore its word length and instruction set cannot be altered. In contrast, a bit-sliced microprocessor can be designed to provide an architecture that fits any given specifications. Its word length can be adjusted to the particular application and its instruction set can be defined by means of a microprogram.

The central component in a bit-sliced design is the bit-sliced processor unit which is organized in a modular form, typically four bits wide. Several identical processor slices can be connected together to achieve a desirable word length. For example, a 4-bit slice IC processor unit contains the registers, ALU, and shifter for manipulating 4-bit data. Two such ICs can be combined to construct an 8-bit processor unit. For a 16-bit processor, it is necessary to use four ICs and connect them in cascade. The output carry from one ALU is connected to the input carry of the next-higher-order ALU and the serial output and input lines of the shifter are connected in cascade.

A microprogrammable bit-sliced CPU has the basic functional block diagram shown in Fig. 8-10. The processor unit is constructed from 4-bit sliced IC components. The diagram shows a 16-bit wide processor unit made up from four ICs. The internal structure of a typical processor unit is shown in Fig. 7-1. The status bits in the processor, such as carry, sign, zero, and overflow, are applied to the microprogram sequencer. The mapping function converts the bits of the instruction code to a control memory address. The microprogram sequencer and control memory are presented in more detail in Fig. 8-9.

The pipeline register inserted between the control memory and the processor is optional. If used, it provides an isolation between the present microinstruction which is available at the output of the register and the next microinstruction which is read from control memory. While the present microinstruction is executing the micro-operations in the processor, the next address can be computed and the next microinstruction can be read from control memory. This allows an overlapping of

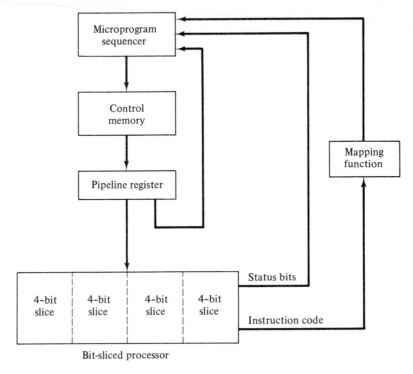

Bit-sliced processor

Fig. 8-10 Block diagram of a bit-sliced CPU.

the microinstruction execution with reading of the next microinstruction. The pipe-line register provides a parallel processing scheme which improves overall system performance and speed.

All the components needed to design a bit-sliced CPU are available in high-speed integrated circuit chips. Bit-sliced microprocessors are designed and manufactured to achieve a high performance level and to satisfy a specific need.

8-5 MICROINSTRUCTION FORMATS

The bits of a microinstruction are usually divided into parts called fields, with each field defining a distinct, separate function. The various fields encountered in micro-instruction formats provide the following functions:

1. A control word that initiates micro-operations in the system. The bits of the control word are sometimes subdivided into separate fields.

2. Control and address bits for the sequencer to specify the way the next micro-instruction address is to be evaluated.

3. Other special fields containing data for transfer to a given destination.

In the computer of Sec. 8-3 we have shown an example of a microinstruction format employing the first two types of fields listed above. The process of introducing data into the system from the output of the control memory is a frequently used technique in many microprogrammed systems. The field in the control word that does this is called *emit* field or a *literal*. Output from the emit field may be used to set up control registers and introduce data into processor registers. For example, a constant in the emit field may be added to a register to increment its content by a specified value. Another use of the emit field is in setting a sequence counter to a constant value. The sequence counter is then used to count the number of times a microprogram loop is traversed, as is usually required in a multiply or divide routine.

The designer who is assigned the task of formulating the microinstruction format for a control memory must be thoroughly familiar with the total system operation and have an insight for any future developments. There are many techniques which are useful in formulating the microinstruction and some of these techniques are discussed below. Usually, a combination of techniques is employed to formulate microinstructions; the ones used depend on the particular application.

Horizontal Microinstructions

The simplest configuration is to use one bit of the microinstruction to control each micro-operation. For example, the 21 micro-operations defined in Fig. 8-8(b) will require a 21-bit field if a horizontal format is adopted. The technique concentrates on the individual control variables that are required in the system and is concerned with the optimum generation of these variables. There can be as many as fifty or more different micro-operations in a computer which may result in an excessively long control word. Horizontal microinstructions with 64 bits or more are common. The term horizontal implies the existence of a long control word that produces a horizontal pattern of 1's and 0's.

Horizontal microinstructions are able to control a variety of components operating in parallel. A horizontal microinstruction may initiate the simultaneous and independent micro-operations for many registers, for a memory-read or memory-write operation and for the generation of the next address, all in one microinstruction. Horizontal microprogramming has the potential advantage of efficient hardware utilization. However, the bits in the control word are not fully utilized and the fact that long words are used makes the control memory very expensive.

Encoding of Control Bits

The number of control bits in a control word can be reduced by grouping mutually exclusive variables into fields and encoding the k bits in each field to provide 2^k micro-operations. Each field requires a hardware decoder to produce the corresponding control signals. This method reduces the size of the control word but requires additional hardware external to the control memory. It also increases the generation time of the control signals because the bits of the microinstruction must propagate through the decoder circuits. The designer must select mutually exclusive operations when grouping control bits into fields.

The encoding of control bits was demonstrated in the programming example of Sec. 8-3. Both the condition (CD) and branch (BR) fields are encoded to give four functions with two bits. The nine bits of the micro-ops fields are divided into three subfields of three bits each and each subfield was encoded to give eight micro-operations. A horizontal format could be established if the micro-ops field were not encoded. In that case, each bit can specify one distinct micro-operation. The horizontal format allows the simultaneous initiation of nine micro-operations, while the encoded format was restricted to specifying three simultaneous micro-operations in one microinstruction. The nine bits of the micro-ops field can be encoded to supply $2^9 = 512$ micro-operations. However, a computer would not have that many distinct micro-operations and a 9 to 512 line decoder would require an excessive number of gates. Moreover, only one micro-operation could be specified in each microinstruction.

Multiple Word Format

In large computers, speed is attained by allowing many operations to proceed simultaneously. The greater the simultaneity, the longer the control word becomes. In slow computers, control decisions are made sequentially and therefore shorter control words can be used. One frequently used technique in small systems is to have a number of different control word formats. Each of these formats will generally be dedicated to one type of major operation. This greatly reduces the length of the control words but also slows down the system performance. For example, in short word-length microprogrammed devices, one microinstruction will be used to add two registers, a second to test the result and a third to branch to an address based on the result of the test. Each of these microinstructions might have a different format, whereas in a longer control word this would be accomplished in one microinstruction word.

A method by which a multiple control word format may be achieved is by encoding the meaning of some fields according to the value of the bits in another field. Thus, one field can specify the way the other fields are interpreted. The use of multiple-bit format can save a significant number of control bits at the expense of more complex decoding circuitry.

An example of a multiple word format is shown in Table 8-4 where an eight-bit control word is used to give five different formats. Bits 1 and 2 provide a field whose purpose is to specify the meaning of the other six bits. When bits 1 and 2 are 00, the other six bits specify one of 64 micro-operations; when 01, the other bits specify the address for an unconditional branch. When 10, the other bits specify an ALU function and when 11, bits 3 and 4 are further used to specify two possible configurations. When bits 3 and 4 are 00, the remaining bits specify one of 16 possible status conditions for a skip microinstruction. When 11, the remaining four bits are interpreted as an emit field whose value is transferred to a sequence counter.

TABLE 8-4   Multiple-Bit Format for an Eight-Bit Control Word

1 2 3 4 5 6 7 8	Control Word Bits
00 X X X X X X	64 micro-operations specified by XXXXXX bits
01 Y Y Y Y Y Y	Branch to address YYYYYY
10 Z Z Z Z Z Z	Perform ALU function specified by ZZZZZZ bits
11 0 0 C C C C	Skip next microinstruction on status condition CCCC
11 1 1 S S S S	Transfer SSSS to sequence counter

Vertical Microinstructions

A microinstruction format that is not horizontal is commonly classified as a vertical microinstruction. This is a term given to a microinstruction that needs decoding circuits external to the control memory. As such, it encompasses the last two techniques discussed above. In the horizontal configuration, there is usually no decoding of control bits since each bit controls one micro-operation. The term "vertical" is derived from the fact that the encoding of fields necessitates decoding circuits that form a vertical pattern. This pattern may consist of one or two levels of decoding.

A *direct* encoding of bits results in a single level of decoding as shown in Fig. 8-11(a). The bits that control the mutually exclusive operations are combined into fields. The circuits that decode the bits in each field form a single level of decoders.

An *indirect* encoding results in a multiple-word format with the meaning of the fields made to depend on the value of a control field in the microinstruction. The circuits that decode this type of control word require two levels of decoding. As shown in Fig. 8-11(b), the two bits of field A control the function of the six bits in field B. Both fields are decoded in the first level. The second level combines each of the four output lines from decoder A with the outputs of decoder B to supply the control signals.

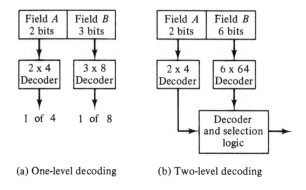

(a) One-level decoding   (b) Two-level decoding

Fig. 8-11 Decoding pattern of vertical microinstructions.

Nanomemory and Nanoinstructions

The decoder circuits in a vertical microprogram memory organization constitute a combinational circuit. It was mentioned in Sec. 2-7 that any combinational circuit can be implemented by means of a read-only memory (ROM). If we replace the decoding circuits with a ROM, we obtain a microprogram control unit with two memory levels: the first level contains the microinstructions and the second level decodes the fields of the microinstructions. Some computers use this mode of operation in which an encoded microinstruction addresses a lower level memory, which is then called a *nanomemory*. The words stored in the nanomemory are called *nanoinstructions*.

    A two-level microprogram memory organization can be viewed as a mechanism that converts a vertical microinstruction format into a horizontal nanoinstruction format. The horizontal nanoinstruction format is usually a long word exceeding 100 bits that includes the control words for all possible micro-operations in the system. Although each word contains a large number of bits, the total number of words in a nanomemory is usually relatively small because there are a finite number of ways that micro-operations can be combined to operate in parallel. The result is that the microprogram memory has a large number of short microinstructions, while the nanomemory contains fewer words with longer nanoinstructions. The short vertical format of the microinstruction provides an address for the nanomemory. The word at that address provides a long horizontal format nanoinstruction. This scheme is attractive in computers that need a large number of bits to specify micro-operations and have the characteristic that the same combination of micro-operations operating in parallel happen to occur frequently.

    To illustrate the concept of a nanomemory with an example, assume that a microprogram needs 2048 microinstructions of 200 bits each. With only one memory in the system, we will require a control memory of $2048 \times 200 = 409{,}600$ bits. Suppose that an investigation reveals that only 256 different microinstruction bit combinations are possible because of conflicts among micro-operations operating in parallel. A more efficient method would be to design the system with two memory levels as shown in Fig. 8-12. A nanomemory of size 256 × 200 is used to store the 256 distinct nanoinstructions. The control memory can be reduced to 2048 × 8 bits. Each of the 2048 microinstructions can now supply an 8-bit address for the nanomemory. In the example shown, the nanomemory requires 256 × 200 = 51,200 bits. The control memory requires 2048 × 8 = 16,384 bits. Thus, the two-level memory system requires a total of 51,200 + 16,384 = 67,584 bits, compared to 409,600 bits in the one-memory scheme. In addition, the control memory word must have one or more extra fields for controlling the address sequence of microinstructions.

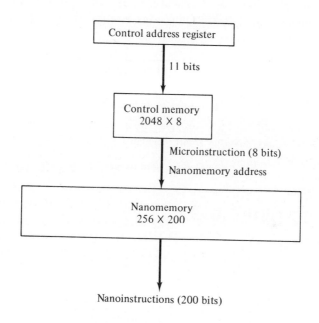

Fig. 8-12   Nanomemory control organization.

Direct Control of Bus System

A CPU is quite often organized around a bus system. A microinstruction that controls a bus organized CPU may be classified as a vertical microinstruction with the decoders for the various fields being placed in the bus system itself. A block diagram of a CPU bus system was presented in Sec.7-1. From Fig. 7-1 we note that the control selection inputs to each of the five components in the system are already decoded within the components. The microinstruction that controls this bus system can be divided into five fields, with each field providing the control bits to select the function in each component.

A control-word format for controlling a bus system is depicted in Fig. 8-13. Two fields LB and RB specify the source registers for the input buses to the ALU. If there are eight registers in the system, each of these fields must contain three bits. These bits are applied directly to the selection inputs of the multiplexer that controls the input bus. The FU field specifies the ALU function and the SH field, the type of shift. The number of bits in these fields are dependent on the number of decoded functions that the units provide. The DB field specifies the destination register for storing the result. In addition to these fields, the control word must have fields for determining the address sequence of microinstructions.

We have discussed here a few methods commonly employed to formulate the control word formats for a control memory. In a practical situation, a combination of techniques is used, taking into consideration the particular application and economic factors.

LB	RB	DB	FU	SH	Address sequence

LB   Specifies the register to be connected to the left bus of ALU
RB   Specifies the register to be connected to the right bus of ALU
DB   Specifies the register where the result is to be transferred
FU   Specifies an ALU function
SH   Specifies a shift function

Fig. 8-13   Control word format for a bus organized CPU.

8-6   SOFTWARE AIDS

Microprograms are considered to be one level lower than machine-language programs. Machine-language programs deal with instructions that specify macro-operations between memory and processor registers. The programmer does not have to be concerned with micro-operations or other control details involved in the execution of the instructions. Microprograms for a control memory deal with the hardware resource of the system and require a familiarity with and knowledge of the hardware organization of components and how they react to each microinstruction. Nevertheless, the two types of programming are conceptually similar and knowledge of one provides valuable experience for working with the other.

Just as in machine language, microprograms can be written in straight binary or in symbolic form. The binary procedure is tedious and error prone. However, for a small control memory to be used in a particular system only once, this would be the most economical method because there is no way to justify the development costs of a symbolic translator program such as an assembler. A simple register transfer language may help in the process of writing binary programs. The microprogram is first written in symbolic form by means of register transfer statements. The translation to binary can be carried out by the programmer himself by inspection without resorting to an automatic translator.

When a large microprogram has to be developed, or when the same system is used to implement various different configurations, the cost of developing an assembler or even a compiler is justified. Programming with familiar symbols is much less tedious and produces microcodes more quickly and with fewer errors. The translation to binary is done by a system program so the programmer does not have to be concerned with strings of 1's and 0's.

When a microprogram is developed for a new system, it is necessary to produce the ROM with the appropriate 1's and 0's and exercise the system to check for errors and to make sure that the system works properly. This is an expensive procedure because the hardware production of ROMs is costly and time-consuming. Every time a 1 has to be changed to a 0 or vice versa, a new ROM must be produced. The best way to check a microprogram is to use a ROM simulator. A ROM simulator is a high-speed special random-access memory that can be operated in a read-only mode to simulate the operation of a ROM. A pattern of 1's and 0's is entered into the simulator RAM by placing the unit in an off-line position and a write mode. Simulation is achieved by placing the unit in an on-line position which extends control of only the read function to the user's equipment. The cables in the simulator have special connectors designed to plug directly into the ROM sockets of the system being checked. The simulator performs under actual working conditions and is used to exercise the system. Changes can be effected by placing the simulator in an off-line position and writing a new pattern. When the design has been proved to work correctly, error-free ROM masks can be generated from the content of the simulator memory.

Simulators facilitate microprogram checkout, but do not simplify the writing of microprograms. They are useful in determining alternate machine architectures and in developing new and experimental systems. To facilitate microprogram preparation, most manufactures of microprogrammable machines develop suitable support software such as assemblers and compilers.

An assembler is a computer program which translates symbolic code into an equivalent binary pattern. Assemblers can be used to translate symbolic microprograms just as they are used to translate machine-language programs. Symbolic microprograms can be written either in a register transfer language or in a conventional assembly language. A register transfer language for writing microprograms would be similar to the one used in this book except that it must be defined precisely. The exact rules for writing symbolic statements must be formulated so one can write a symbolic program that can be translated correctly without any ambiguity. Each register transfer statement would have an equivalent bit or a group of bits in a microinstruction that defines the relation between the symbolic statement and its equivalent binary pattern. Any special character employed in the register transfer language (such as an arrow) must be available in the input device used to prepare the program (such as a teletypewriter or punch cards). If not available, it would be necessary to replace it by another available character. An example of a register transfer microprogramming language is presented in Sec. 9-8.

An assembly microprogramming language provides the capability to express microinstructions in symbolic form similar to a machine-language assembler. A fixed format in which certain columns are reserved for each field is characteristic of such languages. The symbols for each field are defined and the assembler translates each symbol to an equivalent binary field. The microinstruction is assembled from the binary fields so obtained.

The translation of an assembly language program to binary is often performed on a separate computer and the resulting microcode is then used for the system that executes the microprogram. This is especially necessary when the development of the hardware and the microprogram is done concurrently. A host computer is employed to translate the microprogram while the hardware of the system that will use the microprogram is being developed.

The use of high-level languages for microprogramming is still in its infancy. The development and use of such languages has been restricted due to the scarcity of user microprogrammable computers and the inefficiency of compiled microcodes. The adoption of microprogramming for the control section of microprocessors and the use of this technique by developers of microcomputer systems will most likely stimulate the development of efficient high-level microprogramming languages.

8-7 ADVANTAGES AND APPLICATIONS

It was shown in previous sections that microprogramming is a method for implementing the control unit of a digital computer. A second alternative is to employ a hard-wired control implementation and design it entirely with hardware, without the use of a control memory. There are many advantages and a few disadvantages to using a microprogrammed control unit as opposed to a hard-wired configuration. Moreover, the microprogramming concept is not unique to a digital computer. There are many other digital systems that can use this concept to obtain an efficient control implementation.

The design of a control unit with a control memory, as opposed to a hard-wired inplementation, may, sometimes, be too costly. This is especially true when the digital system is very simple and does not require many micro-operations or many control decisions. If only a few identical units are to be produced, the cost of the ROM may be higher than the few gates and flip-flops that a hard-wired control may require. One must realize that the price to be paid for a control memory is not only the cost of the ROM itself but also the time and cost involved in the hardware production for masking the microprogram bits. In other words, the vendor will usually add on an extra charge for every new ROM configured by the customer, in addition to the price of each IC package. However, for a system with a rather complex set of instructions, the investment in the control memory is often justified.

The use of a control memory may decrease the speed of the computer if the access time of the ROM is longer than the time that signals would take to propagate if a hard-wired control were used. Control decisions in a hard-wired implementation are available as soon as the control signals propagate. In a microprogrammed control unit, the time it takes to execute a micro-operation includes the access time of ROM. However, if the access time of ROM is relatively short, a control memory may not markedly affect the speed of the computer.

The most important advantage of microprogramming is that it provides a well-structured control organization. A hard-wired control unit is generally quite random. It contains counters, special flip-flops, decoders, and assorted combinational circuits. In microprogramming, control functions are systematized into a kind of programming discipline and a regular memory replaces most of the random combinational circuits. The more regular a machine organization, the fewer miscellaneous parts must be implemented with small-scale integration, low density, logic circuits.

A microprogrammed control unit is more adaptable to changes. During the design of a system, new ideas always come up to improve it and frequently one discovers that some portions have been left out. With microprogramming many additions and changes can be made by changing the microprogram in control memory. Final system definition can be postponed to a later time in the design cycle since it is possible to alter the instruction set without affecting the hardware design. Because of the nature of the control memory organization, it is possible to introduce rather complex instructions into the instruction set with no additional hardware. The required micro-operation steps can be provided by simply using additional locations in the control memory.

Microprogramming has many economic advantages. Although hard-wired logic is a more economical way of implementing very simple systems, as the complexity of the system increases, the cost of the control logic increases at a fairly rapid rate. In microprogrammed implementations, the cost of the simplest system is somewhat higher, but adding new features only requires additional control memory. In general, replacing most of the control logic with a ROM affords substantial hardware savings because of the high-density packaging of ROM arrays. It is estimated that about 16 bits of ROM can be used to replace a gate in the control logic. Thus, a 4096-bit ROM organized as a 256 by 16 array is capable of replacing 256 gates connected randomly.

The problem of servicing and maintaining a computer system is facilitated when microprogramming is used. Every computer system requires a diagnostic package of routines for checking, locating, and isolating hardware malfunctions. These software routines are supplied by the manufacturer for each specific system to help maintenance personnel repair malfunctions in the equipment. If the system does not employ microprogramming, these routines would be written in machine language and use the main memory for their execution. With microprogramming, it is possible to use routines which reside in control memory. They are usually called microdiagnostic routines and their purpose is to provide the necessary diagnostic procedures for checking malfunctions in the system. A given data path is diagnosed by forcing a sequence of micro-operations by means of predetermined bit test patterns stored in control memory. The output from the data path is analyzed in order to select a finer set of test patterns to isolate an error in a particular unit. The control memory that contains microdiagnostics may employ a ROM or a writable control memory. In the former case, special ROM units containing the microdiagnostic routines must be inserted manually. With a writable control memory, the microdiagnostic routines may be loaded in small segments with each segment being able to check a different portion of the hardware.

Because of the regulartiy of the control memory, computer-aided methods can be utilized to reduce the design cost of the system. The designer can specify the microprogram in symbolic language and employ a computer to translate it into the binary configuration of each control word. Microprogramming also simplifies the documentation and serivice training of the system, resulting in reduced total system cost.

By changing the content of control memory it is possible to change the meaning of the coded bits of computer instructions. The simulation of the instruction set of one computer in another computer is called *emulation*. By changing the microprogram it is possible to emulate one computer in another. Microprogrammable machines have been used to emulate a variety of computers so that one host computer with several emulators can economically replace several different target computers. Also, emulation provides a research facility to experiment with different computer architectures.

Implementing commonly used routines directly in microcode can result in significant performance improvement. Microprogramming simple routines such as multiply, square root, matrix inversion, and table look-up saves the hardware which would be required in a hard-wired implementation or the memory space that will be occupied by a software implementation. Micro-programming is typically more efficient than software and more flexible than hardware in many applications.

Not only a central processor may be controlled by a microprogram, but also other parts of a general-purpose computer. An example would be an input-output processor whose function is to control the transfer of data between a number of specialized devices and main memory. A data communication processor supervises the transfer of information between a computer and many remote terminals. Microprogramming data communication processors provides efficiency and flexibility of implementation because they can be microprogrammed to suit the particular needs of each terminal.

For some time, special, dedicated digital systems have been implemented by hard-wired methods. Because microprogramming offers direct low-level control over the hardware components, as well as the flexibility to alter the design, it is replacing the hard-wired configurations of many special purpose systems. System efficiency is achieved by using instructions which are particularly suited to the specific application. A significant impact on consumer electronics has been the application of microprogramming to the implementation of electronic calculators. Microprogrammed calculator ICs can be modified in function by changes in the content of the read-only memory in the chip.

The use of a writable control memory whose microprogram content can be changed by conventional programming procedures under processor control offers a number of advantages. Multiple sets of microprograms can make the same computer appear at different times as a different logical machine. It can increase performance for certain specialized functions in such areas as scientific applications and compilers. In many scientific applications, a computer may spend the major portion of its processing time executing a given function. Savings in speed may be achieved if a special microprogram is used to execute the repetitive function.

Efficient language translation and compilation can be achieved through microprogramming, as opposed to conventional software compilers. Writable control memory can support a multiplicity of architectures within a single computer. A computer may have a number of different machine codes, say one suitable for scientific calculations and another for commercial use. It can also include different specialized instructions that are efficient for the process of compilation. In a dynamic microprogrammed computer, the microprogram can be changed by the operating system. One microprogram may be used to compile a Fortran program, and another for executing machine instructions. When a Fortran program is to be compiled, the operating system would load into control memory a microprogram which is efficient for compilation. A different microprogram would be loaded during the machine-language program execution.

Many of the functions once performed by hardware are shifting into the domain of microprogramming. The development of integrated circuit memories, both ROM and RAM, is encouraging this trend since these units provide a satisfactory component for the control memory.

REFERENCES

1. MANO, M. M., *Digital Logic and Computer Design*. Englewood Cliffs, N.J.: Prentice-Hall, Inc., 1979.

2. AGRAWALA, A. K., AND T. G. RAUSCHER, *Foundations of Microprogramming, Architecture*. New York: Academic Press, Inc., 1976.

3. AGRAWALA, A. K., AND T. G. RAUSCHER, "Microprogramming Perspective and Status," *IEEE Trans. on Computers*, Vol. C-23 (August 1974), pp. 817–837.

4. HUSSON, S. S., *Microprogramming: Principles and Practices*. Englewood Cliffs, N.J.: Prentice-Hall, Inc., 1970.

5. ALEXANDRIDIS, N. A., "Bit-Sliced Microprocessor Architecture," *Computer*, Vol. 11 (June 1978), pp. 56–80.

6. POWERS, V. M., AND J. H. HERNANDEZ, "Microprogram Assemblers for Bit-Sliced Microprocessors," *Computer*, Vol. 11 (July 1978), pp. 108–120.

7. Advanced Micro Devices, *Microprogramming Handbook*, Sunnyvale, Calif., 1977.

8. SALISBURY, A. B., *Microprogrammable Computer Architecture*. New York: Elsevier, 1976.

9. MICK, J., AND J. BRICK, *Bit-Slice Microprocessor Design*. New York: McGraw-Hill Book Company, 1980.

10. KATZAN, H., JR., *Microprogramming Primer*. New York: McGraw-Hill Book Company, 1977.

PROBLEMS

8-1. Define the following terms in your own words: (a) control memory; (b) hard-wired control; (c) dynamic microprogramming; (d) control word; (e) microinstruction; (f) microprogram; (g) microcode; (h) micro-operation; (i) macro-operation.

8-2. The microinstructions stored in the control memory of Fig. 8-3 have a width of 24 bits. Each microinstruction is divided into three fields: a micro-operation field of 13

bits, a next address field, and a MUX select field. There are eight status bits in the inputs of the multiplexer.
(a) How many bits are there in the MUX select field?
(b) How many bits are there in the next address field?
(c) What is the size of the control memory?
(d) How many bits are there in the control address register?
(e) Draw a detailed block diagram of the circuit showing all interconnections between the blocks. Use a multiplexer similar to the one shown in Fig. 2-11, a counter with parallel load as in Fig. 2-15, and a ROM like Fig. 2-22.

8-3. The MUX shown in Fig. 8-3 has 16 input status bits numbered 0 through 15. Input 0 is connected to a logic 0 signal and input 15 is connected to a logic 1 signal.
(a) Formulate a procedure for an unconditional branch microinstruction.
(b) Formulate a procedure for incrementing the control address register unconditionally.

8-4. List four alternatives for achieving a conditional branch operation in a control memory.

8-5. Using the mapping process defined in Fig. 8-4, give the first microinstruction address for the following macro-operation codes: (a) 0001; (b) 1110; (c) 1010.

8-6. Formulate a mapping process that will provide eight control words for each macro-operation routine. The macro-operation code has five bits and the control memory has 1024 words.

8-7. Suppose that we want to achieve the mapping specified in Fig. 8-4 by means of a mapping memory as described in Fig. 8-5.
(a) What is the size of the mapping memory, i.e., how many words and how many bits per word?
(b) Tabulate the bits of each word in each address.
(c) Show how any routine may be assigned any number of words.

8-8. Add the following instructions to the computer defined in Sec. 8-3. Obtain the symbolic microprogram for each routine as in Table 8-1.

Symbol	Op-code	Symbolic Function*	Description
AND	0011	$AC \leftarrow AC \wedge M$	AND M to AC
XCHG	0100	$AC \leftarrow M, M \leftarrow AC$	Exchange AC and M
SUB	0101	$AC \leftarrow AC - M$	Subtract M from AC
ADM	0110	$M \leftarrow M + AC$	Add AC to memory operand (*AC* does not change)
BTCL	0111	$AC \leftarrow AC \wedge \overline{M}$	AND complemented memory word to AC (Bit clear)
BZ	1000	If $(AC = 0)$ then $(PC \leftarrow EA)$	Branch if AC is zero
SEQ	1001	If $(AC = M)$ then $(PC \leftarrow PC + 1)$	Skip if AC equals M (*AC* does not change)
BPNZ	1010	If $(AC > 0)$ then $(PC \leftarrow EA)$	Branch if AC is positive and non-zero

*EA is the effective address; M is the memory word stored at the effective address.

8-9. Translate the microprogram routines from Prob. 8-8 to binary and tabulate them as in Table 8-2.

8-10. The following is a symbolic microprogram routine for an instruction in the computer defined in Sec. 8-3.

ORG 40

NOP	S	JMP	FETCH
NOP	Z	JMP	FETCH
NOP	I	CALL	INDRCT
BRTPC	U	JMP	FETCH

(a) Give a name to the instruction and specify what it does.
(b) Convert the four microinstructions into their equivalent binary form.

8-11. The first microinstruction in the ADD routine of Table 8-1 has no micro-operations. The ADD routine can be reduced to two microinstructions if the first microinstruction contains the micro-operation READ. Follow this suggestion and show all necessary changes in the ADD and INDRCT routines. Is the modified INDRCT subroutine valid when called by the microinstructions in location OVER and STORE?

8-12. Change the INDRCT subroutine in Table 8-1 to a multiple-level indirect address. In multiple-level indirect addressing, bit I must be successively checked in all words read from memory and every time it is a 1, a new operand address is read. Memory access terminates and the address of the operand is available when I = 0.

8-13. Write the symbolic microprogram for the seven memory reference instructions listed in Table 5-3 for the basic computer. Use the microinstruction format defined in Fig. 8-8 and the fetch and indirect routines of Table 8-1. (Note that $MBR = 0$ status is not available in the CD field. Swap AC and MBR and check Z when implementing the ISZ instruction.)

8-14. Table 7-11 lists six branch instructions useful after a comparison of two unsigned numbers. Problem 7-30 gives the condition of status bits C and Z in each case. Assume that the CD field in Fig. 8-8 has an additional status bit symbolized by C. Using the computer defined in Sec. 8-3, write the symbolic microprogram routines for the conditional branch instructions BHI, BHE, BLO, BLOE, BE, and BNE.

8-15. Assume that the input logic of the microprogram sequencer of Fig. 8-9 has four inputs, $I_2, I_1, I_0,$ and T and three outputs, $S_1, S_0,$ and L. The operations that can be performed in the unit are as follows:

I_2	I_1	I_0	Operation
X	0	0	Increment CAR unconditionally
0	0	1	JMP to ADF if $T = 1$, increment CAR if $T = 0$
1	0	1	CALL subroutine if $T = 1$, increment CAR if $T = 0$
0	1	0	Return from subroutine if $T = 1$, increment CAR if $T = 0$
1	1	0	MAP external address if $T = 1$, increment CAR if $T = 0$
X	1	1	JMP to ADF unconditionally

Design the input logic circuit using a minimum number of gates.

8-16. (a) Design a 7-bit combinational circuit incrementer for the microprogram sequencer of Fig. 8-9.
(b) Design an incrementer with one control line P. When $P = 0$, the circuit increments by 1, but when $P = 1$, the circuit increments by 2.

8-17. A microprogram sequencer uses a register stack eight levels deep.
(a) Draw a block diagram of the sequencer.
(b) Formulate the sequence of internal operations which are required to implement the call and return from subroutine microinstructions.

8-18. Insert an exclusive-OR gate between MUX 2 and the input logic of Fig. 8-9. One input to the gate comes from the test output of the multiplexer. The other input to the gate comes from a bit labeled P (for polarity) in the microinstruction stored in control memory. The output of the gate goes to input T in the input logic circuit. What does the polarity control P accomplish?

8-19. The microprogrammed CPU of Fig. 8-10 has a control address register (CAR) inside the microprogram sequencer. CAR is located in the input of the control memory. The pipeline register (PLR) is located in the output of the control memory. Compare the speed of operation by comparing the propagation delay encountered during the interval between two consecutive clock pulses when the system uses:
(a) A CAR without a PLR
(b) A PLR without a CAR

8-20. What is the difference between hardware, software, and firmware implementation? Consider the multiplication of two binary numbers and explain how this operation is implemented in each of the three methods. Discuss the advantages and disadvantages between the three implementations.

8-21. Show how a 9-bit micro-operation field in a microinstruction can be divided into subfields to specify 46 micro-operations. How many micro-operations can be specified in one microinstruction?

8-22. Show how a conditional branch operation is to be handled by the multiple control-word format of Table 8-4.

8-23. Show all the decoding circuits necessary for the microinstruction defined in Fig. 8-8. Indicate how these circuits are connected to the output of the control memory.

8-24. A microprogram control unit contains 1024 words of 100 bits each. If only 120 different bit combinations are used, how many bits can be saved by using a nanomemory? What would be the sizes of the micromemory and nanomemory?

8-25. A CPU has 16 registers, an ALU with 16 logic and 16 arithmetic functions and a shifter with 8 operations, all connected with a common bus system.
(a) Formulate a control word to specify the various micro-operations for the CPU.
(b) Specify the number of bits for each field and give a general encoding scheme for each.
(c) Show the bits of a control word that specify the micro-operation $R7 \leftarrow R1 + R14$.

8-26. Under what conditions would it be more feasible to use a hard-wired control than a microprogrammed control unit?

8-27. State five advantages of the microprogrammed control unit organization.

8-28. The basic computer of Chap. 5 uses a hard-wired control unit. It is necessary to redesign it with a microprogrammed control unit. Define a control memory and any suitable control word format and then write the microprogram for the control memory. You may find it convenient to leave the register-reference and input-output instructions in their hard-wired form.

Arithmetic Processor Design

9-1 INTRODUCTION

Arithmetic instructions in digital computers manipulate data to produce results necessary for the solution of computational problems. These instructions perform arithmetic calculations and are responsible for the bulk of activity involved in processing data in a computer. The four basic arithmetic operations are: addition, subtraction, multiplication, and division. From these four basic operations, it is possible to formulate other arithmetic functions and solve scientific problems by means of numerical analysis methods.

An arithmetic processor is the part of a processor unit that executes arithmetic operations. The data type assumed to reside in processor registers during the execution of an arithmetic instruction is specified in the definition of the instruction. An arithmetic instruction may specify binary or decimal data and in each case the data may be in fixed-point or floating-point form. Fixed-point numbers may represent integers or fractions. Negative numbers may be in signed-magnitude or signed-complement representation. The arithmetic processor is very simple if only a binary fixed-point *add* instruction is included. It would be more complicated if it includes all four arithmetic operations for binary and decimal data in fixed-point and floating-point representation.

At an early age we are taught how to perform the basic arithmetic operations in signed-magnitude representation. This knowledge is valuable when the operations are to be implemented by hardware. However, the designer must be thoroughly familiar with the sequence of steps to be followed in order to carry out the operation and achieve a correct result. The solution to any problem which is stated by a finite number of well defined procedural steps is called an *algorithm*. An algorithm was stated in Sec. 3-2 for the addition of two fixed-point binary numbers when negative numbers are in signed-2's complement representation. This is a simple algorithm since all it needs for its implementation is a parallel binary adder. When negative numbers are in signed-magnitude representation, the algorithm is slightly more complicated and its implementation requires circuits to add and subtract, and to compare the signs and the magnitudes of the numbers. Usually, an algorithm will contain a number of procedural steps which are dependent on results of previous steps. A convenient method for presenting algorithms is a flow chart. The computational steps are specified in the flow chart inside rectangular boxes. The decision steps are indicated inside diamond-shaped boxes from which two or more alternate paths emerge.

The purpose of this chapter is to develop the algorithms and show a procedure for the design of an arithmetic processor. The arithmetic processor performs the four basic operations of addition, subtraction, multiplication, and division. The type of data to be employed is *binary, fixed-point, signed-magnitude, integer* numbers. Algorithms for signed-complement representation and floating-point or decimal data are presented in the following chapter.

Each of the three representations for negative numbers (signed-magnitude, signed-1's complement and signed-2's complement) produce a different set of steps for carrying out the various arithmetic operations. A different algorithm will require a different sequence of micro-operations when the operation is implemented with hardware. The designer must adopt one, and only one, representation and design the hardware according to the algorithm of the adopted representation. The hardware will produce correct results if, and only if, negative numbers are stored in memory and processor registers in the adopted representation. Results generated by the hardware will also be in the adopted representation.

It is important to realize that the adopted representation for negative numbers refers to the representation of numbers in the registers before and after the execution of the arithmetic operation. It does not mean that complement arithmetic is used in an intermediate step. For example, it is convenient to employ complement arithmetic when performing a subtraction operation with numbers in signed-magnitude representation. As long as the initial minuend and subtrahend, as well as the final difference, are in signed-magnitude form the fact that complements have been used in an intermediate step does not alter the fact that the representation is in signed-magnitude.

9-2 COMPARISON AND SUBTRACTION OF UNSIGNED BINARY NUMBERS

The algorithms for addition and subtraction of binary numbers in signed-complement representation treat the sign bit as an extended bit of the number. In contrast, the arithmetic algorithms for numbers in signed-magnitude representation treat the sign bit and the magnitude of the numbers separately. For this reason, it is convenient to consider the magnitude part alone as being an unsigned binary number. The operations performed with the magnitude of the numbers are comparison, subtraction, and addition. In this section we consider a few alternatives for comparing and subtracting unsigned binary numbers. These procedures are useful for deriving the arithmetic algorithms for numbers in signed-magnitude representation.

Magnitude Comparator

The comparison of two numbers is an operation that determines if one number is greater than, less than, or equal to the other number. A magnitude comparator is a combinational circuit that compares two numbers A and B and determines their relative magnitude. The outcome of the comparison is specified by three binary variables that indicate whether $A > B$, $A = B$, or $A < B$.

The circuit of a magnitude comparator can be derived from the procedure most commonly used to compare the relative magnitude of numbers. Consider two numbers A and B with four digits in each. Let $A = A_3 A_2 A_1 A_0$ and $B = B_3 B_2 B_1 B_0$ where each subscripted letter represents one of the digits in the number. The two numbers are equal if all pairs of significant digits are equal, that is, if $A_3 = B_3$ and $A_2 = B_2$ and $A_1 = B_1$ and $A_0 = B_0$. When the numbers are binary, the digits are either 1 or 0 and the equality relation of the individual bits can be expressed by the following Boolean function:

$$x_i = A_i B_i + A_i' B_i' \qquad i = 0, 1, 2, 3$$

where $x_i = 1$ if the pair of bits in position i are equal, that is, if both are 1's or both are 0's.

The equality of numbers A and B is specified by a binary variable which we designate by the symbol $(A = B)$. This binary variable is equal to 1 if A is arithmetically equal to B and is 0 otherwise. For the *binary* variable $(A = B)$ to be equal to 1 we must have all x_i variables equal to 1. This dictates an AND Boolean function as follows:

$$(A = B) = x_3 x_2 x_1 x_0$$

To determine if A is greater than or less than B, we inspect the relative magnitude of pairs of significant digits starting from the most significant position. If the two digits are equal, we compare the next lower significant pair of digits. This comparison is continued until a pair of unequal digits is reached. If the corresponding digit of A is greater than that of B we have $A > B$. If the corresponding digit of B is greater, we have $A < B$. In the case of binary digits, the sequential comparison can be expressed by the following Boolean functions:

$$(A > B) = A_3 B_3' + x_3 A_2 B_2' + x_3 x_2 A_1 B_1' + x_3 x_2 x_1 A_0 B_0'$$
$$(A < B) = A_3' B_3 + x_3 A_2' B_2 + x_3 x_2 A_1' B_1 + x_3 x_2 x_1 A_0' B_0$$

The symbols $(A > B)$ and $(A < B)$ are *binary* output variables which are equal to 1 when $A > B$ or $A < B$, respectively.

The logic diagram of a 4-bit magnitude comparator is shown in Fig. 9-1. The

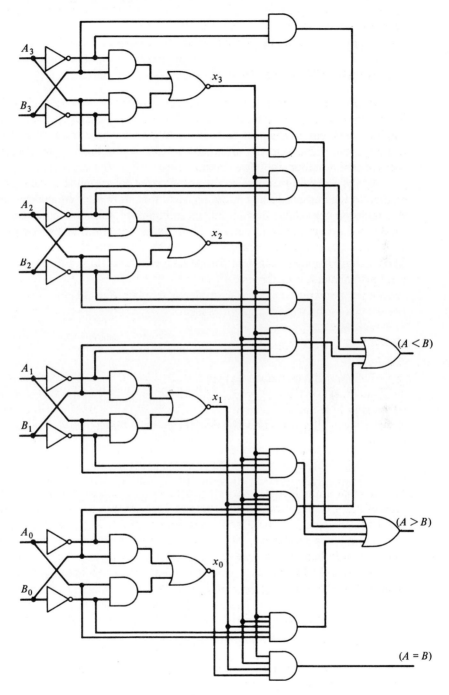

Fig. 9-1 4-bit magnitude comparator.

x outputs are generated by an exclusive-NOR circuit and applied to a 4-input AND gate to produce the binary output variable ($A = B$). The other two outputs are generated according to the Boolean functions listed above. The procedure for obtaining magnitude comparator circuits for binary numbers with more than four bits is obvious. Four-bit magnitude comparators are available in integrated circuit packages.

Complements

Complements were introduced in Sec. 3-2. We review here some of the properties of complements and extend the discussion to obtain additional properties that will be useful in the development of comparison and subtraction algorithms.

In the following discussion, A and B refer to unsigned binary numbers and n refers to the number of bits in the registers that store their equivalent binary value. It is important to realize that 2^n is equal in binary to a number consisting of a 1 followed by n zeros. $2^n - 1$ is represented in binary as n 1's. The 2's complement of an unsigned integer B is defined as $2^n - B$. The 1's complement is defined as $2^n - 1 - B$. These definitions are convenient for proving arithmetic algorithms involving complement arithmetic.

As a numerical example, consider a number $B = 20$. For $n = 6$, the binary equivalents of the various quantities are:

$$B = 010100$$
$$2^6 = 1000000$$
$$2^6 - 1 = 111111$$
$$2^6 - B = 101100 = \text{2's complement of } B$$
$$2^6 - 1 - B = 101011 = \text{1's complement of } B$$

From the definitions above it is easily shown that the 1's complement is obtained by complementing each bit. The 2's complement is obtained by either one of the following simple procedures: (1) take the 1's complement of the number and add 1: or (2) leave all least significant 0's and the first 1 unchanged and then complement the remaining bits.

Straight Subtraction

The subtraction of two unsigned binary numbers may be implemented by means of hardware with n full-subtractors in cascade. The output-borrow of each full-subtractor is connected to the input-borrow of the full-subtractor on its left. The output-borrow of the most significant stage will be referred to as the end-borrow. When an unsigned number B is subtracted from another unsigned number A, the difference $A - B$ will appear at the D (difference) outputs of the full-subtractors. If the end-borrow is a 0, it means that $A \geq B$ and the difference is the correct number. The difference is equal to zero if $A = B$. If the end-borrow is a 1, it signifies that 2^n has been borrowed to form the difference $2^n + A - B$. This will occur if $A < B$. The result of this operation can be represented as $2^n - (B - A)$ which, by definition, is the 2's complement of $(B - A)$. To obtain the correct difference, we take the 2's complement again and obtain: $2^n - (2^n + A - B) = B - A$. A negative sign must be transferred to the sign flip-flop when the number is represented in sign-magnitude. The results of the discussion above are tabulated in the first entry of Table 9-1.

TABLE 9-1   Subtraction and Comparison of Unsigned Binary Numbers

Operation	if	E is	Result is	if	E is	Result is	If $A = B$ result contains
$A - B$	$A \geq B$	0	$A - B$	$A < B$	1	2's complement of $(B - A)$	All 0's
$A + \bar{B}$	$A \leq B$	0	1's complement of $(B - A)$	$A > B$	1	$A - B - 1$	All 1's
$A + \bar{B} + 1$	$A < B$	0	2's complement of $(B - A)$	$A \geq B$	1	$A - B$	All 0's

E is the end-carry for addition or end-borrow for subtraction.

The relative magnitude of two unsigned numbers A and B may be determined from the subtraction of B from A and a check of the end-borrow. If the end-borrow is 0, the difference $A - B$ is positive and $A \geq B$. If it is 1, the difference is negative and $A < B$. The two numbers are equal if the end-borrow is 0 and the difference is also 0. This comparison algorithm follows from the previous discussion.

Subtraction with Complements

The subtraction implementation presented above requires n full-subtractors and a complementer (to complement the result if $A < B$). A more practical method would be to use a parallel-adder composed of n full-addres and a complementer. The addition operation can be done by the parallel-adder. The subtraction can be implemented by complementing the subtrahend and adding it to the minuend. The advantage of this method is that it uses the parallel-adder for implementing both addition and subtraction.

The subtraction of two unsigned binary numbers by means of 2's complements or 1's complements is summarized in Table 9-1. The operation $A + \bar{B}$ designates the addition of A to the 1's complement of B. The operation $A + \bar{B} + 1$ designates the addition of A to the 2's complement of B. In each case, E designates the end-carry out of the last, most significant, stage.

The proof for the 1's complement subtraction will be left as an exercise. The proof for the 2's complement subtraction follows. The addition of $A + \bar{B} + 1$ is equivalent to $A + (2^n - B) = 2^n + (A - B)$. When the end-carry E is equal to 1, it means that a 1 is available in the $n + 1$ position of the result. This value is equal to 2^n because it represents a number consisting of a 1 followed by n zeros. Now, if $A \geq B$ then $(A -$

B) must be a positive number and $2^n + (A - B) \geq 2^n$. If we remove the end-carry we obtain $A - B$. Note also that when $A = B$ the result of the operation gives 2^n which indicates that $E = 1$ and the remaining bits consists of all zeros.

If $A < B$, then $(A - B)$ must be a negative number. Therefore, $2^n + (A - B) < 2^n$ and E must be 0. The result of this operation can be written as $2^n - (B - A)$, where $B - A$ is a positive number. This is equivalent to the 2's complement of $(B - A)$. To obtain the magnitude of the difference we must complement again to obtain $2^n - (2^n + A - B) = B - A$, and the result is negative.

The relative magnitude of A and B can be determined from the above operation. If $E = 1$, the difference $A - B$ is positive and $A \geq B$. If $E = 0$, the difference is negative and $A < B$. The two numbers are equal if $E = 1$ and all the bits of the result are zeros.

It is worth emphasizing again that the above algorithms are for unsigned binary numbers. These algorithms are useful for implementing the subtraction and comparison operations with the magnitude part of binary numbers when they are in signed-magnitude representation. When the numbers are represented in signed-2's complement form, the addition and subtraction algorithms treat the sign bit as an extended bit of the number.

9-3 ADDITION AND SUBTRACTION ALGORITHMS

The representation of numbers in signed-magnitude is familiar because it is used in every day arithmetic calculations. The procedure for adding or subtracting two signed binary numbers with paper and pencil is simple and straightforward. A review of this procedure will be helpful for deriving the hardware algorithm.

We designate the magnitude of the two numbers by A and B. When the signed numbers are added or subtracted, we find that there are eight different conditions to consider, depending on the sign of the numbers and the operation performed. These conditions are listed in the first column of Table 9-2. The other columns in the table show the actual operation to be performed with the *magnitude* of the numbers. The last column is needed to prevent a negative zero. In other words, when two equal numbers are subtracted, the result should be $+0$ not -0.

The algorithms for addition and subtraction are derived from the table and can be stated as follows (the words inside parentheses should be used for the subtraction algorithm):

Addition (subtraction) algorithm: when the signs of A and B are identical (different) add the two magnitudes and attach the sign of A to the result. When the signs of A and B are different (identical), compare the magnitudes and subtract the smaller number from the larger. Choose the sign of the result to be the same as A if $A > B$ or the complement of the sign of A if $A < B$. If the two magnitudes are equal, subtract B from A and make the sign of the result a plus.

TABLE 9-2   Addition and Subtraction of Signed-Magnitude Numbers

Operation	Add Magnitudes	Subtract Magnitudes		
		When $A > B$	When $A < B$	When $A = B$
$(+A) + (+B)$	$+(A + B)$			
$(+A) + (-B)$		$+(A - B)$	$-(B - A)$	$+(A - B)$
$(-A) + (+B)$		$-(A - B)$	$+(B - A)$	$+(A - B)$
$(-A) + (-B)$	$-(A + B)$			
$(+A) - (+B)$		$+(A - B)$	$-(B - A)$	$+(A - B)$
$(+A) - (-B)$	$+(A + B)$			
$(-A) - (+B)$	$-(A + B)$			
$(-A) - (-B)$		$-(A - B)$	$+(B - A)$	$+(A - B)$

The two algorithms are similar except for the sign comparison. The procedure to be followed for identical signs in the addition algorithm is the same as for different signs in the subtraction algorithm, and vice-versa.

Hardware Implementation

To implement the two arithmetic operations with hardware, it is first necessary that the two numbers be stored in registers. Let A and B be two registers that hold the magnitudes of the numbers, and A_s and B_s be two flip-flops that hold the corresponding signs. The result of the operation may be transferred to a third register: however, a saving is achieved if the result is transferred into A and A_s. Thus A and A_s together form an accumulator register.

Consider now the hardware implementation of the above algorithms. First, a parallel-adder is needed to perform the micro-operation $A + B$. Second, a comparator circuit is needed to establish if $A > B$, $A = B$, or $A < B$. Third, two parallel-subtractor circuits are needed to perform the micro-operations $A - B$ and $B - A$. The sign relationship can be determined from an exclusive-OR gate with A_s and B_s as inputs.

This procedure requires a magnitude comparator, an adder and two subtractors. However, from the discussion of the previous section we know that a different procedure can be found that requires less equipment. First of all, we know that subtraction can be accomplished by means of complement and add. Second, the result of a comparison can be determined from the end-carry after the subtraction. Careful investigation of the alternatives reveals that the use of 2's complement for subtraction and comparison is an efficient procedure that requires only an adder and a complementer.

Figure 9-2 shows a block diagram of the hardware for implementing the addition and subtraction operations. It consists of registers A and B and sign flip-flops A_s and B_s. Subtraction is done by adding A to the 2's complement of B. The end-carry is transferred to flip-flop E where it can be checked to determine the relative magnitudes of the two numbers. The add-overflow flip-flop AVF holds the overflow bit when A and B are added. The A register provides other micro-operations that may be needed when we specify the sequence of steps in the algorithm.

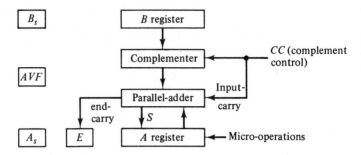

Fig. 9-2   Block diagram of hardware for addition and subtraction.

The addition of A and B is done through a binary parallel-adder. The S outputs of the adder are applied to the inputs of the A register for their transfer with a parallel-load micro-operation. The complementer provides an output of B or $\bar{B}$ depending on the state of the binary variable CC (complement control). The complementer consists of exclusive-OR gates and the parallel-adder consists of full-adder (FA) circuits. One typical stage of the complementer and adder is shown in Fig. 9-3. From the truth

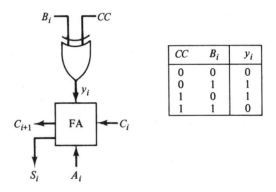

CC	B_i	y_i
0	0	0
0	1	1
1	0	1
1	1	0

Fig. 9-3   One stage of complementer and parallel-adder.

table of the exclusive-OR gate it is clear that input y_i to the full-adder is equal to B_i when $CC = 0$. But $y_i = B_i'$ if $CC = 1$. The CC variable also supplies the input carry to the binary parallel-adder. When $CC = 0$, B is applied to the adder, the input-carry is 0, and the output of the parallel-adder is equal to $A + B$. When $CC = 1$, $\bar{B}$ is applied to the adder, the input-carry is 1, and $S = A + \bar{B} + 1$. This is equal to A plus the 2's complement of B.

Hardware Algorithm

The flow chart for the hardware algorithm is presented in Fig. 9-4. The two signs A_s and B_s are compared by an exclusive-OR gate. If the output of the gate is 0, the signs are identical; if it is 1, the signs are different. For an *add* operation, identical signs dictate that the magnitudes be added. For a *subtract* operation, different signs dictate that the magnitudes be added. The magnitudes are added with a micro-operation $EA \leftarrow A + B$, where EA is a register that combines E and A. The carry in E after the addition constitutes an overflow if it is equal to 1. The value of E is transferred into the add-overflow flip-flop AVF.

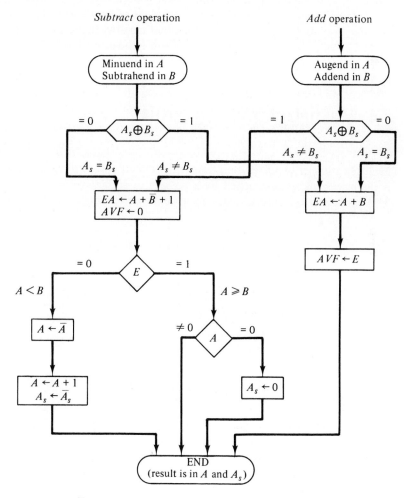

Fig. 9-4 Flow chart for add and subtract operations.

The two magnitudes are subtracted if the signs are different for an *add* operation or identical for a *subtract* operation. The magnitudes are subtracted by adding A to the 2's complement of B. No overflow can occur if the numbers are subtracted so AVF is cleared to 0. A 1 in E indicates that $A \geq B$ and the number in A is the correct result. If this number is zero, the sign A_s must be made positive to avoid a negative zero. A 0 in E indicates that $A < B$. For this case, it is necessary to take the 2's complement of the value in A. This operation can be done with one micro-operation $A \leftarrow \bar{A} + 1$. However, we assume that the A register has circuits for micro-operations *complement* and *increment*, so the 2's complement is obtained from these two micro-operations. In other paths of the flow chart, the sign of the result is the same as the sign of A, so no change in A_s is required. However, when $A < B$, the sign of the result is the complement of the original sign of A. It is then necessary to complement A_s in order to obtain the correct sign. The final result is found in register A and its sign in A_s. The value in AVF provides an overflow indication. The final value of E is immaterial.

9-4 MULTIPLICATION ALGORITHM

Multiplication of two fixed-point binary numbers in signed-magnitude representation is done with paper and pencil by a process of successive shift and add operations. This process is best illustrated with a numerical example as shown in Fig. 9-5. The

```
 23        10111    Multiplicand
 19     x  10011    Multiplier
 __        10111
           10111
           00000    +
           00000
           10111
437     110110101   Product
```

Fig. 9-5 Example of binary multiplication.

process consists of looking at successive bits of the multiplier, least significant bit first. If the multiplier bit is a 1, the multiplicand is copied down; otherwise, zeros are copied down. The numbers copied down in successive lines are shifted one position to the left from the previous number. Finally, the numbers are added and their sum forms the product.

The sign of the product is determined from the signs of the multiplicand and multiplier. If they are alike, the sign of the product is plus. If they are unlike, the sign of the product is minus.

Hardware Implementation

When multiplication is implemented in a digital computer, it is convenient to change the process slightly. First, instead of providing registers to store and add simultaneously as many binary numbers as there are bits in the multiplier, it is convenient to provide an adder for the summation of only two binary numbers and successively accumulate the partial products in a register. Second, instead of shifting the multiplicand to the left, the partial product is shifted to the right, which results in leaving the partial product and the multiplicand in the required relative positions. Third, when the corresponding bit of the multiplier is 0, there is no need to add all zeros to the partial product since it will not alter its value.

The hardware for multiplication consists of the equipment shown in Fig. 9-2 plus two more registers. These registers together with registers A and B are shown in Fig. 9-6. The multiplier is stored in the Q register and its sign in Q_s. The sequence counter SC is initially set to a number equal to the number of bits in the multiplier. The counter is decremented by 1 after forming each partial product. When the content of the counter reaches zero, the product is formed and the process stops.

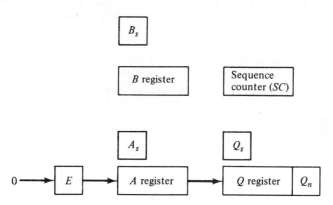

Fig. 9-6 Register EAQ and sequence counter needed for multiplication and division.

Initially, the multiplicand is in register B and the multiplier in Q. The sum of A and B forms a partial product which is transferred to the EA register. Both partial product and multiplier are shifted to the right. This shift will be denoted by the statement shr EAQ to designate the right shift depicted in Fig. 9-6. The least significant bit of A is shifted into the most significant position of Q; the bit from E is shifted into the most significant position of A; and 0 is shifted into E. After the shift, one bit of the partial product is shifted into Q, pushing the multiplier bits one position to the right. In this manner, the right-most flip-flop in register Q, designated by Q_n, will hold the bit of the multiplier which must be inspected next.

Hardware Algorithm

Figure 9-7 is a flow chart of the hardware multiply algorithm. Initially, the multiplicand is in B and the multiplier in Q. Their corresponding signs are in B_s and Q_s, respectively. The signs are compared, and both A and Q are set to correspond to the sign of the product since a double-length product will be stored in registers A and Q. Registers A and E are cleared and the sequence counter SC is set to a number equal to the number of bits of the multiplier. We are assuming here that operands are transferred to registers from a memory unit that has words of n bits. Since an operand must be stored with its sign, one bit of the word will be occupied by the sign and the magnitude will consist of $n - 1$ bits.

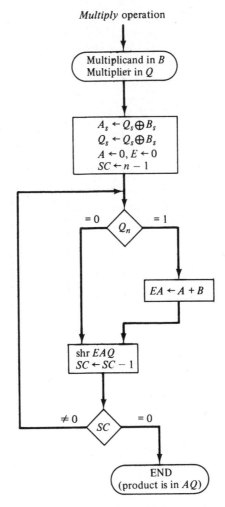

Fig. 9-7 Flow chart for multiply operation.

After the initialization, the low-order bit of the multiplier in Q_n is tested. If it is a 1, the multiplicand in B is added to the present partial product in A. If it is a 0, nothing is done. Register EAQ is then shifted once to the right to form the new partial product. The sequence counter is decremented by 1 and its new value checked. If it if not equal to zero, the process is repeated and a new partial product is formed. The process stops when $SC = 0$. Note that the partial product formed in A is shifted into Q one bit at a time and eventually replaces the multiplier. The final product is available in both A and Q, with A holding the most significant bits and Q holding the least significant bits.

The previous numerical example is repeated in Fig. 9-8 to clarify the hardware multiplication process. The procedure follows the steps outlined in the flow chart.

Multiplicand: B = 10111	E	A	Q	SC
Multiplier in Q:		00000	10011	5
$Q_n = 1$; add B		10111		
First partial product	0	10111		
shr EAQ	0	01011	11001	4
$Q_n = 1$; add B		10111		
Second partial product	1	00010		
shr EAQ	0	10001	01100	3
$Q_n = 0$; shr EAQ	0	01000	10110	2
$Q_n = 0$; shr EAQ	0	00100	01011	1
$Q_n = 1$; add B		10111		
Fifth partial product	0	11011		
shr EAQ; final product:		01101	10101	0

Fig. 9-8   Example of binary multiplication with digital hardware.

9-5   DIVISION ALGORITHM

Division of two fixed-point binary numbers in signed-magnitude representation is done with paper and pencil by a process of successive compare, shift, and subtract operations. Binary division is simpler than decimal division because the quotient digits are either 0 or 1 and there is no need to estimate how many times the dividend or partial remainder fits into the divisor. The division process is illustrated by a numerical example in Fig. 9-9. The divisor B consists of five bits and the dividend A, of ten bits. The five most significant bits of the dividend are compared with the divisor. Since the 5-bit number is smaller than B, we try again by taking the six most significant bits of A and compare this number with B. The 6-bit number is greater than B so we place a 1 for the quotient bit in the sixth position above the dividend. The divisor is then shifted once to the right and subtracted from the dividend. The difference is called a *partial remainder* because the division could have stopped here to obtain a quotient of 1 and a remainder equal to the partial remainder. The process is continued by com-

```
Divisor:                        11010        Quotient = Q
B = 10001         )0111000000             Dividend = A
                   01110                  5 bits of A < B, quotient has 5 bits
                   011100                 6 bits of A ⩾ B
                  −10001                  Shift right B and subtract; enter 1 in Q

                  −010110                 7 bits of remainder ⩾ B
                  −−10001                 Shift right B and subtract; enter 1 in Q

                  −−001010                Remainder < B; enter 0 in Q; shift right B
                  −−−010100               Remainder ⩾ B
                  −−−−10001               Shift right B and subtract; enter 1 in Q

                  −−−−000110              Remainder < B; enter 0 in Q
                  −−−−−00110              Final remainder
```

Fig. 9-9 Example of binary division.

paring a partial remainder with the divisor. If the partial remainder is greater than or equal to the divisor, the quotient bit is equal to 1. The divisor is then shifted right and subtracted from the partial remainder. If the partial remainder is smaller than the divisor, the quotient bit is 0 and no subtraction is needed. The divisor is shifted once to the right in any case. Note that the result gives both a quotient and a remainder.

Hardware Implementation

When the division is implemented in a digital computer, it is convenient to change the process slightly. Instead of shifting the divisor to the right, the dividend, or partial remainder, is shifted to the left, thus leaving the two numbers in the required relative position. Subtraction may be achieved by adding A to the 2's complement of B. The information about the relative magnitudes is then available from the end-carry.

The hardware for implementing the division operation is identical to that required for multiplication and consists of the components shown in Fig. 9-6. Register EAQ is now shifted to the left with 0 inserted into Q_n and the previous value of E lost. The numerical example is repeated in Fig. 9-10 in order to clarify the proposed division process. The divisor is stored in the B register and the double-length dividend is stored in registers A and Q. The dividend is shifted to the left and the divisor is subtracted by adding its 2's complement value. The information about the relative magnitude is available in E. If $E = 1$, it signifies that $A \geq B$. A quotient bit 1 is inserted into Q_n and the partial remainder is shifted to the left to repeat the process. If $E = 0$, it signifies that $A < B$ so the quotient in Q_n remains a 0 (inserted during the shift). The value of B is then added to restore the partial remainder in A to its previous value. The partial remainder is shifted to the left and the process is repeated again until all five quotient bits are formed. Note that while the partial remainder is shifted left, the quotient bits are shifted also and after five shifts, the quotient is in Q and the final remainder is in A.

Before showing the algorithm in flow chart form, we have to consider the sign of the result and a possible overflow condition. The sign of the quotient is determined

Divisor $B = 10001$, $\bar{B} + 1 = 01111$

	E	A	Q	SC
Dividend:		01110	00000	5
shl EAQ	0	11100	00000	
add $\bar{B} + 1$		01111		
$E = 1$	1	01011		
Set $Q_n = 1$	1	01011	00001	4
shl EAQ	0	10110	00010	
Add $\bar{B} + 1$		01111		
$E = 1$	1	00101		
Set $Q_n = 1$	1	00101	00011	3
shl EAQ	0	01010	00110	
Add $\bar{B} + 1$		01111		
$E = 0$; leave $Q_n = 0$	0	11001	00110	
Add B		10001		
				2
Restore remainder	1	01010		
shl EAQ	0	10100	01100	
Add $\bar{B} + 1$		01111		
$E = 1$	1	00011		
Set $Q_n = 1$	1	00011	01101	1
shl EAQ	0	00110	11010	
Add $\bar{B} + 1$		01111		
$E = 0$; leave $Q_n = 0$	0	10101	11010	
Add B		10001		
Restore remainder	1	00110	11010	0
Neglect E				
Remainder in A:		00110		
Quotient in Q:			11010	

Fig. 9-10 Example of binary division with digital hardware.

from the signs of the dividend and the divisor. If the two signs are alike, the sign of the quotient is plus. If they are unlike, the sign is minus. The sign of the remainder is the same as the sign of the dividend.

Divide Overflow

The division operation may result in a quotient with an overflow. This is not a problem when working with paper and pencil, but is crtical when the operation is implemented with hardware. This is because the lenght of registers is finite and will not hold a number that exceeds the standard length. To see this, consider a system that has 5-bit registers. We use one register to hold the divisor and two registers to hold the dividend. From the example of Fig. 9-9 we note that the quotient will consist of six bits if the five most significant bits of the dividend constitute a number greater than the divisor. The quotient is to be stored in a standard 5-bit register so the overflow bit will require one more flip-flop for storing the sixth bit. This divide overflow condition must be avoided in normal computer operations because the entire quotient will be too long for transfer into a memory unit which has words of standard length, that is, the same as the length of registers. Provisions to insure that this condition is detected must be included in either the hardware or software of the computer, or in a combination of the two.

When the dividend is twice as long as the divisor, the condition for overflow can be stated as follows:

> *A divide-overflow condition occurs if the high-order half bits of the dividend constitute a number greater than or equal to the divisor.*

Another problem associated with division is the fact that a division by zero must be avoided. The divide-overflow condition stated above takes care of this condition as well. This occurs because any dividend will be greater than or equal to a divisor which is equal to zero. Overflow condition is usually detected when a special flip-flop is set. We will call it a divide-overflow flip-flop and label it DVF.

The occurrence of a divide overflow can be handled in a variety of ways. In some computers it is the responsibility of the programmer to check if DVF is set after each divide instruction. He then branches to a subroutine that takes a corrective measure such as rescaling the data to avoid overflow. In some older computers, the occurrence of a divide overflow stopped the computer and this condition was referred to as a *divide stop*. Stopping the operation of the computer is not recommended because it is time-consuming. The procedure in most computers is to provide an interrupt request when DVF is set. The interrupt causes the computer to suspend the current program and branch to a service routine to take a corrective measure. The most common corrective measure is to remove the program and type an error message explaining the reason why the program could not be completed. It is then the responsibilty of the user who wrote the program to rescale his data or take any other corrective measure. The best way to avoid a divide overflow is to use floating-point data. We will see in the next chapter that a divide overflow can be handled very simply if numbers are in floating-point representation.

Hardware Algorithm

The hardware divide algorithm is shown in the flow chart of Fig. 9-11. The dividend is in A and Q and the divisor in B. The sign of the result is transferred into Q_s to be part of the quotient. A constant is set into the sequence counter SC to specify the number of bits in the quotient. As in multiplication, we assume that operands are transferred to registers from a memory unit that has words of n bits. Since an operand must be stored with its sign, one bit of the word will be occupied by the sign and the magnitude will consists of $n - 1$ bits.

A divide-overflow condition is tested by subtracting the divisor in B from half of the bits of the dividend stored in A. If $A \geq B$, the divide-overflow flip-flop DVF is set and the operation is terminated prematurely. If $A < B$, no divide overflow occurs so the value of the dividend is restored by adding B to A.

The division of the magnitudes starts by shifting the dividend in AQ to the left

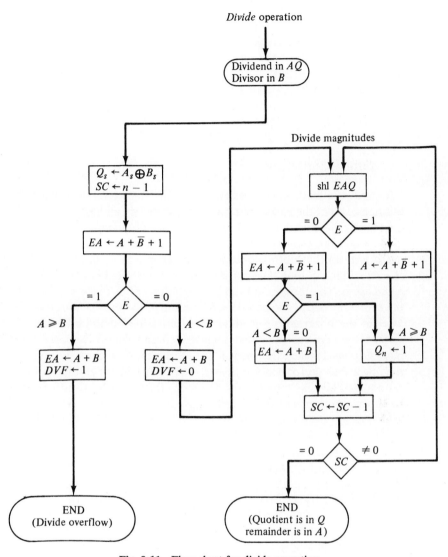

Fig. 9-11 Flow chart for divide operation.

with the high-order bit shifted into E. If the bit shifted into E is 1, we know that $EA > B$ because EA consists of a 1 followed by $n - 1$ bits while B consists of only $n - 1$ bits. In this case, B must be substracted from EA and 1 inserted into Q_n for the quotient bit. Since register A is missing the high-order bit of the dividend (which is in E), its value is $EA - 2^{n-1}$. Adding to this value the 2's complement of B results in

$$(EA - 2^{n-1}) + (2^{n-1} - B) = EA - B$$

The carry from this addition is not transferred to E if we want E to remain a 1.

If the shift-left operation inserts a 0 into E, the divisor is subtracted by adding its 2's complement value and the carry is transferred into E. If $E = 1$, it signifies that $A \geq B$, therefore, Q_n is set to 1. If $E = 0$, it signifies that $A < B$ and the original number is restored by adding B to A. In the latter case, we leave a 0 in Q_n (0 was inserted during the shift).

This process is repeated again with register A holding the partial remainder. After $n - 1$ times, the quotient magnitude is formed in register Q and the remainder is found in register A. The quotient sign is in Q_s and the sign of the remainder in A_s is the same as the original sign of the dividend.

Other Algorithms

The hardware method just described is called the *restoring method*. The reason for this name is that the partial remainder is restored by adding the divisor to the negative difference. Two other methods are available for dividing numbers, the *comparison* method and the *nonrestoring* method. In the comparison method A and B are compared *prior* to the subtraction operation. Then if $A \geq B$, B is subtracted from A. If $A < B$ nothing is done. The partial remainder is shifted left and the numbers are compared again. The comparison can be determined prior to the subtraction by inspecting the end-carry out of the parallel-adder prior to its transfer to register E.

In the nonrestoring method, B is not added if the difference is negative but instead, the negative difference is shifted left and then B is added. To see why this is possible consider the case when $A < B$. From the flow chart in Fig. 9-11 we note that the operations performed are $A - B + B$, that is B is subtracted and then added to restore A. The next time around the loop, this number is shifted left (or multiplied by 2) and B subtracted again. This gives: $2(A - B + B) - B = 2A - B$. This result is obtained in the non-restoring method by leaving $A - B$ as is. The next time around the loop, the number is shifted left and B *added* to give: $2(A - B) + B = 2A - B$ which is the same as before. Thus, in the nonrestoring method, B is subtracted if the previous value of Q_n was a 1 but B is added if the previous value of Q_n was a 0 and no restoring of the partial remainder is required. This process saves the step of adding the divisor if A is less than B but it requires special control logic to remember the previous result. The first time the dividend is shifted, B must be subtracted. Also, if the last bit of the quotient is 0, the partial remainder must be restored to obtain the correct final remainder.

9-6 PROCESSOR CONFIGURATION

The part of a digital computer devoted to processing arithmetic operations is identified as an arithmetic processor. A stand-alone arithmetic processor is called a calculator. The difference between an electronic calculator and a digital computer lies in their overall capability: a calculator is a dedicated device that performs arithmetic operations only; a general-purpose computer can perform other data processing functions as well. Input data and arithmetic operations in a calculator are entered through a keyboard and output data are displayed visually. Some expensive calculators come close to resembling a digital computer by having printing capabilities and programmable facilities, but all programs are concerned with arithmetic functions. Calculators use decimal arithmetic with floating-point numbers to facilitate the communication with the user. General-purpose computers may, sometimes, have hardware for processing decimal floating-point numbers. However, if a computer has hardware for fixed-point binary arithmetic operations only, it can be programmed to do calculations with floating-point binary or decimal numbers.

This section introduces a computer configuration for processing fixed-point arithmetic operations. In the next section we show a method for the design of a hardwired control for this processor. Section 9-8 demonstrates a procedure for the design of a microprogram controlled arithmetic processor. Although the microprogrammed version is used to describe a binary calculator, it can be easily applied to a general-purpose computer.

The position of the arithmetic processor among other computer components is shown in the block diagram of Fig. 9-12. The arithmetic processor consists of four registers: *BR*, *AC*, *QR*, and *SC*, and three flip-flop: *E*, *AVF*, and *DVF*. It also has

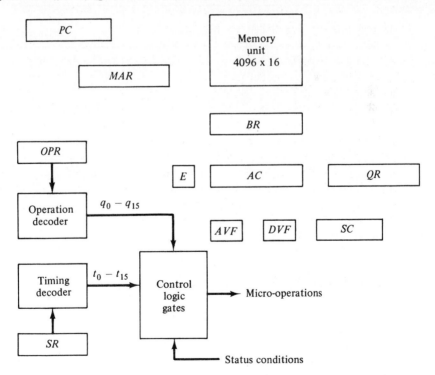

Fig. 9-12 Block diagram of computer with arithmetic processor.

combinational circuits for implementing various micro-operations. The AC register consists of 16 bits with the high-order bit designated by A_s and the other 15 bits by A. Thus, A_s and A together constitute the AC. Similarly, the memory buffer register BR is subdivided into B_s and B and register QR into Q_s and Q. A 16-bit operand read from memory is transferred into BR with the high-order bit going to B_s and the other 15 bits to B. A word in BR is stored in memory from B_s (one bit) and B (15 bits). Transfers between BR and AC or QR are 16-bit transfers and include both the magnitude and sign.

The other components of the computer are: a memory unit; a program counter PC; an address register MAR; and an operation register OPR to hold the operation code of the instruction. The hard-wired control consists of two decoders, control logic gates and a sequence register SR. The design of the control unit is discussed in the next section.

The instruction format is chosen to be as simple as possible in order not to complicate the example. It consists of four bits for the operatin code and 12 bits for the address. This computer uses the same instructions as the basic computer of Chap. 5 with additional arithmetic instructions. The 16 instructions are listed in Table 9-3.

TABLE 9-3 Computer Instructions

Symbol	Instruction Code		Description	Function
ADD	0000	m	Add	$AC \leftarrow AC + M$
SUB	0001	m	Subtract	$AC \leftarrow AC - M$
MUL	0010	m	Multiply	$AC\&QR \leftarrow QR * M$
DIV	0011	m	Divide	$QR \leftarrow AC\&QR/M$, $AC \leftarrow$ remainder
LDA	0100	m	Load AC	$AC \leftarrow M$
LDQ	0101	m	Load QR	$QR \leftarrow M$
STA	0110	m	Store AC	$M \leftarrow AC$
STQ	0111	m	Store QR	$M \leftarrow QR$
BAF	1000	m	Branch on AVF	If $(AVF = 1)$ then $(PC \leftarrow m)$
BDF	1001	m	Branch on DVF	If $(DVF = 1)$ then $(PC \leftarrow m)$
AND	1010	m	Logical AND	$AC \leftarrow AC \wedge M$
ISZ	1011	m	Increment and skip if 0	$M \leftarrow M + 1$, if $(M + 1 = 0)$ then $(PC \leftarrow PC + 1)$
BSA	1100	m	Branch and save address	$M \leftarrow PC, PC \leftarrow m + 1$
BUN	1101	m	Branch unconditionally	$PC \leftarrow m$
	1110		Register reference instructions	
	1111		Input-output instructions	

The symbol m designates a 12-bit address field. M is the memory word specified by the address m. The first four instructions are arithmetic instructions for fixed-point signed-magnitude binary numbers. The next four are needed for transfer of operands to and from memory and processor registers. The next two are branch instructions to special routines that take care of overflow conditions. The last six instructions are the same as the basic computer of Chap. 5.

The operands must be available in processor registers before an arithmetic instruction is executed. The following instructions add two operands from memory and transfer the result back to memory:

LDA	X	Transfer augend to AC
ADD	Y	Transfer addend to BR and add to AC
STA	Z	Transfer result back to memory
BAF	AF	Branch to routine AF if overflow occurs

Operand transfers to and from registers and memory are 16-bit transfers and include both sign and magnitude. Although the processor manipulates the signs and magnitudes separately, the initial operands and final results are always transferred as signed numbers with the most significant bit representing the sign and the other 15 bits representing the magnitude.

To subtract two numbers stored in memory and transfer the result back to memory we need the following instructions:

LDA	X	Transfer minuend to AC
SUB	Y	Transfer subtrahend to BR and subtract from AC
STA	Z	Store result back in memory
BAF	AF	Branch to a program that takes care of overflow

In this example, and all others listed here, it is assumed that the operands are in memory. If the augend in the previous example or the minuend in this example is already in the AC (from a previous operation), it is not necessary to use the instructions that load them into the AC.

After two numbers are multiplied, the product is of double length with both A_s and Q_s holding the sign, and A and Q holding the magnitude. The double-length product in AC and QR must be stored in memory in two words. The following is a program that multiplies two operands and stores their product in memory:

LDQ	X	Transfer multiplier to QR
MUL	Y	Transfer multiplicand to BR and multiply
STA	Z1	Store most significant bits of product
STQ	Z2	Store least significant bits of product

To divide two numbers, we must transfer the double-length dividend into AC and QR and then store both the quotient from QR and the remainder from AC:

LDA	X1	Transfer high-order bits of dividend to AC
LDQ	X2	Transfer low-order bits of dividend to QR
DIV	Y	Transfer divisor to BR and divide
BDF	DF	Branch to DF if overflow occurs
STQ	ZQ	Store quotient in memory
STA	ZR	Store remainder in memory

If the dividend has only one memory word, it must be placed in QR and the AC must be cleared. The sign of the dividend must be placed in the sign bit of the AC. This can be accomplished by the following instructions:

LDQ	X	Transfer dividend to QR
LDA	X	Transfer dividend to AC
AND	MASK	Mask the magnitude but leave the sign
DIV	Y	Transfer divisor to BR and divide
.		
.		
.		
MASK, HEX	8000	Operand for clearing magnitude of AC

The mask operand does not change the sign bit in the high-order position of the AC but clears the magnitude bits to all zeros.

9-7 DESIGN OF CONTROL

The basic computer of Chap. 5 is controlled by four cycles with four timing sequences in each cycle. A short timing sequence in the execute cycle may not be sufficient for executing complicated operations such as the arithmetic operations considered here. The longest sequence of timing signals for a computer is determined from the instruction with the most time-consuming sequence of micro-operations. Moreover, it is not mandatory for the control to distinguish between the fetch and execute cycles. The timing signals for executing the instruction can follow the fetch micro-operations as soon as they are completed. A careful investigation reveals that the most time-consuming instruction in the arithmetic processor requires more than eight but less than sixteen timing sequences to fetch the instruction from memory and execute it.

The control unit of the arithmetic processor employs a sequence register SR as shown in Fig. 9-12. This register has four flip-flops that can be in any one of 16 possible states. The timing decoder attached to this register provides outputs for 16 distinct timing signals. The sequence register functions as a binary counter most of the time to produce an orderly numerical sequence of timing signals. Once in awhile, the content of SR is forced out of sequence by a parallel transfer of a constant value. Moreover, SR is cleared as soon as the execution of an instruction is completed causing a return to the beginning of the fetch cycle. In this manner, the control has a maximum of 16 timing signals t_0–t_{15} for each instruction, but the normal sequence can be altered or terminated at any time.

The instruction fetch cycle is common to all instructions and is activated during timing sequences t_0–t_2 as shown in Table 9-4. Note that SR is incremented at the same

TABLE 9-4 Register Transfer Statements for Fetch Cycle

t_0:	$MAR \leftarrow PC$,	$SR \leftarrow SR + 1$
t_1:	$BR \leftarrow M$, $\quad PC \leftarrow PC + 1$,	$SR \leftarrow SR + 1$
t_2:	$MAR \leftarrow BR(AD)$, $OPR \leftarrow BR(OP)$,	$SR \leftarrow SR + 1$

time that the other micro-operations are executed and causes control to go to the next timing sequence. After time t_2, the operation code of the instruction is available in OPR. This register is decoded to provide 16 outputs q_0 to q_{15}, one for each of the operation codes in the computer.

Each instruction has its own set of control gates that generate the control functions for its micro-operations. Each control function receives one input from the operation decoder (to specify the operation), one input from the timing decoder (to specify the timing sequence) and, sometimes, inputs from other registers in the processor (to specify a status condition). The gates generate the control functions for the micro-operations and for SR as well. The control functions are determined from the list of register transfer statements that are written for each instruction.

The list of all control functions for the computer is too lengthy and will not be undertaken here. A few examples will be presented to show how they can be derived.

The register transfer statements for the ADD and SUB instructions are listed in Table 9-5. The operations decoded are either q_0 for ADD or q_1 for SUB. The steps

TABLE 9-5 Register Transfer Statements for ADD and SUB

$(q_0 + q_1)t_3$:	$BR \leftarrow M$,	$SR \leftarrow SR + 1$	Read operand, go to t_4
$(x'q_0 + xq_1)t_4$*:	$EA \leftarrow A + B$,	$SR \leftarrow SR + 1$	Add magnitudes, go to t_5
$(xq_0 + x'q_1)t_4$:	$EA \leftarrow A + \bar{B} + 1$, $AVF \leftarrow 0$,	$SR \leftarrow 0110$	Subtract magnitudes, go to t_6
$(q_0 + q_1)t_5$:	$AVF \leftarrow E$,	$SR \leftarrow 0$	Set overflow and return to t_0
$E(q_0 + q_1)t_6$:	If $(A = 0)$ then $(A_s \leftarrow 0)$,	$SR \leftarrow 0$	Set sign and return to t_0
$E'(q_0 + q_1)t_6$:	$A \leftarrow \bar{A}$,	$SR \leftarrow SR + 1$	Complement A, go to t_7
$(q_0 + q_1)t_7$:	$A \leftarrow A + 1$, $A_s \leftarrow \bar{A}_s$,	$SR \leftarrow 0$	Increment and return to t_0

*$x = A_s \oplus B_s$.

follow the algorithm developed in Fig. 9-4. The operand is read from memory at time t_3 and placed in BR. The control functions at time t_4 determine whether to add or subtract the magnitudes. The signs of the operands are compared by an exclusive-OR gate whose output is $x = A_s \oplus B_s$. If $x = 0$ (signs alike) during the ADD instruction ($q_0 = 1$) or if $x = 1$ (signs unlike) during the SUB instruction ($q_1 = 1$), then the magnitudes are added. Otherwise, the magnitudes are subtracted. SR is incremented if the magnitudes are added but is set to a constant value of 6 (binary 0110) if the magnitudes are subtracted. In this way, the present control function can determine the next timing sequence. Incrementing SR at time t_4 gives t_5 as the next timing signal. The add-overflow flip-flop AVF receives the carry value from E and the instruction execution is completed by clearing SR to 0. The next timing sequence becomes t_0 and control returns to the beginning of the fetch cycle. If control moved from t_4 to t_6, the next micro-operation depends on the value of the carry in E. If $E = 1$, the instruction execution is completed after t_6. If $E = 0$. The magnitude in A is complemented and incremented and the instruction execution is completed after t_7. Note that the decision boxes in the flow chart of Fig. 9-4 are implemented by the control functions. If two decision boxes follow each other (as when $E = 1$ followed by $A = 0$), both conditions are included as part of the control condition.

Table 9-6 lists the register transfer statements needed to execute the multiply operation. The steps follow the algorithm developed in Fig. 9-7. The initialization

TABLE 9-6   Register Transfer Statements for MUL

q_2t_3:	$BR \leftarrow M$, $SR \leftarrow SR + 1$
q_2t_4:	$A_s \leftarrow Q_s \oplus B_s$, $Q_s \leftarrow Q_s \oplus B_s$, $A \leftarrow 0$, $E \leftarrow 0$, $SC \leftarrow 15$, $SR \leftarrow SR + 1$
$Q_nq_2t_5$:	$EA \leftarrow A + B$
q_2t_5:	$SC \leftarrow SC - 1$, $SR \leftarrow SR + 1$
q_2t_6:	shr EAQ, if $(SC = 0)$ then $(SR \leftarrow 0)$, if $(SC \neq 0)$ then $(SR \leftarrow 0101)$

is done during t_4. A partial product is formed during t_5 and t_6 and the sequence counter SC is decremented. At t_6 control goes back to t_5 if $SC \neq 0$ to form a new partial product. The execution terminates and SR is set to 0 when $SC = 0$.

The register transfer statements for the other 14 instructions of the computer may be derived in a similar manner. The set of control functions thus obtained gives the Boolean functions for the gates in the control logic network. All those control functions that activate an identical micro-operation are ORed together and the output is applied to the corresponding register. It is obvious that this type of control requires a multitude of gates forming a most irregular logic network. Because of its irregular pattern, the hard-wired control is said to have "random logic."

9-8   MICROPROGRAMMED CALCULATOR

Chapter 8 presents a procedure for implementing a microprogrammed control unit in a digital computer. It was also mentioned there that the microprogram concept is not unique to a digital computer. Any special purpose digital system can be microprogrammed for a dedicated application. An electronic calculator is a special-purpose digital system controlled by a microprogram and devoted to the calculation of arithmetic functions. The microprogram controls the arithmetic operations as well as the input data and arithmetic functions entered through the keyboard. In this section we discuss the microprogram aspect of calculators and present a few microprogram routines. The arithmetic routines for the calculator are applicable for use in a digital computer and they can be easily incorporated into the control memory of a general-purpose computer.

A commerical calculator has a keyboard with keys for the ten decimal digits and a decimal point, and for a certain number of arithmetic operations and functions. Signed decimal numbers are displayed with a moving decimal point indicator. When the number of digits exceeds the capacity of the display, some calculators display an overflow symbol and others change the display to a floating-point representation. Internally the calculator has one or more LSI circuits commonly referred to as *chips*. Within the chips are the electronic circuits for processor registers, a decimal arithmetic unit, and a ROM control memory. In order to manipulate decimal numbers with decimal points, the processor must employ floating-point data and the control memory must be microprogrammed to implement decimal floating-point arithmetic operations.

A discussion of the internal operation of commercial calculators would take us too far afield. We may simplify the presentation by considering instead a binary calculator that performs arithmetic operations with fixed-point binary numbers. Obviously, this is not a practical device, but because it is a simplified version, the basic functions of a microprogrammed calculator will be easier to demonstrate. The extension of the principle to a practical decimal calculator should be apparent from this example and after studying the decimal algorithms in the next chapter.

Calculator Configuration

The arithmetic processor for the binary calculator is similar to the one used for the computer in the previous section. As shown in the block diagram of Fig. 9-13, the arithmetic processor consists of registers BR, AC, QR, SC, and flip-flops E, AVF, DVF as before. The keyboard is very simple and consists of eight keys. Since the calculator processes binary numbers in fixed-point integer representation, data entry consists of the digits 0 and 1 only (instead of the ten decimal digits and decimal point in a commercial calculator). There is a key for each of the four arithmetic operations. The "equals" key functions as a command for executing and dispalying the result of the calculation. The key marked C is used for clearing the display.

Four registers are needed for communicating with the keyboard and display:

DSR A display register of 16 bits

INR An input register of 3 bits

OPR An operation register of 3 bits

KBE A keyboard entry flip-flop of 1 bit

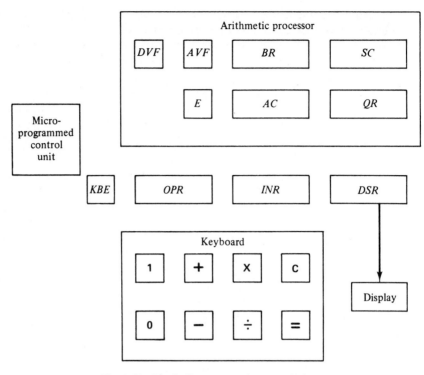

Fig. 9-13 Block diagram of a binary calculator.

DSR holds the binary number presently being displayed. *INR* holds a 3-bit code of the last item entered from the keyboard. The binary code for each item is listed in Table 9-7. The conversion of a keyboard entry to its 3-bit code representation in *INR* is accomplished by means of a combinational circuit. The *KBE* flip-flop is set to 1 every time a key is depressed. It is cleared to 0 after the keyboard entry in *INR* is processed by the control. *OPR* holds the binary code of the last operation entered. This code is the same as the one used for *INR*.

TABLE 9-7 Bit Assignment for *INR* and *OPR*

Key Depressed	Content of INR or OPR
C	000
+	001
−	010
×	011
÷	100
=	101
0	110
1	111

The numbers entered from the keyboard are first displayed in *DSR*. When an operation is executed, the numbers are transferred to processor registers. Results are transferred back to *DSR* for display. The registers in the arithmetic processor that hold the various operands are listed in Table 9-8. The registers employed are as speci-

TABLE 9-8   Registers for Operands and Results

	First Operand		Second Operand		Answer	
Operation	*Register*	*Operand*	*Register*	*Operand*	*Register*	*Result*
$+$	AC	Augend	BR	Addend	AC	Sum
$-$	AC	Minuend	BR	Subtrahend	AC	Difference
$\times$	QR	Multiplier	BR	Multiplicand	QR	Product
$\div$	QR	Dividend	BR	Divisor	QR	Quotient

fied by the algorithms developed in previous sections except that single precision (16 bits) is used. For multiplication, the result may be up to 30 bits and a sign but only the least 15 significant bits and the sign are displayed. If the product exceeds 16 bits, an overflow symbol is displayed. The dividend has only 16 bits when entered from the keyboard and is placed in *QR*. The *AC* must be cleared at the beginning of the division operation. This must be done because the calculator cannot enter or display numbers that exceed 16 bits.

Keyboard Entry

A keyboard entry sets *KBE* to 1 and transfers a binary code into *INR*. The control unit processes each entry as shown in Table 9-9. Pressing the C key clears the display register. When one of the operation keys is depressed, the operation code entered in *INR* is transferred to *OPR*. For plus and minus, the number in *DSR* is transferred to the *AC*. For times and divide, the number in *DSR* is transferred to *QR*, and the *AC* is cleared. *DSR* is cleared to prepare it for the next data entry. Depressing the equals key causes a transfer of the binary number from *DSR* to *BR* and the last operation stored in *OPR* is then executed. The result of the operation is transferred to *DSR* for display. Binary digits entered through the keyboard are shifted into *DSR* one at a time.

TABLE 9-9   Micro-Operations for Keyboard Entry

Key Depressed	Micro-Operations
C	$DSR \leftarrow 0$
$+$ *or* $-$	$OPR \leftarrow INR, AC \leftarrow DSR, DSR \leftarrow 0$
$\times$ *or* $\div$	$OPR \leftarrow INR, QR \leftarrow DSR, AC \leftarrow 0, DSR \leftarrow 0$
$=$	$BR \leftarrow DSR$, perform operation and display result
0 *or* 1	shl $DSR, DSR(16) \leftarrow INR(3)$

This is done by shifting *DSR* left and entering the least significant bit in *INR* into the least significant bit of *DSR*. Depressing the 0 or 1 key at the beginning of data entry will insert a sign bit into the high-order position of *DSR*. If more than 16 bits are entered, the display shows an overflow symbol and further entry is inhibited.

The keyboard entry must follow the following sequence.

1. Depress C to clear display.
2. Enter first operand.
3. Depress an operation key.
4. Enter second operand.
5. Depress the equals key.

For example, to multiply 9 by 6 the keyboard entry would be:

$$\text{C } 1001 \times 110 =$$

and the result $54 = (110110)_2$ will be transferred to *DSR* and displayed. For chain operations, the user will then enter a new operation followed by the next operand. For example, to add 8 to 54 which is presently displayed, the user will enter:

$$+ 1000 =$$

and binary 62 will be displayed.

The first operand in *DSR* may come from the keyboard (after Clear) or from the result of a previous operation (after =). When an operation key is depressed, the number in *DSR* is taken as the first operand and is transferred to *AC* (if + or −) or to *QR* (if × or ÷). When the equals key is depressed, the number in *DSR* is taken as the second operand and is transferred to *BR*. The operation is executed and displayed. If an overflow occurs in any calculation, the overflow flip-flop sets the overflow symbol in the display.

The Control Unit

The various micro-operations and branch decisions are controlled by a microprogram residing in a read-only memory. The microprogram must include microinstructions for the execution of arithmetic operations as well as for controlling the flow of information from keyboard and display. A microprogram must be capable of sequencing its own next address and specifying the sequence of micro-operations in the system. A multiple control word format that provides these capabilities is shown in Table 9-10. We are assuming a control memory of 128 words, 8 bits per word. If bit 1 of the word is a 1, the other seven bits are taken as the address for an unconditional *branch* micro-

TABLE 9-10 Control Word Format for Binary Calculator

1 2 3 4 5 6 7 8	8 bits of control word
1 X X X X X X X	Branch to address XXXXXXX
0 1 Y Y Y Y Y Y	Skip next microinstruction if condition YYYYYY is met
0 0 Z Z Z Z Z Z	Perform micro-operation specified by ZZZZZZ

instruction. If bit 1 of the word is 0, bit 2 specifies either a *skip* microinstruction or a *micro-operation* microinstruction. In both cases, bits 3 to 8 are encoded to give up to 64 different conditions. The skip microinstruction is similar to a skip instruction in a computer, but is implented differently. In a skip instruction, the program counter is incremented to cause a skip of the next instruction. The skip microinstruction in control memory is accomplished by inhibiting all outputs from ROM on the next clock pulse (if the condition is met). This causes the next microinstruction to be ignored and have no effect.

A partial encoding of the skip microinstructions is shown in Table 9-11. The last 6 bits of the control word can be encoded to specify 64 different conditions. The conditions used in the succeeding microprogram examples have been listed in the table but other conditions can be added to the list. A table for encoding the 64 micro-operations is not provided but the reader can very easily formulate such a table.

TABLE 9-11 Partial Encoding of Skip Microinstructions

Control Word	Skip Next Microinstruction If:
01 000001	$E = 1$
01 000010	$E = 0$
01 000011	$A_s \oplus B_s = 0$
01 000100	$A \neq 0$
01 000101	$SC = 0$
01 000110	$Q_n = 0$
01 000111	$KBE = 1$
01 001000	$INR \neq 000$
01 001111	$INR \neq 111$
01 010001	$OPR \neq 001$
01 010100	$OPR \neq 100$

A block diagram of the control memory and its associated logic is shown in Fig. 9-14. The skip microinstruction is applied to a multiplexer to select one of 64 conditions. If the condition is met (if it is equal to 1) the output of the multiplexer is 1, so on the next clock pulse the flip-flop is set making $Q' = 0$ and all microinstructions are disabled causing the next microinstruction to be inhibited during the next clock pulse. The same next clock pulse clears the flip-flop since the output of the multiplexer is 0. The flip-flop remains cleared (with $Q' = 1$) at all times except during one clock

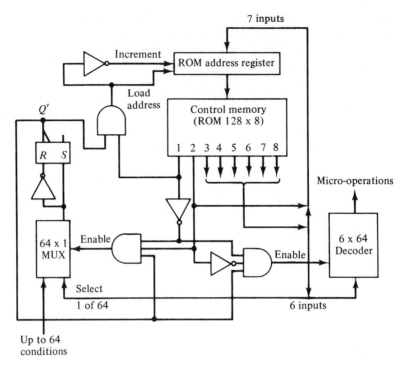

Fig. 9-14 Control memory and associated logic for binary calculator.

pulse interval after the skip microinstruction is executed and only if the specified condition has been met. The ROM address register is incremented with every clock pulse execept during a branch condition, provided it is enabled by the flip-flop. When ROM bits 1 and 2 are both 0 and $Q' = 1$, a 6 by 64 decoder is enabled to provide one of 64 different micro-operations.

The Microprogram

We are now ready to write the microprogram for the calculator. To facilitate the writing of the microprogram we will employ symbolic names for the microinstructions. Each line of microcode may have a symbolic address in a label field. The second field in the microcode must contain a symbol which specifies one of the following types of microinstructions:

branch to address

skip if condition

micro-operation

The *branch to* symbol is translated to an 8-bit control word 1XXXXXXX where the bits designated by X speicfy a binary address. The symbolic address after *branch to* must also occur in the label field to specify its binary value. A *skip if* symbol designates a skip microinstruction and is translated to an 8-bit word 01YYYYYY where the bits designated by Y are determined from Table 9-11 for each specified condition. A *micro-operation* microinstruction is specified by a register transfer statement and is translated into binary as 00ZZZZZZ, where the bits designated by Z must be encoded in some convenient manner.

When power is turned on in the binary calculator, the display register *DSR* and the operation register *OPR* are cleared. Control branches to a routine that scans the keyboard for an entry. This routine, called KBRD, is listed in Table 9-12. The first micro-instruction clears *KBE* to 0. Remember that every time a key is depresses, *KBE* is set to 1 and the 3-bit code specified in Table 9-7 enters the input register *INR*. The

TABLE 9-12   Microprogram for Keyboard Entry

KBRD	$KBE \leftarrow 0$	Clear *KBE*
KD	Skip if $KBE = 1$	Check keyboard entry
	branch to KD	$KBE = 0$, go to check again
	Skip if $INR \neq 000$	$KBE = 1$, check entry
	Branch to CLEAR	Go to service C entry
	Skip if $INR \neq 001$	
	Branch to POM	Go to service "plus" entry
	Skip if $INR \neq 010$	
	Branch to POM	Go to service "minus" entry
	Skip if $INR \neq 011$	
	Branch to TOD	Go to service "times" entry
	Skip if $INR \neq 100$	
	Branch to TOD	Go to service "divide" entry
	Skip if $INR \neq 101$	
	Branch to EQUALS	Go to service an "equals" entry
	Branch to ONZ	Go to service a numeric entry
CLEAR	$DSR \leftarrow 0$	
	Branch to KBRD	
POM	$OPR \leftarrow INR$	
	$AC \leftarrow DSR$	
	$DSR \leftarrow 0$	
	Branch to KBRD	
TOD	$OPR \leftarrow INR$	
	$QR \leftarrow DSR$	
	$AC \leftarrow 0$	
	$DSR \leftarrow 0$	
	Branch to KBRD	
ONZ	shl *DSR*	
	$DSR(16) \leftarrow INR(3)$	
	Branch to KBRD	

second microinstruction checks if $KBE = 1$, and if not, control returns to KD to check KBE again. If $KBE = 1$, the next microinstruction is skipped and INR is scanned for the keyboard entry. If key C was depressed, control branches to routine CLEAR. If the plus or minus keys are depressed, control branches to routine POM. The KBRD routine continues to scan all eight entries and branches to one of five routines.

Four of the routines that process the keyboard entry are listed next. The micro-operations for each routine are as specified in Table 9-9. The CLEAR routine clears the display. POM (Plus Or Minus) transfers the first operand from DSR to AC. TOD (Times Or Divide) transfers the first operand from DSR to QR and clears the AC. In each case, the 3-bit code from INR is transferred to OPR. ONZ (One or Zero) causes a left shift of DSR and a transfer of the input bit from INR into the least significant position of DSR. When the processing of the keyboard is terminated, control goes back to the KBRD routine to process the next entry.

Assume now that two binary operands have been entered, together with an operation in between. Depressing the equals key should cause the execution of the operation and display of the result. This routine, called EQUALS, is listed in Table 9-13. The first microinstruction is a micro-operation that transfers the second operand

TABLE 9-13   Microprogram for Routine EQUALS

EQUALS	$BR \leftarrow DSR$	Transfer second operand to BR
	Skip if $OPR \neq 001$	Check if plus operation
	Branch to ADD	Go to ADD routine
	Skip if $OPR \neq 010$	Check if minus operation
	Branch to SUB	Go to SUB routine
	Skip if $OPR \neq 011$	Check if times operation
	Branch to MUL	Go to MUL routine
	Skip if $OPR \neq 100$	Check if divide operation
	Branch to DIV	Go to DIV routine
	$DSR \leftarrow 0$	Clear display
	Branch to KBRD	Branch to scan keyboard

from DSR into BR. The routine then scans the OPR register for the operation and branches to one of four arithmetic routines. If OPR holds an unacceptable code, DSR is cleared and no operation is executed.

The four arithmetic routine ADD, SUB, MUL, and DIV are derived from the algorithms for addition, subtraction, multiplication, and division given in flow chart form in previous sections. The ADD and SUB routines are listed in Table 9-14; the other two are left for exercises. The microprogram follows the algorithm of Fig. 9-4 and should be self-explanatory. Note that at the end control returns to routine KBRD to scan the next entry from the keyboard.

TABLE 9-14 Microprogram Routine for ADD and SUB

ADD	Skip if $A_s \oplus B_s = 0$	Check signs
	branch to SB1	Go to SB1 if signs unlike
AD1	$EA \leftarrow A + B$	Add magnitudes
	$AVF \leftarrow E$	Set overflow
	Branch to COMP	Operation completed
SUB	Skip if $A_s \oplus B_s = 0$	Check signs
	Branch to AD1	Go to AD1 if signs unlike
SB1	$EA \leftarrow A + \bar{B} + 1$	Subtract magnitudes
	$AVF \leftarrow 0$	No overflow
	Skip if $E = 0$	Check end-carry
	Branch to SB2	Go to SB2 if $E = 1$
	$A \leftarrow \bar{A}$	Complement A
	$A \leftarrow A + 1$	Increment A
	$A_s \leftarrow \bar{A}_s$	Complement sign
	Branch to COMP	Operation completed
SB2	Skip if $A \neq 0$	Check for zero content
	$A_s \leftarrow 0$	Make sign plus if $A = 0$
COMP	$DSR \leftarrow AC$	Display result
	$DSR(OVF) \leftarrow AVF$	Display overflow
	Branch to KBRD	Go to scan keyboard

REFERENCES

1. MANO, M. M., *Digital Logic and Computer Design.* Englewood Cliffs, N.J.: Prentice-Hall, Inc., 1979.

2. CHU, Y., *Computer Organization and Microprogramming.* Englewood Cliffs, N.J.: Prentice-Hall, Inc., 1972.

3. RICHARDS, R. K., *Arithmetic Operations in Digital Computers.* Princeton, N.J.: D. Van Nostrand, 1955.

4. HWANG, K., *Computer Arithmetic: Principles, Architecture, and Design.* New York: John Wiley & Sons, Inc., 1979.

5. GSCHWIND, H. W., AND E. D. MCCLUSKEY, *Design of Digital Computers.* New York: Springer-Verlag, 1975.

PROBLEMS

9-1. The magnitude comparator of Fig. 9-1 does not have the facility for expansion to numbers of more than 4 bits. Modify the circuit by using three more inputs that will indicate the status of any external lower-significance bits and show how the three inputs are to be connected internally to provide an expansion capability. Draw a block diagram showing how several modified 4-bit comparator packages can be connected to produce a comparator for numbers of eight or more bits.

9-2. Prove the comparison and subtraction relations listed in Table 9-1 for $A + \bar{B}$.

9-3. Consider the following pairs of unsigned *binary* numbers:
(a) $A = 25$, $B = 18$
(b) $A = 15$, $B = 22$
(c) $A = 20$, $B = 20$
For each pair, perform the operation $A + \bar{B}$ and justify the result obtained.

9-4. Derive an algorithm in flow chart form for the addition and subtraction of fixed-point binary numbers in signed-magnitude representation with subtraction done by a parallel-subtractor ($EA \leftarrow A - B$). Show one stage of the adder-subtractor circuit with an add-subtract control (ASC).

9-5. The complementer shown in Fig. 9-2 is not needed if instead of performing $A + \bar{B} + 1$ we perform $B + \bar{A}$ (B plus the 1's complement of A). Derive an algorithm in flow chart form for addition and subtraction of fixed-point binary numbers in signed-magnitude representation with the magnitudes subtracted by the two micro-operations $A \leftarrow \bar{A}$ and $EA \leftarrow A + B$.

9-6. Mark each individual path in the flow chart of Fig. 9-4 by a number and then indicate the overall path that the algorithm takes when the following numbers are computed. In each case give the value of AVF. The leftmost bit denotes the sign. A seventh bit in the magnitude constitutes an overflow.
(a) $0\ 101101 + 0\ 011111$
(b) $1\ 011111 + 1\ 101101$
(c) $0\ 101101 - 0\ 011111$
(d) $0\ 101101 - 0\ 101101$
(e) $1\ 011111 - 0\ 101101$

9-7. Prove that the multiplication of two n-digit numbers in base r gives a product of no more than $2n$ digits in length. Show that this statement implies that no overflow can occur in the multiplication operation.

9-8. Show the contents of registers A, E, Q, and SC (as in Fig. 9-8) during the process of multiplication of two binary numbers, 11111 (multiplicand) and 10101 (multiplier). The signs are not included.

9-9. Show the contents of registers A, E, Q, and SC (as in Fig. 9-10) during the process of division of (a) 10100011 by 1011 and (b) 1111 by 0011. (Use a dividend of eight bits.)

9-10. Show that adding B after the operation $A + \bar{B} + 1$ restores the original value of A. What should be done with the end-carry?

9-11. Why should the sign of the remainder after a division be the same as the sign of the dividend?

9-12. The algorithms for the four arithmetic operations presented in this chapter assume integer representation. List all changes necessary in the algorithms (if any) when the fixed-point numbers are assumed to be fractions.

9-13. In the comparison method of binary division the partial remainder in EA is compared with the divisor in B prior to the subtract operation. Then if $A \geq B$, B is subtracted from A; but if $A < B$ nothing is done. Derive the flow chart for binary division by the comparison method.

9-14. Derive an algorithm in flow chart form for the non-restoring method of fixed-point binary division.

9-15. Derive an algorithm for evaluating the square root of a binary fixed-point number.

9-16. Write a program using the computer instructions of Table 9-3 that calculates:

(a) $\dfrac{X * Y}{Z}$ (b) $\dfrac{X - Y}{Z}$ (c) $\dfrac{W + X}{Y - Z}$

9-17. From Tables 9-4, 9-5, and 9-6, determine the time it takes to process the ADD, SUB, and MUL instructions (including the fetch cycle). Assume that each timing signal is T sec long.

9-18. Explain why the sequence counter SC is decremented at time t_5 (Table 9-6) and not at time t_6 together with the shift as indicated in the flow chart of Fig. 9-7.

9-19. List the register transfer statements for the divide instruction (similar to Table 9-6). Minimize the total number of timing signals required to process the instruction.

9-20. List the register transfer statements (similar to Table 9-5) for the following four instructions listed in Table 9-3: (a) LDA; (b) LDQ; (c) STA; (d) STQ.

9-21. List the register transfer statements (similar to Table 9-5) for the following two instructions listed in Table 9-3: (a) ISZ; (b) BSA.

9-22. List all micro-operations executed in the Q register. What kind of register is needed for Q?

9-23. List all the control functions that execute the micro-operations $EA \leftarrow A + B$ and $EA \leftarrow A + \bar{B} + 1$. Show how these control functions are to be connected to the CC (complement control) and to the load function: $A \leftarrow S$, $E \leftarrow$ carry, shown in Fig. 9-2.

9-24. Show that the BR register in the calculator of Sec. 9-8 can function as the display register and that DSR can be removed. Modify the necessary micro-operations to take care of this change.

9-25. Design a combinational circuit that accepts eight inputs from the keyboard of Fig. 9-13 and generates a 3-bit code for INR as specified in Table 9-7. Generate also the signal for flip-flop KBE.

9-26. Write the microprogram for the MUL routine in symbolic form, for the calculator of Sec. 9-8.

9-27. Write the microprogram for the DIV routine in symbolic form, for the calculator of Sec. 9-8.

9-28. (a) List all micro-operations used in the examples of Table 9-14. Encode these micro-operations and assign a control word for each.
      (b) Translate the symbolic microprogram of Table 9-14 to its equivalent binary form. Assume that the ROM location for ADD is binary 32 and that of KBRD, binary 0.

9-29. Formulate a microprogram control unit for the computer specified in Sec. 9-6 and write the microprogram for the fetch cycle and a few typical instructions.

Arithmetic Algorithms

10

10-1 INTRODUCTION

The design and analysis of digital systems is a complex undertaking especially since the development of IC technology. Many installations develop special software automation techniques to facilitate the design process. Design-automation programs are extensively used to perform such tasks as logic minimization and simplification; assignment of logic circuits from a list of register transfer statements; generation of wiring lists; simulation of the system prior to construction; and generation of documents for manufacturing and maintenance.

However, the specifications for a system and the development of algorithmic procedures for achieving the various data processing tasks cannot be automated and require the reasoning of a human designer. The most challenging and creative part of the design is the establishment of objectives and the formulation of algorithms and procedures for achieving these objectives. This task requires a considerable amount of experience and ingenuity on the part of the designer.

An algorithm is a procedure for obtaining a solution to a problem. A design algorithm is an algorithm for implementing the procedure with a given piece of equipment. The development of a design algorithm cannot start unless the designer has knowledge of two things. First, the problem at hand must be thoroughly understood and fully defined. Second, the designer must be familiar with the tools and methods available for expressing algorithms such as Boolean algebra, flow charts, register transfer languages and programming languages. The particular method employed would depend on the way the algorithm is to be expressed for its implementation.

Arithmetic algorithms are not difficult to define because we are all familiar with arithmetic operations. On the other hand, to define a procedure for an interface between a computer and an input device would be more complicated because one must be thoroughly familiar with the terminal behavior of the components. Nevertheless, the design procedure in each case is similar. Starting from the problem requirements and equipment availability, a solution must be found and an algorithm formed. The algorithm is stated by a finite number of well-defined procedural steps.

Because arithmetic algorithms are simpler to define, we use them here to demonstrate the procedures for deriving design algorithms. Other digital design algorithms will require a similar creative endeavor and reasoning ability. However, they may be more difficult to design because of the additional effort involved in formulating the exact specifications.

Many algorithms and especially arithmetic algorithms may be implemented in a computer by means of software, hardware, firmware, or a combination of the three methods. Some small computers have only one hardware arithmetic operation such as addition of two fixed-point binary numbers. The *add* instruction, together with *complement*, *shift*, and other instructions, is then used to generate subroutines for other arithmetic operations. These subroutines constitute a software implementation for the arithmetic operations. A subroutine occupies memory space for storing its instructions and the computational process is time-consuming because many instructions have to be executed for one operation. Software implementation saves hardware at the expense of memory space and time of execution.

An arithmetic operation is implemented by hardware if the computer has an instruction for the operation. In hardware implementation, the registers receive control signals from the control unit and generate a sequence of micro-operations for executing the operation specified by the instruction. Hardware implementation requires special circuits which would not be needed if the operation were to be implemented by software. On the other hand, hardware methods provide higher computation speed and occupy memory space for only one instruction.

The control unit in a hardware implementation may be either hard-wired or microprogrammed. In the latter case, the micro-operations are programmed in a control memory and constitute a microprogram for the instruction. Operations that are implemented by means of a microprogram are said to be implemented by firmware.

Algorithms for arithmetic operations are very important for the design of the arithmetic unit of a digital computer or for the development of arithmetic software routines. Software implementation of arithmetic operations was discussed in Sec. 6-6. Algorithms for fixed-point signed-magnitude data were introduced in Chap. 9. This chapter presents arithmetic algorithms for the following types of data.

1. Fixed-point binary data in signed-2's complement representation.

2. Floating-point binary data.

3. Binary-coded decimal data.

The algorithms presented here assume the availability of a parallel arithmetic unit capable of performing addition and subtraction of numbers in parallel. The same algorithms can be easily adapted for serial operations. They can also be used as a basis for software subroutines or for a microprogram. The method by which an algorithm is implemented in a particular situation depends on the equipment availability and on the particular application.

10-2 ARITHMETIC WITH SIGNED-2's COMPLEMENT NUMBERS

The signed-2's complement representation of numbers together with some arithmetic algorithms are introduced in Sec. 3-2. They are summarized here for easy reference. The left-most bit of a binary number in signed-2's complement form represents the sign bit: 0 for plus and 1 for minus. If the sign bit is minus, the entire number is represented in 2's complement form. Thus, $+9$ is represented as 001001 and -9 as 110111. Note that 110111 is the 2's complement of 001001, and vice versa.

The 2's complement of a binary number can be obtained by taking the 1's complement and then adding 1. This requires two simple computational steps. The 2's complement can be formed in one step by leaving all least significant 0's and the first 1 unchanged, and then complementing the remaining bits. For example, the 2's complement of 10100 (-14) is 01100 ($+14$). It is obtained by leaving the two low-order 0's and the first 1 unchanged, and then complementing the two most significant bits.

The addition of two numbers in signed-2's complement form consists of adding the numbers with the sign bits treated the same as the other computational bits. Any carry out of the sign-bit position is discarded. The subtraction consists of first taking the 2's complement of the subtrahend and then adding it to the minuend. The addition in both cases assumes that there is no overflow.

When two numbers of n digits each are added and the sum occupies $n + 1$ digits, we say that an overflow occurs. The effect of an overflow on the sum of two signed-2's complement numbers is discussed in Sec. 3-2. We summarize here the most important points: (1) An overflow condition occurs when the exclusive-OR of the last two carries is equal to 1. (See Fig. 7-14 for the hardware implementation.) (2) An overflow produces a sign reversal in the highest-order bit position which represents the sign bit. (3) The correct $n + 1$ bit answer can be obtained from the n-bit sum plus an appended sign bit in the $(n + 1)$ position given by the output carry (which is normally discarded if there is no overflow).

Hardware Implementation

The register configuration for the hardware implementation of the four arithmetic operations with signed-2's complement numbers is shown in Fig. 10-1. This is the same configuration as was used in Chap. 9. The AC (accumulator) register is subdivided into two parts. The highest-order bit in the register represents the sign bit and is designated by A_s. The rest of the register is designated by the symbol A. Thus, A_s together with A constitute the AC register. Similarly, register BR is subdivided into B_s (for the sign bit) and B and register QR into Q_s and Q. The least significant bit in register Q is designated by Q_n.

The sequence counter SC is used during multiplication and division for counting the number of times that a computational loop must be repeated. Not shown in the

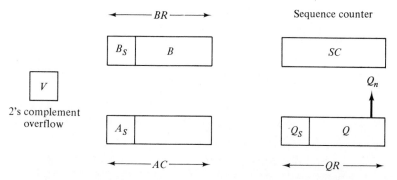

Fig. 10-1 Registers for signed-2's complement arithmetic operations.

diagram are a complementer and parallel adder used for adding and subtracting two numbers stored in AC and BR. The function of this circuit is explained in conjunction with Fig. 9-2. The overflow bit V is set to 1 if the exclusive-OR of the last two carries out of the parallel adder are equal to 1; otherwise, it is cleared to 0.

Addition and Subtraction with Signed-2's Complement Numbers

The algorithm for adding and subtracting two binary numbers in signed-2's complement representation is shown in the flow chart of Fig. 10-2. The sum is obtained by adding the content of AC and BR (including the sign bits). V is set if there is an overflow. The subtraction operation is accomplished by adding the content of AC to the 2's complement of BR. Taking the 2's complement of BR has the effect of changing a positive number to negative, or vice versa. An overflow must be checked during this operation because the two numbers added could have the same sign.

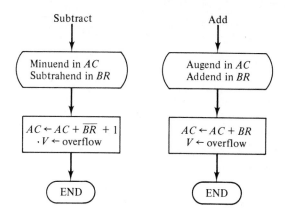

Fig. 10-2 Algorithm for adding and subtracting numbers in signed-2's complement representation.

Obviously, if an overflow occurs, the AC has an erroneous result and something must be done if $V = 1$.

Comparing this algorithm with its signed-magnitude counterpart, we note that it is much simpler to add and subtract numbers if negative numbers are maintained in signed-2's complement representation. For this reason many computers adopt this representation over the more familiar signed-magnitude. However, we will see in the next section that multiplication and division have a reverse property. It is simpler to multiply and divide numbers in signed-magnitude than it is in signed-2's complement representation.

Arithmetic Shifts

An arithmetic shift is an operation that shifts a signed number to the left or right. An arithmetic shift-right divides the number by 2 and an arithmetic shift-left multiplies it by 2. Arithmetic shifts must leave the sign-bit unchanged because the sign of the number remains the same when it is multiplied or divided by 2. We now consider the arithmetic shifts for binary numbers in signed-2's complement representation.

Consider first the arithmetic shift-left that multiplies a number by 2. The entire number must be shifted to the left and a 0 inserted in the least significant position. A number shifted to the left may cause an overflow. An overflow occurs as a result of a left shift if the sign-bit value after the shift is not the same as the sign bit was before the shift.

Consider now the arithmetic shift-right that divides a number by 2. The entire number must be shifted to the right but the sign bit must remain unchanged. This is because a positive number must remain positive and must insert a 0 into the most significant position of the number bits. A negative number must remain negative and must insert a 1 into the most significant position of the number bits. Thus, the sign bit must be shifted right together with all other bits but the sign-bit position remains unaltered.

We have seen in Chap. 9 that the multiplication algorithm is implemented by means of repeated addition-and-shift operations. The addition in signed-2's complement representation may cause an overflow. Therefore, the subsequent shift-right operation must take into consideration a previous overflow condition. Consider the addition of two numbers with their sum transferred into the AC register of Fig. 10-1. V represents the overflow condition and A_s designates the sign bit. The sum can be shifted to the right by shifting the entire AC once to the right and inserting the correct sign into A_s. The sign-bit value after the shift depends on the sign-bit value before the shift and the overflow condition in V as shown in Table 10-1. If there was no overflow in the previous addition, the value of A_s does not change. If there was an overflow, there was also a sign reversal, so A_s must be complemented. From the table we see that A_s after the shift is equal to the exclusive-OR of A_s before the shift and the value in V. The arithmetic shift-right operation can be symbolized with the following statement:

$$\text{shr } AC, \qquad A_s \leftarrow A_s \oplus V$$

TABLE 10-1 Sign-Bit Value for Arithmetic Shift-Right

Overflow, V	Sign bit A_s before shift	Sign bit A_s after shift	Comments
0	0	0	No overflow, sign remains positive
0	1	1	No overflow, sign remains negative
1	0	1	Overflow, needs sign reversal
1	1	0	Overflow, needs sign reversal

The entire AC is shifted to the right and the value inserted into the sign-bit position comes from an exclusive-OR gate with V and A_s as inputs.

10-3 MULTIPLICATION AND DIVISION

In Chap. 9 we presented algorithms for multiplying and dividing binary numbers in signed-magnitude representation. This section presents some alternatives for multiplying and dividing fixed-point binary numbers.

Array Multiplier

Checking the bits of the multiplier one at a time and forming partial products is a sequential operation that requires a sequence of add and shift micro-operations. The multiplication of two binary numbers can be done with one micro-operation by means of a combinational circuit that forms the product bits all at once. This is a fast way of multiplying two numbers since all it takes is the time for the signals to propagate through the gates that form the multiplication array. However, an array multiplier requires a large number of gates and for this reason it was not economical until the development of integrated circuits. Combinational circuit binary multipliers are available in IC packages.

To get an idea how an array binary multiplier is formed, consider the multiplication of two 2-bit numbers as shown in Fig. 10-3. The multiplicand bits are b_1 and b_0, the multiplier bits are a_1 and a_0 and the product is $c_3 c_2 c_1 c_0$. The first partial product is formed by multiplying a_0 by $b_1 b_0$. The multiplication of two bits such as a_0 and b_0 produces a 1 if both bits are 1; otherwise, it produces a 0. This is identical to an AND operation and can be implemented by hardware with an AND gate. As shown in the diagram, the first partial product is formed by means of two AND gates. The second partial product is formed by multiplying a_1 by $b_1 b_0$ and adding this product to the first partial product. This is achieved by two more AND gates and a parallel binary adder. The binary adder in this case consists of two half-adders (HA) since only two bits are added in each circuit. If more partial products are needed, we will have to use full-adder circuits to add two bits and a previous carry. Note

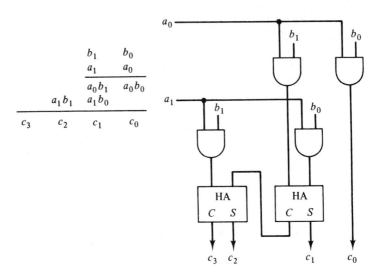

$$
\begin{array}{cccc}
 & & b_1 & b_0 \\
 & & a_1 & a_0 \\
\hline
 & & a_0 b_1 & a_0 b_0 \\
 & a_1 b_1 & a_1 b_0 & \\
\hline
c_3 & c_2 & c_1 & c_0
\end{array}
$$

Fig. 10-3 2 by 2 binary array multiplier.

that the least significant bit does not have to go through an adder since it is formed by the output of the first AND gate.

An array binary multiplier with more bits can be constructed in a similar fashion. A bit of the multiplier is ANDed with each bit of the multiplicand in as many levels as there are bits in the multiplier. The binary output in each level of AND gates is added in parallel to the partial product of the previous level to form a new partial product. For j multiplier bits and k multiplicand bits we need jk AND gates and $(j - 1)$ parallel-adders.

Instead of using a large number of AND gates and a number of parallel adders, the array multiplier can be more conveniently implemented by means of a read-only memory. The ROM can implement any combinational circuit and as such it can implement a binary multiplier circuit. Thus, a 4-bit by 3-bit multiplier requires 7 inputs and 7 outputs. A 128 by 7 ROM will have 7 address lines and 7 output lines. Four of the address lines receive the multiplicand bits and the other three receive the multiplier bits. The multiplication truth table for each of the 128 words is then used to mask the required bits in the ROM. It may be worth noting that the least significant product bit can be obtained from one AND gate. This fact can be utilized to reduce the number of ROM outputs by one.

Multiplication with Signed-2's Complement Numbers

The multiplication of two binary numbers when negative numbers are in signed-2's complement representation is complicated by the fact that the function of the multiplier bits is not always the same when forming partial products. The bits are treated as in signed-magnitude when the multiplier is positive. When it is negative, the mul-

370

tiplier is in its 2's complement form. Any least significant zeros and the first 1 must be considered as in a positive multiplier but the rest of the bits have an opposite effect because they are complemented. Although it is possible to formulate a multiplication algorithm that operates with 2's complement numbers directly, most of these algorithms require special control functions that sense the sign bits to determine how the partial products are to be formed.

The simplest way to solve this complication would be to employ an algorithm which complements a negative multiplier or multiplicand prior to the operation. Thus only positive numbers would be multiplied just as in the sign-magnitude case. The positive product obtained would then be complemented only if the product is to be negative. The correct sign can be determined as simply as in the sign-magnitude case.

A more convenient procedure is to change only the multiplier to a positive number and leave the multiplicand either positive or negative. If the original multiplier and multiplicand are both positive, no complementing is required. If the multiplier is positive but the multiplicand is negative, the product should be negative. If we add a negative multiplicand in the proper complement form to a negative partial product in the proper complement form, the result will be a negative product in the proper complement form. So it makes no difference whether the multiplicand is positive or negative. In the first case we form positive partial products and in the second case we form negative partial products.

The multiplier, however, must always be positive. If it is negative, both the multiplier and multiplicand are complemented. This is equivalent to multiplying both numbers by minus one which does not change the product but makes the multiplier positive.

The algorithm that follows this procedure is shown in Fig. 10-4. The multiplicand is in BR and the multiplier in QR. The sign bit of QR is designated by Q_s, the magnitude bits by Q and the least significant bit by Q_n (See Fig. 10-1). The partial products are formed in the AC and if negative, they are in signed-2's complement representation. The AC is first cleared to hold a zero partial product and the sequence counter SC is set to a number equal to the number of bits in the magnitude part of the multiplier. If the multiplier sign is negative, both QR and BR are complemented. This ensures that the multiplier is always positive at the start of the operation. If the least significant bit of the multiplier is 1, the multiplicand in BR is added to the present partial product in the AC. The overflow bit V is set if there is an overflow and cleared otherwise. If $Q_n = 0$, no addition is performed and the overflow bit V remains a 0. The partial product in AC and Q is shifted once to the right. The least significant bit of AC is shifted into Q, bypassing the sign bit Q_s. The sign bit in the AC, designated by A_s, remains unchanged if $V = 0$ but is complemented if $V = 1$. This is according to the arithmetic shift-right procedure established in the preceding section. The add-and-shift loop is repeated for all bits of the multiplier. The final double-length product is formed in the AC and Q. The sign of the product is already available in the first bit of the AC. The sign of QR must have the same sign as the product. The last operation in the flow chart transfers the sign bit from AC into QR.

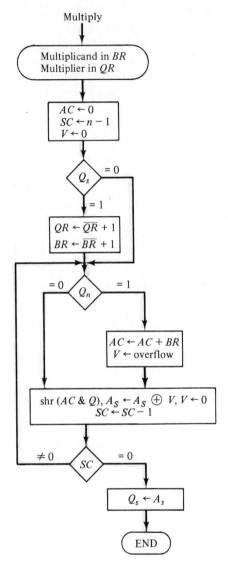

Fig. 10-4 Multiply algorithm for binary numbers in signed-2's complement representation.

Booth's Multiplication Algorithm

The multiplication technique presented in Fig. 10-4 requires that the multiplier always be positive. Booth's algorithm treats a positive and negative multiplier uniformly and is more suitable for multiplication of signed-2's complement numbers. It operates on the fact that strings of 0's in the multiplier require no addition but just shifting, and a string of 1's in the multiplier from bit weight 2^u to weight 2^v can be treated as $2^{u+1} - 2^v$. For example, if the multiplier is 001110 (+14), then $u = 3$ and $v = 1$ and $2^4 - 2^1 = 14$. As in all multiplication schemes, the algorithm requires the examination of the multiplier bits and shifting of the partial product. Prior to the shifting, the multiplicand may be either added to, or subtracted from, or may not change the partial product according to the following rules:

1. The multiplicand is subtracted from the partial product upon encountering the first 1 in a string of 1's in the multiplier.

2. The multiplicand is added to the partial product upon encountering the first 0 (provided that there was a previous 1) in a string of 0's in the multiplier.

3. The partial product does not change when the bit is identical to the previous multiplier bit.

The algorithm works for positive or negative multipliers in 2's complement representation. This is because a negative multiplier ends with a string of 1's and the last operation will be a subtraction of the appropriate weight. For example, a multiplier equal to -14 is represented as 110010 and treated as $-2^4 + 2^2 - 2^1 = -14$.

The hardware implementation of Booth's algorithm requires the register configuration of Fig. 10-1. As shown in the figure, Q_n designates the least significant bit of the multiplier in register QR. An extra flip-flop Q_{n+1} must be appended to QR to facilitate a double-bit inspection of the multiplier. The flow chart for Booth's algorithm in shown in Fig. 10-5. The AC and the appended bit Q_{n+1} are initially cleared to 0 and the sequence counter SC is set to a number equal to the number of bits in the multiplier. The two bits of the multiplier in Q_n and Q_{n+1} are inspected. If the two bits are equal to 10, it means that the first 1 in a string of 1's has been encountered. This requires a subtraction of the multiplicand from the partial product in the AC. If the two bits are equal to 01, it means that the first 0 in a string of 0's has been encountered. This requires the addition of the multiplicand to the partial product. When the two bits are equal, the partial product does not change. The next step is to shift-right the partial product and the multiplier (including bit Q_{n+1}). This is an arithmetic shift-right (ashr) which requires no change in the AC sign bit. An overflow cannot occur because the addition and subtraction of the multiplicand follow each other. As a consequence, the two numbers that are added have always opposite signs, a condition that excludes an overflow. The sequence counter is decremented and the computational loop is repeated n times.

A numerical example of Booth's algorithm is shown in Table 10-2 for $n = 5$. It shows the step-by-step multiplication of $(-9) \times (-13) = +117$. Note that the multiplier in QR is negative and the multiplicand in BR is also negative. The 10-bit product appears in the AC and QR and is positive. The final value of Q_{n+1} is the original sign bit of the multiplier and should not be taken as part of the product.

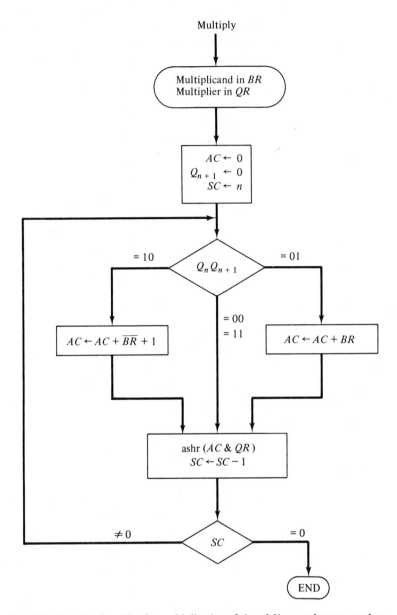

Fig. 10-5 Booth's algorithm for multiplication of signed-2's complement numbers.

TABLE 10-2 Example of Multiplication with Booth's Algorithm

$$BR = 10111$$
$$\overline{BR} + 1 = 01001$$

$Q_n Q_{n+1}$		AC	QR	Q_{n+1}	SC
	Initial	00000	10011	0	5
1 0	Subtract BR	01001			
		01001			
	ashr	00100	11001	1	4
1 1	ashr	00010	01100	1	3
0 1	Add BR	10111			
		11001			
	ashr	11100	10110	0	2
0 0	ashr	11110	01011	0	1
1 0	Subtract BR	01001			
		00111			
	ashr	00011	10101	1	0

Division with Signed-2's Complement Numbers

The division of two binary numbers when negative numbers are in signed-2's complement representation is more complicated than multiplication. This is because the quotient bits must be generated in the adopted representation and the dividend may be either added or subtracted from the partial remainder, depending on the relative signs of the dividend and divisor. It is sometimes convenient to convert the negative numbers to positive, divide the two positive numbers as in signed-magnitude, and then complement the result if it is negative.

An algorithm that performs the division with converted positive numbers is shown in Fig. 10-6. The double length dividend is in AC and QR and the divisor in BR. The sign of the quotient is first determined from the signs of the dividend and divisor. The sign of the dividend in A_s is checked and if it is negative, the dividend in A and Q is changed to positive by complementing the number. Similarly, the divisor in BR is complemented if it is negative. In this way, both numbers become positive but the sign bit in Q_s is the correct sign of the quotient. The two positive magnitudes are then divided as in the signed-magnitude case. When the divide operation is terminated, the positive remainder is in A and the positive quotient in Q. The sign in Q_s is checked and if negative, the quotient in Q is complemented. The original sign of the dividend in A_s is checked and if negative, the remainder in A is complemented.

The algorithm requires that all three registers have a 2's complement capability. This is not a problem if the processor has a common ALU with all registers connected to it by a common bus sustem. Each complement micro-operation can be executed

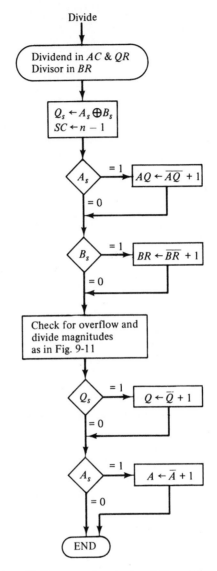

Fig. 10-6 Division with binary numbers in signed-2's complement representation.

in the common ALU. There is no need to provide individual complement circuits for each register.

The algorithms presented in this and the previous section are for signed-2's complement representation. They can be easily modified to provide algorithms for performing arithmetic operations with numbers in signed-1's complement representation. When numbers in signed-1's complement representation are added, it is necessary to check the end-carry out of the sign position. The result in the *AC* must be incremented if the end-carry is a 1.

10-4 FLOATING-POINT ARITHMETIC OPERATIONS

Many high-level programming languages have a facility for specifying floating-point numbers. The most common way is to specify them by a *real* declaration statement as opposed to fixed-point numbers which are specified by an *integer* declaration statement. Any computer that has a compiler for such high-level programming language must have a provision for handling floating-point arithmetic operations. The operations are quite often included in the internal hardware. If no hardware is available for the operations, the compiler must be designed with a package of floating-point software subroutines. Although the hardware method is more expsnsive, it is so much more efficient than the software method that floating-point hardware is included in most computers and is omitted only in very small ones.

Basic Considerations

Floating-point representation of data was introduced in Sec. 3-3. A floating-point number in computer registers consists of two parts: a mantissa *m* and an exponent *e*. The two parts represent a number obtained from multiplying *m* times a radix *r* raised to the value of *e*, thus:

$$m \times r^e$$

The mantissa may be a fraction or an integer. The location of the radix point and the value of the radix *r* are assumed and are not included in the registers. For example, assume a fraction representation and a radix 10. The decimal number 537.25 is represented in a register with $m = 53725$ and $e = 3$ and is interpreted to represent the floating-point number

$$.53725 \times 10^3$$

A floating-point number is normalized if the most significant digit of the mantissa is non-zero. In this way, the mantissa contains the maximum possible number of significant digits. A zero cannot be normalized because it does not have a non-zero digit. It is represented in floating-point by all 0's in the mantissa and exponent.

Floating-point representation increases the range of numbers that can be accomodated in a given register. Consider a computer with 48-bit words. Since one bit must be reserved for the sign, the range of fixed-point integer number will be $\pm(2^{47} - 1)$ which is approximately $\pm 10^{14}$. The 48 bits can be used to represent a floating-point number with 36 bits for the mantissa and 12 bits for the exponent. Assuming fraction representation for the mantissa and taking the two sign bits into consideration the range of numbers that can be accommodated is

$$\pm(1 - 2^{-35}) \times 2^{2047}$$

This number is derived from a fraction that contains 35 1's, an exponent of eleven bits (excluding its sign), and the fact that $2^{11} -1 = 2047$. The largest number that can be accommodated is approximately 10^{615} which is an astronomical number. The mantissa can accommodate 35 bits (excluding the sign) and if considered as an integer it can store a number as large as $(2^{35} - 1)$. This is approximately equal to 10^{10}, which is equivalent to a decimal number of ten digits.

Computers with shorter word lengths use two or more words to represent a floating-point number. An 8-bit microcomputer may use four words to represent one floating-point number. One word of 8 bits is reserved for the exponent and the 24 bits of the other three words are used for the mantissa.

Arithmetic operations with floating-point numbers are more complicated than with fixed-point numbers and their execution takes longer and requires more complex hardware. Adding or subtracting two numbers requires first an alignment of the radix point since the exponent parts must be made equal before adding or subtracting the mantissas. The alignment is done by shifting one mantissa while its exponent is adjusted until it is equal to the other exponent. Consider the sum of the following floating-point numbers.

$$.5372400 \times 10^2$$

$$+ .1580000 \times 10^{-1}$$

It is necessary that the two exponents be equal before the mantissas can be added. We can either shift the first number three positions to the left, or shift the second number three positions to the right. When the mantissas are stored in registers, shifting to the left causes a loss of most significant digits. Shifting to the right causes a loss of least significant digits. The second method is preferable because it only reduces the accuracy while the first method may cause an error. The usual alignment procedure is to shift the mantissa that has the smaller exponent to the right by a number of places equal to the difference between the exponents. After this is done, the mantissas can be added:

$$
\begin{array}{r}
.5372400 \times 10^2 \\
+ .0001580 \times 10^2 \\
\hline
.5373980 \times 10^2
\end{array}
$$

When two normalized mantissas are added, the sum may contain an overflow digit. An overflow can be corrected easily by shifting the sum once to the right and incrementing the exponent. When two numbers are subtracted, the result may contain most significant zeros as shown in the following example:

$$
\begin{array}{r}
.56780 \times 10^5 \\
- .56430 \times 10^5 \\
\hline
.00350 \times 10^5
\end{array}
$$

A floating-point number that has a 0 in the most significant position of the mantissa is said to have an *underflow*. To normalize a number that contains an underflow, it is necessary to shift the mantissa to the left and decrement the exponent until a nonzero digit appears in the first position. In the above example, it is necessary to shift left twice to obtain $.35000 \times 10^3$. In most computers, a normalization procedure is performed after each operation to ensure that all results are in a normalized form.

Floating-point multiplication and division do not require an alignment of the mantissas. The product can be formed by multiplying the two mantissas and adding the exponents. Division is accomplished by dividing the mantissas and subtracting the exponents.

The operations performed with the mantissas are the same as in fixed-point numbers so the two can share the same registers and circuits. The operations performed with the exponents are compare and increment (for aligning the mantissas), add and subtract (for multiplication and division), and decrement (to normalize the result). The exponent may be represented in any one of the three representations: signed-magnitude, signed-2's complement, or signed-1's complement.

A fourth representation employed in many computers is known as a *biased* exponent. In this representation, the sign bit is removed from being a separate entity. The bias is a positive number which is added to each exponent as the floating-point number is formed, so that internally all exponents are positive. The following example may clarify this type of representation. Consider an exponent that ranges from -50 to 49. Internally it is represented by two digits (without a sign) by adding to it a bias of 50. The exponent register contains the number $e + 50$ where e is the actual exponent. This way, the exponents are represented in registers as positive numbers in the range of 00 to 99. Positive exponents in registers have the range of numbers from 99 to 50. The subtraction of 50 gives the positive values from 49 to 0. Negative exponents are represented in registers in the range from 49 to 00. The subtraction of 50 gives the negative values in the range of -1 to -50.

The advantage of biased exponents is that they contain only positive numbers. It is then simpler to compare their relative magnitude without being concerned with their signs. As a consequence, an IC magnitude comparator (Fig. 9-1) can be used to compare their relative magnitude during the alignment of the mantissa. Another advantage is that the smallest possible biased exponent contains all zeros. The floating-point representation of zero is then a zero mantissa and the smallest possible exponent.

In the examples above, we used decimal numbers to demonstrate some of the concepts that must be understood when dealing with floating-point numbers. Obviously, the same concepts apply to binary numbers as well. The algorithms developed in this section are for binary numbers. Decimal computer arithmetic is discussed in the next section.

Register Configuration

The register configuration for floating-point operations is quite similar to the layout for fixed-point operations. As a general rule, the same registers and adder used for fixed-point arithmetic are used for processing the mantissas. The difference lies in the way the exponents are handled.

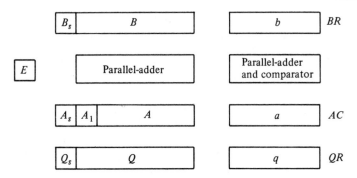

Fig. 10-7 Registers for floating-point arithmetic operations.

The register organization for floating-point operations is shown in Fig. 10-7. There are three registers BR, AC, and QR. Each register is subdivided into two parts. The mantissa part has the same upper case letter symbols as in fixed-point representation. The exponent part uses the corresponding lower case letter symbol.

It is assumed that each floating-point number has a mantissa in signed-magnitude representation and a biased exponent. Thus the AC has a mantissa whose sign is in A_s and a magnitude which is in A. The exponent is in the part of the register denoted by the lower case letter symbol a. The diagram shows explicitly the most significant bit of A, labeled by A_1. The bit in this position must be a 1 for the number to be normalized. Note that the symbol AC represents the entire register, that is, the concatenation of A_s, A, and a.

Similarly, register BR is subdivided into B_s, B, and b, and QR into Q_s, Q, and q. A parallel-adder adds the two mantissas and transfers the sum into A and the carry into E. A separate parallel-adder is used for the exponents. Since the exponents are biased, they do not have a distinct sign bit but are represented as a biased positive quantity. It is assumed that the floating-point numbers are so large that the chance of an exponent overflow is very remote and for this reason the exponent overflow will be neglected (see Prob. 10-25). The exponents are connected also to a magnitude comparator that provides three binary outputs to indicate their relative magnitude.

The number in the mantissa will be taken as a *fraction* so the binary point is assumed to reside to the left of the magnitude part. Integer representation for floating-point causes certain scaling problems during multiplication and division. To avoid these problems, we adopt a fraction representation (see Prob. 10-26).

The numbers in the registers are assumed to be initially normalized. After each arithmetic operation, the result will be normalized. Thus all floating-point operands coming from and going to the memory unit are always normalized.

Addition and Subtraction

During addition or subtraction, the two floating-point operands are in AC and BR. The sum or difference is formed in the AC. The algorithm can be divided into four consecutive parts.

1. Check for zeros.

2. Align the mantissas.

3. Add or subtract the mantissas.

4. Normalize the result.

A floating-point number that is zero cannot be normalized. If this number is used during the computation, the result may also be zero. Instead of checking for zeros during the normalization process we check for zeros at the beginning and terminate the process if necessary. The alignment of the mantissas must be carried out prior to their operation. After the mantissas are added or subtracted, the result may be un-normalized. The normalization procedure insures that the result is normalized prior to its transfer to memory.

The flow chart for adding or subtracting two floating-point binary numbers is shown in Fig. 10-8. If BR is equal to zero, the operation is terminated with the value in the AC being the result. If AC is equal to zero, we transfer the content of BR into AC and also complement its sign if the numbers are to be subtracted. If neither number is equal to zero, we proceed to align the mantissas.

The magnitude comparator attached to exponents a and b provides three outputs that indicate their relative magnitude. If the two exponents are equal, we go to perform the arithmetic operation. If the exponents are not equal, the mantissa having the smaller exponent is shifted to the right and its exponent incremented. This process is repeated until the two exponents are equal.

The addition and subtraction of the two mantissas is identical to the fixed-point addition and subtraction algorithm presented in Sec. 9-3. The magnitude part is added or subtracted depending on the operation and the signs of the two mantissas. If an overflow occurs when the magnitudes are added it is transferred into flip-flop E. If E is equal to 1, the bit is transferred into A_1 and all other bits of A are shifted right. The exponent must be incremented to maintain the correct number. No underflow may occur in this case because the original mantissa that was not shifted during the alignment was already in a normalized position.

If the magnitudes were subtracted, the result may be zero or may have an underflow. If the mantissa is zero, the entire floating-point number in the AC is made zero. Otherwise, the mantissa must have at least one bit that is equal to 1. The mantissa has an underflow if the most significant bit in position A_1 is 0. In that case, the mantissa is shifted left and the exponent decremented. The bit in A_1 is checked again and the process is repeated until it is equal to 1. When $A_1 = 1$, the mantissa is normalized and the operation is completed.

Multiplication

The multiplication of two floating-point numbers requires that we multiply the mantissas and add the exponents. No comparison of exponents or alignment of mantissas is necessary. The multiplication of the mantissas is performed in the same way as in fixed-point to provide a double-precision product. The double-precision

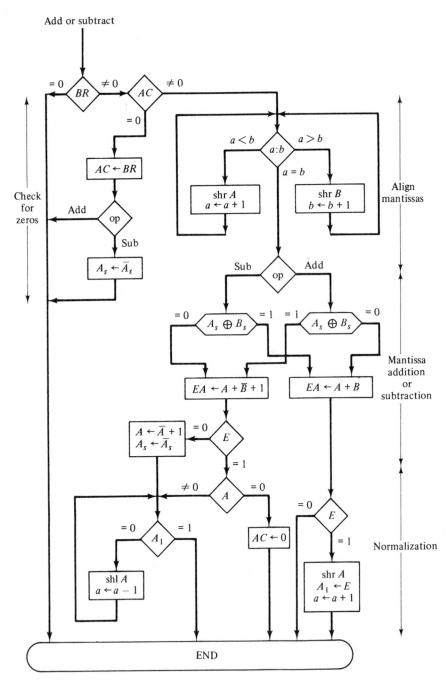

Fig. 10-8 Addition and subtraction of floating-point numbers.

answer is used in fixed-point numbers to increase the accuracy of the product. In floating-point, the range of a single-precision mantissa combined with the exponent is usually accurate enough so that only single precision numbers are maintained. Thus, the half most significant bits of the mantissa product and the exponent will be taken together to form a single-precision floating-point product.

The multiplication algorithm can be subdivided into four parts.

1. Check for zeros.
2. Add the exponents.
3. Multiply the mantissas.
4. Normalize the product.

Steps 2 and 3 can be done simultaneously if separate adders are available for the mantissas and exponents.

The flow chart for floating-point multiplication is shown in Fig. 10-9. The two operands are checked to determine if they contain a zero. If either operand is equal to zero, the product in the AC is set to zero and the operation is terminated. If none of the operands are equal to zero, the process continues with the exponent addition.

The exponent of the multiplier is in q and the adder is between exponents a and b. It is necessary to transfer the exponents from q to a, add the two exponents and transfer the sum into a. Since both exponents are biased by the addition of a constant, the exponent sum will have double this bias. The correct biased exponent for the product is obtained by subtracting the bias number from the sum.

The multiplication of the mantissas is done as in the fixed-point case with the product residing in A and Q. Overflow cannot occur during multiplication so there is no need to check for it.

The product may have an underflow so the most significant bit in A is checked. If it is a 1, the product is already normalized. If it is a 0, the mantissa in AQ is shifted left and the exponent decremented. Note that only one normalization shift is necessary. The multiplier and multiplicand were originally normalized and contained fractions. The smallest normalized operand is 0.1 so the smallest possible product is 0.01. Therefore, only one leading zero may occur.

Although the low-order half of the mantissa is in Q, we do not use it for the floating-point product. Only the value in the AC is taken as the product.

Division

Floating-point division requires that the exponents be subtracted and the mantissas divided. The mantissa division is done as in fixed-point except that the dividend has a single precision mantissa which is placed in the AC. Remember that the mantissa dividend is a fraction and not an integer. For integer representation, a single-precision dividend must be placed in register Q and register A must be cleared. The

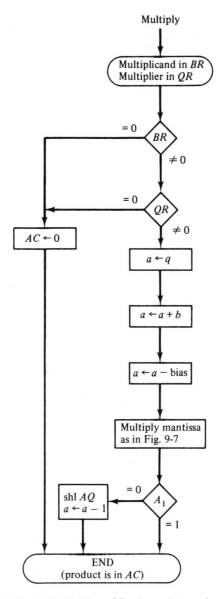

Fig. 10-9 Multiplication of floating-point numbers.

zeros in A are to the left of the binary point and have no significance. In fraction representation, a single precision dividend is placed in register A and register Q is cleared. The zeros in Q are to the right of the binary point and have no significance.

The check for divide-overflow is the same as in fixed-point representation. However, with floating-point numbers the divide-overflow imposes no problems.

If the dividend is greater than or equal to the divisor, the dividend fraction is shifted to the right and its exponent incremented by 1. For normalized operands this is a sufficient operation to insure that no mantissa divide-overflow will occur. The above operation is referred to as a *dividend alignment*.

The division of two normalized floating-point numbers will always result in a normalized quotient provided a dividend alignment is carried out before the division (see Prob. 10-23). Therefore, unlike the other operations, the quotient obtained after the division does not require a normalization.

The division algorithm can be subdivided into five parts.

1. Check for zeros.

2. Initialize registers and evaluate the sign.

3. Align the dividend.

4. Subtract the exponents.

5. Divide the mantissas.

The flow chart for floating-point division is shown in Fig. 10-10. The two operands are checked for zero. If the divisor is zero, it indicates an attempt to divide by zero, which is an illegal operation. The operation is terminated with an error message. An alternative procedure would be to set the quotient in QR to the most positive number possible (if the dividend is positive) or to the most negative possible (if the dividend is negative). If the dividend in AC is zero, the quotient in QR is made zero and the operation terminates.

If the operands are not zero, we proceed to determine the sign of the quotient and store it in Q_s. The sign of the dividend in A_s is left unchanged to be the sign of the remainder. The Q register is cleared and the sequence counter SC is set to a number equal to the number of bits in the quotient.

The dividend alignment is similar to the divide-overflow check in the fixed-point operation. The proper alignment requires that the fraction dividend be smaller than the divisor. The two fractions are compared by a subtraction test. The carry in E determines their relative magnitude. The dividend fraction is restored to its original value by adding the divisor. If $A \geq B$, it is necessary to shift A once to the right and increment the dividend exponent. Since both operands are normalized, this alignment insures that $A < B$.

Next, the divisor exponent is subtracted from the dividend exponent. Since both exponents were originally biased, the subtraction operation gives the difference without the bias. The bias is then added and the result transferred into q because the quotient is formed in QR.

The magnitudes of the mantissas are divided as in the fixed-point case. After the operation, the mantissa quotient resides in Q and the remainder in A. The floating-point quotient is already normalized and resides in QR. The exponent of the remainder should be the same as the exponent of the dividend. The binary point for the remainder mantissa lies $(n - 1)$ positions to the left of A_1. The remainder can be converted

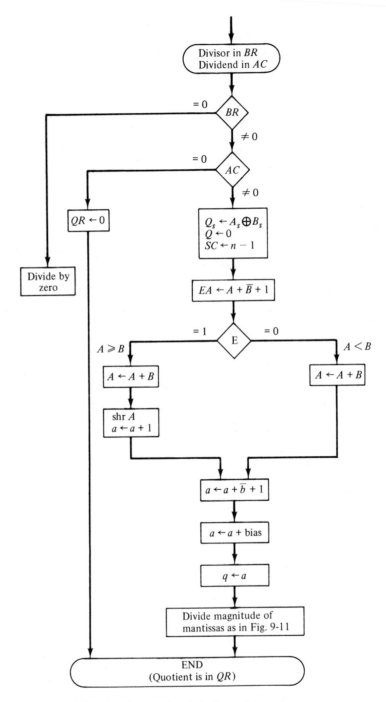

Fig. 10-10 Division of floating-point numbers.

to a normalized fraction by subtracting $n - 1$ from the dividend exponent and by shift and decrement until the bit in A_1 is equal to 1. This is not shown in the flow chart and is left as an exercise (see Prob. 10-24).

10-5 DECIMAL ARITHMETIC UNIT

The user of a computer prepares his data with decimal numbers and receives his results in decimal form. A CPU with an arithmetic logic unit can perform arithmetic micro-operations with binary data. To perform arithmetic operations with decimal data, it is necessary to convert the input decimal numbers to binary, to perform all calculations with binary numbers, and then to convert the results into decimal. This may be an efficient method in applications requiring a large number of calculations and a relatively smaller amount of input and output data. When the application calls for a large amount of input-output and a relatively smaller number of arithmetic calculations, it becomes convenient to do the internal arithmetic directly with the decimal numbers. Computers capable of performing decimal arithmetic must store the decimal data in binary-coded form. The decimal numbers are then applied to a decimal arithmetic unit capable of executing decimal arithmetic micro-operations.

Electronic calculators invariably use an internal decimal arithmetic unit since inputs and outputs are frequent. There does not seem to be a reason for converting the keyboard input numbers to binary and again converting the displayed results to decimal, since this process requires special circuits and also takes a longer time to execute. Many computers have hardware for arithmetic calculations with both binary and decimal data. The user can specify by programmed instructions whether he wants the computer to perform calculations with binary or decimal data.

A decimal arithmetic unit is a digital function that performs decimal micro-operations. It can add or subtract decimal numbers, usually by forming the 9's or 10's complement of the subtrahend. The unit accepts coded decimal numbers and generates results in the same adopted binary code. A single-stage decimal arithmetic unit consists of nine binary input variables and five binary output variables, since a minimum of four bits are required to represent each coded decimal digit. Each stage must have four inputs for the augend digit, four inputs for the addend digit and an input-carry. The outputs include four terminals for the sum digit and one for the output-carry. Of course, there is a wide variety of possible circuit configurations dependent upon the code used to represent the decimal digits.

BCD Adder

Consider the arithmetic addition of two decimal digits in BCD, together with a possible carry from a previous stage. Since each input digit does not exceed 9, the output sum cannot be greater than $9 + 9 + 1 = 19$, the 1 in the sum being an input-carry. Suppose that we apply two BCD digits to a 4-bit binary adder. The adder will form the sum in *binary* and produce a result which may range from 0 to 19. These binary numbers are listed in Table 10-3 and are labeled by symbols K, Z_8, Z_4, Z_2, and Z_1. K is the carry and the subscripts under the letter Z represent the weights 8, 4, 2, and 1 that can be assigned to the four bits in the BCD code. The first column in the table lists the binary sums as they appear in the outputs of a 4-bit *binary* adder. The output sum of two *decimal* numbers must be represented in BCD and should appear in the form listed in the second column of the table. The problem is to find a simple rule by which the binary number in the first column can be converted to the correct BCD digit representation of the number in the second column.

TABLE 10-3   Derivation of BCD Adder

Binary Sum $K\ Z_8\ Z_4\ Z_2\ Z_1$	BCD Sum $C\ S_8\ S_4\ S_2\ S_1$	Decimal
0 0 0 0 0	0 0 0 0 0	0
0 0 0 0 1	0 0 0 0 1	1
0 0 0 1 0	0 0 0 1 0	2
0 0 0 1 1	0 0 0 1 1	3
0 0 1 0 0	0 0 1 0 0	4
0 0 1 0 1	0 0 1 0 1	5
0 0 1 1 0	0 0 1 1 0	6
0 0 1 1 1	0 0 1 1 1	7
0 1 0 0 0	0 1 0 0 0	8
0 1 0 0 1	0 1 0 0 1	9
0 1 0 1 0	1 0 0 0 0	10
0 1 0 1 1	1 0 0 0 1	11
0 1 1 0 0	1 0 0 1 0	12
0 1 1 0 1	1 0 0 1 1	13
0 1 1 1 0	1 0 1 0 0	14
0 1 1 1 1	1 0 1 0 1	15
1 0 0 0 0	1 0 1 1 0	16
1 0 0 0 1	1 0 1 1 1	17
1 0 0 1 0	1 1 0 0 0	18
1 0 0 1 1	1 1 0 0 1	19

In examining the contents of the table, it is apparent that when the binary sum is equal or less than 1001, the corresponding BCD number is identical and therefore no conversion is needed. When the binary sum is greater than 1001, we obtain a nonvalid BCD representation. The addition of binary 6 (0110) to the binary sum converts it to the correct BCD representation and also produces an output-carry as required.

One method of adding decimal numbers in BCD would be to employ one 4-bit binary adder and perform the arithmetic operation one digit at a time. The low-order pair of BCD digits are first added to produce a binary sum. If the result is equal or greater than 1010, it is corrected by adding 0110 to the binary sum. This second operation will automatically produce an output-carry for the next pair of significant digits. The next higher-order pair of digits, together with the input-carry, are then added to produce their binary sum. If this result is equal or greater than 1010, it is corrected by adding 0110. The prodecure is repeated again until all decimal digits are added.

The logic circuit that detects the necessary correction can be derived from the table entries. It is obvious that a correction is needed when the binary sum has an output carry $K = 1$. The other six combinations from 1010 to 1111 that need a correction have a 1 in position Z_8. To distinguish them from binary 1000 and 1001 which also have a 1 in position Z_8, we specify further that either Z_4 or Z_2 must have a 1. The condition for a correction and an output-carry can be expressed by the Boolean function

$$C = K + Z_8 Z_4 + Z_8 Z_2$$

When $C = 1$, it is necessary to add 0110 to the binary sum and provide an output-carry for the next stage.

A BCD adder is a circuit that adds two BCD digits in parallel and produces a sum digit also in BCD. A BCD adder must include the correction logic in its internal construction. To add 0110 to the binary sum, we use a second 4-bit binary adder as shown in Fig. 10-11. The two decimal digits, together with the input-carry, are

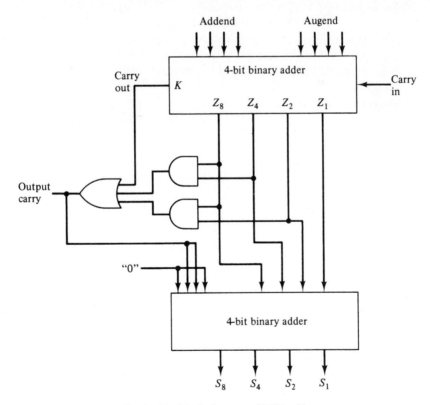

Fig. 10-11 Block diagram of BCD adder.

first added in the top 4-bit binary adder to produce the binary sum. When the output-carry is equal to 0, nothing is added to the binary sum. When it is equal to 1, binary 0110 is added to the binary sum through the bottom 4-bit binary adder. The output-carry generated from the bottom binary adder may be ignored, since it supplies information already available in the output-carry terminal.

A decimal parallel-adder that adds n decimal digits needs n BCD adder stages with the output-carry from one stage connected to the input-carry of the next higher-order stage. To achieve shorter propagation delays, IC BCD adders include the necessary circuits for carry look-ahead. Furthermore, the adder circuit for the correction does not need all four full-adders and this circuit can be optimized within the IC package.

BCD Subtraction

A straight subtraction of two decimal numbers will require a subtractor circuit which will be somewhat different from a BCD adder. It is more economical to perform the subtraction by taking the 9's or 10's complement of the subtrahend and adding it to the minuend. Since the BCD is not a self-complementing code, the 9's complement cannot be obtained by complementing each bit in the code. It must be formed by a circuit that subtracts each BCD digit from 9.

The 9's complement of a decimal digit represented in BCD may be obtained by complementing the bits in the coded representation of the digit provided a correction is included. There are two possible correction methods. In the first method, binary 1010 (decimal 10) is added to each complemented digit and the carry discarded after each addition. In the second method, binary 0110 (decimal 6) is added before the digit is complemented. As a numerical illustration, the 9's complement of BCD 0111 (decimal 7) is computed by first complementing each bit to obtain 1000. Adding binary 1010 and discarding the carry, we obtain 0010 (decimal 2). By the second method, we add 0110 to 0111 to obtain 1101. Complementing each bit, we obtain the required result of 0010. Complementing each bit of a 4-bit binary number N is identical to the subtraction of the number from 1111 (decimal 15). Adding the binary equivalent of decimal 10 gives $15 - N + 10 = 9 - N + 16$. But 16 signifies the carry that is discarded so the result is $9 - N$ as required. Adding the binary equivalent of decimal 6 and then complementing gives $15 - (N + 6) = 9 - N$ as required.

The 9's complement of a BCD digit can be obtained also through a combinational circuit. When this circuit is attached to a BCD adder, the result is a BCD adder/subtractor. Let the subtrahend (or addend) digit be denoted by the four binary variables B_8, B_4, B_2, and B_1. Let M be a mode bit that controls the add/subtract operation. When $M = 0$, the two digits are added; when $M = 1$, the digits are subtracted. Let the binary variables x_8, x_4, x_2, and x_1 be the outputs of the 9's complementer circuit. By an examination of the truth table for the circuit, it may be observed (see Prob. 10-30) that B_1 should always be complemented; B_2 is always the same in the 9's complement as in the original digit; x_4 is 1 when the exclusive-OR of B_2 and B_4 is 1; and x_8 is 1 when $B_8 B_4 B_2 = 000$. The Boolean functions for the 9's complementer circuit are:

$$x_1 = B_1 M' + B_1' M$$
$$x_2 = B_2$$
$$x_3 = B_4 M' + (B_4' B_2 + B_4 B_2') M$$
$$x_4 = B_8 M' + B_8' B_4' B_2' M$$

From these equations we see that $x = B$ when $M = 0$. When $M = 1$, the x outputs produce the 9's complement of B.

One stage of a decimal arithmetic unit that can add or subtract two BCD digits is shown in Fig. 10-12. It consists of a BCD adder and a 9's complementer. The mode M controls the operation of the unit. With $M = 0$, the S outputs form the sum of A and B. With $M = 1$, the S outputs form the sum of A plus the 9's complement of B. For numbers with n decimal digits we need n such stages. The output-carry C_{i+1} from one stage must be connected to the input-carry C_i of the next-higher-order stage. The best way to subtract the two decimal numbers is to let $M = 1$ and apply a 1 to the input-carry C_1 of the first stage. The outputs will form the sum of A plus the 10's complement of B, which is equivalent to a subtraction operation if the carry out of the last stage is discarded.

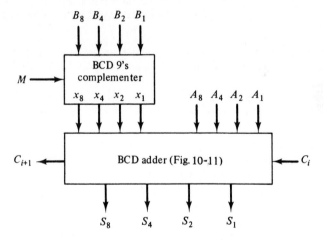

Fig. 10-12 One stage of a decimal arithmetic unit.

10-6 DECIMAL ARITHMETIC OPERATIONS

The algorithms for arithmetic operations with decimal data are similar to the algorithms for the corresponding operations with binary data. In fact, except for a slight modification in the multiplication and division algorithms, the same flow charts can be used for both types of data provided we interpret the micro-operation symbols properly. Decimal numbers in BCD are stored in computer registers in groups of four bits. Each 4-bit group represents a decimal digit and must be taken as a unit when performing decimal micro-operations.

For convenience, we will use the same symbols for binary and decimal arithmetic micro-operations but give them a different interpretation. As shown in Table 10-4, a bar over the register letter symbol denotes the 9's complement of the decimal number stored in the register. Adding 1 to the 9's complement produces the 10's complement. Thus, for decimal numbers, the symbol $A \leftarrow A + \bar{B} + 1$ denotes a transfer of the decimal sum formed by adding the original content A to the 10's complement of B. The use of identical symbols for the 9's complement and the 1's complement may be confusing if both types of data are employed in the same system. If this is the case, it may be better to adopt a different symbol for the 9's complement. If only one type of data is being considered, then the symbol would apply to the type of data used.

TABLE 10-4   Decimal Arithmetic Micro-operation Symbols

Symbolic Designation	Description
$A \leftarrow A + B$	Add decimal numbers and transfer sum into A
$\bar{B}$	9's complement of B
$A \leftarrow A + \bar{B} + 1$	Content of A plus 10's complement of B into A
$Q_L \leftarrow Q_L + 1$	Increment BCD number in Q_L
dshr A	Decimal shift-right register A
dshl A	Decimal shift-left register A

Incrementing or decrementing a register is the same for binary and decimal except for the number of states that the register is allowed to have. A binary counter goes through 16 states, from 0000 to 1111, when incremented. A decimal counter goes through ten states from 0000 to 1001 and back to 0000, since 9 is the last count. Similarly, a binary counter sequences from 1111 to 0000 when decremented. A decimal counter goes from 1001 to 0000.

A decimal shift right or left is preceded by the letter d to indicate a shift over the four bits that hold the decimal digits. As a numerical illustration consider a register A holding decimal 7860 in BCD. The bit pattern of the 12 flip-flops is:

$$0111 \quad 1000 \quad 0110 \quad 0000$$

The micro-operation *dshr* A shifts the decimal number one digit to the right to give 0786. This shift is over the four bits and changes the content of the register into

$$0000 \quad 0111 \quad 1000 \quad 0110$$

Addition and Subtraction

The algorithm for addition and subtraction of binary signed-magnitude numbers applies also to decimal signed-magnitude numbers provided we interpret the micro-operation symbols in the proper manner. Similarly, the algorithm for binary signed-2's complement numbers applies to decimal signed-10's complement numbers. The binary data must employ a binary adder and a complementer. The decimal data must employ a decimal arithmetic unit capable of adding two BCD numbers and forming the 9's complement of the subtrahend as shown in Fig. 10-12.

Decimal data can be added in three different ways as shown in Fig. 10-13. The parallel method uses a decimal arithmetic unit composed of as many BCD adders as there are digits in the number. The sum is formed in parallel and requires only one micro-operation. In the digit-serial bit-parallel method, the digits are applied to a single BCD adder serially while the bits of each coded digit are transferred in parallel. The sum is formed by shifting the decimal numbers through the BCD adder one at a time. For k decimal digits, this configuration requires k micro-operations, one for each decimal shift. In the all serial adder, the bits are shifted one at a time through a full-adder. The binary sum formed after four shifts must be corrected into a valid BCD digit. This correction, discussed in Sec. 10-5, consists of checking the binary sum. If it is greater than or equal to 1010, the binary sum is corrected by adding to it 0110 and generating a carry for the next pair of digits.

The parallel method is fast but requires a large number of adders. The digit-serial bit-parallel method requires only one BCD adder which is shared by all the digits. It is slower than the parallel method because of the time required to shift the digits. The all serial method requires a minimum amount of equipment but is very slow.

Multiplication

The multiplication of fixed-point decimal numbers is similar to binary except for the way the partial products are formed. A decimal multiplier has digits that range in value from 0 to 9 whereas a binary multiplier has only 0 and 1 digits. In the binary case, the multiplicand is added to the partial product if the multiplier bit is 1. In the decimal case, the multiplicand must be multiplied by the digit multiplier and the result added to the partial product. This operation can be accomplished by adding the multiplicand to the partial product a number of times equal to the value of the multiplier digit.

The registers organization for the decimal multiplication is shown in Fig. 10-14. We are assuming here four-digit numbers with each digit occupying four bits for a total of 16 bits for each number. There are three registers, A, B, and Q, each having a corresponding sign flip-flop A_s, B_s, and Q_s. Registers A and B have four more bits designated by A_e and B_e that provide an extension of one more digit to the registers. The BCD arithmetic unit adds the five digits in parallel and places the sum in the 5-digit A register. The end-carry goes to flip-flop E. The purpose of digit A_e is to accommodate an overflow while adding the multiplicand to the partial product during multiplication. The purpose of digit B_e is to form the 9's complement of the divisor when subtracted from the partial remainder during the division operation. The least significant digit in register Q is denoted by Q_L. This digit can be incremented or decremented.

A decimal operand coming from memory consists of 17 bits. One bit (the sign)

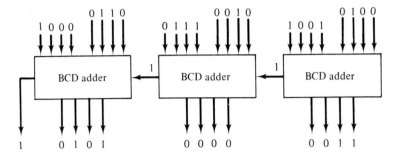

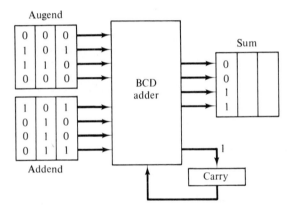

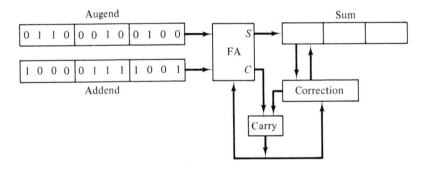

(a) Parallel decimal addition: 624 + 879 = 1503

(b) Digit-serial, bit-parallel decimal addition

(c) All serial decimal addition

Fig. 10-13 Three ways of adding decimal numbers.

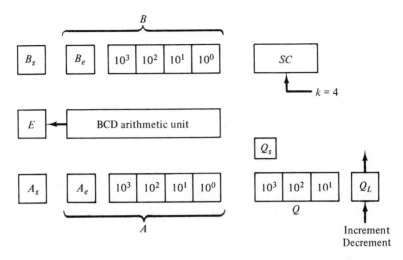

Fig. 10-14 Registers for decimal arithmetic multiplication and division.

is transferred to B_s and the magnitude of the operand is placed in the lower 16 bits of B. Both B_e and A_e are cleared initially. The result of the operation is also 17 bits long and does not use the A_e part of the A register.

The decimal multiplication algorithm is shown in Fig. 10-15. Initially, the entire A register and B_e are cleared and the sequence counter SC is set to a number k equal to the number of digits in the multiplier. The low-order digit of the multiplier in Q_L is checked. If it is not equal to 0, the multiplicand in B is added to the partial product in A once and Q_L is decremented. Q_L is checked again and the process is repeated until it is equal to 0. In this way, the multiplicand in B is added to the partial product a number of times equal to the multiplier digit. Any temporary overflow digit will reside in A_e and can range in value from 0 to 9.

Next, the partial product and the multiplier are shifted once to the right. This places zero in A_e and transfers the next multiplier quotient into Q_L. The process is then repeated k times to form a double-length product in AQ.

Division

Decimal division is similar to binary division except of course that the quotient digits may have any of the ten values from 0 to 9. In the restoring division method, the divisor is subtracted from the dividend or partial remainder as many times as necessary until a negative remainder results. The correct remainder is then restored by adding the divisor. The digit in the quotient reflects the number of subtractions up to but excluding the one that caused the negative difference.

The decimal division algorithm is shown in Fig. 10-16. It is similar to the algorithm with binary data except for the way the quotient bits are formed. The dividend

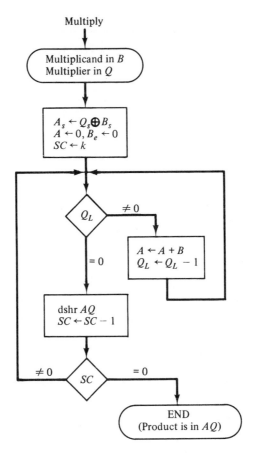

Multiply

Multiplicand in B
Multiplier in Q

$A_s \leftarrow Q_s \oplus B_s$
$A \leftarrow 0, B_e \leftarrow 0$
$SC \leftarrow k$

Q_L $\neq 0$

$A \leftarrow A + B$
$Q_L \leftarrow Q_L - 1$

$= 0$

dshr AQ
$SC \leftarrow SC - 1$

$\neq 0$ SC $= 0$

END
(Product is in AQ)

Fig. 10-15 Flow chart for decimal multiplication.

(or partial remainder) is shifted to the left with its most significant digit placed in A_e. The divisor is then subtracted by adding its 10's complement value. Since B_e is initially cleared, its complement value is 9 as required. The carry in E determines the relative magnitude of A and B. If $E = 0$, it signifies that $A < B$. In this case, the divisor is added to restore the partial remainder and Q_L stays at 0 (inserted there during the shift). If $E = 1$, it signifies that $A \geq B$. The quotient digit in Q_L is incremented once and the divisor subtracted again. This process is repeated until the subtraction results in a negative difference which is recongnized by E being 0. When this occurs, the quotient digit is not incremented but the divisor is added to restore the positive remainder. In this way, the quotient digit is made equal to the number of times that the partial remainder "goes" into the divisor.

The partial remainder and the quotient bits are shifted once to the left and the process is repeated k times to form k quotient digits. The remainder is then found in register A and the quotient is in register Q. The value of E is neglected.

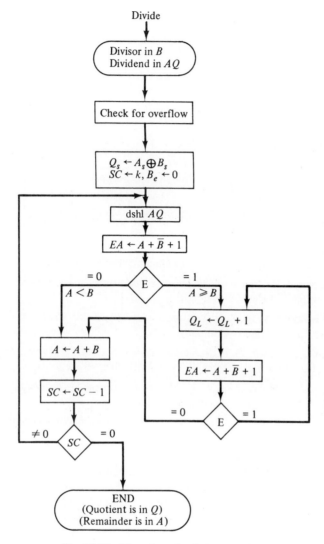

Fig. 10-16 Flow chart for decimal division.

Floating-Point Operations

Decimal floating-point arithmetic operations follow the same procedures as binary operations. The algorithms in Sec. 10-4 can be adopted for decimal data provided the micro-operation symbols are interpreted correctly. The multiplication and division of the mantissas must be done by the methods decribed above.

REFERENCES

1. GSCHWIND, H. W., AND E. D. McCLUSKEY, *Design of Digital Computers*. New York: Springer-Verlag, 1975.

2. FLORES, I., *The Logic of Computer Arithmetic*. Englewood Cliffs, N.J.: Prentice-Hall, Inc., 1962.

3. RICHARDS, R. K., *Arithmetic Operations in Digital Computers*. Princeton, N.J.: D. Van Nostrand, 1955.

4. HWANG, K., *Computer Arithmetic: Principles, Architecture and Design*. New York: John Wiley & Sons, Inc., 1979.

5. CHU, Y., *Digital Computer Design Fundamentals*. New York: McGraw-Hill Book Company, 1962.

6. CHU, Y., *Computer Organization and Microprogramming*. Englewood Cliffs, N.J.: Prentice-Hall, Inc., 1972.

7. COONEN, J. T., "An Implementation Guide to a Proposed Standard for Floating-Point Arithmetic," *Computer*, Vol. 13 (January 1980), pp. 68–79.

8. HAYES, J. P., *Computer Architecture and Organization*. New York: McGraw-Hill Book Company, 1978.

9. HAMACHER, V. C., Z. G. VRANESIC, AND S. G. ZAKY, *Computer Organization*. New York: McGraw-Hill Book Company, 1978.

10. HILL, F. J., AND G. R. PETERSON, *Digital Systems: Hardware Organization and Design*, 2nd ed. New York: John Wiley & Sons, Inc., 1978.

11. KULISCH, U. W., AND W. L. MIRANKER, *Computer Arithmetic in Theory and Practice*. New York: Academic Press, Inc., 1980.

12. SCHMID, H., *Decimal Arithmetic*. New York: John Wiley & Sons, Inc., 1979.

PROBLEMS

10-1. Perform the arithmetic operations below with binary numbers and with negative numbers in signed-2's complement representation. Use seven bits to accomodate each number together with its sign. In each case, determine if there is an overflow by checking the carries into and out of the sign bit position.
   (a) $(+35) + (+40)$
   (b) $(-35) + (-40)$
   (c) $(-35) - (+40)$

10-2. Consider the binary numbers when they are in signed-2's complement representation. Each number has n bits: one for the sign and $k = n - 1$ for the magnitude. A negative number $-X$ is represented as $2^k + (2^k - X)$, where the first 2^k designates the sign bit and $(2^k - X)$ is the 2's complement of X. A positive number is represented as $0 + X$, where the 0 designates the sign bit, and X, the k-bit magnitude. Using these generalized symbols, prove that the sum $(\pm X) + (\pm Y)$ can be formed by adding the numbers including their sign bits and discarding the carry out of the sign-bit position. In other words, prove the algorithm for adding two binary numbers in signed-2's complement representation.

10-3. Formulate a hardware procedure for detecting an overflow by comparing the sign of the sum with the signs of the augend and addend. The numbers are in signed-2's complement representation.

10-4. (a) Perform the operation $(-9) + (-6) = -15$ with binary numbers in signed-1's complement representation using only five bits to represent each number (including the sign). Show that the overflow detection procedure of checking the inequality of the last two carries fails in this case.
(b) Suggest a modified procedure for detecting an overflow when signed-1's complement numbers are used.
(c) Is the procedure suggested in Prob. 10-3 valid for signed-1's complement numbers?

10-5. Derive an algorithm in flow chart form for adding and subtracting two fixed-point binary numbers when negative numbers are in signed-1's complement representation.

10-6. Show the diagram of a 3 by 3 array multiplier using nine AND gates, three full-adders and three half-adders.

10-7. Obtain the diagram of a 4 by 3 array multiplier using 12 AND gates and two 4-bit binary parallel adders.

10-8. List a few typical entries of the truth table for a 64 by 5 ROM that implements a 3 by 3 array multiplier. The least significant bit of the product is formed by an AND gate without using the ROM.

10-9. An array multiplier can be used to multiply two binary numbers in signed-2's complement representation if the sign bit is determined separately and the other bits are multiplied through an array multiplier. However, the product out of the array multiplier must be corrected. The correction algorithm depends on whether X (multiplicated) or Y (multiplier) or both are negative: If X is negative, add the 2's complement of Y to the most significant half of the product. If Y is negative, add the 2's complement of X to the most significant half of the product. If both X and Y are negative, add X plus Y to the most significant half of the product and discard the carry.
(a) Show that this procedure is valid by performing the multiplication of binary (± 101) by (± 110) four times, each time with a different set of signs and with negative numbers being in their 2's complement form.
(b) Prove that the stated corrections will produce the correct product for any two numbers of n bits each.

10-10. A momentary overflow may occur while forming a partial product during multiplication with signed-2's complement numbers. Show that the arithmetic shift right in Fig. 10-4 can be implemented as follows:
(a) If $V = 0$, shift AC & Q without changing A_s.
(b) If $V = 1$, shift AC & Q, complement A_s and clear V.

10-11. Derive a flow chart algorithm for multiplying two binary numbers in signed-2's complement representation. Both multiplier and multiplicand are changed to positive numbers at the beginning. The positive product is 2's complemented if it is to be negative.

10-12. Show the step-by-step multiplication process as given in the flow chart of Fig. 10-4 when the following numbers are multiplied. Assume 5-bit registers that hold both sign and magnitude. The multiplicand in each case is $+15$.

(a) $(+15) \times (+13)$

(b) $(+15) \times (-13)$

10-13. The following operation is encountered in the flow chart of Fig. 10-6:

$$AQ \leftarrow \overline{AQ} + 1$$

where AQ is a combined register made up of registers A and Q. Assume that only one register at a time can be 1's complemented or incremented. Specify the sequence of micro-operations in flow chart form for implementing the above operation.

10-14. Repeat Prob. 10-12 using Booth's algorithm. Give your answers in tabular form as in Table 10-2.

10-15. Show the step-by-step division process as given in the flow chart of Fig. 10-6 when $(-160)/(+12)$ is computed. Assume 5-bit registers that hold both sign and magnitude.

10-16. (a) Prove that if 2^x is equal to 10^y then $y = 0.3x$.

(b) Using this relation, show that a 36-bit register can accomodate an integer signed binary number equivalent to 11 decimal digits.

(c) What would be the largest positive number that can be accomodated if the 36-bit register holds a floating-point number with eight exponent bits and integer representation for the mantissa?

10-17. A binary floating-point number has seven bits for a biased exponent. The constant used for the bias is 64.

(a) List the biased representation of all exponents from -64 to $+63$.

(b) Show that a 7-bit magnitude comparator can be used to compare the relative magnitude of the two exponents.

(c) Show that after the addition of two biased exponents it is necessary to subtract 64 in order to have a biased exponents sum. How would you subtract 64 by adding its 2's complement value?

(d) Show that after the subtraction of two biased exponents it is necessary to add 64 in order to have a biased exponent difference.

10-18. Derive an algorithm in flow chart form for the comparison of two signed binary numbers when negative numbers are in signed-2's complement representation:

(a) By means of a subtraction operation with the signed-2's complement numbers.

(b) By scanning and comparing pairs of bits from left to right.

10-19. Repeat Prob. 10-18 for signed-magnitude binary numbers.

10-20. Let n be the number of bits of the mantissa in a binary floating-point number. When the mantissas are aligned during the addition or subtraction, the exponent difference may be greater than $n - 1$. If this occurs, the mantissa with the smaller exponent is shifted entirely out of the register. Modify the mantissa alignment in Fig. 10-8 by including a sequence counter SC that counts the number of shifts. If the number of shifts is greater than $n - 1$, the larger number is then used to determine the result.

10-21. The procedure for aligning mantissas during addition or subtraction of floating-point numbers can be stated as follows:

Subtract the smaller exponent from the larger and shift right the mantissa having the smaller exponent a number of places equal to the difference between the exponents. The exponent of the sum (or difference) is equal to the larger exponents.

Without using a magnitude comparator, assuming biased exponents, and taking into account that only the AC can be shifted, derive an algorithm in flow-chart form for aligning the mantissas and placing the larger exponent in the AC.

10-22. Show that there can be no mantissa overflow after a multiplication operation.

10-23. Show that the division of two normalized floating-point numbers with fractional mantissas will always result in a normalized quotient provided a dividend alignment is carried out prior to the division operation.

10-24. Extend the flow chart of Fig. 10-10 to provide a normalized floating-point remainder in the AC. The mantissa should be a fraction.

10-25. The algorithms for the floating-point arithmetic operations in Sec. 10-4 neglect the possibility of exponent overflow or underflow.
(a) Go over the three flow charts and find where an exponent overflow may occur.
(b) Repeat (a) for exponent underflow. An exponent underflow occurs if the exponent is more negative than the smallest number that can be accommodated in the register.
(c) Show how an exponent overflow or underflow can be detected by the hardware.

10-26. If we assume integer representation for the mantissa of floating-point numbers, we encounter certain scaling problems during mulitplication and division. Let the number of bits in the mangitude part of the mantissa be $(n - 1)$. For integer representation:
(a) Show that if a single-precision product is used, then $(n - 1)$ must be added to the exponent product in the AC.
(b) Show that if a single precision mantissa dividend is used then $(n - 1)$ must be subtracted from the exponent dividend when Q is cleared.

10-27. Show the hardware to be used for the addition and subtraction of two decimal numbers in signed-magnitude representation. Indicate how an overflow is detected.

10-28. Show that $673 - 356$ can be computed by adding 673 to the 10's complement of 356 and discarding the end carry. Draw the block diagram of a three-stage decimal arithmetic unit and show how this operation is implemented. List all input bits and output bits of the unit.

10-29. Show that the lower 4-bit binary adder in Fig. 10-11 can be replaced by one full-adder and two half-adders.

10-30. Using combinational circuit design techniques (Sec. 1-4), derive the Boolean functions for the BCD 9's complementer of Fig. 10-12. Draw the logic diagram.

10-31. It is necessary to design an adder for two decimal digits represented in the excess-3 code (Table 3-6). Show that the correction after adding two digits with a 4-bit binary adder is as follows:
(a) The output-carry is equal to the uncorrected carry.
(b) If output-carry = 1, add 0011.
(c) If output-carry = 0, add 1101 and ignore the carry from this addition. Show that the excess-3 adder can be constructed with seven full-adders and two inverters.

10-32. Derive the circuit for a 9's complementer when decimal digits are represented in the excess-3 code (Table 3-6). A mode control input determines whether the digit is complemented or not. What is the advantage of using this code over BCD?

10-33. Show the hardware to be used for the addition and subtraction of two decimal numbers with negative numbers in signed-10's complement representation. Indicate how an overflow is detected. Derive the flow chart algorithm and try a few numbers to convince yourself that the algorithm produces correct results.

10-34. Show the content of registers A, B, Q, and SC during the decimal multiplication (Fig. 10-15) of (a) 470 $\times$ 152 and (b) 999 $\times$ 199. Assume 3-digit registers and take the second number as the multiplier.

10-35. Show the content of registers A, E, Q, and SC during the decimal division (Fig. 10-16) of 1680/32. Assume 2-digit registers.

10-36. Show that sub-register A_e in Fig. 10-14 is zero at the termination of (a) the decimal multiplication as specified in Fig. 10-15 and (b) the decimal division as specified in Fig. 10-16.

10-37. Change the floating-point arithmetic algorithms in Sec. 10-4 from binary to decimal data. In a table, list how each micro-operation symbol should be interpreted.

Input-Output
Organization

11-1   PERIPHERAL DEVICES

The input-output subsystem of a computer provides an efficient mode of communication between the central system and the outside environment. Programs and data must be entered into computer memory for processing and results obtained from computations must be recorded or displayed for the user. A computer serves no useful purpose without the ability to receive information from an outside source and to transmit results in a meaningful form. The simplest and cheapest way to communicate with a computer is by means of a typewriter keyboard and printer. However, this is a very slow process and wastes computer time. A central processor is an extremely fast device capable of performing operations at very high speed. When input and output information are transferred to the processor via a slow terminal, the processor will be idle most of the time while waiting for the information to arrive. To use a computer efficiently, a large amount of programs and data must be prepared in advance and entered into a storage medium such as magnetic tapes or disks. The information in the disk is then transferred into computer memory at a rapid rate. Results of programs should also be transferred into a high-speed storage, such as disks, from which they can be transferred later into a printer to provide a printed output of results.

Devices that are under the direct control of the processor are said to be connected *on-line*. These devices are designed to read information into or out of the memory unit upon command from the CPU and are considered to be part of the computer system. A device is *off-line* when it is operated independently of the computer. Off-line equipment devices are useful for preparing programs and data. For example, a key-punch is an off-line device where the operator prepares his program and data on punched cards. A line printer may be operated off-line to print results of programs from a magnetic tape. Input or output devices attached to the computer on-line or available off-line are called *peripherals*.

Among the most common peripherals are card readers and punches, paper-tape readers and punches, keyboards, printers, plotters, and display devices. Peripherals that provide auxiliary storage for the system are magnetic tapes, disks, and drums. Peripherals are electromechanical and electromagnetic devices of some complexity. Only a very brief discussion of their function will be given here without going into detail of their internal construction.

Magnetic tapes are used mostly for storing files of data, for example, a company's payroll record. Access is sequential and consists of records which can be accessed one after another as the tape moves along a stationary read-write mechanism. It is one of the cheapest and slowest methods for storage and has the advantage that tapes can be removed when not in use. *Magnetic disks* and *drums* have high-speed rotational surfaces coated with magnetic material. Access is achieved by moving a read/write mechanism to a track in the magnetized surface. Disks and drums are used mostly for bulk storage of programs and data. Tapes, disks, and drums are discussed further in Sec. 12-1 in conjunction with their role as auxiliary memory.

Programs and data are often prepared on punched cards for input to a computer. Of the different cards that are in use, the Hollerith card is the most common. A punched card consists of 80 columns of 12 rows each. Each column represents an alphanumeric character of 12 bits by punching holes in the appropriate rows. A hole is sensed as a 1 and the absence of a hole as a 0. Punched cards offer a great convenience because they carry a complete record in a single separable card. The deletion of unwanted cards or the insertion of new cards in a card deck is a very simple process. For this reason, punched cards are very convenient for correcting errors in a program or for using different data for the same program. The 12-bit character code employed in punched cards is inefficient with respect to the number of bits used. Most computers convert the card into an internal 6-bit code to conserve bits of storage.

A *card reader* is an electromechanical input device that senses holes in cards and produces electrical signals. The sensing is done by brush contacts which develop signals as they detect holes in the card that slides over them. The cards can be moved past the brushes to sense one column at a time or one row at a time. Cards can be read in this manner at speeds of a few hundred per minute. Higher reading speeds are attainable by using photo-electric sensing cells. Holes in the cards allow light to pass through to energize the photo cell that, in response to the light, produces electrical signals. Cards can be read in this manner at speeds of 1000 to 2000 per minute.

A *card punch* is an electromechanical output device that punches holes in cards. The holes in each column are specified by the alphanumeric binary code presented to a buffer register. Cards are seldom used for output since people prefer to obtain results in printed form. They are sometimes used to punch a binary program after it is translated by a compiler. The binary program can then be used again without the need of a repeated compilation.

A *paper-tape reader and punch* provide a relatively inexpensive method of input and output for a computer. The paper tape commonly used is a one-inch wide strip of paper with eight hole positions along the tape width. In addition, a single strip of small holes along the paper provides sprockets that are used to hold the paper properly in place and to sense when the tape is in a reading position. Binary information is punched in the eight information channels in each row with a hole representing a

1 and no hole a 0. Each row of eight bits may represent the code of one alphanumeric character or part of a binary program. Paper tapes are also available with five, six, or seven hole positions per row. Often a paper-tape reader and punch are mounted on a teletypewriter. As the operator types characters on the key-board, the unit can be made to punch the character on paper tape. When the computer prints results on the typewriter, the paper punch may be turned on to punch the characters being printed. In this way, a permanent record is produced and the paper tape can be used off-line to type a duplicate record.

A *teletypewriter* is basically an electric typewriter which, in addition, has a capability of sending keyboard information and receiving printed information remotely via electric wires. The information is transmitted by a series of pulses representing the binary code of the character whose key is struck or the character that is printed. A teletypewriter is sometimes called a *teleprinter* or *Teletype*. The keyboard is used as an input terminal and the printer as an output terminal. The transfer rate of teletypewriters is very low, ranging from 10 to 100 characters per second. They are sometimes used in very small computers as a primary input and output device. In many computers, they are used as an operator's console or as remote terminals for time-sharing systems.

An *interactive display* device is similar to a teletypewriter except that characters are displayed on a cathode-ray tube instead of being printed. These devices commonly offer editing capabilities and a local storage. The text entered from the keyboard is stored in the local memory for later transmission to the computer. A characteristic feature of display devices is a cursor which marks the position in the screen where the next character will be inserted. The cursor can be moved to any position in the screen, to a single character, the beginning of a word, or to any line. Edit keys add or delete information based on the cursor position. The display terminal can operate in a Teletype mode where each character entered on the screen through the keyboard is simultaneously transmitted to the computer. In the block mode, the edited text is first stored off-line in the local memory and when ready, it is transferred to the computer as a block of information.

Teletypewriters and display devices can print or display one character at a time across a line. For faster printing, a high-speed *line printer* is commonly employed. This type of printer can print entire lines of up to 120 characters at a rate of up to 1000 lines per minute. All characters for a line are transferred to the printer at electronic speed and stored in a buffer memory until a complete line is assembled. The characters for the line stored in the buffer memory are then printed with one mechanical operation. The paper moves at a uniform speed so that when the next set of characters is assembled, it is printed in the next line. Mechanical printers are limited in their speed by the mechanical motion of the parts. When multiple copies are not required, an electrostatic printer can be used to print lines at a speed of thousands of lines per minute. Electrostatic printers require special paper with electrical conductive material. The characters are produced by charging the special paper with small dot patterns by means of electrodes.

Other input and output devices encountered in computer systems are digital incremental plotters, optical and magnetic character readers, analog to digital converters and various data acquisition equipment. Computers can be used to control various processes in real time such as machine tooling, assembly line procedures and chemical and industrial processes. For such applications, a method must be provided for sensing status conditions in the process and sending control signals to the process being controlled.

The input-output organization of a computer is a function of the size of the computer and the devices connected to it. The difference between a small and large system is largely dependent on the amount of hardware the computer has available for communicating with peripheral units and the number of peripherals connected to the system. Since each peripheral behaves differently from any other, it would be prohibitive to dwell on the detailed interconnections needed between the computer and each peripheral. Certain techniques common to most peripherals are presented in this chapter.

11-2   I/O INTERFACE

Input-output (I/O) interface provides a method for transferring binary information between internal storage, such as memory and CPU registers, and external I/O devices. Peripherals connected on-line to a computer need special communcation links for interfacing them with the central processor. The purpose of the communication link is to resolve the differences that exist between the central computer and each peripheral. The major differences are:

1. Peripherals are electromechanical devices and their manner of operation is different from the operation of the CPU and memory which are electronic devices.

2. The data transfer rate of peripherals is much slower then the transfer rate in the central computer.

3. The operation of the peripherals must be synchronized with the operation of the CPU and memory unit.

4. Data formats in peripherals differ from the word format in the central processor.

5. The operation of each peripheral must be controlled so as not to disturb the operation of the central computer and other peripherals connected to the system.

To resolve these differences, computer systems invariably include special hardware components between the central computer and peripherals to supervise all input and output transfers. Large computers include an I/O processor in the system to provide a pathway for the transfer of information passing between input and output devices and internal memory. The I/O processor is sometimes called a *data channel controller*, since it controls and regulates the flow of data to and from the internal and external parts of the computer. To keep the price low, small computers come without an I/O processor but instead, an interface module is provided for each peripheral that is attached to the computer.

I/O Bus and Interface Module

A typical communication link between the CPU and several peripherals is shown in Fig. 11-1. The CPU has an I/O control that supervises the flow of information in the I/O bus. The computer I/O control receives instructions from program memory and proceeds to execute them by communicating with the peripheral through its interface. Each peripheral has associated with it an interface module. The interface logic decodes the commands received from the I/O bus, interprets them for the peripheral and provides signals for the peripheral controller. It also synchronizes the data flow and supervises the transfer rate between peripheral and computer. Each peripheral has its own controller that operates and controls the particular electromechanical device. For example, a line-printer controller controls the paper motion, the print timing, and the selection of printing characters. A controller may be housed separately or may be physically integrated with the peripheral. Several peripherals of the same type may sometimes share a common controller.

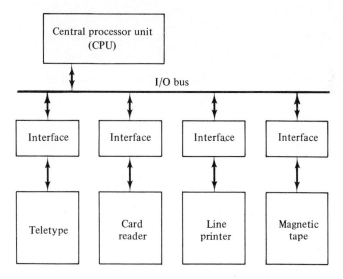

Fig. 11-1   I/O communication link.

The I/O bus is a common bus attached to all peripheral interfaces. To commnunicate with a particular device, the CPU places a device address on a set of lines in the bus. Each interface attached to the common bus contains an address decoder which monitors continuously the address lines. When the interface detects its own address code, it activates the paths between the I/O bus lines and the peripheral attached to it. All peripherals whose code does not correspond to the address code in the bus are disabled by their interface.

At the same time that the address is made available in the address lines, the computer I/O control provides a function code on another set of lines in the bus. The selected interface decodes the function code and proceeds to execute it. The function code is often called a *command* and is in essence an instruction that is executed in the interface module.

To see how the computer generates commands for the peripheral, consider the I/O instruction format as shown in Fig. 11-2. The instruction is read from memory during the fetch cycle and placed in an instruction register. The instruction has three fields. The operation code field distinguishes the instruction as an I/O type. The device address field can specify up to 16 peripherals. The function code specifies the command for the I/O interface. In this example, we assume that all I/O instructions have an operation code 1111. The instruction specifies the peripheral with assigned address 1101 and the function code is a command for this peripheral.

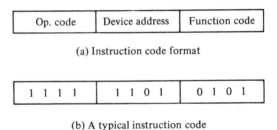

(a) Instruction code format

(b) A typical instruction code

Fig. 11-2 Typical I/O instruction.

The connection of the I/O bus to the computer is shown in Fig. 11-3. It consists of the address lines, the function code lines and bidirectional data lines for data transfer to and from the accumulator register and the interface. The sense lines detect the status of the peripheral as for example, the status of the flag that indicates the readiness of the peripheral for data transfer.

The connection of the I/O bus to an interface is shown in Fig. 11-4. The address bits are decoded through an AND gate and the output of the gate enables the control section of the interface. It is assumed that the assigned device address for this peripheral is 1101 so the output of the gate is 1 only when the address lines contain these bits; otherwise, the output of the gate is 0. The function code bits are decoded in the command decoder. The decoded function is then applied to the interface control to activate the specified command. The interface has a buffer register for holding the data being transferred through the I/O bus. A second register is used to transfer data to the output peripheral device. The status register stores the flags that notify the computer of important conditions in the interface. These include conditions that data has been received from the peripheral, that the interface is ready to receive data from

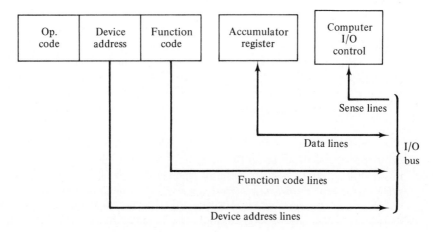

Fig. 11-3 Connection of I/O bus to computer.

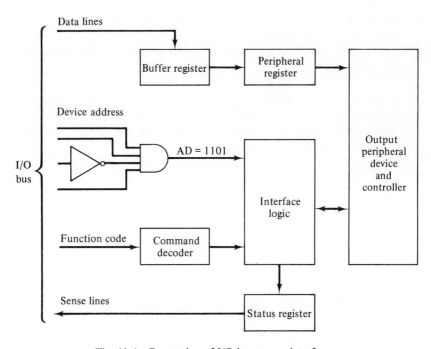

Fig. 11-4 Connection of I/O bus to one interface.

the computer, as well as error indications such as parity error, or device power being off.

An interface is assigned the task of synchronizing the data flow between computer and peripheral. For data input synchronization the interface receives an item of data at the rate that the peripheral can provide and transfers it to the computer through the I/O bus whenever it is available. For output synchronization, the interface receives an item of data from the I/O bus and holds it in its buffer register. It is then transferred to the peripheral at the rate it can be accepted. The interface must have specialized control signals to communicate with the particular peripheral to which it is attached.

Types of Commands

The computer issues commands through its function code bits. The interpretation of the command depends on the peripheral that it is addressing. There are four types of commands that an interface may receive when it is addressed by the CPU. They are classified as *control*, *test*, *data-output* and *data-input* commands.

A *control* command is issued to activate the peripheral and to inform it what to do. For example, a magnetic-tape unit may be instructed to back-space the tape by one record, to rewind the tape, or to start the tape moving in the forward direction. The particular control command issued depends upon the peripheral and each peripheral receives its own distinguished sequence of control commands dependent on its own mode of operation.

A *test* command is used to test various status conditions in the interface or the peripheral. Before a transfer of data is made, the computer may want to test the path to the peripheral to see if power is on and if the selected peripheral is connected on-line to the computer. The command decoder in the interface recognizes the conditions being tested, checks these conditions and transfers a response back to the computer via the sense lines in the I/O bus. The binary response in the sense lines is checked by the computer to determine what to do next. For example, if the status report indicates that the peripheral is available and ready, the computer then initiates a data transfer. If the device is not ready, the computer may either remain in a program loop checking the status of the peripheral or branch to some other program. A status response does not necessarily need special sense lines. The status bits may be transferred by the interface to the accumulator via the data lines. After issuing a sense command, the computer checks the bits of the accumulator and interprets the status bits according to some adopted convention.

A *data-output* command causes the interface to respond by taking an item of data, say one character, from the data lines in the I/O bus. Consider an example with a tape unit: the computer starts the tape moving by issuing a control command. The processor then monitors the status of the tape by means of test commands. When the tape is in the correct position, the computer issues a data-output command. The interface responds to the address and command lines and transfers the data from the I/O bus data lines to its buffer register. The interface then communicates with the peripheral controller to accept a new item of data to be stored on tape.

A *data-input* command is just the opposite of a data-output. In this case, the interface receives an item of data from the peripheral and places it in its buffer register. The processor checks if data is available by means of a test command and then issues a data-input command. The interface puts the data into the I/O data bus where it is accepted by the CPU and placed in the accumulator register.

Microprocessor Interface

Some computer systems use two separate buses, one to communicate with memory and the other with I/O interfaces. The memory bus is used to communicate between the CPU and the memory unit. A separate I/O bus is employed for transfers between the CPU and I/O devices through their interface. The I/O bus described in Fig. 11-3 assumes this type of configuration. Some minicomputers and all microprocessors use a common single bus system for both the memory and interface units. If an interface has a number of registers, each register is selected by its own address, just as a memory word is selected. The microprocessor is introduced in Sec. 7-8 and its bus connection to memory and I/O interface is shown in Fig. 7-15.

The communication between the microprocessor and all interface units is via a common data bus. An interface connected to a peripheral device may have a number of data registers, a control register, and a status register. A command is passed to the peripheral by sending a word to the appropriate interface register. In a system like this, the function code and sense lines of the I/O bus are not needed because commands are sent to a register and status information is received from another register just as data are transferred, except that the register address is different. Thus, the transfer of data, control, and status information is always via the common data bus. The distinction between data and control or status information is determined from the particular interface register with which the CPU is communicating.

Manufacturers of microprocessors supplement their product with a set of interface chips suitable for communication between the microprocessor and a variety of standard input and output peripheral devices. Interface components are usually designed to operate with a particular microprocessor system bus with no additional logic besides address decoding. A typical example of an interface unit for a microprocessor is shown in Fig. 11-5. It consists of three data registers called *ports*, a control register, tri-state buffers for the data bus, and timing and control circuits.

The interface registers communicate with the microprocessor through the data bus. The address bus selects the interface unit through the chip select and the two register select lines. A circuit must be inserted externally (usually a decoder or an AND gate) to detect the address assigned to the interface. This circuit enables the chip select (CS) input when the interface is selected by the address bus. The two register select inputs RS1 and RS0 are usually connected to the two lowest-order lines of the address bus. These two inputs select one of the four registers in the interface, as specified in the table accompanying the diagram. The content of the selected register is transferred into the microprocessor via the data bus when the I/O read input is enabled. The microprocessor transfers binary information into the selected register via the data bus when the I/O write input is enabled.

The peripheral unit attached to the interface communicates with the data in each

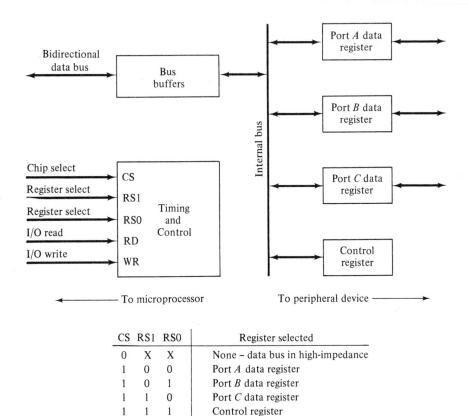

CS	RS1	RS0	Register selected
0	X	X	None – data bus in high-impedance
1	0	0	Port A data register
1	0	1	Port B data register
1	1	0	Port C data register
1	1	1	Control register

Fig. 11-5 Interface unit for microprocessor.

of the three ports. The binary information in each port can be assigned a meaning depending on the mode of operation of the peripheral unit. For example, Port A can be assigned the task of transferring data to and from the CPU and the I/O device. Port B can be used to specify a command for the peripheral unit and Port C could function as a status register which accumulates status bit conditions to be read by the CPU at a later time.

The microprocessor initializes each port by transferring a byte to the control register in the interface. By loading appropriate bits into the control register at system initialization, the microprocessor can define the mode of operation of each port. Most interface chip components can be initialized to accommodate a variety of combinations of operating modes. For example, each port can be placed in an input or an output mode. Some individual lines in one of the ports may be assigned the task of synchronizing the transfer of data in other lines. By changing the bits in the control register, it is possible to change the interface characteristics. For this reason, interface chips are said to be *programmable* because their mode of operation can be specified by means of program instructions. The instructions that transfer binary data into the control register are included in the microprocessor program and are used to initialize the interface for a particular mode of operation.

Isolated versus Memory-Mapped I/O

As mentioned previously, microprocessors use a common bus system for selecting memory words and interface registers. The distinction between a memory transfer and I/O transfer is made through separate read and write lines. The microprocessor specifies whether the address on the address bus is for a memory word or for an interface register by enabling one of two possible read or write lines. For example, the I/O read and I/O write input lines shown in Fig. 11-5 are enabled during an I/O transfer. Some microprocessors provide two more control lines for specifying separate memory-read and memory-write operations. This configuration isolates all I/O interface addresses from the addresses assigned to memory and is referred to as the *isolated* I/O method of address assignment.

In the isolated I/O configuration, the microprocessor has distinct input and output instructions, and each of these instructions is associated with the address of an interface register. When the microprocessor fetches and decodes the operation code of an input or output instruction, it places the address associated with the instruction into the address bus. At the same time, it enables the I/O read (for input) or I/O write (for output) control line. This informs the external components that the address is for an interface register and not for a memory word. On the other hand, during a fetch cycle or a memory-reference execute cycle, the microprocessor places an address on the address bus and enables the memory-read or memory-write control line. This informs the external components that the address is for a memory word and not for an I/O interface.

The isolated I/O method isolates memory and I/O addresses so that memory address range is not affected by interface address assignment. The other alternative is to assign memory addresses to interface registers. This is the case in those microprocessors that employ only one set of read and write signals and thus do not distinguish between memory and I/O addresses. This configuration is referred to as *memory-mapped* I/O. The microprocessor treats an interface register as being part of the memory system. The assigned addresses for interface registers cannot be used for memory words, which reduces the memory address range available.

In a memory-mapped I/O organization there are no specific input or output instructions. The CPU can manipulate I/O data residing in interface registers with the same instructions that are used to manipulate memory words. Each interface is organized as a set of registers that respond to read and write requests in the normal address range. Typically, a segment of the total address range is reserved for interface registers, but in general, they can be located at any address as long as there is not also a memory word that responds to that address.

Memory-mapped I/O allows the use of memory-type instructions to access I/O data. It allows the processor to use the same instructions for input-output transfers as it does for memory transfers. The advantage is that the same set of instructions used for reading and writing memory can be used to input and output data. In a typical computer, there are many more memory instructions than I/O instructions. With memory-mapped I/O all memory instructions are also available for I/O data.

Modes of Transfer

Data transfer between the central computer and peripherals is handled in one of three possible modes:

1. Data transfer under program control.
2. Interrupt initiated data transfer.
3. Direct memory access (DMA) transfer.

Program-controlled operations are the result of I/O instructions written in the computer program. Each data item transfer is initiated by an instruction in the program. Usually, the transfer is to and from a processor register such as accumulator and peripheral. Another instruction is needed to transfer the data to and from accumulator and memory. Transferring data under program control requires constant monitoring of the peripheral by the processor. Once a data transfer is initiated, the processor is required to monitor the peripheral flag to see when a transfer can again be made. It is up to the processor to keep close tabs on everything that is taking place in the interface unit. Examples of program controlled input-output operations can be found in Sec. 6-8.

In the program-controlled transfer, the processor stays in a program loop until the I/O unit indicates that it is ready. This is a time-consuming process since it keeps the processor busy needlessly. It can be avoided by using an interrupt facility and special commands to inform the interface to issue an interrupt request when the peripheral becomes available. The processor then goes to execute another program. The interface meanwhile keeps monitoring the peripheral. When the interface determines that the peripheral is ready for data transfer, it generates an interrupt request to the processor. Upon detecting an interrupt, the processor stops momentarily the task it is doing, branches to a service routine to process the data transfer, and then returns to the task it was performing. Interrupt-inititated I/O transfers are discussed in more detail in Sec. 11-5.

Transfer of data under program control is through the I/O bus and between processor and peripheral. In direct memory access (DMA), the interface transfers data into and out of the memory unit through the memory bus. The CPU initiates this type of transfer by supplying the interface with a starting memory address and the number of words and then proceeds to other tasks. When a transfer is made, the interface requests a memory cycle through the memory bus. When the request is granted by the memory controller, the interface transfers a data word directly into memory. Such a transfer is said to *steal* a memory cycle from the processor. The processor merely delays its operation for one memory cycle to allow the direct memory I/O transfer. Since peripheral speed is much slower then processor speed, I/O memory transfers are infrequent compared to processor access to memory. An example of a direct memory access is presented in Sec. 11-4.

Many computers combine the interface logic with the requirements for a direct memory access into one unit and call it a data channel. A data channel is an I/O processor that can handle many peripherals through a DMA and interrupt facility. In such a system, the central computer can be divided into three separate modules: the memory unit, the CPU and the I/O processor. I/O processors are discussed in Sec. 11-6.

Software Considerations

The previous discussion was concerned with the basic hardware needed to interface peripherals to a computer system. A computer must also have software routines for controlling peripherals and for transfer of data between the processor and peripherals. I/O routines must issue control commands to activate the peripheral and to check the device status to determine when it is ready for data transfer. Once ready, information is transferred item by item until all the data are transferred. In some cases, a control command is then given to execute a device function such as stop tape or print characters. Error checking and other useful steps often accompany the transfers. In interrupt controlled transfers, the I/O software must issue commands to the peripheral to interrupt when ready and to service the interrupt when it occurs. In DMA transfer, the I/O software must initiate the DMA channel to start its operation.

Software control of input-output equipment is a complex undertaking. For this reason I/O routines for standard peripherals are provided by the manufacturer as part of the computer system. Quite often they are included within the operating system. Most operating systems are supplied with a variety of I/O programs to support the particular line of peripherals offered for a computer. I/O routines are usually available as macros or subroutines and the programmer uses the established routines to specify the type of transfer required without going into detailed machine-language programs.

11-3 ASYNCHRONOUS DATA TRANSFER

The internal operations in a digital system are synchronized by means of clock pulses supplied by a common pulse generator. Clock pulses are applied to all registers within a unit and all data transfers among internal registers occur simultaneously during the occurrence of a clock pulse. Two units, such as a CPU and an I/O interface, are designed independently of each other. If the registers in the interface share a common clock with the CPU registers, then the transfer between the two units is said to be synchronous. In most cases, the internal timing in each unit is independent from the other in that each uses its own private clock pulses for internal registers. In that case, the two units are said to be asynchronous to each other. This approach is widely used in most computer systems.

Asynchronous data transfer between two independent units requires that control signals be transmitted between the communicating units to indicate the time at which data is being transmitted. One way of achieving this is by means of a *strobe* pulse supplied by one of the units to indicate to the other unit when the transfer has to occur. Another method commonly used is to accompany each data item being transferred with a control signal that indicates the presence of data in the bus. The unit receiving the data item responds with another control signal to acknowledge receipt of the data. This type of agreement between two independent units is referred to as *handshaking*.

The strobe pulse method and the handshaking method of asynchronous data transfer are not restricted to I/O transfers. In fact, they are used extensively in numerous occasions requiring the transfer of data between two independent units. In the general case we consider the transmitting unit as the source and the receiving unit as the destination. For example, the CPU is the source unit during an output or a write transfer and it is the destination unit during an input or a read transfer. It is customary to specify the asynchronous transfer between two independent units by means of a timing diagram that shows the timing relationship that must exist between the control signals and the data in the buses. The sequence of control during an asynchronous transfer depends on whether the transfer is initiated by the source or by the destination unit.

Strobe Control

The strobe control method of asynchronous data transfer employs a single control line to time each transfer. The strobe may be activated by either the source or the destination unit. Figure 11-6(a) shows a source-initiated transfer. The data bus

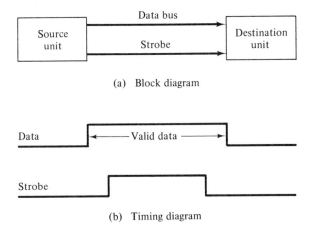

(a) Block diagram

(b) Timing diagram

Fig. 11-6 Source-initiated strobe for data transfer.

carries the binary information from source unit to the destination unit. Typically, the bus has multiple lines to transfer an entire byte or word. The strobe is a single line that informs the destination unit when a valid data word is available in the bus.

As shown in the timing diagram of Fig. 11-6(b), the source unit first places the data on the data bus. After a brief delay to ensure that the data settles to a steady value, the source activates the strobe pulse. The information on the data bus and the strobe signal remain in the active state for a sufficient time period to allow the destination unit to receive the data. Often, the destination unit uses the falling edge of the strobe pulse to transfer the contents of the data bus into one of its internal registers. The source removes the data from the bus a brief period after it disables its strobe pulse. Actually, the source does not have to change the information in the data bus. The fact that the strobe signal is disabled indicates that the data bus does not contain valid data. New valid data will be available only after the strobe is enabled again.

Figure 11-7 shows a data transfer initiated by the destination unit. In this case the destination unit activates the strobe pulse, informing the source to provide the data. The source unit responds by placing the requested binary information on the data bus. The data must be valid and remain in the bus long enough for the destination unit to accept it. The falling edge of the strobe pulse can be use again to trigger a destination register. The destination unit then disables the strobe and the source removes the data.

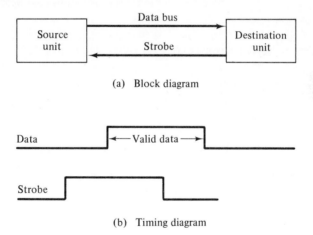

(a) Block diagram

(b) Timing diagram

Fig. 11-7 Destination-initiated strobe for data transfer.

The transfer procedure like that just described is used in most microprocessors. In microprocessor systems it is common to find that what we have called a strobe pulse is actually one of the clock signals which is used to time the CPU. The CPU is always in control of the buses and informs the external units how to transfer data. For example, the strobe of Fig. 11-6 could be a memory-write control signal from the CPU to a memory unit. The source, being the CPU, places a word on the data bus and informs the memory unit, which is the destination, that this is a write operation.

Similarly, the strobe of Fig. 11-7 could be a memory-read control signal from the CPU to a memory unit. The destination, being the CPU initiates the read operation to inform the memory, which is the source, to place a selected word into the data bus.

The transfer of data between the CPU and an interface unit is similar to the memory transfer just described. Data transfer between an interface and an I/O device is commonly controlled by a set of handshake lines.

Handshaking

The disadvantage of the strobe method is that the source unit that initiates the transfer has no way of knowing whether the destination unit has actually received the data item that was placed in the bus. Similarly, a destination unit that initiates the transfer has no way of knowing whether the source unit has actually placed the data on the bus. The handshake method solves this problem by introducing a second control signal that provides a reply to the unit that initiates the transfer. The basic principle of the two-wire handshaking method of data transfer is as follows. One control line is in the same direction as the data flow in the bus from the source to the destination. It is used by the source unit to inform the destination unit whether there is valid data in the bus. The other control line is in the other direction from the destination to the source. It is used by the destination unit to inform the source whether it can accept data. The sequence of control during the transfer depends on the unit that initiates the transfer.

Figure 11-8 shows the data transfer procedure when initiated by the source. The two handshaking lines are *data valid*, which is generated by the source unit, and *data accepted*, generated by the destination unit. The timing diagram shows the exchange of signals between the two units. The sequence of events listed in part (c) shows the four possible states that the system can be at any given time. The source unit initiates the transfer by placing the data on the bus and enabling its *data valid* signal. The *data accepted* signal is activated by the destination unit after it accepts the data from the bus. The source unit then disables its *data valid* signal, which invalidates the data on the bus. The destination unit then disables its *data accepted* signal and the system goes into its initial state. The source does not send the next data item until after the destination unit shows its readiness to accept new data by deactivating its *data accepted* signal. This scheme allows arbitrary delays from one state to the next and perimits each unit to respond at its own data tansfer rate. The rate of transfer is determined by the slowest unit.

The destination-initiated transfer using handshaking lines is shown in Fig. 11-9. Note that the name of the signal generated by the destination unit has been changed to *ready for data* to reflect its new meaning. The source unit in this case does not place data on the bus until after it receives the *ready for data* signal from the destination unit. From there on, the handshaking procedure follows the same pattern as in the source-initiated case. Note that the sequence of events in both cases would be identical if we consider the *ready for data* signal as the complement of *data accepted*. In fact,

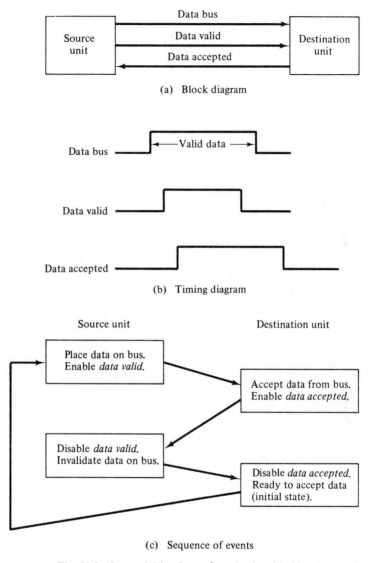

(a) Block diagram

(b) Timing diagram

(c) Sequence of events

Fig. 11-8 Source-initiated transfer using handshaking.

the only difference between the source-initiated and the destination-initiated transfer is in their choice of initial state.

The handshaking scheme provides a high degree of flexibility and reliability because the successful completion of a data transfer relies on active participation by both units. If one unit is faulty, the data transfer will not be completed. Such an error can be detected by means of a *timeout* mechanism, which produces an alarm if the

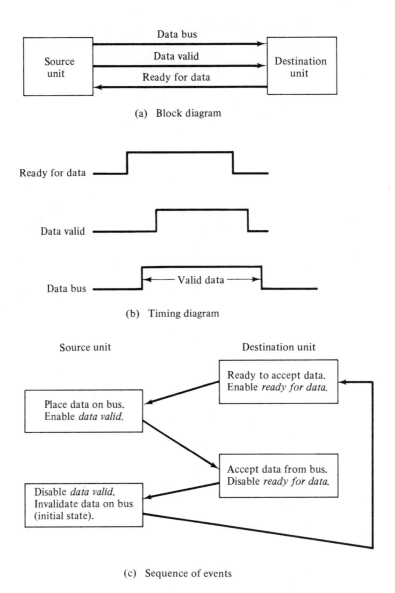

(a) Block diagram

(b) Timing diagram

(c) Sequence of events

Fig. 11-9 Destination-initiated transfer using handshaking.

data transfer is not completed within a predetermined time. The timeout is implemented by means of an internal clock that starts counting time when the unit enables one of its handshaking control signals. If the return handshake signal does not respond within a given time period, the unit assumes that an error has occurred. The timeout signal can be used to interrupt the processor and hence execute a service routine that takes appropriate error recovery action.

Three-Wire Handshaking

The two-wire handshaking procedure just described is suitable for transfer between a source unit and a single destination unit. There are occasions where a source unit transfers data to two or more destination units. In such a case, the source must ensure that all destination units are ready for the transfer before validating the data on the bus. Moreover, the source must ensure that all destination units have accepted the data before it invalidates the data in the bus. These two requirements dictate the need for three control signals for the handshake procedure.

The three-wire handshake procedure is part of a standard that defines a general-purpose interface bus (GPIB). This standard, known as the IEEE Standard 488, defines a bus system that contains 16 signal lines. Eight lines are used to carry a byte of data and the other eight are used for control. Three of the control lines are used for handshaking procedure to effect the transfer of each byte of data.

Figure 11-10 demonstrates the three-wire handshake protocol. The system shown consists of one source and three destination units. The source places the data on the bus and enables the data valid (DAV) signal. Note the bar on top of the symbol, which designates the fact that the signal is enabled when in the low-level state. Each destination unit can generate a request for data (RFD) signal and a data accepted (DAC) signal. Each of these two control wires is tied together and applied to the source unit. The wires are assumed to come from open-collector circuits that form a wire-AND connection (see Sec. 2-1). In this scheme, all destination units must have the signal in the high-level state for the input to the source to be in the high-level state. If any unit has its signal in the low-level state, the source unit detects a low-level signal at the input.

The timing diagram in Fig. 11-10(b) shows the sequence of control signals required for transferring one byte from the source unit to all destination units. The source checks the RFD line to make sure that all units are requesting data. The dashed lines in the RFD waveform give an indication concerning the sequence by which the units change their signal to the high-level state. The source does not recognize RFD until all units respond with a high-level signal. When RFD is recognized, the source enables DAV to inform all units that a data byte is available on the bus. Each unit accepts the data at its own rate of transfer. When a destination unit accepts the data in the bus, it disables its RFD signal and enables its DAC signal. Note that RFD goes to the low-level state as soon as one destination unit brings the signal down. The DAC line goes to the high-level state only after all units have enabled this signal. The source leaves the data on the bus until the DAC signal goes high. The source then disables DAV and all destination units disable their DAC line. The cycle can now be repeated to transfer a new byte of data.

Asynchronous Serial Transfer

The transfer of data between two units may be done in parallel or serial. In parallel data transmission, each bit of the message has its own path and the total message is transmitted at the same time. This means that an n-bit message must be transmitted

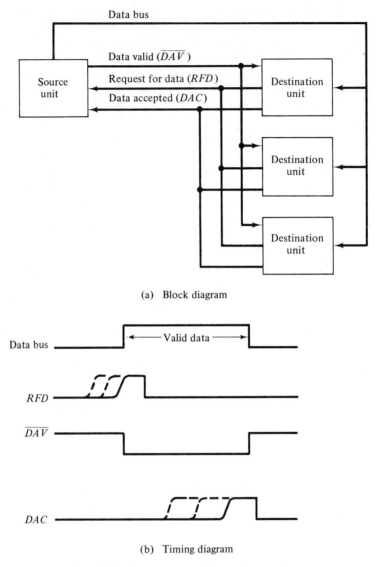

(a) Block diagram

Data bus

Valid data

RFD

$\overline{DAV}$

DAC

(b) Timing diagram

Fig. 11-10 Three-wire handshake data transfer.

through *n* separate conductor paths. In serial data transmission, each bit in the message is sent in sequence one at a time. This method requires the use of one pair of conductors or one conductor and a common ground. Parallel transmission is faster but requires many wires. It is used for short distances and where speed is important. Serial transmission is slower but is less expensive since it requires only one pair of conductors.

Serial transfer of data can be synchronous or asynchronous. In sychronous trans-

422

mission, the two units share a common clock frequency and bits are transmitted continuously at the rate dictated by the clock pulses. In long-distant serial transmission, each unit is driven by a separate clock of the same frequency. Synchronization signals are transmitted periodically between the two units to keep their clocks in step with each other. In asynchronous transmission, binary information is sent only when it is available and the line remains idle when there is no information to be transmitted. This is in contrast to synchronous transmission, where bits must be transmitted continuously to keep the clock frequency in both units synchronized with each other. Synchronous serial transmission is discussed further in Sec. 11-8.

A serial asynchronous data transmission technique used in most interactive terminals, such as Teletypes, employs special bits which are inserted at both ends of the character code. With this technique, each character consists of three parts: a start bit, the data bits, and stop bits. An example of this format is shown in Fig. 11-11.

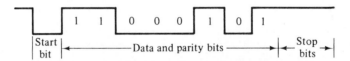

Fig. 11-11   Asynchronous serial transmission.

The convention in these terminals is that the transmitter rests at the 1-state when no message is transmitted. The first bit, called the start bit, is always a 0 and is used to indicate the beginning of a character. A character can be detected by the receiver from knowledge of four rules:

1. When data are not being sent, the line is kept in the 1 state.

2. The initiation of a character transmission is detected by a start bit, which is always a 0.

3. The character bits always follow the start bit.

4. After the last character bit is transmitted, a stop bit is detected when the line returns to the 1-state for at least 1 bit time.

Using these rules, the interface can detect the start bit when the line goes from 1 to 0. A clock in the receiver interface then allows examination of the line at proper bit times. The receiver knows the transfer rate of the bits and the number of information bits to expect. After the character bits are transmitted, one or two stop bits are sent. The stop bits are always in the 1-state and frame the end of character to signify the idle or wait state.

At the end of the message the line is held at the 1-state for a period of at least 1 or 2 bit times so that both the transmit and receive terminals can resynchronize. The length of time that the line stays in this state depends on the amount of time required for the equipment to resynchronize. Most electromechanical equipment uses 2 stop bits but some newer terminals use 1 stop bit. The line will remain in the 1-state until another character is transmitted. The stop time insures that a new character will not follow for 1 or 2 bit times.

As an illustration, let us consider the serial transmission in the Model 33 Teletype. This unit is popular because of its low cost compared to other interactive terminals. The transfer rate is 10 characters per second. Each transmitted character consists of a start bit, seven information bits, a parity bit, and 2 stop bits, for a total of 11 bits. The information bits specify a character according to the ASCII code.

Ten characters per second means that each character takes 0.1 second for transfer. Since there are eleven bits to be transmitted, it follows that the bit time is 9.09 msec. The receiver that accepts the message must have an internal clock that produces pulses at this interval. The *baud* rate is defined as the rate at which serial information is transmitted and is equivalent to the data transfer rate in bits per second. Ten characters per second with an 11-bit format gives a transfer rate of 110 baud.

A Teletype has a keyboard and a printer. Every time a key is depressed, the Teletype sends an 11-bit message along a wire. To print a character in the Teletype, an 11-bit message must be received along another wire. The Teletype interface consists of a transmitter and a receiver. The transmitter accepts an 8-bit character from the computer and proceeds to send a serial 11-bit message into the printer line. The receiver accepts a serial 11-bit message from the keyboard line and forwards the 8-bit character code to the computer. Integrated circuits are available which are specifically designed to provide the interface between computer and a Teletype or any other similar interactive terminal. Such a circuit is called *asynchronous communication interface* or *universal asynchronous receiver-transmitter* (UART).

The block diagram of an asynchronous communication interface which can be connected to a microprocessor is shown in Fig. 11-12. It functions as both a transmitter and a receiver. The interface is initialized for a particular mode of transfer by means of a control byte which is loaded into its control register. The transmitter register accepts a data byte from the microprocessor through the data bus. This byte is transferred to a shift register for serial transmission. The receiver portion receives serial information into another shift register, and when a complete data byte is accumulated, it is transferred to the receiver register. The microprocessor can select the receiver register to read the byte through the data bus. The bits in the status register are used for input and output flags and for recording certain errors that may occur during the transmission. The microprocessor can read the status register to check the status of the flag bits and to determine if any errors have occurred. The chip select and the read and write control lines communicate with the microprocessor. The chip select (CS) input is used to select the interface through the address bus. The register select (RS) is associated with the read (RD) and write (WR) controls. Two registers are write-only and two are read-only. The register selected is a function of the RS value and the RD and WR status, as listed in the table accompanying the diagram.

The operation of the asynchronous communication interface is initialized by the CPU by sending a byte to the control register. The initialization procedure places the interface in a specific mode of operation as it defines certain parameters such as the baud rate to use, how many bits are in each character, whether to generate and check

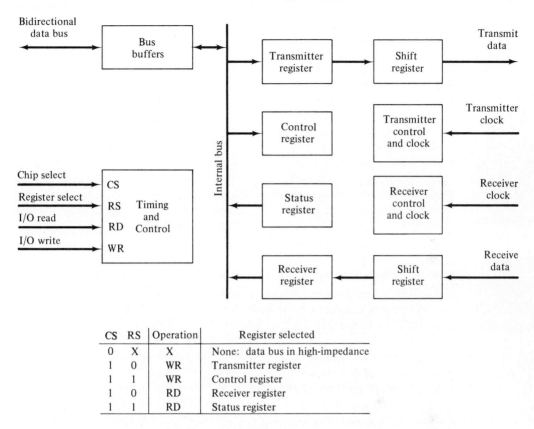

CS	RS	Operation	Register selected
0	X	X	None: data bus in high-impedance
1	0	WR	Transmitter register
1	1	WR	Control register
1	0	RD	Receiver register
1	1	RD	Status register

Fig. 11-12 Block diagram of a typical asynchronous communication interface.

parity, and how many stop bits are appended to each character. Two bits in the status register are used as flags. One bit is used to indicate whether the transmitter register is empty and another bit is used to indicate whether the receiver register is full.

The operation of the transmitter portion of the interface is as follows. The CPU reads the status register and checks the flag to see if the transmitter register is empty. If it is empty, the CPU transfers a character to the transmitter register and the interface clears the flag to mark the register full. The first bit in the transmitter shift register is set to 0 to generate a start bit. The character is transferred in parallel from the transmitter register to the shift register and the appropriate number of stop bits are appended into the shift register. The transmitter register is then marked empty. The character can now be transmitted one bit at a time by shifting the data in the shift register at the specified baud rate. The CPU can transfer another character to the transmitter register after checking the flag in the status register. The interface is said to be *double buffered* because a new character can be loaded as soon as the previous one starts transmission.

The operation of the receiver portion of the interface is similar. The receive-data input is in the 1-state when the line is idle. The receiver control monitors the receive-data line for a 0 signal to detect the occurrence of a start bit. Once a start bit has been detected, the incoming bits of the character are shifted into the shift register at the prescribed baud rate. After receiving the data bits, the interface checks for the parity and stop bits. The character without the start and stop bits is then transferred in parallel from the shift register to the receiver register. The flag in the status register is set to indicate that the receiver register is full. The CPU reads the status register and checks the flag, and if set, it reads the data from the receiver register.

The interface checks for any possible errors during transmission and sets appropriate bits in the status register. The CPU can read the status register at any time to check if any errors have occurred. Three possible errors that the interface checks during transmission are parity error, framing error, and overrun error. Parity error occurs if the number of 1's in the received data is not the correct parity (see Sec. 3-5). A framing error occurs if the right number of stop bits are not detected at the end of the received character. An overrun error occurs if the CPU does not read the character from the receiver register before the next one becomes available in the shift register. Overrun error results in a loss of characters in the received data stream.

First-In First-Out (FIFO) Buffer

A first-in first-out buffer is a memory unit that stores information in such a manner that the item first in is the item first out. A FIFO buffer comes with separate input and output terminals. The important feature of this buffer is that it can input data and output data at two different rates and the output data are always in the same order in which the data entered the buffer. When placed between two units, the FIFO can accept data from the source unit at one rate of transfer and deliver the data to the destination unit at another rate. If the source unit is slower than the destination unit, the buffer can be filled with data at a slow rate and later emptied at the higher rate. **If the source is faster than the destination, the FIFO is useful for those cases where the source data arrives in bursts that fill out the buffer but the time between bursts is long enough for the destination unit to empty some or all the information from the buffer. Thus, a FIFO buffer can be useful in some applications when data is transferred asynchronously. It piles up data as it comes in and gives it away in the same order when the data is needed.**

The logic diagram of a typical 4×4 FIFO buffer is shown in Fig. 11-13. It consists of four 4-bit registers RI, $I = 1, 2, 3, 4$, and a control register with flip-flops F_i, $i = 1, 2, 3, 4$, one for each register. The FIFO can store four words of four bits each. The number of bits per word can be increased by increasing the number of bits in each register and the number of words can be increased by increasing the number of registers.

A flip-flop F_i in the control register that is set to 1 indicates that a 4-bit data word is stored in the corresponding register RI. A 0 in F_i indicates that the corresponding register does not contain valid data. The control register directs the move-

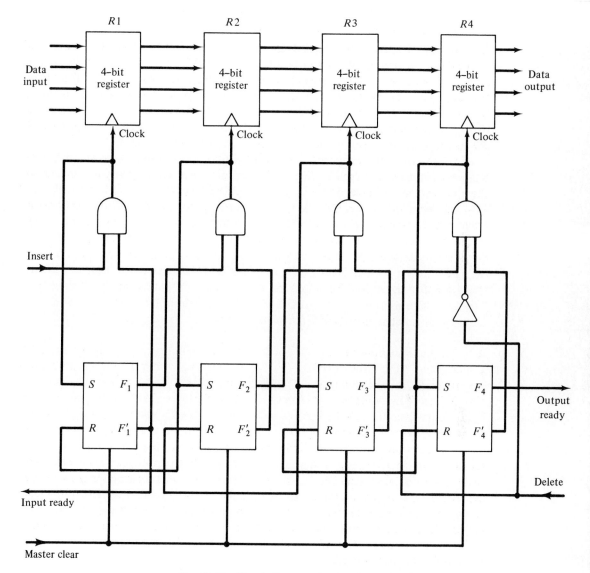

Fig. 11-13 Circuit diagram of a 4 × 4 FIFO buffer.

ment of data through the registers. Whenever the F_i bit of the control register is set ($F_i = 1$) and the F_{i+1} bit is reset ($F'_{i+1} = 1$), a clock is generated causing register $R(I + 1)$ to accept the data from register RI. The same clock transition sets F_{i+1} to 1 and resets F_i to 0. This causes the control flag to move one position to the right together with the data. Data in the registers move down the FIFO toward the output as long as there are empty locations ahead of it. This ripple-through operation stops when the data reach a register RI with the next flip-flop F_{i+1} being set to 1, or at the

427

last register *R4*. An overall master clear is used to initialize all control register flip-flops to 0.

Data is inserted into the buffer provided that the *input ready* signal is enabled. This occurs when the first control flip-flop F_1 is reset, indicating that register *R1* is empty. Data is loaded from the input lines by enabling the clock in *R1* through the *insert* control line. The same clock sets F_1, which disables the *input ready* control, indicating that the FIFO is now busy and unable to accept more data. The ripple-through process begins provided that *R2* is empty. The data in *R1* is transferred into *R2* and F_1 is cleared. This enables the *input ready* line, indicating that the inputs are now available for another data word. If the FIFO is full, F_1 remains set and the *input ready* line stays in the 0 state. Note that the two control lines *input ready* and *insert* constitute a destination-initiated pair of handshake lines.

The data falling through the registers stack up at the output end. The *output ready* control line is enabled when the last control flip-flop F_4 is set, indicating that there is valid data in the output register *R4*. The output data from *R4* is accepted by a destination unit, which then enables the *delete* control signal. This resets F_4, causing *output ready* to disable, indicating that the data on the output is no longer valid. Only after the *delete* signal goes back to 0 can the data from *R3* move into *R4*. If the FIFO is empty, there will be no data in *R3* and F_4 will remain in the reset state. Note that the two control lines *output ready* and *delete* constitute a source-initiated pair of handshake lines.

11-4 DIRECT MEMORY ACCESS

Direct memory access (DMA), as the name implies, is an interface that provides I/O transfer of data directly to and from the memory unit and peripheral. The CPU initializes the DMA by sending a memory address and the number of words to be transferred. The actual transfer of data is done directly between peripheral and the memory unit through the DMA, freeing the CPU for other tasks. The major difference between an I/O program controlled transfer and DMA is that data transfer does not employ the registers of the CPU. The transfer is done in the DMA interface by first checking if the memory unit is not used by the CPU and then the DMA *steals* one memory cycle to access a word in memory. DMA is the preferred form of data transfer for use with high-speed peripheral devices such as magnetic disks or tapes. An entire record is usually transferred between memory and peripheral. This is stored in memory as a block of consecutive locations in a reserved space. The position of a DMA interface with other components of the computer is illustrated in Fig. 11-14.

A DMA system needs the usual circuits of an interface such as a device address decoder, a command decoder, and special control logic. In addition, it needs a separate memory address register, a memory buffer register and a word count register. The address and buffer registers are used for direct communication with the memory unit. The word-count register specifies the number of words to be transferred. A

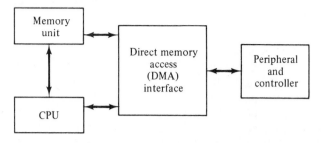

Fig. 11-14 Block diagram of computer with DMA.

computer with a DMA facility must include a special control section for the memory unit to communicate with both the CPU and DMA on a priority basis.

The DMA interface is first initialized by the CPU. After that, the DMA starts and continues to transfer data between memory and peripheral until an entire block is transferred. When the transfer is completed, the DMA prepares for the CPU a status report and then sends an interrupt request. When the CPU services the interrupt, it receives the status message and checks if the transfer was satisfactory.

The initialization process is essentially a program consisting of I/O instructions that include the device address and command codes for the DMA interface. The CPU checks the status of the peripheral and DMA and if all is in order, it sends the following information through the I/O communication lines:

1. The starting address of the memory block where data are available (for output) or where data are to be stored (for input).

2. The word count, which is the number of words in the memory block.

3. One bit specifying an input or output transfer.

4. A command to start the DMA.

The starting address, word count, and the bit specifying the direction of transfer are stored in designated registers in the DMA. The CPU then stops communicating with the DMA. The DMA does all the housekeeping operations such as packing characters into words (for input) or unpacking words into characters (for output) and checks the status of the peripheral. When a word is ready to be read or written in memory the DMA communicates directly with the memory and receives a memory cycle for a word access.

DMA Transfer Example

The communication between memory and CPU must be modified to take into consideration direct memory access transfers. The position of the CPU and DMA in relation to the memory unit is illustrated in Fig. 11-15. Both the CPU and DMA communicate with the memory unit (MU), but DMA has priority over the CPU. Each of the three units have an address register (AR) and a buffer register (BR). A request flip-flop RF,

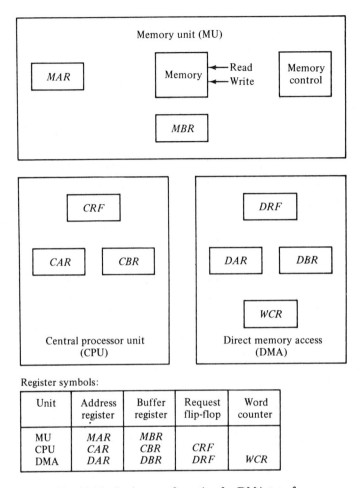

Fig. 11-15 Register configuration for DMA transfer.

one in the CPU and one in the DMA is set when the corresponding unit requests a memory cycle. The memory control services both units and resolves conflicts between the two requests. The word count register WCR in the DMA holds the number of words that must be transferred.

A flow chart for the memory operations with DMA is shown in Fig. 11-16. Initially, both request flip-flops are cleared. The DMA request flip-flop DRF is checked first because the DMA has higher priority. If $DRF = 0$, the CPU request flip-flop CRF is checked. If it is 0, the memory control continues to check the request flip-flops until one of them is set. When the CPU requests a memory access (during the fetch or execute cycle), it sets CRF to 1. The memory control checks the operation requested by the CPU. For a write operation, the address and data from CPU registers are transferred to memory registers and the word is stored in memory. For a read operation, the address is transferred from CAR to MAR, the word is read into

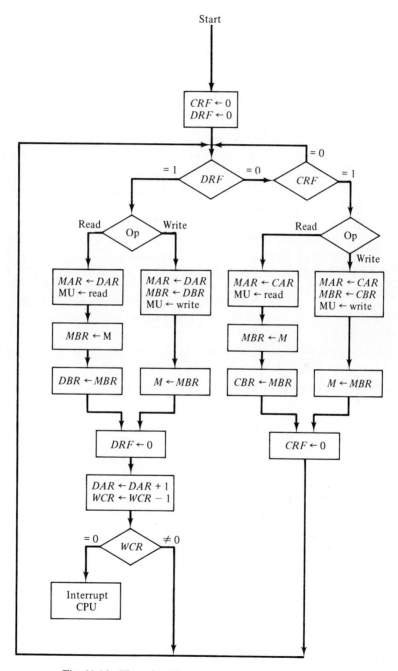

Fig. 11-16 Flow chart for memory operations with DMA.

MBR and then transferred to the CPU register *CBR*. At the completion of the operation, the request bit is cleared and the memory control goes back to check for further requests.

When the DMA request flip-flop *DRF* is set, the memory control communicates with the DMA registers in the same manner to write or read a word from memory. After each DMA transfer, the DMA address register is incremented and the word count decremented simultaneously (this is done by the DMA control, not the memory control). When the word count reaches zero, the DMA stops the transfer and informs the CPU of the termination by means of an interrupt request.

Microprocessor DMA Transfer

When two or more units communicate with the same memory unit, the data and address lines must form a common bus system. The address and data lines from the registers in the CPU and DMA as depicted in Fig. 11-15 must be connected through multiplexers to form a common memory bus. (Figure 4-6 shows a block diagram of such a bus system.) Instead of using multiplexers, the common bus system can be constructed with tri-state buffers. In this way, the CPU and DMA data and address lines can be connected to one common set of lines. The unit that communicates with the memory has its tri-states buffers active while the inactive unit has its tri-state buffers in the high-impedance state. Most microprocessors buses function in this manner. (Figure 7-17 shows a pair of tri-state buffers connected to a bidirectional bus line.)

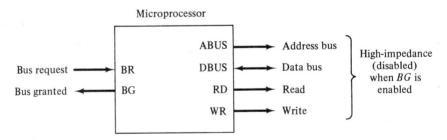

Fig. 11-17   Microprocessor signals for DMA transfer.

Microprocessors are designed to operate in parallel with a DMA unit. Figure 11-17 shows two control signals in a typical microprocessor which can be used in conjunction with DMA transfer. The bus request (BR) input, when enabled, informs the microprocessor that an external unit such as DMA is requesting control of the system buses. The microprocessor terminates the execution of the current instruction and then places its address and data buses, as well as the read and write lines, into the high-impedance state. When this is done, the microprocessor enables its bus granted (BG) line. As long as the bus granted line is enabled, the microprocessor is idle and its buses are disabled. The DMA unit that originated the bus request can now take control of the buses to conduct memory transfers without processor intervention.

When the DMA terminates the transfer, it disables the BR line. The microprocessor then disables its BG line and takes control of the buses. The bus request line is sometimes called a *hold* signal, and the bus granted a *hold acknowledge*.

The position of a DMA unit among other components in a microcomputer system is illustrated in Fig. 11-18. The microprocessor communicates with the DMA unit through the address and data buses as with any I/O interface unit. The DMA has its own address, which activates the CS (chip select) and RS (register select) input lines. The microprocessor initializes the DMA through the data bus by transferring the starting address and word count to appropriate DMA registers. The microprocessor then sends a control byte to inform the DMA to start its operation when it is ready.

When the peripheral device sends a DMA request, the DMA activates its BR line, informing the processor to relinquish the buses. The microprocessor responds with its BG line, informing the DMA that its buses are disabled. The DMA then puts the current value of its address register on the address bus, initiates the RD or WR signal, and sends a DMA acknowledge to the peripheral device. Note that the

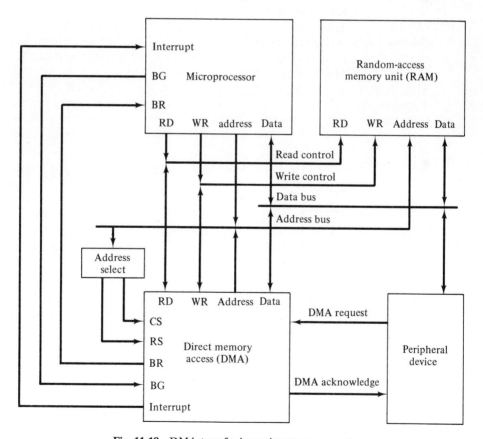

Fig. 11-18 DMA transfer in a microprocessor system.

RD and WR lines in the DMA are bidirectional. The direction of the signals depends on the status of the BG line. When BG = 0, the RD and WR are input signals allowing the microprocessor to communicate with the DMA registers through the data bus to read from or write into the DMA registers. When BG = 1, the RD and WR are output signals from the DMA that go into the random-access memory (RAM) to specify a read or write operation for the data.

When the peripheral device receives a DMA acknowledge, it puts a word on the data bus (for write) or receives a word from the data bus (for read). Thus, the DMA controls the read or write operation and supplies the address for the memory. The peripheral unit can then communicate with the RAM through the data bus for direct transfer between the two units while the microprocessor is momentarily disabled. The transfer can be made for an entire block of memory words, suspending the processor operation until the whole block is transferred or the transfer can be made one word at a time in between microprocessor instruction execution. When the DMA stops transferring data, it disables its BR signal, which disables the BG signal in the microprocessor, returning control of the buses to the microprocessor.

11-5 PRIORITY INTERRUPT

Data transfers between the CPU and an I/O device must be initiated by the CPU. However, the CPU cannot start the transfer unless the device is ready to communicate with the CPU. The readiness of the device can be determined from the status of a control line or a flag. The CPU can monitor the flag to check the status, but this is a time-consuming process since it keeps the CPU busy needlessly. The alternative is for the device interface to interrupt the CPU every time the flag is enabled. The CPU responds to the interrupt signal by storing the return address from *PC* (program counter) into a memory stack and then branching to a service routine that processes the required transfer. As discussed in Sec. 7-7, some processors push also the current PSW (program status word) into the stack and then load a new PSW for the service routine. We will neglect the PSW here in order not to complicate the discussion of I/O interrupts.

The way that the processor chooses the branch address of the service routine varies from one unit to another. In principle, there are two methods for accomplishing this. One is called *vectored* and the other *nonvectored* interrupt. In a nonvectored interrupt, the branch address is assigned to a fixed location in memory. In a vectored interrupt, the interrupting source itself supplies the branch information to the processor. This information is called an *interrupt vector*. In some computers, the interrupt vector gives the beginning address of the service routine. In other computers, the interrupt vector is an address that points to a location in memory where the beginning address of the service routine is stored.

In a typical application there are a number of I/O devices that are attached to the CPU. Each is allowed to originate an interrupt request. The first task of the interrupt system is to identify the source of the interrupt. There is also the possibility that several sources will request service simultaneously. In this case, the system must also decide which device to service first.

A *priority interrupt* is an interrupt system that establishes a priority over the various sources to determine which condition is to be serviced first when two or more requests arrive simultaneously. It can also be designed to determine which conditions are permitted to interrupt the processor while another interrupt is being serviced. Higher-priority interrupt levels are assigned to requests which, if delayed or interrupted, could have serious consequences. I/O devices with high-speed transfers such as magnetic disks are given a high priority and slow-speed devices receive a lower priority. When two devices interrupt the processor at the same time, the processor services the device with the higher priority first.

Establishing the priority of simultaneous interrupts can be done by software or hardware. A *polling* procedure is used to identify the highest-priority source by software means. In this method, there is one common branch address for all interrupts. The common service program begins at the branch address and polls the interrupt sources in sequence. The order in which they are tested determines the priority of each interrupt request. The highest-priority source is tested first and if its interrupt signal is on, control branches to a service routine for this source. Otherwise, the next-lower-priority source is tested, and so on. Thus, the initial service routine for all interrupts consists of a program that tests the interrupt sources in sequence and branches to one of many possible service routines. The particular service routine reached belongs to the highest-priority device among all devices that interrupt the processor. The disadvantage of the software method is that if there are many interrupts, the time required to poll them can exceed the time available to service the I/O device. In this situation, a hardware priority interrupt unit can be used to speed up the operation.

A hardware priority interrupt unit functions as an overall manager in an interrupt system environment. It accepts interrupt requests from many sources, determines which of the incoming requests is of the highest priority, and issues an interrupt signal to the processor based on this determination. To speed up the operation, each interrupt source has its own interrupt vector to access directly to its own service routine. Thus, no polling is required because all the decisions are established by the hardware priority interrupt unit. The hardware priority function can be established either by a serial or a parallel connection of the interrupt lines. The serial connection is also known as the daisy-chain method.

Daisy-Chain Priority Interrupt

The daisy-chain method of priority selection consists of a serial connection of all devices that request an interrupt from the processor. The device with the highest priority is placed in the first position, followed by lower-priority devices up to the device with the lowest priority, which is placed last in the chain. This method of connection between three devices and the CPU is shown in Fig. 11-19. The interrupt

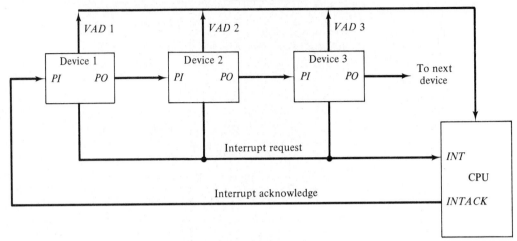

Processor data bus

VAD 1   VAD 2   VAD 3

| Device 1 | | Device 2 | | Device 3 | |
| PI | PO | PI | PO | PI | PO |

To next device

Interrupt request

INT

CPU

Interrupt acknowledge

INTACK

Fig. 11-19 Daisy chain priority interrupt.

request line is common to all devices and forms a wired logic connection. If any device has its interrupt signal in the low-level state, the interrupt line goes to the low-level state and enables the interrupt input in the CPU. When no interrupts are pending, the interrupt line remains in the high-level state and no interrupts are recognized by the CPU. The CPU responds to an interrupt request by enabling the interrupt acknowledge line. This signal is received by device 1 at its PI (priority in) input. The acknowledge signal passes on to the next device through the PO (priority out) terminal only if device 1 is not requesting an interrupt. If device 1 has a pending request for interrupt, it blocks the acknowledge signal from the next device by placing a 0 in its PO output. It then proceeds to put its interrupt vector address (VAD) in the data bus for the processor to use during the interrupt cycle.

A device with a 0 in its PI input generates a 0 in its PO output to inform the next-lower-priority device that the acknowledge signal has been blocked. A device with a 1 in its PI input which is requesting an interrupt will intercept the acknowledge line by placing a 0 in its PO output. If the device does not have a pending interrupt, it transmits the acknowledge signal to the next device by placing a 1 in its PO output. Thus, the device with $PI = 1$ and $PO = 0$ is the one with the highest priority that is requesting an interrupt and this is the device that places its VAD on the data bus. The daisy-chain arrangement gives the highest priority to the device that receives the interrupt acknowledge signal directly from the CPU. The farther the device is from this position, the lower its priority level.

Figure 11-20 shows the internal logic that must be included within each device when connected in the daisy-chain priority scheme. The device sets its RF flip-flop when it wants to interrupt the CPU. The output of the RF flip-flop goes through an open-collector inverter (see Sec. 2-1) to provide the wired logic for the common interrupt line. If $PI = 0$, then both PO and the VAD enable signals are equal to 0,

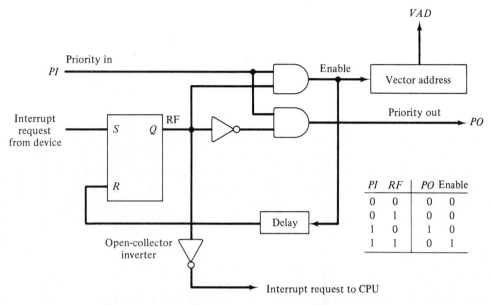

Fig. 11-20 One stage of the daisy chain priority arrangement.

irrespective of the value of *RF*. If $PI = 1$ and $RF = 0$, then $PO = 1$ and the vector address is disabled. This condition passes the acknowledge signal to the next device through *PO*. The device is active when $PI = 1$ and $RF = 1$. This condition places a 0 in *PO* and enables the vector address for the data bus. It is assumed that each device has its own distinct vector address. The *RF* flip-flop is reset after a sufficient delay to ensure that the CPU has received the vector address.

Parallel Priority Interrupt

The parallel priority interrupt method uses a register whose bits are set separately by the interrupt requests from each device. Priority is established according to the position of the bits in the register. In addition to the interrupt register the circuit may include a mask register whose purpose is to control the status of each interrupt request. The mask register can be programmed to disable lower-priority interrupts while a higher-priority device is being serviced. It can also provide a facility that allows a high-priority device to interrupt the CPU while a lower-priority device is being serviced.

The priority logic for a system of four interrupt sources is shown in Fig. 11-21. It consists of an interrupt register whose individual bits are set by external conditions and cleared by program instructions. The magnetic disk, being a high-speed device, is given the highest priority. A line printer has the next priority, followed by a card reader and a Teletype keyboard. The mask register has the same number of bits as the

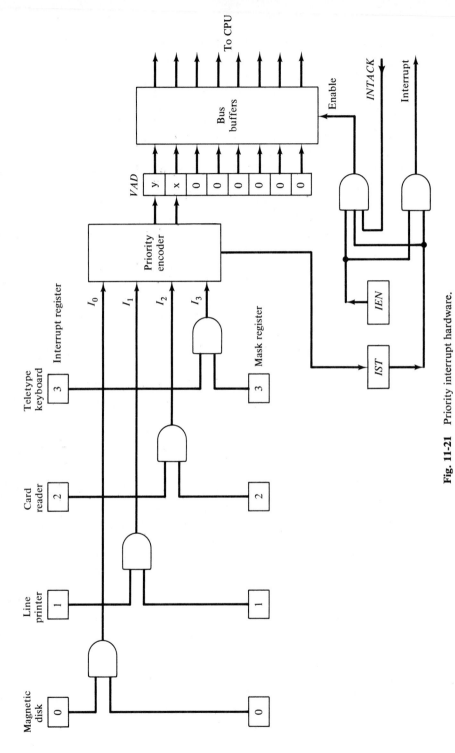

Fig. 11-21 Priority interrupt hardware.

interrupt register. By means of program instructions, it is possible to set or clear any bit in the mask register. Each interrupt bit and its corresponding mask bit are applied to an AND gate to produce the four inputs to the priority encoder. In this way, an interrupt is recognized only if its corresponding mask bit is set to 1 by the program. The priority encoder generates two bits of the vector address (VAD), which is then transferred to the CPU via the tri-state bus buffers. Two flip-flops and the interrupt acknowledge ($INTACK$) signal from the CPU are used to enable the bus buffers. The *interrupt status IST* is set if an interrupt that is not masked has occured. The output of IST provides a common interrupt signal for the CPU. The *interrupt enable IEN* can be set or cleared by the program to provide overall control over the interrupt system. We will now explain the priority encoder circuit and then discuss the interaction between the priority interrupt unit and the CPU.

The priority encoder is a basic circuit that implements the priority function. The logic of the priority encoder is such that, if two or more inputs arrive at the same time, the input having the highest priority will take precedence. The truth table of a four-input priority encoder is given in Table 11-1. The X's in the table designate don't-

TABLE 11-1   Priority Encoder Truth Table

I_0	I_1	I_2	I_3	x	y	IST	Boolean functions
\multicolumn{4}{c}{Inputs}	\multicolumn{3}{c}{Outputs}	

Inputs				Outputs			
I_0	I_1	I_2	I_3	x	y	IST	Boolean functions
1	X	X	X	0	0	1	
0	1	X	X	0	1	1	$x = I_0' I_1'$
0	0	1	X	1	0	1	$y = I_0' I_1 + I_0' I_2'$
0	0	0	1	1	1	1	$(IST) = I_0 + I_1 + I_2 + I_3$
0	0	0	0	X	X	0	

care conditions. Input I_0 has the highest priority; so regardless of the values of other inputs, when this input is 1, the output generates an output $xy = 00$. I_1 has the next priority level. The output is 01 if $I_1 = 1$ provided that $I_0 = 0$, regardless of the values of the other two lower-priority inputs. The output for I_2 is generated only if higher-priority inputs are 0, and so on down the priority level. The interrupt status IST is set only when one or more inputs are equal to 1. If all inputs are 0, IST is cleared to 0 and the other outputs of the encoder are not used, so they are marked with don't-care conditions. This is because the vector address is not transferred to the CPU when $IST = 0$. The Boolean functions listed in the table specify the internal logic of the encoder. Usually, a computer will have more than four interrupt sources. A priority encoder with eight inputs, for example, will generate an output of three bits.

The output of the priority encoder is used to form part of the vector address for each interrupt source. The other bits of the vector address can be assigned any value. For example, the vector address can be formed by appending six zeros to the x and y outputs of the encoder. With this choice the interrupt vectors for the four I/O devices are assigned binary numbers 0, 1, 2, and 3.

Interrupt Cycle

The interrupt enable flip-flop *IEN* shown in Fig. 11-21 can be set or cleared by program instructions. When *IEN* is cleared, the interrupt request coming from *IST* is neglected by the CPU. The program-controlled *IEN* bit allows the programmer to choose whether to use the interrupt facility. If an instruction to clear *IEN* has been inserted in the program, it means that the user does not want his program to be interrupted. An instruction to set *IEN* indicates that the interrupt facility will be used while the current program is running. Most computers include internal hardware that clears *IEN* to 0 every time an interrupt is acknowledged by the processor.

At the end of each execute cycle the CPU checks *IEN* and the interrupt signal from *IST*. If either is equal to 0, control continues with the next fetch cycle. If both *IEN* and *IST* are equal to 1, the CPU goes to an interrupt cycle. During the interrupt cycle the CPU performs the following sequence of micro-operations:

$SP \leftarrow SP + 1$	Increment stack pointer
$M[SP] \leftarrow PC$	Push *PC* into stack
$INTACK \leftarrow 1$	Enable interrupt acknowledge
$PC \leftarrow VAD$	Transfer vector address to *PC*
$IEN \leftarrow 0$	Disable further interrupts
Go to fetch cycle	

The CPU pushes the return address from *PC* into the stack. It then acknowledges the interrupt by enabling the *INTACK* line. The priority interrupt unit responds by placing a unique interrupt vector into the CPU data bus. The CPU transfers the vector address into *PC* and clears *IEN* prior to going to the next fetch cycle. The instruction read from memory during the next fetch cycle will be the one located at the vector address.

Software Routines

A priority interrupt system is a combination of hardware and software techniques. So far we have discussed the hardware aspects of a priority interrupt system. The computer must also have software routines for servicing the interrupt requests and for controlling the interrupt hardware registers. Figure 11-22 shows the programs that must reside in memory for handling the interrupt system. Each device has its own service program that can be reached through a jump (JMP) instruction stored at the assigned vector address. The symbolic name of each routine represents the starting address of the service program. The stack shown in the diagram is used for storing the return address after each interrupt.

To illustrate with a specific example assume that the Teletype keyboard sets its interrupt bit while the CPU is executing the instruction in location 749 of the main program. At the end of the execute cycle, the computer goes to an interrupt cycle. It stores

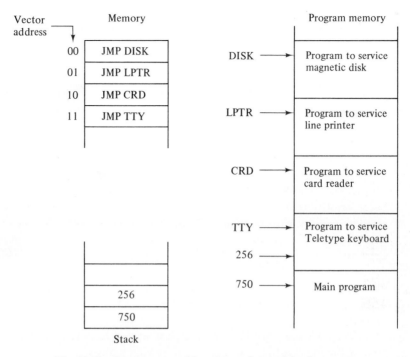

Fig. 11-22 Programs stored in memory for servicing interrupts.

the return address 750 in the stack and then accepts the vector address 00000011 from the bus and transfers it to *PC*. The instruction in location 11 is executed next, resulting in transfer of control to the TTY routine. Now suppose that the disk sets its interrupt bit when the CPU is executing the instruction at address 255 in the TTY program. Address 256 is pushed into the stack and control is transferred to the DISK service program. The last instruction in each routine is a return from interrupt instruction. When the disk service program is completed, the return instruction pops the stack and places 256 into *PC*. This returns control to the TTY routine to continue servicing the Teletype. At the end of the TTY program, the last instruction pops the stack and returns control to the main program at address 750. Thus, a higher-priority device can interrupt a lower-priority device. It is assumed that the time spent in servicing the high-priority interrupt is short compared to the transfer rate of the low-priority device so that no loss of information takes place.

Initial and Final Operations

Each interrupt service routine must have an initial and final set of operations for controlling the registers in the hardware interrupt system. Remember that the interrupt enable *IEN* is cleared at the end of an interrupt cycle. This flip-flop must be set again to enable higher priority interrupt requests, but not before lower priority interrupts are disabled. The initial sequence of each interrupt service routine must have instructions to control the interrupt hardware in the following manner.

1. Clear lower level mask register bits.
2. Clear interrupt status bit *IST*.
3. Save contents of processor registers.
4. Set interrupt enable bit *IEN*.
5. Proceed with service routine.

The lower level mask register bits (including the bit of the source that interrupted) are cleared to prevent these conditions from enabling the interrupt. Although lower priority interrupt sources are assigned to higher numbered bits in the mask register, priority can be changed if desired since the programmer can use any bit configuration he wishes for the mask register. The interrupt status bit must be cleared so it can be set again when a higher priority interrupt occurs. The contents of processor registers are saved because they may be needed by the program which has been interrupted after control returns to it. The interrupt enable *IEN* is then set to allow other (higher priority) interrupts and the computer proceeds to service the interrupt request.

The final sequence in each interrupt service routine must have instructions to control the interrupt hardware in the following manner:

1. Clear interrupt enable bit *IEN*.
2. Restore contents of processor registers.
3. Clear the bit in the interrupt register belonging to the source that has been serviced.
4. Set lower level priority bits in the mask register.
5. Restore return address into *PC* and set *IEN*.

The bit in the interrupt register belonging to the source of the interrupt must be cleared so it will be available again for the source to interrupt. The lower priority bit in the mask register (including the bit of the source being interrupted) are set so they can enable the interrupt. The return to the interrupted program is accomplished by restoring the return address to PC. Note that the hardware must be designed so that no interrupts occur while executing steps 2-5; otherwise the return address may be lost and the information in the mask and processor registers may be ambiguous if an interrupt is acknowledged while executing the operations in these steps. For this reason *IEN* is initially cleared and then set after the return address is transferred into *PC*.

The initial and final operations listed above are referred to as *overhead* operations or *housekeeping* chores. They are not part of the service program proper but are essential for processing interrupts. All overhead operations can be implemented by software. This is done by inserting the proper instructions at the begining and at the end of each service routine. Some of the overhead operations can be done automatically by the hardware. The contents of processor registers can be pushed into a stack by the hardware before branching to the service routine. Other initial and final operations can be assigned to the hardware. In this way, it is possible to reduce the time between receipt of an interrupt and the execution of the instruction that services the interrupt source.

11-6   INPUT-OUTPUT PROCESSOR (IOP)

Instead of having each interface communicate with the CPU, a computer may incorporate one or more external processors and assign them the task of communicating directly with all I/O devices. An input-output processor (IOP) may be classified as a processor with direct memory access that can communicate with I/O devices. In this configuration, the computer system can be divided into a memory unit and a number of processors comprised of the CPU and one or more IOPs. Each IOP takes care of input-output tasks, relieving the CPU from the housekeeping chores involved in I/O transfers. Processors that communicate directly with I/O devices are also called *data channels*. A processor that communicates with remote terminals over telephone wires and other communication media is called a *data communication processor*. Data communication processors are presented in Sec. 11-8.

The block diagram of a computer system with two different processors is shown in Fig. 11-23. The memory unit occupies a central position and can communicate with each processor by means of direct memory access. The CPU is responsible for processing data needed in the solution of computational tasks. The IOP provides a path for transfer of data between various peripheral devices and the memory unit. The CPU is usually assigned the task of initiating the I/O transfer. Once the IOP is initiated,

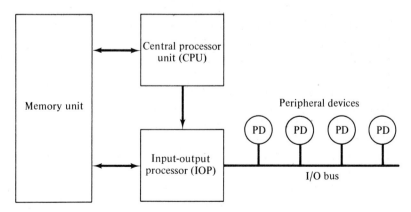

Fig. 11-23   Block diagram of a computer with I/O processor.

it operates independently of the CPU and continues to transfer data from external devices and memory.

The data format of peripheral devices differs from the memory and CPU data formats. The IOP must structure data words from many different sources. For example, it may be necessary to take four 8-bit characters from an input device and pack them into one 32-bit word before the transfer to memory. Data are gathered in the IOP at the device rate and bit capacity while CPU is executing its own program. After the input data is assembled into a memory word, it is transferred from the IOP directly into memory by stealing one memory cycle from the CPU. Similarly, an output word transferred from memory to the IOP is directed from the IOP to the output device at the device rate and bit capacity.

The communication between the IOP and the devices attached to it is similar to the I/O interface transfer as described in Secs. 11-2 and 11-3. Communication with the memory unit is by direct memory access as described in Sec. 11-4. The method by which the CPU and the IOP communicate depends on the level of sophistication included in the system. In a few very large computers, each processor is independent of all others and either can initiate an operation. In most computer systems, the CPU is assigned the task of initiating all operations but I/O instructions initiated in the CPU are executed in the IOP. CPU instructions provide operations to start an I/O transfer and also to test I/O status conditions to aid in making decisions on various I/O activities. The IOP, in turn, typically asks for CPU attention by means of an interrupt. It also responds to CPU requests by placing a status word in a prescribed memory location which can be examined by CPU instructions. When an I/O operation is desired, the CPU transfers one instruction to the IOP, indicating which peripheral is to be used and the location in memory where to find further instructions, and then leaves the transfer details to the IOP.

Instructions that are read from memory by an IOP are called *commands*, to distinguish them from instructions that are read from the CPU. Otherwise, an instruction and a command have similar functions. Command words are prepared by the user and stored in memory. The command words constitute the program for the IOP. The CPU informs the IOP where to find the command words in memory when it is time to execute the I/O program.

CPU-IOP Communication

The communication between CPU and IOP may take different forms depending on the particular computer considered. In most cases, the memory unit acts as a message center where each processor leaves information for the other. To appreciate the operation of a typical IOP, we will illustrate by a specific example the method by which the CPU and IOP can communicate. This is a simplified example that omits many operating details in order to provide an overview of basic concepts. Later in this section we investigate the CPU-IOP communication in two commercial computers.

The CPU initiates an I/O operation by transferring an I/O instruction to the IOP. A possible format for this instruction is shown in Fig. 11-24. The IOP receives the instruction word and proceeds to execute it. The instruction code has three fields:

1. An *operation code* field that specifies an operation. Some typical operations are listed in the figure.

2. A *device address* field that specifies the address of a particular I/O device attached to the IOP.

3. A *memory address* for the IOP to use when it responds to the CPU instruction.

The sequence of operations may be carried out as shown in the flow chart of Fig. 11-25. The CPU sends a test I/O instruction to the IOP. The IOP responds by inserting a status word in memory at the location specified by the memory address field of the instruction. The bits in the status word indicate the condition of the IOP and I/O device, such as IOP overload, device busy with another transfer, or device ready for I/O transfer.

Operation code	Device address	Memory address

Operation code	Operation
001	Test I/O
010	Start I/O
100	Read I/O status

Fig. 11-24   Example of CPU I/O instruction format.

The CPU refers to the status word in memory to decide what to do next. If all is in order, the CPU sends the instruction to start I/O transfer. The memory address received with this instruction tells the IOP where to find the first command word for the I/O operation. The command words consitute a program for the IOP. The program may consist of one word or many words.

The CPU can now continue with another program while the IOP is busy with the I/O program. Both refer to memory by means of DMA transfers. When the IOP terminates its program, it sends an interrupt request to the CPU. The CPU responds to the interrupt by issuing the instruction to read the status from the IOP. The IOP responds to the instruction by placing the contents of its status report into the memory location specified by the memory address field of the instruction. The status word indicates whether the transfer has been completed by the IOP or if any errors occurred during the transfer. From inspection of the bits in the status word, the CPU determines if the I/O operation was completed satisfactorily without any errors.

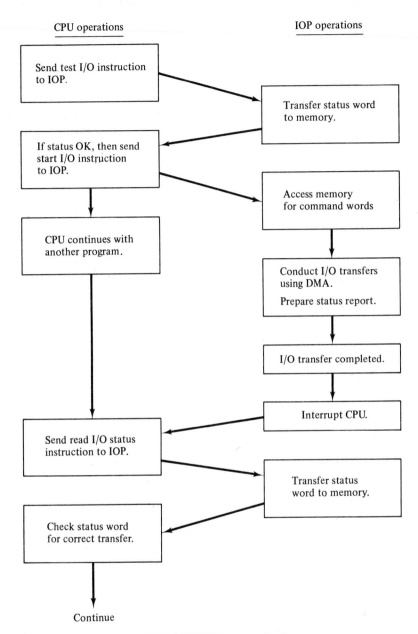

CPU operations

IOP operations

Send test I/O instruction
to IOP.

Transfer status word
to memory.

If status OK, then send
start I/O instruction
to IOP.

Access memory
for command words

CPU continues with
another program.

Conduct I/O transfers
using DMA.

Prepare status report.

I/O transfer completed.

Interrupt CPU.

Send read I/O status
instruction to IOP.

Transfer status
word to memory.

Check status word
for correct transfer.

Continue

Fig. 11-25 CPU-IOP communication.

IOP Operation

The command words specify the program that is executed in the IOP. The address of the command words is given to the I/O processor by the CPU with a *start I/O* instruction. A command word format usually specifies the memory buffer area associated with the operation and the actions to be taken during the transfer. A typical command word format is illustrated in Fig. 11-26. This command may be placed in one memory word (if all its bits fit into one word) or in two or more words. The command word has four fields:

1. The *buffer address* field specifies a memory address for the beginning of a buffer area in memory.

2. The *word count* field indicates the length of the buffer, i.e., the number of words it contains.

3. The *operation* field specifies the operation to be performed.

4. The *special* field specifies a particular function and is different for each I/O device.

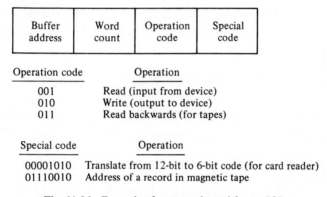

| Buffer address | Word count | Operation code | Special code |

Operation code	Operation
001	Read (input from device)
010	Write (output to device)
011	Read backwards (for tapes)

Special code	Operation
00001010	Translate from 12-bit to 6-bit code (for card reader)
01110010	Address of a record in magnetic tape

Fig. 11-26 Example of command word for an IOP.

The memory buffer is an area in memory where data from an input device are to be stored or where data are available for transfer to an output device. The operation field specifies an input, output, or other operations. The special field is unique for each device and may specify a variety of functions, a few of which are listed in the figure.

To continue with a specific example, assume that a CPU *start I/O* instruction specifies a device address of a card reader. The command word in the specified memory address contains a buffer address, a word count, a read operation code, and the special code for translating the 12-bit card code to an internal 6-bit code. The IOP first activates the card reader and goes to fulfill other I/O tasks while waiting for a signal from the card reader to indicate that it is ready to transfer information. When the ready signal is received, the IOP starts receiving data from cards. The 12-bit character code from each card column is converted to an internal 6-bit code by the IOP. Characters are then packed into a word length suitable for memory storage. When a word is ready to be stored, the IOP *steals* a memory cycle and stores the word in the assigned buffer. The buffer address is then incremented and the word count decremented, preparing the next word for storage. If the count reaches 0, the IOP stops receiving data; otherwise, data transfer continues until the card reader has no more cards.

While data are being transferred, the IOP prepares a status word that indicates all error conditions that occur. The status word may also contain the number of words in the buffer that have been used since there may not have been enough cards to fill the buffer. When the transfer terminates, the IOP sets the card reader interrupt bit in the interrupt register and interrupts the CPU. The CPU then asks for the status word and examines it to determine if the transfer was satisfactory.

When the IOP is reading information from a low-speed unit such as a card reader, the actual data transfer does not take much processor time. If it has several registers for addresses and counters, it can handle several units simultaneously. These units would actually be staggered in their transmission times. Several card readers and printers, for example, could each be transmitting characters at the same time.

The IOP provides the transfer of data between several I/O units and the memory while the CPU is processing its own program. The IOP and CPU are competing for the use of memory so the number of units that can be in operation is limited by the access time of the memory. It is not possible to saturate the memory by I/O devices on most systems, as the speed of most devices is much slower than memory. However, some very fast units, such as magnetic disks, can use an appreciable number of the available memory cycles. In that case, the speed of the CPU is decreased because it will often have to wait for the IOP to finish a memory reference before it can use the memory.

IBM 370 I/O Channel

The I/O processor in the IBM-370 computer is called a *channel*. A typical computer system configuration includes a number of channels with each channel attached to one or more I/O devices. There are three types of channels: multiplexer, selector, and block-multiplexer. The multiplexer channel can be connected to a number of slow- and medium-speed devices and is capable of operating with a number of I/O devices simultaneously. The selector channel is designed to handle one I/O operation at a time and is normally used to control one high-speed device. The block-multiplexer channel combines the features of both the multiplexer and selector channels. It provides a connection to a number of high-speed devices, but all I/O transfers are conducted with an entire block of data as compared to a multiplexer channel, which can transfer only one byte at a time.

The CPU communicates directly with the channels through dedicated control lines and indirectly through reserved storage areas in memory. Fig. 11-27 shows the word formats associated with the channel operation. The I/O instruction format has three fields: operation code, channel address, and device address. The computer system may have a number of channels and each is assigned an address. Similarly, each channel may be connected to several devices and each device is assigned an address. The operation code specifies one of eight I/O instructions. They are: start

Operation code	Channel address	Device address

(a) I/O instruction format

Key	Address	Status	Count

(b) Channel status word format

Command code	Data address	Flags	Count

(c) Channel command word format

Fig. 11-27 IBM-370 I/O related word formats.

I/O, start I/O fast release, test I/O, clear I/O, halt I/O, halt device, test channel, and store channel identification. The addressed channel responds to each of the I/O instructions and executes it. It also sets one of four condition codes in a processor register called PSW (processor status word). The CPU can check the condition code in the PSW to determine the result of the I/O operation. The meaning of the four condition codes is different for each I/O instruction. But, in general, they specify whether the channel or the device is busy, whether or not it is operational, whether interruptions are pending, if the I/O operation had started successfuly, and whether a status word was stored in memory by the channel.

The format of the channel status word is shown in Fig. 11-27(b). It is always stored in location 64 in memory. The key field is a protection mechanism used to prevent unauthorized access by one user to information that belongs to another user or to the operating system. The address field in the status word gives the address of the last command word used by the channel. The count field gives the residual count when the transfer was terminated. The count field will show zero if the transfer was completed successfully. The status field identifies the conditions in the device and the channel and any errors that occurred during the transfer.

The difference between the start I/O and start I/O fast release instructions is that the latter requires less CPU time for its execution. When the channel receives one of these two instructions, it refers to memory location 72 for the address of the first channel command word (CCW). The format of the channel command word is shown in Fig. 11-27(c). The data address field specifies the first address of a memory buffer and the count field gives the number of bytes involved in the transfer. The command field specifies an I/O operation and the flag bits provide additional information for the channel. The command field corresponds to an operation code that specifies one of six basic types of I/O operations:

1. *Write.*   Transfer data from memory to I/O device.
2. *Read.*   Transfer data from I/O device to memory.
3. *Read backwards.*   Read magnetic tape with tape moving backwards.
4. *Control.*   Used to initiate an operation not involving transfer of data, such as rewinding of tape or positioning a disk-access mechanism.
5. *Sense.*   Informs the channel to transfer its channel status word to memory location 64.
6. *Transfer in channel.*   Used instead of a jump instruction. Here the data address field specifies the address of the next command word to be executed by the channel.

An example of a channel program is shown in Table 11-2. It consists of three command words. The first causes a transfer into a magnetic tape of 60 bytes from

TABLE 11-2   IBM-370 Channel Program Example

Command	Address	Flags	Count
Write tape	4000	100000	60
Write tape	6000	010000	20
Write tape	3000	000000	40

memory starting at address 4000. The next two command words perform a similar function with a different portion of memory and byte count. The six flags in each control word specify certain interrelations between the command words. The first flag is set to 1 in the first command word to specify "data chaining." It results in combining the 60 bytes from the first command word with the 20 bytes of its successor into one record of 80 bytes. The 80 bytes are written on tape without any separation or gaps even though two memory sections were used. The second flag is set to 1 in the second command word to specify "command chaining." It informs the channel that the next command word will use the same I/O device, in this case, the tape. The channel informs the tape unit to start inserting a record gap on the tape and proceeds to read the next command word from memory. The 40 bytes of the third command word are then written on tape as a separate record. When all the flags are equal to zero, it signifies the end of I/O operations for the particular I/O device.

A memory map showing all pertinent information for I/O processing is illustrated in Fig. 11-28. The operation begins when the CPU program encounters a start I/O instruction. The IOP then goes to memory location 72 to obtain a channel address word. This word contains the starting address of the I/O channel program. The channel then proceeds to execute the program specified by the channel command

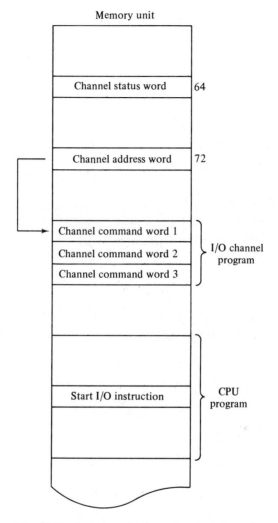

Fig. 11-28 Location of information in memory for
I/O operations in the IBM-370.

words. The channel constructs a status word during the transfer and stores it in
location 64. Upon interruption, the CPU can refer to memory location 64 for the
status word.

Intel 8089 IOP

The Intel 8089 I/O processor is contained in a 40-pin integrated circuit package.
Within the 8089 are two independent units called *channels*. Each channel combines
the general characteristics of a processor unit with those of a direct memory access

controller. The 8089 is designed to function as an IOP in a microcomputer system where the Intel 8086 microprocessor is used as the CPU. The 8086 CPU initiates an I/O operation by building a message in memory that describes the function to be performed. The 8089 IOP reads the message from memory, carries out the operation, and notifies the CPU when it has finished.

In contrast to the IBM-370 channel, which has only six basic I/O commands, the 8089 IOP has 50 basic instructions that can operate on individual bits, on bytes, or 16-bit words. The IOP can execute programs in a manner similar to a CPU except that the instruction set is specifically chosen to provide efficient input-output processing. The instruction set includes general data transfer instructions, basic arithmetic and logic operations, conditional and unconditional branch operations, and subroutine call and return capabilities. The set also includes special instructions to initiate DMA transfers and issue an interrupt request to the CPU. It provides efficient data transfer between any two components attached to the system bus, such as I/O to memory, memory to memory, or I/O to I/O.

A microcomputer system using the Intel 8086/8089 pair of integrated circuits is shown in Fig. 11-29. The 8086 functions as the CPU and the 8089 as the IOP. The two units share a common memory through a bus controller connected to a system bus, which is called a "multibus" by Intel. The IOP uses a local bus to communicate with various interface units connected to I/O devices. The CPU communicates with the IOP by enabling the *channel attention* line. The *select* line is used

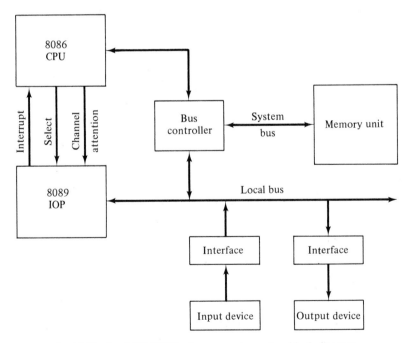

Fig. 11-29   Intel 8086/8089 microcomputer system block diagram.

by the CPU to select one of two channels in the 8089. The IOP gets the attention of the CPU by sending an interrupt request.

The CPU and IOP communicate with each other by writing messages for one another in system memory. The CPU prepares the message area and signals the IOP by enabling the channel attention line. The IOP reads the message, performs the required I/O functions, and executes the appropriate channel program. When the channel has completed its program, it issues an interrupt request to the CPU.

The communication scheme consists of program sections called "blocks," which are stored in memory as shown in Fig. 11-30. Each block contains control and parameter information as well as an address pointer to its successor block. The address of the control block is passed to each IOP channel during initialization. The busy flag indicates whether the IOP is busy or ready to perform a new I/O operation. The CCW (channel command word) is specified by the CPU to indicate the type of operation required from the IOP. The CCW in the 8089 does not have the same meaning as the command word in the IBM channel. The CCW here is more like an I/O instruction that specifies an operation for the IOP, such as: start operation, suspend operation, resume operation, and halt I/O program. The parameter block contains variable data that the IOP program must use in carrying out its task. The task block contains the actual program to be executed in the IOP.

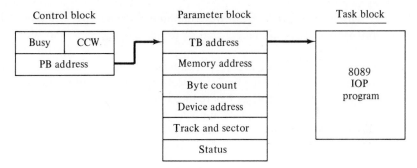

Fig. 11-30 Location of information in memory for I/O operations in the Intel 8086/8089 microcomputer system.

The CPU and IOP work together through the control and parameter blocks. The CPU obtains use of the shared memory after checking the busy flag to ensure that the IOP is available. The CPU then fills in the information in the parameter block and writes a "start operation" command in the CCW. After the communication blocks have been set up, the CPU enables the channel attention signal to inform the IOP to start its I/O operation. The CPU then continues with another program. The IOP responds to the channel attention signal by placing the address of the control block into its program counter. The IOP refers to the control block and sets the busy flag. It then checks the operation in the CCW. The PB (parameter block) address and TB (task block) address are then transferred into internal IOP registers. The IOP starts executing the program in the task block using the information in the parameter block. The entries in the parameter block depend on the I/O device. The parameters listed in Fig. 11-30 are suitable for data transfer to or from a magnetic disk. The memory address specifies the beginning address of a memory buffer. The byte count gives the number of bytes to be transferred. The device address specifies the particular I/O device to be used. The track and sector numbers locate the data on the disk. When the I/O operation is completed, the IOP stores its status bits in the status word location of the parameter block and interrupts the CPU. The CPU can refer to the status word to check if the transfer has been completed satisfactorily.

11-7 MULTIPROCESSOR SYSTEM ORGANIZATION

A multiprocessor system is an interconnection of two or more CPUs sharing common memory and input-output equipment. The term "processor" in multiprocessor can mean either a central processor unit (CPU) or an input-output processor (IOP). However, a system with a single CPU and one or more IOPs is usually not included in the definition of a multiprocessor system unless the IOP has computational facilities comparable to a CPU. As it is most commonly defined, a multiprocessor system implies the existence of multiple CPUs, although usually there will be one or more IOPs as well.

Although a few large-scale computers include two or more CPUs in their overall system, it is the emergence of the microprocessor that has been the major motivation for multiple processor systems. The fact that microprocessors take very little physical space and are very inexpensive brings about the feasibility of interconnecting a large number of microprocessors into one composite system. Large-scale integrated circuit technology has reduced the cost of computer components to such a low level that the concept of applying multiple processors to meet system performance requirements has become an attractive design possibility.

The benefit derived from a multiprocessor organization is an improved system performance. It is achieved through partitioning an overall function into a number of tasks that each processor can handle individually. System tasks may be allocated to special-purpose processors whose design is optimized to perform certain types of processing efficiently. An example is a computer system where one processor performs the computations for an industrial process control while others monitor and control the various parameters, such as temperature and flow rate. Another example is a computer where one processor performs high-speed floating-point mathematical computations and another takes care of routine data processing tasks. Performance can be improved also if a program can be decomposed into parallel executable tasks. The system function can be distributed among separate concurrently executing processors operating in parallel, thus reducing the overall execution time.

Multiprocessing improves the reliability of the system so that a failure or error in one part has a limited effect on the rest of the system. If a fault causes one processor to fail, a second processor can be assigned to perform the functions of the disabled processor. The system as a whole can continue to function correctly with perhaps some loss in efficiency.

Interconnection between Processors

The components that form a multiprocessor system are CPUs, IOPs connected to input-output devices, and a memory unit that may be partitioned into a number of separate modules. The interconnection between the components can have different physical configurations, depending on the number of transfer paths that are available between the processors and memory. Four interconnection schemes that have been used are:

1. Multiport memory.
2. Crossbar switch.
3. Time-shared common bus.
4. Dual-bus structure.

A multiport memory system employs separate buses between each memory module and each CPU or IOP. This is shown in Fig. 11-31 for two CPUs, two IOPs,

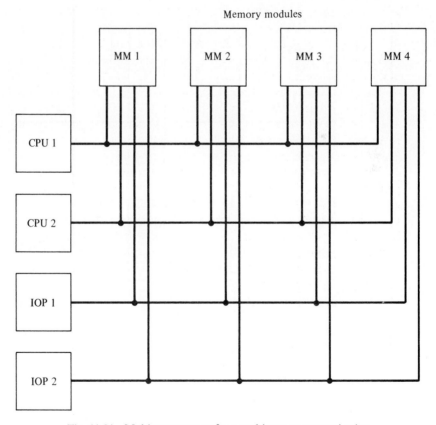

Memory modules

Fig. 11-31 Multiport memory for a multiprocessor organization.

and four memory modules (MM). Each processor bus is connected to each memory module. A processor bus consists of the address, data, and control lines required to communicate with memory. The module is said to have four ports and each port accommodates one of the buses. The module must have internal control logic to determine which port will have access to memory at any given time. Memory access conflicts are resolved by assigning fixed priorities to each memory port. The priority for memory access associated with each processor may be established by the physical port position that its bus occupies in each module. Thus, IOP 2 would have priority over IOP 1 and IOP 1 will have priority over CPU 2 and with CPU 1 having the lowest priority. The advantage of the multiport memory organization is the high transfer rate that can be achieved because of the multiple paths between processors and memory. The disadvantage is that it requires expensive memory control logic and a large number of cables and connectors.

The crossbar switch organization consists of a number of crosspoints that are placed at intersections between processor buses and memory module paths. Figure 11-32 shows a crossabar switch interconnection between two CPUs, two IOPs,

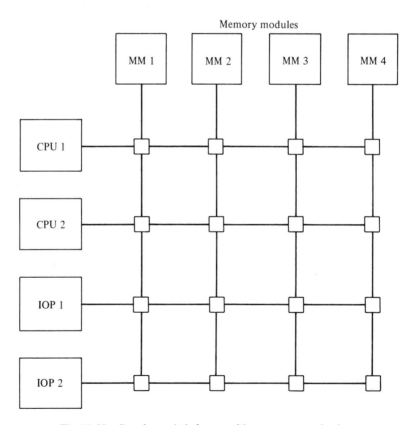

Fig. 11-32   Crossbar switch for a multiprocessor organization.

and four memory modules. The small squares in each crosspoint is a switch that determines the path from a processor to a memory module. Each switch point has control logic to set up the transfer path between a processor and memory. It examines the address that is placed in the bus to determine whether its particular module is being addressed. It also resolves multiple requests for access to the same memory module on a predetermined priority basis. A crossbar switch organization supports simultaneous transfers from all memory modules. However, the hardware required to implement the switch can become quite large and complex.

The common bus multiprocessor system consists of a number of processors connected through a common path to a memory unit. A time-shared common bus for four processors is shown in Fig. 11-33. Only one processor can communicate with the memory at any given time. Transfer operations are conducted by the processor that is in control of the bus at the time. Any other processor wishing to initiate a transfer must first determine the availability status of the bus, and only after the bus becomes available can the processor address the memory unit to initiate the transfer. The system may exhibit memory access conflicts since one common bus is shared by all processors. Memory contention must be resolved with a bus controller that establishes priorities among the requesting units.

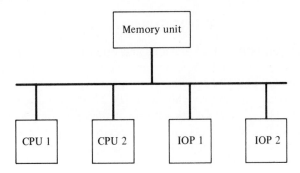

Fig. 11-33   Time-shared common bus multiprocessor organization.

A single common bus system is restricted to one transfer at a time. This means that when one processor is communicating with the memory, all other processors are either busy with internal operations or must be idle waiting for the bus. The processors in the system can be kept busy more often through the implementation of a dual-bus structure as depicted in Fig. 11-34. Here we have a number of local buses each connected to its own local memory and to one or more processors. Each local bus may be connected to a CPU, an IOP, or any combination of processors. A system bus controller links each local bus to a common system bus. The I/O devices connected to the local IOP and the local memory as well are available to the local processors only. The memory connected to the common system bus is shared by all processors. If an IOP is connected directly to the system bus, the I/O devices attached to it may be made available to all processors. Only one processor can com-

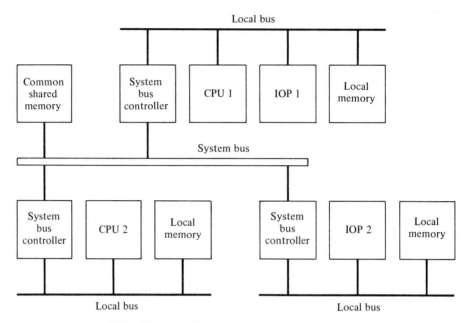

Fig. 11-34 Dual-bus multiprocessor organization.

municate with the shared memory and other common resources through the system bus at any given time. The other processors are kept busy communicating with their local memory and I/O devices.

Although the system shown in Fig. 11-34 qualifies as a multiprocessor system, it can be classified more correctly as a multiple-computer system. This is because a CPU, IOP, and memory, when connected together with a local bus, constitute a computer system in their own right. This type of multiprocessor organization is the one most commonly employed in the design of multiple-microprocessor systems.

Interprocessor Communication

The various processors in a multiprocessor system must be provided with a facility for communicating with each other. A communication path can be established through common input-output channels. However, the most common procedure is to set aside a portion of memory which is accessible to all processors. The primary use of the common memory is to act as a message center similar to a mailbox, where each processor can leave messages for other processors and pick up messages intended for it.

The sending processor structures a request, a message, or a procedure, and places it in the memory mailbox. Status bits residing in common memory are generally used to indicate the condition of the mailbox, whether it has meaningful information and for which processor intended. The receiving processor can check the mailbox periodically to determine if there are valid messages for it. The response time of this

458

procedure can be time consuming since a processor will recognize requests only when it does its next polling of messages. A better procedure is for the sending processor to alert the receiving processor directly by means of an interrupt signal. This can be accomplished through a software-initiated interprocessor interrupt. It is done by an instruction in the program of one processor which, when executed, produces an external hardware interrupt signal in a second processor. This alerts the interrupted processor of the fact that a new message was inserted in memory by the interrupting processor.

In addition to a shared memory, a multiprocessor system would have other shared resources. For example, a disk storage unit connected to an IOP may be available to all CPUs. This provides a facility for sharing of systems programs stored in a magnetic disk. A communication path between two CPUs can be established also through a link between two IOPs associated with two different CPUs. This type of link allows each CPU to treat the other as an I/O device so that I/O operations can be used to transfer information between the local memories of the two CPUs.

A multiprocessor system that employs a shared memory interconnection and uses common I/O system resources is said to be a *tightly coupled* system. This is characteristic of a multiprocessor system that has all its major components, such as CPUs, IOPs, and I/O devices, in close proximity. In contrast, a *loosely coupled* system is a multicomputer interconnection with each computer communicating with all others through remote communication lines. The systems considered in this section are classified as tightly coupled. The communication between loosely coupled computers over communication lines is based on the use of protocols as discussed in Sec. 11-8.

Bus Arbitration

Each processor in a multiprocessor system requests access to common memory or other common resources through a common bus system. If no other processor is currently utilizing the common bus, the requesting processor may be granted access immediately. However, the requesting processor must wait if another processor is currently utilizing the system bus. Furthermore, other processors may also request the system bus at the same time. Arbitration must then be performed to resolve this multiple contention for the shared resources. The arbitration logic would be part of the system bus controller placed between the local bus and the system common bus as shown in Fig. 11-34.

Arbitration procedures service all processor requests on the basis of established priorities. The bus priority arbitration technique bears a strong resemblance to the priority interrupt logic discussed in Sec. 11-5. A hardware bus priority resolving technique can be established by means of a serial or parallel connection of the units requesting control of the system bus.

The serial priority resolving technique is obtained from a daisy-chain connection of bus arbiters as shown in Fig. 11-35. It is assumed that each processor has its own bus arbiter logic. The priority out (*PO*) of each arbiter is connected to the priority in (*PI*) of the next-lower-priority arbiter. The *PI* of the highest-priority unit is main-

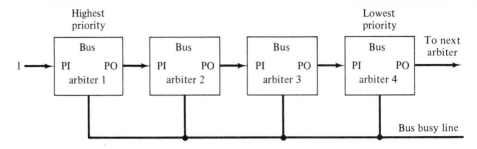

Fig. 11-35 Serial (daisy chain) arbitration.

tained at a logic 1 value. The highest-priority unit in the system will always receive access to the system bus when it requires it. The *PO* output for a particular arbiter is equal to 1 if its *PI* input is equal to 1 and the processor associated with the arbiter logic is not requesting control of the bus. This is the way that priority is passed to the next unit in the chain. If the processor requests control of the bus and the corresponding arbiter finds its *PI* input equal to 1, it sets its *PO* output to 0. Lower-priority arbiters receive a 0 in *PI* and generate a 0 in *PO*. Thus, the processor whose arbiter has a *PI* = 1 and *PO* = 0 is the one that is given control of the system bus.

A processor may be in the middle of a bus operation when a higher-priority processor requests the bus. The lower-priority processor must complete its bus operation before it relinquishes control of the bus. The bus busy line shown in Fig. 11-35 provides a mechanism for an orderly transfer of control. The busy line comes from open-collector circuits in each unit and provides a wire-OR logic connection. When an arbiter receives control of the bus (because its *PI* = 1 and *PO* = 0), it examines the busy line. If the line is inactive, it means that no other processor is using the bus. The arbiter enables the busy line and its processor takes control of the bus. However, if the arbiter finds the busy line active, it means that another processor is currently using the bus. The arbiter keeps examining the busy line while the lower-priority processor that lost control of the bus completes its operation. When busy returns to its inactive state, the higher-priority arbiter enables the busy line and its corresponding processor can then conduct the required bus transfers.

The parallel bus arbitration technique uses an external priority encoder and a decoder as shown in Fig. 11-36. Each bus arbiter in the parallel scheme has a bus request output line and a bus acknowledge input line. Each arbiter enables the request line when its processor is requesting access to the system bus. The processor takes control of the bus if its acknowledge input line is enabled. The bus busy line provides an orderly transfer of control, as in the daisy-chain case.

Fig. 11-36 shows the request lines from four arbiters going into a 4 × 2 priority encoder. The output of the encoder generates a 2-bit code which represents the highest-priority unit among those requesting the bus. The truth table of the priority encoder is presented in Table 11-1 (Sec. 11-5). The 2-bit code drives a 2 × 4 decoder which enables the proper acknowledge line to grant bus access to the highest-priority unit. The circuit of the decoder is shown in Fig. 2-8.

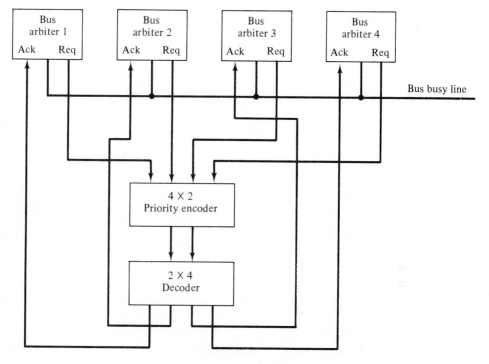

Fig. 11-36 Parallel arbitration.

Mutual Exclusion

A properly functioning multiprocessor system must provide a mechanism that will guarantee an orderly access to shared memory and other shared resources. This is necessary to protect data from being changed simultaneously by two or more processors. This mechanism has been termed mutual exclusion. Mutual exclusion must be provided in a multiprocessor system to enable one processor to exclude or lock out access to a share resource by other processors when it is in a critical program section. A *critical program section* is a program sequence that, once begun, must complete execution before another processor accesses the same shared resource.

A binary variable called *semaphore* is often used to indicate whether or not a processor is executing a critical program section. A semaphore is a software-controlled flag that is stored in a memory location that all processors can access. When the semaphore is equal to 1, it means that a processor is executing a critical program, so the shared memory is not available to other processors. When the semaphore is equal to 0, the shared memory is available to any requesting processor. Processors that share the same memory segment agree by convention not to use the memory segment unless the semaphore is equal to 0, indicating that memory is available. They also agree to set the semaphore to 1 when they are executing a critical program section and to clear it to 0 when they are finished.

Testing and setting the semaphore is itself a critical operation and must be performed as a single indivisible operation. If it is not, two or more processors may test the semaphore simultaneously and then each set it, allowing them to enter a critical program section at the same time. This action would allow simultaneous execution of critical programs, which can result in erroneous initialization of control parameters and a loss of essential information.

A semaphore can be initialized by means of a *test and set* instruction in conjuction with a hardware *lock* mechanism. A hardware lock is a processor-generated signal which serves to prevent other processors from using the system bus as long as the signal is active. The test and set instruction tests and sets a semaphore and activates the lock mechanism during the time that the instruction is being executed. This prevents other processors from changing the semaphore between the time that the processor is testing it and the time that it is setting it. Assume that the semaphore is a bit in the least significant position of a memory word whose address is symbolized by SEM. Let the mnemonic TSL designate the "test and set while locked" operation. Then the instruction

$$\text{TSL} \qquad \text{SEM}$$

will be executed in two memory cycles without interference as follows:

$$R \leftarrow M[SEM] \qquad \text{Test semaphore}$$
$$M[SEM] \leftarrow 1 \qquad \text{Set semaphore}$$

The semaphore is tested by transferring its value into a processor register R and then it is set to 1. The value in R determines what to do next. If the processor finds that $R = 1$, it knows that the semaphore was originally set. (The fact than R is set again does not change the semaphore value.) That means that another processor is executing a critical program section, so the processor that checked the semaphore does not access the shared memory. If $R = 0$, it means that the common memory (or the shared resource that the semaphore represents) is available. The semaphore is set to 1 to prevent other processors from accessing memory. The processor can now execute the critical program section. The last instruction in the program must clear location SEM to zero to release the shared resource to other processors.

Note that the lock signal must be active during the execution of the test and set instruction. It does not have to be active once the semaphore is set. Thus, the lock mechanism prevents other processors from accessing memory while the semaphore is being set. The semaphore itself, when set, prevents other processors from accessing shared memory while one processor is executing a critical program section.

11-8 DATA COMMUNICATION PROCESSOR

A data communication processor is an I/O processor that distributes and collects data from many remote terminals connected through telephone and other communication lines. It is a specialized I/O processor designed to communicate directly with data communication networks. A communication network may consist of any of a wide variety of devices such as teletypewriters, printers, interactive display devices, digital sensors, or a remote computing facility. With the use of a data communication processor, the computer can service fragment of each network demand in an interspersed manner and thus have the apparent behavior of serving many users at once. In this way the computer is able to operate efficiently in a time-sharing environment.

The most striking difference between an I/O processor and a data communication processor is in the way the processor communicates with the I/O devices. An I/O processor communicates with the peripherals through a common I/O bus which is comprised of many data and control lines. All peripherals share the common bus and use it to transfer information to and from the I/O processor. A data communication processor communicates with each terminal through a single pair of wires. Both data and control information are transferred in a serial fashion with the result that the transfer rate is much slower. The task of the data communication processor is to transmit and collect digital information to and from each terminal, determine if the information is data or control and respond to all requests according to predetermined established procedures. The processor, obviously, must also communicate with the CPU and memory in the same manner as any I/O processor.

The way that remote terminals are connected to a data communication processor is via telephone lines or other public or private communication facilities. Since telephone lines were originally designed for voice communication and computers communicate in terms of digital signals, some form of conversion must be used. The converters are called *data sets*, *acoustic couplers*, or *modems* (from modulator-demodulator). A modem converts digital signals into audio tones to be transmitted over telephone lines and also converts audio tones from the line to digital signals for machine use. Various modulation schemes as well as different grades of communication media and transmission speeds are used.

A block diagram showing the various units that are connected to a data communication processor is presented in Fig. 11-37. Each remote terminal (or a group of terminals) is connected to the communication line via a modem. The other side of the line is also connected to a modem. The two modems receive and transmit audio tones along the line but convert them to digital signals for the terminal and interface. The interface converts characters from serial to parallel and vice-versa as they are transferred to and from the processor. The data communication processor scans the interface units in order to send or receive binary information. This scan is called *multiplexing* and is analogous to a rotary switch rotating at a high speed while sampling each interface in sequence. The data communication processor comes with an extensive bit comparison logic which is used during input operations to examine the incoming data stream. The binary information received by the processor is assembled into words and transferred into the memory unit or a magnetic disk for storage. The data communication processor prepares outgoing data for transmission by inserting control and address bits into a message according to established procedures.

A line may be connected to a synchronous or asynchronous interface, depending on the transmission method of the remote terminal. An asynchronous interface receives serial data with start and stop bits in each character as shown in Fig. 11-11.

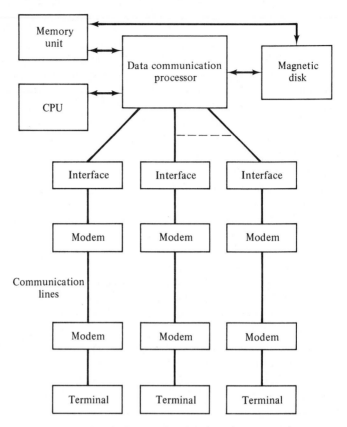

Fig. 11-37 Block diagram showing the units connected to a data communication processor.

This type of interface is similar to the asynchronous communication interface unit presented in Fig. 11-12.

Synchronous transmission does not use start-stop bits to frame characters and therefore makes more efficient use of the communication link. High-speed devices use synchronous transmission to realize this efficiency. The modems used in synchronous transmission have internal clocks that are set to the frequency that bits are being transmitted in the communication line. For proper operation, it is required that the clocks in the transmitter and receiver modems remain synchronized at all times. The communication line, however, contains only the data bits from which the clock information must be extracted. Frequency synchronization is achieved by the receiving modem from the signal transitions that occur in the received data. Any frequency shift that may occur between the transmitter and receiver clocks is continuously adjusted by maintaining the receiver clock at the frequency of the incoming bit stream. The modem transfers the received data together with the clock to the interface unit. The interface or terminal on the transmitter side also uses the clock information from its modem. In this way, the same bit rate is maintained in both transmitter and receiver.

Contrary to asynchronous transmission, where each character can be sent separately with its own start and stop bits, synchronous transmission must send a continuous message in order to maintain synchronism. The message consists of a group of bits transmitted sequentially as a block of data. The entire block is transmitted with special control characters at the beginning and end of the block. The control characters at the beginning of the block supply the information needed to separate the incoming bits into individual characters.

One of the functions of the data communication processor is to check for transmission errors. An error can be detected by checking the parity in each received character. Another procedure used in asynchronous terminals involving a human operator is to *echo* the character. The character transmitted from the keyboard to the computer is recognized by the processor and retransmitted to the terminal printer. The operator would realize that an error occurred during transmission if the character printed is not the same as the character whose key he has struck.

In synchronous transmission, where an entire block of characters is transmitted, each character has a parity bit for the receiver to check. After the entire block is sent, the transmitter sends one more character that constitutes a parity over the length of the message. This character is called a longitudinal redundancy check (LRC) and is the accumulation of the exclusive-OR of all transmitted characters. The receiving station calculates the LRC as it receives characters and compares it with the transmitted LRC. The calculated and received LRC should be equal for error-free messages. If the receiver finds an error in the transmitted block, it informs the sender to retransmit the same block once again. Another method used for checking errors in transmission is the cyclic redundancy check (CRC). This is a polynomial code obtained from the message bits by passing them through a feedback shift register containing a number of exclusive-OR gates. This type of code is suitable for detecting burst errors occurring in the communication channel.

Data can be transmitted between two points in three different modes: simplex, half duplex, or full duplex. A *simplex* line carries information in one direction only. This mode is seldom used in data communication because the receiver cannot communicate with the transmitter to indicate the occurrence of errors. Examples of simplex transmission are radio and television broadcasting.

A *half-duplex* transmission system is one that is capable of transmitting in both directions but data can be transmitted in only one direction at a time. A pair of wires is needed for this mode. A common situation is for one modem to act as the transmitter and the other as the receiver. When transmission in one direction is completed, the role of the modems is reversed to enable transmission in the reverse direction. The time required to switch a half-duplex line from one direction to the other is called the turnaround time.

A *full-duplex* transmission can send and receive data in both directions simultaneously. This can be achieved by means of a four-wire link, with a different pair of wires dedicated to each direction of transmission. Alternatively, a two-wire circuit can support full-duplex communication if the frequency spectrum is subdivided into two nonoverlapping frequency bands to create separate receive and transmit channels in the same physical pair of wires.

The communication lines, modems, and other equipment used in the transmission of information between two or more stations is called a *data link*. The orderly transfer of information in a data link is accomplished by means of a *protocol*. A data link control protocol is a set of rules that are followed by interconnecting computers and terminals to ensure the orderly transfer of information. The purpose of a data link protocol is to establish and terminate a connection between two stations, to identify the sender and receiver, to ensure that all messages are passed correctly without errors, and to handle all control functions involved in a sequence of data transfers. Protocols are divided into two major categories according to the message framing technique used. These are character-oriented protocol and bit-oriented protocol.

Character-Oriented Protocol

The character-oriented protocol is based on the binary code of a character set. The code most commonly used is ASCII (American Standard Code for Information Interchange). It is a 7-bit code with an eighth bit used for parity. The code has 128 characters, of which 95 are graphic characters and 33 are control characters. The graphic characters include the upper- and lowercase letters, the ten numerals, and a variety of special symbols. A partial list of the ASCII graphic characters can be found in Table 3-4. The control characters are used for the purpose of routing data, arranging the test in a desired format, and for the layout of the printed page. The characters that control the transmission are called *communication control* characters. These characters are listed in Table 11-3. Each character has a 7-bit code and is

TABLE 11-3 ASCII Communication Control Characters

Code	Symbol	Meaning	Function
0010110	SYN	Synchronous idle	Establishes synchronism
0000001	SOH	Start of heading	Heading of block message
0000010	STX	Start of text	Precedes block of text
0000011	ETX	End of text	Terminates block of text
0000100	EOT	End of transmission	Concludes transmission
0000110	ACK	Acknowledge	Affirmative acknowledgement
0010101	NAK	Negative acknowledge	Negative acknowledgement
0000101	ENQ	Inquiry	Inquire if terminal is on
0010111	ETB	End of transmission block	End of block of data
0010000	DLE	Data link escape	Special control character

referred to by a three-letter symbol. The role of each character in the control of data transmission is stated briefly in the function column of the table.

The SYN character serves as synchronizing agent between the transmitter and receiver. When the 7-bit ASCII code is used with an odd parity bit in the most significant position, the assigned sync character has the 8-bit code 00010110 which has the property that, upon circular shifting, it repeats itself only after a full 8-bit cycle. When the transmitter starts sending 8-bit characters, it sends a few sync characters first and then sends the actual message. The initial continuous string of bits accepted by the receiver is checked for a sync character. In other words, with each clock pulse, the receiver checks the last eight bits received. If they do not match the bits of the sync character, the receiver accepts the next bit, rejects the previous high-order bit, and again checks the last eight bits received for a sync character. This is repeated after each clock pulse and bit received until a sync character is recognized. Once a sync character is detected, the receiver has framed a character. From here on the receiver counts every eight bits and accepts them as a single character. Usually, the receiver checks two consecutive sync characters to remove any doubt that the first sync character did not occur as a result of a noise signal on the line. Moreover, when the transmitter is idle and does not have any message characters to send, it sends a continous string of sync characters. The receiver recognizes all sync characters as a condition for synchronizing the line and goes into a synchronous idle state. In this state, the two units maintain bit and character synchronism even though no meaningful information is communicated.

Messages are transmitted through the data link with an established format consisting of a header field, a text field, and an error-checking field. A typical message format for a character-oriented protocol is shown in Fig. 11-38. The two sync characters assure proper synchronization at the start of the message. Following the sync characters is the header, which starts with an SOH (start of heading) character. The header consists of address and control information. The STX character terminates the header and signifies the beginning of the text transmission. The text portion of the message is variable in length and may contain any ASCII characters except the communication control characters. The text field is terminated with the ETX character. The last field is a block check character (BCC) used for error checking. It is usually either a longitudinal redundancy check (LRC) or a cyclic redundancy check (CRC).

The receiver accepts the message and calculates its own BCC. If the BCC transmitted does not agree with the BCC calculated by the receiver, the receiver responds with a negative acknowledge (NAK) character. The message is then retransmitted and checked again. Retransmission will be typically attempted serveral times before it is assumed that the line is faulty. When the transmitted BCC matches the one calculated by the receiver, the response is a positive acknowledgment using the ACK character.

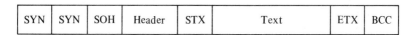

Fig. 11-38   Typical message format for character-oriented protocol.

Transmission Example

In order to appreciate the function of a data communication processor, let us illustrate by a specific example the method by which a terminal and the processor communicate. The communication with the memory unit and CPU is similar to any I/O processor.

A typical message that might be sent from a terminal to the processor is listed in Table 11-4. A look at this message reveals that there are a number of control characters used for message formation. Each character, including the control characters, is transmitted serially as an 8-bit binary code which consists of the 7-bit ASCII code plus an odd parity bit in the eighth most signifiicant position. The two SYN characters are used to synchronize the receiver and transmitter. The heading

TABLE **11-4**   Typical Transmission from a Terminal to Processor

Code	Symbol	Comments
0001 0110	SYN	First sync character
0001 0110	SYN	Second sync character
0000 0001	SOH	Start of heading
0101 0100	T	Address of terminal is T4
0011 0100	4	
0000 0010	STX	Start of text transmission
0101 0010		
0100 0101	request	Text sent is a request to respond with the balance of
.	balance	account number 1234
.	of account	
.	No. 1234	
1011 0011		
0011 0100		
1000 0011	ETX	End of text transmission
0111 0000	LRC	Longitudinal parity character

starts with the SOH character and continues with two characters that specify the address of the terminal. In this particular example, the address is T4, but in general it can have any set of two or more graphic characters. The STX character terminates the heading and signifies the beginning of the text transmission. The text data of concern here is "request balance of account number 1234." The individual characters for this message are not listed in the table because they will take too much space. It must be realized, however, that each character in the message has an 8-bit code and that each bit is transmitted serially. The ETX control character signifies the termination of the text characters. The next character following ETX is a logitudinal redundancy check (LRC). Each bit in this character is a parity bit calculated from all the bits in the same column in the code section of the table.

The data communication processor receives this message and proceeds to analyze it. It recognizes terminal T4 and stores the text associated with the message. While receiving the characters, the processor checks the parity in each character and also computes the longitudinal parity. The computed LRC is compared with the LRC character received. If the two match, a positive acknowledgment (ACK) is sent back to the terminal. If a mismatch exists, a negative acknowledgment (NAK) is returned to the terminal, which would initiate a retransmission of the same block.

If the processor finds the message without errors, it transfers the message into memory and interrupts the CPU. When the CPU acknowledges the interrupt, it analyzes the message and prepares a text message for responding to the request. The CPU sends an instruction to the data communication processor to send the message to the terminal.

A typical response from processor to terminal is listed in Table 11-5. After two SYN characters, the processor acknowledges the previous message with an ACK

TABLE 11-5   Typical Transmission from Processor to Terminal

Code	Symbol	Comments
0001 0110	SYN	First sync character
0001 0110	SYN	Second sync character
1000 0110	ACK	Processor acknowledges previous message
0001 0110	SYN	Line is idling
.	.	
.	.	
.	.	
0001 0110	SYN	Line is idling
0000 0001	SOH	Start of heading
0101 0100	T	Address of terminal is T4
0011 0100	4	
0000 0010	STX	Start of text transmission
1100 0010		
1100 0001	balance	Text sent is a response from the computer giving the
.	is	balance of account
.	$100.00	
.		
.		
1011 0000		
1000 0011	ETX	End of text transmission
1101 0101	LRC	Longitudinal parity character

character. The line continues to idle with SYN character waiting for the response to come. The message received from the CPU is arranged in the proper format by the processor by inserting the required control characters before and after the text. The message has the heading SOH and the address of the terminal T4. The text message informs the terminal that the balance is $100. An LRC character is computed and sent to the terminal. If the terminal responds with a NAK character, the processor retransmits the message.

While the processor is taking care of this terminal it is busy processing other terminals as well. Since the characters are received in a serial fashion, it takes a certain amount of time to receive and collect an 8-bit character During this time the processor is multiplexing all other communication lines and services each one in turn. The speed of most remote terminals is extremely slow compared to the processor speed. This property allows multiplexing of many users to achieve greater efficiency in a time-sharing system. This also allows many users to operate simultaneously while each is being sampled at speeds comparable to normal human response.

Data Transparency

The character-oriented protocol was originally developed to communicate with keyboard, printer, and display devices that use alphanumeric characters exclusively. As the data communication field expanded, it became necessary to transmit binary information which is not ASCII text. This happens, for example, when two remote computers send programs and data to each other over a communication channel. An arbitrary bit pattern in the text message becomes a problem in the character-oriented protocol. This is because any 8-bit pattern belonging to a communication control character will be interpreted erroneously by the receiver. For example, if the binary data in the text portion of the message has the 8-bit pattern 10000011, the receiver will interpret this as an ETX character and assume that it reached the end of the text field When the text portion of the message is variable in length and contains bits that are to be treated without reference to any particular code, it is said to contain transparent data. This feature requires that the character recognition logic of the receiver be turned off so that data patterns in the text field are not accidentally interpreted as communication control information.

Data transparency is achieved in character-oriented protocols by inserting a DLE (data link escape) character before each communication control character. Thus, the start of heading is detected from the double character DLE SOH, and the text field is terminated with the double character DLE ETX. If the DLE bit pattern 00010000 occurs in the text portion of the message, the transmitter inserts another DLE bit pattern following it. The receiver removes all DLE characters and then checks the next 8-bit pattern. If it is another DLE bit pattern, the receiver considers it as part of the text and continues to receive text. Otherwise, the receiver takes the following 8-bit pattern to be a communication control character.

The achievement of data transparency by means of the DLE character is inefficient and somewhat complicated to implement. Therefore, other protocols have been developed to make the transmission of transparent data more efficient. One protocol used by Digital Equipment Corp. employs a byte count field that gives the number of bytes in the message that follows. The receiver must then count the number of bytes received to reach the end of the text field. The protocol that has been mostly used to solve the transparency problem (and other problems associated with the character-oriented protocol) is the bit-oriented protocol.

Bit-Oriented Protocol

The bit-oriented protocol does not use characters in its control field and is independent of any particular code. It allows the transmission of serial bit stream of any length without the implication of character boundaries. Messages are organized in a specific format called a frame. In addition to the information field, a frame contains

address, control, and error-checking fields. The frame boundaries are determined
from a special 8-bit number called a flag. Examples of bit-oriented protocols are
SDLC (synchronous data link control) used by IBM, HDLC (high-level data link
control) adopted by the International Standard Organization, and ADCCP (advanced
data communication control procedure) adopted by the American National Standards
Institute.

Any data communication link involves at least two participating stations The
station that has responsibility for the data link and issues the commands to control
the link is called the primary station. The other station is a secondary station. Bit-
oriented protocols assume the presence of one primary station and one or more
secondary stations. All communication on the data link is from the primary station
to one or more secondary stations, or from a secondary station to the primary station.

The frame format for the bit-oriented protocol is shown in Fig. 11-39. A frame
starts with the 8-bit flag 01111110 followed by an address and control sequence.
The information field is not restricted in format or content and can be of any length.
The frame check field is a CRC (cyclic redundancy check) sequence used for detecting
errors in transmission. The ending flag indicates to the receiving station that the 16

Flag 01111110	Address 8 bits	Control 8 bits	Information any number of bits	Frame check 16 bits	Flag 01111110

Fig. 11-39 Frame format for bit-oriented protocol.

bits just received constitute the CRC bits. The ending frame can be followed by
another frame, another flag, or a sequence of consecutive 1's. When two frames
follow each other, the intervening flag is simultaneously the ending flag of the first
frame and the beginning flag of the next frame. If no information is exchanged,
the transmitter sends a series of flags to keep the line in the active state. The line is
said to be in the idle state with the occurrence of 15 or more consecutive 1's. Frames
with certain control messages are sent without an information field. A frame must
have a minimum of 32 bits between two flags to accommodate the address, control,
and frame check fields. The maximum length depends on the condition of the communication channel and its ability to transmit long messages error-free.

To prevent a flag from occurring in the middle of a frame, the bit-oriented
protocol uses a method called *zero insertion*. This requires that a 0 be inserted by
the transmitting station after any succession of five continuous 1's. The receiver
always removes a 0 that follows a succession of five 1's. Thus, the bit pattern 0111111
is transmitted as 01111101 and restored by the receiver to its original value by the
removal of the 0 following the five 1's. As a consequence, no pattern of 01111110
is ever transmitted between the beginning and ending flags.

Following the flag is the address field, which is used by the primary station
to designate the secondary station address. When a secondary station transmits a
frame, the address tells the primary station which secondary station originated the
frame. An address field of eight bits can specify up to 256 addresses. Some bit-oriented

protocols permit the use of an extended address field. To do this, the least significant bit of an address byte is set to 0 if another address byte follows. A 1 in the least significant bit of a byte is used to recognize the last address byte.

Following the address field is the control field. The control field comes in three different formats, as shown in Fig. 11-40. The information transfer format is used for ordinary data transmission. Each frame transmitted in this format contains send and receive counts. A station that transmits sequenced frames counts and numbers each frame. This count is given by the send count N_s. A station receiving sequenced frames counts each error-free frame that it receives. This count is given by the receive count N_r. The N_r count advances when a frame is checked and found to be without errors. The receiver confirms accepted numbered information frames by returning its N_r count to the transmitting station.

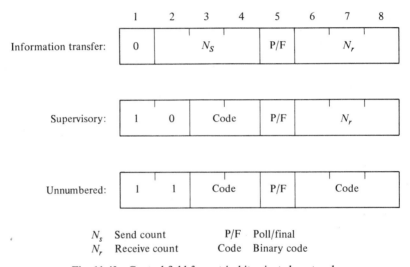

Fig. 11-40   Control field format in bit-oriented protocol.

The P/F bit is used by the primary station to poll a secondary station to request that it initiate transmission. It is used by the secondary station to indicate the final transmitted frame. Thus, the P/F field is called P (poll) when the primary station is transmitting but is designated as F (final) when a secondary station is transmitting. Each frame sent to the secondary station from the primary station has a P bit set to 0. When the primary station is finished and ready for the secondary station to respond, the P bit is set to 1. The secondary station then responds with a number of frames in which the F bit is set to 0. When the secondary station sends the last frame, it sets the F bit to 1. Therefore, the P/F bit is used to determine when data transmission from a station is finished.

The supervisory format of the control field is recognized from the first two bits being 1 and 0. The next two bits indicate the type of command. This follows by a P/F bit and a receive sequence frame count. The frames of the supervisory format do not carry an information field. They are used to assist in the transfer of information in that they confirm the acceptance of preceding frames carrying information, convey ready or busy conditions, and report frame numbering errors.

The unnumbered format is recognized from the first two bits being 11. The five code bits available in this format can specify up to 32 commands and responses. The primary station uses the control field to specify a command for a secondary station. The secondary station uses the control field to transmit a response to the primary station. Unnumbered-format frames are employed for initialization of link functions, reporting procedural errors, placing stations in a disconnected mode, and other data link control operations.

REFERENCES

1. HAYES, J. P., *Computer Architecture and Organization*. New York: McGraw-Hill Book Company, 1978.

2. LIPPIATT, A. G., *The Architecture of Small Computer Systems*. London: Prentice-Hall International, 1979.

3. HAMACHER, V. C., Z. G. VRANESIC, AND S. G. ZAKY, *Computer Organization*. New York: McGraw-Hill Book Company, 1978.

4. ARTWICK, B. A., *Microcomputer Interfacing*. Englewood Cliffs, N.J.: Prentice-Hall, Inc., 1980.

5. HOFFMAN, A. A., R. L. FRENCH, AND G. M. LANG, "Minicomputer Interfaces: Know More, Save More," *IEEE Spectrum*, Vol. 11 (February 1974), pp. 64–68.

6. BUZEN, J. P., "I/O Subsystem Architecture," *Proc. IEEE*, Vol. 63 (June 1975), pp. 871–879.

7. IBM CORP., *IBM System /370 Principle of Operations*, Publ. GA22-7000-5, Poughkeepsie, N.Y., 1976.

8. INTEL CORP., *The 8086 Family User's Manual*. Santa Clara, Calif., 1980.

9. EL-AYAT, K. A., "The Intel 8089: An Integrated I/O Processor," *Computer*, Vol. 12 (June 1979), pp. 67–78.

10. WEITZMAN, C., *Distributed Micro/Minicomputer Systems*. Englewood Cliffs, N.J.: Prentice-Hall, Inc., 1980.

11. ENSLOW, P. H., JR. "Multiprocessor Organization—A Survey," *ACM Comp. Surveys*, Vol. 9 (March 1977), pp. 103–129.

12. ADAMS, G., AND T. ROLANDER, "Design Motivation for Multiple Processor Microcomputer Systems," *Computer Design*, Vol. 17 (March 1978), pp. 81–89.

13. SATYANARAYANAN, M., "Commercial Multiprocessing Systems," *Computer*, Vol. 13 (May 1980), pp. 75–96.

14. McNAMARA, J. E., *Technical Aspects of Data Communication*. Maynard, Mass.: Digital Equipment Corp., 1977.

15. DOLL, D. R., *Data Communications*. New York: Wiley-Interscience, 1978.

PROBLEMS

11-1. List three different ways for preparing a program off-line. What peripherals will be used?

11-2. List four peripheral devices that produce an acceptable output for a person to understand.

11-3. What is the difference between I/O program-controlled transfer and DMA transfer?

11-4. Why does I/O interrupt make more efficient use of the CPU?

11-5. What is the difference between isolated I/O and memory-mapped I/O? What are the advantages and disadvantages of each?

11-6. Indicate whether the following constitute a test, control, or data transfer commands.
(a) Skip next instruction if flag is set.
(b) Seek a given record on a magnetic disk.
(c) Check if I/O device is ready.
(d) Move paper tape to next character position.
(e) Read status register.

11-7. How many I/O devices can be attached to a computer with an instruction code format as shown in Fig. 11-2(a) if the address field contains six bits?

11-8. Six interface units of the type shown in Fig. 11-5 are connected to a microprocessor that uses isolated I/O with an address of eight bits. Each one of the six chip select (CS) inputs is connected to one, and only one, address line. The two low-order address lines are connected to RS1 and RS0 of all interface units. Determine the 8-bit address of each register in each interface. (Total of 24 addresses.)

11-9. A microprocessor with a 300-ns clock period is connected to a memory with an access time of 500 ns. Formulate a read and write timing diagram using a read strobe and a write strobe from the microprocessor.

11-10. An interface unit has two handshake lines: an input line labeled STB (strobe), and an output line labeled IBF (input buffer full). A low signal on STB loads data from the bus to an interface register. A high signal on IBF indicates that the data have been accepted by the interface. IBF goes low after an I/O read signal from the CPU.
(a) Draw a block diagram showing the pertinent interconnections between the CPU, the interface, and the I/O device.
(b) Draw a timing diagram for the handshaking transfer.
(c) Obtain a sequence-of-events flow chart for the transfer.

11-11. Derive a sequence-of-events flow chart (as in Fig. 11-9c) for the three-wire handshake described in Fig. 11-10.

11-12. How many characters per second can be transmitted over a 1200-baud line in each of the following modes? (Assume a character code of eight bits.)
(a) Synchronous serial transmission.
(b) Asynchronous transmission with two stop bits.
(c) Asynchronous transmission with one stop bit.

11-13. Give at least six status conditions for setting bits in the status register of an asynchronous communication interface.

11-14. How many bits are there in the transmitter shift register of Fig. 11-12 when the interface is attached to a terminal that needs two stop bits? List the bits in the shift register when the letter F is transmitted using the ASCII code with even parity.

11-15. Draw a flow chart that describes the sequence of operations in the transmitter portion of an asynchronous communication interface.

11-16. A Teletype receiver interface accepts bits from the input line at an interval of 9.09 ms (110 baud). To ensure that the bits in the line are not in transition but have achieved a steady value, the line is sampled by the receiver at a time midway between two bit transitions. Show how this can be done using a clock frequency of 1760 Hz and a 4-bit counter. (Note that $110 \times 16 = 1760$.)

11-17. Information is inserted into a FIFO buffer at a rate of m bytes per second. The information is deleted at a rate of n bytes per second. The maximum capacity of the buffer is k bytes.
(a) How long does it take for an empty buffer to fill up when $m > n$?
(b) How long does it take for a full buffer to empty when $m < n$?
(c) Is the FIFO buffer needed if $m = n$?

11-18. The bits in the control register of the FIFO shown in Fig. 11-13 are: $F_1 F_2 F_3 F_4 = 0011$. Give the sequence of internal operations when an item is deleted from the FIFO and a new item is inserted.

11-19. What are the values of "input ready," "output ready," and control bits F_1 through F_4 in Fig. 11-13 when:
(a) The buffer is empty?
(b) The buffer is full?
(c) The buffer contains two data items?

11-20. Why does DMA have priority over the CPU when both request a memory transfer?

11-21. A DMA unit connected as in Fig. 11-15 receives characters of 8 bits from a peripheral device, packs four characters in a 32-bit word, and then stores words of 32 bits in memory.
(a) Define a set of registers for the DMA unit. (Shift registers should not be used because they are too slow.)
(b) Define a set of handshake lines for the DMA to communicate with the peripheral device.
(c) Obtain a flow chart showing the sequence of operations in the DMA during the transfer of data.

11-22. Assume that the CPU shown in Fig. 11-15, which defines a DMA facility, is part of the computer defined in Sec. 9-6. Derive a flow chart or formulate the register transfer statements in the modified CPU for fetching and executing the Load AC instruction. Do not include the operations from Fig. 11-16, as these are done by the memory controller.

11-23. Consider the possibility of connecting two microprocessors to a common set of data and address buses. How can an orderly transfer of information be established between the microprocessors and the common memory? How can the bus request and grant lines shown in Fig. 11-17 be of use for this purpose?

11-24. Some computers use the configuration shown in Fig. P11-24 for the daisy-chain priority interrupt. *PI*, *PO*, and *VAD* have the same meaning as in Fig. 11-19.
(a) Explain how the system operates to provide a priority interrupt.
(b) Draw the circuit diagram (similar to Fig. 11-20) of one stage in the chain.

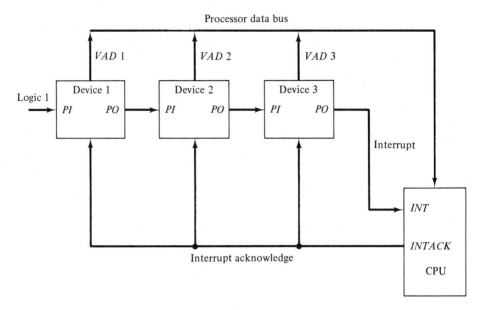

Fig. P11-24   Daisy chain priority interrupt.

11-25. Using combinational circuit design techniques, derive the Boolean functions listed in Table 11-1. Draw the logic diagram of the priority encoder.

11-26. Design a parallel priority interrupt hardware for a system with eight interrupt sources.

11-27. (a) Obtain the truth table of an 8 × 3 priority encoder.
(b) The three outputs x, y, z from the priority encoder are used to provide an 8-bit vector address of the form $101xyz00$. List the eight addresses in hexadecimal starting from the one with the highest priority.

11-28. What is the basic advantage of priority interrupt over a nonpriority system? Is it possible to have a priority interrupt without a mask register?

11-29. What programming steps are required to check when a source interrupts the computer while it is still being serviced by a previous interrupt request from the same source?

11-30. Consider a computer without priority interrupt hardware. Any interrupt request results in storing the return address in memory location 0 and branching to location 1. Explain how a priority can be established by software means.

11-31. A program for an I/O processor may consist of a variable number of command words. How would you design the control word format so the IOP knows if there are more command words in its program?

11-32. The I/O processor responds to three of the CPU instructions listed in Fig. 11-24 by placing a word in a specified memory location. Devise a method by which the CPU will know that the word in that memory location is indeed the one requested.

11-33. Formulate a command word (Fig. 11-26) when the I/O device is a magnetic tape. It is necessary to specify the number of blocks to be read or written on tape, the address of the first block, and the number of characters in each block. What should be done if all the bits of the command code do not fit in one memory word?

11-34. Draw a flow chart similar to the one in Fig. 11-25 that describes the CPU-I/O channel communication in the IBM 370.

11-35. Draw the circuit diagram (similar to Fig. 11-20) of one bus arbiter stage in the daisy-chain arbitration scheme shown in Fig. 11-35.

11-36. The bus controlled by the parallel arbitration logic shown in Fig. 11-36 is initially idle. Devices 2 and 3 then request the bus at the same time. Specify the input and output binary values in the encoder and decoder and determine which bus arbiter is acknowledged.

11-37. Explain why the busy flag in the control block of Fig. 11-30 must be designed to function in conjunction with a semaphore.

11-38. List a possible line procedure and the character sequence for the communication between a data communication processor and a remote terminal. The processor inquires if the terminal is operative. The terminal responds with yes or no. If the response is yes, the processor sends a block of text.

11-39. The address of a terminal connected to a data communication processor consists of two letters of the alphabet or a letter followed by one of the 10 numerals. How many different addresses can be formulated?

11-40. The longitudinal redundancy check (LRC) character is computed by the exclusive-OR of the bits along the longitudinal bits of a block. Show that the total bits in a column including the LRC bit has an even parity.

11-41. A data communication link employs the character-oriented protocol with data transparency using the DLE character. The message that the transmitter sends between STX and ETX is as follows:

DLE   STX   DLE   DLE   ETX   DLE   DLE   ETX   DLE   ETX

What is the binary value of the transparent text data?

11-42. What is the minimum number of bits that a frame must have in the bit-oriented protocol?

11-43. Show how the zero insertion works in the bit-oriented protocol when a zero followed by the 10 bits that represent the binary equivalent of 1023 are transmitted.

Memory Organization

12

12-1 AUXILIARY MEMORY

The memory unit is an essential component in any digital computer since it is needed for storing the programs that are executed by the CPU. A very small computer with a limited application may be able to fulfil its intended task without the need of additional storage capacity. However, most computers would run more efficiently if they are supplied with additional storage beyond the capacity of the main memory. There is just not enough space in one memory unit to accommodate all the systems programs written for a typical computer. Moreover, most computer installations accumulate and continue to accumulate large amounts of information. Not all accumulated information is needed by the processor at the same time. Therefore, it is more economical to use lower-cost storage devices to serve as a backup for storing the information that is not currently used by the CPU. The memory unit that communicates directly with the CPU is called the *main memory*. Devices that provide backup storage are called *auxiliary memory*. Only programs and data currently used by the processor reside in main memory. All other information is stored in auxiliary memory and is transferred to main memory on a demand basis.

The most common auxiliary memory devices used in computer systems are magnetic drums, magnetic disks, and magnetic tapes. Other components used, but not as frequently, are large-capacity core memories, magnetic bubble, and charge-coupled devices. To understand fully the physical mechanism of auxiliary memory devices one must have a knowledge of magnetics, electronics, and electro-mechanical systems. Although the physical properties of these storage devices can be quite complex, their logical properties can be characterized and compared by a few parameters. The important characteristics of any device are its access mode, access time, transfer rate, capacity, and cost.

The average time required to reach a storage location in memory and obtain its contents is called the access time. In electromechanical devices with moving parts such as drums, disks, and tapes, the access time consists of a *seek* time required to position the read-write head to a location and a *transfer* time required to transfer data to or from the device. Because the seek time is usually much longer than the transfer time, auxiliary storage is organized in records or blocks. A record is a specified number of characters or words. Reading or writing is always done on entire records. The transfer rate is the number of characters or words that the device can transfer per second, after it has been positioned at the beginning of the record.

Magnetic drums and disks are quite similar in operation. Both consist of high-speed rotating surfaces coated with a magnetic recording medium. The rotating surface of the drum is a cylinder and that of the disk, a round flat plate. The recording surface rotates at uniform speed and is not started or stopped during access operations. Bits are recorded as magnetic spots on the surface as it passes a stationary mechanism called a *write head*. Stored bits are detected by a change in magnetic field produced by a recorded spot on the surface as it passes through a *read head*. The amount of surface available for recording in a disk is greater than in a drum of equal physical size. Therefore, more information can be stored on a disk than on a drum of comparable size. For this reason, disks are employed more frequently than drums.

Magnetic Drum

The cylindrical surface of a drum is divided into tracks as shown in Fig. 12-1. Each track can accommodate a large number of magnetized spots. The read-write head is mounted on a movable arm near the surface of the cylinder. A drum may have one head which can be moved mechanically to any one track position, or may have several heads over several tracks for simultaneous access to a number of bits at one time. The

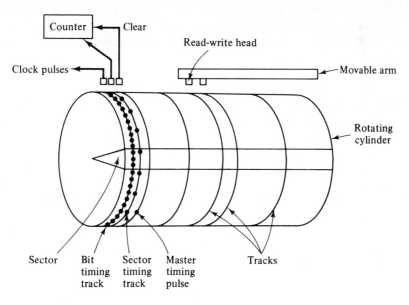

Fig. 12-1 Magnetic drum.

bit timing track has permanent bits recorded in its surface at equal intervals. These bits are used to generate clock pulses and to synchronize the bits in each track. A typical drum may have as many as 500 tracks with 30,000 magnetized spots or bits around each track.

Each track is divided into sectors with each sector specifying a given number of bits. A typical sector may have 32 bits. The sectors are identified by counting permanent stored bits in the sector timing track. This track has one bit at the end of each sector. These permanently recorded bits are applied to a counter to provide the address of the sector presently being scanned by the read/write heads. A master timing pulse on a separate track is used to clear the counter once every revolution.

A drum is addressed by specifying a track and sector number. For example, **256 tracks can be specified with 8 bits and 1024 sectors with 10 bits. An address** of 18 bits is needed to specify a particular sector (of 32 bits) in a particular track. The high-order 8 bits of the address go to a control mechanism that physically moves the read/write head to the specified track. The 10 low-order bits of the address are compared with the content of the counter that counts the pulses coming out of the sector timing track. When the count is equal to the desired sector address, the bits from the specified track are read and transferred to a shift register one after another until the whole sector is assembled. The 32 bit sector is then ready to be transferred to main memory.

Magnetic Disk

The storage organization of a magnetic disk is similar to that of a drum except that a flat surface is used instead of a cylinder. A disk unit is an electromechanical assembly, containing a flat disk coated with magnetic material. Often both sides of the disk are used and several disks may be stacked on one spindle with read/write heads available in each surface. All disks rotate together at high speed and are not stopped or started for access purposes. Bits are stored in the magnetized surface in spots along concentric circles called tracks. The tracks are commonly divided into sections called sectors. In most systems, the minimum quantity of information which can be transferred is a sector. The subdivision of one disk surface into tracks and sectors is shown in Fig. 12-2.

Some units use a single read-write head for each disk surface. In this type of unit, the track address bits are used by a mechanical assembly to move the head into the specified track position before reading or writing. In other disk systems, separate read/write heads are provided for each track in each surface. The address bits can then select a particular track electronically through a decoder circuit. This type of unit is more expensive and is found only in very large computer systems.

Permanent timing tracks are used in disks as in drums to synchronize the bits and recognize the sectors. A disk system is addressed by address bits that specify the disk number, the disk surface, the sector number and the track within the sector. After the read/write heads are positioned in the specified track, the system has to wait until the rotating disk reaches the specified sector under the read/write head. Information transfer is very fast once the beginning of a sector has been reached. Both drums

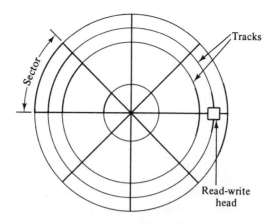

Fig. 12-2 Magnetic disk.

and disks may have multiple heads and simultaneous transfer of bits from several tracks at the same time.

A track in a given sector near the circumference is longer than a track near the center of the disk. If bits are recorded with equal density, some tracks will contain more recorded bits than others. To make all the records in a sector of equal length, some disks use a variable recording density with higher density on tracks near the center than on tracks near the circumference. This equalizes the number of bits on all tracks of a given sector.

Very often, the disks are permanently attached to the unit assembly and cannot be removed by the occasional user. A different type of unit called a *disk-pack* is also available which allows the disk to be removed easily. A relatively recent innovation in disk storage is the *flexible* or *floppy* disk that replaces the more conventional rigid disk. The flexible disk is made of plastic coated with a magnetic recording medium and is approximately the size and shape of a 45-rpm record. The flexible disk can be inserted and removed about as easily as a tape cartridge.

Magnetic Tape

A magnetic tape transport consists of the electrical, mechanical, and electronic components to provide the parts and control mechanism for a magnetic-tape unit. The tape itself is a strip of plastic coated with a magnetic recording medium. Bits are recorded as magnetic spots on the tape along several tracks. Usually 7 or 9 bits are recorded simultaneously to form a character together with a parity bit. Read/write heads are mounted one in each track so that data can be recorded and read as a sequence of characters.

Magnetic tape units can be stopped, started to move forward or in reverse, or can be rewound. However, they cannot be started or stopped fast enough between individual characters. For this reason, information is recorded in blocks referred to as records. Gaps of unrecorded tape are inserted between records where the tape can be stopped. The tape starts moving while in a gap and attains its constant speed by the time it reaches the next record. Each record on tape has an identification bit pattern at the beginning and end. By reading the bit pattern at the beginning, the tape control identifies the record number. By reading the bit pattern at the end of the record, the control recognizes the beginning of a gap. A tape unit is addressed by specifying the record number and the number of characters in the record. Records may be of fixed or variable length.

12-2 MICROCOMPUTER MEMORY

The memory unit is an integral part of a typical computer and is supplied by the manufacturer as part of the total computer system. In contrast, when the design of a special-purpose microcomputer system is undertaken, it is quite often necessary to determine the amount and type of memory that must be allocated to the microprocessor. The connection of integrated circuit memory chips through the data and address bus of a microprocessor is illustrated in block diagram form in Fig. 7-15. There are two types of memory chips used in microcomputer systems: RAM (random-access memory) and ROM (read-only memory). RAM is used for storing data, variable parameters, and intermediate results that need updating and are subject to change. ROM is used for storing programs and table of constants that do not change in value once the production of the microcomputer system is completed.

The size of the memory attached to a microprocessor depends on the size of the program and data words needed for the particular application. A typical microprocessor has an address bus of 16 lines and a data bus of 8 lines to accommodate up to 64K bytes of memory. In many applications, the amount of memory needed may be less than 64K bytes. RAM and ROM chips are available in a variety of sizes and the individual chips must be interconnected to form the required memory capacity.

RAM and ROM Chips

A RAM chip is better suited for communicating with a microprocessor if it has one or more control inputs for selecting and enabling the unit upon request. Another convenient feature is a bidirectional data bus to avoid inserting external bus buffers between the RAM and the data bus. The block diagram of a RAM chip suited for microcomputer applications is shown in Fig. 12-3. The capacity of the memory is 128 words of 8 bits each. This requires a 7-bit address and an 8-bit bidirectional data bus. The read and write inputs specify the memory operation and the two chips select (CS) control inputs are for enabling the chip only when it is selected by the microprocessor. The availability of more than one control input to select the chip facilitates the decoding of the address lines when multiple chips are used in the microcomputer. The read and write inputs are sometimes combined into one line labeled R/W. When the chip is selected, the two binary states in this line specify the two operations of read or write.

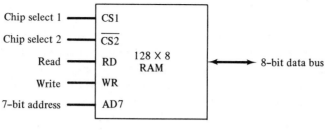

(a) Block diagram

CS1	$\overline{CS2}$	RD	WR	Memory function	State of data bus
0	0	X	X	Inhibit	High-impedance
0	1	X	X	Inhibit	High-impedance
1	0	0	0	Inhibit	High-impedance
1	0	0	1	Write	Input data to RAM
1	0	1	X	Read	Output data from RAM
1	1	X	X	Inhibit	High-impedance

(b) Function table

Fig. 12-3 Typical RAM chip.

The function table listed in Fig. 12-3(b) specifies the operation of the RAM chip. The unit is in operation only when CS1 = 1 and $\overline{CS2}$ = 0. The bar on top of the second select variable indicates that this input is enabled when it is equal to 0. If the chip select inputs are not enabled, or if they are enabled but the read or write inputs are not enabled, the memory is inhibited and its data bus is in a high-impedance state. When CS1 = 1 and $\overline{CS2}$ = 0, the memory can be placed in a write or read mode. When the WR input is enabled, the memory stores a byte from the data bus into a location specified by the address input lines. When the RD input is enabled, the content of the selected byte is placed into the data bus. The RD and WR signals control the memory operation as well as the bus buffers associated with the bidirectional data bus.

A ROM chip is organized externally in a similar manner. However, since a ROM can only read, the data bus can only be in an output mode. The block diagram of a ROM chip is shown in Fig. 12-4. For the same-size chip, it is possible to have more

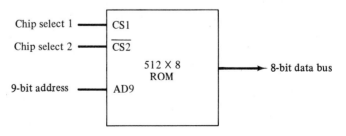

Fig. 12-4 Typical ROM chip.

bits of ROM than of RAM, because the internal binary cells in ROM occupy less space than in RAM. For this reason, the diagram specifies a 512-byte ROM, while the RAM has only 128 bytes.

The 9 address lines in the ROM chip specify any one of the 512 bytes stored in it. The two chip select inputs must be CS1 $= 1$ and $\overline{\text{CS2}} = 0$ for the unit to operate. Otherwise, the data bus is in a high-impedance state. There is no need for a read or write control because the unit can only read. Thus, when the chip is enabled by the two select inputs, the byte selected by the address lines appears on the data bus.

Memory Address Map

The designer of a microcomputer system must calculate the amount of memory required for the particular application and assign it to either RAM or ROM. The interconnection between memory and microprocessor is then established from knowledge of the size of memory needed and the type of RAM and ROM chips available. The addressing of memory can be established by means of a table that specifies the memory address assigned to each chip. The table, called a *memory address map*, is a pictorial representation of assigned address space for each chip in the system.

To demonstrate with a particular example, assume that a microcomputer system needs 512 bytes of RAM and 512 bytes of ROM. The RAM and ROM chips to be used are specified in Figs. 12-3 and 12-4. The memory address map for this configuration is shown in Table 12-1. The component column specifies whether a RAM or a

TABLE 12-1   Memory Address Map for Microprocomputer

Component	Hexadecimal address	Address bus									
		10	9	8	7	6	5	4	3	2	1
RAM 1	0000–007F	0	0	0	x	x	x	x	x	x	x
RAM 2	0080–00FF	0	0	1	x	x	x	x	x	x	x
RAM 3	0100–017F	0	1	0	x	x	x	x	x	x	x
RAM 4	0180–01FF	0	1	1	x	x	x	x	x	x	x
ROM	0200–03FF	1	x	x	x	x	x	x	x	x	x

ROM chip is used. The hexadecimal address column assigns a range of hexadecimal equivalent addresses for each chip. The address bus lines are listed in the third column. Although there are 16 lines in the address bus, the table shows only 10 lines because the other 6 are not used in this example and are assumed to be zero. The small x's under the address bus lines designate those lines that must be connected to the address inputs in each chip. The RAM chips have 128 bytes and need 7 address lines. The ROM chip has 512 bytes and needs 9 address lines. The x's are always assigned to the low-order bus lines: lines 1 through 7 for the RAM and lines 1 through 9 for the ROM. It is now necessary to distinguish between four RAM chips by assigning to each a different address. For this particular example we choose bus lines 8 and 9 to represent four distinct binary combinations. Note that any other pair of unused bus lines can be chosen for this purpose. The table clearly shows that the nine low-order bus lines constitute a memory space for RAM equal to $2^9 = 512$ bytes. The distinction between a RAM and ROM address is done with another bus line. Here we choose line 10 for this purpose. When line 10 is 0, the microprocessor selects a RAM, and when this line is equal to 1, it selects the ROM.

The equivalent hexadecimal address for each chip is obtained from the information under the address bus assignment. The address bus lines are subdivided into groups of four bits each so that each group can be represented with a hexadecimal digit. The first hexadecimal digit represents lines 13 to 16 and is always 0. The next hexadecimal digit represents lines 9 to 12, but lines 11 and 12 are always 0. The range of hexadecimal addresses for each component is determined from the x's associated with it. These x's represent a binary number that can range from an all-0's to an all-1's value.

Memory Connection to Microprocessor

RAM and ROM chips are connected to a microprocessor through the data and address buses. The low-order lines in the address bus select the byte within the chips and other lines in the address bus select a particular chip through its chip select inputs. The connection of memory chips to the microprocessor is shown in Fig. 12-5. This configuration gives a memory capacity of 512 bytes of RAM and 512 bytes of ROM. It implements the memory map of Table 12-1. Each RAM receives the seven low-order bits of the address bus to select one of possible 128 bytes. The particular RAM chip selected is determined from lines 8 and 9 in the address bus. This is done through a 2×4 decoder whose outputs go to the CS1 inputs in each RAM chip. Thus, when address lines 8 and 9 are equal to 00, the first RAM chip is selected. When 01, the second RAM chip is selected, and so on. The RD and WR outputs from the microprocessor are applied to the inputs of each RAM chip.

The selection between RAM and ROM is achieved through bus line 10. The RAMs are selected when the bit in this line is 0, and the ROM when the bit is 1. The other chip select input in the ROM is connected to the RD control line for the ROM chip to be enabled only during a read operation. Address bus lines 1 to 9 are applied to the input address of ROM without going through the decoder. This assigns addresses 0 to 511 to RAM and 512 to 1023 to ROM. The data bus of the ROM has only an output capability, whereas the data bus connected to the RAMs can transfer information in both directions.

The example just shown gives an indication of the interconnection complexity that can exist between memory chips and the microprocessor. The more chips that are connected, the more external decoders are required for selection among the chips. The designer must establish a memory map that assigns addresses to the various chips from which the required connections are determined. Since microprocessors com-

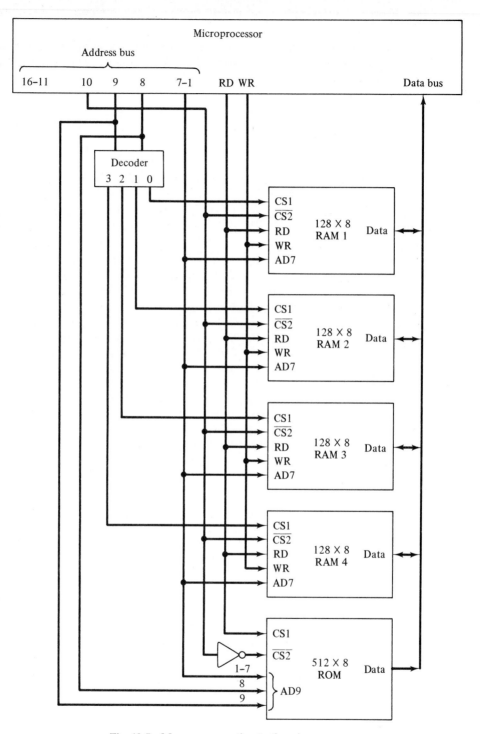

Fig. 12-5 Memory connection to the microprocessor.

municate also with interface units, it is necessary to assign addresses to each interface as well. The communication between the microprocessor and interface units was discussed in Sec. 11-2 in conjunction with Fig. 11-5.

12-3 MEMORY HIERARCHY

The total memory capacity of a computer can be visualized as being a hierarchy of components. The memory hierarchy system consists of all storage devices employed by a computer system from the slow but high-capacity auxiliary memory devices, to a relatively faster main memory, to an even smaller and very fast buffer memory accessible to the high-speed processing logic. Figure 12-6 illustrates the components in a typical memory hierarchy. At the bottom of the hierarchy are the relatively slow magnetic tapes used to store removable files. Above it are the magnetic disks or drums used as backup storage. The main memory occupies a central position by being able to communicate directly with the CPU and with auxiliary devices through an I/O processor. When programs not residing in main memory are needed by the CPU, they are brought in from auxiliary memory. Programs not currently needed in main memory are transferred into auxiliary memory to provide space for currently used programs and data.

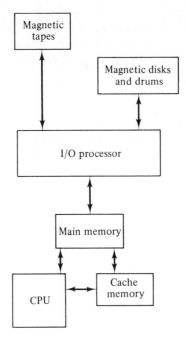

Fig. 12-6   Storage hierarchy in a large computer system.

A special very high-speed memory is sometimes used to increase the speed of processing by making current programs and data available to the CPU at a rapid rate. The cache memory shown in Fig. 12-6 is sometimes employed in large computer systems to compensate for the speed differential between main memory access time and processor logic. Processor logic is usually faster than main memory access time with the result that processing speed is mostly limited by the speed of main memory. A technique used to compensate for the mismatch in operating speeds is to employ an extremely fast, small memory between CPU and main memory whose access time is close to processor logic propagation delays. This type of memory is called a *buffer* and sometimes a *cache* memory. It is used to store segments of programs currently being executed in the CPU and temporary data frequently needed in the present calculations. By making programs and data available at a rapid rate, it is possible to increase the performance rate of the processor.

In a computer system where the demand for service is high, it is customary to run all programs in one of two possible modes: a *batch* mode or *time-sharing* mode (some computers are capable of operating in both modes). In a batch mode, each user prepares his program off-line and submits it to the computer center. An operator loads all programs into the computer where they are executed. The operator retrieves the printed output and returns it to the user. What makes the batch mode efficient is the fact that programs can be fed into the computer as fast as they can be processed. In this way it is insured that the computer is busy processing information most of the time.

In a *time-sharing* mode, many users communicate with the computer via remote terminals. Because of slow human response compared to computer speeds, the computer can respond to multiple users at, seemingly, the same time. This is accomplished by having many programs reside in memory while the system allocates a time-slice to each program for execution in the CPU.

A major concept common to both batch and time-sharing modes is their use of *multiprogramming*. Multiprogramming refers to the existence of many programs in different parts of main memory at the same time. In this way, it is possible to keep all parts of the computer busy by working with several programs in sequence. For example, suppose a program is being executed in the CPU and an I/O transfer is required. The CPU initiates the I/O processor to start executing the transfer. This leaves the CPU free to execute another program. In a multiprogramming system, when one program is waiting for input or output transfer, there is another program ready to utilize the CPU.

With multiprogramming systems the need arises for running partial programs, for varying the amount of main memory in use by a given program, and for moving programs around in the memory hierarchy. Application programs are sometimes too long to be accomodated in the total space available in main memory. Bearing in mind that a computer system uses not only application programs but also many system programs, it becomes apparent that all programs cannot reside in main memory at all times. A program with its data normally resides in auxiliary memory. When the program or a segment of the program is to be executed, it is transferred to main memory to be executed by the CPU. Thus, one may think of auxiliary memory as containing the totally of information stored in a computer system. It is the task of the operating system to maintain in main memory a portion of this information that is currently active. The part of the operating system that supervises the flow of information between all storage devices is called the *memory management* system.

The most important reason for a memory hierarchy is economic. The cost per bit of storage is roughly proportional to the memory's level in the hierarchy. It would be prohibitively expensive to maintain all programs and data in main memory especially during a time when they are not needed by the processor. The memory management system distributes programs and data to various levels in the memory hierarchy according to their expected frequency of usage. The objective of the memory management system is to adjust the frequency with which the various memories are referenced to provide an efficient method of transfers between levels so as to maximize the utilization of all computer components.

12-4 ASSOCIATIVE MEMORY

Many data processing applications require the search of items in a table stored in memory. An assembler program searches the symbol address table in order to extract the symbol's binary equivalent. An account number may be searched in a file to determine the holder's name and account status. The established way to search a table is to store all items where they can be addressed in sequence. The search procedure is a strategy for choosing a sequence of addresses, reading the content of memory at each address, and comparing the information read with the item being searched until a match occurs. The number of accesses to memory depends on the location of the item and the efficiency of the search algorithm. Many search algorithms have been developed to minimize the number of accesses while searching for an item in a random or sequential access memory.

The time required to find an item stored in memory can be reduced considerably if stored data can be identified for access by the content of the data itself rather than by an address. A memory unit accessed by content is called an *associative memory* or *content addressable memory* (CAM). This type of memory is accessed simultaneously and in parallel on the basis of data content rather than by specific address or location. When a word is written in an associative memory, no address is given. The memory is capable of finding an empty unused location to store the word. When a word is to be read from an associative memory, the content of the word, or part of the word, is specified. The memory locates all words which match the specified content and marks them for reading.

Because of its organization, the associative memory is uniquely suited to do parallel searches by data association. Moreover, searches can be done on an entire word or on a specific field within a word. An associative memory is more expensive than a random access memory because each cell must have storage capability as well as logic circuits for matching its content with an external argument. For this reason, associative memories are used in applications where the search time is very critical and must be very short.

Hardware Organization

The block diagram of an associative memory is shown in Fig. 12-7. It consists of a memory array and logic for m words with n bits per word. The argument register A and key register K each have n bits, one for each bit of a word. The match register M has m bits, one for each memory word. Each word in memory is compared in parallel with the content of the argument register. The words that match the bits of the argument register set a corresponding bit in the match register. After the matching process, those bits in the match register that have been set indicate the fact that their corresponding words have been matched. Reading is accomplished by a sequential access to memory for those words whose corresponding bits in the match register have been set.

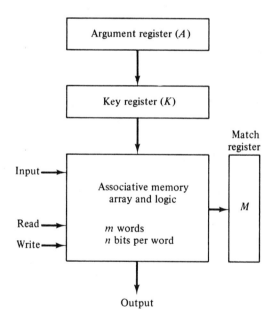

Fig. 12-7   Block diagram of associative memory.

The key register provides a mask for choosing a particular field or key in the argument word. The entire argument is compared with each memory word if the key register contains all 1's. Otherwise, only those bits in the argument that have 1's in their corresponding position of the key register are compared. Thus, the key provides a mask or identifying piece of information which specifies how the reference to memory is made. To illustrate with a numerical example, suppose that the argument register A and the key register K have the bit configuration shown below. Only the three leftmost bits of A are compared with memory words because K has 1's in these positions.

A	101 111100	
K	111 000000	
word 1	100 111100	no match
word 2	101 000001	match

Word 2 matches the unmasked argument field because the three left-most bits of the argument and the word are equal.

The relation between the memory array and external registers in an associative memory is shown in Fig. 12-8. The cells in the array are marked by the letter C with two subscripts. The first subscript gives the word number and the second specifies the

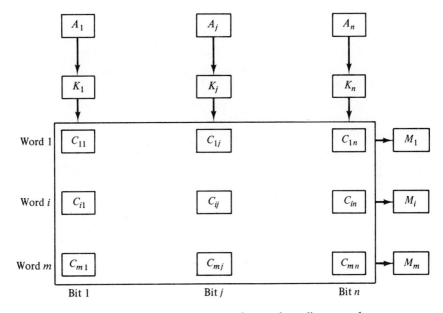

Fig. 12-8 Associative memory of m word, n cells per word.

bit position in the word. Thus, cell C_{ij} is the cell for bit j in word i. A bit A_j in the argument register is compared with all the bits in column j of the array provided $K_j = 1$. This is done for all columns $j = 1, 2, \ldots, n$. If a match occurs between all the unmasked bits of the argument and the bits in word i, the corresponding bit M_i in the match register is set to 1. If one or more unmasked bits of the argument and the word do not match, M_i is cleared to 0.

The internal organization of a typical cell C_{ij} is shown in Fig. 12-9. It consists of a flip-flop storage element F_{ij} and the circuits for reading, writing, and matching

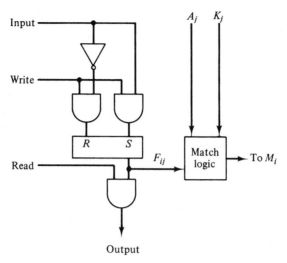

Fig. 12-9 One cell of associative memory.

the cell. The input bit is transferred into the storage cell during a write operation. The bit stored is read out during a read operation. The match logic compares the content of the storage cell with the corresponding unmasked bit of the argument and provides an output for the decision logic that sets the bit in M_i.

Match Logic

The match logic for each word can be derived from the comparison algorithm for two binary numbers. First, we *neglect* the key bits and compare the argument in A with the bits stored in the cells of the words. Word i is equal to the argument in A if $A_j = F_{ij}$ for $j = 1, 2, \ldots, n$. Two bits are equal if they are both 1 or both 0. The equality of two bits can be expressed logically by the Boolean function:

$$x_j = A_j F_{ij} + A'_j F'_{ij}$$

where $x_j = 1$ if the pair of bits in position j are equal; otherwise, $x_j = 0$.

For a word i to be equal to the argument in A we must have all x_j variables equal to 1. This is the condition for setting the corresponding match bit M_i to 1. The Boolean function for this condition is

$$M_i = x_1 x_2 x_3 \ldots x_n$$

and constitutes the AND operation of all pairs of matched bits in a word.

We now include the key bit K_j in the comparison logic. The requirement is that if $K_j = 0$, the corresponding bits of A_j and F_{ij} need no comparison. Only when $K_j = 1$ must they be compared. This requirement is achieved by ORing each term with K'_j, thus:

$$x_j + K'_j = \begin{cases} x_j \text{ if } K_j = 1 \\ 1 \text{ if } K_j = 0 \end{cases}$$

When $K_j = 1$, we have $K'_j = 0$ and $x_j + 0 = x_j$. When $K_j = 0$, then $K'_j = 1$ and $x_j + 1 = 1$. A term $(x_j + K'_j)$ will be in the 1 state if its pair of bits are not compared. This is necessary because each term is ANDed with all other terms so that an output of 1 will have no effect. The comparison of the bits has an effect only when $K_j = 1$.

The match logic for word i in an associative memory can be now expressed by the following Boolean function:

$$M_i = (x_1 + K'_1)(x_2 + K'_2)(x_3 + K'_3) \ldots (x_n + K'_n)$$

Each term in the expression will be equal to 1 if its corresponding $K_j = 0$. If $K_j = 1$, the term will be either 0 or 1 depending on the value of x_j. A match will occur and M_i will be equal to 1 if all terms are equal to 1.

If we substitute the original definition of x_j, the above Boolean function can be expressed as follows:

$$M_i = \prod_{j=1}^{n} (A_j F_{ij} + A'_j F'_{ij} + K'_j)$$

where $\prod$ is a product symbol designating the AND operation of all n terms. We need m such functions, one for each word $i = 1, 2, 3, \ldots, m$.

The circuit for matching one word is shown in Fig. 12-10. Each cell requires two

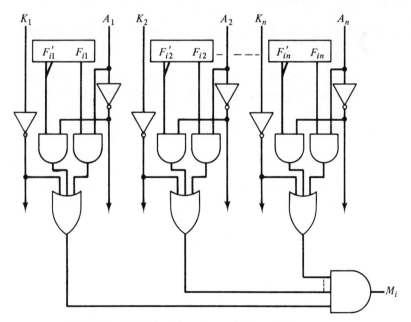

Fig. 12-10　Match logic for one word of associative memory.

AND gates and one OR gate. The inverters for A_j and K_j are needed once for each column and are used for all bits in the column. The output of all OR gates in the cells of the same word go to the input of a common AND gate to generate the match signal for M_i. M_i will be logic 1 if a match occurs and 0 if no match occurs. Note that if the key register contains all 0's, output M_i will be a 1 irrespective of the value of A or the word. This occurrence must be avoided during normal operation.

Read Operation

If more than one word in memory matches the unmasked argument field, all the matched words will have 1's in the corresponding bit position of the match register. It is then necessary to scan the bits of the match register one at a time. The matched words are read in sequence by applying a read signal to each word line whose corresponding M_i bit is a 1.

In most applications, the associative memory stores a table with no two identical items under a given key. In this case, only one word may match the unmasked argument field. By connecting output M_i directly to the read line in the same word position (instead of the M register), the content of the matched word will be presented automatically at the output lines and no special read command signal is needed. Furthermore, if we exclude words having a zero content, then an all zero output will indicate that no match occurred and that the searched item is not available in memory.

Write Operation

An associative memory must have a write capability for storing the information to be searched. Writing in an associative memory can take different forms, depending on the application. If the entire memory is loaded with new information at once prior to a search operation then the writing can be done by addressing each location in sequence. This will make the device a random-access memory for writing and a content addressable memory for reading. The advantage here is that the address for input can be decoded as in a random access memory. Thus, instead of having m address lines, one for each word in memory, the number of address lines can be reduced by the decoder to d lines where $m = 2^d$.

If unwanted words have to be deleted and new words inserted one at a time, there is a need for a special register to distinguish between active and inactive words. This register, sometimes called a *tag* register, would have as many bits as there are words in the memory. For every active word stored in memory, the corresponding bit in the tag register is set to 1. A word is deleted from memory by clearing its tag bit to 0. Words are stored in memory by scanning the tag register until the first 0 bit is encountered. This gives the first available inactive word and a position for writing a new word. After the new word is stored in memory it is made active by setting its tag bit to 1. An unwanted word when deleted from memory can be cleared to all 0's if this value is used to specify an empty location. Moreover, the words that have a tag bit of 0 must be masked (together with the K_j bits) with the argument word so that only active words are compared.

Associative Processor

The advantages of associative memories are numerous and many applications have been found for their use. A considerable amount of research activity has been conducted to include such a memory in the design of general-purpose computers. A computer with an associative memory (instead of a random-access memory) is called an *associative processor*. In an associative processor each cell is "associated" with its neighboring cells for handling the usual arithmetic, logic, and shift operations. The operations are performed in parallel instead of having to bring the operands one by one to the CPU for processing. A group of operations that would be programmed as a routine in a conventional computer can be executed in parallel in an associative processor. However, as may be evident from the previous discussion, an associative memory requires a considerable number of logic circuits within its individual cells and in its environment. Because of economic reasons, associative memories have been used mostly in specialized applications.

12-5 VIRTUAL MEMORY

In a memory hierarchy system, programs and data are first stored in auxiliary memory. Portions of a program or data are brought into main memory as they are needed by the CPU. *Virtual memory* is a concept used in some large computer systems that permit the user to construct his programs as though he had a large memory space, equal to the totality of auxiliary memory. Each address which is referenced by the CPU goes through an address mapping from the so-called virtual address to an actual address in main memory. Virtual memory is used to give the programmer the illusion that he has a very large memory at his disposal, even though the computer actually has a relatively small main memory. A virtual memory system provides a mechanism for translating program-generated addresses into correct main memory locations. This is done dynamically, while programs are being executed in the CPU. The translation or mapping is handled automatically by the hardware by means of a mapping table.

Address Space and Memory Space

An address used by a programmer will be called a *virtual* address, and the set of such addresses the *address space*. An address in main memory is called a *location* or *physical address*. The set of such locations is called the *memory space*. Thus, the address space is the set of addresses generated by programs as they reference instructions and data; the memory space consists of the actual main memory locations directly addressable for processing. In most computers the address and memory spaces are identical. The address space is allowed to be larger than the memory space in computers with virtual memory.

As an illustration, consider a computer with a main-memory capacity of 32K words (K = 1024). Fifteen bits are needed to specify a physical address in memory since 32K = 2^{15}. Suppose that the computer has available auxiliary memory for storing 2^{20} = 1024K words. Thus, auxiliary memory has a capacity for storing information equivalent to the capacity of 32 main memories. Denoting the address space by N and the memory space by M, we then have for this example $N = 1024K$ and $M = 32K$.

In a multiprogram computer system, programs and data are transferred to and from auxiliary memory and main memory based on demands imposed by the CPU. Suppose that program 1 is currently being executed in the CPU. Program 1 and a portion of its associated data are moved from auxiliary memory into main memory as shown in Fig. 12-11. Portions of programs and data need not be in contiguous locations in memory since information is being moved in and out, and empty spaces may be available in scattered locations in memory.

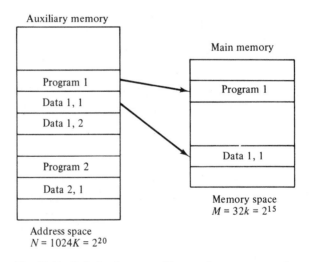

Fig. 12-11 Relation between address and memory space in a virtual memory system.

In a virtual memory system, the programmer is told that he has the total address space at his disposal. Moreover, the address field of the instruction code has a sufficient number of bits to specify all virtual addresses. In our example, the address field of an instruction code will consists of 20 bits but physical memory addresses must be specified with only 15 bits. Thus CPU will reference instructions and data with a 20-bit address but the information at this address must be taken from physical memory because access to auxiliary storage for individual words will be prohibitively long. (Remember that for efficient transfers, auxiliary storage moves an entire record to the main memory.) A table is then needed, as shown in Fig. 12-12, to map a virtual address of 20 bits to a physical address of 15 bits. The mapping is a dynamic operation which means that every address is translated immediately as a word is referenced by CPU.

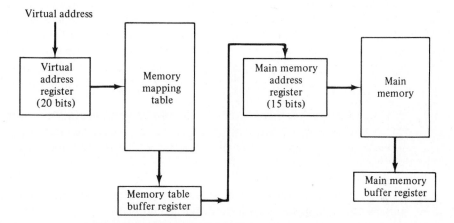

Fig. 12-12   Memory table for mapping a virtual address.

The mapping table may be stored in a separate memory as shown in Fig. 12-12 or in main memory. In the first case, an additional memory unit is required as well as one extra memory access time. In the second case, the table takes space from main memory and two accesses to memory are required with the program running at half speed. A third alternative is to use an associative memory as explained below.

Address Mapping

The table implementation of the address mapping is simplified if the information in the address space and the memory space are each divided into groups of fixed size. The physical memory is broken down into groups of equal size called *blocks*, which may range from 64 to 4096 words each. The term *page* refers to groups of address space of the same size. For example, if a page or block consists of 1K words then, using the previous example, address space is divided into 1024 pages and main memory is divided into 32 blocks. Although both a page and a block are split into groups of 1K words, a page refers to the organization of address space, while a block refers to the organization of memory space. The programs are also considered to be split into pages. Portions of programs are moved from auxiliary memory to main memory in records equal to the size of a page.

Consider a computer with an address space of 8K and a memory space of 4K. If we split each into groups of 1K words we obtain 8 pages and 4 blocks as shown in Fig. 12-13. At any given time, up to four pages of address space may reside in main memory in any one of the four blocks.

The mapping from address space to memory space is facilitated if each virtual address is considered to be represented by two numbers: a page number address and

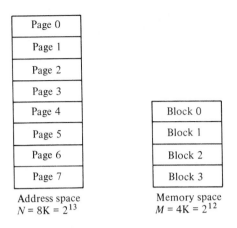

| Page 0 |
| Page 1 |
| Page 2 |
| Page 3 |
| Page 4 |
| Page 5 |
| Page 6 |
| Page 7 |

| Block 0 |
| Block 1 |
| Block 2 |
| Block 3 |

Address space
$N = 8K = 2^{13}$

Memory space
$M = 4K = 2^{12}$

Fig. 12-13 Address space and memory space split into groups of $1K$ words.

a line within the page. In a computer with 2^p words per page, p bits are used to specify a line address and the remaining high-order bits of the virtual address specify the page number. In the example of Fig. 12-13, a virtual address has 13 bits. Since each page consists of $2^{10} = 1024$ words, the high-order three bits of a virtual address will specify one of the eight pages and the low-order 10 bits give the line address within the page. Note that the line address in address space and memory space is the same; the only mapping required is from a page number to a block number.

The organization of the memory mapping table in a paged system is shown in Fig. 12-14. The memory-page table consists of eight words, one for each page. The adress in the page table denotes the page number and the content of the word gives the block number where that page is stored in main memory. The table shows that pages 1, 2, 5 and 6 are now available in main memory in blocks 3, 0, 1, and 2, respectively. A presence bit in each location indicates whether the page has been transferred from auxiliary memory into main memory. A 0 in the presence bit indicates that this page is not available in main memory. The CPU reference a word in memory with a virtual address of 13 bits. The three high-order bits of the virtual address specify a page number and also an address for the memory-page table. The content of the word in the memory-page table at the page number address is read out into the memory table buffer register. If the presence bit is a 1, the block number thus read is transferred to the two high-order bits of the main memory address register. The line number from the virtual address is transferred into the 10 low-order bits of the memory address register. A read signal to main memory transfers the content of the word to the main memory buffer register ready to be used by the CPU. If the presence bit in the word read from the page table is 0, it signifies that the content of the word referenced by the virtual address does not reside in main memory. A call to the operating system is then generated to fetch the required page from auxiliary memory and place it into main memory before resuming computation.

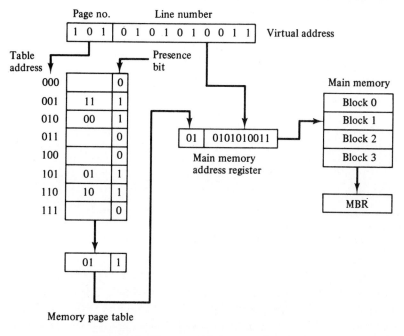

Fig. 12-14 Memory table in a paged system.

Associative Memory-Page Table

A random access memory-page table is inefficient with respect to storage utilization. In the example of Fig. 12-14 we observe that eight words of memory are needed, one for each page, but at least four words will always be marked empty because main memory cannot accommodate more than four blocks. In general, a system with n pages and m blocks would require a memory-page table of n locations of which up to m blocks will be marked with block numbers and all others will be empty. As a second numerical example, consider an address space of 1024K words and memory space of 32K words. If each page or block contains 1K words then the number of pages is 1024 and the number of blocks 32. The capacity of the memory-page table must be 1024 words and only 32 locations may have a presence bit equal to 1. At any given time, at least 992 locations will be empty and not in use.

A more efficient way to organize the page table would be to construct it with a number of words equal to the number of blocks in main memory. In this way, the size of the memory is reduced and each location is fully utilized. This method can be implemented by means of an associative memory with each word in memory containing a page number together with its corresponding block number. The page field in each word is compared with the page number in the virtual address. If a match occurs, the word is read from memory and its corresponding block number is extracted.

Consider again the case of eight pages and four blocks as in the example of Fig.

12-14. We replace the random access memory-page table with an associative memory of four words as shown in Fig. 12-15. Each entry in the associative memory array consists of two fields. The first three bits specify a field for storing the page number. The last two bits constitute a field for storing the block number. The virtual address is placed in the argument register. The page number bits in the argument register are compared with all page numbers in the page field of the associative memory. If the page number is found, the 5-bit word is read out from memory. The corresponding block number, being in the same word, is transferred to the main memory address register. If no match occurs, a call to the operating system is generated to bring the required page from auxiliary memory.

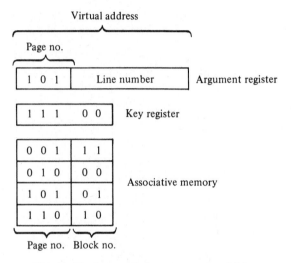

Fig. 12-15   An associative memory page table.

Page Replacement

A virtual memory system is a combination of hardware and software techniques. The memory management software system handles all the software operations for the efficient utilization of memory space. It must decide: (1) which page in main memory ought to be removed to make room for a new page; (2) when a new page is to be transferred from auxiliary memory to main memory; and (3) where the page is to be placed in main memory. The hardware mapping mechanism and the memory management software together constitute the architecture of a virtual memory.

When a program starts execution, one or more pages are transferred into main memory and the page table is set to indicate their position. The program is executed from main memory until it attempts to reference a page that is still in auxiliary memory. This condition is called *page fault*. When page fault occurs, the execution of the present program is suspended until the required page is brought into main memory. Since loading a page from auxiliary memory to main memory is basically an I/O operation, the operating system assigns this task to the I/O processor. In the meantime, control is transferred to the next program in memory that is waiting to be processed in the CPU. Later, when the memory block has been assigned and the transfer completed, the original program can resume its operation.

When a page fault occurs in a virtual memory system, it signifies that the page referenced by the CPU is not in main memory. A new page is then transferred from auxiliary memory to main memory. If main memory is full, it would be necessary to remove a page from a memory block to make room for the new page. The policy for choosing pages to remove is determined from the replacement algorithm that is used. The goal of a replacement policy is to try to remove the page least likely to be referenced in the immediate future.

Two of the most common replacement algorithms used are the *first-in first-out* (FIFO) and the *least recently used* (LRU). The FIFO algorithm selects for replacement the page that has been in memory the longest time. Each time a page is loaded into memory, its identification number is pushed into a FIFO stack. FIFO will be full whenever memory has no more empty blocks. When a new page must be loaded, the page least recently brought in is removed. The page to be removed is easily determined because its identification number is at the top of the FIFO stack. The FIFO replacement policy has the advantage of being easy to implement. It has the disadvantage that under certain circumstances pages are removed and loaded from memory too frequently.

The LRU policy is more difficult to implement but has been more attractive on the assumption that the least recently used page is a better candidate for removal than the least recently loaded page as in FIFO. The LRU algorithm can be implemented by associating a counter with every page that is in main memory. When a page is referenced, its associated counter is set to zero. At fixed intervals of time, the counters associated with all pages presently in memory are incremented by 1. The least recently used page is the page with the highest count. The counters are often called *aging registers*, as their count indicates their age, that is, how long ago their associated pages have been referenced.

12-6   CACHE MEMORY

Analysis of a large number of typical programs has shown that the references to memory at any given interval of time tend to be confined within a few localized areas in memory. This phenomenon is known as the property of *locality of reference*. The reason for this property may be understood considering that a typical computer program flows in a straight-line fashion with program loops and subroutine calls encountered frequently. When a program loop is executed, the CPU repeatedly refers to the set of instructions in memory that constitute the loop. Every time a given subroutine is called, its set of instructions are fetched from memory. Thus, loops and subroutines tend to localize the references to memory for fetching instructions. To a lesser degree, memory references to data also tend to be localized. Table-lookup procedures repeatedly refer to that portion in memory where the table is stored. Iterative procedures refer to common memory locations and array of numbers are confined within a local portion of memory. The result of all these observations is the locality of reference property, which states that, over a short interval of time, the addresses generated by a typical program refer to a few localized areas of memory repeatedly while the remainder of memory is accessed relatively infrequently.

If the active portions of the program and data are placed in a fast small memory, the average memory access time can be reduced, thus reducing the total execution time of the program. Such a fast small memory is referred to as a *cache* memory. It is placed between the CPU and main memory as illustrated in Fig. 12-6. The cache memory access time is less than the access time of main memory by a factor of 5 to 10. The cache is the fastest component in the memory hierarchy and approaches the speed of CPU components.

The fundamental idea of cache organization is that by keeping the most frequently accessed instructions and data in the fast cache memory, the average memory access time will approach the access time of the cache. Although the cache is only a small fraction of the size of main memory, a large fraction of memory requests will be found in the fast cache memory because of the locality of reference property of programs.

The basic operation of the cache is as follows. When the CPU needs to access memory, the cache is examined. If the word is found in the cache, it is read from the fast memory. If the word addressed by the CPU is not found in the cache, the main memory is accessed to read the word. A block of words containing the one just accessed is then transferred from main memory to cache memory. The block size may vary from one word (the one just accessed) to about 16 words adjacent to the one just accessed. In this manner, some data is transferred to cache so that future references to memory find the required words in the fast cache memory.

While a virtual memory system manages data transfers between auxiliary memory and main memory, the cache organization is concerned with the transfer of information between main memory and CPU. Thus each is involved with a different level in the memory hierarchy system. The reason for having two or three levels of memory hierarchy is economics. As the storage capacity of the memory increases, the cost per bit for storing binary information decreases, and the access time of the memory becomes longer. The auxiliary memory has a large storage capacity, is relatively inexpensive, but has a low access speed compared to main memory. The cache memory is very small, relatively expensive, and has very high access speed. Thus, as the memory access speed increases, so does its relative cost. The overall goal of virtual and cache memories is to obtain the highest possible average access speed while minimizing the total cost of the entire memory system.

Although virtual memory and cache memory are similar in principle, they are used for different purposes. The cache holds those parts of the program and data that are most heavily used, while the auxiliary memory holds those parts that are not presently used by the CPU. Moreover, the CPU has direct access to both cache and main memory. In a virtual memory system, the CPU has access to main memory only; the transfer from auxiliary to main memory is usually done by an I/O processor that transfers large blocks of data. A typical access-time ratio between cache and main memory is about 1:7. For example, a typical cache memory may have an access time of 100 ns while main memory access time may be 700 ns. Auxiliary memory average access time is usually 1000 times that of main memory. Block size in virtual memory typically ranges from 64 to 4096 words, while cache block size is typically from 1 to 16 words. The memory management in virtual memory is implemented with a combination of hardware and software procedures. In cache memory, all transfer decisions are made by a hardware controller in order to achieve the maximum possible speed of operation.

The performance of cache memory is frequently measured in terms of a quantity called *hit ratio*. When the CPU refers to memory and finds the word in cache, it is said to produce a *hit*. If the word is not found in cache, then it is in main memory and it counts as a *miss*. The ratio of the number of hits divided by the total CPU references to memory (hits plus misses) is the hit ratio. The hit ratio is best measured experimentally by running representative programs in the computer and measuring the number of hits and misses during a given interval of time. Hit ratios of 0.9 and higher have been reported. This high ratio verifies the validity of the locality of reference property.

The average memory access time of a computer system can be improved considerably by use of a cache. If the hit ratio is high enough so that most of the time the CPU accesses the cache instead of main memory, the average access time is closer to the access time of the fast cache memory. For example, a computer with cache access time of 100 ns, a main memory access time of 1000 ns, and a hit ratio of 0.9 produces an average access time of 200 ns. This is a considerable improvement over a similar computer without a cache memory, whose access time is 1000 ns.

The basic characteristic of cache memory is its fast access time. Therefore, very little or no time must be wasted when searching for words in the cache. The transformation of data from main memory to cache memory is referred to as a *mapping* process. Three types of mapping procedures are of practical interest when considering the organization of cache memory.

1. Associative mapping.

2. Direct mapping.

3. Set-associative mapping.

To help in the discussion of these three mapping procedures we will use a specific example of a memory organization as shown in Fig. 12-16. The main memory can store 32K words of 12 bits each. The cache is capable of storing 512 of these words at any given time. For every word stored in cache, there is a duplicate copy in main memory. The CPU communicates with both memories. It first sends a 15-bit address to cache. If there is a hit, the CPU accepts the 12-bit data from cache. If there is a

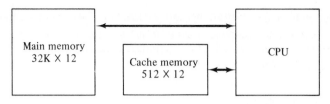

Fig. 12-16 Example of cache memory.

miss, the CPU reads the word from main memory and the word is then transferred to cache.

Associative Mapping

The fastest and most flexible cache organization uses an associative memory. This organization is illustrated in Fig. 12-17. The associative memory stores both the address and content (data) of the memory word. This permits any location in cache to store any word from main memory. The diagram shows three words presently stored in the cache. The address value of 15 bits is shown as a 5-digit octal number and its corresponding 12-bit word is shown as a 4-digit octal number. A CPU address of 15 bits is placed in the argument register (see Fig. 12-7) and the associative memory is searched for a matching address. If the address is found, the corresponding 12-bit data is read and sent to the CPU. If no match occurs, the main memory is accessed for the word. The address-data pair is then transferred to the associative cache memory. If the cache is full, then an address-data pair must be displaced to make room for a pair that is needed and not presently in the cache. The decision as to what pair is

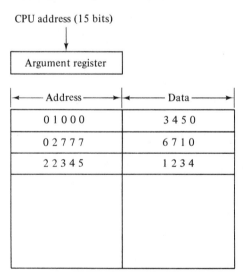

Fig. 12-17 Associative mapping cache (all numbers are in octal).

504

replaced is determined from the replacement algorithm that the designer chooses for the cache. A simple procedure is to replace cells of the cache in round-robin order whenever a new word is requested from main memory. This constitutes a first-in first-out (FIFO) replacement policy.

Direct Mapping

Associative memories are expensive compared to random-access memories because of the added logic associated with each cell. The possibility of using a random-access memory for the cache is investigated in Fig. 12-18. The CPU address of 15 bits is divided into two fields. The nine least significant bits constitute the *index* field and the remaining six bits form the *tag* field. The figure shows that main memory needs an address that includes both the tag and the index bits. The number of bits in the index field is equal to the number of address bits required to access the cache memory.

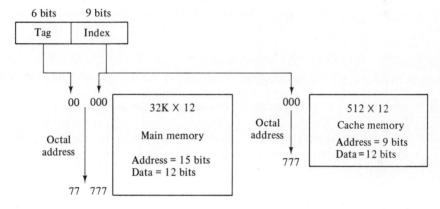

Fig. 12-18 Addressing relationships between main and cache memories.

In the general case, there are 2^k words in cache memory and 2^n words in main memory. The n-bit memory address is divided into two fields: k bits for the index field and $n - k$ bits for the tag field. The direct mapping cache organization uses the n-bit address to access the main memory and the k-bit index to access the cache. The internal organization of the words in the cache memory is as shown in Fig. 12-19(b). Each word in cache consists of the data word and its associated tag. When a new word is first brought into the cache, the tag bits are stored alongside the data bits. When the CPU generates a memory request, the index field is used for the address to access the cache. The tag field of the CPU address is compared with the tag in the word read from the cache. If the two tags match, there is a hit and the desired data word is in cache. If there is no match, there is a miss and the required word is read from main memory. It is then stored in the cache together with the new tag, replacing the previous value. The disadvantage of direct mapping is that the hit ratio can drop considerably if two or more words whose addresses have the same index but different tags are accessed

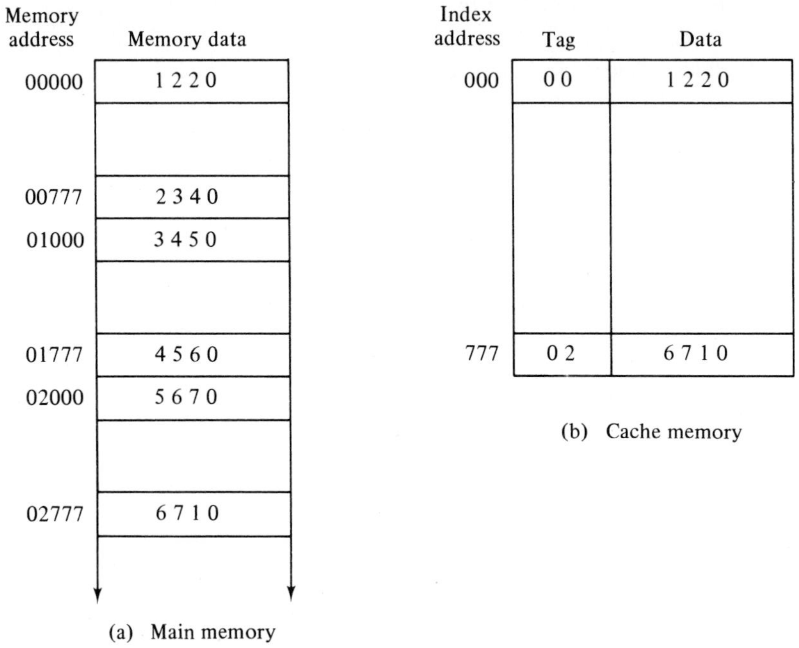

Memory address	Memory data
00000	1 2 2 0
00777	2 3 4 0
01000	3 4 5 0
01777	4 5 6 0
02000	5 6 7 0
02777	6 7 1 0

(a) Main memory

Index address	Tag	Data
000	0 0	1 2 2 0
777	0 2	6 7 1 0

(b) Cache memory

Fig. 12-19 Direct mapping cache organization.

repeatedly. However, this possibility is minimized by the fact that such words are relatively far apart in the address range (multiples of 512 locations in this example.)

To see how the direct-mapping organization operates, consider the numerical example shown in Fig. 12-19. The word at address zero is presently stored in the cache (index = 000, tag = 00, data = 1220). Suppose that the CPU now wants to access the word at address 02000. The index address is 000, so it is used to access the cache. The two tags are then compared. The cache tag is 00 but the address tag is 02, which does not produce a match. Therefore, the main memory is accessed and the data word 5670 is transferred to the CPU. The cache word at index address 000 is then replaced with a tag of 02 and data of 5670.

The direct-mapping example just described uses a block size of one word. The same organization but using a block size of 8 words is shown in Fig. 12-20. The index field is now divided into two parts: the block field and the word field. In a 512-word cache there are 64 blocks of 8 words each, since $64 \times 8 = 512$. The block number is specified with a 6-bit field and the word within the block is specified with a 3-bit field. The tag field stored within the cache is common to all 8 words of the same block. Every time a miss occurs, an entire block of 8 words must be transferred from main memory to cache memory. Although this takes extra time, the hit ratio will most likely improve with a larger block size because of the sequential nature of computer programs.

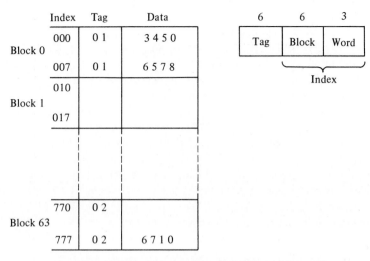

Fig. 12-20 Direct mapping cache with block size of 8 words.

Set-Associative Mapping

It was mentioned previously that the disadvantage of direct mapping is that two words with the same index in their address but with different tag values cannot reside in cache memory at the same time. A third type of cache organization, called set-associative mapping, is an improvement over the direct-mapping organization in that each word of cache can store two or more words of memory under the same index address. Each data word is stored together with its tag and the number of **tag-data** items in one word of cache is said to form a set. An example of a set-associative cache organization for a set size of two is shown in Fig. 12-21. Each index address refers to

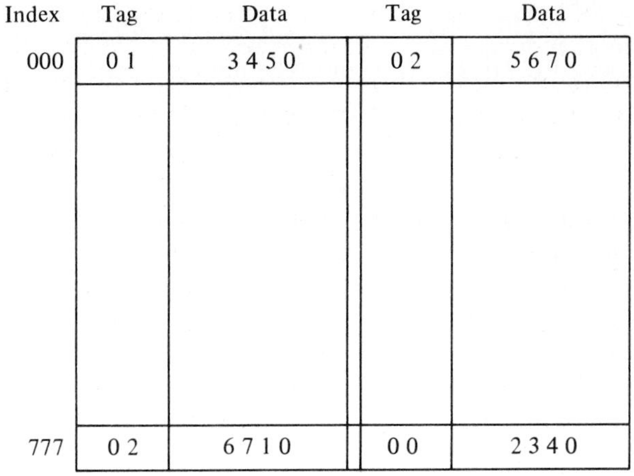

Index	Tag	Data	Tag	Data
000	0 1	3 4 5 0	0 2	5 6 7 0
777	0 2	6 7 1 0	0 0	2 3 4 0

Fig. 12-21 Set-associative mapping cache with set size of two.

two data words and their associated tags. Each tag requires six bits and each data word has 12 bits, so the word length is $2(6 + 12) = 36$ bits. An index address of nine bits can accommodate 512 words. Thus, the size of cache memory is 512×36. It can accommodate 1024 words of main memory since each word of cache contains two data words. In general, a set-associative cache of set size k will accommodate k words of main memory in each word of cache.

The octal numbers listed in Fig. 12-21 are with reference to the main memory contents illustrated in Fig. 12-19(a). The words stored at addresses 01000 and 02000 of main memory are stored in cache memory at index address 000. Similarly, the words at addresses 02777 and 00777 are stored in cache at index address 777. When the CPU generates a memory request, the index value of the address is used to access the cache. The tag field of the CPU address is then compared with both tags in the cache to determine if a match occurs. The comparison logic is done by an associative search of the tags in the set similar to an associative memory search: thus the name "set-associative". The hit ratio will improve as the set size increases because more words with the same index but different tags can reside in cache. However, an increase in the set size increases the number of bits in words of cache and requires more complex comparison logic.

When a miss occurs in a set-associative cache and the set is full, it is necessary to replace one of the tag-data items with a new value. The most common replacement algorithms used are: random replacement, first-in first-out (FIFO), and least recently used (LRU). With the random replacement policy the control chooses one tag-data item for replacement at random. The FIFO procedure selects for replacement the item that has been in the set the longest. The LRU algorithm selects for replacement the item that has been least recently used by the CPU. Both FIFO and LRU can be implemented by adding a few extra bits in each word of cache (see Prob. 12-26).

Writing into Cache

An important aspect of cache organization is concerned with memory write requests. When the CPU finds a word in cache during a read operation, the main memory is not involved in the transfer. However, if the operation is a write, there are two ways that the system can proceed.

The simplest and most commonly used procedure is to update main memory with every memory write operation, with cache memory being updated in parallel if it contains the word at the specified address. This is called the *write-through* method. This method has the advantage that main memory always contains the same data as the cache. This characteristic is important in systems with direct memory access transfers. It ensures that the data residing in main memory is valid at all times so that an I/O device communicating through DMA would receive the most recent updated data.

The second procedure is called the *write-back* method. In this method only the cache location is updated during a write operation. The location is then marked by a flag so that later when the word is removed from the cache it is copied into main memory. The reason for the write-back method is that during the time a word resides in the cache, it may be updated several times; however, as long as the word remains in the cache, it does not matter whether the copy in main memory is out of date, since requests from the word are filled from the cache. It is only when the word is displaced from the cache by a different word that an accurate copy need be rewritten into main memory. Analytical results indicate that the number of memory writes in a typical program ranges between 10 and 30% of the total references to memory.

Cache Initialization

One more aspect of cache organization that must be taken into consideration is the problem of initialization. The cache is initialized when power is applied to the computer or when the main memory is loaded with a complete set of programs from auxiliary memory. After initialization the cache is considered to be empty, but in effect it contains some nonvalid data. It is customary to include with each word in cache a *valid bit* to indicate whether or not the word contains valid data.

The cache is initialized by clearing all the valid bits to 0. The valid bit of a particular cache word is set to 1 the first time this word is loaded from main memory and stays set unless the cache has to be initialized again. The introduction of the valid bit means that a word in cache is not replaced by another word unless the valid bit is set to 1 and a mismatch of tags occurs. If the valid bit happens to be 0, the new word automatically replaces the invalid data. Thus, the initialization condition has the effect of forcing misses from the cache until it fills with valid data.

12-7 MEMORY MANAGEMENT HARDWARE

In a multiprogramming environment where many programs reside in memory it becomes necessary to move programs and data around the memory, to vary the amount of memory in use by a given program and to prevent a program from changing other programs. The demands on computer memory brought about by multiprogramming have created the need for a memory management system. A memory management system is a collection of hardware and software procedures for managing the various programs residing in memory. The memory management software is part of an overall operating system available in many computers. Here we are concerned with the hardware unit associated with the memory management system.

The basic components of a memory management unit are:

1. A facility for dynamic storage relocation that maps logical memory references into physical memory addresses.

2. A provision for sharing common programs stored in memory by different users.

3. Protection of information against unauthorized access between users and preventing users from changing operating system functions.

The dynamic storage relocation hardware is a mapping process similar to the paging system described in Sec. 12-5. The fixed page size used in the virtual memory system causes certain difficulties with respect to program size and the logical structure of programs. It is more convenient to divide programs and data into logical parts called segments. A *segment* is a set of logically related instructions or data elements associated with a given name. Segments may be generated by the programmer or by the operating system. Examples of segments are a subroutine, an array of data, a table of symbols, or a user's program.

The sharing of common programs is an integral part of a multiprogramming system. For example, several users wishing to compile their Fortran programs should be able to share a single copy of the compiler rather than each user having a separate copy in memory. Other system programs residing in memory are also shared by all users in a multiprogramming system without having to produce multiple copies.

The third issue in multiprogramming is protecting one program from unwanted interaction with another. An example of unwanted interaction is one user's unauthorized copying of another user's program. Another aspect of protection is concerned with preventing the occasional user from performing operating system functions and thereby interrupting the orderly sequence of operations in a computer installation. The secrecy of certain programs must be kept from unauthorized personnel to prevent abuses in the confidential activities of an organization.

The address generated by a segmented program is called a *logical address*. This is similar to a virtual address except that logical address space is associated with variable-length segments rather than fixed-length pages. The logical address may be larger than the physical memory address as in virtual memory, but it may also be equal, and sometimes even smaller than the length of the physical memory address. In addition to relocation information, each segment has protection information associated with it. Shared programs are placed in a unique segment in each user's logical address space so that a single physical copy can be shared. The function of the memory management unit is to map logical addresses into physical addresses similar to the virtual memory mapping concept. Two mapping procedures will be presented. The first is called a segmented-page mapping and is similar to the one used in the IBM-370 computer. It requires two mapping tables in conjunction with a small associative memory. The second mapping procedure employs a number of segment registers and is similar in operation to the one used in the PDP-11 and Z8000 computers.

Segmented-Page Mapping

It was already mentioned that the property of logical space is that it uses variable-length segments. The length of each segment is allowed to grow and contract according to the needs of the program being executed. One way of specifying the length of a segment is by associating with it a number of equal-size pages. To see how this is done, consider the logical address shown in Fig. 12-22. The logical address is partitioned into three fields. The segment field specifies a segment number. The page field specifies

Logical address

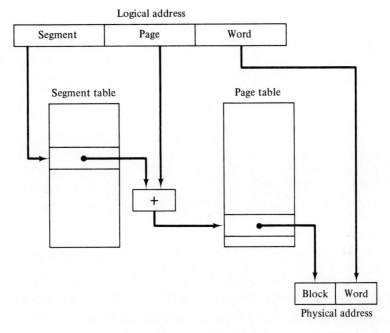

(a) Logical to physical address mapping

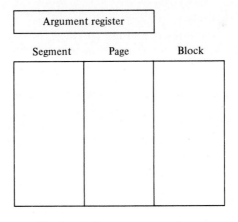

(b) Associative memory mapping

Fig. 12-22 Mapping in segmented-page memory management unit.

the page within the segment and the word field gives the specific word within the page. A page field of k bits can specify up to 2^k pages. A segment number may be associated with just one page or with as many as 2^k pages. Thus, the length of a segment would vary according to the number of pages that are assigned to it.

The mapping of the logical address into a physical address is done by means of two tables, as shown in Fig. 12-22(a). The segment number of the logical address specifies the address for the segment table. The entry in the segment table is a pointer address for a page table base. The page table base is added to the page number given in the logical address. The sum produces a pointer address to an entry in the page table. The value found in the page table provides the block number in physical memory. The concatenation of the block field with the word field produces the final physical mapped address.

The two mapping tables may be stored in two separate small memories or in main memory. In either case, a memory reference from the CPU will require three accesses to memory: one from the segment table, one from the page table, and the third from main memory. This would slow the system significantly when compared to a conventional system that requires only one reference to memory. To avoid this speed penalty, a fast associative memory is used to hold the most recently referenced table entries. The first time a given block is referenced, its value together with the corresponding segment and page numbers are entered into the associative memory as shown in Fig. 12-22(b). Thus, the mapping process is first attempted by associative search with the given segment and page numbers. If it succeeds, the mapping delay is only that of the associative memory. If no match occurs, the slower table mapping of Fig. 12-22(a) is used and the result transformed into the associative memory for future reference.

Numerical Example

A numerical example may clarify the operation of the memory management unit. Consider the 20-bit logical address specified in Fig. 12-23(a). The 4-bit segment number specifies one of 16 possible segments. The 8-bit page number can specify up

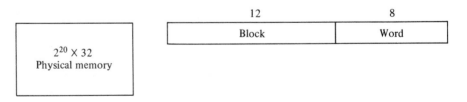

4	8	8
Segment	Page	Word

(a) Logical address format: 16 segments of 256 pages each, each page has 256 words

	12	8
$2^{20} \times 32$ Physical memory	Block	Word

(b) Physical address format: 4096 blocks of 256 words each, each word has 32 bits

Fig. 12-23 An example of logical and physical addresses.

to 256 pages, and the 8-bit word field implies a page size of 256 words. This configuration allows each segment to have any number of pages up to 256. The smallest possible segment will have one page or 256 words. The largest possible segment will have 256 pages, for a total of $256 \times 256 = 64K$ words.

The physical memory shown in Fig. 12-23(b) consists of 2^{20} words of 32 bits each. The 20-bit address is divided into two fields: a 12-bit block number and an 8-bit word number. Thus, physical memory is divided into 4096 blocks of 256 words each. A page in a logical address has a corresponding block in physical memory. Note that both the logical and physical address have 20 bits. In the absence of a memory management unit, the 20-bit address from the CPU can be used to access physical memory directly.

Consider a program loaded into memory that requires five pages. The operating system may assign to this program segment 6 and pages 0 through 4, as shown in Fig. 12-24(a). The total logical address range for the program is from hexadecimal 60000 to 604FF. When the program is loaded into physical memory, it is distributed among five blocks in physical memory where the operating system finds empty spaces. The correspondence between each memory block and logical page number is then entered in a table as shown in Fig. 12-24(b). The information from this table is entered in the segment and page tables as shown in Fig. 12-25(a).

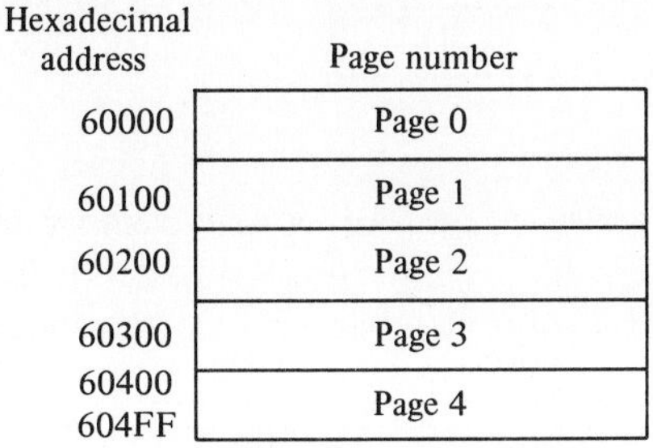

Hexadecimal address	Page number
60000	Page 0
60100	Page 1
60200	Page 2
60300	Page 3
60400 / 604FF	Page 4

Segment	Page	Block
6	00	012
6	01	000
6	02	019
6	03	053
6	04	A61

(a) Logical address assignment

(b) Segment-page versus memory block assignment

Fig. 12-24 Example of logical and physical memory address assignment.

Now consider the specific logical address given in Fig. 12-25. The 20-bit address is listed as a 5-digit hexadecimal number. It refers to word number 7E of page 2 in segment 6. The base of segment 6 in the page table is at address 35. Segment 6 has associated with it 5 pages, as shown in the page table at addresses 35 through 39. Page 2 of segment 6 is at address $35 + 2 = 37$. The physical memory block is found in the page table to be 019. Word 7E in block 19 gives the 20-bit physical address 0197E. Note that page 0 of segment 6 maps into block 12 and page 1 maps into block 0. The associative memory in Fig. 12-25(b) shows that pages 2 and 4 of segment 6 have been referenced previously and therefore their corresponding block numbers are stored in the associative memory.

Logical address (in haxadecimal)

6	02	7E

Segment table
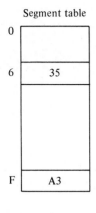

Page table
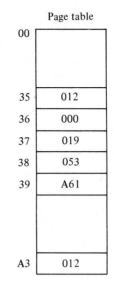

Physical memory
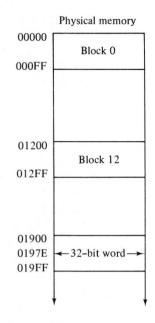

(a)   Segment and page table mapping

Segment	Page	Block
6	02	019
6	04	A61

(b)   Associative memory mapping

Fig. 12-25   Logical to physical memory mapping example (all numbers are in hexadecimal).

From this example it should be evident that the memory management system can assign any number of pages to each segment. Each logical page can be mapped into any block in physical memory. Pages can move to different blocks in memory depending on memory space requirements. The only updating required is the change of the block number in the page table. Segments can grow or shrink independently without affecting each other. Different segments can use the same block of memory if it is required to share a program by many users. For example, block number 12 in physical memory can be assigned a second logical address F0000 through F00FF. This specifies segment number 15 and page 0, which maps to block 12 as shown in Fig. 12-25(a).

Mapping with Segment Registers

As discussed in Sec. 12-5, virtual memory is used to provide an address space that is larger than the physical memory unit. There are occasions when the reverse situation exists; that is, the computer physical memory is larger than the processor can directly address. This can happen if the number of bits available to specify a memory address in the instruction format is less than the number of bits required to address physical memory. An example of this situation is the PDP-11 computer. The PDP-11 processor uses a 16-bit address to specify up to 64K bytes. The physical memory attached to some versions of the PDP-11 can accommodate $2^{18} = 256K$ bytes of memory. Thus, a transformation is needed from a CPU address of 16 bits to a physical address of 18 bits. This is done by means of segment registers which are part of the memory management unit available in the computer. In this case the logical address has 16 bits and is smaller than the physical address of 18 bits. The logical address in the PDP-11 is sometimes referred to as a virtual address by the vendor.

The time it takes to map a logical address into a physical address can be reduced if a small number of high-speed registers are used instead of two memory-mapping tables. The segment number in the logical address selects one of the registers where a page address base is stored. The base address is then added to the logical page number to obtain the physical memory block number. An example of mapping with segment registers is shown in Fig. 12-26. The logical address contains 15 bits and the physical address has 18 bits. There are eight segment registers each containing a 12-bit base address. The mapping of a logical address to a physical address is as follows. The 3-bit segment field in the logical address is used to select one of the eight segment registers. The base address contained in the selected register is added to the page number in the logical address to give a 12-bit block number. The block number is concatenated with the word number to obtain the 18-bit physical address. A numerical example is shown in Fig. 12-26(b) to clarify this process.

Note that because page numbers add directly to the base address, it is necessary to load consecutive pages in contiguous locations in physical memory. This is in contrast to the segmented-page mapping procedure where pages can be distributed among nonconsecutive memory blocks.

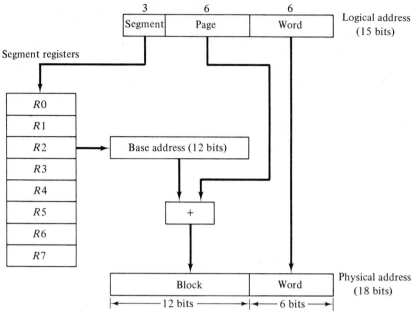

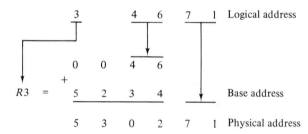

(a) Logical to physical address mapping

(b) Numerical example (all numbers are in octal)

Fig. 12-26 Mapping with segment registers.

Memory Protection

Memory protection can be assigned to the physical address or the logical address. The protection of memory through the physical address can be done by assigning to each block in memory a number of protection bits that indicate the type of access allowed to its corresponding block. Every time a page is moved from one block to another it would be necessary to update the block protection bits. A much better place to apply protection is in the logical address space rather than the physical address space. This can be done by including protection information within the segment table or segment register of the memory management hardware.

The content of each entry in the segment table or a segment register is called a

516

descriptor. A typical descriptor would contain, in addition to a base address field, one or two additional fields for protection purposes. A typical format for a segment descriptor is shown in Fig. 12-27. The base address field gives the base of the page table address in a segmented-page organization or the block base address in a segment register organization. This is the address used in mapping from a logical to the physical address. The length field gives the segment size by specifying the maximum number of pages assigned to the segment. The length field is compared against the page number in the logical address. A size violation occurs if the page number falls outside the segment length boundary. Thus, a given program and its data cannot access memory not assigned to it by the operating system.

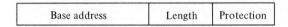

Fig. 12-27 Format of a typical segment descriptor.

The protection field in a segment descriptor specifies the access rights available to the particular segment. In a segmented-page organization, each entry in the page table may have its own protection field to describe the access rights of each page. The protection information is set into the descriptor by the master control program of the operating system. Some of the access rights of interest that are used for protecting the programs residing in memory are:

1. Full read and write privileges.

2. Read only (write protection).

3. Execute only (program protection).

4. System only (operating system protection).

Full read and write privileges are given to a program when it is executing its own instructions. Write protection is useful for sharing system programs such as utility programs and other library routines. These system programs are stored in an area of memory where they can be shared by many users. They can be read by all programs, but no writing is allowed. This protects them from being changed by other programs.

The execute-only condition protects programs from being copied. It restricts the segment to be referenced only during the instruction fetch cycle but not during the execute cycle. Thus, it allows the users to execute the segment program instructions but prevents them from reading the instructions as data for the purpose of copying their content.

Portions of the operating system will reside in memory at any given time. These system programs must be protected by making them inaccessible to unauthorized users. The operating system protection condition is placed in the descriptors of all operating system programs to prevent the occasional user from accessing operating system segments.

REFERENCES

1. HAYES, J. P., *Computer Architecture and Organization*. New York: McGraw-Hill Book Company, 1978.

2. HAMACHER, V. C., Z. G. VRANESIC, AND S. G. ZAKY, *Computer Organization*. New York: McGraw-Hill Book Company, 1978.

3. WATSON, R. W., *Timesharing System Design Concepts*. New York: McGraw-Hill Book Company, 1970.

4. HELLERMAN, H., AND T. F. CONROY, *Computer System Performance*. New York: McGraw-Hill Book Company, 1975.

5. MADNICK, S. E., AND J. J. DONOVAN, *Operating Systems*. New York: McGraw-Hill Book Company, 1974.

6. TANENBAUM, A. S., *Structure Computer Organization*. Englewood Cliffs, N.J.: Prentice-Hall, Inc., 1976.

7. HANLON, A. G., "Content-Addressable and Associative Memory Systems—A Survey," *IEEE Trans. on Electronic Computers*, Vol. EC-15 (August 1966), pp. 509–521.

8. DENNING, P. J., "Virtual Memory", *Computing Surveys*, Vol. 2 (September 1970), pp. 153–187.

9. BELL, J., D. CASASENT, AND C. G. BELL, "An Investigation of Alternative Cache Organizations," *IEEE Trans. on Computers*, Vol. C-23 (April 1974), pp. 346–351.

10. CONTI, C. J., "Concepts for Buffer Storage," *IEEE Computer Group News*, Vol. 2 (March 1969), pp. 9–13.

11. IBM CORP., *IBM System/370 Principles of Operation*, Publ. GA22–7000–5, Poughkeepsie, N.Y. 1976.

12. "AmZ8010 Memory Management," Advanced Micro Devices, Sunnyvale, Calif., 1979.

13. DIGITAL EQUIPMENT CORP., *PDP-11 Processor Handbook*, Maynard, Mass., 1975.

PROBLEMS

12-1. Explain the need for auxiliary memory devices. How are they different from main memory and from other peripheral devices?

12-2. Explain the need for memory hierarchy. What is the main reason for not having a large enough main memory for storing the totality of information in a computer system?

12-3. Give at least four differences between a magnetic-drum and a magnetic-tape unit.

12-4. Why is it that more binary information can be stored in a disk unit than a drum unit of comparable size?

12-5. A magnetic disk unit has eight disks with recording on both surfaces of each disk. Each surface has 16 tracks and 8 sectors. Each sector in a track contains one record. How many bits are needed to address a record in the disk?

12-6. Draw a block diagram for the address selection logic of a drum unit.

12-7.   (a) How many 128 × 8 RAM chips are needed to provide a memory capacity of 2048 bytes?

      (b) How many lines of the address bus must be used to access 2048 bytes of memory? How many of these lines will be common to all chips?

      (c) How many lines must be decoded for chip select? Specify the size of the decoders.

12-8.   A microprocessor uses RAM chips of 1024 × 1 capacity.

      (a) How many chips are needed and how should their address lines be connected to provide a memory capacity of 1024 bytes?

      (b) How many chips are needed to provide a memory capacity of 16K bytes? Explain in words how the chips are to be connected to the address bus.

12-9.   A ROM chip of 1024 × 8 bits has four select inputs and operates from a 5-V power supply. How many pins are needed for the IC package? Draw a block diagram and label all input and output terminals in the ROM.

12-10. Extend the memory system of Fig. 12-5 to 4096 bytes of RAM and 4096 bytes of ROM. List the memory-address map and indicate what size decoders are needed.

12-11. A microprocessor employs RAM chips of 256 × 8 and ROM chips of 1024 × 8. The microcomputer system needs 2K bytes of RAM, 4K bytes of ROM, and four interface units, each with four registers. A memory-mapped I/O configuration is used. The two highest-order bits of the address bus are assigned 00 for RAM, 01 for ROM, and 10 for interface registers.

      (a) How many RAM and ROM chips are needed?

      (b) Draw a memory-address map for the system.

      (c) Give the address range in hexadecimal for RAM, ROM, and interface.

12-12. An 8-bit microprocessor has a 16-bit address bus. The first 15 lines of the address are used to select a bank of 32K bytes of memory. The high-order bit of the address is used to select a register which receives the contents of the data bus. Explain how this configuration can be used to extend the memory capacity of the system to 8 banks of 32K bytes each, for a total of 256K bytes of memory.

12-13. The memory unit of large computers is sometimes partitioned into separate modules. Each module contains a memory array with its own address and data registers. An example of a memory unit organized in four modules is shown in Fig. 7-24. Show how the particular module can be selected from the address available in the address bus.

12-14. Obtain the complement function for the match logic of one word in an associative memory. In other words show that M_i' is the sum of exclusive-OR functions. Draw the logic diagram for M_i' and terminate it with an inverter to obtain M_i.

12-15. Obtain the Boolean function for the match logic of one word in an associative memory taking into consideration a tag bit that indicates whether the word is active or inactive.

12-16. What additional logic is required to give a no-match result for a word in an associative memory when all key bits are zeros?

12-17. (a) Draw the logic diagram of all the cells of one word in an associative memory. Include the read and write logic of Fig. 12-9 and the match logic of Fig. 12-10.

      (b) Draw the logic diagram of all cells along one vertical column (column j) in an associative memory. Include a common output line for all bits in the same column.

(c) From the diagrams in (a) and (b) show that if output M_i is connected to the *read* line of the same word, then the matched word will be read out, provided only one word matches the masked argument.

12-18. Describe in words and by means of a block diagram how multiple matched words can be read out from an associative memory.

12-19. Derive the logic of one cell and of an entire word for an associative memory that has an output indicator when the unmasked argument is greater than (but not equal to) the word in the associative memory.

12-20. An address space is specified by 16 bits and the corresponding memory space by 12 bits.
(a) How many words are there in the address space?
(b) How many words in the memory space?
(c) If a page consists of 256 words, how many pages and blocks are there in the system?

12-21. A virtual memory has a page size of 1K words. There are eight pages and four blocks. The associative memory page table contains the following entries:

Page	Block
0	3
1	1
4	2
6	0

Make a list of all virtual addresses (in decimal) that will cause a page fault if used by the CPU.

12-22. A virtual memory system has an address space of 8K words, a memory space of 4K words, and page and block sizes of 1K words (see Fig. 12-13). The following page reference changes occur during a given time interval. (Only page changes are listed. If the same page is referenced again, it is not listed twice.)

$$4 \quad 2 \quad 0 \quad 1 \quad 2 \quad 6 \quad 1 \quad 4 \quad 0 \quad 1 \quad 0 \quad 2 \quad 3 \quad 5 \quad 7$$

Determine the four pages that are resident in main memory after each page reference change if the replacement algorithm used is (a) FIFO; (b) LRU.

12-23. A digital computer has a memory unit of 64K $\times$ 16 and a cache memory of 1K words. The cache uses direct mapping with a block size of four words.
(a) How many bits are there in the tag, index, block, and word fields of the address format?
(b) How many bits are there in each word of cache, and how are they divided into functions? Include a valid bit.
(c) How many blocks can the cache accommodate?

12-24. A set-associative mapping cache has a block size of 4 words and a set size of 2. The cache can accommodate a total of 2048 words from main memory. The main memory size is 128K $\times$ 32.

(a) Formulate all pertinent information required to construct the cache memory.

(b) What is the size of the cache memory?

12-25. The access time of a cache memory is 100 ns and that of main memory 1000 ns. It is estimated that 80% of the memory requests are for read and the remaining 20% for write. The hit ratio for read accesses only is 0.9. A write-through procedure is used.

(a) What is the average access time of the system considering only memory read cycles?

(b) What is the average access time of the system for both read and write requests?

(c) What is the hit ratio taking into consideration the write cycles?

12-26. A set-associative cache memory uses a set size of 4 words. A replacement procedure based on the least recently used (LRU) algorithm is implemented by means of 2-bit counters associated with each word in the set. A value in the range 0 to 3 is thus recorded for each word. When a hit occurs, the counter associated with the referenced word is set to 0, those counters with values originally lower than the referenced one are incremented by 1, and all others remain unchanged. If a miss occurs, the word with counter value 3 is removed, the new word is put in its place, and its counter is set to 0. The other three counters are incremented by 1. Show that this procedure works for the following sequence of word reference: A, B, C, D, B, E, D, A, C, E, C, E. (Start with A, B, C, D as the initial four words, with word A being the least recently used.)

12-27. Define multiprogramming and explain the function of a memory management unit in computers that use the multiprogramming organization.

12-28. The logical address space in a computer system consists of 128 segments. Each segment can have up to 32 pages of 4K words each. Physical memory consists of 4K blocks of 4K words each. Formulate the logical and physical address formats.

12-29. Determine the two logical addresses from Fig. 12-25(a) that will access physical memory at hexadecimal address 012AF.

12-30. The logical address for the system described in Fig. 12-26 is octal 53706. Segment register R5 contains the octal value 471. Determine the 18-bit physical address.

12-31. The PDP-11 memory management unit maps a 15-bit logical address to a 17-bit physical address using segment registers as shown in Fig. 12-26. The logical address has a 3-bit segment field, a 7-bit page field, and a 5-bit word field. Each segment register contains a base address of 12 bits. Assume that the logical address is given by the octal number 46735 and that segment register 4 contains the octal number 3257.

(a) What are the segment, page, and word numbers in octal?

(b) Determine the physical block number in octal.

(c) What is the physical address in octal?

Index

C

T

U